U.S. PRESIDENTS
FACTBOOK

ELIZABETH JEWELL

RANDOM HOUSE
REFERENCE

New York Toronto London Sydney Auckland

For my sister, who taught me to read
BONNIE JEWELL VIDOU (1950-2005)

Library of Congress Cataloging-in-Publication Data
Jewell, Elizabeth.
U.S. presidents factbook / Elizabeth Jewell.
p.   cm.
Includes index.
ISBN: 0-375-72073-1 (pbk.)
1. Presidents—United States—Miscellanea.   I. Title:
United States presidents factbook.   II. Title.

E176.1.J49 2005
973'.09'9—dc22   2005044935

Cover design by Nora Rosansky
Text design by Tina Malaney
Text composition by North Market Street Graphics

Printed in the United States of America

10 9 8 7 6 5 4 3 2 1

CONTENTS

Introduction

It has been impossible to approach the task of researching the lives and administrations of America's forty-three presidents without gaining in several ways: first, an appreciation for the characters and abilities of these men. They are, by and large, individuals of ability and intellect who have frequently risen to the challenges presented by the highest office in the land. And they are also human, with the interests, foibles, and faults that make them sometimes likable, sometimes despicable.

One also gains an appreciation for the ebb and flow of recurring political themes throughout the more than two centuries of our national government. Whether we should have more or less government—in terms of regulation, taxation, or assistance; whether more power should be vested in the federal government or the states; whether we should be actively engaged with the other countries of the world or more isolated from international conflicts; and whether the executive, legislative, or judicial should be the strongest branch of government, or a balance be maintained among the three, these are all questions that have not lost their power to divide us.

Yet there are also stirring questions of the past that we may consider as settled—whether our money should be backed by silver or gold; whether we should have a national bank; whether a president should be limited to two terms; and whether slavery ought to be allowed in the United States.

Indeed, the question of slavery must be considered when discussing the first fifteen presidents, and it often seems to outweigh any other factors in evaluating them. Of the first fifteen, nine were themselves slaveholders—Washing-ton, Jefferson, Madison, Monroe, Jackson, Harrison, Tyler, Polk, and Taylor. Others, such as Pierce, supported Southern slaveholders and upheld their right to own slaves in the face of a growing abolitionist movement in the North. It is worth noting that both John Adams and John Quincy Adams were opposed to slavery. John Quincy Adams repeatedly urged Congress to repeal the "gag rule" that made the discussion of slavery and its abolition impossible in the legislative branch for many years. He also acted as the lawyer for the Africans held onboard the *Amistad* who had seized the ship and subsequently landed in the United States; Adams successfully argued before the Supreme Court that these Africans were not personal property and should not be handed over to those who claimed to own them.

On the other hand, even many of those presidents who were personally opposed to slavery believed sincerely that the Constitution prohibited federal action in the matter—that it was purely a question for the states to decide. The sixteenth president, Abraham Lincoln, opposed slavery but, although he assumed the presidency in 1861, he did not issue the Emancipation Proclamation until 1863. The Proclamation was limited to slaves in the states of the Confederacy that had not yet fallen to Union control; slave states that had remained loyal to the Union were not touched. The rationale was that the Confederacy used slaves in the fight against the Union, and Lincoln's Proclamation was made for military and propaganda purposes. It was not until the Thirteenth Amendment was ratified in December 1865 that slavery was outlawed throughout the United States.

SPECIFIC NOTES ON THE TEXT

Every attempt has been made to give accurate, verifiable information on the presidents, their families, and their administrations. Because many of the presidents rose from obscure beginnings, it is often difficult to be sure of basic facts. Two different places claim to be the birthplace of Andrew Jackson—one in North Carolina, one in South Carolina—and I have given the weight to South Carolina largely on the basis that this is where Jackson claimed he was born. Chester Alan Arthur's birthdate is in doubt; apparently, he himself may have offered the wrong year in order to pass himself off as younger. Other historians suggest that Arthur may have obscured the truth because he was, in fact, born in Canada and would have thus been ineligible for the presidency.

One of the most difficult areas to research is that of presidential siblings. Reports vary for some families concerning the number of children; this becomes more understandable when one takes into account the high rate of infant and child mortality in centuries past. Further muddying the waters was the custom of using the name of a deceased child for one born later. In addition, as the future president moved onto the national stage, his siblings may have receded in relative importance to him, and their lives may have played little part in his. Thus, it was very difficult in some cases to find dates of death for siblings.

For other parts of the text, inclusion became a matter of choice. For example, where the selected works written by a particular president are presented, recent editions are frequently given rather than the original dates of publication. For the earliest presidents particularly, there exist many collections and selected works of material culled from what may have originally been intended as a pamphlet, newspaper article, diary, or personal letter. For a prolific writer, such as Thomas Jefferson, these selected works, edited in the years since his death, number in the hundreds or even thousands. For later presidents, the decision was made not to include audio recordings. However, microfilm collections are included, especially where the complete papers of a president may not be readily available in published form.

Please note that sources vary in the numbers given for popular vote totals.

In the early years of the nation, presidents carefully balanced their cabinets by selecting members from different states, especially taking care to balance the Northern manufacturing free states and the Southern agricultural slave states. It is, therefore, interesting to observe from which state each cabinet member of the early administrations hails. In recent years, however, state affiliation has become less of a factor and simultaneously less clear-cut to determine. Every attempt has been made to appropriately identify the home state of cabinet members, but people who grew up in one state, attended college in one or two other states, and went on to careers that took them to yet another state or two or three, cannot always be definitively identified with a "home" state. Those who became Washington insiders during many administrations may have lived in D.C., Virginia, or Maryland, but still identified themselves as being "from" the state in which they were reared. Some, too, are identified with the state in which they had a flourishing post-political career or retirement.

The three bulleted lists that are included in each profile are not meant to be comprehensive. The listing of events for every presidency highlights significant legislation, Supreme Court decisions, and executive orders, as well as treaties, conferences, conflicts, territorial changes, and, rarely, significant personal events, such as the death of a spouse or child. The list of US and world events is idiosyncratic at best and is meant to provide perspective. The author freely admits a bias toward including literature (and, since the early twentieth century, film) as these are areas of personal interest—but no less valuable for helping to paint a picture of the time in which the president served. These lists also became longer as the history of our country continued, simply because inhabitants of the modern age are more intimately connected with the rest of the world than our forebears were, who did not have the immediacy of televised images and Internet communication to connect them with events thousands of miles beyond our shores.

The quotations given generally lean toward famous quotations—as there is usually good reason that these particular words have been remembered. I have tried to put them into context with brief explanations. In some cases—Lincoln, Franklin D. Roosevelt, and Kennedy spring to mind—there was an embarrassment of riches from which to choose.

Finally, the biographical essays are deliberately evenhanded in treating the president's entire life. The early years and education are fascinating given the hindsight provided by knowledge of the boy's destiny. With specifics about the events of the presidency provided in the bulleted list that follows, the essay instead tries to examine some of the larger issues and challenges facing the administration, as well as give an evaluation of the president. I have attempted to treat scandals fairly, neither ignoring them nor passing judgment, but recognizing that accusations affected the man, the administration, public perception, and history's assessment.

ACKNOWLEDGMENTS

For initial planning about the approach and format of this book, I have to thank Christine Lindberg and Frank Abate, former colleagues and current friends. Additional research and writing were provided by Debra Argosy, Suzanne Evans, Ian Jackman, and Patti Brecht, all of whom have my heartfelt thanks and deep appreciation. I cannot say enough about the patience and professionalism shown by my editor at Random House, Jena Pincott, and her consistently helpful assistant, Laura Neilson. Their understanding of the trying personal circumstances under which this book was written passes all bounds.

George Washington

Nickname: Father of His Country
Presidency: 1st president, 1789–1797
Party: Federalist (Washington disliked the idea of political parties, but
Washington and Adams came to be identified with the Federalist
party, and the opposition, led by Thomas Jefferson, with the
Republican, or Democratic-Republican, party.)
Life Dates: February 22, 1732–December 14, 1799 (67 years, 295 days)
[Note: Washington's birth date was February 11 under the Julian
calendar and February 22 under the Gregorian calendar adopted in
1751–1752.]

EARLY LIFE AND EDUCATION

George Washington was born on February 22, 1732, at Pope's Creek, Virginia. His father, Augustine Washington, had four children in his first marriage; his second marriage, to Mary Ball Washington, produced six more, of whom George was the eldest. George had a basic education, but the plan to send him to England for further education ended with his father's death, which occurred when George was eleven. George apparently had a close relationship with his older half-brother, Lawrence, who had joined an American regiment in the British army.

George grew to an impressive stature, eventually topping six feet, two inches in height. He was a good rider and hunter who came to the attention of the neighboring aristocratic Fairfax family. Through their patronage, and owing to his talent for mathematics, he began a career in surveying at sixteen. He embraced the western frontier—at that time, just over the Blue Ridge Mountains—and took to the rough conditions and untamed wilderness with enthusiasm.

EARLY MILITARY CAREER

Washington took what would be his only trip outside the country that would become the United States when he accompanied the ailing Lawrence to Barbados. Shortly after the brothers returned to Virginia, Lawrence died from tuberculosis. Following in Lawrence's military footsteps, Washington became a major in the Virginia militia at the age of twenty. He also acquired Lawrence's property, Mount Vernon, first as a leaseholder and eventually as owner.

When the French began laying claim to the Ohio Valley, which the British and the American colonists also claimed, Washington was sent as an envoy to the French. He made an arduous but inconclusive trip to the region in November 1753, and then again in the spring of 1754, when he and his small band of troops encountered a small band of French and decisively defeated them. Unfortunately, the French were outraged by the attack on what they said was a diplomatic mission and the killing of Joseph Coulon, the Sieur de Jumonville, the head of the French mission.

During the ensuing French and Indian War, Washington demonstrated courage and steadfastness, and, moreover, seemed to be the recipient of divine protection. During his long military career he repeatedly rode into the thick of the firing—causing great concern to his aides—and had his horses shot from under him, but never suffered even a minor wound. His military reputation was enhanced by the disastrous expedition led by General Braddock; the British commander ignored Washington's advice about wilderness fighting and was subsequently killed in battle. Washington led the tattered remnants of the expedition in the retreat to safety.

"He is polite with dignity, affable without familiarity, distant without haughtiness, grave without austerity, modest, wise, and good."

Abigail Adams on President Washington, 1789

Despite the military fame he gained in the colonies, Washington was left with feelings of resentment toward the British, who refused to put colonial officers on the same footing as British officers. At the close of the war, he left the military behind and returned to his life as a planter at Mount Vernon.

MARRIAGE
Washington maintained a lifelong friendship and correspondence with Sally Fairfax, the wife of his friend and neighbor George William Fairfax. Although he assured her he loved no one else more, at the age of twenty-seven he married Martha Dandridge Custis, a widow with two children and a large fortune.

Washington enthusiastically immersed himself in managing his large estate; as the owner of a Virginia plantation, he used slave labor. He spent hours each day in the saddle riding through his lands, investigated various aspects of the growing of crops and the breeding of animals, and kept meticulous records of his farming activities. Acting as his own architect, he enlarged the house at Mount Vernon. He enjoyed entertaining a nearly constant stream of guests and was known to appreciate the company of pretty women with whom he could flirt. Like most men of his class, he enjoyed gambling and fox hunting.

CONTINENTAL CONGRESS
Washington entered into colonial politics by becoming a member of Virginia's House of Burgesses and attaining several other local positions. In 1774 he was one of the Burgesses sent to Philadelphia as a delegate to the Continental Congress. When the Second Continental Congress gathered in 1775, after the first battle shots had been fired at Lexington and Concord, Washington said little, but his dress spoke volumes: He appeared in his military uniform, indicating his willingness to fight. John Adams of Massachusetts nominated Washington as leader of the colonial military forces. Adams knew of Washington's military reputation and recognized the need for a southerner in such a position—to secure southern support for armed action against the British. Washington accepted—but refused payment for his services.

THE AMERICAN REVOLUTION
The new general hastened to the besieged city of Boston, which was under British control. He found unorganized and undisciplined troops, as well as problems with supplies, including food, clothing, and arms. Although he imposed a strict order—including the use of corporal punishment—he was known as a fair leader who rewarded his soldiers on the basis of merit (rather than social class). His efforts to mold the men into an army of efficient soldiers were greatly hampered by the fact that the soldiers' terms of service usually lasted for only a few months. And often the Continental Congress was either unwilling or unable to pay the soldiers, making it more difficult for Washington to convince them to re-enlist.

In January 1776 the American forces finally acquired some artillery by hauling guns captured at Fort Ticonderoga over frozen ground to Boston. The guns were mounted on Dorchester Heights above Boston, and in March the British withdrew their forces, escaping by ship. That following summer, the British under the command of General Howe landed in Manhattan and easily defeated the Americans in a skirmish, but Washington managed, as he was to do so repeatedly, to withdraw his troops to safety. In July 1776 the Declaration of Independence arrived from Philadelphia and was read to the troops.

"I heard the bullets whistle and, believe me, there is something charming in the sound."

Colonel Washington after his first skirmish against the French in the Ohio Valley, 1754

Knowing that his untrained troops would be unlikely to prevail against the British in a pitched battle, Washington avoided a confrontation as much as possible. But in late December 1776, Washington faced the irresistible temptation to take the enemy by surprise. Crossing the Delaware River and marching at night through severe winter weather, the Americans took the Hessian troops at Trenton, New Jersey by surprise and won a stunning victory. Washington's troops caught more than nine hundred men without losing a single American soldier.

During 1777 Washington was unable to win a decisive victory over the British. There was a battle at Brandywine Creek, which failed to prevent the British from taking Philadelphia, and another at Germantown, during which troops ran out of ammunition and retreated in a fog that obscured targets. But in northern New York, troops led by General Horatio Gates halted the British advance from Canada at Saratoga and forced the commanding officer, General Burgoyne, to surrender more than 5,000 troops. One American officer who distinguished himself at the Battle of Saratoga was Benedict Arnold.

In winter quarters at Valley Forge, Pennsylvania, Washington struggled to hold his army together under difficult conditions, battling not only the severe weather and the lack of basic supplies, but also an attempt by Gates to either replace Washington or discredit him. Gates was joined in this effort by an Irish-born French soldier, General Thomas Conway, who had volunteered to join the American cause. The so-called "Conway Cabal" against Washington was ultimately defeated because Washington had the support of the Congress.

An alliance with France finally materialized, when France officially declared war against Britain on July 10, 1778, but the arrival of French troops failed to have the expected effect. For the most part, the French were unwilling to put themselves entirely under the command of Washington. Concerted action between the two armies nearly always failed, and French naval help was intermittent at best.

The next three years saw a series of inconclusive battles, including that at Monmouth, New Jersey, in June 1778, at which General Charles Lee, who considered himself a superior tactician to Washington, disregarded Washington's orders (Lee was subsequently court-martialed). At the battle at Camden, South Carolina, in August 1780, the British forces led by General Charles Cornwallis defeated the Americans under General Horatio Gates.

During more punishing winters, Washington endured a mutiny among the troops, as well as Benedict Arnold's treachery in attempting to turn West Point over to the British. Ultimately, the British could not overcome their many disadvantages: Men and supplies had to arrive by ship from a great distance, the war was expensive, they were never able to subdue the citizens or hold territory for any length of time. Furthermore, the American soldiers steadily learned from the mistakes of the British to become experienced soldiers. The Americans were also willing to undergo tremendous hardships and deprivations, to march long distances, and adapt their style of fighting to the terrain. Washington's strengths as a commander included his ability to inspire loyalty from his troops, as well as his recognition that the ability to endure military hardships was more important than risking everything for a chancy victory.

General George Washington crossing the Delaware in December, 1776.

Finally, in 1781, the French fleet under de Grasse forced the British fleet to retreat from the Chesapeake Bay, and French forces under Rochambeau joined Washington's troops in surrounding Cornwallis at Yorktown. Besieged by these troops and deprived of support or a means of escape by the now-absent British fleet, Cornwallis surrendered on October 19, 1781. The war dragged on a while longer, but in 1782 the peace negotiations were underway and in April 1783 an armistice was announced in advance of the peace treaty being signed.

During the relative inaction of the winter of 1782–1783, some of Washington's officers, impatient with the failure of Congress to pay the army, contemplated seizing power. Washington addressed a meeting of the officers, appealing to their love of country. Endeavoring to read a letter from a member of Congress, he pulled out a pair of eyeglasses and said, "Gentlemen, you will permit me to put on my spectacles, for I have grown not only gray but almost blind in the service of my country." Greatly moved by this more than by his arguments, the officers agreed to wait, and Washington managed to secure some money from Congress to pay them, granted leaves of absence to many, and

averted yet another disaster for the fledgling country.

BRIEF RETURN TO PRIVATE LIFE

At the close of the war, Washington astonished the world by resigning his commission. No victorious and popular general had, at the successful conclusion of a revolution, ever voluntarily handed power over to civilian authorities. But Washington believed sincerely in the democratic ideals of the Revolution and desired nothing more than a return to his wife, his home, and his peacetime occupation of farming. He returned to Mount Vernon on December 24, 1783, envisioning for himself a few years surrounded by family and friends before the coming of his demise—he had already passed the age at which his father had died. Mount Vernon itself, now stretching for ten miles along the Potomac River, gave him ample scope for his energies, as he resumed his riding around his properties, engaging in agricultural experiments, and entertaining the many visitors who made their way to his home.

But the next few years of independence made it abundantly clear that the thirteen states needed a central authority stronger than that provided for by the Articles of Confederation. In issues of trade, taxation, payment of the national debt, issuance of currency, defense, transportation, and relationships with other countries, a strong central government was required. As circumstances stood, there was no way to raise money still owed to the soldiers of the Revolution and those who had supplied the army with goods, much less to fund an army or navy to protect the new country. The worst fears of concerned Americans seemed to be realized by Shays' Rebellion in 1786–1787, a large uprising in western Massachusetts which demanded relief from debt, taxes, currency fluctuations, and other ills of the unregulated economy. The rebellion was quashed by militia and private troops, but many took it as a warning of the anarchy that could arise from the loose confederation of states.

Washington was convinced to leave Mount Vernon for Philadelphia to preside over the Constitutional Convention in 1787, where the new Constitution was written. It embodied many ideas that Washington espoused, although he offered little direct comment during discussions. His greatest influence on the proceedings and the document produced by them may have been that it was universally assumed that the chief executive of the new government could be no other man than George Washington. His presiding over the proceedings and his signature on the new Constitution were powerful inducements for the various states to ratify the Constitution.

Following the procedures outlined in the new Constitution, the Electoral College unanimously elected Washington to the presidency. Each elector actually cast two votes, without differentiating between the offices of president and vice president, but every one of the sixty-nine electors cast one vote for Washington. The second highest number of votes, thirty-four, was received by John Adams, who therefore became vice president.

PRESIDENCY

President Washington was aware, from the moment he began considering the office into which he was inaugurated on April 30, 1789, that he

would be establishing precedents for every subsequent president. As soon as the Congress established the various departments of government, he set about making appointments to fill the newly created positions. After trying to gather advice in a variety of ways, such as corresponding with the heads of the departments and visiting Congress, he settled on forming a cabinet and holding meetings with these men as his advisors, a practice that has continued into the twenty-first century. Washington soon found that he could not welcome visitors without appointments, as he had begun to receive such a steady stream of visitors that he could not get his work done. As a result, he founded a tradition of three different types of weekly gatherings: a levee for men only, tea parties given by Martha Washington for men and women, and dinner parties. Another decision made early into Washington's first term was the location of the new nation's capital in the District of Columbia, on the Potomac River.

One of the first orders of business for the new government, undertaken by Secretary of the Treasury Alexander Hamilton, was to resolve the national debt that had been incurred, some of it as far back as pre-revolutionary days. Hamilton urged the creation of a national bank, but this issue raised a storm of controversy. There was the argument that, by strict interpretation, the Constitution did not allow for the creation of institutions; those in favor of the bank argued that the Constitution implied the power to do so—and the dichotomy between "strict construction" and the "implied powers" of loose construction also persists to the present day. Hamilton eventually gained Washington's support and the bank was created.

Washington had hoped to retire after one term as president, but the country seemed too unsettled, both domestically and in its foreign relations, for him to take this step (and in the face of pleas for him to stay on). This period was also marked by the French Revolution and the question of which position the United States should take in the matter. Many Americans were warmly enthusiastic about the revolutionary government of France, seeing it as a parallel to their own recent history. But the new government of France was also at war with Great Britain in the wake of the execution of the French monarchs, and Washington perceived that there would be a danger if his own country were to ally itself with either side in the European conflict. Accordingly, soon after the start of his second term, Washington issued the Neutrality Proclamation in April 1793. This represented a position he espoused repeatedly—that the United States should avoid foreign entanglements.

The new French minister to the United States, Edmond Charles Genet, assumed from the enthusiastic reception he received in the United States that he could defy Washington with impunity. In defiance of the US government, he began outfitting privateers to attack British shipping. Washington asked the French government to recall Genet, but when Genet's replacement, Joseph Fauchet, arrived with a warrant for Genet's arrest, Washington gave Genet asylum in the United States, fearing that he would be guillotined if he returned to France.

Washington obtained a more positive result when he sent General Anthony Wayne to deal with conflicts between American settlers and Native Americans over land ownership, which resulted in a battle and "Mad Anthony's" victory at Fallen Timbers in 1794. Because the British did not aid their Native American allies, this also served to fracture the alliance.

But because Britain ruled the seas, it was imperative for the US government to make an agreement with the British that would protect American ships. Accordingly, Washington sent John Jay to London. When the Jay Treaty arrived in the United States in 1795, it unleashed a storm of protest from the faction led by Jefferson and Madison. Under the treaty, the British agreed to evacuate forts they held in the Great Lakes region and to compensate some US ship owners for ships that the British had seized. However, the treaty did not recognize US neutrality and offered such restrictive terms of trade with the West Indies—a prime American market—that the US Senate rejected that part of the treaty as it accepted the other provisions.

A further complication arose when the House of Representatives demanded that Washington turn over to it all papers relevant to the treaty. Washington categorically refused, arguing that secrecy was sometimes necessary in the handling of foreign affairs, and that the legislative branch had no constitutional right to his papers.

> "With me, a predominant motive has been to endeavor to gain time to our country to settle and mature its yet recent institutions, and to progress without interruption to that degree of strength and consistency, which is necessary to give it, humanly speaking, the command of its own fortunes."
>
> President Washington,
> *Farewell Address*, 1796

A treaty with Spain was more popular. It opened the Mississippi to American shipping at last, making the prospect for settlement and prosperity on the frontier much more promising.

Washington, with the aid of Hamilton, prepared a Farewell Address at the end of his second term. In it he repeated his views on the importance of national union and his conviction that the greatest threats to union were foreign entanglements and party politics. He noted that a form of protection for the US government existed in the system of checks and balances provided for in the Constitution, and he urged the joint guidance of religion and morality for the nation's citizens. Washington was firm in his desire to leave the presidency after two terms and have the next president chosen as the Constitution provided; accordingly, John Adams was elected to the presidency and Thomas Jefferson, with the second highest number of votes, became vice president.

WASHINGTON IN RETIREMENT

Returning to Mount Vernon, Washington set about making repairs to the house, putting the plantation in order, and marshalling his business affairs. He had invested in western lands since his youth, but like most southern plantation owners, he was rich in land but cash-poor. In making his will, he provided for the freeing of his slaves and the support of those who were underage and elderly, for as long as was necessary.

In 1798, confronted by the possibility that the United States might be facing a French invasion, President John Adams appointed Washington as the commander in chief of the army. Washington worried a good deal about the selection of the officers who would serve under him, but eventually diplomatic channels served to smooth relations with France and he was not required to embark on a military campaign.

In December 1799 Washington rode out to inspect his farms (as he did nearly every day). He rode through snow, hail, and rain. A day later he had developed a sore throat and soon became seriously ill. As treatment, various physicians bled him and applied poultices. It is unknown whether his final illness was a streptococcal infection, diphtheria, or some other infection of the throat, but he died on December 14, 1799. He was buried in a simple brick crypt he had ordered to be constructed at Mount Vernon.

CONCLUSION

During his presidency, Washington faced, and protected his fledgling country from, a wide array of potential threats. He remained firm in his conviction that the United States must avoid foreign entanglements, and he refused to be drawn into the conflict between France and Great Britain. The need for a treaty with Great Britain was driven by the need to ensure American prosperity via the protection of American shipping and trade. He upheld the importance of national union, both by regular appointments of men from northern and southern states (so that neither part of the country would claim favoritism toward the other), and by his strong action in suppressing the Whiskey Rebellion, thus simultaneously upholding the rule of law and negating the possibility of secession. He carefully outlined the role and duties of the executive office by offering strong leadership without a hint of monarchical pretension, and by deferring to the legislative branch when he deemed that the Constitution required him to do so, but without needlessly conceding any of the executive power (as when he refused to turn over his papers to Congress).

"To the memory of the man, first in war, first in peace, and first in the hearts of his countrymen."

Eulogy on Washington, December 1799, by Colonel Henry Lee, father of Robert E. Lee

During the more than two centuries that have passed since his presidency, he has consistently been considered one of the greatest US presidents and one of history's greatest Americans. It is impossible to conceive of the birth of the nation absent his contributions. Without his integrity, determination, and character, the history of the United States as an independent, democratic nation might not have occurred at all.

Birthplace: Pope's Creek, Westmoreland County, VA
Residency: Virginia
Religion: Episcopalian
Education: limited formal schooling; no college
Place of Death: Mount Vernon, VA
Burial Site: Family vault, Mount Vernon, VA
Dates in Office: April 30, 1789–March 3, 1797 (7 years, 3 days)
Age at Inauguration: 57 years, 67 days

FAMILY

Father: Augustine Washington (1694–1743)
Mother: Mary Ball Washington (1708–1789)
Siblings: George Washington's father had four children by his first wife: Butler Washington (1716–1716); Lawrence Washington (1718–1752); Augustine Washington (1720–1762); Jane Washington (1722–1735). Mary Ball Washington was Augustine Washington's second wife, by whom he had six children—George was the eldest of these, and his other siblings were Elizabeth "Betty" Washington (1733–1797); Samuel Washington (1734–1781); John Augustine Washington (1736–1787); Charles Washington (1738–1799); Mildred Washington (1739–1740).
Wife: Martha Dandridge Custis Washington (1731–1802), married January 6, 1759, at New Kent County, VA. Before her marriage to Washington, Martha was the widow of Daniel Parke Custis, by whom she had had four children—two of whom died in infancy.
Children: none; two stepchildren: John Parke Custis ("Jackie"; 1754–1781) and Martha Parke Custis ("Patsy"; 1757–1773)

CAREER

Private: Surveyor, planter
Military: Major in the VA militia (1752); colonel in the VA regiment (1754); aide-de-camp to General Braddock in the French and Indian War (1754–1763); after a battle near Fort Duquesne, PA, in which Braddock was killed, he led the remaining troops in retreat; colonel in the VA regiment (1755–1758) and leader of VA forces in the defense of the western border; general and commander-in-chief of the Continental forces during the American Revolutionary War (1775–1783)
Political: Virginia House of Burgesses (1758); justice of the peace, Fairfax County (1770); delegate to the Williamsburg Convention (1771); delegate to the First Continental Congress (1774); delegate to the Second Continental Congress (1775); delegate and president of the Constitutional Convention 1787); president of the United States (1789–1797)
Selected Works: *Rules of Civility: The 110 Precepts that Guided Our First President in War and Peace*, ed. and with commentary by Richard Brookhiser (Charlottesville: University of Virginia Press, 2003); *The Writings of George Washington from the Original Manuscript Sources 1746–1799*, 39 vols., ed. by John C. Fitzpatrick (Westport, CT: Greenwood Press, 1970)

PRESIDENCY

Nomination: No formal nomination process existed; during the Constitutional Convention that convened in 1787 to draft the Constitution, it was assumed by all that Washington was the only choice for president.
Election: 1789: unanimously elected by the newly formed Electoral College on February 4, 1789

1792: unanimously elected on February 13, 1793, by the Electoral College
Opponent: Washington had no opponent.
Vote Totals: 1789: Each of the 69 electors cast two votes without making a distinction between voting for president and vice president; Washington received 69 votes, or one from each elector; the next highest number of votes was received by John Adams of MA, with 34 votes, who became vice president; among others who received votes were John Jay of NY (9 votes); Robert Harrison of MD (6 votes); and John Rutledge of SC (6 votes).

1792: Each of the 132 electors voting cast one vote for Washington, thus electing him unanimously; the next highest number of votes was again John Adams of MA, who continued as vice president, having received 77 votes; among others who received votes were George Clinton of NY (50 votes); Thomas Jefferson of VA (4 votes); and Aaron Burr of NY (1 vote).
Inauguration: April 30, 1789, in New York City, and March 4, 1793, in Philadelphia
Vice President: John Adams, MA (1789–1797)

CABINET

Secretary of State: Thomas Jefferson, VA (1789–1793); Edmund Randolph, VA (1794–1795); Timothy Pickering, MA (1795–1797)
Secretary of the Treasury: Alexander Hamilton, NY (1789–1795); Oliver Wolcott, Jr., CT (1795–1797)

Secretary of War: Henry Knox, MA (1789–1794); Timothy Pickering, MA (1795–1796); James McHenry, MD (1796–1797)
Attorney General: Edmund Randolph, VA (1789–1794); William Bradford, PA (1794–1795); Charles Lee, VA (1795–1797)
Postmaster General: Samuel Osgood, MA (1789–1791); Timothy Pickering, MA (1791–1795); Joseph Habersham, GA (1795–1797)

CONGRESS

1st Congress (1789–1791); Speaker of the House: Frederick A. C. Muhlenberg (PA, Federalist)
2nd Congress (1791–1793); Speaker of the House: Jonathan Trumbull, Jr. (CT, Federalist)
3rd Congress (1793–1795); Speaker of the House: Frederick A. C. Muhlenberg (PA, Republican)
4th Congress (1795–1797); Speaker of the House: Jonathan Dayton (NJ, Federalist)

SUPREME COURT APPOINTEES

John Jay, NY; Chief Justice (1789–1795)
James Wilson, PA; Associate Justice (1789–1798)
John Rutledge, SC; Associate Justice (1790–1791), Chief Justice (1795)
William Cushing, MA; Associate Justice (1790–1810)
John Blair, VA; Associate Justice (1790–1795)
James Iredell, NC; Associate Justice (1790–1799)
Thomas Johnson, MD; Associate Justice (1792–1793)
William Paterson, NJ; Associate Justice (1793–1806)
Oliver Ellsworth, CT; Chief Justice (1796–1800)
Samuel Chase, MD; Associate Justice (1796–1811)

MAJOR EVENTS OF THE WASHINGTON ADMINISTRATION

◆ Congress creates the departments of State, War, and Treasury, 1789.
◆ Congress passes the Federal Judiciary Act, 1789, which authorizes creation of the Supreme Court and the federal judicial system.
◆ Vermont becomes a state, March 4, 1791.
◆ The Bill of Rights is ratified, December 15, 1791.

◆ Kentucky becomes a state, June 1, 1792.
◆ Washington issues a Neutrality Proclamation, 1793, stating that the United States would not side with either Great Britain or revolutionary France in the conflict between the two powers.
◆ The Fugitive Slave Act, 1793, which enforces Article IV, Section 2, of the US Constitution, authorizes any federal district judge, circuit court judge, or state magistrate to decide (without a jury trial) the status of any slave alleged to be a fugitive.
◆ Washington lays the cornerstone of the US Capitol, September 18, 1793.
◆ The Whiskey Rebellion, 1794, a protest by farmers in western Pennsylvania against the whiskey excise tax, is put down by a force of more than 10,000 militiamen called by Washington.
◆ The Battle of Fallen Timbers, August 20, 1794, at which General Anthony Wayne defeats a Native American force of more than 1,000 men, helps to secure the Ohio territory for American settlers.
◆ The Jay Treaty with Great Britain, 1795, in which Britain agrees to leave posts in the Great Lakes area and to restore some of the property it acquired during its seizure of US ships, causes an uproar, especially among Americans who sympathize with the French revolutionaries.
◆ The Treaty with Spain, 1795, gives Americans access to the lower Mississippi.
◆ The Naturalization Act, 1795, makes a residency of five years a requirement for US citizenship.
◆ Tennessee becomes a state, June 1, 1796.
◆ Washington refuses to turn his papers regarding the Jay Treaty over to the House of Representatives, 1796.
◆ Washington's *Farewell Address*, 1796

MAJOR US AND WORLD EVENTS, 1789–1797

◆ The French Revolution begins, 1789.
◆ William Blake publishes *Songs of Innocence*, 1789.
◆ First US census estimates population at 4 million people, 1790.

◆ Thomas Paine publishes *The Rights of Man*, 1791.

◆ Boswell publishes *The Life of Samuel Johnson*, 1791.

◆ The New York Stock Exchange is organized, 1792.

◆ The Treaty of Jassy ends the Russo-Turkish War, 1792.

◆ Mozart conducts the first performance of *The Magic Flute*, 1791; he dies later that same year.

◆ Eli Whitney invents the cotton gin, 1793.

◆ King Louis XVI and Queen Marie Antoinette of France are executed by guillotine, 1793.

◆ Robert Burns composes "Auld Lang Syne," 1794.

◆ Napoleon Bonaparte commands troops that put down a royalist uprising in France, 1795.

◆ English physician Edward Jenner uses cowpox to create an inoculation against smallpox, 1796.

FAST FACTS ABOUT GEORGE WASHINGTON

◆ Many of the popular (but purely imaginary) stories about Washington, including the fable about the cherry tree, are based on biographies written by Mason Locke Weems (Parson Weems) after Washington's death.

◆ The wooden teeth Washington supposedly wore are another fiction; he did wear false teeth in his later years, but these were made of such materials as hippopotamus ivory—which became badly stained from red wine.

◆ As a young man, Washington was ready to join the British navy, but at the last minute was dissuaded by his mother, possibly because she had heard that colonials did not advance in the British navy.

◆ The only time Washington left the area that would become the United States was when he accompanied his ill half-brother Lawrence to Barbados; Washington himself contracted smallpox on the trip, which gave him immunity later in his life, when so many Revolutionary War soldiers succumbed to that disease.

◆ One of Washington's contributions to agriculture was the breeding of generations of strong and hardy mules from a jackass named Royal Gift, given to Washington by the king of Spain; after Royal Gift had sired mules at Mount Vernon, Washington hired him out, eventually sending him on a thousand-mile tour of the southern states.

◆ When Washington became president, the executive branch of government consisted of two people: himself and his vice president, John Adams.

◆ Washington was the only president inaugurated in two different cities, New York in 1789 and Philadelphia in 1793.

◆ Washington established a number of presidential customs, including that of addressing the US chief executive as simply "Mr. President."

◆ Washington was a member of the Freemasons, an international fraternal organization that is known for its highly secretive ceremonies.

John Adams

Nickname: Atlas of Independence, Architect of the Revolution,
Colossus of Debate, Colossus of Independence, His Rotundity,
Duke of Braintree
Presidency: 2nd president, 1797–1801
Party: Federalist
Life Dates: October 30, 1735–July 4, 1826 (90 years, 247 days)
[Note: Adams's birth date was October 19 under the Julian calendar
and October 30 under the Gregorian calendar adopted in 1751–1752.]

EARLY LIFE AND EDUCATION

John Adams was born on October 30, 1735, in Braintree (a section of town later renamed Quincy), Massachusetts. He was the first of three sons born to John Adams and Susanna Boylston Adams. The family lived on a farm not far from the ocean that had been in the Adams family for generations. The elder John Adams was well respected locally and served as a deacon of the church and a selectman of the town; he worked as a farmer and a shoemaker. The future president was educated first at a dame school (taught by a woman in her own home), then at another local school where he lost interest in his studies and decided he would rather be a farmer. His father, after allowing him to dig ditches for a day, gently but firmly sent him back to school. When the boy indicated he disliked his teacher rather than the schooling, his father arranged for him to go to school elsewhere. At age fifteen he enrolled at Harvard College, from which he graduated in 1755.

Young Adams enjoyed his college days and developed a love of books and learning that remained with him throughout his life—even when traveling, he generally carried a book in his pocket. His family had hoped he would be-come a clergyman, but Adams recognized he was not suited for that profession. He decided to study law and took a teaching position in Worcester, Massachusetts, to earn the fee he would need to pay an established attorney for the privilege of studying in his law office. Adams was bored by teaching and spent much of his time dreaming about a more glorious career for himself. After a year he began studying with a lawyer named James Putnam; he continued teaching during the day while spending his nights immersed in books. In 1758 he returned home to Braintree, helping on the family farm while preparing to be admitted to the bar, which occurred later that year.

EARLY CAREER

Adams's list of clients grew slowly, but as he developed his law practice, he gained a reputation as an effective orator. He was elected a selectman in Braintree, but his practice kept him traveling throughout the Boston area. Among his friends were other young lawyers, including Samuel Quincy. Adams met Samuel's sister Hannah Quincy and was attracted to her, but during an evening when he was thinking of proposing, another couple came into the room and the opportunity vanished. Hannah married another of Adams's friends a year later. Yet another friend began courting Mary Smith, the daughter of the Reverend William Smith of Weymouth, and he introduced Adams to Mary's sisters, Abigail and Elizabeth. Five years later, in 1764, Abigail and John were married in a ceremony performed by her father. Throughout their long marriage, they exchanged many letters, which have revealed not only Abigail's lively, well-informed mind and interest in politics, but also their tender affection for each other and their children.

"Let us read and recollect and impress upon our souls the views and ends of our own more immediate forefathers, in exchanging their native country for a dreary, inhospitable wilderness. . . . Let us recollect it was liberty, the hope of liberty for themselves and us and ours, which conquered all discouragements, dangers, and trials."

John Adams, *A Dissertation on the Canon and Feudal Law*, 1765

In 1765 the British Parliament imposed the Stamp Act on the American colonies. It demanded that a special stamp appear on virtually every piece of printed matter in the colonies (and was thus a tax on all printed matter), and was intended to raise money to defray the costs of defending the colonies, especially the frontier and certain trading posts. It aroused a storm of protest in the colonies because the colonial legislatures had not been consulted or allowed to vote on the act. In the wake of the popular protest, Adams wrote a series of essays that appeared in the *Boston Gazette* newspaper; the es-

says were then collected and published as *A Dissertation on the Canon and Feudal Law*. Adams surveyed the transition from medieval to modern forms of law, noting that, in English law, the rights enjoyed by English citizens were a gift from God, not a favor bestowed by a king or parliament. He noted that a well-educated, politically active populace was necessary for liberty to be maintained.

Adams was well known for his patriot views in Boston, but in 1770, when British soldiers opened fire on a mob of protesters and killed five men, Adams agreed to defend the soldiers and suffered harsh public criticism for his decision. Six of the eight soldiers as well as the captain who commanded them were found innocent; two were found guilty of manslaughter. Adams had taken the case in part because he believed that everyone had the right to a fair trial, but he also used his summation to make the point that the real problem was the unpopular practice of quartering British soldiers in civilian households.

POLITICAL CAREER

In 1770 Adams was elected as a representative to the Massachusetts legislature. Owing to the demands of politics and those of his law career, his health was seriously affected, but the family moved from Boston back to Braintree and his health improved. In 1774 he was chosen by the legislature as a representative to the first Continental Congress, although that meeting accomplished little beyond an agreement by its members not to import goods from Great Britain unless the Coercive Acts, which had closed the port of Boston, were repealed.

In late 1774 and early 1775, Adams wrote articles and pamphlets under the pen name "Novanglus," arguing that Americans were only trying to maintain their traditional rights and liberties in the face of unreasonable demands from Great Britain.

At the second Continental Congress in 1776, Adams advocated naming George Washington as commander of the Continental Army. He then plunged into tireless work on various committees, including his acting as head of the important Board of War. He spoke often and persuasively in favor of declaring independence, while some delegates continued to hope for a reconciliation with Great Britain. When the decision was made, Adams was on the committee to prepare the Declaration of Independence, though committee members agreed that Thomas Jefferson should draft the document. Adams himself wrote *Thoughts on Government* early in 1776, advocating a system of government with two legislative houses and an independent judiciary.

"We have not men fit for the times. We are deficient in genius, education, in travel, fortune—in everything. I feel unutterable anxiety."

John Adams in his diary, June 25, 1774

Adams spent a few months at home at the end of 1777 before leaving, in early 1778, for Paris, where he would act as a commissioner and attempt to enlist the aid of the French in the American cause. He took ten-year-old John Quincy Adams, his second child and eldest son, with him. Left at home with Abigail were the other children: Abigail (nicknamed Nabby), and two more sons, Charles and Thomas. Another daughter, Susanna, had lived only two years and died in 1770.

By the time he arrived in Paris, Adams learned that the French had already agreed to aid the Americans. While there, Adams visited and stayed with Benjamin Franklin. Although he did not approve of Franklin's dissolute lifestyle and thought that Franklin was too friendly with the French for his liking, Adams recognized that Franklin was nonetheless the man best suited to deal with them. Adams and his son returned home in 1779, Franklin having been appointed as sole minister to France by the Congress.

Back in Massachusetts, Adams was selected as a delegate to the state constitutional convention and wrote the new state constitution almost entirely by himself. Advocating a "government of laws, not men," the document provided for three independent branches of government—executive, legislative, and judicial. It also provided for two legislative houses and for appointed, rather than elected, judges for the state Supreme Court.

ADAMS RETURNS TO EUROPE

Late in 1779, Adams received word that Congress had appointed him minister plenipotentiary and was asking him to return to France, this time to negotiate a peace treaty with Great Britain and to arrange for a trade agreement as well. Taking both John Quincy and Charles Adams with him, Adams set off. In February 1780 they finally reached Paris.

Adams's mission was complicated by his instructions to work closely with the French foreign minister, Comte Charles de Vergennes, who was irritated by Adams's blunt style and his insistence that the United States was an equal of France, not a client state. Adams continually asked for the promised naval aid, certain that it was essential to the successful conclusion of the war (correctly: the victory at Yorktown was, in fact, dependent on the presence of the French fleet).

Having made himself unpopular in France, Adams went to the Netherlands in the spring of 1781, seeking recognition of the United States as a sovereign country and hoping to arrange a loan. He was extremely ill during the late summer, probably with malaria or typhus, but slowly recovered. In June 1782 he secured a $5 million loan from several Dutch financiers, and in October he signed a treaty of commerce with the Dutch Republic.

As soon as the treaty was signed, Adams returned to Paris to join the other American envoys, including John Jay, in the ongoing negotiations for peace with Great Britain. On September 3, 1783, the treaty with Great Britain was at last signed, by Adams, Franklin, and Jay on behalf of the new nation.

In early 1784 Abigail and Nabby sailed to Europe to join Adams, who had been asked to conclude a commercial treaty with Great Britain. They settled in Paris, where they were soon joined by Thomas Jefferson and his daughter Martha (called Patsy). During this time, Jefferson became a friend to the whole Adams family, working with John but dining often with John, Abigail, Nabby, and John Quincy (Thomas having returned home to continue his schooling).

MINISTER TO GREAT BRITAIN

In April 1785 word came from Congress that Adams had been appointed minister to Great Britain and Jefferson had been appointed to succeed Franklin as minister to France. The Adams family, somewhat regretfully, left behind happy times in France and moved to London; John Quincy Adams returned to the United States to enter Harvard.

> "I must study politics and war that my sons may have liberty to study mathematics and philosophy. My sons ought to study mathematics and philosophy, geography, natural history, naval architecture, navigation, commerce and agriculture, in order to give their children a right to study painting, poetry, music, architecture, statuary, tapestry, and porcelain."
>
> John Adams in a letter to Abigail Adams, May 12, 1780

Although formally received at court, Adams found himself ridiculed in the British press and unable to make headway in his objectives. America asked Britain to comply with the terms of the Treaty of Paris and withdraw from various forts in the northwestern United States (in the Ohio Valley), and made it clear that it was vitally important that trade between the United States and the British West Indies be restored. Britain, in its turn, asked America to pay British creditors.

Despite the frustration of his official position, Adams was able to enjoy a visit from Jefferson in the spring of 1786; the two men took a week-long tour of English gardens. In June, Nabby Adams married William Stephens Smith, a New Yorker who had been appointed as secretary to the American legation in London. And in the late summer, Abigail accompanied Adams to the Netherlands, where he signed a trade agreement with Prussia. The following January, Adams and Jefferson signed a pact with Morocco, agreeing that the United States would pay for their mutual protection against the Barbary pirates who were seizing commercial ships in Mediterranean waters near North Africa.

Adams wrote and published *A Defence of the Constitutions of Government of the United States of America*, putting forth his arguments for three branches of government: a strong executive branch, a bicameral legislature, and an independent judiciary. The work was well received in the United States and would be cited by delegates to the Constitutional Convention, which began in late May 1787. By December, Adams finally received word that his request to be recalled had been approved, and the family arrived back in the United States in June 1788.

VICE PRESIDENCY

Adams returned to a hero's welcome in Massachusetts. He bought another home in Quincy and settled into improving the property and farming amidst rumors about his future. In February 1789 the presidential electors met and chose Washington as president. With the second-highest number of votes, Adams became vice president.

The new government gathered in New York, and Adams took his place in presiding over the Senate. Remaining on the sidelines while others debated the issues did not come naturally to Adams, but after a time he settled into his role, which included casting the deciding vote when there was a tie in the Senate. His decisions were invariably in favor of a strong federal government and a strong executive, which made some accuse him of wanting to impose a monarchy. The Congress was considering such questions as how to address the president and whether to sit or stand when he came into their presence; Adams tended to prefer greater formality, as he wished to enhance the power of the office. When he suggested that Washington be addressed as "His Majesty the President," though, critics ridiculed Adams by dubbing him "His Rotundity."

"He means well for his country, is always an honest man, often a wise one, but sometimes and in some things, absolutely out of his senses."

Benjamin Franklin about John Adams, in a letter to Robert Livingston, July 22, 1783

Despite the similarity of their views, Washington rarely consulted Adams. Shortly after Washington became persuaded to serve another term, and he and Adams had been reelected in 1792, Adams wrote to Abigail, "My country in its wisdom has contrived for me the most insignificant office that ever the invention of man contrived or his imagination conceived." In March 1793 the second inauguration took place in Philadelphia, as the government had moved there in 1790. During Washington's second term a new site for the nation's capital (along the Potomac River) was chosen, as a concession to the southern states and in exchange for their acceptance of Alexander Hamilton's economic plan.

Adams was accused of being pro-British just as the French Revolution began (in late 1789), and a wave of pro-French enthusiasm swept across America. Revolutionary France was soon at war with Great Britain; despite the bond between France and the United States, Washington was firmly convinced that to side with France against Great Britain would be disastrous for the young United States, and he issued a proclamation of neutrality in 1793.

The differing viewpoints among members of the government began to crystallize along party lines. Although Washington abhorred the idea of party politics, Washington, Adams, and Hamilton were identified with the Federalist party, which favored a strong federal government that could override the decisions of the state legislatures and which hoped to improve relations—especially trade relations—with Great Britain. Thomas Jefferson and James Madison were among those known as Republicans or Democratic-Republicans; they supported states' rights and were generally enthusiastic about the French Revolution.

Abigail remained at home during much of the time that Adams was vice president, partly so that she could run the farm and ensure the family's income, and partly because she was sometimes ill and found traveling difficult. During the summers, when Congress was not in session and Philadelphia was prone to devastating outbreaks of yellow fever, Adams would return home, welcoming the chance to be with Abigail and spend time farming.

PRESIDENCY

Washington left office after two terms, hoping to establish the precedent of a peaceful transition of power. In 1796 Adams won the presidency seventy-one to sixty-eight, having received three more electoral votes than Jefferson. Despite the fact that they belonged to different political parties, Jefferson became Adams's vice president—a situation not foreseen by the framers of the Constitution, who had not provided for political parties as part of the American system.

The leading concern of Adams's presidency was the situation in Revolutionary France and the conflict between France and Great Britain, into which it seemed the United States would be drawn. Republicans assumed that Adams and the Federalists would join Great Britain against France, and many Federalists wanted to do just that. But Adams pursued diplomacy, appointing three envoys to France—Charles C. Pinckney, John Marshall, and Elbridge Gerry.

In what came to be called the XYZ Affair, the American envoys in Paris were visited by three agents (referred to in coded messages to the United States as X, Y, and Z) of the French foreign minister, Charles Maurice de Talleyrand-Perigord. The French agents demanded bribes—both for Talleyrand and in the form of loans to France—before the Americans would be received by Talleyrand. The Americans refused; both Pinckney and Marshall left Paris.

> **"I will never send another minister to France, without assurances that he will be received, respected, and honored, as the representative of a great, free, powerful, and independent nation."**
>
> John Adams in a message to Congress in the wake of the XYZ Affair, 1798

The news of the XYZ Affair enflamed the United States and many considered war with France inevitable. Adams called for increased military preparations, appointing George Washington as commander of the army and urging the development of an American navy. And, in the most widely criticized move of his presidency, Adams signed into law the Alien and Sedition Acts of 1798, which increased the time to become a naturalized citizen from five to fourteen years; empowered the president to deport any alien considered dangerous; made it a crime to write anything "false, scandalous, or malicious" about the president, Congress, or the government; and made attempts to stir up sedition a crime.

Though Adams later defended the Acts as "war measures," Republicans were aghast at what they saw as a violation of the First Amendment guarantee of free speech. Madison and Jefferson responded by writing the Virginia and Kentucky Resolutions, respectively, which argued that states had the right to nullify any federal law deemed unconstitutional.

Adams continued to await further news from France and hope for a diplomatic solution. Elbridge Gerry, who had stayed behind in Paris when Pinckney and Marshall left, eventually returned to the United States with the welcome news that the French wished to avoid a war.

Adams then appointed the minister to The Hague, William Vans Murray, as a special envoy to the French Republic. The Hamiltonian Federalists (nominally Adams's own party) objected strenuously, and Adams compromised by agreeing to appoint a commission. The commission concluded a treaty with France on September 30, 1800—although the news didn't reach the United States until too late to aid Adams in the election. He was defeated by Jefferson in 1800.

In January 1801 Adams made a fortuitous choice in naming John Marshall as the new Chief Justice of the Supreme Court. Less successful, perhaps, were other judicial appointments made shortly before his term expired—criticized as the "midnight judges," the last-minute appointments of Federalists to newly created judgeships was resented by Jefferson. Adams then left Washington, DC, without attending Jefferson's inauguration.

AFTER THE PRESIDENCY

In early 1801, before leaving Washington, Adams received word that his son Charles, who had long been a worry to his parents as a ne'er-do-well and alcoholic, had died. The grieving parents returned to Quincy and their farm called Stoneyfield; Charles's widow and two daughters moved in with them.

Although professing himself content to be "farmer John" for the rest of his life, Adams kept a lively interest in politics—fed at least in part by his pride in the career of John Quincy Adams, which included a stint in Congress, his appointments as minister to Russia and to Great Britain, service as secretary of state under James Monroe, and election to the presidency in 1824.

Adams expressed his opinions freely in letters to his friend Benjamin Rush, who urged him to write to Jefferson. In 1812 Adams and Jefferson resumed their correspondence after an estrangement that had lasted eleven years. Witty, opinionated, erudite, and affectionate, the two old friends created one of the great political correspondences in American history.

In 1813 John and Abigail suffered another wrenching loss when their daughter Nabby died of cancer. Five years later, in 1818, Abigail died of typhoid fever.

Adams continued in good health through most of his life, gradually losing his sight and mobility when very old. In 1826, the year marking the fiftieth anniversary of the signing of the Declaration of Independence, both he and Jefferson were asked to appear at various celebrations. Neither was well enough to leave home. On July 4, 1826, ninety-year-old Adams died at home; nearly his last words were "Jefferson survives"—although, unbeknownst to him, Jefferson had died earlier the same day.

Birthplace: Braintree (now Quincy), MA
Residency: Massachusetts
Religion: Unitarian
Education: Harvard College, graduated 1755
Place of Death: Quincy, MA
Burial Site: United First Parish Church, Quincy, MA
Dates in Office: March 4, 1797–March 3, 1801 (4 years)
Age at Inauguration: 61 years, 125 days

FAMILY
Father: John Adams (1691–1761)
Mother: Susanna Boylston Adams (1699–1797)
Siblings: John Adams had two younger brothers, Peter Boylston Adams (1738–1823) and Elihu Adams (1741–1776).
Wife: Abigail Smith Adams (1744–1818), married October 25, 1764, at Weymouth, MA. The marriage was performed by the bride's father, William Smith, a Congregational minister.
Children: Abigail Amelia Adams ("Nabby"; 1765–1813); John Quincy Adams (1767–1848); Susanna Adams (1768–1770); Charles Adams (1770–1800); Thomas Boylston Adams (1772–1832)

CAREER
Private: Schoolmaster, lawyer, farmer
Political: MA delegate to the Continental Congress (1774–1777); chairman of the Continental Board of War and Ordnance (1776–1777); commissioner to France (1778); minister to the Netherlands (1780); minister to England (1785); vice president under George Washington (1789–1797); president of the United States (1797–1801)
Military: none; acted as president of the Continental Board of War and Ordnance (1776–1777); considered the founder of the US navy
Selected Works: Numerous collections of Adams's writings exist. Among them are *The Adams-Jefferson Letters: The Complete Correspondence Between Thomas Jefferson and Abigail and John Adams,* 2 vols., ed. by Lester J. Cappon (Chapel Hill: University of North Carolina Press, 1988); *Book of Abigail and John: Selected Letters of the Adams Family, 1762–1784,* ed. and with an introduction by L. H. Butterfield, Marc Friedlaender, and Mary-Jo Kline, with a new foreword by David McCullough (Boston: Northeastern University Press, 2002); *Diary and Autobiography,* ed. by Lyman H. Butterfield et al. (Cambridge: Belknap Press of Harvard University Press, 1961) [this is part of a projected 100-volume series collectively known as *The Adams Papers,* ed. by Lyman H. Butterfield et al. (Cambridge: Belknap Press of Harvard University Press, 1961–)]; *The Life and Works of John Adams,* ed. by Charles Francis Adams (Washington, DC: Ross and Perry, 2002).

PRESIDENCY
Nomination: No formal nomination process then existed; the Federalist Party that represented the existing government, meeting in congressional caucus, agreed to support Adams, while the opposition Republican Party's congressional caucus agreed to support Thomas Jefferson.

Election: 1796: elected president (election took place in November but voting occurred on different days in different states before 1845, when Congress mandated a uniform election day)

1800: lost election to Thomas Jefferson

Opponent: 1796: Thomas Jefferson, VA, Democratic-Republican; Thomas Pinckney, SC, Federalist; Aaron Burr, NY, Democratic-Republican; Samuel Adams, MA, Federalist; Oliver Ellsworth, CT, Federalist; George Clinton, NY, Democratic-Republican; John Jay, NY, Federalist

1800: Thomas Jefferson, VA, Democratic-Republican; Charles C. Pinckney, SC, Federalist; Aaron Burr, NY, Democratic-Republican; John Jay, NY, Federalist

Vote Totals: 1796: John Adams was elected president with 71 electoral votes; Thomas Jefferson became vice president with 68 electoral votes; among others who received votes were T. Pinckney (59 votes); Burr (30 votes); S. Adams (15 votes); Ellsworth (11 votes); Clinton (7 votes); and Jay (5 votes).

1800: Thomas Jefferson was elected president with 73 electoral votes; Aaron Burr became vice president with 73 electoral votes; among others receiving votes were J. Adams (65 votes); C. Pinckney (64 votes); and Jay (1 vote). Because Jefferson and Burr had the same number of electoral votes, the election was decided in the House of Representatives, where Jefferson was supported by ten of the sixteen states.

Inauguration: March 4, 1797, in Philadelphia

Vice President: Thomas Jefferson, VA (1797–1801)

CABINET

Secretary of State: Timothy Pickering, MA (1797–1800); John Marshall, VA (1800–1801)

Secretary of the Treasury: Oliver Wolcott, Jr., CT (1797–1801); Samuel Dexter, MA (1801)

Secretary of War: James McHenry, MD (1797–1800); Samuel Dexter, MA (1800–1801)

Attorney General: Charles Lee, VA (1797–1801)

Postmaster General: Joseph Habersham, GA (1797–1801)

Secretary of the Navy: Benjamin Stoddert, MD (1798–1801)

CONGRESS

5th Congress (1797–1799); Speaker of the House: Jonathan Dayton (NJ, Federalist)

6th Congress (1799–1801); Speaker of the House: Theodore Sedgwick (MA, Federalist)

SUPREME COURT APPOINTEES

Bushrod Washington, VA; Associate Justice (1799–1829)

Alfred Moore, NC; Associate Justice (1800–1804)

John Marshall, VA; Chief Justice (1801–1835)

MAJOR EVENTS OF THE ADAMS ADMINISTRATION

◆ In the XYZ Affair of 1797, American envoys to France (Charles C. Pinckney, John Marshall, and Elbridge Gerry) are visited by three agents (referred to as X, Y, and Z) of the French foreign minister, Charles Maurice de Talleyrand-Perigord. The agents demand a bribe before the Americans will be received by Talleyrand. The Americans refuse; both Pinckney and Marshall leave Paris.

◆ Congress passes and Adams signs the Naturalization, Alien, and Sedition Acts of 1798, which increase the time for an immigrant to become a naturalized citizen from five to fourteen years; empower the president to deport any alien he deems dangerous; make it a crime to write anything "false, scandalous, or malicious" about the president, Congress, or government; and make attempts to stir up sedition a crime.

◆ Kentucky and Virginia Resolutions are passed in 1798; these resolutions protest the Sedition Acts and assert the right of the states to nullify federal laws.

◆ Creation of the Navy Department and the Marine Corps, 1798.

◆ In February 1799 Adams appoints William Vans Murray as special envoy to France; a treaty with France is finally signed on September 30, 1800.

◆ Fries's Rebellion is staged by PA farmers in 1799 to protest taxes; instigators are sentenced to death for treason but pardoned by Adams in 1800.

◆ The US government moves from Philadelphia to Washington, DC, in 1800; Adams becomes the first president to live in the president's house on Pennsylvania Avenue.

◆ The Library of Congress is established and initially housed in the new Capitol building, 1800.

◆ Adams names John Marshall as Chief Justice of the Supreme Court, 1801.

◆ The Judiciary Act of 1801, an act passed in February 1801 provides for additional judges. Just before leaving office, Adams signs papers appointing Federalist judges to these positions. They are called the "midnight judges."

MAJOR US AND WORLD EVENTS, 1797–1801

◆ Haydn composes the *Emperor Quartet*, 1797.

◆ English astronomer Caroline Herschel discovers her eighth comet, 1797.

◆ French army under Napoleon advances into Rome, Switzerland, and Egypt, 1798.

◆ British fleet under Horatio Nelson defeats the French fleet in Abukir Bay, 1798.

◆ Charles Brockden Brown, considered the first American novelist, publishes *Wieland,* 1798.

◆ William Wordsworth and Samuel Taylor Coleridge publish *Lyrical Ballads*, 1798.

◆ Robert Fulton designs the *Nautilus*, a submarine that holds four people, in 1797; it is successfully tested in France in 1800.

◆ Edward Jenner publishes the results of his vaccinations against smallpox with cowpox virus, 1798.

◆ Napoleon Bonaparte overthrows the French Directory and sets up the Consulate, with himself as First Consul, 1799.

◆ The Rosetta Stone is found near Rosetta, Egypt, by Napoleon's troops in July 1799. The stone contains hieroglyphics, hitherto unreadable, and the same message in Greek, which, as a known language, makes possible the translation of the hieroglyphics and the unlocking of the ancient Egyptian written language.

◆ Napoleon conquers Italy, 1800.

◆ Alessandro Volta invents the electric battery, 1799–1800.

◆ Census of 1800 shows US population to be 5.3 million.

◆ John Chapman sows apple seeds and plants saplings throughout the Ohio Valley, tends his orchards, and sells or gives seeds and saplings to pioneer settlers from 1797 until his death in 1845; he becomes a folk hero known as "Johnny Appleseed."

◆ Great Britain and Ireland become the United Kingdom, January 1, 1801.

FAST FACTS ABOUT JOHN ADAMS

◆ John Adams and Samuel Adams were second cousins.

◆ It was Adams who nominated George Washington as commander of the Continental Army.

◆ When Adams first went to France in 1778, he lived with Benjamin Franklin.

◆ John Adams was the first president to live in what would be called the White House; both the building and the city of Washington were still under construction when he moved there.

◆ Although often at odds politically, John Adams and Thomas Jefferson were lifelong friends and both John and Abigail Adams frequently corresponded with Jefferson. After an estrangement that began just after Jefferson became president in 1801, Adams and Jefferson reconciled in 1812 and corresponded until they both died in 1826.

◆ During Adams's frequent absences from home, Abigail Adams ran the family farm.

◆ Among the steady stream of visitors that John Adams received until the last year of his life was Ralph Waldo Emerson.

◆ The son of John Adams, John Quincy Adams, became the sixth president in 1825, a family accomplishment not repeated until the presidencies of George H. W. Bush (41st president, 1989–1993) and George W. Bush (43rd president, 2001–).

◆ John Adams and Thomas Jefferson died on the same day, July 4, 1826.

Thomas Jefferson

Nickname: Sage of Monticello, Man of the People
Presidency: 3rd president, 1801–1809
Party: Republican (also referred to as Democratic-Republican)
Life Dates: April 13, 1743–July 4, 1826 (83 years, 82 days) [Note:
Jefferson's birth date was April 2 under the Julian calendar and April
13 under the Gregorian calendar adopted in 1751–1752.]

EARLY LIFE AND EDUCATION

Thomas Jefferson was born April 13, 1743, in a farmhouse on the Rivanna River in Goochland County, Virginia. The modest estate was named Shadwell by his father, Peter Jefferson, after the parish in England where his mother, Jane Randolph Jefferson, had been born. The year after Thomas's birth, Goochland County was divided and the area containing Shadwell became part of Albemarle County.

Peter Jefferson was a physically strong, imposing man who was not only a planter but also a surveyor and mapmaker, a colonel in the county militia, a member of the Virginia House of Burgesses, and a justice of the peace. Jane Randolph Jefferson came from a wealthy and powerful Virginia family. When Thomas was two, Peter Jefferson was named as executor of the estate of his friend William Randolph (Jane Randolph Jefferson's cousin). The Jefferson family left Shadwell for Tuckahoe, fifty miles away; Thomas later said one of his earliest memories was of being handed on a pillow to a slave on horseback for this journey. At Tuckahoe, the Randolph family occupied one wing of the large plantation house and the Jefferson family the other. Thomas received his earliest schooling with the Randolph children and his sisters from a tutor at Tuckahoe.

After seven years at Tuckahoe, the Jefferson family returned to Shadwell. Thomas, at nine years old, was sent to nearby Dover Church to board with the Reverend William Douglas, who tutored him; he spent weekends at home. Thomas spent five years with the Reverend Douglas, learning Greek, Latin, and French, and practicing the violin.

When Thomas was fourteen, in the summer of 1757, his father died at age forty-nine, leaving his wife and eight children. Thomas, as the eldest male, was the heir, but the estate was controlled by his mother and five executors until he turned twenty-one.

In February 1758 Thomas went to the Reverend James Maury to continue his education. He continued his study of languages, practiced the violin three hours a day, and copied extracts from his reading into a "Literary Commonplace Book," a practice he followed throughout his life. In March 1760 he went to Williamsburg, 150 miles from Shadwell, to attend William and Mary College. Stopping to visit at a plantation during the journey to Williamsburg, he met Patrick Henry for the first time. Arriving in Williamsburg, he started college in late May and spent two years in study. One of his teachers was Dr. William Small, a Scots professor of mathematics who soon appreciated Jefferson's intellect and became a friend as well as teacher.

> "We hold these truths to be self-evident, that all men are created equal, that they are endowed by their Creator with certain un-alienable Rights, that among these are Life, Liberty and the pursuit of Happiness."
>
> Thomas Jefferson, in the *Declaration of Independence*, 1776

After college, Jefferson began to study law in 1762 with George Wythe. He not only read law books extensively but also accompanied Wythe to court to assist him. Jefferson referred to Wythe as his "second father" and "beloved mentor." Wythe would have other famous students—including John Marshall, James Monroe, and Henry Clay—but Jefferson remained a lifelong friend. When Wythe died, he left his impressive library to Jefferson.

In the same year Jefferson began studying with Wythe he met Rebecca Burwell. His letters to friends were full of his love for her—although he referred to her in a kind of code, calling her variously Becca, Belinda, or Adnelab—but he was shy about approaching her directly and tongue-tied in her presence. He contemplated an extended trip to Europe and wondered if Rebecca would wait for him, but in 1764, the year Jefferson turned twenty-one and came into his inheritance, she married another man. The next year, 1765, saw the marriage of Jefferson's sister Martha to his friend Dabney Carr, and the death of his beloved older sister Jane.

EARLY CAREER

In 1767 Jefferson joined the elite group of lawyers—only eight in Virginia—who were admitted to the practice of law before the General Court, the court to which county court cases were appealed. He practiced law for five years, building himself a good reputation but not finding the law financially rewarding. In 1768 he was elected to the Virginia House of Burgesses; the same year he directed the beginning of the leveling of the mountaintop on which he planned to build his home—called Monticello, which means "little mountain."

In the summer of 1768 Jefferson's friend Jack Walker left for a business trip of four months' duration, asking Jefferson to look after his home, wife, and child. Becky Walker apparently told her husband years later that Jefferson had made advances toward her; many years later, when Jefferson had risen to national importance, the allegations became public. Jefferson apologized to the husband and made it clear that Mrs. Walker had not behaved with any impropriety.

In 1770 Shadwell burned; Jefferson moved to Monticello and began the construction of his home there, initially with a fairly modest bachelor's home in mind. But in the spring of 1770 he began courting a young widow, Martha Wayles Skelton, and on New Year's Day in 1772 they were married. Later that year their daughter Martha, called Patsy, was born. In the same year, Jefferson's friend and brother-in-law Dabney Carr died and was buried at Monticello.

As tensions between America and Britain grew, Jefferson in 1774 wrote *A Summary View of the Rights of British America,* in which he denied the power of the British Parliament to pass laws such as the Stamp Act and decried Britain's closing of Boston Harbor (which Britain had done in response to the Boston Tea Party). In the same year, he received a large inheritance of land and slaves when his father-in-law, John Wayles, died. Among the slaves acquired from the Wayles estate were Betty Hemings and several of her children, some of whom were alleged to have been fathered by John Wayles. Sally Hemings, the same age as

Jefferson's daughter Patsy, may have been a half-sister to his wife Martha.

Another death in 1774 was of Jefferson's twenty-nine-year-old mentally retarded sister, Elizabeth. In 1774 the Jeffersons had another daughter, Jane Randolph Jefferson, who died the next year.

POLITICAL CAREER

In 1775 Jefferson was elected to the Continental Congress. He traveled to Philadelphia, where the Congress was meeting, and at this time first became acquainted with John Adams. In the summer of 1776 he and Adams were both members of the committee selected to prepare the Declaration of Independence, and Adams—with his powers of oratory—had been instrumental in persuading the Congress of its necessity. But when the time came to write the document, Jefferson's skill as a writer, coupled with his position as a representative of the populous and powerful state of Virginia, made him the more obvious choice to write the declaration.

In a little more than two weeks during the month of June, Jefferson drafted the document and it was then reviewed by the other committee members. The committee's revision was presented to the Congress on June 28, 1776; after further revisions, it was adopted on July 4, 1776. Among the passages written by Jefferson—but deleted in the revisions—was a denunciation of the evils of the slave trade. What remained, however, was a simply worded and concise document that enumerated the continuing offenses of the king toward the colonies and stated the authors' intention to consider themselves free and independent. The document was published in newspapers throughout the colonies and read to Washington's troops.

In that same year, Jefferson was elected to the Virginia House of Delegates and appointed to revise Virginia laws. In 1777 he drafted the Virginia Statute for Religious Freedom. It mandated the complete separation of church and state, as well as the freedom for people to worship as they liked. However, it was not passed by the General Assembly until 1786. Jefferson was behind the law that abolished primogeniture, or the practice whereby the eldest son inherited his father's entire estate. Another piece of Jefferson's proposed legislation, the Bill for More General Diffusion of Knowledge, provided for free public schools but did not pass. Jefferson continued to espouse the importance of public schools, believing that educated citizens were necessary in a democracy.

In 1776 Jefferson lost his mother, who died at age fifty-six. In 1777 a son was born to Martha and Thomas Jefferson, but died eighteen days later. In 1778 their only other child who would survive to adulthood, a daughter named Mary but called Marie or Polly, was born. Two more daughters, both named Lucy Elizabeth Jefferson, were born; the first, born in 1780, died in 1781 at the age of five months; the second, born in 1782, died in 1785.

From 1779 to 1781 Jefferson served as the governor of Virginia. In 1781 British troops were advancing on Monticello and Jefferson fled; though he was later criticized for this action, it is difficult to imagine what other course of action might have been open to him.

After the birth of their last child, Martha never recovered her full strength, dying in 1782 after only ten years of marriage. Jefferson was devastated by the loss. For months after her death he wrote very little and stayed at Monticello, venturing forth only for long horseback rides with his daughter Patsy as his companion. During this period of relative isolation at Monticello, he wrote his only complete book, *Notes on the State of Virginia*, describing everything about the state from its flora and fauna to its cities and towns and its constitution.

JEFFERSON IN PARIS

In 1783 Jefferson was elected as a delegate to the new US Congress and recommended the dollar as the main unit of the new nation's currency and the decimal system as the basis for the currency. Jefferson had earlier refused appointments abroad because of obligations to his family, but in 1784 he accepted the position offered by Congress and went to France as a trade commissioner. He took his daughter Martha (Patsy) with him and later sent for Mary (Polly); the girls were educated at a convent school in Paris.

Jefferson spent five years in France, eventually succeeding Benjamin Franklin as minister to France. In Paris he exercised his gift for making friends (including renewing his acquaintance with John Adams); enjoyed French culture and music; bought books, furniture, and artwork; learned about wine and cuisine; and studied French architecture. He became friends with an English artist, Richard Cosway, and his wife Maria, for whom he evidently felt great affection. The correspondence between Jefferson and Maria Cosway includes a famous letter by Jefferson, "A Dialogue Between My Head and My Heart," written after Maria's departure from Paris.

Jefferson signed a commercial treaty with Prussia in 1785. He received a copy of the proposed Constitution of the United States and urged its adoption, but also advocated the addition of a Bill of Rights. Jefferson observed the events in France that were to lead to the French Revolution, but left the country to return to the United States at the start of that revolution, in late 1789. On landing in Norfolk, Virginia, he learned that he had been appointed as the new nation's first secretary of state.

SECRETARY OF STATE

Jefferson served as secretary of state from 1790 to 1793 under Washington. He gradually found himself at the head of the opposition to the policies of Alexander Hamilton, the secretary of the treasury. Jefferson saw Hamilton's financial plans for the young country as supporting the merchants of New England to the detriment of the farmers and planters of the South. He feared that Hamilton, and others who had become identified with the Federalist Party, favored a monarchy. Although this was not generally the case, the Federalists did favor a strong national government, while Jefferson favored the rights of the individual states. The party that formed around Jefferson and that included James Madison and James Monroe became known as the Democratic-Republican Party, or simply as the Republican Party.

In 1793 Jefferson resigned as secretary of state after Washington issued the Proclamation of Neutrality in the Anglo-French war. He returned to Monticello, where he privately (in letters) criticized Jay's Treaty with Great Britain, which provided for settling conflicts between Great Britain and France. He also began extensive renovations to Monticello, enlarging the house and changing it to reflect design ideas he had acquired in Europe. Several months after returning to the United States, Patsy had married her second cousin, Thomas Mann Randolph, in early 1790. In 1797 Polly married another cousin, John Wayles Eppes. Both daughters and their families, as well as other family connections, were frequent visitors to Monticello.

VICE PRESIDENCY

In the election of 1796, it became clear that the new Constitution had failed to provide for some of the consequences of partisan politics. Although they were of different parties, John Adams became president and Jefferson became his vice president. From 1797 to 1801 Jefferson served as vice president, but was never in close consultation with Adams about policies and plans.

During these years, the United States found itself at odds with the French government that had come into power as a result of the French Revolution. Jefferson viewed the French with sympathy, seeing them as similar to the Americans in their fight to establish a democracy and escape an unjust monarchy. Jefferson, like others in the government, was shocked by what had been the attempt to bribe the American emissaries to France in the XYZ Affair, but he was perhaps even more appalled by the passage of the Alien and Sedition Acts in 1798. He secretly worked with James Madison to prepare the Virginia and Kentucky Resolutions (the first written by Madison and the second by Jefferson), which declared the Alien and Sedition Acts unconstitutional and defended the right of the states to ignore such laws.

PRESIDENCY

In the election of 1800, Jefferson defeated John Adams, but the electoral votes cast resulted in a tie between Aaron Burr, intended as Jefferson's

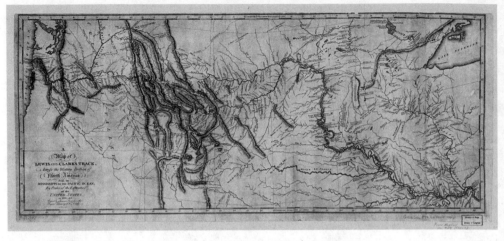

A map of Lewis and Clark's exploratory trek across western North America.

vice president, and Jefferson. The election was decided in the House of Representatives after thirty-six ballots (the first thirty-five had failed to achieve a majority for either of the two candidates). Jefferson was inaugurated in Washington, the new capital. He made a conciliatory inaugural address and set about what he sometimes called "the revolution of 1800"—reducing the number of government employees, cutting army enlistments, and cutting the national debt.

In the midst of his first term, Jefferson faced an unexpected problem. In September 1802 the Richmond *Recorder* newspaper carried an article by James Callender, a journalist who had sought to obtain an official position from Jefferson and had been refused by him. The article alleged that Jefferson kept one of his slaves, Sally Hemings, as his mistress and that he had fathered children by her. The question of whether he had such a relationship and whether he fathered Sally's six children has been a matter of intense interest from his own time to the present. Recent DNA evidence has established that at least one of Sally's children was fathered by a member of the Jefferson clan.

Those who argue against the relationship assert that another Jefferson male, such as Thomas's younger brother Randolph or one of Randolph's sons, could have been the father of Sally Heming's children, and emphasize that Jefferson's daughter Martha Jefferson Randolph denied the relationship on her deathbed in the

presence of her two sons. Those on this side of the controversy find the idea that Jefferson had such a relationship to be inconsistent with his character.

Current evidence makes it impossible to know the truth. Arguments that maintain that the relationship did take place include the DNA evidence, the fact that Jefferson was at Monticello when Sally's children were conceived, the fact that Sally's children were freed upon Jefferson's death (Sally was granted an informal freedom by Jefferson's daughter and went to live with two of her children), and the strong oral tradition in the families descending from Sally Hemings, which upholds that Thomas Jefferson was the father of her children. It was a guiding principle of Jefferson's (which he certainly adhered to in this instance) to make no response to personal attacks.

Perhaps the single greatest success of Jefferson's presidency occurred in 1803, when Jefferson exercised a power not expressly granted him in the Constitution and made the Louisiana Purchase from the French government, led at this time by Napoleon Bonaparte. For $15 million dollars, the area of the United States was doubled and access to the Mississippi was secured—a "conquest" made without a drop of blood being spilled.

Jefferson then set in motion a journey that began in the summer of 1803, when Meriwether Lewis and William Clark led an expedition across the continent. After the transfer of Louisiana was formalized at St. Louis in March 1804, the expedition left from there and headed west. Along the way, Lewis and Clark gained the invaluable services of a Shoshone woman, Sacagawea, who guided them westward, stopping to give birth to a son on the journey. They reached the Pacific in November 1805, and after building a fort in which to spend the winter, returned by an easier route and arrived in St. Louis in September 1806.

"Here was buried Thomas Jefferson, Author of the Declaration of American Independence, of the Statute of Virginia for Religious Freedom, and Father of the University of Virginia."

Thomas Jefferson's epitaph, written by him

In 1804 Jefferson's daughter, Maria (Polly) Jefferson Eppes died. In the same year, Jefferson's vice president, Aaron Burr, challenged Alexander Hamilton to a duel and shot him to death. Burr was charged with murder but never arrested, and he resumed his duties as vice president for the remainder of the term. For the second term, however, Jefferson replaced him with George Clinton, another New Yorker; the two men were elected by an overwhelming margin. Jefferson faced further problems having to do with Burr several years later, when, in 1807, Burr was tried (and acquitted) on charges of treason for attempting to form another country west of the Appalachians from US territory and territory that Burr planned to seize from the Spanish.

During Jefferson's second term, he continued to strive for neutrality in the face of the conflict between Britain and France. Threats to American shipping were frequent; another source of conflict was the harassment of US sailing vessels by pirates of the Barbary Coast, just off northern Africa. The Congress, in 1802, had declared that it would protect its ships in this area, and in 1804, the fledgling navy fought in the harbor of Tripoli (destroying an American frigate that had been captured). After the city of Derna (in present-day Libya) was taken by American forces, a treaty signed in 1805 offered US ships safe passage.

Taking on the Tripolitans was one thing, but the United States was not prepared to battle either Great Britain or France, both of which were liable to engage American ships on the high seas as the conflict between the two countries intensified. The British had also impressed thousands of American sailors, forcing them into British service and claiming that they were in reality British sailors who had abandoned their country. In 1806 Congress passed the Embargo Act, prohibiting international trade from any US port, and hoped that by depriving France and Britain of American trade a peaceful resolution could be reached. The Embargo Act was wildly unpopular, particularly in New England, where merchants lost a great deal by being unable to trade; it also failed to have the desired effect abroad. In 1809, just before the end of Jefferson's term of office, the Embargo Act was replaced by the Non-Intercourse Act, which allowed the resumption of international trade with countries other than France and Great Britain.

RETIREMENT AT MONTICELLO

Jefferson returned home, believing the government to be safe and secure in the hands of his former secretary of state, the newly elected James Madison. His daughter Patsy managed the house, which was filled with grandchildren and frequent guests. He managed his farms, had a wide correspondence, and read extensively, as always. In 1812 he began again to correspond with John Adams; the two old friends had lost none of their passion for political discussion.

Jefferson's interest in education bore fruit with the founding of the University of Virginia, for which he designed both buildings and curriculum, recruited professors, and acquired the library. The cornerstone was laid in 1817 and the university opened in 1825.

"I think this is the most extraordinary collection of talent, of human knowledge, that has ever been gathered together at the White House—with the possible exception of when Thomas Jefferson dined alone."

President John F. Kennedy, at a dinner for Nobel laureates, April 29, 1962

Toward the end of his life, Jefferson suffered from poor health and mounting debts. He was concerned about the growth of power in both the executive and judicial branches of government. On July 4, 1826, he died at Monticello, fifty years to the day after the adoption of the Declaration of Independence, and on the same day that John Adams died. There are few men for whom the sobriquet "Renaissance Man" is more appropriate; Jefferson's wide range of interests and abilities were recognized by his peers and by succeeding generations. He was a highly effective president, and he greatly influenced the two men who followed him in the office.

Birthplace: Shadwell Plantation, Goochland County, VA [Note: Goochland County was divided in late 1744, and Shadwell Plantation was within the newly created Albemarle County.]
Residency: Virginia
Religion: no church affiliation
Education: College of William and Mary, graduated 1762
Place of Death: Monticello, (near Charlottesville), VA
Burial Site: Monticello, (near Charlottesville), VA
Dates in Office: March 4, 1801–March 3, 1809 (8 years)
Age at Inauguration: 57 years, 325 days

FAMILY
Father: Peter Jefferson (1708–1757)
Mother: Jane Randolph Jefferson (1720–1776)

Siblings: Thomas Jefferson was the third of ten children and the eldest son. His siblings were Jane Jefferson (1740–1765); Mary Jefferson (1741–1760); Elizabeth Jefferson (1744–1774); Martha Jefferson (1746–1811); Peter Field Jefferson (1748–1748); an unnamed male infant (1750; died at birth); Lucy Jefferson (1752–1811); Anna Scott Jefferson (1755; twin, died at birth); Randolph Jefferson (1755–1815; twin).
Wife: Martha Wayles Skelton Jefferson (1748–1782), married January 1, 1772, at The Forest, the Wayles family estate in Williamsburg, VA. At her marriage to Jefferson, Martha Wayles Skelton was the widow of Bathurst Skelton, by whom she had had a son who died in infancy.
Children: Martha Washington Jefferson ("Patsy"; 1772–1836); Jane Randolph Jefferson (1774–1775); an infant son (died at birth; 1777); Mary Jefferson ("Maria" or "Polly"; 1778–1804); Lucy Elizabeth Jefferson (1780–1781); Lucy Elizabeth Jefferson (1782–1785)

CAREER
Private: Planter, lawyer
Political: member, Virginia House of Burgesses (1769–1774); delegate to the Continental Congress (1775–1776; 1783–1785); delegate to the Virginia House of Delegates (1776–1779); governor of Virginia (1779–1781); commissioner and minister to France (1784–1789); secretary of state under George Washington (1790–1793); vice president under John Adams (1797–1801); president of the United States (1801–1809)
Military: none
Selected Works: The Princeton University Press, as of 2003, has published thirty volumes, covering 1760 to 1799, of *The Papers of Thomas Jefferson*, ed. by Barbara B. Oberg (Princeton, NJ: University of Princeton Press, 1950–); a multitude of individual and selected works exist, including *The Adams-Jefferson Letters: The Complete Correspondence Between Thomas Jefferson and Abigail and John Adams*, ed. by Lester J. Cappon (Chapel Hill: University of North Carolina Press, 1988); *The Declaration of Independence: Thomas Jefferson's Manuscript Draft from the Collections of the American Philosophical Society* (Philadelphia: American Philosophical Society, 2000); *The*

Jefferson Bible: The Life and Morals of Jesus of Nazareth: with selected writings (Las Vegas, NV: Classic Americana, 1999); *Jefferson's Literary Commonplace Book,* ed. by Douglas L. Wilson (Princeton, NJ: Princeton University Press, 1989); *Jefferson in Love: Love Letters Between Thomas Jefferson and Maria Cosway,* ed. by John P. Kaminski (Madison, WI: Madison House, 1999); *A Manual of Parliamentary Practice for the Use of the Senate of the United States* (Washington, DC: Government Printing Office, 1993); *Notes on the State of Virginia,* ed. and with an introduction by David Waldstreicher (New York: Palgrave, 2002); *The Republic of Letters: The Correspondence Between Thomas Jefferson and James Madison, 1776–1826,* ed. by James Morton Smith (New York: Norton, 1995); *A Summary View of the Rights of British America,* facsimile reproduction, with an introduction by Thomas P. Abernethy (Delmar, NY: Scholars' Facsimiles and Reprints, 1976); *Thomas Jefferson's Farm Book, with commentary and relevant extracts from other writings,* ed. by Edwin Morris Betts (Charlottesville, VA: Thomas Jefferson Memorial Foundation, 1999); *Thomas Jefferson's Garden Book, 1766–1824, with relevant extracts from his other writings,* annotated by Edwin Morris Betts, with introduction by Peter J. Hatch (Charlottesville, VA: Thomas Jefferson Memorial Foundation, 1999).

PRESIDENCY

Nomination: 1800: Jefferson was chosen by the Republican congressional caucus, which also agreed to support Aaron Burr (presumably as vice president, but the fact that electors did not vote separately for president and vice president led those who supported the Republicans to cast one vote for each man, leading to the tie between Jefferson and Burr).

1804: In February 1804 the Republican (Democratic-Republican) congressional caucus agreed to support Jefferson for president again and George Clinton for vice president. Because of the 12th Amendment to the Constitution, the electors would cast separate votes for president and vice president for the first time in the 1804 election.

Election: 1800: elected president (election took place in November but voting occurred on different days in different states before 1845, when Congress mandated a uniform election day)

1804: elected president (election took place in November but voting occurred on different days in different states before 1845, when Congress mandated a uniform election day)

Opponent: 1800: John Adams, MA, Federalist; Charles C. Pinckney, SC, Federalist; Aaron Burr, NY, Democratic-Republican; John Jay, NY, Federalist

1804: Charles C. Pinckney, SC, Federalist

Vote Totals: 1800: Thomas Jefferson was elected president with 73 electoral votes; Aaron Burr became vice president with 73 electoral votes; others receiving votes included Adams (65 votes); C. Pinckney (64 votes); and Jay (1 vote). Because Jefferson and Burr received the same number of electoral votes, the election was decided in the House of Representatives, whose members voted from February 11, 1801, to February 17, 1801. Jefferson finally received the support of ten of the states; Burr was supported by four, and two states cast blank ballots.

1804: Thomas Jefferson was reelected president with 162 electoral votes; C. Pinckney received 14 electoral votes.

Inauguration: 1800: March 4, 1801, in Washington, DC; all subsequent inaugurations have taken place in Washington, DC

1804: March 4, 1805

Vice President: Aaron Burr, NY (1801–1805); George Clinton, NY (1805–1809)

CABINET

Secretary of State: James Madison, VA (1801–1809)

Secretary of the Treasury: Samuel Dexter, MA (1801); Albert Gallatin, PA (1801–1809)

Secretary of War: Henry Dearborn, MA (1801–1809)

Attorney General: Levi Lincoln, MA (1801–1804); John Breckinridge, KY (1805–1806); Caesar A. Rodney, DE (1807–1809)

Postmaster General: Joseph Habersham, GA (1801); Gideon Granger, CT (1801–1809)

Secretary of the Navy: Benjamin A. Stoddert, MD (1801); Robert Smith, MD (1801–1809)

CONGRESS

7th Congress (1801–1803); Speaker of the House: Nathaniel Macon (NC, Republican)
8th Congress (1803–1805); Speaker of the House: Nathaniel Macon (NC, Republican)
9th Congress (1805–1807); Speaker of the House: Nathaniel Macon (NC, Republican)
10th Congress (1807–1809); Speaker of the House: Joseph Bradley Varnum (MA, Republican)

SUPREME COURT APPOINTEES

William Johnson, SC; Associate Justice (1804–1834)
Henry Brockholst Livingston, NY; Associate Justice (1807–1823)
Thomas Todd, KY; Associate Justice (1807–1826)

MAJOR EVENTS OF THE JEFFERSON ADMINISTRATION

◆ Congress establishes the United States Military Academy at West Point, NY, 1802.
◆ Congress repeals the Naturalization Act, which extended the time for immigrants to become citizens from five to fourteen years, and the Judiciary Act, which had allowed John Adams to appoint the so-called "midnight judges." The Alien and Sedition Acts are allowed to expire, 1802.
◆ Congress in 1802 declares the intent of the United States to protect its ships against the Barbary pirates (the conflict is called the Tripolitan War).
◆ *Marbury v. Madison* establishes the right of the Supreme Court to review laws passed by Congress and declare them unconstitutional, 1803.
◆ Ohio becomes a state, March 1, 1803.
◆ The United States purchases the Louisiana Territory (828,000 square miles) from France for $15 million, 1803.
◆ Meriwether Lewis and William Clark lead an expedition from St. Louis to the Pacific Ocean, 1804–1806.
◆ US naval forces under Stephen Decatur enter the harbor of Tripoli and destroy the former US frigate *Philadelphia*, which had been captured by the Tripolitans, 1804.
◆ 12th Amendment to the Constitution, 1804,

provides that voters will vote separately for president and vice president.
◆ Vice president Aaron Burr challenges Alexander Hamilton to a duel and kills him, 1804.
◆ In the election of 1804, Jefferson is reelected in a landslide, with George Clinton as his vice president.
◆ US forces take Derna in North Africa; as part of the ensuing treaty Tripoli offers safe passage to US ships in the Mediterranean, 1805. However, piracy continues until 1815.
◆ Congress passes the Embargo Act, which prohibits international trade from any US port, 1806. The act is especially aimed against England in protest of British seizures of American ships and impressments of American sailors.
◆ Aaron Burr is charged with (and later acquitted of) treason in relation to his alleged participation in a conspiracy to establish an independent country from lands west of the Appalachians, including Mexican territory to be conquered, 1807.
◆ Congress prohibits the importation of African slaves, effective January 1, 1808.
◆ Non-Intercourse Act, March 1, 1809, prohibits trade between the United States and both Great Britain and France. International trade with countries other than Great Britain and France that had been stopped by the Embargo Act is allowed to begin again.

MAJOR US AND WORLD EVENTS, 1801–1809

◆ Czar Paul I of Russia, the son of Catherine the Great, is murdered, March 12, 1801; he is succeeded by his son, Czar Alexander I.
◆ Alexander Hamilton founds *The New York Evening Post* newspaper, 1801.
◆ Beethoven composes *Piano Sonata in C Sharp Minor* (the *Moonlight Sonata*), 1801.
◆ Napoleon becomes First Consul for life in France, 1802.
◆ The French suppress the revolt of blacks in Haiti, led by Toussaint L'Ouverture, 1802; L'Ouverture is seized and taken to France, where he dies in 1803.

◆ Napoleon becomes emperor of France, 1804, and has himself crowned before the pope.

◆ Haitians defeat the French; Haiti declares its independence, 1804.

◆ Napoleon proclaims himself King of Italy; wins battles against the Austrians at Ulm and against the Austrians and Russians at Austerlitz, 1805.

◆ The British fleet under Horatio Nelson defeats the French at Trafalgar, October 5, 1805; Nelson is killed in action.

◆ Sir Walter Scott publishes "The Lay of the Last Minstral," 1805.

◆ Noah Webster publishes the *Compendious Dictionary of the English Language*, 1806, a precursor of his later *American Dictionary of the English Language* (1828).

◆ Lieutenant Zebulon Montgomery Pike explores the southwestern territory and sees a mountain he calls "Grand Peak," but which is called Pikes Peak by later explorers, near what is now Colorado Springs, CO, 1806.

◆ Robert Fulton's steamboat, the *Clermont*, travels up the Hudson River from New York to Albany, moving against the current, and takes thirty-two hours to complete the trip, 1807.

◆ John Jacob Astor charters the American Fur Company, 1808.

◆ Napoleon occupies Spain, 1808.

◆ Beethoven composes the *Fifth Symphony* and the *Pastoral Symphony*, 1808.

FAST FACTS ABOUT THOMAS JEFFERSON

◆ At college, Jefferson shared rooms with John Tyler, who would become the father of future president John Tyler.

◆ Jefferson studied law with George Wythe; later students of Wythe included John Marshall, James Monroe, and Henry Clay.

◆ Jefferson was an accomplished violinist; when he was young, he practiced for three hours daily.

◆ Jefferson was the architect of his mountaintop home, Monticello. He also created labor-saving devices for his home, improving on existing designs for dumbwaiters and a device that would hold two pens and allow him to make a copy of a letter as he was writing it. He designed a unique revolving bookstand and, while Secretary of State, designed a "cipher roll" that allowed the sending and receiving of coded messages.

◆ After the Library of Congress was burned by British troops in 1814, Jefferson donated his own library to form the basis for the new Library of Congress.

◆ Jefferson was the founder of the University of Virginia (opened March 1825 with 123 students) and the architect of several of its buildings. Jefferson regularly invited students to Sunday dinner at Monticello, including Edgar Allan Poe, a student from 1826 to 1827. Poe was among the students attending Jefferson's funeral in 1826.

◆ Jefferson agreed to support the Constitution on the condition that a Bill of Rights was added to it.

◆ John Marshall, the Chief Justice of the Supreme Court from 1801 to 1835, was Jefferson's distant cousin; Marshall's great-grandfather and Jefferson's grandfather were brothers.

◆ Jefferson began the presidential custom of shaking hands rather than bowing to others.

◆ Jefferson was known for careless, casual dressing, and once received the British ambassador in his nightwear and slippers.

◆ Jefferson was the first president to serve ice cream in the White House.

◆ The first child born in the White House was James Madison Randolph, the son of Jefferson's daughter, Martha ("Patsy") Jefferson Randolph, and her husband, Thomas Mann Randolph, Jr.

◆ Jefferson was the first president whose election was decided by the House of Representatives.

◆ Jefferson is the only vice president to be elected president and serve two full terms in office.

◆ Jefferson's was the first inauguration to take place in Washington, DC.

◆ Thomas Jefferson and John Adams died on the same day, July 4, 1826.

James Madison

Nickname: Father of the Constitution, The Great Little Madison
Presidency: 4th president, 1809–1817
Party: Democratic-Republican (also called Republican)
Life Dates: March 16, 1751–June 28, 1836 (85 years, 104 days)

EARLY LIFE AND EDUCATION

James Madison was born on March 5, 1751, the first of twelve children (some sources say ten children, but apparently two infants died at birth) of James Madison and Eleanor (Nelly) Conway Madison. He was born in King George County, Virginia, at the home of his maternal grandmother. The family's home was in Orange County, Virginia, where his father, in addition to owning a large plantation and many slaves, was a justice of the peace, vestryman of the church, and commander of the county militia. Named after his father, young James was called "Jemmy"—to distinguish him from the elder James Madison. He was born into a very well-connected family and was related on both sides to many prominent Virginians, including future president Zachary Taylor.

Madison was sent to boarding school at age eleven; his schoolmaster was Donald Robertson. After five years at school, he returned home and was tutored for two years by the Reverend Thomas Martin. As the College of William and Mary in Williamsburg, Virginia, was regarded by some at that time as an institution of academic mediocrity, the Reverend Martin convinced Madison and his parents that he should

attend Martin's alma mater, the College of New Jersey (later known as Princeton). The Madisons may also have been influenced by having heard the president of the College of New Jersey, the Presbyterian minister John Witherspoon, advocate religious freedom during a tour of Virginia.

Witherspoon, an immigrant from Scotland who would be one of the signers of the Declaration of Independence, brought the ideals of the Scottish enlightenment, including the works of Adam Smith and David Hume, to the College of New Jersey. Madison had been well-prepared for academic pursuit and studied diligently; he completed the college's course in only two years but stayed an additional year to study, while considering a career as a clergyman. He also needed to rest and restore his health, which troubled him throughout his long life.

In 1771 he returned home and continued his studies, reading widely. He considered training for the law but ultimately decided against it. He tutored his younger brothers and sisters and learned something of plantation management from his father. As tensions with Great Britain grew, he joined the county militia under his father's command and trained with the troops, although he was not physically suited for a soldier's life.

EARLY POLITICAL CAREER

In 1776, at the age of twenty-five, he was elected as a delegate to the Virginia Convention. His first public contribution was a slight but important rewording of language in the new state constitution to replace the guarantee of religious "toleration" with a guarantee that "all men are equally entitled to the free exercise of religion, according to the dictates of conscience." He failed at his bid for reelection the next year, however, because he refused to provide the usual drinks at the polls on election day.

But the connections he had made served him well; he was appointed to the Virginia Governor's Council and served from 1777 to 1779, under Patrick Henry and Thomas Jefferson. Madison and Jefferson would be both lifelong friends and political allies. Much of the Council's work concerned raising men and supplies for the Continental Army. Madison learned a great deal about practical committee work and the compromises necessary in government.

From 1780 to 1783, Madison served as a delegate to the Continental Congress. Frustrated by the mounting debts of the new government and the runaway inflation, Madison proposed the somewhat radical idea of authorizing Congress to use military force to make the states pay what they owed in connection with the war, including the seizure of goods and blockading of ports. Not surprisingly, Congress tabled this idea. However, Madison supported the amendment to the Articles of Confederation that allowed Congress to impose new taxes and duties to raise necessary monies.

In the spring of 1783, while in a boardinghouse in Philadelphia, Madison became acquainted with another boarder, William Floyd, a delegate from New York, and his three daughters. Madison became attracted to the youngest, sixteen-year-old Catherine (called Kitty). They entered into an informal engagement, but soon thereafter she disappointed Madison and chose to marry a young doctor.

From 1784 to 1787, Madison served in the Virginia House of Delegates, where he urged the passage of Jefferson's bill for religious freedom. He continued to advocate Virginia's support for the national government, which then existed under the loose Articles of Confederation. But during these years, the nation continued to have trouble collecting money and paying debts, as each state enacted laws and attempted to deal with foreign powers on its own, frequently ending up at cross-purposes with neighboring states.

In 1786 Madison attended the Annapolis Convention, which was intended to address the need for Congress to regulate American commerce. Not all states sent delegates and not all delegates arrived on time, but those who met took the opportunity to plan for a more general meeting, with the stated view of amending the Articles of Confederation. The meeting was set for May 1787 in Philadelphia. Madison, accompanied by James Monroe and his wife, returned to Virginia, stopping on the way home to visit George Washington.

At Mount Vernon, Madison rendered one of his many services to the future Constitution by convincing Washington to lead the Virginia delegation to the convention being planned, knowing that Washington's prestige would do more than anything else to convince other states to send delegates and support the proceedings.

CONSTITUTIONAL CONVENTION

Madison and the rest of the Virginia delegation arrived early in Philadelphia in May 1787; the entire Virginia delegation was present by May 17, though the convention was not scheduled to begin until May 25. Madison used this week to present the other delegates from Virginia with what became known as the "Virginia Plan," whereby the radical suggestion was made to scrap the Articles of Confederation (instead of amending them) and to draft an entirely new constitution—decidedly not what they had been authorized to do by the states.

Drafted by Madison and reflecting many of his ideas, the Virginia Plan advocated a federal government with three branches that would provide checks and balances of power and a bi-cameral legislature with proportional represen-tation based on population, as well as provide for ratification of the proposed constitution and procedures for admitting new states into the union. The Virginia Plan was presented to the assembled delegates on May 29 by Virginia's governor, Edmund Randolph, and adopted.

One of the first issues to present itself was how to satisfy the need of larger states to be represented according to the sizes of their pop-ulations without depriving smaller states of their voices. The compromise eventually reached was that representation would be equal for all states in the upper house, the Senate, but proportional in the lower house, the House of Representatives. The convention also tackled the matter of how to choose the man to occupy the highest office in the executive branch, finally deciding on a mechanism that would be known as the Electoral College as the best means of electing the holder of this position. Yet another service performed by Madison was the taking of detailed notes of the proceedings—the best record that remains of the birth of the US Con-stitution is by the man deemed its father.

Madison was by no means entirely happy with the document that emerged from these weeks of discussion, but as time went by he be-came ever more committed to its ratification. The first step toward ratification was to travel to New York and urge the Congress to transmit it to the state legislatures for their ratification without their first amending it; from almost the beginning, calls for a Bill of Rights came from many (like Jefferson) who otherwise supported the Constitution.

In 1788 Madison served as a delegate to the Continental Congress, during which time he wrote twenty-nine of the eighty-five *Federalist* ar-ticles that appeared first in newspapers and urged adoption of the Constitution. The other articles were written by Alexander Hamilton and John Jay.

From 1789 to 1797, during all of George Washington's first term as president and half of his second term, Madison was a member of the House of Representatives. In the earliest days of the new legislative body, he drafted the Bill of Rights and helped to enact the first revenue leg-islation, but he opposed the financial proposals of Alexander Hamilton, the secretary of the treasury, feeling that they would give undue ad-vantage to northern businessmen at the ex-pense of farmers and southerners. He also wrote Washington's inaugural address and the House of Representatives' response to it, as well as Washington's thank you for the re-sponse!

> **"It will be of little avail to the people, that the laws are made by men of their own choice, if the laws be so voluminous that they cannot be read, or so incoherent that they cannot be understood; if they be repealed or revised before they are prom-ulgated, or undergo such inces-sant changes that no man, who knows what the law is today, can guess what it will be tomorrow."**
>
> James Madison, *The Federalist* No. 62, as published in the *Independent Journal*, February 27, 1788

In May 1794 Madison asked Aaron Burr to introduce him to Dolley Payne Todd, a widow seventeen years his junior who had lost her hus-band and one of her two sons in the yellow fever epidemic of 1793. The lively and charming widow referred to her suitor as the "great little Madison," but his persistence was rewarded by her acceptance of his proposal, and on Septem-ber 15, 1794, they were married at the home of her sister Lucy, who had married George Wash-ington's nephew, George Steptoe Washington. The newlyweds settled in Philadelphia. Because Dolley had been raised a Quaker and Madison was an Episcopalian, Dolley was "read out" of the Quaker meeting (expelled) for marrying outside her faith.

> "[Exchange] the galling burden of bachelorship for the easy yoke of matrimony."
>
> James Madison to J. K. Paulding, c. 1830

Owing in part to his opposition to Hamilton and the many areas in which he was in agreement with Thomas Jefferson, Madison found himself a leading figure of one of the two political parties that had come into existence, the Republicans (also called Democratic-Republicans). Individually and as a group, they opposed the Jay Treaty of 1795, believing that it was too conciliatory to Great Britain and bound to offend (as it did) the French government.

The Republicans were shocked when the difficulties that continued to plague the United States in its relations with the French culminated in the XYZ Affair, in which French governmental agents tried to extract bribes from American envoys. When the Congress, anticipating imminent conflict with France, passed the Alien and Sedition Acts (which were signed by President John Adams), Madison and Jefferson were appalled. Madison, who had retired from Congress in 1797 and returned to Montpelier, drafted the Virginia Resolutions in 1798, in which he argued that states had the right to declare federal laws unconstitutional and to refuse to follow them; Jefferson drafted the similar Kentucky Resolutions. In 1800 Madison published his *Report on the Virginia Resolutions,* in which he addressed objections to the Resolutions.

With the long-awaited triumph of the Republicans in the election of 1800, in which Jefferson ascended to the presidency, Madison was named secretary of state, although he had never traveled outside the United States. He served from 1801 to 1809. He supported the Louisiana Purchase in 1801 and advised the president on the nation's troubled relationships with Great Britain and France. Madison supported the embargo against trade with the European powers, and in 1806 he published *An Examination,* which condemned British maritime practices.

PRESIDENCY

Elected in 1808, Madison brought not only his formidable intellect and wide-ranging experience to the White House, he also brought Dolley— one of the most popular and influential of all the presidents' wives. She decorated the White House (work that was destroyed when the British burned the building in 1814) and established a tradition of warm, gracious hospitality.

Madison inherited the nation's continuing difficulties with the French and the British. The Embargo Act was repealed and replaced by the Non-Intercourse Act in March 1809, just before Madison took office. Owing to a series of misunderstood messages, trade with Britain was restored in 1809, and again banned in 1810.

In 1811 William Henry Harrison met with an uprising of Shawnee Indians led by their charismatic leader Tecumseh, and defeated them at Tippecanoe (in what would become Indiana). Most Americans were suspicious of the British government's support for the Indians in the American West, and considered an invasion by British troops coming down from Canada a genuine threat.

With no progress having been made in relations with Great Britain in the wake of the embargoes, Madison, on June 1, 1812, sent Congress his war message; Congress obligingly declared war on Great Britain. From the beginning, the war did not go well—the American navy was ill-prepared, funds were insufficient, and the support of the citizens, who dubbed the war "Mr. Madison's War," was far from universal. In 1812 Detroit surrendered to British forces, and an American invasion of Canada failed. One bright spot in the war news, however, was the American naval victories, which included those of the USS *Constitution,* a frigate that gained the nickname "Old Ironsides" after it had defeated two British ships.

"In republics, the great danger is, that the majority may not sufficiently respect the rights of the minority."

James Madison, speech at the Virginia Convention, 1829

In 1813 Russia's Tsar Alexander tried unsuccessfully to negotiate an end to the war. The navy continued to give Americans hope, as Oliver Hazard Perry had scored a victory on Lake Erie. The next year, 1814, saw the inconclusive battles of Chippewa and Lundy's Lane, both near the US–Canadian border. The British installed a force in Maryland, composed of veterans of the war against Napoleon Bonaparte in France; it marched on Washington. After defeating the American forces at the Battle of Bladensburg, the British captured Washington and burned the Capitol and the White House. Madison was away when the troops arrived, but Dolley Madison, leaving behind a table set for dinner, gathered what papers and valuables she could, including a portrait of George Washington, and fled.

Fort McHenry in Baltimore withstood a British attack in the war; the battle was later commemorated by Francis Scott Key's composition, "The Star Spangled Banner," inspired in part by the sight of an American flag still standing after a night of artillery fire. The US navy achieved yet another victory at Plattsburgh on Lake Champlain, and Andrew Jackson defeated the Creek Indians at Horseshoe Bend (in what is now Alabama).

In New England there was such strong discontent over the war and the administration's policies that in late 1814 and early 1815, Federalist leaders met in what is known as the Hartford Convention to denounce the war and to discuss secession and the making of a separate peace with Great Britain. But the question became moot as the United States entered into peace talks held at Ghent, Belgium. The peace agreement entailed a return to the status quo of the period prior to the war.

In 1815 the peace treaty was ratified, but before news of the peace had reached New Orleans, Andrew Jackson led his troops in what turned out to be the greatest American victory of the conflict, the Battle of New Orleans. It ended the conflict on a high note for Americans, who felt a flush of national pride and considered the war a second war for independence.

After the war James and Dolley Madison moved into a friend's home in Washington and awaited the rebuilding of the White House. Madison turned his attention to domestic affairs, and in 1816 the second Bank of the United States was chartered and a protective tariff was passed. He also recommended strengthening America's defenses and the country's infrastructure (e.g., roads and canals). Other recommendations, such as the one for a national university, were introduced to the legislature but were rejected; however, Madison retired from the presidency as a popular and highly respected man.

RETIREMENT AT MONTPELIER

Like Jefferson before him, Madison left the presidency in the hands of his secretary of state (in Madison's case, James Monroe). Madison returned to Montpelier with Dolley and lived in peaceful retirement from 1817 until his death in 1836. He continued his correspondence with Jefferson and worked with him on the establishment of the University of Virginia. His strong sentiments in favor of states' rights in the South induced him to defend the Virginia Resolutions, which had been, in effect, attempts to bolster states' autonomous privileges. Like the other founding fathers, he grappled with the question of slavery, and joined the American Colonization Society, which strove to free slaves and transport them to western Africa (to the area that became the nation of Liberia).

Madison's last public service came in 1829, when he was elected as a delegate to the Virginia State Convention for the purpose of revising the state constitution. He spoke at the convention, and the delegates gathered around him to catch the sound of his voice, which was growing faint at this time.

"Nothing more than a change of mind, my dear."

James Madison's last words,
to his niece Nelly Willis on being
asked whether anything was wrong,
June 28, 1836

He died on June 28, 1836; he had been the last surviving signer of the Constitution. After Madison's death, Dolley remained at Montpelier until she was forced to sell it in 1844—in part because of the expenses incurred by her son John Payne Todd, a reckless spender. She moved to Washington, DC, and lived there until her death in 1849, a much honored woman whom Zachary Taylor would describe as a "first lady."

Birthplace: Port Conway, King George County, VA (at the home of his maternal grandmother)
Residency: Virginia
Religion: Episcopalian
Education: College of New Jersey (now Princeton University), graduated 1771
Place of Death: Montpelier, VA
Burial Site: Montpelier, VA
Dates in Office: March 4, 1809–March 3, 1817 (8 years)
Age at Inauguration: 57 years, 353 days

FAMILY

Father: James Madison (1723–1801)
Mother: Eleanor Rose ("Nelly") Conway Madison (1731–1829)
Siblings: James was the eldest of twelve children. His siblings were Francis (or Frances?) Madison (1753–1800); Ambrose Madison (1755–1793); Catlett Madison (1758; died a little over a month after birth); Nelly Conway Madison

(1760–1802); William Madison (1762–1843); Sarah Madison (1764–1843); an unnamed infant (1766; died at birth); Elizabeth Madison (1768–1775); an unnamed infant (1770; stillborn); Reuben Madison (1771–1775); Frances Taylor Madison (1774–1823).
Wife: Dolley Dandridge Payne Todd Madison (1768–1849), married on September 15, 1794, at Harewood, Jefferson County, VA. At the time of her marriage to Madison she was the widow of John Todd, by whom she had had two sons. Her husband and her second son, William Temple Todd (1793), both died in the yellow fever epidemic of 1793. Her elder son was John Payne Todd (1792–1852).
Children: none

CAREER

Private: lawyer, planter
Political: member of the VA Constitutional Convention (1776); member of the Continental Congress (1780–1783); member of the VA legislature (1784–1786); member of the Constitutional Convention (1787); member of the US House of Representatives (1789–1797); secretary of state under Jefferson (1801–1809); president of the United States (1809–1817)
Military: commissioned as a colonel in the county militia (1775–1776); trained with the militia but did not see action
Selected Works: There are many editions of the Federalist papers, which were written jointly by Alexander Hamilton, James Madison, and John Jay and published under the pseudonym Publius, available both in editions of selected numbers and in their entirety (as follows): *The Federalist*, with *The Letters of Brutus*, [both works] ed. by Terence Ball (New York: Cambridge University Press, 2003). Other works by Madison include *James Madison, A Biography in His Own Words*, ed. by Merrill D. Peterson, with an introduction by Robert A. Rutland, pictures editor Joan Paterson Kerr (New York: Newsweek, distributed by Harper & Row, 1974); *Journal of the Federal Convention*, ed. by E. H. Scott (Union, NJ: Lawbook Exchange, 2002); *The Papers of James Madison: Presidential Series*, ed. by Robert A. Rutland et al. (Charlottesville: University Press of

Virginia, 1984–); *The Republic of Letters: The Correspondence Between Thomas Jefferson and James Madison, 1776–1826*, ed. by James Morton Smith (New York: Norton, 1995); *Writings*, selection of contents and notes by Jack N. Rakove (New York: Library of America, 1999).

PRESIDENCY

Nomination: nominated by a congressional caucus of Democratic-Republicans

Election: 1808: elected president (election took place in November but voting occurred on different days in different states before 1845, when Congress mandated a uniform election day)

1812: elected president (election took place in November but voting occurred on different days in different states before 1845, when Congress mandated a uniform election day)

Opponent(s): 1808: Charles C. Pinckney, SC, Federalist; George Clinton, NY, Democratic-Republican

1812: DeWitt Clinton, NY, Federalist

Vote Totals: 1808: James Madison was elected president with 122 electoral votes; C. Pinckney received 47 votes; G. Clinton received 6 votes; 1 electoral vote was not cast.

1812: James Madison was elected president with 128 electoral votes; D. Clinton received 89 votes; 1 electoral vote was not cast.

Inauguration: 1808: March 4, 1809

1812: March 4, 1813

Vice President: George Clinton, NY (1809–1812)

Elbridge Gerry, MA (1813–1814)

CABINET

Secretary of State: Robert Smith, MD (1809–1811); James Monroe, VA (1811–1817)

Secretary of the Treasury: Albert Gallatin, PA (1809–1814); George W. Campbell, TN (1814); Alexander J. Dallas, PA (1814–1816); William H. Crawford, GA (1816–1817)

Secretary of War: William Eustis, MA (1809–1812); John Armstrong, NY (1813–1814); James Monroe, VA (1814–1815); William H. Crawford, GA (1815–1816)

Attorney General: Caesar A. Rodney, DE (1809–1811); William Pinkney, MD (1812–1814); Richard Rush, PA (1814–1817)

Postmaster General: Gideon Granger, CT (1809–1814); Return J. Meigs, Jr., OH (1814–1817)

Secretary of the Navy: Paul Hamilton, SC (1809–1812); William Jones, PA (1813–1814); Benjamin W. Crowninshield, MA (1815–1817)

CONGRESS

11th Congress (1809–1811); Speaker of the House: Joseph Bradley Varnum (MA, Republican)

12th Congress (1811–1813); Speaker of the House: Henry Clay (KY, Republican)

13th Congress (1813–1815); Speaker of the House: Henry Clay (KY, Republican); Langdon Cheves (SC, Republican)

14th Congress (1815–1817); Speaker of the House: Henry Clay (KY, Republican)

SUPREME COURT APPOINTEES

Gabriel Duvall, MD; Associate Justice (1811–1835)

Joseph Story, MA; Associate Justice (1812–1845)

MAJOR EVENTS OF THE MADISON ADMINISTRATION

❖ The Non-Intercourse Act of 1809 is repealed, 1810; it is replaced by the Macon Act, which lifts restrictions on trade with both Great Britain and France but provides that if either nation will agree to respect American neutrality and not hinder US shipping, the United States will institute an embargo against the other.

❖ Madison allows the charter of the Bank of the United States to lapse, 1811.

❖ William Henry Harrison defeats Native Americans led by Chief Tecumseh at the Battle of Tippecanoe (north of present-day Lafayette, Indiana), November 7, 1811.

❖ Louisiana becomes a state, April 30, 1812.

❖ War against England is declared, June 18, 1812.

❖ The frigate USS *Constitution* earns the nickname "Old Ironsides" by first defeating the British frigate *Guerrière* in the waters off Nova Scotia; then destroying the British frigate *Java* near the coast of Brazil, 1812.

❖ Naval forces under Commodore Oliver Hazard Perry defeat the British on Lake Erie,

September 10, 1813, forcing British ships to retreat to Canada.

◆ American forces under General Andrew Jackson defeat the Creeks in the Battle of Horseshoe Bend (on the Tallapoosa River in Alabama), March 27, 1814, ending the Creek War.

◆ Washington, DC, is captured; the White House and the Capitol are burned by the British, August 24, 1814.

◆ The "Star Spangled Banner" is written by Francis Scott Key, who is inspired by the sight of the US flag during a battle at Fort McHenry, Baltimore, on September 14, 1814.

◆ At the Hartford Convention, December 15, 1814, to January 4, 1815, Federalist leaders from New England denounce the war and Madison's leadership; the possibility of seceding from the Union and making a separate peace with Great Britain is discussed and rejected. The end of the war makes the question irrelevant, and the Federalist Party loses most of its prestige and influence thereafter.

◆ The Treaty of Ghent, December 24, 1814, ends the war with an agreement to return to "status quo ante bellum," the same state of affairs that existed before the war. The British practice of impressment (forcing American sailors into British service), which was a leading cause of the war, had become moot as the ending of the war between Great Britain and France meant the British no longer needed more sailors.

◆ After war officially ends in 1814, Andrew Jackson defeats the British in the Battle of New Orleans on January 8, 1815 (word of the treaty had not yet reached New Orleans).

◆ The Capitol and White House are rebuilt under the direction of architect Benjamin Henry Latrobe, 1815.

◆ Indiana becomes a state, December 11, 1816.

◆ A second Bank of the United States is chartered, April 10, 1816.

◆ The first protective tariff passes in 1816, and is designed to protect developing American industries, such as textiles and the iron industry.

MAJOR US AND WORLD EVENTS, 1809–1817

◆ British forces under Arthur Wellesley (later the Duke of Wellington) invade the Iberian Peninsula and with the aid of Portuguese and Spanish forces defeat the French at the Battle of Talavera, July 27–28, 1809.

◆ Washington Irving publishes the satirical Diedrich Knickerbocker's A History of New-York, which purports to cover New York history "from the beginning of the world until the end of the Dutch dynasty," 1809.

◆ George Gordon, Lord Byron, publishes English Bards and Scotch Reviewers in response to savage reviews of his work in the Edinburgh Review, 1809.

◆ Napoleon Bonaparte marries Marie Louise, the daughter of Francis I of Austria, to help solidify his role as emperor of France and in hopes of having a male heir, 1810.

◆ The Yale Medical School is established, 1810.

◆ US census figures show a population of 7.2 million, 1810.

◆ John Dalton publishes the first part of his New System of Chemical Philosophy, 1810, which sets forth his theory that elements are composed of tiny particles that he names "atoms."

◆ Muhammed Ali massacres the Mamluk rulers of Egypt, who had ruled since 1250, and makes himself ruler, 1811.

◆ Jane Austen anonymously publishes Sense and Sensibility, 1811.

◆ Construction of the Cumberland Road (also called the National Road) in Cumberland, MD, is begun, 1811; the road terminates in Vandalia, IL, and is used by many settlers on their westward journey.

◆ Jacob and Wilhelm Grimm publish Grimm's Fairy Tales, 1812.

◆ British forces under Wellington defeat the French at the Battle of Salamanca, in Spain, 1812.

◆ Napoleon Bonaparte invades Russia with more than half a million men. He meets Russians at the Battle of Borodino on September 7, 1812, at which both sides suffer serious losses. After the battle the Russians retreat and Napoleon is able to take Moscow (much of which is burned the same night). However, the French are forced to retreat after encountering scorched earth and the Russian winter. Fewer than 30,000 soldiers make it back to France.

◆ Jane Austen publishes *Pride and Prejudice*, 1813.

◆ The alliance of Austria, Russia, Prussia, Britain, Spain, Portugal, and Sweden defeats Napoleon at the Battle of Leipzig, 1813.

◆ Napoleon abdicates and is exiled to Elba; the Bourbon monarchy is restored in France under Louis XVIII, 1814.

◆ Napoleon returns from exile and rules for the "Hundred Days" before being defeated by British forces under Wellington and Prussian forces under Blücher at the Battle of Waterloo, June 18, 1815; Napoleon is then exiled to St. Helena, where he lives until his death in 1821.

◆ Rossini's opera *The Barber of Seville* is first performed, 1816.

FAST FACTS ABOUT JAMES MADISON

◆ James Madison and Zachary Taylor were second cousins.

◆ Madison was the first president who had served as a congressman before becoming president.

◆ Madison was the smallest president; he stood about five feet five inches tall and weighed just a hundred pounds.

◆ Madison was the first president to wear long trousers rather than knee breeches.

◆ The first inaugural ball was held after Madison's inauguration.

◆ The nickname "White House" is of unknown origin but early use; the story that the building was first painted white to hide the scorch marks from its burning by the British is fiction.

◆ Aaron Burr introduced James Madison to Dolley Payne Todd.

◆ The first White House wedding was held on March 29, 1812, when Lucy Payne Washington, Dolley Madison's sister, married Thomas Todd, an associate justice of the US Supreme Court.

◆ Both of Madison's vice presidents died in office.

◆ Madison was among the leaders of the American Colonization Society, founded in 1819, which endeavored to free slaves and transport them to the west coast of Africa; it is estimated that as many as 20,000 blacks were transported during the 19th century to the area that would become Liberia.

◆ Madison helped Thomas Jefferson to found the University of Virginia and was its second rector, from 1826. He helped to guide the university through its early years. He bequeathed to the university $1,500 and his personal library.

◆ Dolley Madison initiated the Easter egg roll on the Capitol lawn.

◆ Dolley Madison was the first person to send a personal message using the Morse telegraph, in 1844.

◆ Dolley Madison lived until 1849; after Madison's death she was forced to sell Montpelier and lived (in increasing poverty) in Washington across from the White House. Important visitors would visit the White House and then cross the street to call on Dolley Madison.

James Monroe

Nickname: Era-of-Good-Feelings President, The Last Cocked Hat
Presidency: 5th president, 1817–1825
Party: Democratic-Republican (also called Republican)
Life Dates: April 28, 1758–July 4, 1831 (73 years, 67 days)

EARLY LIFE AND EDUCATION

James Monroe was born on April 28, 1758, in Westmoreland County, Virginia. His father, Spence Monroe, was from a respectable family of modest holdings; little is known of his mother, Elizabeth Jones Monroe. James was the eldest son and was sent at age eleven as a day student to the Campbelltown Academy, which was headed by the Reverend Archibald Campbell. In 1774, when James was sixteen, he entered the College of William and Mary. In the same year, his father died. James was assisted in providing for his two brothers and his sister by his uncle, Judge Joseph Jones, who was a member of Virginia's House of Burgesses.

James arrived at college in Williamsburg just after the Royal Governor of Virginia had dissolved the House of Burgesses, whose members had promptly reconvened at the nearby Raleigh Tavern and issued a call for the first Continental Congress. The college students took part in demonstrations and began drilling with rifles. In June 1775 Monroe joined in a surprise attack on the governor's palace that removed hundreds of muskets and swords and turned them over to the militia.

REVOLUTIONARY WAR SERVICE

In the spring of 1776, Monroe and his college friend John Mercer enlisted in the Third Virginia Infantry and became commissioned lieutenants. They were trained by General Andrew Lewis, who had led expeditions against Native Americans—making them better prepared as fighters than many of the colonial troops. They marched from Virginia to New York to join Washington's army.

Many of Monroe's regiment fell ill in the next few months, but Monroe remained healthy and was able to take part in the surprise attack on Trenton in December 1776. Monroe was part of an advance detachment of fifty men who were given the task of preventing word of the advancing Continental Army from reaching the Hessian troops at Trenton. While capturing two field cannons, Monroe and Captain William Washington were both seriously wounded.

After convalescing and returning briefly to Virginia to attempt recruiting for the army, Monroe returned to service as an aide-de-camp to William Alexander, Lord Stirling, an American-born claimant to a Scottish earldom. In this position, Monroe became friendly with General

Charles Lee, Alexander Hamilton, Aaron Burr, the Marquis de Lafayette, and Pierre Du Ponceau, the secretary to Baron Steuben. With Du Ponceau, Monroe exchanged books and ideas, finding himself attracted to the philosophy of the Stoics.

"Turn his soul wrong side outwards and there is not a speck on it."

Thomas Jefferson, commenting about James Monroe in a letter to James Madison, 1787

Monroe wintered at Valley Forge and fought in the battle of Monmouth Court House in the summer of 1778. As a young officer, Monroe also socialized with his fellow officers. During that same summer, at the home of Mrs. Theodosia Prevost, the future wife of Aaron Burr, Monroe allegedly fell in love with a young lady to whom he had been introduced, but told her that he planned to study in France after his military service. Nothing came of the romance.

Monroe continually tried to obtain a field command, but was unable to do so, despite his having received a recommendation from Washington himself. Returning to Virginia and trying to recruit a regiment, Monroe became friends with Thomas Jefferson, who advised him to study law. In 1780 Monroe reentered the College of William and Mary, but read law under Jefferson's direction. Despite his involvement in his studies, Monroe, in May 1780, was sent by Jefferson to North Carolina to assess the readiness of the state to repel the expected British invasion.

POLITICAL CAREER

In the spring of 1782, Monroe was elected a member of the Virginia House of Delegates, to the seat vacated by his uncle Judge Jones, who had been sent to the Continental Congress. In 1783 he was elected to the new US Congress, formed under the Articles of Confederation, where he served until 1786.

In New York, then the nation's capital, Monroe met Elizabeth Kortright, the daughter of Lawrence Kortright, a merchant and a British officer who had become wealthy as a British privateer during the French and Indian War, but suffered reverses during the Revolutionary War. The couple met in 1785 and were married in 1786, when she was seventeen and he was twenty-seven. A beautiful, well-dressed woman, many found her reserved and formal manners off-putting, but the marriage appeared to have been a happy one. The couple had three children—two daughters, Eliza Kortright and Maria Hester, and a son, Spence, who died as an infant.

After his service in Congress, the Monroes settled in Fredericksburg, Virginia, where Monroe began his law practice. After a few years the family moved to Albermarle County to be near Jefferson.

In 1788 Monroe was elected to the Virginia convention called to consider ratification of the new Constitution; he opposed ratification, believing that too much power had been given to the federal government at the expense of the states. He also thought that it should include a bill of rights. However, after the Constitution had been ratified, he ran for a seat in the US House of Representatives and was defeated by James Madison. In 1790 he was elected to the US Senate, where he served until 1794.

With Jefferson and Madison, Monroe became a leading figure in the Republican (also called Democratic-Republican) Party that had formed in opposition to the Federalist policies of George Washington, John Adams, and Alexander Hamilton. Nonetheless, the fair-minded Washington appointed Monroe as minister to France in 1794. Monroe, like most of the Republicans, was sympathetic toward the French—so much so that Washington recalled him in 1796. Monroe felt betrayed, especially when the treaty between the United States and Great Britain that had been negotiated by John Jay seemed to favor the British at the expense of the French.

Monroe was elected governor of Virginia in 1799 and served until 1802. During this period he suggested settling free blacks in the West, hoping thereby to encourage manumission and the end of slavery, but there was no federal support for this plan.

> "National honor is national property of the highest value."
>
> James Monroe, First Inaugural Address, March 4, 1817

Monroe's friend Thomas Jefferson had been elected president in 1800, and in 1803 he sent Monroe back to France, with instructions to assist the minister to France, Robert Livingston, in his effort to acquire a port on the Mississippi River. But as Napoleon was finding himself short of money, he offered the whole Louisiana Territory to the Americans. Despite their having no authority to make such a purchase, Livingston and Monroe concluded the deal, doubling the size of the nation.

Monroe then became the minister to England, remaining there until 1807. He returned home and vied with Madison for the presidential nomination; Madison won both the nomination and the White House. Monroe was again elected governor of Virginia in 1811, but later the same year was appointed by Madison as secretary of state.

SECRETARY OF STATE

As secretary of state, Monroe was able to support Madison and the "War Hawks" in their eagerness to stop British interference with American ships. Defense measures were passed, and in 1812 war was declared. When, after the capture of the city of Washington by the British in 1814, Secretary of War John Armstrong was forced to resign, Monroe was named to that post as well. As secretary of war, he organized his department, though his efforts had little effect on the conduct of the war.

In 1813 the Monroes moved to an estate called Oak Hill in Loudon County, Virginia, to be closer to Washington. In the early 1820s Monroe began construction of the mansion in which he would spend the bulk of his retirement.

PRESIDENCY

Although Monroe seemed a natural candidate to follow Madison in the election of 1816, members of his party who thought that the "Virginia dynasty" had gone on long enough supported William H. Crawford, who had become secretary of war after Monroe. Monroe won only a narrow victory in the Democratic-Republican caucus, but in the election defeated the Federalist candidate for president, Rufus King, by a wide margin. The Federalist party had little effect on national politics after this defeat.

> "Attacks on me will do no harm, and silent contempt is the best answer to them."
>
> James Monroe in a letter to George Hay, April 29, 1808

When the new president and his family moved into the White House, it had been reconstructed after being burned by the British in 1814. The Monroes had developed an abiding love of French style when living abroad and furnished the White House accordingly. Both Monroe and his wife adopted a much more formal manner than the Madisons had displayed; Mrs. Monroe established a precedent for future First Ladies when she refused to return social calls in Washington society. This was, in part, because she was frequently ill, but also because the growth of the city and the government had made such a practice very difficult to sustain. Washington society found her cold and overly formal, though, and thought the same of her daughter Eliza, who, with her husband George Hay, also lived in the White House. When the Monroes' younger daughter, Maria Hester, married Samuel L. Gouveneur in the first White

"We owe it, therefore, to candor and to the amicable relations existing between the United States and those powers to declare that we should consider any attempt on their part to extend their system to any portion of this hemisphere as dangerous to our peace and safety. With the existing colonies or dependencies of any European power we have not interfered and shall not interfere. But with the Governments who have declared their independence and maintain it, and whose independence we have, on great consideration and on just principles, acknowledged, we could not view any interposition for the purpose of oppressing them, or controlling in any other manner their destiny, by any European power in any other light than as the manifestation of an unfriendly disposition toward the United States."

James Monroe, his address to Congress on December 2, 1823, enunciating what became known as the Monroe Doctrine; much of the document was written by John Quincy Adams, the Secretary of State

House wedding of a presidential daughter, the wedding was private, and Washington society again felt slighted.

Monroe did not aggressively pursue a domestic agenda in Congress, believing as a Republican that less federal involvement in states' affairs was preferable to more. In the realm of foreign affairs, however, he and his secretary of state, John Quincy Adams, were much more active. The Rush-Bagot Agreement between the United States and Great Britain led to naval demilitarization on the Great Lakes, with each side agreeing to maintain one ship on Lake Ontario and one on Lake Champlain, and two ships each on Lakes Huron, Michigan, Erie, and Superior.

In 1817 and 1818 Andrew Jackson had attacked Seminole Native Americans in Florida, ostensibly because they harbored runaway slaves belonging to Americans. In addition, he claimed the region for the United States, and was angry when President Monroe returned Pensacola to the Spanish. The matter was resolved in the Adams-Onis Treaty (also called the Transcontinental Treaty), signed February 22, 1819, by which Spain agreed to sell Florida to the United States and the border between Louisiana and Mexico was established.

In the Panic of 1819, the prosperity that had followed the War of 1812 was eroded by the harsh fiscal policies of the Second Bank of the United States. The bank called in its loans, creating difficulties—especially for the western banks, which had loaned money liberally for land speculation. Mortgages were foreclosed, banks failed, and unemployment grew. The westerners blamed the banks; northern manufacturers wanted an increase in tariffs and southerners wanted a decrease in tariffs. Monroe was not inclined to take corrective action, but in 1824 protective tariffs were increased. The economy began to improve by 1824 and gradually grew stronger.

The issue that would eventually divide the Union was being fiercely debated when Missouri requested admission as a state. There was an equal number of slave and free states, and the admission of Missouri as either slave or free was going to tip the balance. The Missouri Compromise of 1820 set a latitude of 36 degrees 30 minutes as the dividing line between the southern slave states and the northern states, where slavery was banned; Missouri was admitted as a slave state and Maine was admitted as a free state, thus maintaining the balance.

From 1818 to 1822, Chile, Venezuela, Mexico, Peru, and Guatemala all became independent. President Monroe proposed that the United States recognize the newly independent countries, and Congress approved the opening of diplomatic relations in 1822. During the same period, Russia was being regarded as a threat to American interests in the American continent's northwest. Both of these international affairs provided impetus for the address given by Monroe before Congress on December 2, 1823, which became known as the Monroe Doctrine. Formulated by Monroe and written in part by John Quincy Adams, it warned European powers that the Americas should no longer be considered as available for colonization. It further stated that the United States would not interfere in European disputes, and any interference by European powers with governments in the Americas that had been recognized as legitimate by the United States would be considered an unfriendly act toward the United States.

Despite the country's economic woes, Monroe's popularity (which had led to his nearly unanimous reelection in 1820) remained strong throughout his two terms.

RETIREMENT

The Monroes retired to Oak Hill. They were left with many debts from the entertaining they had felt was necessary while they were residents of the White House, and Monroe applied to Congress for a reimbursement of monies he had spent as a diplomat, but with limited success. Elizabeth Monroe suffered from declining health for years before her death on September 23, 1830. After her death, Monroe sold Oak Hill and moved to New York City to live with his daughter, Maria Hester Monroe Gouverneur. He died there on July 4, 1831.

Birthplace: Westmoreland County, VA
Residency: Virginia
Religion: Episcopalian
Education: College of William and Mary, graduated 1776
Place of Death: New York, NY
Burial Site: Second Street Cemetery, New York, NY; his remains were moved in 1858 to Hollywood Cemetery, Richmond, VA
Dates in Office: March 4, 1817–March 3, 1825 (8 years)
Age at Inauguration: 58 years, 310 days

FAMILY

Father: Spence Monroe (c. 1724–1774)
Mother: Elizabeth (Eliza) Jones Monroe (c. 1727–1774?) [Note: It is assumed that Elizabeth Monroe died before her husband because she is not mentioned in his will.]
Siblings: Family information for the Monroes is sketchy at best. James Monroe was the eldest or the second eldest of five children; his siblings were Elizabeth Monroe (life dates unknown, though she grew up and married); Andrew Monroe (?–1826); Joseph Jones Monroe (c. 1770–1824); Spence Monroe (?).
Wife: Elizabeth "Eliza" Kortright Monroe (1768–1830), married on February 16, 1786, in New York, NY
Children: Eliza Kortright Monroe (1786–1835); James Spence Monroe (1799–1800); Maria Hester Monroe (1803–1850)

CAREER

Private: lawyer
Political: member of the Continental Congress (1783–1786); US senator (1790–1794); minister to France (1794–1796); governor of VA (1799–1802); minister to France and England (1803–1807); secretary of state under Madison (1811–1817); secretary of war under Madison (1814–1815); president of the United States (1817–1825)
Military: joined the Continental Army in 1776 as a lieutenant; fought at Trenton (where he was seriously wounded), Monmouth, Brandywine, and Germantown; promoted to major, but left the army in December 1778 when he could not obtain an active command; appointed (by

Thomas Jefferson) military commissioner of Virginia with the rank of lieutenant colonel
Selected Works: *The Papers of James Monroe*, ed. by Daniel Preston (Westport, CT: Greenwood Press, 2003–); *The People, The Sovereigns: Being a Comparison of the Government of the United States with Those of the Republics Which Have Existed Before, with the Causes of Their Decadence and Fall*, ed. by Samuel L. Gouverneur (Cumberland, VA: James River Press, 1987)

PRESIDENCY

Nomination: 1816: nominated by a Republican congressional caucus

1820: Monroe's popularity after his first term of office meant his candidacy was considered a foregone conclusion by the members of his party, so very few bothered to attend the nominating caucus. Those who did attend did not wish to leave him with such a small number of votes, so they declined to nominate a candidate at all—and he ran unopposed.

Election: 1816: elected president (election took place in November but voting occurred on different days in different states before 1845, when Congress mandated a uniform election day)

1820: elected president (election took place in November but voting occurred on different days in different states before 1845, when Congress mandated a uniform election day)

Opponent: 1816: Rufus King, NY, Federalist Party

1820: John Quincy Adams, MA, Independent/Republican Party [Note: John Quincy Adams was not nominated and did not run in opposition to Monroe, whose secretary of state he was, but Adams did receive one electoral vote, cast by New Hampshire's Governor George Plummer, who disliked Monroe.]

Vote Totals: 1816: James Monroe was elected president with 183 electoral votes; Rufus King received 34 electoral votes; 4 electoral votes were not cast.

1820: James Monroe was elected president with 231 electoral votes; John Quincy Adams received 1 electoral vote; 3 electoral votes were not cast.

Inauguration: 1816: March 4, 1817

1820: March 5, 1821 (The inauguration was held on March 5 because March 4 fell on a Sunday.)

Vice President: Daniel D. Tompkins, NY (1817–1825)

CABINET

Secretary of State: John Quincy Adams, MA (1817–1825)

Secretary of the Treasury: William H. Crawford, GA (1817–1825)

Secretary of War: John C. Calhoun, SC (1817–1825)

Attorney General: Richard Rush, PA (1817); William Wirt, VA (1817–1825)

Postmaster General: Return J. Meigs, OH (1817–1823); John McLean, OH (1823–1825)

Secretary of the Navy: Benjamin W. Crowninshield, MA (1817–1818); Smith Thompson, NY (1819–1823); Samuel L. Southard, NJ (1823–1825)

CONGRESS

15th Congress (1817–1819); Speaker of the House: Henry Clay (KY, Republican)

16th Congress (1819–1821); Speaker of the House: Henry Clay (KY, Republican), John W. Taylor (NY, Republican)

17th Congress (1821–1823); Speaker of the House: John W. Taylor (NY, Republican)

18th Congress (1823–1825); Speaker of the House: John W. Taylor (NY, Republican)

SUPREME COURT APPOINTEES

Smith Thompson, NY; Associate Justice (1823–1843)

MAJOR EVENTS OF THE MONROE ADMINISTRATION

❖ The Anglo-American Convention in 1818 leads to the signing of the Rush-Bagot Agreement between the United States and Great Britain, which limits for each side the number of ships that would be maintained on the Great Lakes.

◆ Mississippi becomes a state, December 10, 1817.

◆ In the First Seminole War, 1817–1818, Andrew Jackson leads troops into Spanish Florida and captures Pensacola. Spain, France, and England protest, and President Monroe repudiates Jackson's actions and returns Pensacola to Spain.

◆ Illinois becomes a state, December 3, 1818.

◆ In 1818 Congress establishes thirteen stripes for the US flag to honor the original thirteen colonies, and decrees that a new star will be added for each new state that joins the Union.

◆ Florida is ceded by Spain to the United States in the Adams-Onis Treaty (also called the Transcontinental Treaty), February 22, 1819; the Treaty also establishes the border between Mexico and the Louisiana Territory.

◆ The Panic of 1819, during which banks fail, mortgages are foreclosed, and unemployment is high, sweeps across the country; prosperity does not return until 1824.

◆ In *McCulloch v. Maryland*, 1819, the Supreme Court upholds the constitutionality of the creation of the Bank of the United States by Congress, and further notes that states cannot pass laws (in this case, taxing the bank) contravening federal laws. The case further establishes the power of the federal government and a loose (as opposed to strict) interpretation of the Constitution.

◆ Alabama becomes a state, December 14, 1819.

◆ Maine becomes a state, March 15, 1820.

◆ The Missouri Compromise of 1820 sets a latitude of 36 degrees 30 minutes as the dividing line between the southern slave states and the northern states, where slavery is banned.

◆ Missouri becomes a state, August 10, 1821.

◆ Monroe proposes that the United States recognize the newly independent countries of Latin America and Congress approves the opening of diplomatic relations, 1822.

◆ Monroe vetoes the Cumberland Road Bill, 1822; the bill would have extended the Cumberland Road to Zanesville, OH, but Monroe believes the bill is unconstitutional because it appropriates taxes for a purpose that would benefit a particular area rather than the whole nation.

◆ The Monroe Doctrine is enunciated by Monroe during an address to Congress, December 2, 1823; it warns European powers that the Americas should no longer be considered as open to new colonization, and that interference by European countries in governments of nations within the Americas that have been recognized as legitimate by the United States would be considered an unfriendly act toward the United States.

◆ The Tariff Act increases protective tariffs, 1824.

◆ The General Survey Bill, 1824, provides for improvements to the nation's roads and waterways.

MAJOR US AND WORLD EVENTS, 1817–1825

◆ Construction begins on the Erie Canal, July 4, 1817; the canal is completed, October 26, 1825.

◆ Chile becomes independent after San Martín defeats the Spanish, 1818.

◆ Mary Wollstonecraft Shelley writes *Frankenstein*, 1818.

◆ Sir Walter Scott publishes *Rob Roy* and *The Heart of Midlothian*, 1818.

◆ Two of Jane Austen's novels, *Northanger Abbey* and *Persuasion,* are published posthumously, 1818.

◆ Simón Bolívar is elected president of Venezuela, 1819.

◆ George Gordon, Lord Byron, publishes the first part of *Don Juan*, 1819.

◆ Arthur Schopenhauer publishes *The World as Will and Idea*, 1819.

◆ The Census of 1820 shows a US population of 9.6 million people; Great Britain has 20.8 million; France 30.4 million; Germany 26 million, and Italy 18 million.

◆ John Keats publishes poems, including "Ode to a Nightingale" and "Ode on a Grecian Urn," 1820.

◆ Washington Irving publishes *The Sketch Book*, a book of short stories that includes "Rip

Van Winkle" and "The Legend of Sleepy Hollow," 1820.

◆ The "Venus de Milo" is discovered on the island of Melos, Greece, 1820.

◆ Mexico, Peru, and Guatemala become independent from Spain, 1821.

◆ The Greeks begin their War of Independence against the Turks, 1821.

◆ British scientist Michael Faraday experiments with electromagnetism and demonstrates the conversion of electrical energy into motive force, thereby inventing the electric motor, 1821.

◆ Emma Willard opens the Troy Female Seminary in New York state, offering college education to American women, 1821.

◆ Brazil becomes independent from Portugal, 1822.

◆ Clement C. Moore writes "'Twas the Night Before Christmas," 1822.

◆ Eleven-year-old Hungarian pianist Franz Liszt debuts in Vienna, Austria, 1822.

◆ James Fenimore Cooper publishes *The Pioneer*, the first of the "Leatherstocking Tales," 1823.

◆ Scottish chemist Charles Macintosh introduces his waterproof material as "Mackintosh," 1824.

◆ War begins between Burma and the British, who capture Rangoon, 1824.

◆ Beethoven, though deaf, composes *Symphony No. 9 in D Minor*, 1824.

◆ Lafayette visits the United States, 1824.

FAST FACTS ABOUT JAMES MONROE

◆ Monroe's daughter was the first president's daughter to be married from the White House; Maria Hester Monroe married Samuel L. Gouverneur on March 9, 1820.

◆ The US Marine Band played at Monroe's 1821 inauguration and has played at every inauguration since.

◆ Monroe was the first president who had served as a US senator.

◆ Monroe was inaugurated on March 5, 1821, because March 4 was a Sunday.

◆ In the election of 1820, Monroe received every electoral vote but one; the sole vote for John Quincy Adams was cast by New Hampshire's Governor George Plummer, who disliked Monroe. The story that Plummer had cast the one vote that was not for Monroe to preserve Washington's status as the only president who had been elected unanimously is untrue.

◆ Monroe, like George Washington, was a member of the Masonic Order.

◆ Monroe was the first president to ride on a steamship.

◆ James and Elizabeth Monroe both attended Napoleon Bonaparte's coronation as emperor of France.

◆ When the wife of the Marquis de Lafayette was imprisoned during the French Revolution, Elizabeth Monroe's visits to her prompted the French government to use Mrs. Monroe's interest—and their desire to avoid offending their American allies—as a reason to release Madame de Lafayette.

◆ Monroe was the third president to die on the Fourth of July.

John Quincy Adams

Nickname: Old Man Eloquent; Defender of the Rights of Man
Presidency: 6th president, 1825–1829
Party: Federalist/Democratic-Republican/National Republican
Life dates: July 11, 1767–February 23, 1848 (80 years, 227 days)

EARLY LIFE AND EDUCATION

John Quincy Adams seemed almost to be destined for the presidency. Born on July 11, 1767, in Braintree (now Quincy), Massachusetts, he was the eldest child of Abigail Smith Adams and John Adams. At the time of his birth his father was a lawyer practicing in the Boston area, but the elder John Adams had already become interested in politics and was eager for America to break away from British rule. When he was eight years old, John Quincy and his mother climbed nearby Penn's Hill to watch the Battle of Bunker Hill.

John Quincy was taught at home by his parents and then tutored by a cousin, John Thaxter. On February 13, 1778, he embarked with his father for France, where the elder Adams was being sent to assist in peace negotiations between the British and Americans after the war. They reached Paris on April 8, and settled in Passy, a suburb of Paris, where they for a time lived with Benjamin Franklin, the American minister to France. John Quincy was then enrolled in a weekday boarding school.

John Adams was called back to the United States, and father and son set off on June 17, 1779. The precocious younger Adams spent much of the journey teaching English to two distinguished French passengers. After only three months at home, John and John Quincy headed back to Paris, this time accompanied by John Quincy's younger brother Charles. Cousin John Thaxter came along as John Adams' secretary, and Francis Dana traveled as a secretary to the peace commission. The leaky ship made the first available landfall at the tip of Spain, where the group embarked on an arduous overland journey to Paris.

John Quincy and Thomas enrolled in school, but in 1780 they moved with their father to Holland, where John Adams hoped to conclude trade agreements and arrange loans for his new country. Because John Quincy could not speak Dutch, he was placed with much younger students; when he complained to his father—and the school's rector complained that John Quincy was rebellious—John Adams withdrew his sons and arranged for private tutoring. John Quincy was soon attending lectures at the University of Leyden and following his father's rigorous curriculum of Greek, Latin, and mathematics—at the same time not forgetting the English poets.

In July 1781, the month he turned fourteen, John Quincy was asked, mostly on the strength of his fluency in French (the language of the

Russian court), to join Francis Dana as his secretary in a diplomatic mission to St. Petersburg, Russia. The mission found that Catherine the Great was not inclined to grant official recognition to the United States, so John Quincy busied himself with visiting bookstores, attending social events, and learning German.

In October 1782 he left St. Petersburg and traveled through Sweden, Denmark, and Germany. In each city he met leading citizens, attended dinners and dances and the theater, and found himself a sought-after guest. It was April 1783 before he reached The Hague (in the Netherlands), pleading the difficulties of travel in the winter as an excuse for his tardiness.

In 1784 Abigail Adams and her daughter Nabby (John Quincy's older sister) arrived in London. John Quincy, almost unrecognizable to his mother and sister, met them and escorted them to Paris, where the family lived for the next nine months. When John Adams was appointed the minister to Great Britain, it was decided that John Quincy needed to return to his native land to attend college.

He landed in New York on July 17, 1785, and after a month, set off for Boston and Braintree. Much to his chagrin, the president of Harvard College thought him deficient in Latin and Greek and insisted on private tutoring as a condition to his being admitted to the school. He lived and studied with his uncle, Reverend John Shaw, and developed a close relationship with his Aunt Elizabeth Shaw, who was more affectionate and less demanding than his parents.

In 1787 he graduated second in his class at Harvard and, with some foreboding, embarked on the study of law—something his parents expected of him. He studied with Theophilus Parsons, a lawyer in Newburyport, about forty miles from Boston. Unexcited by the law, he thought about writing poetry, wishing to make his mark in literature. He suffered an episode of depression at this time. He returned to Braintree. His Aunt Elizabeth took care of him during this episode, which lasted from October 1788 until March 1789.

Back at his studies, he became infatuated with a young resident of Newburyport, Mary

Frazier. Even after he had begun his law practice in 1790, he only wanted to come to an informal arrangement with her, knowing that he was not yet prepared to support a wife. When Mary pressed him for a formal engagement, they separated.

EARLY CAREER
In the summer of 1791, he began publishing the "Letters of Publicola" in a Boston newspaper, as a response to Thomas Jefferson's approval of Thomas Paine's *Rights of Man*. In further essays, he defended the American concept of a balance of powers, in part by citing the excesses of the government of revolutionary France.

> **"I wish I could have been consulted before it was irrevocably made. I rather wish it had not been made at all."**
>
> John Quincy Adams, 1794, in response to the news of his appointment as US minister to the Netherlands

In 1794, somewhat to his surprise, he was appointed by President Washington as the US minister to the Netherlands. He had little to do at The Hague, but he enjoyed being financially independent and having plenty of time for study. In 1795 he made an extended visit to London, where he met Louisa Catherine Johnson, the daughter of the American consul, Joshua Johnson. He again became infatuated, and after a certain amount of clumsiness and embarrassment on his part (the young woman's family thought at first that he preferred her older sister), he declared his intentions.

At the start of what was never an easy relationship, Louisa Catherine and John Quincy differed over when to be married, and he even received cautionary letters from home after news of his engagement had reached his family. He then got word that he had been given another diplomatic post: he had been appointed the new minister to Portugal. Before he reached London (on his way to Lisbon), however, he learned that his father had been elected the US president and was assigning him instead to Berlin, to the court of the king of Prussia. The couple was married in London and honeymooned there, saying goodbye to Louisa's family (who were returning to the United States under the cloud of a financial scandal).

The couple stayed in Berlin until 1801, when the senior Adams's term of office ended. After several miscarriages, Louisa Catherine delivered a son, George Washington Adams, in 1801; the couple would have two more sons, John Adams in 1803 and Charles Francis Adams in 1807, as well as a daughter, Louisa Catherine, in 1811, who died in 1812.

POLITICAL CAREER

In 1801 the family of John Quincy Adams returned to the United States. Adams again undertook the practice of law, but he was in very short order immersed in politics once again, being elected a Massachusetts state senator in 1802, and then selected as a US senator by his state's legislature in 1803, serving until 1808. He also, from 1805 to 1829, served as a professor of rhetoric and oratory at Harvard.

Despite his Federalist pedigree, Adams often found himself in agreement with Thomas Jefferson; he supported the Louisiana Purchase as well as Jefferson's extremely unpopular trade embargo. His support of Republican policies led to a break with the Federalists, and there was an attempt to replace him as a US senator. Adams resigned in June 1808, when a successor to his seat was chosen several months before the usual time of filling a vacant seat.

Less than a year later, James Madison was elected president and he appointed Adams as minister to Russia in 1809; Adams served until 1814, obtaining some trade concessions and forming a close relationship with Czar Alexander I. In 1810 he was offered a seat on the US Supreme Court, but he invoked Louisa Catherine's pregnancy as the reason he was unable to travel and to accept the position, which he did

not really want. The baby daughter, named Louisa Catherine, died in 1812 after a year of life.

In 1814 President Madison asked Adams to join the peace negotiations with the British at Ghent, Belgium. Adams soon found himself at odds with his fellow Americans, who included Speaker of the House Henry Clay and Secretary of the Treasury Albert Gallatin. Finally, the opposing parties managed to arrive at a treaty that restored the relationship between the United States and Great Britain to what it had been before the war; this was hailed by Americans, grateful that the war was over, as a great victory.

Adams was then appointed as minister to Great Britain and was joined in London, first by Louisa Catherine, and then by their two sons, who had been cared for by relatives in America during the years their parents were in Russia. At the end of 1816, the rumor reached Adams that the newly elected President Monroe would appoint him as secretary of state. After an eight-year absence, Adams returned to the United States in 1817.

SECRETARY OF STATE

From 1817 to 1825, Adams held the post at which his talents were displayed to their fullest. He worked well with Monroe, who outlined the broad policy that Adams then implemented through negotiation and treaty. In an agreement with Great Britain in 1818 he acquired valuable fishing rights off Newfoundland, which he had long sought; the Adams-Onís Treaty of 1819 allowed the United States to acquire Florida from Spain and defined the western border of the Louisiana Territory. Adams wrote much of the address that President Monroe delivered to Congress, which became known as the Monroe Doctrine. It asserted that the American continents were no longer open to colonization, and that European interference in the affairs of the independent nations that had been recognized by the United States would be interpreted as an unfriendly act toward the United States. The Monroe Doctrine had no immediate effect on European powers and could not always be enforced in practice, but over time it became the guiding policy for the United States, as a member nation of the Americas, and provided justification for US protection of the interests of Central and South American republics in particular.

PRESIDENCY

The presidential election of 1824 was hotly contested and became a four-way contest. None of the four candidates (Andrew Jackson, John Quincy Adams, William Crawford, and Henry Clay) had won the necessary majority of electoral votes, and the election was thrown to the House of Representatives, where Henry Clay was Speaker. With the lowest number of electoral votes, Clay was removed from consideration. However, he used his influence to throw his support to Adams (Jackson had received both more popular and more electoral votes than Adams), and Adams was ultimately elected president.

Adams then named Clay as his secretary of state, giving rise to accusations of a "corrupt bargain"—the charge that Adams had traded the position to Clay in exchange for Clay's support in the House. Jackson's many supporters were particularly incensed, and spent the next four years planning to unseat Adams in the next election. This also made Adams's relationship with Congress a difficult one, and he had little success in getting his programs passed. He urged sweeping programs of domestic improvements, particularly improvements to roads and canals, the majority of which met with rebuff and rejection by the Congress.

Under his direction, there were some international successes: a reciprocal trade treaty with the Federation of Central America (Guatemala, San Salvador [modern El Salvador], Honduras, Nicaragua, and Costa Rica) in 1825 and agreements with Great Britain in 1826 and 1827 for the restitution of property lost in the War of 1812 and joint occupation of the Oregon Territory. Less successful was Adams's desire to send delegates to the Panama Congress in 1826, which was an attempt to strengthen commercial interests between the United States and South American countries; southern foes feared that the United States would be drawn into supporting antislavery provisions. By the time the

US Congress gave its approval to the sending of delegates, the Panama Congress had disbanded. Better luck attended the Adams administration's attempts to form trading agreements with Sweden, Denmark, Norway, and the Hanseatic cities of Germany, all concluded between 1824 and 1828.

> "I implore the mercy of God to control my temper, to enlighten my soul, and to give me utterance, that I may prove myself in every respect equal to the task."
>
> John Quincy Adams, in his diary, October 1840, after being asked to defend the freedom of the slaves taken from the slave ship *Amistad*

On July 4, 1826, both John Adams and Thomas Jefferson died on the fiftieth anniversary of the signing of the Declaration of Independence; the deaths were cause for national mourning and, for Adams, personal mourning.

A series of protective tariffs had been introduced in earlier years, but a higher tariff, in part designed to counteract the effect of the dumping of cheap British goods on the American market in the wake of the War of 1812, was passed in 1828 and dubbed the "Tariff of Abominations" by southerners. The bill had been proposed by Adams's vice president, John C. Calhoun, who assumed the bill would not be accepted by Adams and that it would bolster support for Jackson. But Adams signed the bill, realizing that by doing so that he was probably dooming his desire for reelection. He was right: in the election of 1828, Jackson won a resounding victory.

"OLD MAN ELOQUENCE"

Adams returned to Massachusetts, but he was unhappy in retirement. Before long, he was back in politics; he was elected to the House of

Representatives, where he served from 1831 until his death in 1848. Here he pursued his interest in civil works and improving the American economy.

He was publicly identified during these years as an opponent of slavery and an antislavery orator (he was given the nickname "Old Man Eloquent"). Congress had instituted a "gag rule," prohibiting discussion of the elimination of slavery. For years Adams campaigned for the repeal of the gag order, which finally occurred in 1844. Another victory for human rights was struck in 1841, when he argued before the Supreme Court the defense of the rebelling slaves who had been aboard the slave ship *Amistad*, which they had seized from their captors before making landfall on Long Island, New York. The ship, with most of the slaves it had been carrying still aboard, was taken into custody and towed to New Haven, Connecticut. The Spanish owners of the vessel requested that their "property"—the slaves—be returned to them. When the case came before the Supreme Court, Adams successfully argued that the men had been free in Africa at the time of their capture and that the slave trade was illegal in the United States. Thus the men could not be slaves. They returned to Africa as free men.

**"This is the last of earth!
I am content."**

John Quincy Adams, last words,
February 21, 1848

Adams collapsed in the House of Representatives from a stroke and died two days later, on February 23, 1848. Louisa Catherine had a stroke a year later, and died three years after that, on May 15, 1852.

Birthplace: Braintree (now Quincy), MA
Residency: Massachusetts
Religion: Unitarian
Education: Harvard College, graduated 1787

Place of Death: Washington, DC
Burial site: United First Parish Church, Quincy, MA
Dates in office: March 4, 1825–March 3, 1829 (4 years)
Age at inauguration: 57 years, 236 days

FAMILY
Father: John Adams (1735–1826)
Mother: Abigail Smith Adams (1744–1818)
Siblings: John Quincy Adams was the second of five children; his siblings were Abigail "Nabby" Adams (1765–1813); Susanna Adams (1768–1770); Charles Adams (1770–1800); Thomas Boylston Adams (1772–1832).
Wife: Louisa Catherine Johnson (1775–1852), married on July 26, 1797, in London, England
Children: George Washington Adams (1801–1829); John Adams (1803–1834); Charles Francis Adams (1807–1886); Louisa Catherine Adams (1811–1812)

CAREER
Private: Lawyer, diplomat
Political: secretary to the US minister to Russia (1781); minister to the Netherlands (1794); minister to Prussia (1797–1801); MA state senator (1802); US senator (1803–1808); minister to Russia (1809–1814); peace commissioner for the Treaty of Ghent (1814); minister to Great Britain (1815–1817); secretary of state under Monroe (1817–1825); president of the United States (1825–1829); member of the US House of Representatives (1831–1848)
Military: none
Selected Works: *Argument of John Quincy Adams Before the Supreme Court of the United States, in the Case of the United States, Appellants, vs. Cinque, and Others, Africans, Captured in the Schooner Amistad . . .* (New York: Negro Universities Press, 1969); *Diary of John Quincy Adams,* ed. by David Grayson Allen, et al. (Cambridge, MA: Belknap Press of Harvard University Press, 1981); *Lectures on Rhetoric and Oratory (1810); A Facsimile Reproduction with an Introduction by Charlotte Downey* (Delmar, NY: Scholars' Facsimiles & Reprints, 1997); *The I of John Adams, Begun by John Quincy Ada*

Completed by Charles Francis Adams.
Philadelphia Lippincott, 1871 (St. Clair Shores, MI: Scholarly Press, 1971); *Report of the Secretary of State upon Weights and Measures, Prepared in Obedience to a Resolution of the House of Representatives of the Fourteenth of December 1819* (New York: Arno Press, 1980); *The Wants of Man, a Poem*, with an introduction by L. H. Butterfield (Barre, MA: Imprint Society, 1972)

PRESIDENCY

Nomination: Adams is nominated as a "favorite son" by the MA legislature in 1824 after the congressional caucus (attended by less than a third of the eligible congressmen) had selected William H. Crawford of GA as a candidate; Henry Clay of KY was nominated as a favorite son by the KY state legislature, and Andrew Jackson had been nominated by the TN legislature two years earlier, in 1822.

Election: 1824: elected president (the election took place in November but voting occurred on different days in different states before 1845, when Congress mandated a uniform election day; the disputed election is settled in the House of Representatives in February of 1825)
1828: lost the election to Andrew Jackson

Opponent: 1824: Andrew Jackson, TN, Democratic-Republican Party; Henry Clay, KY, Democratic-Republican Party; William H. Crawford, GA, Democratic-Republican Party
1828: Andrew Jackson, TN, Democratic Party

Vote Totals: 1824: Adams, 108,740 popular, 84 electoral; Jackson, 153,544 popular, 99 electoral; Clay, 47,136 popular, 37 electoral; Crawford, 46,618 popular, 41 electoral
1828: Jackson, 647,286 popular, 178 electoral; Adams, 508,064 popular, 83 electoral

Inauguration: March 1825

Vice President: John C. Calhoun, SC (1825–1829)

CABINET

Secretary of State: Henry Clay, KY (1825–1829)
Secretary of the Treasury: Richard Rush, PA (1825–1829)
Secretary of War: James Barbour, VA (1825–; Peter B. Porter, NY (1828)

Attorney General: William Wirt, VA (1825–1829)
Postmaster General: John McLean, OH (1825–1829)
Secretary of the Navy: Samuel L. Southard, NJ (1825–1829)

CONGRESS

19th Congress (1825–1827); Speaker of the House: John W. Taylor (NY, Democrat [later Taylor was an organizer of the National Republican Party and then the Whig Party])
20th Congress (1827–1829); Speaker of the House: Andrew Stevenson (VA, Democrat)

SUPREME COURT APPOINTEES

Robert Trimble, KY; Associate Justice (1826–1828)

MAJOR EVENTS OF THE ADAMS ADMINISTRATION

◆ The Erie Canal is completed, 1825.
◆ Although Andrew Jackson receives more electoral votes than Adams, none of the four candidates (Jackson, Adams, William Crawford, and Henry Clay) attains a majority, so the election is decided in the House of Representatives. Henry Clay, as speaker of the House, throws his support to Adams—despite instructions from the KY legislature to vote for Jackson—and thus gains him the presidency in February of 1825. Jackson is furious.
◆ Adams appoints Henry Clay as secretary of state, 1825; political opponents, supporters of Andrew Jackson, charge that Adams and Clay made a "corrupt bargain" by exchanging the appointment of Clay for Clay's support of Adams in the House of Representatives during the resolution of the 1824 election.
◆ The United States signs a reciprocal trade treaty with the Federation of Central America (Guatemala, San Salvador [modern El Salvador], Honduras, Nicaragua, and Costa Rica), 1825.
◆ The newly independent states of Central America convene the Panama Congress, 1826; Adams asks that two US delegates be sent, but this arouses a storm of protest among

southerners, who fear that the United States will be urged to join the Central American nations in outlawing slavery. Approval for the delegates is eventually given by the US Congress, but the Panama Congress has disbanded by the time they arrive.

◆ John Adams and Thomas Jefferson die, July 4, 1826.

◆ The United States and Great Britain finally conclude an agreement in 1826 for restitution of property damages incurred by the United States during the War of 1812.

◆ The United States and Great Britain agree to their joint occupation of the Oregon territory, 1827.

◆ Favorable trading agreements are concluded with Sweden, Denmark, Norway, and the Hanseatic cities, 1824–1828.

◆ Ground is broken for the Chesapeake and Ohio Canal, 1828; intended to connect the Chesapeake Bay to the Ohio River along the Potomac River, it is completed as far as Cumberland, MD, but railroads make the remainder of the planned canal unnecessary.

◆ The Baltimore & Ohio railroad is chartered in 1827 and ground is broken in 1828.

◆ Joel Poinsett, the US minister to Mexico, accedes to the Mexican Boundary Settlement, 1828, which confirms the Sabine River as the US-Mexican boundary.

◆ A protectionist tariff is passed and dubbed the "Tariff of Abominations" by southerners, 1828. Adams's vice president, John C. Calhoun, undermines the bill (which he had proposed to bolster support for Jackson) by secretly writing the "South Carolina Exposition and Protest," in which he advocates a state's right to nullify federal laws it deems unconstitutional.

MAJOR US AND WORLD EVENTS, 1825–1829

◆ Thomas Cole establishes the Hudson River School of landscape painting, 1825.

◆ Bolivia proclaims its independence, 1825.

◆ James Fenimore Cooper publishes *The Last of the Mohicans*, 1826.

◆ Georg Ohm publishes *Die galvanische Kette,*

mathematisch bearbeitet, 1827, in which he explains his theory of electricity, as well as the unusual mathematical approach he took in developing it.

◆ John James Audubon publishes *Birds of America*, 1827.

◆ Nathaniel Hawthorne publishes his first novel, *Fanshawe*, 1828.

◆ Russia declares war on the Ottoman Empire, 1828; the truce that ends the war in 1829 puts the entire Caucasus under Russian control. Ethnic Armenians generally opt to live in the area dominated by Russia, while Muslims generally move into areas under Ottoman control.

◆ Noah Webster publishes *An American Dictionary of the English Language* in two volumes, 1828.

◆ Greeks are victorious in their war of independence with the Ottoman Empire, 1828.

FAST FACTS ABOUT JOHN QUINCY ADAMS

◆ When only fourteen years old, John Quincy Adams traveled from Paris to St. Petersburg, Russia, accompanying Francis Dana on a diplomatic mission; Adams acted as secretary and translator as he was fluent in French.

◆ John Quincy Adams was the first president whose father was also president (George W. Bush is the second).

◆ Adams was the first president elected with neither the largest number of popular votes nor the largest number of electoral votes (the third president, Thomas Jefferson, had tied with Aaron Burr in the number of electoral votes received)—the election was decided in the House of Representatives.

◆ As president, Adams was in the habit of rising before dawn for exercise. Sometimes he walked or rode, and sometimes he went down to the Potomac River, took off his clothes, and went for a swim. On one occasion, reporter Anne Royall followed him and sat on his clothes, refusing to move until he answered her questions.

◆ Adams was the first president to be photographed.

◆ Adams is the only president to serve in the House of Representatives after his presidency.

◆ In 1791 Adams injured his eyes by viewing an eclipse of the sun; he had forgotten to bring along a piece of smoked glass to protect his eyes.

◆ Adams was the first president whose son was married at the White House.

◆ Adams wrote poetry and regretted that he did not have a distinguished literary career.

◆ Adams began a journal at age eleven that he kept for most of his life.

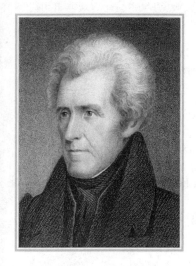

Andrew Jackson

Nickname: Old Hickory, King Andrew
Presidency: 7th president (1829–1837)
Party: Democratic
Life dates: March 15, 1767–June 8, 1845 (78 years, 85 days)

EARLY LIFE AND EDUCATION

Elizabeth Hutchinson Jackson and Andrew Jackson and their two young sons, Hugh and Robert, were a Scotch-Irish family from Northern Ireland that emigrated in 1765. They settled as farmers near family members in the Waxhaw Settlement, near the boundary of North Carolina and South Carolina. Andrew Jackson died in March 1767, just before his wife bore their third son on March 15, 1767; the baby was named Andrew Jackson after his father. The widow moved with her three sons into the home of her invalid sister, Jane Crawford, and her husband, James Crawford. Elizabeth Jackson acted as her sister's housekeeper and sent her boys to local schools. She hoped that young Andrew would become a Presbyterian minister, so she sent him to an academy run by Dr. William Humphries and then to a school run by James White Stephenson, a Presbyterian minister.

It is doubtful that anyone but his mother thought Andrew would become a minister. He was an active youngster with a mean temper who received little education before quitting school during the Revolutionary War, when British troops were invading South Carolina. An-

drew joined the regiment commanded by Colonel William Richardson Davie and was present at the battle of Hanging Rock, on August 1, 1780. The following year, Andrew and his brother Robert were captured by the British. Ordered to clean an officer's boots, he refused and was struck with a sword. The injury left him with permanent scars. Imprisoned in Camden, both boys contracted smallpox. Their mother arranged for a prisoner exchange and obtained their release. Hugh, the eldest son, had died in 1779; Robert died on the journey home but Andrew slowly recovered. After he recovered, his mother went to Charleston to nurse prisoners of war on prison ships; she died from cholera in 1781. Andrew, at the age of fourteen, became an orphan.

Andrew lived with various relatives, held down a variety of jobs, and attended a school run by Robert McCulloch. For a time he taught school in Waxhaw, from 1783 to 1784. He then decided to study law and moved to Salisbury, North Carolina, where he studied under Spruce McCay for two years. During his days as a law student, Jackson was rather wild, spending his spare time drinking, fighting, and racing horses. He continued his law studies under Colonel

John Stokes and passed the bar on September 26, 1787.

EARLY CAREER

For the next year Jackson practiced law and tended a store in Martinsville, North Carolina, before being appointed as public prosecutor for the Western District of North Carolina. He moved west to Jonesborough, in the eastern part of what would become Tennessee. On August 12, 1788, he fought his first duel, with Waightstill Avery, who had questioned Jackson's legal knowledge. Neither man was injured in the affair.

"[H]is decisions were short, untechnical, unlearned, sometimes ungrammatical, and generally right."

James Parton, an early biographer of Andrew Jackson, describing Jackson as a judge, 1866

About a month later, Jackson moved to Nashville and moved into a boardinghouse kept by a widow, Mrs. Donelson. Jackson was introduced to her daughter, Rachel Donelson Robards, who had recently separated from a jealous and abusive husband. They fell in love and, believing (erroneously) that Rachel was legally divorced, married in August 1791. They lived together for two years before Rachel's husband challenged the legality of their divorce, accused her of adultery and bigamy, and subsequently divorced her. Rachel and Andrew married again, on January 17, 1794. At intervals for the rest of their married life, Rachel was distressed by rumors about herself, believed to have been set in motion by her ex-husband, and Andrew was always quick to defend her honor, by offering a duel if necessary.

Jackson was appointed attorney general for Tennessee's Mero District in 1791, and judge advocate for the Davidson County militia in 1792. The Jacksons moved to an estate called Poplar Grove. Like most men who lived on the frontier, Jackson engaged in land speculation throughout his career.

POLITICAL CAREER

Jackson was elected as a delegate to the Tennessee Constitutional Convention in 1795 and attended the convention in January and February of 1796. That same year, he was elected the first member of the US House of Representatives from the new state of Tennessee. The following year he was elected to the US Senate, but he resigned the seat after only a year.

Returning home to the property he had purchased in 1796, Hunter's Hill, he was soon elected a judge of the Superior Court of Tennessee, a position he held for six years. In 1802 he was elected major general of the Tennessee militia, and in 1804 he resigned his position of judge. On August 4, 1804, he purchased the Hermitage property, on which he would later build a mansion. Jackson was a landowner and slave owner who engaged in trade and land speculation, sometimes coming dangerously close to bankruptcy.

A guest at the Hermitage was Aaron Burr, who shared with Jackson his plans for an "adventure" in the southwest. Jackson viewed favorably Burr's plans to attack the Native Americans and the Spanish; he was later surprised and disbelieving when President Thomas Jefferson charged that Burr's plans were treasonable.

On May 30, 1806, Jackson shot and killed Charles Dickinson in a duel provoked by an argument over a wager on a horse race. Dickinson was reputedly the best shot in Tennessee and wounded Jackson near the heart before Jackson returned his fire and killed him. The bullet caused Jackson pain and occasional hemorrhaging for the rest of his life.

In 1809 Rachel and Andrew adopted their nephew, the son of Elizabeth and Severn Donelson, naming the child Andrew Jackson, Jr.

MILITARY CAREER

The War of 1812 made Jackson a national hero. He led the Tennessee militia against the Creek tribe of Native Americans, winning a series of victories, notably the one at Horseshoe Bend, on March 27, 1814. He made peace treaties with Native Americans that actually deprived them of massive tracts of land. His arduous campaigns prompted his troops to nickname him "Old Hickory." Jackson met with threats of desertion from his starving, undisciplined troops, but managed to maintain command and win the respect of the troops. On May 28, 1814, the US government recognized his military successes by commissioning him as a major general in the US Army.

In October 1814 Jackson began invading Florida, capturing Pensacola in November. He left Pensacola to march for New Orleans, where in mid-December he imposed martial law on the city. The war had officially ended but the news had not reached New Orleans prior to the battle that took place on January 8, 1815, in which he commanded in a stunning defeat of the British. The British lost more than 2,000 men, while the American losses were just 13 men. After a war in which America had won few victories, the capital city had been captured and the White House burned, and the treaty that ended the war had had little effect in changing the conditions that prevailed prior to the war, Jackson's victory was an occasion for national pride.

In late 1817 Jackson assumed command of the Seminole War and invaded Spanish Florida. He captured Pensacola a second time, on May 24, 1818, and executed two British subjects. Initially criticized by the federal government for his actions, he was defended by Secretary of State John Quincy Adams, who blamed the incident on the Spanish neglect of their colony and eventually brokered with Spain to sell Florida to the United States. In 1821 Jackson was appointed governor of the Florida Territory and he resigned his army commission. On July 17, 1821, he officially received the command of Florida from the Spanish and in November he resigned as governor. He returned to Tennessee, where he had begun building a mansion on the Hermitage property.

PRESIDENTIAL ASPIRATIONS

Jackson's friends and supporters began to urge him to consider the presidency. In 1822, two years before the election, the Tennessee state legislature nominated him as a candidate. To enhance his prospects for the presidency, his supporters also arranged for him to be elected to the US Senate in 1823.

In the election of 1824, Jackson received more popular votes than anyone else, but because the opposition was composed of three other candidates, no-one received a majority. The fourth-place candidate, Henry Clay, was excluded from consideration when it came time for members of the House of Representatives to vote for the top three candidates—Jackson, John Quincy Adams, and William Crawford— but, as Speaker of the House, Clay may have had a deciding influence on the vote. Clay threw his support to Adams, who was elected president. Jackson's supporters accused Adams and Clay of making "a corrupt bargain" when Adams later appointed Clay as his secretary of state.

"There are no necessary
evils in government.
Its evils exist only in its abuses."

Andrew Jackson, his veto of the
Second National Bank, July 10, 1832

Jackson formed new political ties with such men as Martin Van Buren, who was instrumental to the formation of the political party that would be known as the Democratic Party. During the next four years, this group focused on Jackson's election in 1828. The campaign was bitterly fought, and the old rumors about Rachel Jackson were used in attempts to discredit Jackson. He was elected by a large majority, but prior to his inauguration, Rachel Jackson died of a heart attack. Jackson blamed his political opponents for her death.

PRESIDENCY

Jackson's niece, Emily Donelson, acted as the White House hostess for most of his presidency. After she left the White House, either in the wake of the Peggy Eaton Affair or because of illness (she died in 1836), the role of White House hostess was filled by Sarah Yorke Jackson, the wife of his nephew and adopted son, Andrew Jackson, Jr.

Andrew Jackson was a wildly popular president for two terms. He was widely seen as representing and espousing the cause of the common man. He set out to reform government; one of his goals was to reduce the national debt, which he did. However, the establishment of the "spoils system," by which government jobs are awarded to party members, has also been attributed to Jackson.

Jackson's use of his influence in Congress and his use of the veto power (he used the veto more than all previous presidents combined) prompted his critics to dub him "King Andrew." Even when the Supreme Court ruled on a question, Jackson refused to support their ruling if it ran counter to his own position.

Several debates enflamed passions during Jackson's presidency: One grew out of southern opposition to protective tariffs, which were thought to protect northern manufacturing interests. The tariffs were imposed on imported goods in order to protect domestic products, but southern agricultural interests objected to the higher prices tariffs forced them to pay. In 1832 Jackson issued a Nullification Proclamation, reaffirming the principle that states could not nullify federal laws. When South Carolina adopted the "Ordinance of Nullification," attempting to nullify federal tariff laws, Jackson threatened to enforce the tariff with arms—a threat backed up by congressional approval. In the wake of this, John C. Calhoun resigned as

vice president and became a senator from South Carolina in 1835. Congress eventually eased the tariffs, averting further conflict on this issue.

"John Marshall has made his decision: now let him enforce it!"

a remark attributed to Andrew Jackson, following an 1832 legal case in which two missionaries from New England living among the Cherokee had refused to take an oath of allegiance to the state of Georgia and been imprisoned; the Supreme Court under Chief Justice John Marshall ordered their release, but the state refused to comply and Jackson supported the state's right to do so

---

Another debate concerned the Second Bank of the United States. Jackson vetoed the recharter of the bank in 1832, and in 1833 moved the bank's monies into state-chartered banks. Ultimately, this probably contributed to the financial panic of 1837; however, that crisis came after Jackson had passed the torch to his second vice president, Martin Van Buren.

A continuing theme of Jackson's life, both before and during his presidency, was the forced removal of Native Americans to lands further west. As a soldier he contributed to this movement of peoples through military defeats and restrictive treaties; during his presidency, the Indian Removal Act, passed by Congress in 1830, sanctioned the forcible removal of tribes to lands west of the Mississippi. The tragic "Trail of Tears" was the expulsion of Creek and Cherokee from their homelands in 1835 to 1838 and the subsequent coerced migration, with many dying from drought, cold, and disease along the way. The Black Hawk War of 1832, a consequence of another endeavor to push Native Americans westward, was precipitated by Sauk and Fox tribes who left the Iowa Territory to return to Illinois, where they were attacked and defeated by the US army and militia.

Another political imbroglio of Jackson's tumultuous presidency was the Peggy Eaton Affair (also called the "petticoat affair"). Margaret "Peggy" Eaton was the wife of a friend and colleague of Jackson's, John Eaton, whom he named as his secretary of war. Peggy Eaton was a lively and popular young woman, and rumors about her liaisons with various men began to circulate. Many of the women in Washington society snubbed her, including the wives of the members of Jackson's cabinet. Always quick to defend a lady's honor, Jackson defended her, and regarded denigration of her as part of a political attack on him. The issue became so heated that Jackson's entire cabinet resigned in 1831, and an entirely new cabinet was appointed for his second term.

RETIREMENT TO THE HERMITAGE

Jackson left the presidency in the hands of his second vice president, Martin Van Buren, and returned to the Hermitage. During his final years, he continued to exert an influence on national politics, but on a personal level he battled poor health and a mountain of debt that had been incurred by his adopted son. He died in 1845 and was buried at the Hermitage next to Rachel Jackson.

Birthplace: Waxhaw, SC (presumably) [Note: The actual place Jackson was born is not precisely known; it was near the border of North Carolina and South Carolina and could have been in either state.]
Residency: Tennessee
Religion: Presbyterian
Education: some schooling as a boy; quit in order to fight in the Revolutionary War
Place of Death: The Hermitage, Nashville, TN
Burial site: The Hermitage, Nashville, TN
Dates in office: March 4, 1829–March 3, 1837 (8 years)
Age at inauguration: 61 years, 354 days

FAMILY

Father: Andrew Jackson (c. 1730–1767)
Mother: Elizabeth Hutchinson Jackson (c. 1735–1781)

Siblings: Andrew Jackson was the third of three sons; his brothers were Hugh Jackson (1762–1779) and Robert Jackson (1765–1781).
Wife: Rachel Donelson Robards Jackson (1767–1828); married in August 1791 and in another ceremony on January 17, 1794. At the time of her marriage she believed herself divorced from Captain Lewis Robards; the couple later learned that the process had not been completed and so married again after the divorce was confirmed.
Children: Andrew Jackson, Jr., adopted (1808–1865)

CAREER

Private: Lawyer
Political: Member of the US House of Representatives (1796–1797); US senator (1797–1798); justice, Tennessee Supreme Court (1798–1804); governor of the Florida Territory (1821); US senator (1823–1825); president of the United States (1829–1837)
Military: joined the Continental Army at age thirteen; captured (with his brother Robert) by the British (1781); imprisoned in Camden, SC; released in an exchange of prisoners arranged by his mother; elected major general of the Tennessee militia (1802); from 1812 to 1815, led troops against Native Americans and British forces (1812–1815); nicknamed Old Hickory; won a victory against Creeks at Tallushatchee (November 3, 1813); won a victory against Native Americans at Talladega, AL (November 9, 1813); defeated Creek at Horseshoe Bend (March 27, 1814); commissioned a major general in the US Army (May 28, 1814); imposed the Treaty of Fort Jackson on the Creek Nation (August 9, 1814); occupied Mobile, AL (August 1814); invaded Florida (October 1814); captured Pensacola (November 1814) but evacuated two days later; arrived in New Orleans (December 1, 1814) and imposed martial law on the city (December 16, 1814); defeated the British in the Battle of New Orleans (January 8, 1815); signed treaties with Cherokees and Chickasaws (September 1816); signed another treaty with Cherokees (July 1817); quarreled with the War Department and General Winfield Scott (late 1817); assumed command of the Seminole War and invaded Spanish Florida

(March 1818); captured Pensacola (again) (May 24, 1818); a Congressional censure of Jackson rejected (February 8, 1819)

Selected Works: *Correspondence of Andrew Jackson*, ed. by John Spencer Bassett (Washington, DC: Carnegie Institute of Washington, 1926–1935); *The Papers of Andrew Jackson*, ed. by Sam B. Smith and Harriet Chappell Owsley; consulting editor Robert V. Remini (Knoxville: University of Tennessee Press, 1980–2002)

PRESIDENCY

Nomination: Jackson was nominated by the Tennessee legislature in 1822; after winning the popular vote (but not a majority of electoral votes) in 1824 and losing when the election was decided in the House of Representatives, Jackson accused Adams and Henry Clay of having made "a corrupt bargain" and dedicated himself to gaining the office he felt had been stolen from him, which he did in 1828; in 1832, the first national nominating conventions took place, with the Democratic Party meeting mainly to confirm Jackson's choice of vice president (Martin Van Buren) for his second term as president.

Election: 1824: lost the election to John Quincy Adams

1828: elected president (election took place in November but voting occurred on different days in different states before 1845, when Congress mandated a uniform election day)

1832: elected president (election took place in November but voting occurred on different days in different states before 1845, when Congress mandated a uniform election day)

Opponent: 1824: John Quincy Adams, MA, Democratic-Republican; Henry Clay, KY, Democratic-Republican; William H. Crawford, GA, Democratic-Republican

1828: John Quincy Adams, MA, National Republican

1832: Henry Clay, KY, National Republican; William Wirt, MD, Anti-Masonic; John Floyd, VA, Republican

Vote Totals: 1824: Adams, 108,740 popular, 84 electoral; Jackson, 153,544 popular, 99 electoral;

Clay, 47,136 popular, 37 electoral; Crawford, 46,618 popular, 41 electoral

1828: Jackson, 647,286 popular, 178 electoral; Adams, 508,064 popular, 83 electoral

1832: Jackson, 687,502 popular, 219 electoral; Clay, 530,189 popular, 49 electoral; Wirt, 7 electoral; Floyd, 11 electoral; votes not cast, 2

Inauguration: 1828: March 4, 1829

1832: March 4, 1833

Vice President: John C. Calhoun, SC (1829–1832); Martin Van Buren, NY (1832–1837)

CABINET

Secretary of State: Martin Van Buren, NY (1829–1831); Edward Livingston, LA (1831–1833); Louis McLane, DE (1833–1834); John Forsyth, GA (1834–1837)

Secretary of the Treasury: Samuel D. Ingham, PA (1829–1831); Louis McLane, DE (1831–1833); William J. Duane, PA (1833); Roger B. Taney, MD (1833–1834); Levi Woodbury, NH (1834–1837)

Secretary of War: John H. Eaton, TN (1829–1831); Lewis Cass, MI (1831–1836)

Attorney General: John M. Berrien, GA (1829–1831); Roger B. Taney, MD (1831–1833); Benjamin F. Butler, NY (1833–1837)

Postmaster General: William T. Barry, KY (1829–1835); Amos Kendall, KY (1835–1837)

Secretary of the Navy: John Branch, NC (1829–1831); Levi Woodbury, NH (1831–1834); Mahlon Dickerson, NJ (1834–1837)

CONGRESS

21st Congress (1829–1831); Speaker of the House: Andrew Stevenson (VA, Democrat)
22nd Congress (1831–1833); Speaker of the House: Andrew Stevenson (VA, Democrat)
23rd Congress (1833–1835); Speaker of the House: John Bell (TN, Whig)
24th Congress (1835–1837); Speaker of the House: James K. Polk (TN, Democrat)

SUPREME COURT APPOINTEES

John McLean, OH; Associate Justice (1830–1861)
Henry Baldwin, PA; Associate Justice (1830–1844)
James Moore Wayne, GA; Associate Justice (1835–1867)

Philip Pendleton Barbour, VA; Associate Justice (1836–1841)
Roger Brooke Taney, MD; Chief Justice (1836–1864)

MAJOR EVENTS OF THE JACKSON ADMINISTRATION

◆ Jackson establishes an informal group of advisors, dubbed the "kitchen cabinet," 1829.
◆ David Walker, a free black man, publishes his antislavery *Appeal*, September 1829, which argues that America belongs to those who have enriched it with their "blood and tears" and, therefore, that the colonization of Africa by freed American slaves is undesirable; he also calls for slaves to revolt against their masters.
◆ The Peggy Eaton Affair (also called the "petticoat affair"), 1828 to 1831, centers on the wife of Jackson's secretary of war, John Eaton. Rumors about the woman's past cause Washington society to snub her, but Jackson defends her honor. Eventually the controversy extends to Jackson's cabinet, as some of its members (and their wives) continue to snub her. The entire cabinet resigns in 1831.
◆ The Indian Removal Act is passed by Congress, 1830; it authorizes the forcible removal of various tribes to lands west of the Mississippi; from 1835 to 1838, the Creek and Cherokee are moved west along the "Trail of Tears" and nearly one-quarter of them die along the way.
◆ Jackson vetoes the Maysville Road Bill, 1830, believing that because the road would lie entirely within one state, it should be paid for locally and not with federal tax dollars.
◆ Nat Turner leads a slave revolt in Southampton County, Virginia, 1831. He is captured and hanged.
◆ Jackson issues a Nullification Proclamation, reaffirming the principle that states are forbidden to nullify federal laws, 1832.
◆ Jackson vetoes the recharter of Second Bank of the United States, 1832.
◆ The Black Hawk War erupts in 1832; Sauk and Fox tribes attempt to leave Iowa Territory and return to Illinois, but are defeated by US regular troops and militia.

◆ With the Force Bill, 1833, Congress authorizes the use of the army, if necessary, to collect tariff revenues in the states.
◆ South Carolina adopts the "Ordinance of Nullification," which attempts to nullify federal tariff laws; John C. Calhoun resigns as vice president and becomes a South Carolina senator, 1835.
◆ In 1835, Richard Lawrence attempts to assassinate Jackson in the Capitol rotunda, but his two pistols misfire; Lawrence is captured and committed to an insane asylum.
◆ The Battle of the Alamo, in which 190 Americans fight 6,000 Mexicans for twelve days, ends in the defeat of the Americans, on March 6, 1836.
◆ Jackson issues the Specie Circular, 1836, which orders that gold and silver are to be the only acceptable currency for the purchase of federal lands.
◆ In the Texas Revolution, 1836, American settlers in Texas declare their independence from Mexico and establish an independent republic; Jackson recognizes Texas independence, 1837.
◆ Arkansas becomes a state, June 15, 1836.
◆ Michigan becomes a state, January 26, 1837.

MAJOR US AND WORLD EVENTS, 1829–1837

◆ The first American encyclopedia, the *Encyclopedia Americana*, is published in Philadelphia, 1829.
◆ Britain's Metropolitan Police are founded by Sir Robert Peel, after whom the police are dubbed "Bobbies," 1829.
◆ James Smithson dies, 1829, and leaves his fortune to the United States for the foundation of a museum (later known as the Smithsonian), provided his heir dies without issue (which he does in 1835). The United States is informed of the bequest and after urging by President Jackson, Congress agrees to accept the bequest in 1838.
◆ Hector Berlioz composes the *Symphonie fantastique*, 1830.
◆ The US census shows a population of 12.8 million people, 1830.

◆ Joseph Smith founds the Church of Jesus Christ of Latter Day Saints (Mormons) in New York state, 1830.

◆ Marie Henri Beyle, a French author who writes under the name Stendhal, publishes *The Red and the Black*, 1830.

◆ Samuel F. Smith writes "My Country, 'tis of Thee," 1831.

◆ Belgium separates from the Netherlands and Leopold I becomes the Belgian king, 1831.

◆ Victor Hugo publishes *The Hunchback of Notre Dame*, 1831.

◆ William Lloyd Garrison founds *The Liberator*, a periodical that urges the abolition of slavery, 1831.

◆ English scientist Michael Faraday demonstrates the principle of induction, producing an electric current from changes in a magnetic field, 1831.

◆ A cholera epidemic, originating in India, reaches Britain and Ireland and spreads from there to American cities, including New York City and New Orleans, 1832.

◆ Antonio López de Santa Anna is elected president of Mexico, 1833.

◆ Felix Mendelssohn composes the *Italian Symphony*, 1833.

◆ Civil war breaks out in Spain between supporters of Queen Isabella II and the Carlists, supporters of Don Carlos, Isabella's uncle, 1834. This first Carlist War continues until 1840.

◆ Edward Bulwer-Lytton publishes *The Last Days of Pompeii*, 1834.

◆ Cyrus McCormick patents his mechanical reaper, 1834, greatly increasing the amount of wheat that could be cut in a day.

◆ Slavery is abolished throughout the British Empire, 1834.

◆ Charles Dickens publishes his first book, *Sketches by Boz*, 1835.

◆ Hans Christian Andersen publishes his first volume of fairy tales, 1835.

◆ French mathematician Gaspard Gustave de Coriolis publishes a paper describing what is now called the Coriolis force, an effect of gravity according to which a moving mass of air, water, or the like appears to be deflected from its course, 1835.

◆ On December 16–17, 1835, a massive fire in New York City destroys 530 buildings.

◆ Ralph Waldo Emerson publishes *Nature*, in which he expounds the basic ideas of the Transcendental movement, 1836.

◆ Robert Schumann composes *Fantasy in C Major*, 1836.

FAST FACTS ABOUT ANDREW JACKSON

◆ As a child, Jackson had a habit described as slobbering—if teased about it, he would immediately fight his tormenter.

◆ Andrew Jackson was thirteen years old when he joined the South Carolina militia during the Revolutionary War. Captured by the British, he received a sword cut across the forehead, leaving a scar, when he refused to clean a British officer's boots.

◆ Jackson was the only president to serve in both the Revolutionary War and the War of 1812.

◆ Both Sam Houston and Davy Crockett served under Andrew Jackson in the campaign against the Creek Native Americans during the War of 1812.

◆ Jackson was the first president who married a divorced woman.

◆ Jackson fought a number of duels, including one fought on May 30, 1806, against Charles Dickinson, over a bet on a horse race. Dickinson was shot and killed by Jackson, who was wounded by a bullet that lodged in the vicinity of his heart and was never removed. It caused him considerable pain for the rest of his life.

◆ Jackson was the first president born in a log cabin.

◆ Jackson smoked a corncob pipe; Rachel Jackson also smoked a pipe.

◆ Jackson was Tennessee's first US congressman.

◆ Jackson is credited with introducing the "spoils system"—the practice of awarding government positions on the basis of party membership and service.

◆ Jackson was the first president whose vice president (Calhoun) resigned.

◆ Jackson was the first president to use the "pocket veto"—which consisted of the president's failing to sign a bill before Congress adjourned, so that it did not become law; he used this form of veto seven times, and an outright veto five times. Jackson used the veto more than all previous presidents combined.

◆ In 1833 Jackson moved funds from the Bank of the United States into various state banks, declaring the Bank of the United States a monopoly. In 1834 he vetoed legislation that would have extended the life of the Bank of the United States, after which the Whig Party asked him for documents relating to the veto. Jackson refused the request, and the Senate voted to censure him. Jackson denied the constitutional power of the Senate to censure him; when Democrats gained control of the Senate in 1836, the censure of Jackson was expunged from the record.

◆ The White House under Jackson had running water for the first time.

◆ Jackson had twenty spittoons placed in the East Room of the White House.

◆ Jackson was the first president to ride on a train.

◆ Jackson survived the first attempt to assassinate a president when Richard Lawrence's pistols misfired in 1835.

◆ Upon seeing a photograph of himself as an old man, Jackson reportedly remarked, "Looks like a monkey."

Martin Van Buren

*Nickname: The Little Magician, The Red Fox of Kinderhook,
Little Van, Martin Van Ruin, Old Kinderhook*
Presidency: 8th president, 1837–1841
Party: Democratic
Life Dates: December 5, 1782–July 24, 1862 (79 years, 231 days)

EARLY LIFE AND EDUCATION

Martin Van Buren was born in Kinderhook, New York, on December 5, 1782. His parents were Abraham Van Buren and Maria Hoes Van Alen Van Buren. His mother had three children from her first marriage, and Martin was the third of five children from this, her second marriage. Abraham Van Buren kept a tavern and was a freehold farmer. Growing up, Martin heard frequent political discussions in his father's tavern. Abraham supported the revolution and the ideals of the Jeffersonian Democratic-Republicans—a party affiliation his son also adopted, despite the influence of the many Federalists that New York boasted.

Dutch was spoken by the family. Martin attended a local one-room school and then the Kinderhook Academy, from which he graduated in 1796 at the age of fourteen. From then until he was twenty-one, he worked in law offices while studying the law, first with a local attorney, Francis Sylvester, and then with an attorney in New York City, William P. Van Ness. He was admitted to the bar in 1803 and joined his half-brother, James Van Alen, in his practice.

EARLY CAREER

Van Buren worked hard as a lawyer and became well-known, moving to a new practice in nearby Hudson, New York, in 1808. But his interest in politics was evident from the very beginning of his career; as early as 1801, while still studying for the bar, he was sent as a delegate to a regional nominating convention in Troy, New York.

In February 1807 Van Buren married Hannah Hoes, a distant cousin whom he had known since childhood. Their first son, Abraham, was born in Kinderhook later that year. After the family moved to Hudson, she gave birth to John and Martin Junior. She also bore a son, named for Van Buren's friend General Winfield Scott, who died in infancy. The family again moved, to the state capital, Albany, in 1816, and the couple had another son, Smith, in 1817. Reportedly a gentle woman who helped her rising politician husband (in part through her willingness to host his friends), Hannah never really recovered her full strength after the birth of her last child and became ill from tuberculosis, dying in 1819 after twelve years of marriage. Van Buren never remarried.

THE YOUNG POLITICIAN

In 1808 Van Buren was appointed by New York Governor Daniel Tompkins to the position of surrogate of Colombia County, a legal post. Continuing to build his law practice and his political connections, he was nominated by the Democrats (as the Democratic-Republicans loyal to Jefferson and Madison had come to be known) for a seat in the New York state senate, an election he won by a narrow margin in 1812. While serving as a state senator, he was simultaneously appointed as New York's attorney general for the period 1815–1819.

> "It is said that he [Van Buren] is a great magician. I believe it, but his only wand is good common sense, which he uses for the benefit of the country."
>
> Andrew Jackson

As the Federalist Party began to lose much of its influence, the Democratic Party split into many factions, even within New York state. Van Buren became known for playing his cards close to his vest, for not declaring his allegiances or opinions unless it became necessary. He gradually became the leader of one of the factions of the Democratic Party, and often found himself in opposition to DeWitt Clinton, governor of New York from 1817 to 1822. Van Buren formed political alliances in Albany as part of a group originally known as the Bucktails, and later as the Albany Regency. As the leader of this group, Van Buren helped to build a political organization that emphasized loyalty to the party. The leaders met often to decide policy and nominate candidates, and their decisions were communicated to newspapers whose editors were members of the group. The party also focused efforts on appointing, or helping to elect, local officials who would support the party goals.

NATIONAL POLITICS

In 1821 Van Buren moved onto the national stage as a US senator, a position he held until 1829. As a member of the Senate, he served on the Finance Committee and chaired the Judiciary Committee. He also set about trying to build the same kind of party organization on a national scale that he had on a state scale in New York. He encountered difficulties, owing to the sectional differences between northern and southern Democrats, but gradually helped to form the coalition that backed Andrew Jackson's bid for the presidency in 1828. Elected governor of New York state in 1828, Van Buren resigned in 1829 when Jackson appointed him secretary of state.

As secretary of state he wrangled with Jackson's vice president, John C. Calhoun, on specific issues and vied with Calhoun for Jackson's favor. Van Buren scored a victory when he supported Jackson's efforts to win social acceptance for Peggy Eaton, the wife of Secretary of War John Eaton, who had been ostracized by the wives of many cabinet members, especially Calhoun's wife. When the Eaton affair led to the breakup of Jackson's cabinet, Jackson appointed Van Buren as minister to Great Britain. Van Buren left for London, but after he arrived in that city he learned that Calhoun and his supporters had gained control of the Senate and were opposed to his confirmation as ambassador. Jackson responded by naming Van Buren as his running mate for his second term.

> "Van Buren is as opposite to General Jackson as dung is to a diamond."
>
> Congressman Davy Crockett, 1835

Jackson and Van Buren won an overwhelming victory in 1832. Van Buren tried to mediate between northern and southern interests in their disputes, including the disputes over tariffs and the threats coming from southern states of their intention to nullify the tariff and secede from the nation. Van Buren put aside his differences with Calhoun to help with the passage of the compromise tariff of 1833. Another debate centered on the second Bank of the United States, which Jackson refused to recharter. He withdrew the deposits from the bank and moved them to various state-controlled banks; Van Buren was not wholeheartedly in support of this move, but Jackson prevailed.

PRESIDENCY

With Jackson's support, Van Buren won the Democratic nomination and then the presidency, in 1836. The biggest problem facing him as president was the financial crisis that began in 1837, which included the closing of banks in New York City and Philadelphia and led to a nationwide depression that lasted most of his term. Van Buren held to his Democratic ideals, believing that federal interference should be limited and states' rights upheld. He was criticized for failing to recommend sweeping aid to the business community during the economic downturn, but his major goal was the establishment of an independent treasury separate from the federal government, which he achieved in 1840.

Van Buren continued many of Jackson's policies, including those that led to the Seminole War in the south and the forced removal of many Native Americans west along the "Trail of Tears," during which thousands of Native Americans died.

Van Buren's experience of working toward political compromise placed him in good stead when tensions between the United States and Great Britain threatened to lead to conflict over the border between the United States and Canada. Van Buren worked to resolve the disputes through diplomatic channels, keeping the United States out of war, but angering those who had advocated more aggressive action in dealing with the problem.

Van Buren's presidency also witnessed the *Amistad* affair, during which slaves aboard a slave ship revolted, took over the ship, and dropped anchor in the United States. Van Buren supported extraditing the slaves to Cuba (the ship had been Cuban), but northern antislavery interests forced a trial that was centered on the question of whether the slaves were property. Former president John Quincy Adams successfully defended the freedom of these slave rebels before the Supreme Court in early 1841, at the end of Van Buren's term. Those who had survived the ordeal were returned to their home in Africa.

> **"In receiving from the people the sacred trust twice confided to my illustrious predecessor, and which he has discharged so faithfully and so well, I know that I can not expect to perform the arduous task with equal ability and success."**
>
> Martin Van Buren, inaugural address, March 4, 1837

Among Van Buren's close advisors during his presidency were his sons, Abraham and Martin, who served as his aides. His eldest son, Abraham, married Angelica Singleton, who had been introduced to the Van Burens by former First Lady Dolley Madison, to whom Singleton was related by marriage. Angelica and Abraham took an extended trip to Europe, but after their return Angelica served as White House hostess for the last two years of Van Buren's presidency.

The opponents of Jacksonian Democrats formed the new Whig Party and chose William Henry Harrison, a war hero, as their candidate. In the election of 1840, Harrison was portrayed as a simple man of the people who had been born in a log cabin, despite the fact that he came from a wealthy family. Van Buren, by contrast, was portrayed as a luxury-loving aristocrat; even his habit of being well-dressed was held up to ridicule. The popular vote was close but Harrison won the electoral vote by 234 to 60.

RETIREMENT TO KINDERHOOK

Van Buren returned to Kinderhook and purchased an estate that he renamed Lindenwald. One of the joys of his life there were the frequent visits from his sons and their families; Van Buren had always had a close relationship with his sons, but he now spent considerable time with his grandchildren, as well.

By no means ready to quit politics, however, Van Buren became the favored candidate for the Democratic nomination for president in 1844, but lost support when he adamantly opposed the proposed annexation of Texas. He had always opposed the spread of slavery, and he feared that the annexation of Texas would mean the entry of an additional slave state into the Union, as well as a possible war with Mexico. Van Buren still seemed the favorite at the beginning of the convention, but was forced to withdraw his candidacy when Democrats from the South and West opposed him. Andrew Jackson, who had come out in favor of the annexation of Texas, threw his support to James K. Polk, who also supported annexation. Polk was nominated and elected. After his defeat at the convention, Van Buren put aside his disappointment and worked diligently for Polk's election. After Polk had been installed as president, Van Buren and his supporters expected Polk to offer Van Buren an important position. Polk did offer Van Buren the position of minister to Great Britain, but Van Buren turned it down.

In the election of 1848, Van Buren was chosen as the presidential candidate by the Free Soil Party, a group of former Democrats and Whigs united by their opposition to slavery. He was soundly defeated by the Whig candidate, Zachary Taylor. He later returned to the Democratic Party and supported the Compromise of 1850, hoping to avoid a split between North and South.

In 1853 he took an extended trip to Europe, spending two years there and working on his autobiography. He returned to Lindenwald and died there on July 24, 1862, at the age of seventy-nine, having seen the differences between the North and South erupt into the Civil War that he had tried so steadfastly to avoid.

Birthplace: Kinderhook, NY
Residency: New York
Religion: Dutch Reformed
Education: Kinderhook Academy, graduated 1796
Place of Death: Kinderhook, NY
Burial Site: Kinderhook Reformed Cemetery, Kinderhook, NY
Dates in Office: March 4, 1837–March 3, 1841 (4 years)
Age at Inauguration: 54 years, 89 days

FAMILY

Father: Abraham Van Buren (1737–1817)
Mother: Maria Hoes Van Alen Van Buren (1747–1817)
Siblings: Martin Van Buren was the third of five children; his siblings were Derike Van Buren (1777–1865); Hannah (Jannetje) Van Buren (1780); Lawrence Van Buren (1786–1868); Abraham Van Buren (1788–1836).

His mother also had three children from her first marriage to Johannes Van Alen (1744?–1773 or 1776): some sources record these children as Marytje Van Alen (1768–1829); Johannes Van Allen (1770–1805); and Jacobus Van Allen (1773–1822); other sources record these children as John Van Alen (1770–?); a daughter, name unknown (1774–?); and James Isaac Van Alen (1776–1870). [Note: Martin Van Buren had a law practice with a half-brother, identified as James Van Alen, who also became a member of the US Congress. If this is the James born in 1776, and that date of birth is correct, the death date for his father, Johannes Van Alen must be 1776, not 1773 as it is given in some sources.]
Wife: Hannah Hoes Van Buren (1783–1819), married February 21, 1807, at Catskill, NY
Children: Abraham Van Buren (1807–1873); John Van Buren (1810–1866); Martin Van Buren (1812–1855); Winfield Scott Van Buren (1813; died in infancy); Smith Thompson Van Buren (1817–1876)

CAREER

Private: lawyer
Political: NY state senator (1813–1821); NY attorney general (1815–1819); US senator (1821–

1829); governor of NY (January–March 1829); secretary of state under Jackson (1829–1831); minister to England (1831); vice president under Jackson (1832–1837); president of the United States (1837–1841)
Military: none
Selected Works: *The Autobiography of Martin Van Buren*, ed. by John C. Fitzpatrick (New York: Da Capo Press, 1973); *Inquiry into the Origin and Course of Political Parties in the United States*, ed. by Abraham and John Van Buren (New York: Hurd and Houghton, 1867); *The Papers of Martin Van Buren* [microfilm], ed. by Lucy Fisher West, Walter L. Ferree, and George W. Franz (Alexandria, VA: Chadwyck-Healey, 1987)

PRESIDENCY

Nomination: Van Buren was nominated, unanimously, by the Democratic convention in Baltimore, MD, in May 1835, largely because of Andrew Jackson's support.
Election: 1836: elected president (election took place in November but voting occurred on different days in different states before 1845, when Congress mandated a uniform election day)
1840: lost the election to William Henry Harrison
Opponent: 1836: William Henry Harrison, OH, Whig; Hugh L. White, TN, Whig; Daniel Webster, MA, Whig; W. P. Mangum, NC, Whig
1840: William Henry Harrison, OH, Whig
Vote Totals: 1836: Van Buren, 765,483 popular, 170 electoral; Harrison, 549,508 popular, 73 electoral; White, 145,352 popular, 26 electoral; Webster, 41,287 popular, 14 electoral; Mangum, 11 electoral
1840: Harrison, 1,274,624 popular, 234 electoral; Van Buren, 1,127,781 popular, 60 electoral
Inauguration: March 4, 1837
Vice President: Richard M. Johnson, KY (1837–1841)

CABINET

Secretary of State: John Forsyth, GA (1837–1841)
Secretary of the Treasury: Levi Woodbury, NH (1837–1841)

Secretary of War: Joel R. Poinsett, SC (1837–1841)
Attorney General: Benjamin F. Butler, NY (1837–1838); Felix Grundy, TN (1838–1839); Henry D. Gilpin, PA (1840–1841)
Postmaster General: Amos Kendall, KY (1837–1840); John M. Niles, CT (1840–1841)
Secretary of the Navy: Mahlon Dickerson, NJ (1837–1838); James K. Paulding, NY (1838–1841)

CONGRESS

25th Congress (1837–1839); Speaker of the House: James K. Polk (TN, Democrat)
26th Congress (1839–1841); Speaker of the House: Robert M. T. Hunter (VA, Republican)

SUPREME COURT APPOINTEES

John Catron, TN; Associate Justice (1837–1865)
John McKinley, AL; Associate Justice (1838–1852)
Peter Vivian Daniel, VA; Associate Justice (1842–1860)

MAJOR EVENTS OF THE VAN BUREN ADMINISTRATION

❖ In the Second Seminole War, which lasts from 1835 to 1842, Seminoles in Florida under Osceola fight US attempts to move them west and/or to exterminate them; they fight a guerilla war from the Everglades. During a truce, Osceola is captured; he dies in captivity in 1838. They fight on until 1842, when the remaining Seminoles accept their being forced to move to Oklahoma.
❖ An act of Congress increases the number of Supreme Court justices from seven to nine, 1837.
❖ The Panic of 1837 befalls the nation. Banks close in Philadelphia and New York City on May 10, 1837, setting in motion a depression that extends throughout Van Buren's term of office.
❖ In the *Caroline* Affair, 1837, Canadians rebelling against British rule in favor of a more democratic government are supplied with provisions and arms by Americans using the steamboat *Caroline*. Canadian militia cross the river and burn the *Caroline*. Americans burn the British steamer *Sir Robert Peel* in return. The tensions are ultimately abated through

diplomacy and the Webster-Ashburton Treaty of 1842 [for details, see the entry for President John Tyler].

◆ The House of Representatives adopts the "gag rule" that prohibits the discussion of petitions from abolitionists to limit or end slavery, 1836; an even stricter rule is adopted in late 1837 and not repealed until 1844. Among the most vocal critics of the gag rule is former president John Quincy Adams.

◆ The Trail of Tears is the name given to the route from Georgia to Oklahoma that is followed by thousands of Cherokees who are forced to leave their homes in the American southeast and march to new lands in the west; about 4,000 die en route, 1838.

◆ The Aroostook War, 1839, stems from a dispute between Maine and New Brunswick, Canada, over lumbering in territory that is claimed by both; the dispute is settled by the Webster-Ashburton Treaty in 1842.

◆ The United States and various European powers recognize Texas independence, 1839–1840.

◆ The Independent Treasury Act is passed in 1840, establishing subtreasuries for the deposit of federal funds in major US cities and providing that all payments made to or by the American government are to be rendered in specie (coined money) by 1843.

◆ The *Amistad* case is tried before the Supreme Court in early 1841; former president John Quincy Adams defends the right of blacks who had been imprisoned on the slave ship *Amistad* and then revolted to be considered free men and not property.

MAJOR US AND WORLD EVENTS, 1837–1841

◆ Samuel F. B. Morse applies for a patent for his electromagnetic telegraph, 1837, and demonstrates it publicly in 1838; introducing the Morse code at the same time.

◆ King William IV dies and his niece Victoria becomes the queen of Great Britain and Ireland, June 20, 1837.

◆ Nathaniel Hawthorne publishes *Twice-Told Tales*, 1837.

◆ Charles Dickens publishes *Oliver Twist*, 1837.

◆ John Deere, a blacksmith, invents a plow with a steel moldboard, 1837; by 1842, 100 of these plows are built; by 1852, more than 4,000 are being built each year.

◆ The Chartist movement in Great Britain, 1839–1848, during which petitions are presented to Parliament (and rejected), urges universal male suffrage, secret ballots, and the abolition of the property requirement for members of Parliament.

◆ The First Opium War between Great Britain and China comes to pass, 1839–1842; the Chinese attempt to end the exchange of opium by the British for Chinese silver and to ease the deleterious effects of opium use by many Chinese; the British are victorious and force the Chinese to continue to trade (including in opium), to allow missionaries into China, and to turn over Hong Kong to the British.

◆ Audubon publishes *Birds of North America*, 1839.

◆ Louis Daguerre, a French physicist, develops one of the first forms of photography, dubbed the "daguerrcotype"; the process is announced publicly in 1839.

◆ The Central American Federation dissolves into the countries of Guatemala, Honduras, Costa Rica, El Salvador, and Nicaragua, 1839.

◆ Samuel Cunard, a Canadian, establishes the first steamship line with scheduled transatlantic crossings, and makes a bid to the British government for regular mail delivery, 1839.

◆ Edgar Allan Poe publishes *Tales of the Grotesque and Arabesque*, which includes such stories as "The Fall of the House of Usher" and "Ms. Found in a Bottle," 1840.

◆ The census of 1840 shows a US population of more than 17 million people.

FAST FACTS ABOUT MARTIN VAN BUREN

◆ Martin Van Buren was the first president born (in 1782) after the signing of the Declaration of Independence.

◆ Van Buren wrote an autobiography, noted for its not mentioning his wife even once.

◆ Van Buren was sometimes called "Old Kinderhook," in reference to his home town of Kinderhook, NY. Clubs that formed to support his campaign for the presidency came to be known as "O.K. Clubs," which eventually led to the use of "O.K." to mean "all right."

◆ After his presidency, Van Buren sought the office three more times, without success.

◆ Because Van Buren's wife Hannah died long before he became president, his son Abraham's wife, Angelica Singleton Van Buren, served as hostess at the White House. Angelica first met the Van Burens when Dolley Madison, to whom she was related by marriage, took her to call at the White House.

◆ Van Buren and Jackson rode to Van Buren's inauguration in a carriage made from the timbers of the USS *Constitution*.

◆ During Van Buren's inauguration, the crowd politely clapped for Van Buren and then gave his predecessor, Andrew Jackson, a standing ovation.

William Henry Harrison

Nickname: Tippecanoe, Old Tip
Presidency: 9th president, 1841
Party: Whig
Life dates: February 9, 1773–April 4, 1841 (68 years, 54 days)

EARLY LIFE AND EDUCATION

William Henry Harrison was born at Berkeley, a plantation on the James River in Virginia that had belonged to his family since his great-grandfather, Benjamin Harrison III, had acquired it. Benjamin's grandson, Colonel Benjamin Harrison V, married Elizabeth Bassett; the couple had seven children, of whom William, born February 9, 1773, was the youngest. Colonel Harrison was a member of Virginia's House of Burgesses, a delegate to the Continental Congress, and a signer of the Declaration of Independence; in 1781 he became governor of Virginia and served until 1785, when he again took up his seat in the House of Burgesses until his death in 1791.

William was originally educated by private tutors at home and then attended the Brandon School before going, at the age of fourteen, to Hampden-Sydney College in Prince Edward County, Virginia. He studied there from 1787 to 1790 (but did not graduate). He briefly took up the study of medicine in Richmond before being sent to Philadelphia to continue his medical studies. After his father's death, he was left with land, but no money, and could not continue to pay for medical school.

EARLY MILITARY CAREER

On his own for the first time, the young man promptly gained a commission as an ensign in the First Infantry of the US Army. He was assigned to Fort Washington at Cincinnati in the Ohio Territory. A serious young officer who decided to eschew the drunkenness and dueling that were common pastimes for officers, he was soon promoted to lieutenant. His new commander, General "Mad Anthony" Wayne, made him his aide-de-camp in June 1793. Harrison served at the Battle of Fallen Timbers on August 20, 1794. He was made commander of Fort Washington after Wayne's death in 1795.

Harrison was introduced to Anna Symmes, the daughter of Judge John Cleves Symmes. She had been raised in New Jersey and New York, but accompanied her father to the Ohio Territory when he acquired land patents there. The Judge thought a military life on the frontier would be too difficult for his daughter, so he opposed Harrison's courtship, but the couple eloped while the Judge was away in November 1795, and Anna's father eventually accepted the marriage.

Harrison was promoted to captain in 1797, but became bored with garrison duty and resigned from the army in 1798. He then moved his family from Fort Washington to North Bend and purchased land for a farm.

HARRISON AND THE INDIANA TERRITORY

Harrison was appointed secretary of the Northwest Territory in 1798 and was elected by the territorial legislature as the territory's delegate to the US Congress in 1799, a position he held for two years. During his tenure, he chaired a committee that recommended the Land Act of 1800, which made the purchase of land in the Northwest Territory easier for settlers. Harrison also urged the division of the Northwest Territory into two territories, Ohio and Indiana.

President John Adams appointed Harrison the territorial governor of Indiana in 1801, a position he held for the next twelve years. Harrison settled his growing family (he and Anna would have ten children) in Vincennes and built a grand house called Grouseland. Harrison's major assignment as governor was to acquire lands from the Native Americans, which he did by various treaties, often concluded after they had been offered large quantities of alcohol. Few Native Americans had a clear concept of land ownership (or understood it as the settlers understood it), and under the treaties they signed away tremendous amounts of land— parts of the present-day states of Illinois, Wisconsin, and Missouri.

HARRISON VERSUS TECUMSEH

Harrison was also responsible for defending settlers in the Indiana territory against Native American attacks. By 1809 settlers had become troubled by the rise of Tecumseh, the most powerful local chief, who had formed a confederacy against the settlers. Harrison signed the Treaty of Fort Wayne with other tribes outside of Tecumseh's confederacy, according to which the United States acquired nearly three million more acres. Tecumseh intensified his efforts to find allies, seeking help from the British as well as other Native Americans. In 1811 Harrison was given permission to attack the confederacy; moreover, he had convinced President James Madison to make him commander of the regu-

lar and militia forces that marched out against the Native Americans.

Tecumseh was away seeking allies when Harrison's troops were advancing on the forces of Tecumseh's growing confederacy in November 1811. In Tecumseh's absence, the Native Americans were commanded by his brother Tenskwatawa, called the Prophet. Harrison's troops camped, and the Native Americans attacked on November 7, 1811. The Battle of Tippecanoe was bloody, with heavy casualties on either side, but Harrison's troops prevailed.

> **"Some folks are silly enough to have formed a plan to make a President of the United States out of this Clerk and Clodhopper!"**
>
> William Henry Harrison, speaking about himself in a letter to General Solomon Van Rensselaer, January 15, 1835

The battle became famous throughout America and Harrison's new fame as a military leader led to his being appointed brigadier general and commander of the Army in the Northwest for the War of 1812. In the wake of Oliver Hazard Perry's victory on Lake Erie, Harrison's forces took Detroit and then met the British and their Native American allies in the Battle of the Thames, north of Lake Erie, on October 5, 1813. With a superior force and some well-trained fighters, Harrison scored another victory, which also saw the death of Tecumseh and the end of his confederacy. Harrison did little more during the war, resigning in 1814 and settling down on his farm in North Bend.

NATIONAL POLITICS

Harrison continually sought political office; he was elected to the US House of Representatives from Ohio in 1816 and served until 1819. He served in the Ohio state senate and then was again elected, as a US senator from Ohio, a position he served in from 1825 to 1828.

Harrison convinced Henry Clay, then secretary of state under John Quincy Adams, to help him secure an appointment as minister to Colombia in 1828. Harrison immediately made himself unpopular in Colombia because of his support for rebels against the government of Simón Bolívar, with the result that the Colombian government planned to expel the American envoy. Before it was able to expel him, Harrison was recalled by the newly elected Andrew Jackson in March 1829; Jackson replaced Harrison with one of his own supporters. Back in Ohio, Harrison finally secured the position of Hamilton county clerk in 1834, needing the position to help him with his mounting debts.

PRESIDENCY

After the immensely popular Andrew Jackson left the presidency, Martin Van Buren, Jackson's vice president, won the presidency in 1836. Van Buren did not have Jackson's popularity and, moreover, faced an economic depression that he did little to alleviate. The Whigs, bearing in mind that much of Jackson's popularity stemmed from his status as a military hero, sought another military hero to run against Van Buren. In 1836 Harrison was one of three Whig candidates put forward for the presidency, but in 1840, at the first national convention for the Whig Party, William Henry Harrison was selected as the Whig candidate. John Tyler of Virginia was chosen as Harrison's running mate, to help ensure the southern vote.

When a newspaper article ridiculed Harrison, saying he should be given a barrel of hard cider and allowed to sit in his log cabin beside the fire, the Whigs seized on this and turned it to advantage, portraying Harrison as a man of the people and circulating the entirely false picture of a man born in a humble log cabin. In contrast, Van Buren was portrayed as a luxury-loving effete—a picture with some elements of truth, as Van Buren did enjoy fine food and comfortable living. Ironically, Van Buren was actually a man whose birth and childhood were considerably humbler than those of Harrison, born a member of the Virginia aristocracy.

The "Log Cabin and Hard Cider" campaign was also the first American political campaign to feature a slogan, "Tippecanoe and Tyler, Too." The campaign featured large rallies with speeches and political songs, as well. Harrison won the popular vote by a narrow margin but received 234 electoral votes to Van Buren's 60.

> **"Give him a barrel of hard cider and settle a pension of two thousand a year on him, and take my word for it, he will sit the remainder of his days in his log cabin by the side of a sea coal fire, and study moral philosophy."**
>
> dismissive editorial comment about Harrison in the *Baltimore Republican* newspaper, seized on by Harrison's supporters to create the "Log Cabin and Hard Cider" campaign

Anna Harrison was too ill to accompany her husband to Washington for his inauguration. When Harrison arrived in the city, Daniel Webster edited his inaugural address, trimming some of its many classical allusions. On a cold, blustery March 4, Harrison delivered the longest inaugural address of all the presidents (8,445 words and 105 minutes), wearing neither a hat nor coat. His address emphasized his vision of government, in which the president deferred to the legislative branch and (in contrast to Jackson) used the presidential veto only if he considered a law that had been passed by Congress to be unconstitutional. Harrison also promised not to seek a second term.

Shortly after the inauguration, on March 9, 1841, the Supreme Court affirmed that the black slaves who had seized the slave ship *Amistad* were free and need not be returned to the Spanish planters in Cuba who claimed them as property.

Harrison came down with a cold that progressed to pneumonia and he died on April 4, 1841, after only one month of service as president. Anna Harrison was packing to join her husband when she received the news of his death. She subsequently remained in North Bend, until her home burned in 1858, at which time she moved in with her son John Scott Harrison, the only one of her ten children to outlive her. She died in 1864 at the age of eighty-eight.

"It is true Democratic feeling, that all the measures of the government are directed to the purpose of making the rich richer and the poor poorer."

William Henry Harrison, 1840

Harrison was succeeded by Vice President John Tyler, who established the precedent of the vice president succeeding to the full powers of the presidency for the remainder of the term.

Birthplace: Berkeley, Charles City County, VA
Residency: Ohio
Religion: Episcopalian
Education: Hampden-Sydney College, VA, attended 1787–1790, did not graduate; briefly studied medicine
Place of Death: Washington, DC
Burial Site: William Henry Harrison Memorial, North Bend, OH
Dates in Office: March 4, 1841–April 4, 1841 (32 days)
Age at Inauguration: 68 years, 23 days

FAMILY

Father: Benjamin Harrison (1726–1791)
Mother: Elizabeth Bassett Harrison (1730–1792)

Siblings: William Henry Harrison was the seventh and youngest child; his siblings were Elizabeth Harrison (1751–1830); Ann Harrison (1753–1821); Benjamin Harrison (1755–1799); Lucy Harrison (1756?–1809); Carter Bassett Harrison (1757–1808); Sarah Harrison (1770–1812).
Wife: Anna Tuthill Symmes Harrison (1775–1864), married November 25, 1795, in North Bend, OH
Children: Elizabeth (Betsey) Bassett Harrison (1796–1846); John Cleves Symmes Harrison (1798–1830); Lucy Singleton Harrison (1800–1826); William Henry Harrison (1802–1838); John Scott Harrison (1804–1878); Benjamin Harrison (1806–1840); Mary Symmes Harrison (1809–1842); Carter Bassett Harrison (1811–1839); Anna Tuthill Harrison (1813–1845); James Findlay Harrison (1814–1817)

CAREER

Private: none (soldier and politician)
Political: secretary of the Northwest Territory (1798); territorial delegate to the US Congress (1799–1801); territorial governor of Indiana (1801–1813); member of the US House of Representatives (1816–1819); US senator (1825–1828); minister to Colombia (1828–1829); clerk of the court of common pleas for Hamilton County, OH (1834–1840); president of the United States (1841)
Military: commissioned as ensign in the First Infantry of the US Army, 1791; assigned to Fort Washington in the Ohio territory; promoted to lieutenant and made aide-de-camp to General "Mad Anthony" Wayne; served at the Battle of Fallen Timbers, August 20, 1794; made captain and commander of Fort Washington after Wayne's death in 1795; resigned from the Army in 1798; as governor of the Indiana Territory, convinced President Madison to make him commander of the regular and militia troops deployed against a Native American uprising in the Battle of Tippecanoe, November 7, 1811; made major general and commander of the Army in the Northwest for the War of 1812; defeated the British and their Native American allies in the

Battle of the Thames, north of Lake Erie, October 5, 1813, which also saw the death of the Native American leader Tecumseh

Selected Works: *Messages and Letters of William Henry Harrison*, ed. by Logan Esarey (New York: Arno Press, 1975); *William Henry Harrison, 1773–1841; John Tyler, 1790–1862; Chronology, Documents, Bibliographical Aids*, ed. by David A. Durfee (Dobbs Ferry, NY: Oceana Publications, 1970)

PRESIDENCY

Nomination: 1836: The newly formed Whig Party chose Harrison as a war hero to counteract the influence of Andrew Jackson's military record, as the candidate of the Democratic Party was Jackson's choice (his vice president, Martin Van Buren). However, two other Whig candidates were also chosen for their strength in various regions.

1840: The Whig convention was held in December 1839 in Harrisburg, PA; although the party considered nominating one of its leaders, Daniel Webster or Henry Clay, its members decided to nominate Harrison, as a military hero and one who would provide contrast to the incumbent Van Buren.

Election: 1836: lost the election to Martin Van Buren

1840: elected president (election took place in November but voting occurred on different days in different states before 1845, when Congress mandated a uniform election day)

Opponent: 1836: Martin Van Buren, NY, Democratic; Hugh L. White, TN, Whig; Daniel Webster, MA, Whig; W. P. Mangum, NC, Anti-Jackson

1840: Martin Van Buren, NY, Democratic

Vote Totals: 1836: Van Buren, 765,483 popular, 170 electoral; Harrison, 549,508 popular, 73 electoral; White, 145,352 popular, 26 electoral; Webster, 41,287 popular, 14 electoral; Mangum, 11 electoral

1840: Harrison, 1,274,624 popular, 234 electoral; Van Buren, 1,127,781 popular, 60 electoral

Inauguration: March 4, 1841

Vice President: John Tyler, VA (1841)

CABINET

Secretary of State: Daniel Webster, MA (1841)

Secretary of the Treasury: Thomas Ewing, OH (1841)

Secretary of War: John Bell, TN (1841)

Attorney General: John J. Crittenden, KY (1841)

Postmaster General: Francis Granger, NY (1841)

Secretary of the Navy: George E. Badger, NC (1841)

CONGRESS

Congress was not in session during the month-long presidency of William Henry Harrison; the 27th Congress convened on May 31, 1841.

> **"But the delicate duty of devising schemes of revenue should be left where the Constitution has placed it—with the immediate representatives of the people. For similar reasons the mode of keeping the public treasure should be prescribed by them, and the further removed it may be from the control of the Executive the more wholesome the arrangement and the more in accordance with republican principle."**
>
> William Henry Harrison, his inaugural address, March 4, 1841

SUPREME COURT APPOINTEES

MAJOR EVENTS OF THE HARRISON ADMINISTRATION

❖ Harrison delivers the longest inaugural address of any president, 8,445 words and 105 minutes, on March 4, 1841, a cold day on which he wore neither a hat nor coat.

◆ The Supreme Court decides on March 9, 1841, to affirm that the black slaves who had seized the slave ship *Amistad* were free and need not be returned to the Spanish in Cuba who claimed them as property.

◆ After only a month in office, Harrison dies of pneumonia, probably contracted while he gave his inaugural address.

MAJOR US AND WORLD EVENTS, 1841

◆ The first US steam fire engine is tested in New York City, March 27, 1841.

◆ The first performance of Robert Schumann's *Symphony No. 1 in B flat major*, called "Spring," is given on March 31, 1841.

FAST FACTS ABOUT
WILLIAM HENRY HARRISON

◆ Harrison's father, Benjamin Harrison, signed the Declaration of Independence; he was also governor of Virginia for three terms.

◆ The "Log Cabin and Hard Cider" campaign of 1840 touted Harrison as a frontiersman born in a log cabin (although he actually came from an aristocratic and wealthy Virginia family). Harrison's opponent, President Martin Van Buren, was portrayed as a luxury-loving effete, although he actually came from the middle class.

◆ Harrison was the first president to have had a campaign slogan: "Tippecanoe and Tyler, too."

◆ Harrison had the shortest term of office of any president—just one month.

◆ Harrison was the grandfather of the 23rd president, Benjamin Harrison.

◆ Harrison was the first president who was born in the same county as his vice president (Charles City County, VA).

◆ At age 68, Harrison was the oldest man to become president, and he held on to that distinction until the election of Ronald Reagan in 1980.

◆ Harrison had a pet goat named "His Whiskers."

◆ American folklore has long circulated the story of a curse, put on US presidents by Tecumseh, in revenge for his defeat at Tippecanoe, or by his half-brother Tenskwatawa, in revenge for Tecumseh's death. The curse is on American presidents elected in years ending with a zero. Harrison, who died shortly after his 1840 election was its first victim, followed by Abraham Lincoln (elected in 1860, assassinated in 1865), James A. Garfield (elected 1880, assassinated in 1881), William McKinley (reelected 1900, assassinated in 1901), Warren G. Harding (elected 1920, died of natural causes in 1923), Franklin Delano Roosevelt (elected 1940, died of natural causes in 1945), and John Fitzgerald Kennedy (elected 1960, assassinated in 1963). Ronald Reagan (elected 1980), survived an assassination attempt in 1981, a feat that some claim may have broken the curse.

John Tyler

Nickname: His Accidency, Honest John
Presidency: 10th president, 1841–1845
Party: Whig [Formerly a Democrat, Tyler, with Henry Clay and Daniel Webster, formed the Whig Party in the mid-1830s in opposition to Andrew Jackson.]
Life dates: March 29, 1790–January 18, 1862 (71 years, 295 days)

EARLY LIFE AND EDUCATION

John Tyler was born in Charles City County, Virginia, on March 29, 1790. He was the fourth of that name in a distinguished family; his father, the third John Tyler, was generally known as Judge Tyler, though he also served in the Virginia House of Delegates and as governor of Virginia for four terms. The Judge was married to Mary Marot Armistead, and the family made its home at a plantation named Greenway. John was the sixth of eight children; he had two brothers and five sisters.

John attended a local school run by a Mr. McMurdo; there is a story that the schoolmaster was so tyrannical that his students, led by John Tyler, rose up against him and left him tied in the schoolhouse one afternoon. In 1802, at age twelve, John was sent to the preparatory school of the College of William and Mary for a year or two before entering the college itself. He was graduated in 1807, when he was seventeen.

After college, John read law under the direction of his father, Judge Tyler, who was elected the Virginia governor the following year. John accompanied the family to Richmond and continued his legal studies under Edmund Randolph, who had served in President Washington's cabinet.

EARLY CAREER

John received a license to practice law before his twentieth birthday and joined a law firm in Richmond. Like his father, John was a strong adherent of Jefferson's Democratic-Republican Party. His first political service came with his election to the Virginia House of Delegates, as the delegate of Charles City County, in 1811; he served until 1815, again from 1823 to 1826, and once more in 1839.

During the War of 1812, Tyler was named captain of a Charles City County militia company that had been raised to defend the state, but he saw no action and resigned after a few months, returning to his law practice. Having built up a respectable practice, Tyler felt he was in a position to court Letitia Christian—whom he married at her family home, Cedar Grove, on March 29, 1813. They had eight children together between 1815 and 1830.

CONGRESS AND GOVERNOR OF VIRGINIA

Tyler was elected to the US House of Representatives and served in that body from 1817 to 1821. Tyler's political views were representative of those of his party—he believed in limited federal power and states' rights, and resisted attempts by the federal government to restrict slavery in southern states. He voted against the second Bank of the United States and the Missouri Compromise of 1820. He fought against protective tariffs.

> "[I am] not disposed to represent the State of Virginia in so poor a condition as to require a *charitable* donation from Congress. . . . The day, it is to be hoped, has passed, in which a national debt was esteemed a national blessing."
>
> John Tyler, a newspaper statement published in the Richmond *Enquirer*, March 17, 1817, in which he explained his opposition to federal funding of internal improvements and his belief that the federal funds should instead be used to pay down the national debt

---

Believing himself to be at odds with the political climate of the day, and stricken with an illness that had left him weak, Tyler declined to run again in 1821 and returned home. He purchased Greenway, his childhood home, for his expanding family. By 1823 he was again in the Virginia state legislature, in 1825 he was selected as Virginia's governor, and in 1826 he was elected as a US senator. Although he had been a supporter of John Quincy Adams, he disliked Adams's program for domestic improvements and became a supporter of Andrew Jackson instead. After Jackson was elected to the presidency in 1828, Tyler supported Jackson's fight against the Bank of the United States, but parted ways with the president when he withdrew the monies of the bank and deposited them in state banks. Tyler believed this action was unconstitutional.

Tyler joined the Whig Party that had been formed by Henry Clay of Kentucky and Daniel Webster of Massachusetts. Initially the party had no platform beyond opposition to Jackson, but gradually, separate groups joined together, from those who supported the Bank of the United States to those who were members of the anti-Masonic movement (originating in New York state, the anti-Masons distrusted the political power of members of the Masonic Order), and a stronger platform was developed.

President Jackson had been asked by the Senate to turn over to it his papers relating to his veto of the recharter of the Bank of the United States. When he refused, the Senate, which was under the control of anti-Jackson supporters at the time, censured him. When the control of the Senate passed back to Jackson's supporters, they put forward a resolution to have the censure removed from the Senate's official record. The Virginia legislature instructed Tyler, as a member of the US Senate, to vote for the resolution. Tyler felt that he could not obey these instructions and, unable to agree with the instructions of those who had placed him in the office of senator, resigned.

The fledgling Whig Party could not agree on a single candidate for the 1836 election and instead offered three candidates from different sections of the country. Martin Van Buren, as Jackson's political heir, won the election easily.

The Whigs were much better organized for the 1840 election, at which time they selected military hero William Henry Harrison as their candidate and John Tyler as the vice presidential candidate. After an aggressive campaign (that included the slogan "Tippecanoe and Tyler, Too!" in reference to the bloody Battle of Tippecanoe, in which Harrison was victorious), the Whigs carried the day.

PRESIDENCY

After only a month in office, President William Henry Harrison died of pneumonia. For the first time, the succession of the vice president to the presidency was tested in the United States. Many in Congress felt that Tyler should only be regarded and addressed as the "Acting President," and that he should hold that position only until new elections could be held. From the first, Tyler firmly insisted that he was actually and fully president; he took the oath of office and even returned mail addressed to the "acting president" without having opened it.

The Whig Party assumed that the new president would follow the platform laid out by Harrison in his inaugural address, but Tyler proved to be his own man. The party supported banking bills that would have revived the Bank of the United States as the Fiscal Bank of the United States, but Tyler vetoed these bills, believing that the federal government had not been granted the power by Congress to establish a bank. Henry Clay and the Whigs were outraged; Tyler was expelled from the Whig Party. His entire cabinet, with the single exception of Secretary of State Daniel Webster, resigned in protest. Tyler was dubbed "the president without a party."

However, with Webster as his secretary of state, Tyler was able to score a few victories in international affairs during his tenure as president. The so-called Aroostook War, a border dispute that took place between Americans in Maine and Canadians in New Brunswick, was settled in 1839 when General Winfield Scott convinced both sides to submit to a boundary commission. The result was the Webster-Ashburton Treaty with Great Britain in 1842, which settled the dispute and delineated the border between the United States and British-held Canada from Maine to as far west as the Rocky Mountains.

Caleb Cushing, the first US commissioner to China, negotiated the Treaty of Wanghia (or Wanghsia) in 1844, which opened trade between the United States and China at five Chinese ports and granted "most favored nation" status to the United States. The provisions of the Treaty of Wanghia were modeled on the arrangement China had made with Great Britain in the Treaty of Nanking in 1842.

The Republic of Texas had applied for admission to the union, and the annexation of Texas by the United States was agreed to, via a treaty between the United States and Mexico, on March 1, 1845. Tyler supported the annexation, which was opposed by many in the north

who objected to Texas's entering the union as a slave state. At the end of his term, Tyler signed the resolution of Congress that sanctioned the annexation, but left it to his successor, James K. Polk, to deal with the threatened war with Mexico.

"My resolution is fixed, and I shall resign. Such, too, seems to be the wish of my friends in Richmond. I cannot look to consequences, but perhaps I am doomed to perpetual exile from the public councils. If so, I am content, nor should I repine at it."

John Tyler, a letter to his son Robert Tyler, February 15, 1836, about his decision to resign from the US Senate

---

In September 1842 Letitia Tyler died; she had been ill since having suffered a stroke several years earlier. After her death, the duties of White House hostess were assumed by Priscilla Cooper Tyler, the wife of the Tylers' son Robert. In late 1842 President Tyler met the beautiful, popular Julia Gardiner, a young woman (thirty years his junior) who was visiting Washington, DC, with her parents.

Julia, allegedly, received a proposal of marriage from the president in no time, but she did not accept his proposal until after tragedy struck. During a pleasure outing on a gunboat, the *Princeton,* on February 24, 1844, a massive gun dubbed "The Peacemaker," was fired several times. On its final firing near Mount Vernon, which was meant to honor the memory of George Washington, the gun exploded and killed several of the passengers, including Julia's father, David Gardiner. Julia, an eyewitness to the accident, fainted in the president's arms; he carried her ashore. She later said that that moment had been a turning point, causing her to harbor feelings for Tyler that she could not imagine herself harboring for a younger man. They were married in June 1844.

Julia's time as first lady was brief, but she enjoyed it immensely and referred to it as her "reign." Young, beautiful, and wealthy, she liked to entertain formally, to dance, and to dress lavishly. However, given the fact that the Whigs had read Tyler out of the party, they were not inclined to nominate him for the presidential election of 1844; Henry Clay was nominated as the Whig candidate. He lost to James K. Polk, the Democratic candidate.

POST-PRESIDENTIAL CAREER

After leaving the presidency, Tyler retired with Julia to his plantation home in Virginia, which he renamed Sherwood Forest—a reference to Henry Clay's criticism that he was an outlaw from his party (Clay had said that Tyler was retiring to his "Sherwood Forest"). He and Julia had seven children. Together, they continued to support such southern causes as states' rights and slavery.

As relations between the North and the South were disintegrating, Tyler acted as the chairman of a peace conference in February 1861 at Washington, D.C. However, when the Southern states seceded and formed the Confederacy, he was elected to the House of Representatives of the Confederate Congress. He died on January 18, 1862, at age seventy-one, before he had been able to take his seat in the congress. No official notice of his death was taken by the US government, as his allegiance to the Confederacy at the time of his demise caused him to be regarded as a sworn enemy.

Julia Tyler supported the Confederacy, but, fearing for her safety at one point during the war, moved to her mother's crowded home in New York City. Eventually, she returned to Sherwood Forest (in the 1870s), while she was facing considerable financial difficulty. In 1881 she was granted a pension as the widow of a president. Late in life she converted to Roman Catholicism and remained a devout Catholic until her death in 1889 at the age of sixty-nine. She

was buried by her husband's side in Richmond, Virginia.

Birthplace: Greenway, Charles City County, VA
Residency: Virginia
Religion: Episcopalian
Education: College of William and Mary, graduated 1807
Place of Death: Richmond, VA
Burial Site: Hollywood Cemetery, Richmond, VA
Dates in Office: April 6, 1841–March 3, 1845 (3 years, 332 days)
Age at Inauguration: 51 years, 8 days

FAMILY

Father: John Tyler (1747–1813)
Mother: Mary Marot Armistead Tyler (1761–1797)
Siblings: John Tyler was the sixth of eight children; his siblings were Anne Contesse Tyler (1778–1803); Elizabeth Armistead Tyler (1780–1824); Martha Jefferson Tyler (1782–1855); Maria Henry Tyler (1784–1843); Wat Henry Tyler (1788–1862); William Tyler (1791–1856); Christiana Booth Tyler (1795–1842)
Wife: Letitia Christian (1790–1842), married March 29, 1813, at Cedar Grove, New Kent County, VA; Julia Gardiner (1820–1889), married June 26, 1844, at the Church of the Ascension, New York City, NY
Children: With Letitia Christian: Mary Tyler (1815–1848); Robert Tyler (1816–1877); John Tyler (1819–1896); Letitia Tyler (1821–1907); Elizabeth Tyler (1823–1850); Anne Contesse Tyler (1825; lived only three months); Alice Tyler (1827–1854); Tazewell Tyler (1830–1874).

With Julia Gardiner: David Gardiner Tyler (1846–1927); John Alexander Tyler (1848–1883); Julia Gardiner Tyler (1849–1871); Lachlan Tyler (1851–1902); Lyon Gardiner Tyler (1853–1935); Robert Fitzwalter Tyler (1856–1927); Pearl Tyler (1860–1947).

CAREER

Private: lawyer
Political: Member of the Virginia House of Delegates (1811–1816); member of the US House

of Representatives (1816–1821); governor of Virginia (1825–1827); member of the US Senate (1827–1829; 1833–1836); vice president under William Henry Harrison (1841); president of the United States (1841–1845); member of the Confederate Congress (1862; elected but did not serve)

Military: made captain of a Charles City County company raised to defend the Richmond area during the War of 1812, but did not see action

Selected Works: *Papers of John Tyler*, archival manuscript on microfilm (Washington, DC: Library of Congress); *William Henry Harrison, 1773–1841; John Tyler, 1790–1862; Chronology, Documents, Bibliographical Aids*, ed. by David A. Durfee (Dobbs Ferry, NY: Oceana Publications, 1970)

PRESIDENCY

Nomination: Tyler was not nominated nor did he run for president; he became president when President William Henry Harrison died in office.

Election: succeeded to the presidency; was not elected

Opponent: none

Vote Totals: n/a

Inauguration: April 6, 1841

Vice President: none

CABINET

Secretary of State: Daniel Webster, MA (1841–1843); Abel P. Upshur, VA (1843–1844); John C. Calhoun, SC (1844–1845)

Secretary of the Treasury: Thomas Ewing, OH (1841); Walter Forward, PA (1841–1843); John C. Spencer, NY (1843–1844); George M. Bibb, KY (1844–1845)

Secretary of War: John Bell, TN (1841); John C. Spencer, NY (1841–1843); James M. Porter, PA (1843–1844); William Wilkins, PA (1844–1845)

Attorney General: John J. Crittenden, KY (1841); Hugh S. Legaré, SC (1841–1843); John Nelson, MD (1843–1845)

Postmaster General: Francis Granger, NY (1841); Charles A. Wickliffe, KY (1841–1845)

Secretary of the Navy: George E. Badger, NC (1841); Abel P. Upshur, VA (1841–1843); David

Henshaw, MA (1843–1844); Thomas W. Gilmer, VA (1844); John Y. Mason, VA (1844–1845)

CONGRESS

27th Congress (1841–1843); Speaker of the House: John White (KY, Whig)

28th Congress (1843–1845); Speaker of the House: John W. Jones (VA, Democratic)

SUPREME COURT APPOINTEES

Samuel Nelson, NY; Associate Justice (1845–1872)

MAJOR EVENTS OF THE TYLER ADMINISTRATION

◆ Following the death of President William Henry Harrison after only a month in office, Tyler sets the precedent for the presidential succession of a vice president, 1841.

◆ The entire cabinet, except for Secretary of State Daniel Webster, resigns in protest after Tyler vetoes banking bills supported by the Whig Party, 1841. The bills would have revived the National Bank of the United States as "the Fiscal Bank of the United States."

◆ The Preemption Act is passed, 1841; it provides that settlers on land that has been surveyed by the government will have the first right to buy the land after a 14-month residence on it.

◆ The Webster-Ashburton Treaty, 1842, settles the Maine-New Brunswick border between the United States and Canada and the border in the west as far as the Rocky Mountains. The treaty is named for Secretary of State Daniel Webster and the British Privy Council member, Alexander Baring, Lord Ashburton, who concluded it.

◆ The Treaty of Wanghia, 1844, opens trade between the United States and China at five Chinese ports and grants "most favored nation" status to the United States, and provides that American citizens in China will be subject only to US laws.

◆ Texas is annexed, March 1, 1845, as part of a treaty between the United States and the Republic of Texas (the annexation leads to the Mexican-American War, 1846–1848).

◆ Florida becomes a state, March 3, 1845.
◆ For the first time, Congress overrides a presidential veto (of a tariff bill), in March 1845.

MAJOR US AND WORLD EVENTS, 1841–1845

◆ James Fenimore Cooper publishes *The Deerslayer*, 1841.
◆ Henry Wadsworth Longfellow publishes *Ballads and Other Poems*, 1841.
◆ Charles Dickens publishes *The Old Curiosity Shop*, 1841.
◆ Horace Greeley begins publication of the *New York Tribune* newspaper, 1841.
◆ The Opium War between Great Britain and China ends with the Treaty of Nanking; China turns Hong Kong over to the British.
◆ The New York Philharmonic Society is founded, 1842.
◆ Christian Doppler presents a paper, "On the coloured light of the double stars and certain other stars of the heavens," to the Royal Bohemian Society on May 25, 1842; the paper contains the first exposition of the Doppler effect.
◆ P. T. Barnum purchases the American Museum in New York City in 1841 and begins exhibiting unusual people, starting with Tom Thumb in 1842.
◆ The Oregon Trail opens; the first settlers, nearly a thousand people, set out in 1843.
◆ Edgar Allan Poe publishes his short stories, including "The Murders in the Rue Morgue" and "The Pit and the Pendulum," 1843.
◆ Charles Dickens publishes *A Christmas Carol*, 1843.
◆ Felix Mendelssohn composes the music for *A Midsummer Night's Dream*, 1843; it includes the "Wedding March."
◆ Alexandre Dumas, père, publishes *The Three Musketeers*, 1844.
◆ France begins a war with Morocco, 1844.
◆ The YMCA is founded in London, England, by George Williams, 1844; the first American YMCA is founded in Boston in 1851.
◆ Friedrich Engels publishes *The Condition of the Working Class* in England, 1844.

◆ Samuel Morse transmits the first telegraph message from Washington to Baltimore in May 1844, saying "What hath God wrought?"
◆ Charles Goodyear patents the process for vulcanizing rubber, 1844.

FAST FACTS ABOUT JOHN TYLER

◆ Tyler was the first vice president to succeed a president who died while in office, setting the precedent for the vice president's succession and his serving out the full remaining term.
◆ Tyler was the first president whose wife died while he was in office.
◆ Tyler was the first president to be married while in the White House.
◆ Tyler had more children (fifteen) than any other president.
◆ The custom of playing "Hail to the Chief" whenever a president arrives at state functions was begun by Tyler's second wife, Julia Gardiner Tyler.
◆ At his graduation from the College of William and Mary, Tyler delivered an address on the subject of female education.
◆ Tyler was threatened with impeachment by both the Democrats and the Whigs; he was known as "the president without a party."
◆ Charles Dickens visited Tyler in the White House in 1842.
◆ Members of Tyler's family suspected that they were descended from Wat Tyler, a fourteenth-century English peasant who led a revolt against the crown under Richard II after a tax collector had assaulted Tyler's daughter.
◆ First Lady Julia Tyler spent her own money redecorating the White House when Henry Clay led Congress in refusing the Tylers' request for funds to redecorate.
◆ Tyler was elected to the Confederate House of Representatives in 1862, but died before he could serve.
◆ Tyler's home was previously known as Walnut Grove. When he was leaving the presidency, he refused to support Henry Clay for the presidency, supporting Polk instead. Henry Clay accused him of being an outlaw from the Whig Party and said that Tyler was

retiring from the presidency to his Sherwood Forest (a reference to the home of the legendary outlaw Robin Hood). Tyler liked the name and renamed his home Sherwood Forest.

◆ Tyler's descendants (his grandson and his grandson's family) continue to live at Sherwood Forest in the twenty-first century, though the home is also open to the public for tours.

◆ Tyler was born in 1790, during Washington's presidency; his youngest daughter, Pearl, died in 1947, during the presidency of Harry S. Truman—a span of 157 years.

James Knox Polk

Nickname: Young Hickory, Napoleon of the Stump, Polk the Plodder
Presidency: 11th president, 1845–1849
Party: Democratic
Life dates: November 2, 1795–June 15, 1849 (53 years, 225 days)

EARLY LIFE AND EDUCATION

James Knox Polk was born November 2, 1795, in Mecklenburg County, North Carolina. His mother was Jane Knox Polk, the daughter of a Revolutionary War captain, and his father was Samuel Polk, a farmer and occasional surveyor. James was the eldest of their ten children. In 1806 the family moved into the valley of the Duck River in Tennessee. James attended school and later had a private tutor. During much of his youth he suffered from poor health; when he was seventeen, he underwent surgery for gallstones. After the surgery his health improved, and in 1815 he entered the University of North Carolina as a sophomore. In 1818 he graduated first in his class.

In 1819 Polk entered the law offices of Felix Grundy to read law; at the same time, he served as chief clerk of the Tennessee Senate. He became acquainted with Andrew Jackson, of whom he would become a staunch supporter.

EARLY CAREER

In 1820 Polk was admitted to the bar and established his law practice in Colombia, Tennessee. He quickly became successful as a lawyer, and as quickly started to be in demand as a public speaker, earning the nickname "Napoleon of the Stump," in part because he was not very tall.

Polk was introduced to and courted Sarah Childress, the daughter of a Murfreesburo merchant and planter, Captain Joel Childress, who had died in 1819. Sarah had been educated at a Moravian academy and was thus better educated than most women of her time. Andrew Jackson reportedly encouraged the romance, and Sarah and James were married in 1824. They had no children, and thus Sarah was able to devote her considerable talents to aiding her husband's political ambitions. She quietly advised him, copied his correspondence, clipped newspaper articles for him, and became popular in social circles in Tennessee and in Washington. She also became well-known as a gracious hostess with a gift for political conversation and political insight.

POLITICAL CAREER

Polk was elected to the Tennessee state legislature in 1823, in which he served for two years. Despite his youth, he emerged as a leader in that legislative body, and he became a strong supporter of Andrew Jackson. In 1825 he was elected to the US House of Representatives. The election of 1824 had seen Andrew Jackson win the popular vote but lose the presidency to John Quincy Adams. (Because none of the candidates had received the necessary majority of Electoral College votes, the election was decided in the House of Representatives.) Polk entered Congress as one of the many Jackson supporters determined to see Jackson elected in 1828. During the years leading up to the 1828 election, Polk often kept Jackson (at his home in Tennessee) informed of Washington political events by letter.

> **"[He was] temperate but not unsocial, industrious but accessible, punctual but patient, moral without austerity, and devotional though not bigoted."**
>
> George M. Dallas,
> Polk's vice president, in his
> "Eulogy on the Life and Character of
> the Late James K. Polk," 1849

In 1828, when Jackson was elected president, Polk served Jackson faithfully in Congress. From 1833 to 1835 (a period that coincided with the controversy over the National Bank), Polk was chairman of the Ways and Means Committee. He supported Jackson's decision to remove deposits from the bank and move them to state banks. He also followed Jackson's lead in opposing the federal funding of improvements to the nation's infrastructure. In 1835 Polk was chosen as Speaker of the House; he held the position until 1839.

The emergence of the new Whig Party under Henry Clay was seen by Polk as a threat to the welfare of his home state, where Whigs were already in control of the state legislature and were thus able to send Whigs to the US Senate. Wishing to challenge Whig power in his state, Polk, a Democrat, ran for governor of Tennessee and was elected in 1839 (but defeated in both

1841 and 1843). As governor, he was able to return the legislature to Democratic control and have Whig senators replaced with Democrats.

Polk's political career seemed to be in decline when he went to the 1844 Democratic nominating convention, although he hoped that he might be nominated for vice president and be put on a ticket with the expected presidential candidate, Martin Van Buren. However, shortly before the convention, a letter by Van Buren, in which he admitted being against the annexation of Texas, appeared in several newspapers. Van Buren consequently lost the support of much of the party, including Andrew Jackson. On the first ballot at the convention, Van Buren failed to gain the necessary two-thirds vote. Lewis Cass, a US senator from Michigan, also failed to get enough votes. In the eighth round of voting, Polk's name was placed in nomination, and on the ninth ballot he received 233 votes—thus becoming the first "dark horse" candidate for the presidency.

PRESIDENCY

Polk narrowly won the election, thanks in part to the antislavery Liberty Party, which took enough votes away from the Whigs in New York state to ensure Polk's victory. From the outset of his presidency, Polk announced that he planned to bring to fruition "four great measures": a reduction of the tariff on exported goods, a reestablishment of the independent treasury, a settlement of the Oregon border dispute, and the acquisition of California. Polk initially worked with a Congress favorable to his programs; in 1846 the Walker Tariff, one of the lowest in US history, was passed. The same year also saw the reestablishment of an independent treasury.

Americans embraced the president's proposed territorial expansion, as they had embraced what was becoming known (in the 1840s) as the doctrine of "Manifest Destiny"— an ideology that held that it was the destiny of the United States to expand its territory to the Pacific Ocean and spread the blessings of liberty.

One of the rallying cries of the campaign had been "Fifty-four forty or fight!"—a reference to the proposed latitude of 54 degrees 40 minutes for the border between the Oregon Territory and Canada. Eventually, however, the border was settled at the forty-ninth parallel—an agreement reached via diplomacy rather than violence in June 1846.

"The public has no idea of the constant accumulation of business requiring the President's attention. No President who performs his duty faithfully and conscientiously can have any leisure. If he entrusts the details and smaller matters to subordinates constant errors will occur. I prefer to supervise the whole operations of the Government myself rather than entrust the public business to subordinates, and this makes my duties very great."

James K. Polk, a diary entry,
December 29, 1848

The formula of diplomacy in lieu of violence carried no weight in the annexation of Texas, however; Polk supported the annexation of Texas, which had been agreed to at the end of the previous administration. But Mexico objected to the annexation (which had occurred in December 1845). Polk sent a diplomatic mission under John Slidell to Mexico to reach a settlement concerning Texas, and authorized Slidell to offer to purchase territories corresponding to New Mexico and California as well. The Mexican government refused to negotiate.

In 1846 US General Zachary Taylor advanced to the Rio Grande, the southern border being claimed by Texas. The Mexicans considered the region to be their territory and viewed Taylor's forces as invaders. When Mexican forces crossed the Rio Grande, the American government claimed that the American troops were being attacked on American soil, and war was declared.

General Taylor defeated the Mexicans at the Battle of Palo Alto on May 8, 1846, and again on May 9 at the Battle of Resaca de la Palma. At the Battle of Buena Vista, in February 1847, General Taylor's forces were engaged by General Antonio Lopéz de Santa Anna. The fighting was fierce, but the Mexicans eventually withdrew.

In March 1847 forces under General Winfield Scott landed at Vera Cruz and took the city after a three-day battle. In September 1847, following a string of hard-fought battles in which the United States was the victor, the Americans took Mexico City. The Treaty of Guadalupe Hidalgo was signed on February 2, 1848; the United States acquired not just Texas and California, but the entire region above the Rio Grande and Gila Rivers (which was to become the southwestern United States). Mexico ceded two-fifths of its territory to the United States, having lost the war—it lost the war not only because of American military prowess, but also in large part because of its own internal political turmoil.

Polk, a southerner and a slaveholder, generally tried to avoid the subject of slavery. He was dismayed when one of his appropriation bills, meant to provide funding for the war with Mexico, had an amendment attached to it that specified that slavery would not be allowed in any lands acquired as a result of the war. This amendment, known as the Wilmot Proviso, after Pennsylvania Senator David Wilmot who proposed it, was defeated, but it turned up in the Congress repeatedly, pushed for by antislavery adherents, but it never passed.

Throughout his presidency Polk was hardworking, putting in long hours and recording his activities in a diary. Sarah Polk, who served as his private secretary and advisor, worried about his health and did all she could to assist him. The Polks were fairly conservative socially; Sarah was a devout Presbyterian who banned dancing and hard liquor at the White House and refused to attend horse races or the theater. The Polks observed the Sabbath faithfully.

POST-PRESIDENTIAL CAREER

Polk refused to run for a second term as president. After Zachary Taylor's inauguration, Polk left Washington to return to Nashville, where he had purchased a new home, Polk Place, for his retirement. The month-long trip through the south left him exhausted and susceptible to cholera, to which he was exposed in New Orleans. Three months after leaving the presidency, at the age of fifty-three, Polk died. He was buried in the garden of Polk Place; in 1893 his remains were moved to the grounds of the state capitol in Nashville.

> "Our patriotic citizens in every part of the Union will readily submit to the payment of such taxes as shall be needed for the support of their Government, whether in peace or in war, if they are so levied as to distribute the burdens as equally as possible among them."
>
> James K. Polk, his inaugural address, March 4, 1845

Sarah Polk lived in their home, Polk Place, for another forty-two years, wearing the black of mourning for the rest of her life. She maintained neutrality during the Civil War and received leaders from both sides in her home, which she rarely left except for church services. She became the guardian of an orphaned great-niece, Sally Polk Jetton, shortly after her husband's death. Sally lived with her aunt for the rest of her aunt's life. Sarah Polk died at age eighty-eight, in 1891, having gained the respect of nearly all who knew her.

Birthplace: Mecklenburg County, NC
Residency: Tennessee
Religion: Presbyterian; baptized as a Methodist on his deathbed
Education: University of North Carolina, graduated 1818
Place of Death: Nashville, TN
Burial Site: State Capitol Grounds, Nashville, TN
Dates in Office: March 4, 1845–March 3, 1849 (4 years)
Age at Inauguration: 49 years, 122 days

FAMILY

Father: Samuel Polk (1772–1827)
Mother: Jane Knox Polk (1776–1852)
Siblings: James was the eldest of ten children; his siblings were Jane Maria Polk (1798–1876); Lydia Eliza Polk (1800–1864); Franklin Ezekiel Polk (1802–1831); Marshall Tate Polk (1805–1831); John Lee Polk (1807–1831); Naomi Tate Polk (1809–1836); Ophelia Clarissa Polk (1812–1851); William Hawkins Polk (1815–1862); Samuel Wilson Polk (1817–1839).
Wife: Sarah Childress Polk (1803–1891), married January 1, 1824, at Murfreesboro, TN
Children: none

CAREER

Private: lawyer
Political: Chief clerk of the TN Senate (1819–1823); member of the TN House of Representatives (1823–1825); member of the US House of Representatives (1825–1839); speaker of the House (1835–1839); governor of TN (1839–1841); president of the United States (1845–1849)
Military: none
Selected Works: *Correspondence of James K. Polk*, ed. by Herbert Weaver; Paul H. Bergeron, assoc. ed. (Nashville, TN: Vanderbilt University Press, 1969–1996); *Papers of James K. Polk*, archival manuscript collection on microfilm (Washington, DC: Library of Congress). [Note: There is also a collection of Polk's papers in the Tennessee State Library.]

PRESIDENCY

Nomination: 1844: At the Democratic convention in Baltimore, former president Martin Van Buren and Lewis Cass were deadlocked, so Polk was suggested as a compromise—a "dark horse" who was

nominated in the hope that both northern and southern Democrats would unite behind him.
Election: 1844: elected president (election took place in November but voting occurred on different days in different states before 1845, when Congress mandated a uniform election day)
Opponent: 1844: Henry Clay, KY, Whig Party
Vote Totals: Polk, 1,338,464 popular, 170 electoral; Clay, 1,300,097 popular, 105 electoral
Inauguration: March 4, 1845
Vice President: George M. Dallas, PA (1846–1849)

CABINET
Secretary of State: James Buchanan, PA (1845–1849)
Secretary of the Treasury: Robert J. Walker, MS (1845–1849)
Secretary of War: William L. Marcy, NY (1845–1849)
Attorney General: John Y. Mason, VA (1845–1849); Nathan Clifford, ME (1846–1848); Isaac Toucey, CT (1848–1849)
Postmaster General: Cave Johnson, TN (1845–1849)
Secretary of the Navy: George Bancroft, MA (1845–1846); John Y. Mason, VA (1846–1849)

CONGRESS
29th Congress (1845–1847); Speaker of the House: John W. Davis (IN, Democrat)
30th Congress (1847–1849); Speaker of the House: Robert C. Winthrop (MA, Whig)

SUPREME COURT APPOINTEES
Levi Woodbury, NH; Associate Justice (1845–1851)
Robert Cooper Grier, PA; Associate Justice (1846–1870)

MAJOR EVENTS OF THE POLK ADMINISTRATION
◆ Texas becomes a state, December 19, 1845.
◆ The US Naval Academy at Annapolis, Maryland, is founded by Secretary of the Navy George Bancroft, 1845.
◆ The Wilmot Proviso, originally put forth in the US Congress as a proposed amendment to an appropriation bill, is introduced in 1846 by Representative David Wilmot of Pennsylvania. Repeatedly voted down in the Senate over the next few years, the Proviso stipulated that slavery would be barred from any lands acquired as a result of the war with Mexico.
◆ The Oregon Treaty, signed in 1846, settles the border of the Oregon territory between the United States and Great Britain at the 49th parallel.
◆ The Walker Tariff Act, 1846, lowers duties on imports.
◆ On June 14, 1846, a small group of settlers take over the fort at Sonoma, California; California is temporarily declared an independent republic, and shortly thereafter claimed for the United States. The settlers raise a rough flag with a figure of a grizzly bear on it; the incident becomes known as the "Bear Flag Revolt."
◆ An act of Congress establishes the Smithsonian Institution, August 10, 1846, eight years after the United States had received James Smithson's bequest of more than $500,000.
◆ Iowa becomes a state, December 28, 1846.
◆ The Mexican-American War is fought, 1846–1848.
◆ Americans defeat Mexicans at Buena Vista (February 22–23, 1847); capture Vera Cruz (March 29, 1847); defeat Mexicans at Cerro Gordo (April 18, 1847), Contreras and Churubusco (August 19–20, 1847), Molino del Rey (September 8, 1847), and Chapultepec (September 13, 1847); and capture Mexico City (September 15, 1847).
◆ The Treaty of 1848 with Mexico gives the United States control over California, New Mexico, Arizona, Nevada, Utah, and parts of Colorado and Wyoming.
◆ Gold is discovered at Sutter's Mill in California, January 1848; the word spreads up and down the west coast and by 1849, gold-seekers from the east flood California.
◆ The first two US postage stamps are issued, 1847; one for five cents features Benjamin Franklin's picture and one for ten cents features George Washington's picture.

◆ The Independent Treasury Act, 1846, essentially reestablishes the provisions of the Independent Treasury Act of 1840, which had been repealed in 1841. The federal government is required to conduct its business in specie (coins, gold, silver, etc., rather than banknotes).

◆ A treaty in 1846 between the United States and New Granada (later Colombia) guarantees that any "right of way or transit across the Isthmus of Panama" will be freely open to the United States and that the United States will guarantee the rights and sovereignty of Colombia over the territory.

◆ An act of Congress establishes a uniform election day, 1845. The first Tuesday following the first Monday of November is selected as election day.

◆ Wisconsin becomes a state, May 29, 1848.

◆ The cornerstone of the Washington Monument is laid, July 4, 1848.

◆ The Home Department, later known as the Department of the Interior, is formed, 1849.

◆ Because March 4, 1849 falls on a Sunday, Polk's term ends but the new president, Zachary Taylor, is not sworn in until March 5—so for one day, the United States has no president.

MAJOR US AND WORLD EVENTS, 1845–1849

◆ The potato famine begins in Ireland, 1845. Within ten years, nearly two million Irish immigrate to the United States.

◆ Alexandre Dumas *père* publishes *The Count of Monte Cristo*, 1845.

◆ Edgar Allan Poe publishes *The Raven and Other Poems*, 1845.

◆ *Scientific American* magazine is founded in 1845; the editors of the magazine found the first branch of the US Patent Agency and aid in the patenting of thousands of inventions.

◆ After the existence of the planet Neptune is postulated by a British mathematician (John Couch Adams) and a French mathematician (Urbain Leverrier), the planet is discovered by German astronomers Johann Galle and Heinrich d'Arrest in 1846.

◆ In 1846 the Liberty Bell is rung on the fiftieth anniversary of Washington's death; an existing crack becomes larger and the bell cannot be rung again.

◆ After a courtship kept secret from her father, poets Elizabeth Barrett and Robert Browning marry, September 12, 1846.

◆ Elias Howe invents a lock-stitch sewing machine in 1845 and takes out a patent on it in 1846.

◆ Using the pseudonyms Currier, Ellis, and Acton Bell, the Brontë sisters publish *Jane Eyre* (Charlotte Brontë), *Wuthering Heights* (Emily Brontë), and *Agnes Grey* (Anne Brontë), 1847.

◆ William Makepeace Thackeray publishes *Vanity Fair*, 1847–1848.

◆ Henry Wadsworth Longfellow writes "Evangeline," 1847.

◆ The Mormons enter the valley of the Great Salt Lake in July of 1847.

◆ In the February Revolution, Louis Philippe of France abdicates and Louis Napoleon Bonaparte (later Napoleon III) is elected president of France, 1848.

◆ After the Austrian Revolution, Emperor Ferdinand I abdicates, and his nephew, Emperor Franz Joseph I, assumes the throne, 1848.

◆ The first women's rights convention is held in Seneca Falls, NY, at the Wesleyan Chapel, on July 18 and 19, 1848.

◆ Karl Marx and Friedrich Engels publish the *Communist Manifesto*, 1848.

◆ British mathematician and physicist William Thomson Kelvin purposes a temperature scale with an absolute zero, 1848; the scale is later called the Kelvin scale.

◆ The Chicago Board of Trade opens, 1848.

◆ Elizabeth Blackwell becomes the first woman physician in the United States, January 23, 1849.

FAST FACTS ABOUT JAMES KNOX POLK

◆ Polk's mother, Jane Knox Polk, was a direct descendant of John Knox, the 16th century Scottish Protestant reformer.

◆ Polk underwent an operation for gallstones when he was seventeen; the operation was performed without anesthesia or antiseptics.

◆ Although, as a strict Presbyterian, Sarah Polk did not serve hard liquor at the White House, the Polks did serve wine and liqueurs to their guests. Sarah Polk also refused to dance (though she attended the Inaugural Ball), attend the theater or horse races, or work on Sunday.

◆ The first photograph taken in the White House was a daguerreotype of Polk and his war cabinet.

◆ Polk is the only president who also served as Speaker of the House of Representatives.

◆ Polk was the first "dark horse" candidate for president—when he attended the 1844 Democratic convention, he supported Martin Van Buren's candidacy, but when Van Buren failed to receive a two-thirds vote on the first round, other candidates were introduced—including Polk, who received one vote in the eighth round and 233 votes in the ninth round, when he was nominated as the Democratic candidate.

◆ When news of Polk's nomination was telegraphed from Baltimore to Washington, some thought the new invention a failure—because they couldn't believe Polk had been nominated.

◆ The phrase "Manifest Destiny" is associated with Polk's presidency; it refers to the idea that it was the destiny of the United States to expand westward to the Pacific.

◆ Polk's nickname of "Young Hickory" was given to him because he was such a strong supporter of "Old Hickory," Andrew Jackson.

◆ While Polk was president, gaslights were installed at the White House.

◆ Sarah Polk hosted the first annual White House Thanksgiving dinner.

◆ Polk was a famously hardworking president; he was the first to spend the summer at the White House (it was not considered healthful in the summertime).

◆ Polk's inaugural address outlined what he hoped to achieve during his presidency; four years later, he had achieved his goals.

◆ Other than presidents who have been assassinated, at 53 years old, Polk was younger at the time of his death than any other president or former president.

◆ A week before his death, Polk became a Methodist.

Zachary Taylor

Nickname: Old Rough and Ready
Presidency: 12th president, 1849–1850
Party: Whig
Life dates: November 24, 1784–July 9, 1850 (65 years, 227 days)

EARLY LIFE AND EDUCATION

Zachary Taylor was born November 24, 1784, at Montebello, a plantation in Virginia belonging to his father's cousin, Valentine Johnson. His mother was Sarah Dabney Strother Taylor, the daughter of an old established Virginia family; his father was Richard Taylor, who also came from an established and prosperous Virginia family. Zachary was related to both James Madison and Robert E. Lee. Richard Taylor had been a lieutenant colonel in the Continental Army during the American Revolution. Shortly before Zachary's birth, Richard had decided to move his family from Orange County in Virginia to the frontier outpost of Louisville, where he had, as a veteran, been granted a thousand acres of land.

Zachary attended two schools in Louisville, but his formal education was limited and his spelling, grammar, and penmanship remained poor throughout his life. In May 1808 he received a commission as a first lieutenant in the 7th Infantry. After a stint as a recruiter, he was assigned to New Orleans, where an attack by British troops was feared. In May and June of 1809 he commanded Fort Pickering near present-day Memphis, Tennessee. He was back

in Louisville in September and October of 1809, possibly recovering from yellow fever.

On June 21, 1810, Taylor married Margaret "Peggy" Mackall Smith, a young woman from Maryland who had been visiting her sister in Louisville. The couple was given a gift of land by his father; it was the start of Taylor's career in land speculation. He eventually amassed a considerable fortune in land and slaves in Kentucky, Mississippi, and Louisiana. In November 1810 Taylor was made a captain of the US Army. In April 1811 the Taylors' first child, Ann Mackall Taylor, was born.

FRONTIER INDIAN FIGHTER

In mid-1811 Taylor received orders to take temporary command at Fort Knox in Vincennes in the Indiana Territory. He oversaw repairs to the fort and restored discipline among the troops stationed there. Taylor did not take part in the Battle of Tippecanoe, led by William Henry Harrison. Taylor was in Maryland at the time to serve as a potential witness in a court martial. After returning to Louisville and his recruiting duties, Taylor was ordered to Fort Harrison, Indiana in 1812, shortly before the declaration of war against Great Britain, in June 1812. In September, Fort Harrison was attacked by Native Americans; Taylor organized the successful defense of the fort, earning a promotion to the rank of major.

"I have no private purposes to accomplish, no party projects to build up, no enemies to punish—nothing to serve but my country."

Zachary Taylor, a letter
to J. S. Allison, April 12, 1848

Taylor's service on the frontier over the next several decades saw him posted in the states (or future states) of Mississippi, Louisiana, Wisconsin, Minnesota, Missouri, Arkansas, and Oklahoma. He was a colonel by the time he fought against the Sauk tribe in the Black Hawk War in 1832. He then took part in the Second Seminole War (1835–1843), which had been triggered by the refusal of Seminoles to relocate from Florida to lands west of the Mississippi. Led by Osceola, the Seminole chief, the Seminoles used guerrilla tactics against the US troops. Resistance among the Native Americans faded after Osceola was captured under a (spurious) flag of truce and placed in a prison, where he died in 1838. Taylor himself respected the Native Americans and worked scrupulously to honor treaties with them, even protecting their lands from incursions by white settlers and establishing a school for them. The Seminoles had runaway slaves living with them; Taylor refused to return slaves to their owners in the absence of absolute proof of ownership, with the result that hundreds of blacks accompanied the Native Americans in the westward movement.

Taylor endured the same hardships as his soldiers, which earned him the nickname "Old Rough and Ready" (it may also have stemmed, in part, from the unkempt appearance that he had become known for). He was generally respected and held in affection by his troops. In 1838 he was made a brigadier general and placed in command of the US troops in Florida.

In 1840 Taylor assumed command of the fort at Baton Rouge, and Margaret Taylor settled in Louisiana—having followed Taylor to most of his frontier commands. Two of their daughters had died of violent fevers while very young; three daughters and a son survived to adulthood. One daughter, Sara Knox Taylor, married Jefferson Davis, who later became president of the Confederate States of America after the southern states seceded from the union. Taylor was well aware of the hardships his wife had endured (as the wife of a career soldier) and did not want his daughters to marry military men. He communicated this bias to the suitor of his daughter Sara, Lieutenant Jefferson Davis, and Davis subsequently resigned from the army in order to marry Sara. However, she contracted cholera and died three months after their marriage.

Another daughter, Mary Elizabeth "Betty" Taylor, in 1848 married Major William W. S. Bliss, who had served under Zachary Taylor at the Battle of Monterey. Bliss, called "Perfect Bliss" by the Taylor family, had advised Taylor in the Battle of Monterey, and Betty served as the hostess at the White House during her father's presidency.

THE MEXICAN-AMERICAN WAR

Taylor's national fame came as a result of his participation in the Mexican-American War (1846–1848). With the annexation of Texas by the United States, war with Mexico seemed inevitable, particularly on the heels of the failure of the diplomatic mission to Mexico under John Slidell, sent by President Polk. In expectation of war, Taylor was ordered to the Rio Grande, which was, according to US claims, the border between Texas and Mexico. Mexico was claiming that the Nueces River was in fact the border, and that US troops were, therefore, intruding on Mexican territory. The Mexican forces attacked the US forces, and the United States declared war after this shedding of "American blood on American soil," in the words of President Polk.

Taylor had to deal with the enemy's numerically superior forces. Nevertheless, he defeated the Mexicans at the Battle of Palo Alto on May 8, 1846, and again on May 9 at the Battle of Resaca de la Palma. Leaving 10,000 men at Matamoras, he took only 6,000 troops with him as he advanced, and still achieved a victory at Monterey. President Polk was angry that Taylor had not pushed even further into Mexico, given his prior successes, and feared the political clout that Taylor was likely to accrue as a military hero. Polk gave General Winfield Scott the task of attacking Vera Cruz, and ordered Taylor to stay where he was. Ignoring the order, Taylor's forces engaged Mexican troops under General Antonio Lopéz de Santa Anna at the Battle of Buena Vista, in February 1847. After fierce and bloody conflict that lasted two days, the Mexican troops withdrew.

Meanwhile, General Winfield Scott landed at Vera Cruz, as ordered, and, in March 1847, took the city in what turned out to be a three-day battle. After a few more battles in which Americans were victorious, the Americans took Mexico City in September. The Treaty of Guadalupe Hidalgo was signed on February 2, 1848; the United States acquired not just Texas and California, but the entire region above the Rio Grande and Gila Rivers.

By the end of 1847 a movement to nominate Taylor for the presidency was well established. Taylor communicated his political positions to members of his party, and he announced that he would run for president if there was "a spontaneous move of the people" to elect him. He identified himself as a Whig, but admitted that he was not a fervent Whig and that he did not know a lot about politics. Taylor ran for president without a defined platform.

PRESIDENCY

Taylor was elected in a narrow victory over Democratic candidate Lewis Cass; he was undoubtedly aided by the third-party candidacy of former president Martin Van Buren, who was the candidate of the Free Soil Party, an antislavery party. In his inaugural address, Taylor avoided mentioning the slavery issue, although it was the most pressing political topic of the time. Those who lived in the northern free states feared that the territory acquired in the Mexican-American War was going to mean that several additional slave states would be added to the Union; the problem was not merely slavery itself, but the impending disturbance to the balance of power between slave and free states.

"It is to be hoped that no international question can now arise which a government confident in its own strength and resolved to protect its own just rights may not settle by wise negotiation; and it eminently becomes a government like our own, founded on the morality and intelligence of its citizens and upheld by their affections, to exhaust every resort of honorable diplomacy before appealing to arms."

Zachary Taylor, his inaugural address, March 5, 1849

Almost immediately, the proposed admission of the states of New Mexico and California focused attention on the slavery issue. Taylor urged Congress to allow New Mexico and California to write their own state constitutions (assuming that they would bar slavery). At the prospect of tipping the balance in favor of free states, southern leaders called for a secession movement. Taylor threatened to hang anyone who disrupted the Union.

Senator Henry Clay of Kentucky proposed

the Compromise of 1850, which was supported by Senator Daniel Webster of Massachusetts and Senator Stephen Douglas of Illinois but opposed by South Carolina's Senator John C. Calhoun. The compromise established that California would be admitted to the Union as a free state, that New Mexico would become a US territory (with the issue of slavery to be decided at a later date), and that there would be tougher fugitive slave laws. Taylor opposed the compromise, which was passed as a series of separate bills, signed after his death by Millard Fillmore.

"I have always done my duty, I am ready to die. My only regret is for the friends I leave behind me."

Zachary Taylor, his last words, July 9, 1850

Taylor scored a success internationally with the Clayton-Bulwer Treaty of 1850, made with Great Britain, which guaranteed access to the future Panama Canal to all nations; both the United States and Great Britain specifically renounced control or dominion over the future canal. Although this was a significant development in amicable Anglo-American relations, some Americans saw the treaty as a weakening of the Monroe Doctrine (which warned European powers not to interfere in the affairs of the Western Hemisphere), and felt that the United States was giving up too much to Great Britain.

On the Fourth of July in 1850, the president listened to a number of speeches while sitting in the hot sun, then took a walk, and returned to the White House, eating a bowl of cherries and drinking ice-cold milk. He soon developed symptoms of severe gastric distress, which continued for five days and were proba-

bly caused by cholera. He died in office on July 9, 1850, and was succeeded by Millard Fillmore.

Margaret Taylor left Washington immediately and spent her final years in Mississippi, dying there in 1852. A quiet, religious woman, she reportedly was unhappy that her husband had been elected president; she maintained a private life during her time in the White House, receiving guests but going out rarely, except to attend church services. No picture or photograph of her survives.

Birthplace: Montebello, near Barboursville, VA [Montebello was a plantation owned by Valentine Johnson, a cousin of Richard Taylor (Zachary's father).]

Residency: Louisiana

Religion: Episcopalian

Education: common school

Place of Death: Washington, DC

Burial Site: Zachary Taylor National Cemetery, near Louisville, KY

Dates in Office: March 5, 1849–July 9, 1850 (1 year, 127 days)

Age at Inauguration: 64 years, 100 days

FAMILY

Father: Richard Taylor (1744–1829)

Mother: Sarah Dabney Strother Taylor (1760–1822)

Siblings: Zachary Taylor was the third of nine children; his siblings were Hancock Taylor (1781–1841); William Dabney Strother Taylor (1782–1808); George Taylor (1790–1829); Elizabeth Lee Taylor (1792–1845); Richard Strother Taylor (1794–1829); Joseph Pannill Taylor (1796–1864); Sarah Bailey Taylor (1799–1851); Emily Richard Taylor (1801–1841 or 1842) [Note: Sources differ about Zachary Taylor's siblings; some list a child who died in infancy, perhaps named Richard and perhaps born in 1780 or 1786; some sources do not list Richard Strother Taylor; some give Joseph Pannill Taylor's birthdate as 1806; some give Sarah Bailey Taylor's name as Sarah Strother Taylor, and so on.]

Wife: Margaret "Peggy" Mackall Smith Taylor (1788–1852), married on June 21, 1810, in Jefferson County, KY
Children: Ann Margaret Mackall Taylor (1811–1875); Sarah Knox Taylor (1814–1835); Octavia P. Taylor (1816–1820); Margaret Smith Taylor (1819–1820); Mary Elizabeth Taylor (1824–1909); Richard Taylor (1826–1879)

CAREER

Private: soldier, planter
Political: president of the United States (1849–1850)
Military: appointed first lieutenant in the 7th Infantry regiment (1808); appointed major in the War of 1812 (1815); made lieutenant colonel (1819); made a colonel in command of the 1st Regiment in the Black Hawk War (1832); led US troops in the Second Seminole War (1835–1843); commanded US forces against the Seminole (1838–1840); led US troops in the Mexican-American War (1846–1848); defeated Mexicans at Palo Alto and Resaca de la Palma; captured Monterrey, Mexico (September 26, 1846); made a brigadier general (1846; he became the second-highest ranking Army officer, second only to Major General Winfield Scott, commanding general of the Army); defeated Mexicans at Buena Vista (February 22–23, 1847)
Selected Works: *Letters of Zachary Taylor, from the battle-fields of the Mexican War* (Rochester, NY: Genesee Press, 1908); *Papers of Zachary Taylor*, archival manuscript collection on microfilm (Washington, DC: Library of Congress); *Zachary Taylor 1784–1850 and Millard Fillmore 1800–1874, chronology, documents, bibliographic aids*, ed. by John J. Farrell (Dobbs Ferry, NY: Oceana Publications, 1971)

PRESIDENCY

Nomination: 1848: At the Whig nominating convention in Philadelphia, Taylor led on the first ballot and gained the nomination on the fourth ballot; Millard Fillmore of NY was selected as the vice presidential candidate in hopes that he would broaden the ticket.

Election: elected president on November 7, 1848 [Note: This was the first election in which the entire nation voted on the same day.]
Opponent: Lewis Cass, MI, Democratic Party
Martin Van Buren, NY, Free Soil Party
Vote Totals: Taylor, 1,360,967 popular, 163 electoral; Cass, 1,222,342 popular, 127 electoral; Van Buren, 291,263 popular, 0 electoral
Inauguration: March 5, 1849
Vice President: Millard Fillmore (1849–1850)

CABINET

Secretary of State: John M. Clayton, DE (1849–1850)
Secretary of the Treasury: William M. Meredith, PA (1849–1850)
Secretary of War: George W. Crawford, GA (1849–1850)
Attorney General: Reverdy Johnson, MD (1849–1850)
Postmaster General: Jacob Collamer, VT (1849–1850)
Secretary of the Navy: William B. Preston, VA (1849–1850)
Secretary of the Interior: Thomas Ewing, OH (1849–1850)

CONGRESS

31st Congress (1849–1851); Speaker of the House: Howell Cobb (GA, Democrat)

SUPREME COURT APPOINTEES

MAJOR EVENTS OF THE TAYLOR ADMINISTRATION

◆ The Clayton-Bulwer Treaty with Great Britain, 1850, guarantees access to the future Panama Canal to all nations; Great Britain and the United States agree not to seek control of the proposed canal.
◆ Senator Henry Clay of Kentucky proposes the Compromise of 1850, which provides for the admission of California into the union as a free state, the formation of New Mexico as a territory (with the option of slavery at the time

of its admission as a state), and harsher fugitive slave laws.

◆ After Fourth of July celebrations on a hot day, Taylor eats a bowl of cherries and drinks iced milk—one or the other of these items is the probable source of the cholera that he contracts. After five days of illness, Taylor dies on July 9, 1850, after sixteen months in office.

MAJOR US AND WORLD EVENTS, 1849–1850

◆ Great Britain annexes the Punjab after defeating the Sikhs at Gujarat, India, 1849.
◆ California holds its state constitutional convention, September 1849.
◆ Harriet Tubman escapes from slavery in Maryland, December 1849.
◆ The Women's Medical College of Pennsylvania, the nation's first medical school for women, is established in March of 1850.
◆ Nathaniel Hawthorne publishes *The Scarlet Letter*, 1850.
◆ The US census of 1850 reports a population of 23.1 million.
◆ Levi Strauss makes his first pair of blue jeans, June 1850.
◆ The first modern safety pin is designed by Walter Hunt, 1850.
◆ Elizabeth Barrett Browning publishes *Sonnets from the Portuguese*, 1850.
◆ The Taiping Rebellion against the Manchu dynasty in China breaks out, 1850.

◆ The first clear photograph (a daguerreotype) of the moon is taken by William Bond, 1850.

FAST FACTS ABOUT ZACHARY TAYLOR

◆ The election of 1848 was the first in which everyone voted on the same day, November 7.
◆ Taylor was mailed notification of his nomination for president, but because there was postage due on the letter, he refused it and did not learn of the nomination for several days.
◆ One of Taylor's daughters, Sarah Knox Taylor, married Jefferson Davis, the future president of the Confederacy. She died only three months after the marriage, in 1835.
◆ Moving around a great deal as an army officer, Taylor had never voted before he became president.
◆ Taylor kept his horse, Whitey, on the White House lawn; visitors would pluck hairs from Whitey's tail as souvenirs.
◆ Taylor was the first president who had never held any prior elective office.
◆ Margaret Mackall Smith Taylor did not care to perform the social duties expected of the first lady; the role of White House hostess was performed by her daughter, Elizabeth "Betty" Bliss.
◆ Taylor's son-in-law, Colonel William W. S. Bliss, was called "Perfect Bliss" by the Taylor family. Fort Bliss, at the border between Texas and New Mexico, is named for him.
◆ Taylor's only son, Richard Taylor, served as a Confederate general during the Civil War.

Millard Fillmore

Nickname: Last of the Whigs, The American Louis-Philippe
Presidency: 13th president, 1850–1853
Party: Anti-Masonic; Whig; American (Know-Nothing)
Life dates: January 7, 1800–March 8, 1874 (74 years, 60 days)

EARLY LIFE AND EDUCATION

Millard Fillmore was born on January 7, 1800, in a log cabin in Locke, New York, a frontier village. His father was Nathaniel Fillmore and his mother was Phoebe Millard Fillmore. They were farmers who had moved from Vermont to New York. Nathaniel was unable to prove his ownership of the land on which he had originally settled in New York state (this was a common problem in the early days of the United States; questions about land deeds and titles formed a large part of the practice of many lawyers), so he moved a few miles away to Sempronius, New York, and became a tenant farmer. Millard, the second of nine children, grew up working the farm. His father was unsuccessful as a farmer and the family was extremely poor; Millard received very little schooling.

Given his own experience, Nathaniel did not want his sons to become farmers, so he apprenticed Millard to a cloth-dresser at the age of fourteen. Millard was unhappy in this situation; he borrowed thirty dollars to pay off his obligation to the man who had taken him on as apprentice, and walked a hundred miles to return home. He was again apprenticed, to one of the owners of a carding and cloth-dressing mill. Eager to learn about the world at large, Millard purchased a share in a circulating library and then bought his first book, a dictionary, in which he looked up words (whose meanings he memorized) during spare moments while he worked at the mill.

When an academy (a private high school) was established at nearby New Hope, New York, Millard enrolled. He was nineteen and his teacher, Abigail Powers, was twenty-one. She encouraged his desire to learn and his ambitions; they fell in love. Millard's father sold his farm tenancy and moved to Montville, New York, becoming the tenant of County Judge Walter Wood. Nathaniel asked Wood to try out Millard as a law clerk. The judge responded affirmatively; when Millard's mother told him the good news, Millard broke down and cried. The judge agreed to give clerical jobs to Millard, to enable him to pay his way as he studied law. First, Millard taught elementary school for three months in order to buy out his mill apprenticeship; he then went to work for Judge Wood.

When the Judge objected to Millard's handling of a small case, Millard quit and returned to his family, which had by this time moved westward to Aurora, New York, near Buffalo. Millard again taught school briefly, before accepting a clerkship with the law firm of Asa Rice and Joseph Clary. Millard alternated teaching, to support himself, with clerking while he studied the law. In 1823 the Court of Common Pleas admitted him to the practice of law.

"The great law of morality ought to have a national as well as a personal and individual application. We should act toward other nations as we wish them to act toward us; and justice and conscience should form the rule of conduct between governments instead of mere power, self-interest, and the desire of aggrandizement."

Millard Fillmore, 1850

EARLY CAREER

Fillmore opened a law office in East Aurora, New York. He was appointed the commissioner of deeds for the region—his first public office. In 1826 he and Abigail were married. They had two children, Millard Powers in 1828 and Mary Abigail in 1832.

In 1830 the family moved to Buffalo, New York; Fillmore became a leading lawyer. He was admitted as an attorney to the state Supreme Court, and took Nathan K. Hall with him as his clerk.

Fillmore became active in local politics in the Anti-Mason Party, which grew out of public suspicion of the Masonic Order, a secretive fraternal organization of freemasons. A stonemason, William Morgan, disappeared and reportedly had been murdered by Masons because he had threatened to publish a book revealing the secrets of the Masons. Thurlow Weed, a newspaper editor, spearheaded the growth of the Anti-Mason Party. Weed became a political boss and a supporter of Fillmore in his early political career. The Anti-Masons allied themselves with the National Republican Party (which later developed into the Whig Party), in opposition to the Jacksonian Democrats then in power.

POLITICAL CAREER

In 1828 Fillmore was elected to the New York legislature. He observed the legislative process in action, and was re-elected for the 1830 session and the 1831 session. He put forth a bill abolishing the imprisonment of debtors and allowing them to declare bankruptcy.

In 1830 the Fillmores moved to Buffalo, which was undergoing rapid growth as a result of the completion of the Erie Canal, which served as a main route for immigrants moving westward. Buffalo had a lively social scene in which the Fillmores took part. They joined the Unitarian Church and attended regularly.

In 1833 Fillmore was elected to the US House of Representatives, and served there until 1835, and then again from 1837 to 1845. The most contentious debate going on in Congress at that time centered on slavery, although the southern-inspired "gag order" that prohibited discussion of slavery was in effect and stymied northern attempts to address the problem. Fillmore presented a petition in Congress to abolish slavery in the District of Columbia (it did not pass), and supported John Quincy Adams in advocating free speech and the right of petition. Generally, Fillmore sided with the Whigs and Henry Clay; the Anti-Masonic Party had for the most part merged with the Whig Party.

After he had served four terms, Fillmore decided not to run again as a Representative. In 1844 he ran for governor of New York but was defeated. In 1847 he was elected comptroller of New York. In 1848 he was selected by the Whigs as General Zachary Taylor's running mate. Taylor was from the South and a slave-owner; Fillmore was nominated as the vice-presidential candidate to balance the ticket. On the heels of Taylor's recent success as a general in the Mexican-American War ensuring his popularity, they won the election.

VICE PRESIDENCY

Taylor and Fillmore met for the first time after the election that made them the leaders of the executive branch of government. Fillmore, who had fought hard for his education and cultivated an elegant appearance, did not enter into a close relationship with "Old Rough and Ready" Taylor.

When Taylor's administration was new, the debate that raged in Congress focused on the territories that had recently been acquired in the Mexican-American War and what effect their admission to the Union would have on the delicate balance of power between slave and free states (at that time there were fifteen slave states and fifteen free states). In this tense atmosphere, Senator Henry Clay of Kentucky proposed several resolutions, from which emerged the Compromise of 1850. Clay proposed that California be admitted as a free state, that the other territories (including New Mexico and Utah) be allowed to determine whether they would allow slavery, that slave trading (though not slavery itself) be ended in the District of Columbia, and that the Fugitive Slave Act, which would provide for runaway slaves to be returned to their owners no matter where they were captured, become law. While the debate was in full swing, President Zachary Taylor died and Millard Fillmore became president.

PRESIDENCY

Fillmore immediately urged acceptance of Clay's proposed compromise, whose proposed laws were passed individually rather then collectively. The country, in effect, became divided along the thirty-seventh parallel, with slave states below and free states above. Although Fillmore supported the compromise in the hopes that it would end the conflict between North and South, it soon became apparent that neither side was really happy with the settlement. In retrospect, it appears that the compromise simply delayed the inevitable (a calamitous war) for a decade.

One of Fillmore's actions as president was to appoint Brigham Young, the leader of the Mormon Church, as governor of the Utah Territory. In Utah under Young, there was little attention paid to federal authority.

> **"God knows that I detest slavery, but it is an existing evil, for which we are not responsible, and we must endure it, and give it such protection as is guaranteed by the Constitution, till we can get rid of it without destroying the last hope of free government in the world."**
>
> Millard Fillmore
> to Daniel Webster, 1850

Fillmore made a more lasting contribution in the area of foreign policy, when he authorized an expedition to Japan in 1852, dispatching a letter to the emperor suggesting closer relations between Japan and the United States. Commodore Matthew C. Perry arrived in Tokyo Bay in 1853; the result was the Treaty of Kanagawa, signed in 1854, which opened two Japanese ports to US trade. Other treaties followed.

During most of Millard Fillmore's presidency, Abigail Fillmore was in frail health. During her tenure as first lady, she fell and injured her foot, which made standing for even short periods extremely painful for her. Her daughter Mary often filled in for her as the White House hostess. Mrs. Fillmore felt strongly that the White House needed a library and asked her husband to request funds from Congress. She took great pleasure in selecting the books that would become the core of the library.

Fillmore lost his party's nomination in 1852, in part because he had alienated the antislavery northern Whigs, and in part because he had replaced the members of Taylor's cabinet with his own supporters. General Winfield Scott won the Whig nomination but lost the election to

Franklin Pierce. Fillmore was, therefore, the "last of the Whigs."

"Let us remember that revolutions do not always establish freedom. Our own free institutions were not the offspring of our Revolution. They existed before."

Millard Fillmore, his third annual message to Congress, 1852

POST-PRESIDENTIAL CAREER

The Fillmores attended the inauguration of Franklin Pierce. Abigail fell ill with pneumonia shortly after the event and died in Washington. Fillmore returned to his law practice in Buffalo, and was plunged into grief again the following year by the death of his daughter Mary, who at the age of twenty-two died from cholera.

Fillmore then traveled extensively in Europe. He returned home in 1856, when he was nominated as a presidential candidate by the American (Know-Nothing) Party. The Know-Nothing name derived from the practice that its members claimed to know nothing pertaining to the secret nativist organizations that comprised the party. The main tenet of the Know-Nothings was their opposition to immigration and to Roman Catholics; Fillmore did not show any interest in these two aspects of their program, but he was accepted as a candidate whose sentiments vis-à-vis slavery—the members of his party believed—fell somewhere in between those of the most passionate antislavery forces and those of the extreme proslavery forces. However, he carried only Maryland in the 1856 election. The Democratic candidate, James Buchanan, became president.

In 1858 Fillmore married Mrs. Caroline Carmichael McIntosh, a wealthy widow from Albany. The couple bought a mansion in Buffalo.

Fillmore was active in Buffalo civic affairs, becoming the founder of the General Hospital in Buffalo, the first president of the historical society, and the chancellor of the University of Buffalo. He was a firm supporter of the Union during the Civil War, although he did not always support Lincoln. He suffered a stroke from which he did not recover, and died in Buffalo on March 8, 1874.

"I am tolerant of all creeds. Yet if any sect suffered itself to be used for political objects I would meet it by political opposition. In my view, Church and State should be separate, not only in form, but fact—religion and politics should not be mingled."

Millard Fillmore, 1856

Fillmore remains one of the least regarded presidents, possibly because much of what was written about him in the wake of his presidency was penned by enemies. His name is associated with a number of questionable movements, notably the Know-Nothing Party, and his support of the Fugitive Slave Act has further marked him as an unfavorable president. If his desire to hold the Union together was laudable, his judgment seems less so.

Birthplace: Locke (now called Summerhill), Cayuga County, NY
Residency: New York
Religion: Unitarian
Education: common school
Place of Death: Buffalo, NY
Burial Site: Forest Lawn Cemetery, Buffalo, NY
Dates in Office: July 10, 1850–March 3, 1853 (2 years, 236 days)
Age at Inauguration: 50 years, 184 days

FAMILY
Father: Nathaniel Fillmore (1771–1863)
Mother: Phoebe Millard Fillmore (1780–1831)
Siblings: Millard Fillmore was the second of
nine children; his siblings were Olive Armstrong
Fillmore (1797–1893); Cyrus Fillmore (1801–
1889); Almon Hopkins Fillmore (1806–1830);
Calvin Turner Fillmore (1810–1872); Julia Fillmore
(1812–? [after 1847]); Darius Ingraham Fillmore
(1814–1837); Charles De Witt Fillmore (1817–
1854); Phoebe Maria Fillmore (1819–1843).
Wife: Abigail Powers Fillmore (1798–1853),
married on February 5, 1826, in Moravia, NY;
Caroline Carmichael McIntosh Fillmore (1813–
1881), married on February 10, 1858, in Albany, NY
Children: Millard Powers Fillmore (1828–1889);
Mary Abigail Fillmore (1832–1854)

CAREER
Private: lawyer
Political: Member of the NY state legislature
(1829–1832); member of the US House of
Representatives (1833–1835; 1837–1843);
comptroller of NY state (1848); vice president
under Zachary Taylor (1849–1850); president of
the United States (1850–1853)
Military: none
Selected Works: *The Early Life of Millard
Fillmore* (Buffalo, NY: Salisbury Club, 1958); *The
Lady and the President: The Letters of Dorothea
Dix and Millard Fillmore*, ed. by Charles M.
Snyder (Lexington: University Press of Kentucky,
1975); *Millard Fillmore Papers*, ed. by Frank H.
Severance (Buffalo, NY: The Buffalo Historical
Society, 1907); *Papers of Millard Fillmore*, archival
collection on microfilm (originals in the Buffalo
and Erie County Historical Society and the State
University of New York in Oswego, NY; copy in
the Library of Congress)

PRESIDENCY
Nomination: 1848: Fillmore, a New Yorker, was
nominated as the vice-presidential candidate by
the Whig Party to balance the ticket of Zachary
Taylor, the southern, slave-holding presidential
candidate.
Election: became president after the death of
President Zachary Taylor

Opponent: n/a
Vote Totals: n/a
Inauguration: not inaugurated; took oath of
office July 10, 1850
Vice President: none

CABINET
Secretary of State: John M. Clayton, DE (1850);
Daniel Webster, MA (1850–1852); Edward Everett,
MA (1852–1853)
Secretary of the Treasury: William M.
Meredith, PA (1850); Thomas Corwin, OH
(1850–1853)
Secretary of War: George W. Crawford, GA
(1850); Charles M. Conrad, LA (1850–1853)
Attorney General: Reverdy Johnson, MD
(1850); John J. Crittenden, KY (1850–1853)
Postmaster General: Jacob Collamer, VT (1850);
Nathan K. Hall, NY (1850–1852); Samuel D.
Hubbard, CT (1852–1853)
Secretary of the Navy: William B. Preston, VA
(1850); William A. Graham, NC (1850–1852);
John P. Kennedy, MD (1852–1853)
Secretary of the Interior: Thomas Ewing, OH
(1850); Thomas M. T. McKennan, PA (1850);
Alexander H. H. Stuart, VA (1850–1853)

CONGRESS
**31st Congress (1849–1851); Speaker of the
House:** Howell Cobb (GA, Democrat)
**32nd Congress (1851–1853); Speaker of the
House:** Linn Boyd (KY, Democrat)

SUPREME COURT APPOINTEES
Benjamin Robbins Curtis, MA; Associate Justice
(1851–1857)

MAJOR EVENTS OF THE
FILLMORE ADMINISTRATION
◆ Abigail Powers Fillmore establishes the
White House Library, 1850–1853.
◆ Fillmore supports and Congress passes the
Compromise of 1850 (September 20, 1850),
which allows California admission to the Union
as a free state and includes the Fugitive Slave
Act, providing for the return of runaway slaves
no matter where in the Union they are found.
The Compromise helps to temporarily relieve

the tensions between North and South that will lead to the Civil War a decade later.

◆ Fillmore names Brigham Young as governor of the Utah Territory, September 28, 1850 (he serves until 1857).

◆ Fillmore sends Commodore Matthew C. Perry to Japan (1852–1854); Perry opens two Japanese ports to American trade.

◆ California becomes a state, September 9, 1850.

◆ The United States ratifies a commercial treaty with El Salvador, January 2, 1851.

◆ The Oregon Territory is divided and the Washington Territory is formed, March 2, 1853.

◆ Congress authorizes the transcontinental rail survey, March 3, 1853; the railway is completed in 1869.

MAJOR US AND WORLD EVENTS, 1850–1853

◆ Richard Wagner's opera *Lohengrin* debuts, 1850.

◆ A national women's rights convention is held in Worcester, MA, from October 23–24, 1850.

◆ Sojourner Truth addresses the first Black Women's Rights Convention in Akron, OH, 1851.

◆ Gail Borden announces the invention of evaporated milk, 1851.

◆ Maine becomes the first US state to ban the sale of alcohol, 1851.

◆ Isaac Singer is granted a patent on a sewing machine, 1851.

◆ The first American YMCA is organized in Boston, 1851.

◆ Artist Emanuel Gottlieb Leutze paints "Washington Crossing the Delaware," 1851.

◆ Australia's first gold rush begins, 1851.

◆ Gold is found in Oregon, July 25, 1851.

◆ The Great Exposition opens in the Crystal Palace in London, 1851.

◆ Fires in May and June destroy much of San Francisco, 1851.

◆ The *New York Times* begins publication, September 18, 1851.

◆ Herman Melville publishes *Moby Dick*, 1851.

◆ Nathaniel Hawthorne publishes *The House of the Seven Gables*, 1851.

◆ Giuseppe Verdi composes *Rigoletto*, 1851.

◆ The yacht *America* wins a sixty-mile race around the Isle of Wight, 1851; the trophy becomes known as the "America's Cup."

◆ Great Britain recognizes the independence of the Transvaal (South African Republic), 1852.

◆ Uncle Sam makes his debut as a cartoon character in the *New York Lantern*, 1852.

◆ Louis Napoleon, president of France, declares himself Emperor Napoleon III, 1852.

◆ Harriet Beecher Stowe publishes *Uncle Tom's Cabin*, 1852.

◆ Stephen Foster publishes "My Old Kentucky Home," 1852.

◆ Charles Dickens publishes *Bleak House*, 1852.

◆ Peter Mark Roget publishes his first *Roget's Thesaurus*, 1852.

◆ Giuseppe Verdi's opera, *Il Trovatore*, premieres, 1853.

FAST FACTS ABOUT MILLARD FILLMORE

◆ Fillmore said that while he was growing up, his family owned three books: a Bible, an almanac, and a hymnbook.

◆ Millard Fillmore was the second vice president to assume the presidency after his predecessor died in office.

◆ Zachary Taylor and Millard Fillmore did not meet until after they had been elected president and vice president, respectively. The two men were very different, and Taylor virtually excluded Fillmore from all decision-making during his presidency.

◆ Fillmore was careful about his health; he did not smoke and did not drink.

◆ Fillmore built a house in East Aurora, NY, in 1826 for himself and his wife Abigail. He is the only president to design and build his own house.

◆ The story that Fillmore installed the first bathtub in the White House originated with a satirical article written by H. L. Mencken in 1917; the fiction has been widely reported as a fact.

◆ During Fillmore's term, the cornerstone of the current House of Representatives chamber was laid.

◆ Fillmore was the first president born in the 1800s.

◆ After his presidency, Fillmore became the chancellor of the University of Buffalo.

◆ Fillmore was one of the founders of the Buffalo Historical Society and the Buffalo General Hospital.

◆ Abigail Fillmore's health was failing during her husband's presidency, so their daughter Mary Abigail performed many of the duties of White House hostess.

◆ Fillmore helped found and served as vice president of the Society for the Prevention of Cruelty to Animals.

Franklin Pierce

Nickname: Young Hickory of the Granite Hills, Handsome Frank, Hero of Many a Bottle
Presidency: 14th president, 1853–1857
Party: Democratic
Life Dates: November 23, 1804–October 8, 1869 (64 years, 319 days)

EARLY LIFE AND EDUCATION

Franklin Pierce was born on November 23, 1804, in Hillsborough, New Hampshire. His father, Benjamin Pierce, had been a major in the Continental Army during the Revolutionary War. After the war the elder Pierce left his native Massachusetts and settled in New Hampshire, where he became the sheriff for the county in which he had settled, a general in the county militia, a state representative, and a governor of New Hampshire for two terms, in 1827 and 1829. He married Elizabeth Andrews Pierce, who died shortly after giving birth to a daughter, in 1788. His second wife, Anna Kendrick Pierce, gave birth to eight children; Franklin was the sixth of these.

For a few years during Franklin's youth, a part of the family home was maintained as a tavern—to help support the family while the land on which they had settled was being cleared for farming. From this lively place, Franklin was sent to a boarding school in Hancock, New Hampshire. He once became so homesick that he walked fourteen miles to his home on a Sunday, waited for his family to return from church, and shared a meal with them. His father then insisted that he make the return trek to the school, accompanying him halfway and making him walk the rest of the way on his own. After that, Franklin stayed in school, later attending an academy in Francestown while living at the home of family friends, the Woodburys.

When he was sixteen, Franklin went to Bowdoin College in Brunswick, Maine. For a time he was at the bottom of his class, but he finally improved in his studies and graduated fifth in his class. At Bowdoin he met Nathaniel Hawthorne, with whom he remained lifelong friends. Hawthorne later wrote a campaign biography of Pierce, and Pierce helped Hawthorne financially.

EARLY CAREER

After Bowdoin, Pierce began to read law in the office of Judge Levi Woodbury in Portsmouth, NH. Woodbury was the son of the family with whom he had lived in Francestown during his school days. He continued his study of the law, first in Northampton, Massachusetts, and then with Judge Edmund Parker in Amherst, New Hampshire. It is likely that he met Jane Means Appleton during the time he spent in Amherst, as she was then living there with her mother, the widow of a former president of Bowdoin

College. Jane's father, Jesse Appleton, had died in 1819, before Pierce's student days. Jane was a petite and introspective woman, deeply religious and shy. Tragedies in her life exacerbated her tendency toward depression.

> **"I find that the remark,
> ''Tis distance lends
> enchantment to the view'
> is no less true of the political
> than the natural world."**
>
> Franklin Pierce, 1832

In 1827 Pierce was admitted to the bar and his father helped him establish a law practice in Hillsborough; this was the same year that his father was first elected governor of New Hampshire. Pierce was not immediately successful as a lawyer, but he persevered in building his law practice while becoming more involved in politics. In 1829 he was elected to the state legislature, where he served until 1833; the last two years of his tenure were spent as speaker of the house.

POLITICAL CAREER

Pierce was elected to the US House of Representatives in 1833 and married Jane Means Appleton on November 19, 1834, at her sister's home in Amherst, New Hampshire. In 1836 their first son, Franklin Pierce, Jr., was born, and died after only three days of life. In 1837 Pierce was elected to the US Senate as the youngest member of that body. He was a strong supporter of Andrew Jackson and the Democratic Party line. Pierce rarely spoke on the floor of Congress, but he was active in committee work and was popular with his peers, especially the southern senators whose views he shared. Pierce believed that the Constitution protected slavery and that abolitionists threatened the Union.

Jane Pierce disliked politics and life in Washington; she spent very little time there even during her husband's years in Congress. She also deplored the heavy drinking that many men in Washington, including her husband, indulged in. Family life took on increased importance when the Pierces' second son, Frank Robert (Frankie) was born in 1839, and their third son, Benjamin (Bennie), in 1841. Jane persuaded her husband to resign from the Senate in 1842, and the family settled in Concord, New Hampshire, where Pierce resumed his law career and joined the temperance movement. In 1843 tragedy struck again when their four-year-old son Frankie died of typhus.

Pierce did not abandon his interest in politics, becoming involved in the Democratic Party in New Hampshire and aiding other candidates, including James Polk, seeking election. In 1845 President Polk asked Pierce to be his attorney general, but Pierce declined because of Jane's poor health; he later also refused the nomination for governor of New Hampshire. But in part owing to his upbringing as the son of a Revolutionary War soldier who also saw two older brothers become soldiers in the War of 1812, Pierce wanted to fight when the Mexican-American War broke out.

MILITARY SERVICE

In 1847 Pierce enlisted as a private but was soon appointed a colonel and then a brigadier general by Polk. He sailed for Vera Cruz, serving under General Winfield Scott, known as "Old Fuss and Feathers" for his devotion to military discipline and protocol. Pierce marched on Mexico City, but in the Battle of Churubusco his leg was crushed. Pierce reportedly fainted from the intense pain, and was subsequently referred to behind his back as "Fainting Frank." This episode would later be used by political foes to discredit his military service.

Pierce returned to Concord and lived fairly quietly; he and Jane cared devotedly for their remaining son, Bennie. Pierce continued to further his successful law career and acted as a member of the New Hampshire state constitutional convention in 1850. Despite his having promised his wife that he would remove his name from the list of presidential candidates,

Pierce was nominated by the Democrats at a meeting in June 1852 in Baltimore. He was considered a compromise candidate, placed in nomination on the thirty-fifth ballot and chosen on the forty-ninth ballot—because he was a northerner with southern sympathies. When Jane Pierce heard the news of her husband's nomination, she fainted. During the campaign, both she and Bennie wrote letters to Pierce in which they said they hoped he would lose.

———◦———

"It is a relief to feel that no heart but my own can know the personal regret and bitter sorrow over which I have been borne to a position so suitable for others rather than desirable for myself. . . . You have summoned me in my weakness; you must sustain me by your strength."

Franklin Pierce, Inaugural Address, March 4, 1853 (Pierce was in deep mourning for his son Benjamin, who had died in a train accident on January 6, 1853)

———◦———

Pierce's opposition was the Whig candidate, his former commander, General Winfield Scott. Pierce did not campaign at all (a not uncommon practice for presidential candidates up until that time) and Scott failed to run a successful campaign. Although the popular vote was close, Pierce won handily with the electoral votes, receiving 254 to Scott's 42. Pierce, at age forty-eight, became the youngest man up to that time to be elected president.

PRESIDENCY

On January 6, 1853, Jane and Franklin Pierce were traveling by train with their eleven-year-old son, Bennie. The train was derailed and, although there were few other injuries, Bennie was thrown the length of the railroad car and suffered severe head injuries. He died there, his parents witness to the tragedy.

Jane Pierce refused to attend her husband's inauguration. He delivered his inaugural address without notes, referring from the outset to the grief that weighed on his mind as he assumed the presidency. Jane Pierce inhabited the upstairs of the White House for two years, refusing to attend social events. She told her husband that Bennie's death was God's price for his election, and that Bennie had died because God had not wanted him to be distracted by his son during his presidency. Hostess duties were performed most often by Abigail Kent Means, Jane's aunt by marriage; the cabinet members' wives—especially Varina Howell Davis (Mrs. Jefferson Davis)—also sometimes acted as hostesses for White House functions.

In April, Vice President Rufus King, who had taken the oath of office in Cuba, died there without ever serving as vice president. Pierce served the rest of his term with no vice president.

Democratic Senator Stephen Douglas put forward the Kansas-Nebraska Act, which proposed that these two territories be allowed to decide the slavery question by popular sovereignty—that the settlers themselves be allowed to vote on the question. However, this was going to violate the previous resolutions to ban slavery above the 36 degrees 30 minutes latitude. Pierce agreed to support the Kansas-Nebraska Act and signed it at the time it passed in 1854. Northern, antislavery Democrats were outraged, and saw the Act as a subterfuge that would allow slavery in territories that should have been free. In Kansas, the Act precipitated violence between proslavery and antislavery settlers, garnering Kansas the nickname of "Bleeding Kansas." Not only did Pierce lose the support of many Democrats, but a new political party, the Republicans, began to coalesce around antislavery forces.

Pierce was somewhat more successful in foreign affairs. He sent James Gadsden as a special envoy to Mexico—to arrange what came to be known as the Gadsden Purchase, finalized in 1854. It provided for a purchase of land from

Mexico, which would become part of the future states of New Mexico and Arizona; the Gadsden Purchase defined, once and for all, the border between the United States and Mexico.

> **"[T]he use of my name . . . before the Democratic National Convention at Baltimore . . . would be utterly repugnant to my tastes and wishes."**
>
> Franklin Pierce, on declining a nomination as a presidential candidate by New Hampshire Democrats, January 1852

Pierce, like many southerners, also hoped to acquire Cuba for the United States; the southerners hoped to add another slave state to the Union in this way. Pierce sent Pierre Soulé as an envoy to Spain, with instructions to purchase Cuba, but Soulé, who became frustrated by his failed attempts to do business with the Spanish, wrote the Ostend Manifesto in 1854, in which he warned that the United States was prepared to intervene militarily in Cuba in the event of a slave revolt there (as such a revolt would serve as provocation to the slaves of the American South and threaten the United States). The Ostend Manifesto was signed not only by Soulé but also by John Mason, the US minister to France, and James Buchanan, the US minister to Great Britain. When the document and its contents became public knowledge, however, both Americans in the North and Europeans in general were immediately appalled by it, and the US Secretary of State, William Marcy, was forced to repudiate it.

Much to Pierce's disappointment, his party failed to nominate him for a second term, choosing instead to nominate career politician James Buchanan.

POST-PRESIDENTIAL CAREER

After the presidency, the Pierces took an extended trip through Europe in hopes of improving Jane Pierce's health—though without any notable success. When they returned to New Hampshire from Europe, Jane stayed for periods of time with her sister Mary Aiken in Andover, Massachusetts, where she died in 1863 at the age of fifty-seven.

Pierce voiced his support for the Union during the Civil War, but openly criticized President Abraham Lincoln, sometimes blaming him for the war. After Lincoln's assassination, a crowd gathered outside Pierce's home and denounced him as a traitor, but he was able to use his powers of oratory to convince them to disperse.

Pierce died on October 8, 1869; his body lay in state at the Capitol in Concord. Although Pierce was and is the only president from New Hampshire, it took his home state forty-five years to raise a statue of him. Pierce was not considered a highly popular president as he, like so many presidents of his era, suffered from an inability to deal with the seemingly insoluble problem of slavery. Pierce's support of proslavery elements in the South and his endorsement of the Kansas-Nebraska Act, which exacerbated rather than moderated the tensions that led to the Civil War, has only dragged him down in the esteem of historians.

Birthplace: Hillsborough [sometimes spelled Hillsboro], NH
Residency: New Hampshire
Religion: Episcopalian
Education: Bowdoin College, Brunswick, ME, graduated 1824
Place of Death: Concord, NH
Burial site: Old North Cemetery, Concord, NH
Dates in Office: March 4,1853–March 3, 1857 (4 years)
Age at Inauguration: 48 years, 101 days

FAMILY
Father: Benjamin Pierce (1757–1839)
Mother: Anna Kendrick Pierce (1768–1838)
Siblings: Franklin Pierce was one of nine children of his father—and one of eight of his

mother. Benjamin Pierce first married Elizabeth Andrews Pierce (1768–1788), with whom he had a daughter, Elizabeth Pierce (1788–1855). By his second wife, Anna Kendrick Pierce, Benjamin had eight children, of whom Franklin was the sixth; his siblings were Benjamin Kendrick Pierce (1790–1850); Nancy Pierce (1792–1837); John Sullivan Pierce (1796–1824); Harriet B. Pierce (1800–1837); Charles Grandison Pierce (1803–1828); Charlotte Pierce (1806?–1837); and Henry Dearborn Pierce (1812–1880).

Wife: Jane Means Appleton Pierce (1806–1863), married November 10, 1834, at Amherst, NH

Children: Franklin Pierce, Jr. (b. 1836; died three days after birth); Frank Robert Pierce (1839–1843); Benjamin Pierce (1841–1853)

CAREER

Private: lawyer

Political: NH state representative (1829–1833); member of the US House of Representatives (1833–1837); US senator from NH (1837–1842); president of the United States (1853–1857)

Military: enlisted in 1847 for service in the Mexican War; appointed colonel and then brigadier general; served nine months, until the conclusion of the Mexican War; wounded in battle at Contreras, August 19, 1847; resigned his commission March 1848

Selected Works: *Franklin Pierce, 1804–1869, chronology, documents, bibliographical aids,* ed. by Irving J. Sloan (Dobbs Ferry, NY: Oceana Publications, 1968); *Papers of Franklin Pierce,* archival collection on microfilm (Washington, DC: Library of Congress)

PRESIDENCY

Nomination: 1852: At the Democratic convention in Baltimore, MD, Pierce went to the convention as a delegate and "favorite son" of NH; his name was not initially placed in nomination, but after the nomination process became badly deadlocked, the VA delegation put Pierce's name in nomination for the thirty-sixth ballot; he was nominated by the party on the forty-ninth ballot.

Election: elected president November 2, 1852

Opponent: Winfield Scott, VA, Whig

Vote Totals: 1852: Pierce, 1,601,274 popular, 254 electoral; Scott, 1,386,580 popular, 42 electoral

Inauguration: March 4, 1853

Vice President: William Rufus De Vane King, AL (King took the oath of office, but died on April 18, 1853, before serving; the position of vice president remained vacant for Pierce's presidency)

CABINET

Secretary of State: William Learned Marcy, NY (1853–1857)

Secretary of the Treasury: James Guthrie, KY (1853–1857)

Secretary of War: Jefferson Davis, MS (1853–1857)

Attorney General: Caleb Cushing, MA (1853–1857)

Postmaster General: James Campbell, PA (1853–1857)

Secretary of the Navy: James Cochran Dobbin, NC (1853–1857)

Secretary of the Interior: Robert McClelland, MI (1853–1857)

CONGRESS

33rd Congress (1853–1855); Speaker of the House: Linn Boyd (KY, Democrat)

34th Congress (1855–1857; Speaker of the House: Nathaniel Prentice Banks (MA, American Party)

SUPREME COURT APPOINTEES

John Archibald Campbell, AL; Associate Justice (1853–1861)

MAJOR EVENTS OF THE PIERCE ADMINISTRATION

◆ The Gadsden Purchase, negotiated by James Gadsden, the US minister to Mexico, is signed December 30, 1853; by its provisions, Mexico agrees to sell to the United States border territory, corresponding to what are now the southernmost portions of Arizona and New Mexico, for 15 million dollars.

◆ The Ostend Manifesto, written by Pierre Soule, the US minister to Spain, in 1854 urges the American acquisition of Cuba, by purchase or, if necessary, by force; this policy is favored by the proslavery faction, whose members fear the creation of an independent black-controlled republic in Cuba and hope that the island can form another slave territory of the United States. The US State Department later disavows any connection with this document.

◆ The opening of Japan to US trade takes place during Pierce's administration, with the successful expedition to Japan by Commodore Matthew Calbraith Perry and the Treaty of Kanagawa, March 31, 1854; the effort was begun under President Fillmore.

◆ Senator Stephen Douglas proposes, Congress passes, and Pierce signs the Kansas-Nebraska Act in May 1854; the act permits new states to decide whether to permit slavery by "popular sovereignty" (voting on the issue), and thus nullifies the Missouri Compromise of 1820.

◆ The Canadian Reciprocity Treaty is signed on June 5, 1854, providing an American market for Canadian timber and fish and commercial rights for the United States on the Great Lakes and in Canadian waters.

◆ The Kansas-Nebraska Act of 1854 is followed by two years of bitter strife in Kansas between proslavery and antislavery settlers; Kansas is dubbed "Bleeding Kansas."

◆ In 1854 the Republican Party is formed in Michigan out of the remnants of the antislavery members of the Whigs and members of the Free Soil and Know-Nothing parties. The new party is united in opposition to the Kansas-Nebraska Act and the prospect of the spread of slavery.

◆ In 1855 abolitionist John Brown and five of his sons join the "Free State" forces—an army formed in Kansas by antislavery settlers.

◆ In 1856 proslavery forces raid Lawrence, Kansas; in retaliation, John Brown and several others massacre five unarmed proslavery Kansas settlers.

◆ On May 22, 1856, US Representative Preston Brooks attacks abolitionist Senator Charles Sumner on the Senate floor with a cane and beats him so severely that Brooks is subsequently arrested and Sumner takes several years to recover from his injuries.

◆ On January 18, 1857, a "State of Disunion" convention is held in Worcester, MA, to discuss the peaceful separation of North and South. The convention is supported by antislavery newspaper editor William Lloyd Garrison and the Massachusetts Emigrant Aid Society.

MAJOR US AND WORLD EVENTS, 1853–1857

◆ The Crimean War (1853–1856) is fought: it eventually involves Russia, Turkey, France, and Britain.

◆ The US Postal Service issues the first stamped envelopes, 1853; the first postal directory, 1855; and the first perforated postage stamps, February 1857.

◆ Henry David Thoreau publishes *Walden; or, Life in the Woods*, 1854.

◆ Large-scale (13,000) Chinese immigration to the United States begins, 1854; the immigrants are mainly employed in building the transcontinental railroad.

◆ Alfred, Lord Tennyson, publishes "The Charge of the Light Brigade," 1854.

◆ British nurse Florence Nightingale goes to Turkey in 1854 to treat British soldiers wounded in the Crimean War.

◆ Johannes Brahms composes *Piano Concerto No. 1 in D Minor*, 1854.

◆ Walt Whitman anonymously publishes *Leaves of Grass*, 1855.

◆ Alexander II becomes Czar of Russia, 1855.

◆ Henry Wadsworth Longfellow publishes "The Song of Hiawatha," 1855.

◆ David Livingstone, a Scottish explorer, discovers Victoria Falls in Africa (between modern-day Zambia and Zimbabwe), 1855.

◆ The first kindergarten in America is established by Margarethe Meyer Schurz in Watertown, Wisconsin, 1856.

◆ Remains of a prehistoric man are found in the Neanderthal Valley in Germany, 1856.

◆ Big Ben, the bell in Parliament Tower in London, is installed, 1856.

FAST FACTS ABOUT FRANKLIN PIERCE

◆ Although Millard Fillmore was born in the year 1800, strictly speaking, Franklin Pierce was the first president born in the nineteenth century.

◆ Pierce is the only president ever to have come from New Hampshire.

◆ Pierce attended college with Nathaniel Hawthorne and Henry Wadsworth Longfellow; Hawthorne later wrote a brief campaign biography of Pierce, *The Life of Franklin Pierce*, in 1852.

◆ In the election of 1852, Pierce defeated his former commander in chief in the Mexican War, General Winfield Scott; he had accompanied Scott at the capture of Mexico City, September 1847.

◆ Pierce's victory over Scott marked the end of the Whig Party as a national presence; the party splintered into several factions, and the Republican Party was formed soon afterward.

◆ Both Jane Pierce and her son Benjamin wrote letters to Franklin Pierce during the presidential campaign, expressing their hope that he would lose.

◆ Pierce's eleven-year-old son, Benjamin—his only surviving child—died tragically in a train derailment after the election but before the inauguration, on January 6, 1853. Both parents were on the train and witnessed their son's death. Jane Pierce did not attend the inauguration and never fully recovered from her grief over this tragedy.

◆ Pierce's vice president, William R. D. King, a prominent US senator from Alabama, had contracted tuberculosis prior to the 1852 election, and had resigned from the Senate and moved to Havana, Cuba, on the advice of his doctor. By special act he was sworn in by the US consul on March 24, 1853, while still in Cuba—the only president or vice president ever to take the inaugural oath on foreign soil. King died shortly thereafter. He never presided over the Senate; Pierce served his term without a vice president.

◆ Pierce is the only president who took the oath of office using the word *affirm* (not *swear*), presumably because of a religious objection; the choice of the two words is offered by the Constitution.

◆ In the election of 1852, Pierce's Whig opponents said of him that he was "a hero of many a well-fought bottle," referring both to the Whig candidate's (Winfield Scott) military record and to Pierce's alcoholism.

◆ Pierce's inaugural address of more than 3,000 words was delivered from memory.

◆ Pierce maintained a strong proslavery position throughout his administration, despite the fact that his native New England was the home of the abolitionist movement.

◆ Pierce's cabinet remained the same for his entire term; his was the only president's cabinet ever to do so.

◆ Pierce is the only elected president whose party did not nominate him for reelection.

◆ Pierce's older brother Benjamin Kendrick Pierce (1790–1850) served in the US Army as a lieutenant colonel; Fort Pierce, FL, is named for him.

◆ It was more than forty years after Pierce's death before a statue of him was raised in New Hampshire.

James Buchanan

Nickname: Old Buck, Ten-Cent Jimmy
Presidency: 15th president, 1857–1861
Party: Democratic
Life dates: April 23, 1791–June 1, 1868 (77 years, 39 days)

EARLY LIFE AND EDUCATION

James Buchanan was born on April 23, 1791, in a log cabin adjacent to a trading post, called Stony Batter in Cove Gap, near Mercersburg, in south-central Pennsylvania. His father, also named James Buchanan, was an immigrant from Ireland who had bought the Stony Batter property in 1787 and married Elizabeth Speer, the daughter of a farmer, in 1788. Their first child, a daughter, was born in 1789 but died in 1791. James was followed by five more daughters, a son born in 1804 who died the same year, and three more sons after that. For most of his childhood, James was the only son, surrounded by sisters and doted on by his mother.

In 1794 the family moved to a farm closer to Mercersburg, and in 1796, to a house in the center of town, part of which became the elder Buchanan's store. James attended the Old Stone Academy in Mercersburg. The pastor of the Presbyterian Church in Mercersburg was Dr. John King, who was also a trustee of Dickinson College in Carlisle, Pennsylvania. Dr. King advised James's father to send James to Dickinson, and in 1807 at the age of sixteen, he entered as a junior.

At Dickinson James was a good student, but he also seems to have explored the college's social life, which generally included smoking (against the college's rules) and drinking. He is alleged to have thought quite well of himself at this time in his life—and this was not lost on those around him, who sometimes found him to be unbearably conceited. He did well academically and returned home for the summer at the end of his first year at Dickinson, only to have his father receive a letter from the college expelling him for disorderly conduct. Despite the college president's statement that they would not have him back under any circumstances, young James went to Dr. King and pledged to behave better; he was subsequently readmitted to the college.

After another year, James graduated and embarked on the study of law in Lancaster (the state capital at the time), in the law offices of James Hopkins. He was admitted to the bar in Lancaster in November 1812.

EARLY CAREER

Buchanan set up his law practice in Lancaster and almost immediately was drawn into the political scene. Like his father, he was a Federalist, a member of the group that favored adoption of the Constitution by the states, and in August 1814 he was nominated as the Federalist candidate from his district for the Pennsylvania State Assembly. When news came of the burning of Washington by British troops, Buchanan registered as a volunteer and joined a company then en route to Baltimore. After a short mission that involved the seizing of horses for use by a cavalry regiment, his group of volunteers was dismissed and he returned to Lancaster, where he was elected to the assembly.

Buchanan headed for Harrisburg, which had become the state capital in 1812. In his first speech, in February 1815, Buchanan held forth against military conscription and in favor of a bill promoting the use of a volunteer army. Other Federalists suggested that he join the Democratic Party, so opposite were his views on this subject from the party line. When it came time for reelection, Buchanan gave a rousing speech, attacking the Jeffersonian Republican-Democrats and affirming his Federalist affiliation. He spent another year in the state assembly and, as it was customary to serve no more than two consecutive terms, returned to his law practice in Lancaster. Gradually, by dint of hard work and careful planning, he became successful. He also joined the local Masonic Lodge. A tall, handsome man with a good career, he soon attracted interest as an eligible bachelor.

Buchanan began courting Ann Caroline Coleman, the daughter of a millionaire ironmaster, and they became engaged in 1819. Her parents were not entirely pleased with the match. Mr. Coleman was a trustee of Dickinson and knew of Buchanan's troubles there, but whether the reservations had to do with Buchanan's past behavior or came from the fear that he was more interested in their daughter's fortune than in their daughter, is unknown.

In the fall of 1819, Buchanan was extremely busy both with his law practice and with local Federalist political concerns, apparently to such an extent that he neglected Ann, who wrote to

him of her suspicions that he was more interested in her money than in her. Matters became worse when he went out of town briefly and, on returning, visited the wife of a friend (and her unmarried sister) before he called on his fiancée. When Ann Coleman learned of this sequence of events, she wrote to Buchanan, breaking off their engagement. After a few days, Ann's mother convinced her to go to Philadelphia to visit her sister and to try to improve her depressed spirits. Ann went to Philadelphia, and is alleged to have there fallen into hysterical convulsions. She died, somewhat mysteriously, on December 9, 1819. Though suicide was suspected, it is unknown what caused her death.

> "There is nothing stable but Heaven and the Constitution."
>
> James Buchanan, May 13, 1856

Buchanan wrote a letter to her family asking for permission to view her body and to take part in the funeral procession, but his letter was refused by her family, who apparently held him responsible. Grief-stricken and the talk of the town, Buchanan retreated to his family's home in Mercersburg for the Christmas holidays. After the holidays he returned to his law practice, which continued to grow. And in August 1820 he was selected as the Federalist candidate for election to the US House of Representatives.

POLITICAL CAREER

Buchanan served in the House of Representatives from 1821 to 1831, during which period he changed his political party—going from the Federalist Party, which was dying out, to the faction of the emerging Democratic Party that supported Andrew Jackson. He found himself gravitating toward the members of Congress who represented southern states. Buchanan was a gifted orator who marshaled his political arguments as he had his legal ones, carefully building a case point by point until his conclusions seemed inevitable to his audience.

Andrew Jackson lost the presidential election in 1824. The election was decided in the House because none of the candidates had a majority of electoral votes. Jackson believed that Buchanan had been part of the "corrupt bargain" that was assumed to have existed between the new president, John Quincy Adams, and Henry Clay, his secretary of state. Before the election, Buchanan had asked Jackson whether he would appoint Adams as secretary of state; Jackson had replied negatively and Buchanan shared that information with others. Despite the feeling on Jackson's part that Buchanan had been underhanded in some way, Buchanan continued to support Jackson, working diligently in Pennsylvania to build the Democratic Party and to ensure support for Jackson's bid for the presidency in the 1828 presidential race, which Jackson did win.

In 1830 Buchanan announced his intention not to run again for his seat in the House. Speculation was rife about the possibility of an appointment for Buchanan, to be made by President Jackson—including the possibility that Jackson would ask Buchanan to run as the vice-presidential candidate for his second term. That honor eventually went to Martin Van Buren, but Jackson rewarded Buchanan's support by appointing him minister to Russia. It did not feel entirely like a reward to Buchanan, as it was a lesser position than he had hoped for, and Russia was far from the center of power.

In Russia he was able to conclude a commercial treaty that had been stalled for some time; it became the first trade agreement between Russia and the United States. He returned to the United States ahead of schedule, arriving just in time to run for and be elected to the US Senate. At around this time, as there would be at several intervals throughout his adult life, there were rumors of romantic attachments, but Buchanan remained a bachelor.

Buchanan served in the Senate from 1835 until 1845, becoming chairman of the Foreign Relations Committee. Buchanan generally tried to occupy the middle ground in instances of a contest or a perceived contest between the power of the federal government and states' rights. He disliked slavery personally but was convinced that the Constitution protected it—a view that placed him on the side of southern senators more often than not, although it was his tendency to seek out compromises to arguments between opposing factions.

> **"It [Russia] was as far as I could send him out of my sight and where he could do the least harm. I would have sent him to the North Pole if we had kept a minister there."**
>
> Andrew Jackson, about Buchanan, after hearing that President Polk had appointed Buchanan as his secretary of state, 1845

Buchanan, like most congressmen in Washington, was at times in need of temporary lodging. He shared living quarters with Alabama Senator William Rufus Devane King (who was later elected vice president under Pierce, but died before serving in that capacity). There was gossip in Washington on the subject of the close friendship between the two men, and King was given such nicknames as "Miss Nancy" and "Aunt Fancy." Speculation that the relationship may have included an amorous and sexual component existed, but without any evidence to confirm such speculation.

In 1845 Buchanan was named secretary of state by President James K. Polk. He did not always agree with Polk. Buchanan worked for a compromise settlement of the Oregon border that put it at the forty-ninth parallel, despite

Polk's campaign slogan of "fifty-four-forty or fight"—which had promised that his administration would gain more territory in this border dispute than it actually gained. Buchanan changed his mind during the course of the Mexican-American War (1846–1848) with respect to how much territory the United States should demand from Mexico after the war. He was clear, however, in his support for the annexation of Cuba, a project dear to the hearts of southerners who hoped for the United States' acquisition of Cuba as a slave-holding state.

In 1848, before the end of his term as secretary of state, he bought a home in Lancaster, Pennsylvania, which he called Wheatland. He retired there in 1849, where he unsuccessfully sought the presidential nomination for the election of 1852. Franklin Pierce was elected president; he named Buchanan as minister to Britain. Buchanan served in that post from 1853 to 1856.

During his tenure in Great Britain, Buchanan teamed up with the US minister to Spain, Pierre Soulé, and the US minister to France, John Mason, in drafting the Ostend Manifesto, which warned that the United States would take Cuba by force if Spain refused to sell it. The ensuing uproar in much of Europe and among northern abolitionists in the United States prompted Secretary of State William L. Marcy to repudiate the manifesto.

Buchanan returned to the United States in 1856 and was selected as the Democratic candidate for the presidency, receiving all of the 296 votes cast on the seventeenth ballot. His three years out of the country had been useful—his name was not strongly associated with either side in the bitter disputes over slavery in the territories (particularly Kansas) that had been dividing the Congress. Buchanan won the election with ease and in November 1856, he entered the office as one of the most well-prepared politicians ever to reach the presidency.

PRESIDENCY

The unmarried president gave his niece, his late sister's daughter Harriet Lane, the role of White House hostess during his term. She was pretty, young, popular, and well-versed in politics—be-

cause of her uncle's influence and because she had accompanied him on one occasion to Great Britain. She brought a gaiety to the White House that the public found very welcome, as no first lady since Julia Tyler had cared much for social life. Harriet was adept at making seating arrangements at dinner tables such that political opposites did not sit next to each other, and as a means of keeping peace, she refused to discuss slavery or allow it to be discussed at her parties.

Buchanan took office expressing the hope that he could suppress northern agitation against slavery, as well as that of the growing Republican Party. He was unequal to the task (though most would argue that the events during his presidency would have overtaken anyone in his position), as the slavery issue continued to widen the gulf between North and South.

> "My dear sir, if you are as happy on entering the White House as I am on leaving, you are a very happy man indeed."
>
> James Buchanan to Abraham Lincoln at Lincoln's inauguration, March 4, 1861

Just two days after Buchanan's inauguration, the Dred Scott decision was handed down, on March 6, 1857. Scott was a slave who had been taken by his owner into free territory. Availing himself of a legal precedent whereby a slave living in free territory and with his master's knowledge was free (whether he remained in free territory or returned to a slave state), Scott sued for his freedom. Scott initially won, but the case was appealed and eventually went before the US Supreme Court, which ruled that blacks were not citizens and therefore had no right to sue, and that, additionally, slavery could not be prohibited in the territories.

Later in 1857, the Kansas situation worsened. Kansas, as a free state, had elected its own legislature, with Robert J. Walker as governor, in

October 1857. The Lecompton Constitution, which was drafted in Lecompton, Kansas by proslavery advocates, and permitted slavery in Kansas, was put to a referendum in December 1857. Even though Buchanan supported the Lecompton Constitution, it was defeated by overwhelming numbers of voters in January 1858. In March, however, the US Senate voted to accept Kansas into the Union under the Lecompton Constitution, and the House of Representatives voted to submit the constitution to Kansas voters once again. In August 1858 the voters of Kansas again rejected the constitution, and Kansas entered the Union as a free state in 1861. As all of this was transpiring, violent clashes occurred between proslavery and antislavery settlers, giving Kansas the nickname "Bleeding Kansas."

Buchanan's support of the Lecompton Constitution led to a break with Illinois Senator Stephen Douglas, who considered the constitution an affront to the principle of popular sovereignty, which he espoused. This break would cost Buchanan politically, as Douglas wielded enormous power within the Democratic Party.

In addition to the turmoil related to slavery, Buchanan's presidency was pummeled by the panic of 1857, an economic recession. To make matters worse (from Buchanan's viewpoint), in 1858, the new Republican Party took control of the House of Representatives. In the Senate race in Illinois, Stephen Douglas and Abraham Lincoln had held a series of debates, with Lincoln arguing against slavery and against the Dred Scott decision. Douglas won the Senate seat, but Lincoln won a national reputation.

Lincoln won the Republican Party's nomination for the presidency in 1860, while the Democrats split into two factions. The popular-sovereignty Democrats nominated Stephen Douglas, whereas the southern Democrats nominated John C. Breckinridge. Another party, the Constitutional Union Party that had grown out of the defunct Whig and American Parties, nominated John Bell.

Lincoln was elected president in November 1860. In December, Senator John Crittenden of Kentucky proposed extending the Missouri Compromise line across the country, allowing slavery everywhere below the line. President-elect Lincoln rejected the Crittenden Compromise, saying that he would not compromise on the slavery issue.

Buchanan's presidency ended on a disturbing note, as South Carolina voted to secede in January 1861—followed by Mississippi, Florida, Alabama, Georgia, and Louisiana.

> **"I have had a hard time of it during my administration, but, upon a careful review of all my conduct, I should not change it in a single important measure if this were now in my power."**
>
> James Buchanan, in a letter to the Philadelphia *Times*, September 21, 1861

The new nation of the Confederate States of America was formed in February, with Jefferson Davis elected as president of the Confederacy on February 9, 1861. Texas seceded in late February; the remaining states that would form the Confederacy (Virginia, Arkansas, North Carolina, and Tennessee) seceded after Lincoln assumed the presidency. Buchanan's view was that the states had no right to secede under the Constitution, but that the Constitution also did not provide any means for the federal government to prevent secession—a legalistic argument that won him no friends on either side.

POST-PRESIDENTIAL CAREER

Buchanan, with his niece Harriet Lane, retired to Wheatland, his estate in Lancaster. He supported the Union during the war, but was vilified as a proslavery advocate who was responsible for its occurrence. Like many of his predecessors, Buchanan had privately expressed his dislike of slavery but did nothing to halt it in his official capacity, maintaining that he was basing his actions on an adherence to the Constitution, and believing that it would not be possible to end slavery without destroying the Union.

Buchanan died on June 1, 1868, at the age of seventy-seven. Harriet Lane had, at her uncle's urging, married two years earlier in 1866. She was passionate about the arts and collected Native American artwork, an interest that led her to try to better the conditions under which Native Americans lived. For her efforts she was dubbed the "great mother of the Indians" by the Chippewa.

Birthplace: Stony Batter, Cove Gap (near Mercersburg), PA
Residency: Pennsylvania
Religion: Presbyterian
Education: Dickinson College, Carlisle, PA; graduated 1809
Place of Death: Wheatland, near Lancaster, PA
Burial Site: Woodward Hill Cemetery, Lancaster, PA
Dates in Office: March 4, 1857–March 3, 1861 (4 years)
Age at Inauguration: 65 years, 315 days

FAMILY

Father: James Buchanan (1761–1821)
Mother: Elizabeth Speer Buchanan (1767–1833)
Siblings: James was the second of eleven children; his siblings were Mary Buchanan (1789–1791); Jane Buchanan (1793–1839); Maria Buchanan (1795–1849); Sarah Buchanan (1798–1825); Elizabeth Buchanan (1800–1801); Harriet Buchanan (1802–1840); John Buchanan (1804); William Speer Buchanan (1805–1826); George Washington Buchanan (1808–1832); Edward Young Buchanan (1811–1895).
Wife: none, Buchanan was unmarried
Children: none

CAREER

Private: lawyer
Political: Member of the PA House of Representatives (1815–1816); member of the US House of Representatives (1821–1831); US minister to Russia (1832–1834); member of the US Senate (1835–1845); secretary of state under Polk (1845–1849); minister to England (1853–1856); president of the United States (1857–1861)
Military: joined as a volunteer during the War of 1812, but saw no action
Selected Works: *James Buchanan, 1791–1868, Chronology, Documents, Bibliographical Aids*, ed. by Irving J. Sloan (Dobbs Ferry, NY: Oceana Publications, 1968); *James Buchanan's Mission to Russia: 1831–1833; His Speeches, State Papers, and Private Correspondence* (New York: Arno Press, 1970); *Mr. Buchanan's Administration on the Eve of the Rebellion* (Freeport, NY: Books for Libraries Press, 1970)

PRESIDENCY

Nomination: Buchanan was nominated at the Democratic convention held the summer of 1856 in Cincinnati; he gained more votes than any of the other candidates in the first ballot and achieved the necessary two-thirds vote in the seventeenth ballot.
Election: 1856: elected president on November 4, 1856
Opponent: 1856: John C. Fremont, CA, Republican; Millard Fillmore, NY, American (Know-Nothing)
Vote Totals: 1856: Buchanan, 1,832,955 popular, 174 electoral; Fremont, 1,339,932 popular, 114 electoral; Fillmore, 871,731 popular, 8 electoral
Inauguration: March 4, 1857
Vice President: John C. Breckinridge, KY (1857–1861)

CABINET

Secretary of State: Lewis Cass, MI (1857–1860); Jeremiah S. Black, PA (1860–1861)
Secretary of the Treasury: Howell Cobb, GA (1857–1860); Philip F. Thomas, MD (1860–1861); John A. Dix, NY (1861)
Secretary of War: John B. Floyd, VA (1857–1860); Joseph Holt, KY (1861)
Attorney General: Jeremiah S. Black, PA (1857–1860); Edwin M. Stanton, PA (1860–1861)
Postmaster General: Aaron V. Brown, TN (1857–1859); Joseph Holt, KY (1859–1861); Horatio King, ME (1861)
Secretary of the Navy: Isaac Toucey, CT (1857–1861)

Secretary of the Interior: Jacob Thompson, MS (1857–1861)

CONGRESS
35th Congress (1857–1859); Speaker of the House: James L. Orr (SC, Republican)
36th Congress (1859–1861); Speaker of the House: William Pennington (NJ: Republican)

SUPREME COURT APPOINTEES
Nathan Clifford, ME; Associate Justice (1858–1881)

MAJOR EVENTS OF THE BUCHANAN ADMINISTRATION
◆ In the Dred Scott decision, handed down from the Supreme Court on March 6, 1857, the Court decides that Dred Scott, a slave who had lived in the free state of Illinois and the free territory of Wisconsin, could not sue for his freedom. The decision holds that blacks were not citizens (and therefore had no legal standing to sue) and that slavery could not be prohibited in the territories.
◆ In September 1857 the Lecompton Constitutional Convention in Kansas frames a constitution that will allow slavery when Kansas becomes a state; voters in Kansas reject this constitution. The US Senate agrees to accept Kansas into the Union under the Lecompton Constitution, while the US House of Representatives proposes putting the constitution to a vote in Kansas. Buchanan supports the Lecompton Constitution, which is resoundingly rejected by the Kansas voters.
◆ Buchanan decides to remove Brigham Young as governor of the Utah Territory; in retaliation, Mormon fanatic John D. Lee and Piute Native Americans massacre nearly 140 westbound settlers in Mountain Meadow, Utah, in September 1857.
◆ Minnesota becomes a state, May 11, 1858.
◆ Oregon becomes a state, February 14, 1859.
◆ At the Southern Commercial Convention in Vicksburg, Mississippi, in March 1859, southern slave owners propose the reopening of the African slave trade, which had been banned by Congress since 1808.

◆ The Kansas Constitutional Convention in 1859 decides that Kansas will enter the Union as a free state.
◆ On October 16, 1859, John Brown and twenty followers raid Harper's Ferry, Virginia, in an effort to establish an abolitionist republic. Brown is captured and hanged in December; considered a traitor in the South, he is viewed by some in the North as a martyr.
◆ Edward Albert, Prince of Wales, visits the White House in 1860.
◆ In April 1860 the Democratic Party holds its convention in Charleston, South Carolina, but fails to nominate a candidate; the party splits between Southern Democrats who wish to enforce slavery in the territories and Northern Democrats who favor popular sovereignty in the territories.
◆ In May 1860 the Constitutional Union Party, formed from the remnants of the Whig and American Parties, nominates John Bell for the presidency.
◆ The Republican Party meets in Chicago in May 1860 and nominates Abraham Lincoln for the presidency.
◆ Part of the Democratic Party meets again in Baltimore in mid-June 1860 and nominates Stephen Douglas as its presidential candidate; the Southern Democrats meet in Charleston in late June and nominate John C. Breckinridge for the presidency.
◆ Lincoln is elected in November 1860; in December, Senator John Crittenden of Kentucky proposes extending the Missouri Compromise line across the country, allowing slavery everywhere below the line, but Lincoln reiterates that he will not compromise on the slavery issue.
◆ South Carolina votes to secede in January 1861, and is followed by Mississippi, Florida, Alabama, Georgia, and Louisiana.
◆ Kansas becomes a state, January 29, 1861.
◆ The Confederate States of America is formed in February 1861.
◆ On February 9, 1861, Jefferson Davis is elected president of the Confederacy.
◆ Texas secedes in late February; Virginia, Arkansas, North Carolina, and Tennessee

secede after the fall of Fort Sumter in April 1861.

MAJOR US AND WORLD EVENTS, 1857–1861

❖ The Sepoy Rebellion begins in India when Sepoy soldiers rebel against British soldiers, 1857.

❖ In November 1857 the first issue of *Atlantic Monthly* magazine appears; the editor is James Russell Lowell.

❖ Gustave Flaubert publishes *Madame Bovary*, 1857.

❖ Charles Baudelaire publishes *Les Fleurs du mal*, 1857, and is fined for offending public morality.

❖ The first Mardi Gras parade of floats in New Orleans occurs in 1857.

❖ Rowland H. Macy opens R.H. Macy & Co., a dry goods store, in New York City, 1858.

❖ Charles Dickens publishes *A Tale of Two Cities*, 1859.

❖ George Eliot (Mary Ann Evans) publishes *Adam Bede*, 1859.

❖ Alfred, Lord Tennyson, publishes the first four books of his Arthurian epic, *The Idylls of the King*, 1859; the remainder of the twelve books are published over a forty-year period.

❖ The Comstock Lode, a major silver strike, is discovered in Nevada, 1859.

❖ Charles Darwin publishes *On the Origin of Species by Means of Natural Selection*, 1859.

❖ Edwin Drake drills the first oil well in Pennsylvania, 1859.

❖ On April 25, 1859, work begins on the Suez Canal under Ferdinand de Lesseps.

❖ Giuseppe Garibaldi leads the "Redshirts" against the Bourbon forces in Sicily and Naples, 1860—the first step in the reunification of Italy.

❖ Wilkie Collins publishes *The Woman in White*, 1860.

❖ George Eliot (Mary Ann Evans) publishes *The Mill on the Floss*, 1860.

❖ The Pony Express is established, 1860, but becomes obsolete a year later when the transcontinental telegraph is completed.

❖ Alexander II, czar of Russia, abolishes serfdom, 1861.

FAST FACTS ABOUT JAMES BUCHANAN

❖ Buchanan was expelled from college for disorderly conduct after his first year, but was allowed back after pledging to do better.

❖ Buchanan was engaged as a young man, but his fiancée, Ann Caroline Coleman, broke off their engagement and then died, possibly by suicide.

❖ Years after Ann Coleman's death, while Buchanan was the US minister to Russia, friends handling his business affairs purchased her father's house for him; he moved into it on his return from Russia.

❖ Buchanan was the only bachelor president; his niece, Harriet Lane, acted as White House hostess.

❖ Buchanan reportedly had one nearsighted eye and one farsighted eye, for which he tried to compensate by changing the position of his head.

❖ Buchanan was close friends with William Rufus Devane King, who was called "Miss Nancy" and "Aunt Fancy" by others in Washington (and who is believed by some historians to have been homosexual). The two men lived together for a number of years; although speculation exists about Buchanan's sexuality, no evidence of a sexual relationship exists.

❖ Buchanan's niece, Harriet Lane, was close to her uncle, for whom she acted as White House hostess. However, she did object to his opening her mail, so she and a friend smuggled their letters to each other in and out of the White House in a butter crock or kettle.

❖ Buchanan received the nickname "Ten-Cent Jimmy" when he said that he thought ten cents a day was an adequate wage for manual laborers.

❖ Buchanan became well off financially from his law practice but was always careful about money, once refusing a check for more than $15,000 because there was an error of ten cents in the amount.

Abraham Lincoln

Nickname: Honest Abe, The Great Emancipator, Spotty Lincoln, The Rail Splitter
Presidency: 16th president, 1861–1865
Party: Whig, Republican
Life dates: February 12, 1809–April 15, 1865 (56 years, 62 days)

EARLY LIFE AND EDUCATION

Just a few months before Abraham Lincoln was born, on February 12, 1809, his parents, Thomas and Nancy Hanks Lincoln, along with their young daughter, Sarah, settled on a site known as Sinking Spring Farm near Hodgenville in Hardin County, Kentucky, and moved into a one-room log cabin. Thomas Lincoln was a farmer and carpenter from Virginia who had settled in Kentucky in 1782; both Thomas and Nancy were uneducated and nearly illiterate (Thomas could just sign his name). When Abraham was two years old, the family moved a few miles away to Knob Creek. In 1811 another son, also named Thomas, was born, but lived only two years.

Abraham spent his youth helping out on the farm; he and his sister Sarah attended school for a few weeks only. At the end of 1816, the family moved to Indiana, where it was possible for one to buy land directly from the government and thus gain a clear title—something Thomas Lincoln had found elusive in the tangled confusion of Kentucky land titles. Abraham continued helping with farm work but was able to attend school in Indiana for just a few months more, which would complete all of the formal schooling he would ever have.

In the fall of 1818, Nancy Hanks Lincoln, her aunt Elizabeth Sparrow, and her aunt's husband Thomas Sparrow all died of "milk sickness," an illness caused by drinking the milk of cows that had grazed on a poisonous plant. The Lincolns lived in very little comfort during the year that followed, after which Thomas Lincoln made a visit to Kentucky and courted a widow, Sarah Bush Johnston, whom he had known previously. Sarah explained that she had debts left from her improvident husband, and Thomas agreed to pay them to ensure their marriage. In future years Lincoln would refer to Nancy Hanks Lincoln as his "Angel Mother," an indication of his love for her and as a way to distinguish her from his stepmother, whom he also loved dearly and called "Mother" or "Mama."

Sarah and her three children joined Thomas and his two children on his farm in Pigeon Creek, Indiana. A cousin, Dennis Hanks, also lived with the family. Sarah's arrival meant an improvement in the family's standard of living, as she brought with her some furniture and comforts, as well as a conviction that the Lincoln children needed to be better dressed. She also supported Abraham's insatiable desire to read—an attitude not shared by Thomas Lincoln, who frequently castigated Abraham for what he saw as lazy behavior. Abraham seems to have resented his father; years later, he would refuse to visit his dying father or attend his funeral.

> "Probably no man since the days of Washington was ever so deeply and firmly embedded and enshrined in the hearts of the people as Abraham Lincoln. Nor was it a mistaken confidence and love. . . . He merited it by his character, by his acts, and by the tenor and tone and spirit of his life."
>
> The Reverend Dr. Phineas D. Gurley, speaking at the funeral of Abraham Lincoln, April 19, 1865

Another cause for resentment on Abraham's part was the legal requirement that, until he came of age, his earnings had to be turned over to his father. Abraham hired out as a rail-splitter, worked as a ferryman, and twice made trips on a flatboat to New Orleans with farm produce. These trips were notable for at least two reasons: one is that Abraham was exposed to the sight of slaves and slave-trading, and the other was his experience on the river. After he entered politics, one of his first concerns was to improve canals necessary for river traffic; he also patented a device designed to lift flatboats over shoals.

EARLY CAREER

In 1830 the family moved to Illinois and settled on the Sangamon River. Abraham helped his father clear the land and hired himself out to split rails for the neighbors. After a harsh winter, the family moved to Coles County, Illinois, but Abraham decided to make his own way in the world. After his second trip to New Orleans, he went

to work as a clerk in a store owned by Denton Offutt in New Salem, Illinois. New Salem was enjoying a brief period of prosperity as a trading town. Abraham's duties at the store were not particularly onerous, and he spent a good deal of time reading, continuing his relentless pursuit of self-education.

Lincoln also became well-known locally for his height (he was six feet, four inches tall), his strength, and his ability to spin humorous tales. He was quickly becoming the center of any gathering. He won a wrestling match against Jack Armstrong, the leader of a local group of rowdies known as the Clary Grove boys. From then on, he was a great favorite of theirs, and they often attended his speeches after he entered politics. This happened soon after he settled in New Salem, at around which time he declared his intention of running for the state legislature.

Immediately after the announcement of his candidacy, in April 1832 the Black Hawk War broke out between the United States and the Native American Sac and Fox tribes over the issue of land settlement. Lincoln volunteered for military service and was elected the captain of his first company. He served three stints total, each time for a different company. He saw no action, but owing to his participation in the war, he was not able to campaign. Little known outside his own town, he lost.

Lincoln continued studying on his own, concentrating on learning the law. He was appointed as the postmaster of New Salem, did some work as a surveyor, and was a partner in a general store for a time. He also met Ann Rutledge, the daughter of a leading citizen and tavern owner, to whom he formed an attachment. The two may have been engaged, but in 1835 she became ill (most likely with typhoid) and died. In the aftermath of her death, Lincoln suffered an episode of the depression to which he was prone. Some historians have disputed whether this romance ever occurred (and conclusions that it did not may have been influenced by the later denials of Mary Todd Lincoln and Robert Lincoln), but evidence seems to substantiate the claim that such a romance did occur, and that Lincoln suffered a real depression over the loss of Ann Rutledge.

However, only a year and a half later Lincoln proposed to Mary Owens, a woman from Kentucky who visited New Salem. After she returned to Kentucky, he realized that he was not ready for marriage—or that he did not wish to marry her—and wrote to her to inform her of this development, pressing her to forget about his proposal and to never write to him again—adding that "it is my sincere wish that you should." After she released him from the engagement, he again became depressed.

Meanwhile, his political career was developing far more robustly than his love life; in 1834, he had run for the state legislature a second time and been elected as a Whig. He was soon in the thick of debates on the subject of proposals to move the state capital to Springfield—a move that he enthusiastically supported. In 1836 he was admitted to the bar, and in 1837, he moved to Springfield. He found lodging with a storekeeper, Joshua Speed, who lived above his store; the two became fast friends as well.

Lincoln was reelected in 1836, 1838, and 1840. He pushed for internal developments in Illinois, including improvements of roadways and canals, although funds for these improvements usually failed to materialize. Lincoln also became his party's floor leader.

LAW CAREER AND MARRIAGE

After Lincoln moved to Springfield he embarked upon his law career, eventually going into partnership with three different men. First he joined his friend John Todd Stuart in a law practice, the partnership lasting from 1837 to 1841, before forming a partnership with Stephen T. Logan, where he remained until 1844. Finally, Lincoln took on a young partner, William Herndon. Much of his work pertained to the Eighth Circuit Court, which covered over 15,000 square miles in rural central Illinois; Lincoln often accompanied the circuit judge in his rounds throughout the counties that comprised the Eighth Circuit.

In Springfield, Lincoln met Ninian Edwards, the son of a former governor of Illinois, and his wife, Elizabeth Todd Edwards. Elizabeth's sister Mary was visiting from Lexington, Kentucky, and eventually moved to Illinois. Mary was pretty, popular, well-educated, and the daughter of a banker and slave owner. She and Lincoln became engaged at the end of 1840, but Lincoln almost immediately had second thoughts on the matter and broke off the engagement, telling her that he did not love her. Another depression followed, with Lincoln taking to his bed for a week.

After avoiding one another for several months, Lincoln and Mary Todd were brought together by a friend, and they cemented their reattachment by writing letters jointly to the *Sangamo Journal* under the pseudonym "Rebecca"—letters that criticized the Illinois state auditor, James Shields. When Shields demanded the name of the author of the letters, Lincoln took the blame for them, protecting Mary Todd. Shields challenged Lincoln to a duel; Lincoln chose broadswords but the two men were convinced at the last minute to shake hands and forget their differences. Lincoln was ashamed of the incident, embarrassed that he had strayed so far from the "cold, calculating reason" he admired.

Lincoln and Mary Todd were married November 4, 1842, at the home of Mary's sister, Elizabeth Edwards. The marriage was a good one, although husband and wife were very different in temperament and background. Mary was high-strung, formal, aristocratic, and social; she had been well-educated and brought up in very comfortable circumstances. Lincoln was of the working class, less formal, and given to bouts of depression; he was also frequently absent from home, leaving his wife to keep house and raise children with (at least at first) fewer resources and comforts than she had been used to.

At the beginning of their married life, the couple boarded at the Globe Tavern in Springfield. Here their first son, Robert Todd Lincoln, was born on August 1, 1843; the family soon afterward moved into a three-room cottage that they rented, and in 1844 they purchased a home. On March 10, 1846, Edward Baker Lincoln, called Eddie, was born.

NATIONAL POLITICAL CAREER

In 1846 Lincoln was elected to the US House of Representatives, and in 1847 the family went to Washington, DC. Mary and the boys stayed only until the end of the first session of Congress, returning to Springfield before the second session began. The new congressman's opposition to the Mexican War earned him the nickname "Spotty Lincoln"—the name deriving from insistence in Congress that President Polk identify the spot where American blood had been spilled at the start of the war. The war was triggered by the pretext of the US government that American blood had been shed on American soil. However, the war's critics, including Lincoln, charged that the bloodshed had occurred on what was in fact Mexican territory. Lincoln also supported the Wilmot Proviso, which attempted to prohibit slavery in the territories acquired as a result of the war.

Having agreed with other members of his party not to run for a second term, Lincoln returned home in May 1849 and went back to his law practice. He built a successful practice, representing, among other clients, the railroads that were growing rapidly in economic importance.

"I do therefore invite my fellow citizens in every part of the United States, and also those who are at sea and those who are sojourning in foreign lands, to set apart and observe the last Thursday of November next, as a day of Thanksgiving and Praise to our beneficent Father who dwelleth in the Heavens."

Abraham Lincoln, his Proclamation of Thanksgiving, October 3, 1863

Lincoln's son Eddie died on February 1, 1850, possibly from tuberculosis. Mary and Abraham's third son, William Wallace Lincoln, called Willie, was born on December 21 of that same year, and their fourth son, Thomas Lincoln, called Tad, was born April 4, 1853.

Lincoln focused more on his law career than on politics for a few years, but he was roused to action by his passionate opposition to the Kansas-Nebraska Act of 1854, which repealed part of the Missouri Compromise of 1820 (as it called for the people of those two territories to decide the question of slavery). The act, sponsored by Illinois Senator Stephen A. Douglas, had a galvanizing effect on antislavery forces in the north. Out of the forces of opposition to the Kansas-Nebraska Act came the nucleus of a new political party, the Republican Party.

Elected to the Illinois state legislature again in 1854, Lincoln immediately resigned in order to run for the US Senate. He nearly garnered the Whig nomination, but failed to win a majority vote in the state legislature, whose members were responsible for electing the US senators for the state at that time. Lincoln gave his support to Lyman Trumbull, a Democrat who opposed the Kansas-Nebraska Act, and Trumbull was elected. By the time of the presidential election, however, Lincoln had abandoned the dissolving Whig Party and had thrown his support to the new Republican Party in Illinois. He supported the Republican candidate, John C. Frémont, who made a strong showing but lost to the Democratic candidate, James Buchanan.

For the 1858 US Senate elections, the Democratic senator from Illinois, Stephen A. Douglas, found himself vying with Abraham Lincoln, as the Republican Party's candidate. Lincoln kicked off his campaign with what became known as the "House Divided" speech, in which he echoed the Bible: "'A house divided against itself cannot stand.' I believe this government cannot endure, permanently *half slave* and *half free*." Lincoln challenged Douglas to a series of seven debates. Douglas defended the principle of popular sovereignty as the final authority in questions of slavery, but Lincoln took the position that slavery was morally wrong and that it should be limited to the states in which it already existed, where it would die a natural death. Because of intense national interest in the subject of slavery and the unprecedented amount of newspaper coverage of the debates, Lincoln gained a national reputation.

The vote was very close, but the composition of the state legislature, a disproportionately large number of whose seats belonged to less populous, heavily Democratic southern Illinois (making more populous, heavily Republican northern Illinois underrepresented), meant a win for Douglas. Lincoln was bitterly disappointed, but soon threw his energies and speaking abilities into supporting Republican candidates throughout the Northern states. Not only did this increase his visibility, it also meant that many powerful Republicans would feel that they had incurred a debt of gratitude to him.

In February 1860 Lincoln spoke in New York City at the Cooper Union before a full house. In his speech he attempted to repudiate the arguments of Stephen Douglas on the subject of popular sovereignty and slavery, as well as the claim of many Southerners that if a Republican were elected, the Union would be dissolved and it would be the fault of the North. He argued for the federal exclusion of slavery in the territories and the containment of slavery in the states in which it existed. His speech was immediately acclaimed by listeners and printed in newspapers.

At the Republican convention in Chicago in May 1860, the leading contender for the presidential nomination was thought to be Senator William Seward of New York, but Lincoln's supporters argued that Seward could not carry Pennsylvania or Indiana, two states that were considered necessary for a Republican victory. Although Seward led on the first ballot, on the third ballot, Lincoln won the nomination.

The Democratic Party could not agree on a candidate and splintered. One faction nominated Stephen A. Douglas and another, the Southern Democrats, nominated John C. Breckinridge. Additionally, the Constitutional Union Party, composed mostly of former Whigs who had found the Republican Party to be too radical, nominated John Bell.

Lincoln won the election with less than 40 percent of the popular vote, but with a majority of electoral votes. Although the total number of popular votes received by all three of his opponents put together exceeded the number of popular votes received by Lincoln, the total number of electoral votes received by all three opponents put together (123) still did not exceed Lincoln's 180 electoral votes.

Taking leave of Springfield, Lincoln traveled to Washington by train, frequently stepping out of the train at stops to greet enthusiastic and curious crowds.

PRESIDENCY

Near the end of President Buchanan's term of office, seven Southern states seceded from the Union: South Carolina, Alabama, Georgia, Mississippi, Florida, Louisiana, and Texas. In February 1861 these states formed the Confederate States of America and chose Jefferson Davis as president. After Lincoln's inauguration in March 1861, he was advised by many to accept the secession and to attempt conciliation with the remaining slave states. However, Lincoln consistently maintained that the Union must be preserved and that the federal government rightfully controlled federal military posts, even those in areas controlled by the new Confederacy. They included Fort Sumter in Charleston, South Carolina—which, Lincoln was advised, was in need of supplies. Lincoln accordingly ordered that supplies be sent to Fort Sumter. On April 12, 1861, Southern forces fired on the fort.

"A house divided against itself cannot stand."

Abraham Lincoln, a speech in Springfield, Illinois, June 16, 1858

On April 15, 1861, Lincoln called for volunteers to enlist in the Union army—an action that spurred the secession of Virginia, Arkansas, North Carolina, and Tennessee. After Virginia had seceded, the Confederate capital was transferred from Montgomery, Alabama, to Richmond, Virginia. In addition, the western part of Virginia broke away and the new state of West Virginia was formed, which was admitted to the Union on June 20, 1863. The border states of Maryland, Missouri, Kentucky, and Delaware stayed in the Union, despite opposition to this within those states.

In April 1861 Robert E. Lee refused an invitation to command the Union army, believing that his allegiance to his home state of Virginia came first. He was then named as the commander of the Virginia forces for the Confederacy.

Lincoln suspended the writ of habeas corpus on April 27, 1861, which meant that individuals could be arrested and held indefinitely without charges being filed or trials ever being held. Lincoln justified the suspension as a necessary expedient of war, and the subsequent uproar over the suspension had less to do with its constitutionality (the Constitution does provide for such actions in wartime) than with whether the executive branch had the power to act as it had (many argued that only Congress had this power).

At the start of the war, the North was significantly more powerful and more strategically advantaged than the South. It had about three times the population, to begin with. The North also had better manufacturing capabilities and better food supplies, as well as two-thirds of the nation's railroads—which enabled both troops and goods to move more efficiently. The South, on the other hand, initially had better military leadership and needed only to defend the newly formed Confederacy (in contrast to the need to fight an offensive war).

However, the question of military leadership was a very troubling one for Lincoln and the North. General Irvin McDowell was in command of the Army of the Potomac, the principal Northern army, which was defeated in the war's first battle, the First Battle of Bull Run (Manassas). Lincoln subsequently appointed General George B. McClellan as commander of the Army of the Potomac. McClellan had genuine talent with regard to the organizing and training of troops, but was woefully inadequate when it

came to the offensive progression of the war. He refused to divulge his strategies to Lincoln, and consistently overestimated the strength of the Confederate forces arrayed against him.

In the midst of wartime gloom, a dearth of news of military successes, and criticism coming from many sides owing to the slowdown of mobilizing troops, Lincoln received another major blow. His son Willie died, on February 22, 1862, probably of typhus, believed to have been contracted via a contamination of the White House water supply. Tad was also very ill but recovered. Mary Todd Lincoln was devastated and went into heavy mourning for a year, during which there were no social activities in the White House. She refused to ever again enter the rooms in which Willie died and lay in his coffin. Lincoln turned increasingly to religion for comfort, whereas Mary consulted spiritualists and mediums, attempting to reach her deceased son.

"And by virtue of the power, and for the purpose aforesaid, I do order and declare that all persons held as slaves within said designated States, and parts of States, are, and henceforward shall be free; and that the Executive government of the United States, including the military and naval authorities thereof, will recognize and maintain the freedom of said persons."

Abraham Lincoln, the Emancipation Proclamation, January 1, 1863

On July 22, 1862, Lincoln read a preliminary draft of the Emancipation Proclamation to his cabinet. Like most presidents before him, Lin-

"Four score and seven years ago our fathers brought forth on this continent, a new nation, conceived in Liberty, and dedicated to the proposition
that all men are created equal. Now we are engaged in a great civil war,
testing whether that nation, or any nation so conceived and so dedicated,
can long endure. We are met on a great battlefield of that war. We have
come to dedicate a portion of that field, as a final resting place for those
who here gave their lives that that nation might live. It is altogether fit-
ting and proper that we should do this. But, in a larger sense, we can not
dedicate—we can not consecrate—we can not hallow—this ground. The
brave men, living and dead, who struggled here, have consecrated it, far
above our poor power to add or detract. The world will little note, nor
long remember what we say here, but it can never forget what they did
here. It is for us the living, rather, to be dedicated here to the unfinished
work which they who fought here have thus far so nobly advanced. It is
rather for us to be here dedicated to the great task remaining before us—
that from these honored dead we take increased devotion to that cause
for which they gave the last full measure of devotion—that we here highly
resolve that these dead shall not have died in vain—that this nation, under God, shall have a new birth of freedom—and that government of the
people, by the people, for the people, shall not perish from the earth."

Abraham Lincoln, the Gettysburg Address, November 19, 1863

coln did not believe that the Constitution gave
the president the power to abolish slavery. However, he personally regarded slavery as a great
evil and had issued the proclamation in part as
a tactic to suppress the continuing rebellion of
the Confederacy and as a tactic of war. The
Emancipation Proclamation, which took effect
on January 1, 1863, abolished slavery only in the
Confederate States of America; slavery persisted
in the border states until the passage of the 13th
Amendment, in 1865.

At the Battle of Antietam, on September 17,
1862, General McClellan again failed to capitalize on his numerical superiority. It was the single bloodiest day of the war, and although the
Union prevailed, McClellan failed to pursue the
retreating Confederates. Lincoln then replaced
McClellan with General Ambrose Burnside, on
November 7, 1862. Burnside commanded at the
Union defeat at Fredericksburg, on December
13, 1862, and then launched an ill-fated offensive, sending his troops over muddy terrain in
wet weather.

On January 26, 1863, Lincoln relieved Burnside of command and replaced him with General Joseph Hooker. Shortly thereafter, Congress
passed a conscription law, introducing the first
military draft in the United States. The law garnered criticism—in part because a draftee could
hire a substitute for $300, making the draft

harder on poor men than men of means. In July 1863, there were demonstrations against compulsory service in New York City that grew into riots.

"With malice toward none, with charity for all, with firmness in the right as God gives us to see the right, let us strive on to finish the work we are in, to bind up the nation's wounds, to care for him who shall have borne the battle and for his widow and his orphan, to do all which may achieve and cherish a just and lasting peace among ourselves and with all nations."

Abraham Lincoln, his second inaugural address, March 4, 1865

The Battle of Chancellorsville in northern Virginia lasted from May 1 to 4, 1863, and resulted in a Confederate victory for General Lee, who had divided his forces and flanked the larger Union forces of General Hooker. General Hooker asked to be relieved of his command and was replaced by General George Gordon Meade in June 1863, just prior to the Battle of Gettysburg. On July 1 to 5, 1863, the Battle of Gettysburg was fought on the fields of Gettysburg, Pennsylvania. General Lee had attempted to infiltrate the Northern states and move toward Washington, DC, but was met with and finally repelled by Union forces under General Meade. Meanwhile, on July 4, 1863, General Ulysses S. Grant captured Vicksburg, cutting the Confederacy forces in two and gaining control of the Mississippi River for the Union.

On November 19, 1863, Lincoln delivered his "Gettysburg Address" at a dedication of the Sol-diers National Cemetery on the grounds of the Battle of Gettysburg.

On March 12, 1864, Lincoln appointed General Ulysses S. Grant commander of all Union armies. Grant decided to headquarter his command with the Army of the Potomac, leaving General William T. Sherman in command of the armies in the West. Grant commanded in the series of engagements known as the Wilderness campaign in May and the subsequent pursuit of the Confederate forces in their retreat toward Richmond. Meanwhile, Sherman's troops cut a swath of destruction through Georgia.

In the midst of the war, Lincoln was nominated for reelection by the Republican Party; his Democratic opponent was General George B. McClellan. Andrew Johnson of Tennessee, the only Southern senator who had remained loyal to the Union, was selected to replace Hannibal Hamlin as the vice-presidential candidate. Lincoln urged voters not to "change horses in midstream" and won a resounding victory, gaining 212 electoral votes to McClellan's 21 votes.

Finally, on April 9, 1865, General Robert E. Lee surrendered to General Ulysses S. Grant at the Appomattox Court House in Virginia, bringing the Civil War to an end.

Final estimates for the toll taken by the war included the more than 110,000 Union soldiers killed (either immediately or following wounds received in battle), and the (approximately) 94,000 Confederate soldiers killed. Additionally, between the two sides, approximately 388,000 soldiers died from infectious diseases.

DEATH OF THE PRESIDENT

Five days after the end of the war, on Good Friday 1865, the Lincolns attended a play at Ford's Theater in Washington—a comedy entitled *Our American Cousin*. During the performance, John Wilkes Booth, an actor and a Southern sympathizer, crept up behind Lincoln and shot him in the head, crying *"Sic semper tyrannis!"* [thus let it ever be with tyrants], and "the South is avenged!"

The president was taken across the street to Petersen's Boarding House, where he died just past seven o'clock on the following morning. Conspirators had also attempted to assassinate

Secretary of State William Seward, entering his private residence and stabbing him. Seward was seriously wounded but recovered.

Booth fled to a farmhouse in Virginia and hid in its barn. He was found there with one of his accomplices, David Herold, who gave himself up. Booth refused to surrender, and the barn was set on fire. Booth was shot and killed while attempting to escape. Herold and three others were hanged in July 1865 for their part in the plot.

A funeral service was held for Abraham Lincoln at the White House on April 19, 1865. Neither Mrs. Lincoln nor Tad felt able to attend. Robert Lincoln, the eldest son, represented the family. After the funeral, the casket was transported in a solemn procession to the Capitol Rotunda for public viewing. Thousands of mourners passed by the casket, which rested on a magnificent catafalque. On April 25, 1865, Lincoln's body, as well as that of his son Willie, who had died in 1862, left Washington on a special funeral train bound for Springfield. The train traveled across many states, stopping in such cities as Baltimore, New York, Philadelphia, Cleveland, Columbus, and Chicago, to enable mourners in those cities to pay their respects. In all, hundreds of thousands passed by the coffin of the fallen president. All along the journey, people lined the tracks, standing in rain for hours with their heads bowed. The former president was buried on May 4, 1865, in Springfield, Illinois; his son Willie was also placed in the family vault.

Mary and Tad Lincoln moved to Chicago, and in 1868 traveled to Europe, where they stayed for more than two years. When they returned to Chicago in 1871, Tad was beginning to feel unwell; he died, probably of tuberculosis, on July 15, 1871, at the age of eighteen.

In 1875 Robert made arrangements for a hearing before a judge, at which Mary was declared legally insane. She spent several months in a private asylum. After her release, the ruling of another hearing reversed the prior ruling and Mary Lincoln was again able to control her own affairs. She spent several more years living in France and traveling in Europe, returning home after injuring her back in a fall. Suffering from a variety of illnesses, she lived with her sister Elizabeth Edwards during her final years, dying on July 16, 1882, in Springfield, Illinois.

Robert Lincoln, the only surviving son of Mary and Abraham, lived to be eighty-two. He served as secretary of war under President Garfield and President Arthur, and was appointed as minister to Great Britain by President Benjamin Harrison. He also became the president of the Pullman Company. His last major public appearance was at the dedication of the Lincoln Memorial, on May 30, 1922.

Birthplace: Sinking Spring Farm, Hardin County, KY
Residency: Illinois
Religion: unaffiliated
Education: grammar schools, for about one year total
Place of Death: Ford's Theater, Washington, DC
Burial Site: Oak Ridge Cemetery, Springfield, IL
Dates in Office: March 4, 1861–April 15, 1865 (4 years, 42 days)
Age at Inauguration: 52 years, 20 days

FAMILY

Father: Thomas Lincoln (1778–1851)
Mother: Nancy Hanks Lincoln (1784–1818) [Note: Thomas Lincoln's second wife, Sarah Bush Johnston Lincoln (1788–1869) became Abraham's stepmother when he was ten.]
Siblings: Abraham was the second of three children; his siblings were Nancy (called Sarah) Lincoln (1807–1828) and Thomas Lincoln (1811–1813). When his father married Sarah Bush Johnston Lincoln, she had three children from her first marriage, who became Abraham's stepsisters and stepbrother: Elizabeth Johnston (1807–?), Matilda Johnston (1811–?), and John D. Johnston (1814–?).
Wife: Mary Ann Todd Lincoln (1818–1882); married November 4, 1842, at the home of the bride's sister, Mrs. Ninian Edwards, in Springfield, IL
Children: Robert Todd Lincoln (1843–1926); Edward ("Eddie") Baker Lincoln (1846–1850); William ("Willie") Wallace Lincoln (1850–1862); Thomas ("Tad") Lincoln (1853–1871)

CAREER

Private: rail-splitter; postmaster of New Salem, IL; storekeeper; surveyor; lawyer
Political: member of the IL legislature (1834–1841); member of the US House of Representatives (1847–1849); president of the United States (1861–1865)
Military: captain in Black Hawk War, did not see action
Selected Works: There are hundreds of editions of Lincoln's works, including letters, speeches, anecdotes, and the Lincoln-Douglas debates. The following are only a few of the available editions: *Abraham Lincoln, 1809–1865, Chronology, Documents, Bibliographical Aids*, ed. by Ian Elliot (Dobbs Ferry, NY: Oceana Publications, 1970); *Collected Works: The Abraham Lincoln Association, Springfield, Illinois*, ed. by Roy P. Basler (New Brunswick, NJ: Rutgers University Press, 1953–1955); *The Emancipation Proclamation* (Bedford, MA: Applewood Books, 1998); *This Fiery Trial: The Speeches and Writings of Abraham Lincoln*, ed. by William E. Gienapp (New York: Oxford University Press, 2002); *The Gettysburg Address*, ed. by Patricia and David Armentrout (Vero Beach, FL: Rourke Publishers, 2004); *The Lincoln-Douglas Debates: The First Complete, Unexpurgated Text*, ed. by Harold Holzer (New York: Fordham University Press, 2004); *The Wit and Wisdom of Abraham Lincoln: A Treasury of More Than 650 Quotations and Anecdotes*, ed. by James C. Humes, with a foreword by Lamar Alexander (New York: HarperCollins Publishers, 1996).

PRESIDENCY

Nomination: 1860: The Republicans met in Chicago in May of 1860; at first, Senator William Seward of New York led in the balloting, but Lincoln won the nomination on the third ballot; Senator Hannibal Hamlin of Maine was selected as the vice-presidential candidate.

1864: The Republicans met in Baltimore in June of 1864; Lincoln won the nomination on the first ballot, and the military governor he had appointed for Tennessee, Andrew Johnson, was chosen as the vice-presidential candidate.

Election: 1860: elected president on November 6, 1860

1864: reelected president on November 8, 1864
Opponent: 1860: Stephen Douglas, IL, Democratic Party; John C. Breckinridge, KY, Democratic Party; John Bell, TN, Constitutional Union Party

1864: George B. McClellan, NJ, Democratic Party
Vote Totals: 1860: Lincoln, 1,865,908 popular, 180 electoral; Douglas, 1,380,202 popular, 12 electoral; Breckinridge, 848,019 popular, 72 electoral; Bell, 590,901 popular, 39 electoral

1864: Lincoln, 2,218,388 popular, 212 electoral; McClellan, 1,812,807 popular, 21 electoral
Inauguration: 1860: March 4, 1861

1864: March 4, 1865
Vice President: 1860: Hannibal Hamlin, ME (1861–1865)

1864: Andrew Johnson, TN (1865)

CABINET

Secretary of State: William H. Seward, NY (1861–1865)
Secretary of the Treasury: Salmon P. Chase, OH (1861–1864); William P. Fessenden, ME (1864–1865); Hugh McCulloch, IN (1865)
Secretary of War: Simon Cameron, PA (1861–1862); Edwin M. Stanton, PA (1862–1865)
Attorney General: Edward Bates, MO (1861–1864); James Speed, KY (1864–1865)
Postmaster General: Montgomery Blair, MO (1861–1864); William Dennison, OH (1864–1865)
Secretary of the Navy: Gideon Welles, CT (1861–1865)
Secretary of the Interior: Caleb B. Smith, IN (1861–1863); John P. Usher, IN (1863–1865)

CONGRESS

37th Congress (1861–1863); Speaker of the House: Galusha A. Grow (PA, Republican)
38th Congress (1863–1865); Speaker of the House: Schuyler Colfax (IN, Republican)

SUPREME COURT APPOINTEES

Noah Haynes Swayne, OH; Associate Justice (1862–1881)

Samuel Freeman Miller, IA; Associate Justice (1862–1890)

David Davis, IL; Associate Justice (1862–1877)

Stephen Johnson Field, CA; Associate Justice (1863–1897)

Salmon Portland Chase, OH; Chief Justice (1864–1873)

MAJOR EVENTS OF THE LINCOLN ADMINISTRATION

◆ The Confederate constitution is adopted, March 11, 1861.

◆ The first shots of the Civil War are fired at Fort Sumter, April 12–13, 1861. Fort Sumter, in the harbor of Charleston, South Carolina, is held by Union forces. When Lincoln informs the governor of South Carolina that provisions are being sent to the troops at Fort Sumter, the Southerners demand that the Union troops leave Fort Sumter and ultimately fire on the fort.

◆ Lincoln calls for volunteer troops, April 15, 1861.

◆ Virginia (on April 17), Arkansas (May 6), North Carolina (May 20), and Tennessee (June 8) secede from the Union and join the Confederacy.

◆ Lincoln suspends the writ of habeas corpus, April 27, 1861.

◆ On May 21, 1861, Richmond, Virginia, becomes the capital of the Confederacy.

◆ The first Battle of Bull Run, July 21, 1861, near Manassas, Virginia, is the first major engagement of the Civil War. Losses: 460 Union, 387 Confederate. [Note: These figures are for those killed; figures for the wounded and captured are much higher.]

◆ The Union naval blockade of Confederate ports begins, July 1861.

◆ Lincoln names George B. McClellan commander in chief of the Union forces, November 1861.

◆ Congress creates the territories of Dakota, Nevada, and Colorado, 1861.

◆ Lincoln's son William Wallace Lincoln ("Willie") dies on February 22, 1862, at age eleven.

◆ The first naval engagement of ironclad ships occurs on March 9, 1862, when the Confederate ironclad *Virginia* (a resurrected USS *Merrimack*) clashes for several hours with the USS *Monitor*. This initial engagement between the two ends in a draw.

◆ In April 1862 David Farragut attacks the Southern position and seizes New Orleans for the Union.

◆ Slavery is abolished in the District of Columbia, April 16, 1862.

◆ On May 15, 1862, Lincoln establishes the Bureau of Agriculture, a precursor of the Department of Agriculture.

◆ Robert E. Lee is appointed commander of the Confederate army (the Army of Northern Virginia) on June 1, 1862.

◆ The Battle of Shiloh, April 6–7, 1862, ends in a Union victory, and in its aftermath much of Tennessee is evacuated by Confederate troops. Losses: 1,754 Union, 1,723 Confederate.

◆ On July 1, 1862, Congress establishes the Bureau of Internal Revenue.

◆ Congress passes the Morrill Act on July 2, 1862. Also called the Land-Grant College Act, it provides for the donation of public lands to the states for the establishment of colleges to teach agriculture and mechanical arts. Among the land-grant universities created by this act are the state universities of Iowa, Kansas, Michigan, Pennsylvania, Vermont, Minnesota, Missouri, Wisconsin, Kentucky, and New Jersey (Rutgers).

◆ On July 22, 1862, Lincoln reads a draft of the Emancipation Proclamation to his cabinet.

◆ In July 1862 the first Union black troops are organized.

◆ On August 29–30, 1862, the second Battle of Bull Run (Manassas) results in a Union loss. Losses: 1,747 Union; 1,552 Confederate.

◆ At the Battle of Antietam, on September 17, 1862, General McClellan again fails to capitalize on his numerical superiority. It is the single bloodiest day of the war. Losses: 2,108 Union, 2,700 Confederate.

❖ Lincoln issues the Emancipation Proclamation, September 22, 1862, to go into effect in January 1863. Under its terms, Confederate slaves are freed, but those in loyal border states are not.

❖ Lincoln replaces McClellan with General Ambrose Burnside, November 7, 1862.

❖ The Battle of Fredericksburg, Virginia, December 13, 1862, results in a Union defeat. Losses: 460 Union, 387 Confederate.

❖ On December 31, 1862, the Union ironclad *Monitor* is sunk, as it founders in a storm off Cape Hatteras, North Carolina.

❖ The Homestead Act of 1862 goes into effect on January 1, 1863; it provides that settlers may claim 160-acre parcels of land after farming them for five years.

❖ On January 1, 1863, the Emancipation Proclamation goes into effect.

❖ The Battle of Murfreesboro is fought, January 2, 1863.

❖ On January 26, 1863, Lincoln relieves Burnside of command and replaces him with General Joseph Hooker.

❖ On February 24, 1863, the Arizona Territory is formed.

❖ On March 3, 1863, Congress passes the Enrollment Act, a conscription (draft) law.

❖ Lasting from May 1 until May 4, 1863, the Battle of Chancellorsville in northern Virginia results in a Confederate victory for General Lee, who divides his forces and flanks the larger Union forces of General Hooker. Losses: 1,606 Union, 1,649 Confederate. Additionally, General Thomas "Stonewall" Jackson is wounded and then contracts pneumonia, dying on May 10.

❖ The Idaho Territory is formed, May 3, 1863.

❖ West Virginia becomes a state, June 20, 1863.

❖ General Hooker asks to be relieved of command and is replaced by General George Gordon Meade in June 1863.

❖ The Battle of Gettysburg, July 1–5, 1863, takes place in Pennsylvania. General Lee attempts to enter the Northern states and move toward Washington, DC, but is met with and finally repelled by Union forces under General Meade. Both sides suffer tremendous losses: 3,155 Union, 3,500 Confederate. (Between the two sides, more than 30,000 men are wounded.)

❖ On July 4, 1863, General Ulysses S. Grant captures Vicksburg, cutting the Confederacy in two and gaining control of the Mississippi River for the Union.

❖ In July 1863 the draft causes riots in New York City.

❖ At the Battle of Chickamauga, September 19–20, 1863, Confederate forces under General James Longstreet split the Union forces under General George Henry Thomas. Losses: 1,657 Union, 2,312 Confederate.

❖ On November 19, 1863, Lincoln gives the "Gettysburg Address" at the dedication of a national cemetery on the site of the Gettysburg battlefield.

❖ At the Battle of Chattanooga, November 23–25, 1863, Union troops under Generals Philip Sheridan and T. J. Wood, on orders from Grant, attack and scatter Confederate troops positioned on Missionary Ridge under General Braxton Bragg. Losses: 753 Union, 361 Confederate.

❖ On December 8, 1863, Lincoln offers a full pardon to Southerners who are willing to take an oath of loyalty to the Union.

❖ On March 12, 1864, Lincoln gives Grant command of the Union armies.

❖ At the Battle of the Wilderness, May 5–6, 1864, Lee and Grant meet for the first time; the battle is a stalemate. The Confederate losses are unknown, while the Union losses are 2,246 men.

❖ In May 1864 General Grant pursues the Confederate troops after the Wilderness campaign; Union forces advance toward Richmond and Confederate forces under Lee and General J. E. B. Stuart defend the Confederate capital; the two sides clash at the Battle of Spotsylvania. Losses: 2,725 Union, unknown Confederate.

❖ Nevada becomes a state, October 31, 1864.

❖ In November and December of 1864, Union General William T. Sherman and his troops burn Atlanta, march from Atlanta to Savannah, capture Savannah, and leave a path of destruction in their wake.

◆ Salmon P. Chase becomes chief justice of the Supreme Court, December 15, 1864.

◆ Congress passes the Thirteenth Amendment to the Constitution, which frees all slaves, January 31, 1865.

◆ On March 13, 1865, the Confederate Congress offers freedom to any slaves (as well as their families) who will volunteer to fight on the side of the Confederacy.

◆ Congress authorizes the Freedman's Bureau to aid newly freed blacks, March 3, 1865.

◆ General Robert E. Lee surrenders to General Ulysses S. Grant at Appomattox Court House in Virginia, April 9, 1865, bringing the Civil War to an end.

◆ Abraham Lincoln is shot at Ford's Theater, April 14, 1865, and dies the next day.

MAJOR US AND WORLD EVENTS, 1861–1865

◆ Italy declares its independence and the Kingdom of Italy, with Victor Emmanuel II as king, is proclaimed, March 17, 1861.

◆ On May 13, 1861, England declares its neutrality in an announcement by Queen Victoria; Britain's position tacitly accepts the Confederate government as having belligerent rights to declare war against the North.

◆ On October 24, 1861, the first transcontinental telegraph is sent from San Francisco to New York; this milestone effectively ends the value of the Pony Express service.

◆ Julia Ward Howe writes the "Battle Hymn of the Republic," 1861; it is published in 1862.

◆ On December 14, 1861, Prince Albert, the consort of Queen Victoria of England, dies. Victoria withdraws from public life for three years.

◆ Photographer Mathew Brady begins his historic photographic coverage of the Civil War, 1861.

◆ Charles Dickens publishes *Great Expectations*, 1861.

◆ George Eliot publishes *Silas Marner*, 1861.

◆ Otto von Bismarck becomes prime minister of Prussia, 1862.

◆ Victor Hugo publishes *Les Misérables*, 1862.

◆ Ivan Turgenev publishes *Fathers and Sons*, 1862.

◆ French actress Sarah Bernhardt makes her theatrical debut, 1862.

◆ Richard Jordan Gatling takes out a patent for a mechanical gun with six barrels mounted on a revolving frame, 1862.

◆ On April 20, 1862, Louis Pasteur and Claude Bernard complete the first trial of pasteurization.

◆ An International Committee that becomes known as the Red Cross is formed, 1863; in 1864 the Geneva Convention adopts a "Convention for the Amelioration of the Wounded in Armies in the Field," which provides for relief to wounded without regard to nationality and neutrality of medical personnel.

◆ On August 11, 1863, Cambodia becomes a French protectorate.

◆ Edouard Manet exhibits "Le Déjeuner sur l'Herbe" at the Salon de Refusées, 1863.

◆ The US National Academy of Science is founded, March 3, 1863.

◆ Jules Verne publishes *A Journey to the Center of the Earth*, 1864.

◆ Fyodor Dostoevsky publishes *Notes from the Underground*, 1864.

◆ Cardinal John Henry Newman publishes *Apologia pro Vita Sua*, 1864.

◆ Rebecca Lee Crumpler graduates from the New England Female Medical College in 1864, the first African-American woman in the United States to earn a medical degree.

◆ The Austrian archduke Maximilian becomes emperor of Mexico, 1864.

◆ British, French, and Dutch fleets attack Japanese ships in the Shimonoseki Straits as a reprisal for Japan's having closed its ports, 1864; Japan subsequently agrees to a truce.

FAST FACTS ABOUT ABRAHAM LINCOLN

◆ Lincoln was the first president born outside of the original thirteen colonies.

◆ Lincoln was six feet, four inches in height.

◆ Lincoln was given to bouts of depression.

◆ Lincoln received the nickname "Honest Abe" because of his efforts to pay off his debts as a young man in Illinois.

◆ Lincoln was given the nickname "Spotty Lincoln" when, as a member of the US House of Representatives, he demanded that President Polk identify the spot on American soil where blood was shed at the start of the Mexican-American War (the inference being that it was Mexican rather than American territory where the first shots were fired).

◆ The US minister to Great Britain under Lincoln was Charles Francis Adams, the son of John Quincy Adams and grandson of John Adams. One of Adams's sons, Charles Francis Adams, Jr., served as a Union officer during the Civil War.

◆ Lincoln is the only president to hold a patent; his patent was for a device to lift boats over shoals or sandbars and was a product of his experiences working on the Sangamon River in Illinois, as well as a later experience of traveling in a boat and becoming stranded on a sandbar. The device was never manufactured.

◆ Stephen A. Douglas, Lincoln's political opponent, was one of Mary Todd's many suitors in Springfield before she married Lincoln.

◆ When Lincoln married Mary Todd, he gave her a gold ring with "Love is eternal" engraved on its inside.

◆ For his important speech given at the Cooper Union in New York City in 1860, Lincoln ordered a new black suit that cost $100.

◆ In a celebrated incident during Lincoln's train trip from Illinois to Washington after winning the election, Lincoln was informed by Allan Pinkerton, who had been hired to provide security, that there was an assassination plot afoot in Baltimore. Lincoln secretly left his hotel in Harrisburg, Pennsylvania, and traveled by night train through Baltimore, trading his customary stovepipe hat for one with a more shallow crown, but not, as later cartoonists suggested, donning a kilt.

◆ Mary Lincoln was the first White House hostess to welcome African Americans as guests at the White House.

◆ Mary Lincoln consulted mediums and held a séance in the White House, hoping to speak to her dead son, Willie.

◆ Lincoln was the first president to be assassinated. He was assassinated only five days after the end of the Civil War.

Andrew Johnson

Nickname: Tennessee Tailor, Sir Veto, Andy, King Andy
Presidency: 17th president, 1865–1869
Party: Democratic
Life dates: December 29, 1808–July 31, 1875 (66 years, 214 days)

EARLY LIFE AND EDUCATION

Andrew Johnson was born on December 29, 1808, in Raleigh, North Carolina. He was the third child of Mary (called Polly) McDonough Johnson and Jacob Johnson. Andrew had an older brother, William, and a sister, Elizabeth, who died in infancy. His mother was a weaver and seamstress. His father worked as a porter at a bank and did odd jobs; at the same time he was a well-respected man in Raleigh who also served as a constable and a captain of the town watch. Both parents were illiterate. Sadly, Jacob died a short time after he plunged into a pond to save several prominent citizens whose boat had capsized. The heroic action may have weakened him. Son Andrew was three years old at the time of his death.

Mary Johnson married again; Andrew's new stepfather was Turner Doughtry. The family members were regarded by more well-to-do citizens of Raleigh as "poor whites"—the lowest class in Raleigh society (excepting black freedmen and slaves). Andrew and his older brother William received no schooling; both were apprenticed to a local tailor, James Selby. It was Selby's responsibility to teach the boys to read and write (as well as the tailoring craft). When Andrew was fifteen,

he and his brother and two other apprentices ran away. Selby posted signs that announced a ten-dollar reward for their return. The signs also promised to pay the same amount for the return of Andrew alone—possibly he was considered the leader of the escapade.

Andrew worked briefly in Carthage, North Carolina. He then moved to Laurens, South Carolina, continuing to work as an apprentice tailor. He also took advantage of his ability to read and, keen for knowledge of all kinds, read constantly. In Laurens he fell in love with a girl whose name was Mary Wood, but his offer of marriage was refused—her mother had little faith in the kind of future the young tailor could offer her daughter. Disappointed, Andrew returned briefly to Raleigh, where he tried (unsuccessfully) to pay off his unfinished apprenticeship. He then headed for Tennessee.

EARLY CAREER

Johnson spent a brief time in Mooresville, Alabama—where he continued to expand his tailoring skills—before heading for Columbia, Tennessee. Six months later, the wandering tailor returned to Raleigh; he returned to Tennessee with his mother and stepfather in the fall of 1826. He settled in Greeneville and began working in George Boyle's tailor shop.

> "His career was remarkable, even in this country; it would have been impossible in any other."
>
> Obituary of Andrew Johnson, from the *New York Times*, August 1, 1875

Johnson met Eliza McCardle, a young woman who reportedly expressed her interest in him the first time she saw him. He then spent time in Rutledge, Tennessee, but soon returned to Greeneville and Eliza. Andrew and Eliza were married May 17, 1827, at Warrensburg, Tennessee. Within seven years, by 1834, the couple had two sons and two daughters; their third son was born eighteen years after the birth of the next-to-last child, in 1852.

In Greeneville, Johnson's tailor shop prospered and, with his wife's help, he continued to read and to educate himself. His newly acquired erudition put him in good stead when he began to engage in local political debates and joined a debating society. He was elected to the position of town alderman in 1828 and remained in that position until 1834, at which time he was elected mayor of Greeneville. He was at that time identified with the Mechanics' Party and informally leaning toward the Whigs.

FURTHER POLITICAL CAREER

Johnson was elected as a member of Tennessee state legislature in 1835. He supported public education but voted against appropriations of funds for internal improvements, and he opposed the railroads—all positions that were unpopular at home in Greeneville. He was defeated in his bid for reelection in 1837. Reelected in 1839, he finally found his political home in the Democratic Party. Long an admirer of Andrew Jackson, Johnson supported Martin Van Buren as Jackson's chosen successor and became acquainted with the governor of Tennessee, James K. Polk.

While back at home in Greeneville, Johnson expanded his business and real estate holdings. Eventually he became the owner of a farm, on which his mother and stepfather came to live, and he bought several slaves. Throughout his life he viewed blacks as inferior beings, an attitude that would influence his decision-making in the White House and put him at odds with the prevailing post–Civil War mood of Congress.

In 1843 he was elected to the US House of Representatives and served there until 1853. He supported the war with Mexico and the Compromise of 1850. Johnson opposed the protective tariff, which reduced duties, and proposed increases in the salaries of elected officials. He sponsored the Homestead Act, which was not passed until 1862. When congressional districts were redrawn in Tennessee in 1852, Johnson thought it unlikely that he would be reelected to Congress, so he ran for governor of Tennessee. He was elected governor in 1853, and again in 1855.

> "The goal to strive for is a poor government but a rich people."
>
> Andrew Johnson, 1845

During most of his political career, Johnson was away from his home and Eliza did not generally accompany him to other cities, preferring to stay at home in Greeneville. However, the two kept in close touch via their correspondence, and he relied on her advice and political opinions. She read widely and clipped newspaper articles she thought would interest him.

In 1857 he was elected to the US Senate. During the period leading up to the 1860 presidential election, Johnson initially supported Stephen A. Douglas, who seemed likely to be the candidate of the Democratic Party. When the party became split, however, Johnson supported the Southern Democratic candidate, John C. Breckenridge. When Abraham Lincoln was elected and the Southern states began to secede, Johnson spoke passionately in the Senate against secession. He then returned to Tennessee to fight against secession. At odds with his former Democratic colleagues, he allied himself with the pro-Unionists. When Tennessee did secede, Johnson became the only Southern senator to remain with the Union. He and his family were forced to leave Tennessee, where he was reviled as a traitor, but in the North, his stand made him a hero.

"I have been informed that part of the business to be transacted on the present occasion is the assassination of the individual who now has the honor of addressing you. . . . Therefore, if any man has come here tonight for the purpose indicated, I do not say to him let him speak, but let him shoot."

Andrew Johnson, 1855, when campaigning for governor; reportedly he prefaced this remark by placing a gun before him on the podium

---

The Union army gained control of central Tennessee, and Lincoln appointed Johnson as the military governor of the state in 1862. Johnson, having returned to Tennessee, sought to bring the state back into the Union and enthusiastically reported to Lincoln that an amendment to the state constitution abolishing slavery had been passed. However, his attempts to form a new government in Tennessee met with limited success.

In 1864 Johnson was placed on the Lincoln ticket as the vice-presidential candidate—as he was expected to attract the votes of the "War Democrats," with whom Johnson was identified. He and Lincoln won handily. Johnson left Tennessee feeling that his task there was unfinished, but arrived in Washington in time for the inauguration. Feeling unwell, he drank whiskey and gave a rambling, incoherent speech. Rumors that he was an alcoholic dogged him, but Lincoln rejected such claims.

At the time that Lincoln was assassinated, Johnson was also being targeted for assassination. But an attack never occurred, as some of the assassins had lost their nerve. On the morning of April 15, 1865, Johnson took the presidential oath of office.

PRESIDENCY

Johnson presided over the country at the start of the Reconstruction period, a time when the country was healing itself from the wounds of the war. He began his presidency by retaining Lincoln's cabinet. As Congress was not in session, he was able to advance a policy that was fairly lenient toward southern states. He issued a proclamation that amnesty would be granted to all former Confederates who would take a loyalty oath—although some would be exempt, including planters who were worth more than $200,000 and men who had been high-ranking officials of the Confederacy. Johnson put provisional governors in place in southern states. As state governments were reestablished, however, elected officials were often the same people who had held office in the Confederacy, and the new governments enacted the severely restrictive Black Codes, under which blacks had virtually the same status that they had had as slaves.

When Congress reconvened at the end of the year, the Radical Republicans were outraged by Johnson's approach. They believed that the former Confederates should be punished and that the rights of the black freedmen needed to be protected. Thus began a battle between Johnson and the Congress. As the members of Congress passed laws, he vetoed them, and they then passed them over Johnson's veto.

Johnson believed that the laws being passed were unconstitutional, in part because the Congress was refusing to seat newly elected southern members until further provisions had been enacted to protect freed slaves.

"I intend to stand by the Constitution . . . as the chief ark of our safety, as the palladium of our civil and religious liberty."

Andrew Johnson, in a speech
given February 22, 1866

In February 1866 Johnson vetoed a bill to extend the powers of the Freedmen's Bureau, a US government agency that had been established for the protection of the rights of black citizens; Congress overrode his veto in July 1866. In March, Johnson vetoed the Civil Rights Act; in April, Congress overrode his veto. The Fourteenth Amendment, establishing the citizenship of blacks, was passed in June and sent to the states for ratification.

In July 1866 Congress enacted legislation to shrink the size of the Supreme Court, reducing it from ten justices to seven (it was later expanded again to nine). The principal motivation behind it was the fact that the Senate did not want Johnson to be able to appoint new justices.

Hoping to influence the 1866 congressional elections, Johnson resurrected a skill that had always served him well in the past: He went on a speaking tour to support moderate candidates, but repeatedly attacked his Radical Republican foes in Congress. At times during the tour, he appeared to be intoxicated. The tour was a disaster and did nothing to enhance his stature among the public or in Congress. The Radical Republicans became an even stronger force in the next Congress.

On March 30, 1867, Johnson's secretary of state, William H. Seward, negotiated the pur-chase of Alaska from Russia. Alaska was purchased for $7.2 million; the US flag was raised over the new territory on October 18, 1867. The deal was mocked, in Congress and elsewhere, and Alaska was dubbed "Seward's Folly," "Seward's Ice Box," "Icebergia," and "Johnson's Polar Bear Garden." More than twenty years later, however, the discovery of gold in Alaska (in 1890) made it clear that Seward had made a good bargain.

In March 1867 Congress overrode Johnson's veto of the Tenure of Office Act, a law that forbade the president to remove any federal office-holder who had been appointed by and with the advice and consent of the Senate unless he gained the further approval of the Senate. In March, Congress also overrode Johnson's vetoes of the First and Second Reconstruction Acts, and in July, of the Third Reconstruction Act. These acts provided for the installation of US military commanders in five southern districts and the eventual transfer of authority to duly elected state governments; voting rights for freedman; and the readmission to the Union of states that ratified the Fourteenth Amendment.

Johnson then reattempted to challenge the Tenure of Office Act. In August 1867 he fired Secretary of War Edwin Stanton and appointed Ulysses S. Grant as the interim secretary, but Grant returned the office to Stanton when the Senate refused to approve Stanton's dismissal. Johnson then appointed General Lorenzo Thomas to the position, and Stanton refused to step down by barricading himself in his office. The dispute between Johnson and the Senate became a case that was tried before the Supreme Court, which refused to rule on it. This led to a resolution in the House of Representatives for Johnson's impeachment (the first for a US president) for "high crimes and misdemeanors"—the crime of his having ignored the Tenure of Office Act (the act was largely repealed in 1887 and declared unconstitutional by the Supreme Court in 1926).

There were eleven articles of impeachment filed. The trial in the Senate lasted three months, but Johnson was acquitted on May 26, 1868, by a vote of thirty-five (for conviction) to nineteen (for acquittal)—one vote shy of the two-thirds vote needed for conviction. Throughout the ordeal, Eliza Johnson supported her husband, always declaring her belief that he would be acquitted. Eliza, who was frequently ill and suffered from tuberculosis, did not take part in social activities at the White House and left those duties to her daughters, but her support for her husband was vital to him.

During the remainder of his term, Johnson had little power.

Post-Presidential Career

After his term expired, Johnson retired to his home in Tennessee. He ran unsuccessfully for the US Senate in 1869 and for the House of Representatives in 1872. In what he considered a vindication of his policies and his record, he was elected as a Democrat to the US Senate in 1874, and served from March 4, 1875, until dying of a stroke on July 31, 1875. Only five months later, on January 15, 1876, Eliza Johnson followed her husband in death.

Better equipped to acquire power than to wield it, Johnson was effectively doomed by his complete opposition to the Radical Republicans and their dominance in Congress. Johnson was content merely to have slavery abolished, but the prejudices he had held since childhood made him resist the movement to make blacks enfranchised citizens. As a southerner loyal to the Union, he apparently wanted to restore the southern states to the Union with as few changes in their traditional power structures as possible, a view widely at variance with the desires of the victorious North, which severely weakened his presidency.

Birthplace: Raleigh, NC
Residency: Tennessee
Religion: unaffiliated
Education: no formal education; taught to read and write by his wife
Place of Death: Carter's Station, TN
Burial Site: Andrew Johnson National Cemetery, Greeneville, TN
Dates in Office: April 15, 1865–March 3, 1869 (3 years, 323 days)
Age at Inauguration: 56 years, 107 days

FAMILY

Father: Jacob Johnson (1778–1812)
Mother: Mary ("Polly") McDonough Johnson (1783–1856)
Siblings: Andrew was the youngest of three children; his siblings were William Johnson (1804–1865) and Elizabeth Johnson (1806–?; died in infancy).
Wife: Eliza McCardle Johnson (1810–1876), married May 17, 1827, at Warrensburg, TN
Children: Martha Johnson (1828–1901); Charles Johnson (1830–1863); Mary Johnson (1832–1883); Robert Johnson (1834–1869); Andrew ("Frank") Johnson (1852–1879)

CAREER

Private: master tailor
Political: alderman of Greeneville, TN (1828–1834); mayor of Greeneville, TN (1834); member of the TN legislature (1835–1836; 1839–1840); member of the TN state senate (1841–1843); member of the US House of Representatives (1843–1853); governor of TN (1853–1857); member of the US Senate (1857–1861); military governor of TN (1862–1865); vice president under Lincoln (1865); president of the United States (1865–1869); member of the US Senate (1875)
Military: military governor of Tennessee, with the rank of brigadier general
Selected Works: *Andrew Johnson, 1808–1875; Chronology, Documents, Bibliographical Aids*, ed. by John N. Dickinson (Dobbs Ferry, NY: Oceana Publications, 1970); *The Impeachment and Trial of Andrew Johnson, President of the United States* (New York: Dover Publications, 1974); *The Papers of Andrew Johnson*, ed. by LeRoy P. Graf and Ralph W. Haskins (Knoxville: University of Tennessee Press, 1967–); *Speeches of Andrew Johnson, President of the United States*, with a biographical introduction by Frank Moore (New York: B. Franklin, 1970)

PRESIDENCY

Nomination: Andrew Johnson was not nominated for the presidency; he was nominated as a vice-presidential candidate for Abraham Lincoln's second term of office.

Election: succeeded to presidency; was not elected
Opponent: none
Vote Totals: n/a
Inauguration: none; took the oath of office on April 15, 1865, the day of Abraham Lincoln's death
Vice President: none

CABINET

Secretary of State: William H. Seward, NY (1865–1869)
Secretary of the Treasury: Hugh McCulloch, IN (1865–1869)
Secretary of War: Edwin M. Stanton, PA (1865–1868); Ulysses S. Grant, IL (1867–1868); John M. Schofield, IL (1868–1869)
Attorney General: James Speed, KY (1865–1866); Henry Stanbery, OH (1866–1868); William M. Evarts, NY (1868–1869)
Postmaster General: William Dennison, OH (1865–1866); Alexander W. Randall, WI (1866–1869)
Secretary of the Navy: Gideon Welles, CT (1865–1869)
Secretary of the Interior: John P. Usher, IN (1865); James Harlan, IA (1865–1866); Orville Browning, IL (1866–1869)

CONGRESS

39th Congress (1865–1867); Speaker of the House: Schuyler Colfax (IN, Republican)
40th Congress (1867–1869); Speaker of the House: Schuyler Colfax (IN, Republican); Theodore M. Pomeroy (NY, Republican)

SUPREME COURT APPOINTEES
none

MAJOR EVENTS OF THE JOHNSON ADMINISTRATION

◆ A funeral service is held for Abraham Lincoln at the White House on April 19, 1865, after which his body is taken to the Capitol Rotunda for viewing. On April 25, 1865, Lincoln's body leaves Washington on a special funeral train, which travels across northern states, stopping in cities along the way for mourners to pay their respects. The former president is buried on May 4, 1865, in Springfield, Illinois.

◆ On May 23 and 24, 1865, the end of the Civil War is celebrated in Washington, DC.

◆ Johnson issues a proclamation on May 29, 1865, granting amnesty to southerners who take an oath of loyalty to the Union. Those who do will have their property restored to them, but high-ranking officials of the Confederate government and planters worth more than $200,000 are exempted from the offer.

◆ Johnson issues another proclamation on May 29, 1865, describing a plan for reconstruction in North Carolina; it provides for a provisional governor and a new constitution that abolishes slavery and denounces secession. The plan serves as a model for other states to rejoin the Union.

◆ During the last two weeks of June 1865, Johnson appoints provisional governors for Mississippi, Georgia, Texas, Alabama, South Carolina, and Florida.

◆ The US Secret Service is established, July 5, 1865, and is initially concerned with preventing counterfeiting.

◆ Starting at the end of 1865, provisional governors are ordered to turn control of state governments over to newly elected officials in southern states.

◆ Beginning with Mississippi, in December 1865, the former Confederate states enact the Black Codes, restricting the rights of the newly freed slaves.

◆ On February 19, 1866, Johnson vetoes a bill that would extend the powers of the Freedmen's Bureau.

◆ On March 27, 1866, Johnson vetoes the Civil Rights Act; Congress overrides his veto in early April. The Act specifically guarantees the rights of freedmen to make contracts, own property, and be punished for crimes in accordance with the law (and not otherwise); the Act also empowers federal troops to enforce the law.

◆ On June 19, 1866, Congress passes the Fourteenth Amendment to the Constitution and sends it to the states for ratification; the amendment establishes the citizenship of

African-Americans, including their right to vote, and bars anyone who has engaged in rebellion against the United States from holding office if that person had previously taken an oath to support the Constitution (e.g., as a member of Congress or the US military). The amendment also prohibits claims for expenses incurred in rebellion against the United States and claims for the value of emancipated slaves.

◆ On July 16, 1866, Congress overrides Johnson's veto of the Freedmen's Bureau Renewal Act.

◆ Tennessee is readmitted to the Union, July 24, 1866.

◆ At the end of August and the beginning of September 1866, Johnson goes on a speaking tour, hoping to contribute to the defeat of some of the Radical Republicans who are up for congressional election in November. Johnson does not impress voters and there are rumors that he has been intoxicated during some of these speeches; the Radical Republicans score major advances in the election and dominate Congress.

◆ Nebraska becomes a state, March 1, 1867.

◆ On March 2, 1867, Congress passes (over Johnson's veto) the Tenure of Office Act, which requires Senate approval for the president's replacement of cabinet officers.

◆ On March 2, 1867, Congress passes the First Reconstruction Act, which sets up five military districts in the South with military commanders appointed by the president and provides that male freedmen will be allowed to vote in elections. The act also provides readmission to the Union for states that ratify the Fourteenth Amendment.

◆ On March 23, 1867, Johnson vetoes the Second Reconstruction Act and Congress overrides his veto; the act calls for military commanders to supervise the elections to be held in the southern states.

◆ Secretary of State William H. Seward makes an agreement on March 30, 1867, to purchase Alaska from Russia for $7,200,000; the purchase is widely ridiculed as "Seward's Folly."

◆ On July 19, 1867, Congress overrides Johnson's veto and passes the Third Reconstruction Act, which gives military commanders in southern states the right to remove elected state officials from office.

◆ On August 12, 1867, in defiance of the Tenure of Office Act, Johnson suspends the secretary of war and appoints Ulysses S. Grant as interim secretary; Grant turns the office back to Stanton, who Johnson then replaces with General Lorenzo Thomas. Stanton barricades himself in his office and the House of Representatives begins impeachment proceedings.

◆ On August 28, 1867, the United States takes possession of the Midway Islands, which had been discovered in 1859 and claimed for the United States by the captain of a Hawaiian ship.

◆ On March 5, 1868, the trial for the impeachment of Johnson for "high crimes and misdemeanors" opens in the Senate; on May 16, 1868, Johnson is acquitted by a vote of 35 to 19, one vote short of the two-thirds necessary for conviction.

◆ In June 1868 Johnson vetoes bills to readmit several southern states to the Union; Congress passes the bills over his vetoes.

◆ The Burlingame Treaty, an amendment to the Treaty of Tientsin between the United States and China, is signed in July 1868. The treaty provides for immigration between the two countries (reversed in the United States by the Chinese Exclusion Act in 1882) and treatment of each country's nationals by the other as citizens of countries enjoying most-favored-nation status.

MAJOR US AND WORLD EVENTS, 1865–1869

◆ Charles Lutwidge Dodgson, using the pseudonym Lewis Carroll, publishes *Alice's Adventures in Wonderland*, 1865.

◆ Edouard Manet displays his nude painting, *Olympia*, in 1865 and provokes a storm of controversy.

◆ The Massachusetts Institute of Technology (MIT) opens, 1866.

◆ Jules Verne publishes *From the Earth to the Moon*, 1866.

◆ The Ku Klux Klan is formed in Tennessee, 1866.

◆ Howard University is founded in 1866 as the Howard Theological Seminary.

◆ Irish-Americans who are part of the Fenian Movement to free Ireland from British rule cross into Canada and defeat Canadian militia, June 1–3, 1866; they are arrested and then released when they return to the United States.

◆ Bedrich Smetana's opera *The Bartered Bride* is produced, 1866.

◆ Fyodor Dostoevsky publishes *Crime and Punishment*, 1866.

◆ On April 10, 1866, the American Society for the Prevention of Cruelty to Animals (ASPCA) is chartered.

◆ Austrian monk Gregor Mendel publishes *Versuche über Pflanzen-Hybride* (*Treatises on Plant Hybrids*), 1866.

◆ In 1867 Horatio Alger publishes *Ragged Dick*, the first of his popular stories about the triumph of young boys against the odds to achieve success.

◆ Johann Strauss, Jr., in 1867 publishes the "Blue Danube," one of the many songs that garner him the nickname of "The Waltz King."

◆ Henrik Ibsen writes and publishes *Peer Gynt*, 1867.

◆ Alfred Nobel obtains a patent on dynamite, 1867.

◆ Karl Marx publishes the first volume of *Das Kapital*, 1867.

◆ In the Meiji Restoration in Japan, 1867–1868, the Emperor Meiji is moved from the former capital of Kyoto to the new capital of Tokyo (Edo); Japan begins to become westernized.

◆ Benjamin Disraeli becomes prime minister of Great Britain briefly, but is soon supplanted by William Gladstone and the Liberal Party, 1868.

◆ Wilkie Collins publishes *The Moonstone*, 1868.

◆ Fyodor Dostoevsky publishes *The Idiot*, 1868.

◆ The first performance is held of Johannes Brahms's *German Requiem*, 1868.

FAST FACTS ABOUT ANDREW JOHNSON

◆ Johnson's father died when Andrew was three years old, shortly after saving the lives of three men whose boat had capsized.

◆ When Eliza McCardle first saw Andrew Johnson, she reportedly said either "There goes my beau, girls," or "There goes the man I am going to marry." They were married within the year; he was eighteen and she was sixteen years old.

◆ Eliza McCardle and Andrew Johnson were married by Mordecai Lincoln, a justice of the peace who was a first cousin to Thomas Lincoln, the father of Abraham Lincoln.

◆ Andrew Johnson was the only southern member of Congress who did not leave the Union at the start of the Civil War.

◆ Eliza Johnson was an invalid during her husband's presidency, so their daughters, Martha Johnson Patterson and Mary Johnson Stover, acted as White House hostesses.

◆ Andrew Johnson was the first president to watch an inter-city baseball game, the first to invite an entire baseball team to the White House, and the guest of honor at the opening of a new ballpark in August 1867, for the National Base Ball Club of Washington.

◆ Johnson was the first and only president to be impeached, until President Clinton was impeached in 1999.

◆ Johnson was the only former president to be elected as a US senator after being president.

Ulysses S. Grant

Nickname: Sam, Hero of Appomattox, Useless, The Butcher,
Unconditional Surrender Grant
Presidency: 18th president, 1869–1877
Party: Republican
Life dates: April 27, 1822–July 23, 1885 (63 years, 87 days)

EARLY LIFE AND EDUCATION

Hiram Ulysses Grant was born on April 27, 1822, in Point Pleasant, Ohio, the eldest of six children of Jesse Root Grant and Hannah Simpson Grant. The year after his birth, the Grant family moved to Georgetown in Brown County, Ohio, where Jesse Grant established a tannery. Ulysses received his earliest education at a grammar school in Georgetown, then attended Maysville Seminary in Maysville, Kentucky, from 1836 to 1838. He then spent a year at a Presbyterian academy in Ripley, Ohio.

Young Ulysses apparently disliked his father's tannery and would have preferred almost any other type of work, including work on the family farm and anything having to do with horses. He had a reputation from his early youth of being able to ride well and break any untrained horse.

In 1839 Jesse Grant arranged to have his son appointed to West Point, the US military academy. Ulysses was not much interested in going, but his father insisted. Ulysses had already decided that he did not want to chance becoming known by his initials, "H.U.G.," so he had decided to reverse his first and second names. But when he arrived at West Point, he found that the congressman who had recommended him had submitted his name as "Ulysses S. Grant," a mistake that had been made probably because of the congressman's knowledge of Grant's mother's maiden name—Simpson. But Grant, accepting the name change, always insisted that the "S" did not stand for anything.

In June 1843 Grant graduated from West Point, twenty-third in his class of thirty-nine, having failed to distinguish himself other than by his horsemanship. Hoping for a cavalry appointment, he was instead assigned as a second lieutenant with the Fourth US Infantry, stationed outside St. Louis, Missouri. Like many of his classmates, Grant did not wish for a career in the military; he hoped to find a job as a professor of mathematics, just as many of his peers planned to use the excellent education they had received at West Point to become engineers.

EARLY MILITARY CAREER

While living in St. Louis, Grant frequently took advantage of the hospitality that had been offered to him by the family of his West Point roommate, Frederick Dent. The Dent family lived on a plantation called White Haven, near St. Louis. In 1844 Frederick's sister, Julia, re-

Lieutenant General Ulysses S. Grant in Cold Harbor, Virginia, circa 1864

turned home from boarding school in St. Louis, and Grant was smitten by the lively, popular Julia. She, too, soon found herself drawn to the dashing young officer.

In May 1844 when Grant found that his regiment had been ordered to Louisiana, he asked Julia to marry him. She agreed, but the engagement was kept secret for a while. Grant joined his regiment, which had been moved south in expectation of conflict with Mexico over the US annexation of Texas.

In 1845 Grant was given leave, which he used to return to St. Louis and ask Julia's father for her hand in marriage. Colonel Dent (the title was honorary) was not in favor of his daughter marrying the poor soldier, but he reluctantly gave his consent.

After he returned to his regiment, Grant and the Fourth Infantry were sent in September of 1845 to New Orleans, and then to Corpus Christi, Texas, on the Nueces River. In March

1846 Grant and his troops, under the command of General Zachary Taylor, began to move across the disputed territory that lay between the Nueces and the Rio Grande Rivers.

When the war finally began in April 1846, Grant experienced battle for the first time, at Palo Alto. Throughout his military career, Grant was noticeably calm under fire, although his personal recollections showed that he experienced normal amounts of fear at these times. He was soon appointed to the position of quartermaster and, as such, not expected to take an active part in battles—a quartermaster's concern being to keep the army provisioned. Although he protested the assignment, it was valuable training for his later command positions. Grant did fight with his regiment at the Battle of Monterrey in September 1846, making a dangerous ride through Monterrey streets under enemy fire while lying along one side of his horse.

In 1847 Grant and the Fourth Infantry were ordered to join General Winfield Scott's troops for the advance into Mexico that led to the capture of Mexico City. Grant, still assigned the quartermaster's duties, fought in the battles that took place prior to the capture of the city, including Vera Cruz, Cerro Gordo, Churubusco, Molino del Rey, and Chapultepec. He was twice promoted, to first lieutenant and then to captain. Grant gained favorable notice when he ordered a howitzer placed in a church belfry, from where it was able to target the enemy very effectively.

In 1848 Grant left Mexico and, from his new post in Mississippi, returned to St. Louis to marry Julia Dent at last, on August 22, 1848. His best man was James Longstreet, who would later become a general in the Confederate army during the Civil War and be among those who surrendered to Grant at Appomattox.

After the Mexican-American War, Grant (becoming part of the peacetime army) was stationed in Sackets Harbor, New York, and then in Detroit, but when he was moved to California in 1852, he had to leave Julia and their children (a son named Frederick, born in 1850, and a son named Ulysses, nicknamed "Buck," born in 1852 shortly after Grant left for California) behind. Grant attempted, unsuccessfully, to make enough money to have his family join him. In California, unhappy with the routine duties, a difficult commanding officer (Colonel Robert Buchanan), and the absence of his family, Grant began drinking. Despite the many accounts of his drinking, Grant was apparently an occasional binge drinker who was much affected by small amounts of alcohol. He generally refrained from drinking when Julia was with him, and there is no evidence that he was ever impaired by alcohol during times of military crisis or during his presidency.

Grant resigned from the US Army in 1854, at virtually the same time he was being promoted to the rank of captain. Although some reports claim that he resigned voluntarily, there is evidence that he resigned at the request of Colonel Buchanan, who had made the request because of his drinking. Grant had been given the choice of resignation or standing trial. As unhappy as he had been in California, Grant worried about supporting his family in the absence of his army career and the salary it guaranteed him.

CIVILIAN LIFE

Grant's worries were justified: As a civilian, he was dogged by failure. He tried farming on a plot of land in Missouri that had been given to the Grants by Julia's father. He dubbed the farm "Hard Scrabble." He built a house and occasionally sold firewood on the streets of St. Louis, but he spent much of 1858 battling an illness that left him too weak to work, and at the end of the year he sold his livestock, crops, and his tools at auction. He again tried farming at White Haven, his father-in-law's home (Colonel Dent having retired), but bad weather ruined his crops.

Grant then went into the real estate business with Harry Boggs, Julia's cousin. Grant was honest but not mercenary; he had trouble demanding rent from those who struggled to pay it, and he was not really enough of a salesman to sell real estate. He next found work as a clerk in the US customs house in St. Louis, a good position that he lost when the collector of customs died and a new appointee replaced Grant.

Grant then swallowed his pride and asked his father for work; he was given a job as a clerk in his father's leather business. The firm had prospered and employed fifty people, including Grant's two younger brothers. Beginning in May 1860, Grant worked in the Galena, Illinois store, handling billing, collections, buying, and selling. He waited on customers reluctantly, but settled into the business, content that at least he could reliably support his family.

"I can't spare this man— he fights!"

President Abraham Lincoln on Ulysses S. Grant, 1862, when critics of Grant's drinking urged Lincoln to replace him

---

When President Lincoln called for volunteers in April 1861, Grant volunteered. He recruited a volunteer infantry company in Galena and helped to organize the volunteers who were pouring into Springfield. Owing to the large number of men jockeying for commissions, at first it seemed that he would not find a place in the army. But he was appointed a colonel of the Twenty-first Illinois Volunteers, a rowdy infantry regiment that had previously resisted discipline, burning down their guardhouse and carousing drunkenly.

THE CIVIL WAR

Grant quickly brought the Twenty-first Illinois under control. On August 7, 1861, President Lincoln promoted Grant to brigadier general of volunteers. In February 1862 Grant led his troops in the capture of two Confederate installations in Tennessee: Fort Henry and Fort Donelson. At each battle, he demanded "unconditional surrender" from the Confederate enemy, earning himself the nickname of "Unconditional Surrender Grant." These victories, the first notable Union victories of the war, opened Tennessee for Union advances. Grant was promoted to major general.

"Let us have peace."

Ulysses S. Grant, writing in his letter of May 29, 1868, accepting the presidential nomination; it was then adopted as a campaign slogan

The Battle of Shiloh in Tennessee, on April 6 and 7 of 1862, was less successful, though ultimately deemed a Union victory. Grant was aided by General William Tecumseh Sherman, on whom he would come to rely for major advances later in the war. Some blamed Grant for the heavy Union losses at Shiloh, and rumors of his drinking were again rampant, although President Lincoln tersely defended Grant, saying, "I can't spare this man—he fights."

From late 1862 through mid-1863, Grant was involved in the slow movement toward Vicksburg, a crucial position held by the Confederates on the Mississippi River. On July 4, 1863, Grant accomplished a stunning victory with the capture of Vicksburg and the surrender of 30,000 Confederate troops. The Confederate forces were split in two and the Mississippi was effectively in Union hands. Grant had become a national hero in the North.

Grant's next major battle was at Chattanooga, in late 1863, toward which he had been advancing in an effort to relieve Union forces that were penned in by Confederates. He first ordered the storming of Lookout Mountain and then was able to defeat the Confederates at Missionary Ridge. In early 1864 Lincoln summoned Grant to Washington, naming him lieutenant general and commander of the Union forces.

Grant changed his location so he could take personal command of the Army of the Potomac, which he used to relentlessly pursue Lee and the Army of Virginia, engaging them in the battles of the Wilderness, Spotsylvania Court House, Cold Harbor, and Petersburg. At the same time, he had sent General William T. Sherman through the South, where Sherman fought and burned his way across Georgia and captured Atlanta and Savannah. Under Grant's direction, for the first time the separate Union armies worked in concert.

Moving toward Richmond, the Confederate capital, and repeatedly fighting battles with horrific losses to both sides, Grant finally forced Lee to abandon the city, and forced the surrender of Lee and the main Confederate army, in April 1865, at the Appomattox Courthouse. Grant's terms of surrender were generous and intended to prevent Confederate commanders from being tried for treason.

"I felt like anything rather than rejoicing at the downfall of a foe who had fought so long and valiantly, and had suffered so much for a cause, though that cause was, I believe, one of the worst for which a people ever fought, and one for which there was the least excuse."

Ulysses S. Grant, writing about the surrender in 1865 by Robert E. Lee at Appomattox, in *Personal Memoirs of U. S. Grant*, 1885

In 1866 Grant was named General of the Armies, a title given to no other general before him except George Washington. Initially supportive of President Andrew Johnson during Reconstruction, Grant was appointed by Johnson as his secretary of war when Johnson was attempting to oust Edwin M. Stanton from the post. But Congress asserted that Johnson did not have the right to replace Stanton, and Grant returned the office to Stanton, thereby incurring Johnson's wrath. Grant found himself more in sympathy with the Radical Republicans after the incident, and became the party's candidate for president in 1868. He won convincingly, gaining 214 electoral votes to the 80 notched by his opponent, Horatio Seymour of New York.

PRESIDENCY

Grant entered the office of president determined to uphold Reconstruction and implement reform in such areas as civil service. With no political experience, though, he was frequently hampered by his poor choice of cabinet officials and advisors. He appointed former military officers and Julia's relatives; some were merely inexperienced, but others were dishonest. Grant himself was not closely implicated in the many scandals that plagued his administration, but he failed to prevent widespread corruption and to deal with it adequately when it was revealed. The scandals became the enduring legacy of his presidency, and have led many historians to consider him among the worst presidents.

In 1869 a number of gold speculators led by Jay Gould and James Fisk tried to corner the gold market. The president's brother-in-law, Abel Corbin, was brought into the plan; he convinced Grant to appoint General Daniel Butterfield as assistant treasurer of the United States. Butterfield, in turn, let Gould and Fisk know when the government intended to sell gold. Using this information, Gould and Fisk drove the price of gold up. When Grant became suspicious, he ordered the government to release $4 million of gold onto the market, causing the price of gold to drop suddenly and ruining numerous speculators. The day the government gold was released, September 24, 1869, became known as "Black Friday."

A positive event of the Grant presidency was the ratification of the Fifteenth Amendment to the Constitution in 1870; it provided that the right to vote should not be denied on account of "race, color, or previous condition of servitude." While the amendment provided Congress with the power to enforce this amendment, in practice, the right to vote was abridged by a variety of means after Reconstruction ended. Southern governments enacted poll taxes, literacy tests (also popular in the north for their ability to keep immigrants from voting), and grandfather clauses (which exempted anyone whose grandfather had voted—therefore virtually any white voter—from the poll taxes and literacy tests) to restrict the ability of blacks to vote. Violence and intimidation were also used to keep blacks from the polls; not until the Civil Rights Act of 1965 were black voters truly enfranchised.

Another blow to newly emancipated black citizens was the fate of the Freedmen's Bureau. Hampered by inadequate funds, the Freedmen's Bureau was limited by Congress in 1869 to efforts in educating the freedmen. Even that effort was ended in 1870, and though the Bureau continued to work for black veterans, in July 1872, Congress ended the Bureau's existence.

Grant supported the Enforcement Acts, a series of laws designed to crack down on the Ku Klux Klan and protect the voting rights of blacks during the 1872 elections. Grant was elected to a second term in 1872, defeating Horace Greeley, who died between the election and the meeting of the electoral college to cast its votes. Grant's first vice president, Schuyler Colfax, did not seek reelection in time to avoid being replaced on the ticket by Henry Wilson, a Massachusetts senator. Wilson died in 1875, after only two years in office; Colfax went on to be implicated in the Crédit Mobilier scandal.

In 1872 and 1873 stockholders in the Union Pacific Railroad formed a company, Crédit Mobilier of America, which was given contracts to build railroads. Several congressmen were sold or given stock in the company; the same congressmen voted that the company be given subsidies, often far in excess of the actual costs of railroad construction. A congressional investigation led to the censure of two members of the House of Representatives, but a number of other prominent politicians were also implicated, including James Garfield, who denied being involved and who was subsequently elected president in 1880.

"I know of no method to secure the repeal of bad or obnoxious laws so effective as their stringent execution."

Ulysses S. Grant, his first inaugural address, March 4, 1869

In 1875 Secretary of the Treasury Benjamin H. Bristow spearheaded an investigation into the Whiskey Ring scandal, in which whiskey distillers bribed Republican politicians to raise taxes on whiskey; the tax monies were generally kept by the distillers, rather than turned over to the government. More than $3 million was recovered, and 110 people were convicted. The president's private secretary, Orville E. Babcock, was indicted but received a presidential pardon, which led to Grant being linked with the corruption, although he was not directly involved.

Secretary of War William W. Belknap was impeached for having taken bribes for the sale of Native American trading posts; he resigned in March 1876 before being brought to trial and was acquitted when the Senate vote fell short of the necessary two-thirds for conviction.

POST-PRESIDENTIAL CAREER

After retirement, Grant traveled for two years with Julia on a triumphal world tour before settling in New York, where he entered into a brokerage business. Like his previous business careers, this one also failed, leaving him in debt.

At a time when he was battling throat cancer, Grant followed the advice of his friend Mark Twain in writing his *Personal Memoirs*, which he finished days before his death, on July 23, 1885. The publication of this autobiography, still considered among the best-written of books authored by US presidents, provided financial security for his family.

Julia Grant was able to live comfortably for the rest of her life. She attended the dedication,

in 1897, of Grant's Tomb in New York City, and she herself was buried there beside her husband after her death in 1902.

Birthplace: Point Pleasant, OH
Residency: Illinois
Religion: Methodist
Education: US Military Academy, West Point, NY, graduated 1843
Place of Death: Mount McGregor, NY
Burial Site: Grant's Tomb, Riverside Park, New York City, NY
Dates in Office: March 4, 1869–March 3, 1877 (8 years)
Age at Inauguration: 46 years, 311 days

FAMILY

Father: Jesse Root Grant (1794–1873)
Mother: Hannah Simpson Grant (1798–1883)
Siblings: Ulysses was the eldest of six children; his siblings were Samuel Simpson Grant (1825–1861); Clara Rachel Grant (1825–1865); Virginia ("Jenny") Paine Grant (1832–1881); Orvil Lynch Grant (1835–1881); Mary Frances Grant (1839–1898).
Wife: Julia Boggs Dent Grant (1826–1902); married on August 22, 1848, in St. Louis, MO
Children: Frederick Dent Grant (1850–1912); Ulysses ("Buck") Simpson Grant, Jr. (1852–1929); Ellen ("Nellie") Wrenshall Grant (1855–1922); Jesse Root Grant (1858–1934)

CAREER

Private: farmer, real estate agent, clerk at leather shop
Political: president of the United States (1869–1877)
Military: graduated from West Point (1843); commissioned second lieutenant with the Fourth Infantry (1843); served in the Mexican-American War (1846–1848); resigned from the army (1854); volunteered at the outbreak of the Civil War and was appointed colonel of the First Illinois Volunteers (1861); promoted to brigadier general (1861); promoted to major general (1862); fought at Shiloh (April 6–7, 1862); commanded the advance on Vicksburg, from late 1862 until the fall of Vicksburg (July 4, 1863); commanded at the

Battle of Chattanooga (November 23–25, 1863); promoted to lieutenant general (March 9, 1864); assigned to command the armies of the United States (March 12, 1864); commanded at battles of Wilderness, Spotsylvania Court House, Cold Harbor, and Petersburg (May–October 1864); accepted the surrender of the Army of Virginia from General Robert E. Lee (April 9, 1865)

Selected Works: *General Grant's Letters to a Friend, 1861–1880*, with an introduction and notes by James Grant Wilson (New York; AMS Press, 1973); *Grant's Tribute to Lincoln*, compiled and ed. by Charles T. White (Brooklyn, NY, 1932 [reprinted from the *New York Christian Advocate*, 1913]); *The Papers of Ulysses S. Grant*, ed. by John Y. Simon (Carbondale: Southern Illinois University Press, 1967–2003); *Personal Memoirs of U. S. Grant*, with an introduction and notes by James M. McPherson (New York: Penguin Books, 1999); *Ulysses S. Grant, 1822–1885, Chronology, Documents, Bibliographical Aids*, ed. by Philip R. Moran (Dobbs Ferry, NY: Oceana Publications, 1968)

PRESIDENCY

Nomination: 1868: Grant was nominated on the first ballot by the Republican Party at their convention in Chicago on May 20, 1868, and Schuyler Colfax of Indiana was chosen as the vice-presidential candidate.

1872: Grant's nomination for a second term was a foregone conclusion when the Republican Party's convention met in Philadelphia in June of 1872, and Henry Wilson of Massachusetts was chosen to replace Schuyler Colfax as the vice-presidential candidate; a splinter group of the Republican Party met separately and dubbed themselves the Liberal Republican Party, nominating Horace Greeley of New York as their candidate—Greeley was then also endorsed as the Democratic Party's candidate.

Election: elected president on November 3, 1868 reelected president on November 5, 1872

Opponent: 1868: Horatio Seymour, NY, Democratic Party

1872: Horace Greeley, NY, Liberal Republican Party and Democratic Party

Vote Totals: 1868: Grant, 3,013,650 popular, 214 electoral; Seymour, 2,708,744 popular, 80 electoral

1872: Grant, 3,598,235 popular, 286 electoral; Greeley, 2,834,761 popular, 66 electoral [Note: Greeley died after the election but before the electoral votes were cast, so his electoral votes were divided among several men: Thomas Hendricks, IN, 42 votes; B. Gratz Brown, MO, 18 votes; Charles Jenkins, GA, 2 votes; David Davis, IL, 1 vote.]

Inauguration: 1868: March 4, 1869
1872: March 4, 1873

Vice President: Schuyler Colfax, IN (1868–1872); Henry Wilson, MA (1873–1875) [Note: Wilson died in 1875, so Grant had no vice president from 1875–1877.]

CABINET

Secretary of State: Elihu B. Washburne, IL (1869); Hamilton Fish, NY (1869–1877)

Secretary of the Treasury: George S. Boutwell, MA (1869–1873); William A. Richardson, MA (1873–1874); Benjamin H. Bristow, KY (1874–1876); Lot M. Morrill, ME (1876–1877)

Secretary of War: John A. Rawlins, IL (1869); William T. Sherman, OH (1869); William W. Belknap, IA (1869–1876); Alphonso Taft, OH (1876); James D. Cameron, PA (1876–1877)

Attorney General: Ebenezer R. Hoar, MA (1869–1870); Amos T. Akerman, GA (1870–1871); George H. Williams, OR (1871–1875); Edwards Pierrepont, NY (1875–1876); Alphonso Taft, OH (1876–1877)

Postmaster General: John A. J. Creswell, MD (1869–1874); James W. Marshall, VA (1874); Marshall Jewell, CT (1874–1876); James N. Tyner, IN (1876–1877)

Secretary of the Navy: Adolph E. Borie, PA (1869); George M. Robeson, NJ (1869–1877)

Secretary of the Interior: Jacob D. Cox, Jr., OH (1869–1870); Columbus Delano, OH (1870–1875); Zachariah Chandler, MI (1875–1877)

CONGRESS

41st Congress (1869–1871); Speaker of the House: James G. Blaine (ME, Republican)
42nd Congress (1871–1873); Speaker of the House: James G. Blaine (ME, Republican)

43rd Congress (1873–1875); Speaker of the House: James G. Blaine (ME, Republican)
44th Congress (1875–1877); Speaker of the House: Michael C. Kerr (IN, Democrat); Samuel J. Randall (PA, Democrat)

SUPREME COURT APPOINTEES
William Strong, PA; Associate Justice (1870–1880)
Joseph P. Bradley, NJ; Associate Justice (1870–1892)
Ward Hunt, NY; Associate Justice (1873–1882)
Morrison Remick Waite, OH; Chief Justice (1874–1888)

MAJOR EVENTS OF THE GRANT ADMINISTRATION
◆ September 24, 1869, is known as "Black Friday," the day that speculators in gold find their plan to corner the gold market ruined when, at Grant's orders, the government releases $4 million worth of gold onto the market, driving the price down.
◆ In 1869 the Wyoming Territory grants women the right to vote.
◆ The Department of Justice is created by act of Congress, June 22, 1870.
◆ The Fifteenth Amendment to the Constitution is ratified, 1870. The Fifteenth Amendment provides that the right to vote should not be denied because of "race, color, or previous condition of servitude."
◆ The Federal Election Law of 1870, one of the Enforcement Acts, calls for the federal supervision of elections in cities with populations of greater than 20,000; the law is designed to protect black voters in southern cities.
◆ The Treaty of Washington is signed between the United States and Great Britain in 1871; it provides for reparations to the United States for damages caused by British-built ships used by the Confederacy.
◆ Grant signs the act establishing the first national park, Yellowstone, 1872.
◆ The Crédit Mobilier of America scandal, 1872–1873, involves congressmen who held shares in a company that built railroads and who also voted on subsidies for the railroads.

◆ The Panic of 1873 begins with the stock market exchange closing for ten days and results in years of financial depression.
◆ The Whiskey Ring, a group of whiskey distillers who engaged in tax fraud and bribery of politicians, is exposed, 1875.
◆ The Specie Resumption Act, 1875, provided for government redemption of notes in specie (gold) and the reduction of greenbacks in circulation.
◆ Vice President Henry Wilson dies, November 22, 1875.
◆ Grant signs the Civil Rights Act of 1875, which guarantees equality in public places for blacks; the bill will be declared unconstitutional in 1883.
◆ Secretary of War William W. Belknap is impeached and resigns, 1876; he is tried but not convicted of taking bribes for the sale of Native American trading posts.
◆ On June 25, 1876, General George A. Custer and the 265 soldiers under him are defeated and killed by the Sioux tribe under Sitting Bull at Little Big Horn, Montana.
◆ Colorado becomes a state, August 1, 1876.
◆ In January 1877 Congress establishes a commission to determine the results of the contested presidential election of 1876 between Rutherford B. Hayes and Samuel J. Tilden.

MAJOR US AND WORLD EVENTS, 1869–1877
◆ Louisa May Alcott publishes *Little Women*, 1869.
◆ Leo Tolstoy completes *War and Peace*, 1869.
◆ Mark Twain publishes *The Innocents Abroad*, 1869.
◆ Richard Blackmore publishes *Lorna Doone*, 1869.
◆ Dmitri Mendeléev publishes *The Principles of Chemistry*, 1869, with the sixty-nine elements then known arranged in a periodic table of elements.
◆ The first all-professional baseball team in America, the Cincinnati Red Stockings, is formed, 1869.
◆ The transcontinental railroad is completed at Promontory Point, Utah, May 10, 1869.

◆ On January 2, 1870, construction begins on the Brooklyn Bridge.

◆ On January 10, 1870, John D. Rockefeller forms the Standard Oil Company of Ohio.

◆ Napoleon III of France is deposed and the Third Republic of France is formed, 1870.

◆ Heinrich Schliemann begins excavations at the site of ancient Troy, 1870.

◆ The United States Weather Bureau is established, February 9, 1870.

◆ Jules Verne publishes *Twenty Thousand Leagues Under the Sea*, 1870.

◆ The US census shows a population of 39.8 million people, 1870.

◆ On November 10, 1871, Henry Morton Stanley finds Dr. David Livingstone in Africa.

◆ Rome becomes the capital of Italy, 1871.

◆ Giuseppe Verdi's *Aida* premieres in Cairo, 1871.

◆ The Great Chicago Fire nearly destroys Chicago, October 8–11, 1871.

◆ George Eliot publishes *Middlemarch*, 1871.

◆ The National Rifle Association is formed, 1871.

◆ Lewis Carroll publishes *Through the Looking Glass*, 1872.

◆ The *Mary Celeste*, a half-brig ship, is discovered at sea in 1872 but there is no sign of the captain, his family, or the crew of eight. What happened to them remains a mystery.

◆ On August 1, 1873, the first cable car is tested in San Francisco.

◆ Jules Verne publishes *Around the World in Eighty Days*, 1873.

◆ In 1873 Boss Tweed (William Marcy Tweed) is convicted of fraud for his illegal activities relating to Tammany Hall, the center of the Democratic Party's political machine in New York City; Rutherford B. Hayes is instrumental in exposing the corruption.

◆ The Women's Christian Temperance Union is founded in Cleveland, Ohio, November 18–20, 1874.

◆ Thomas Hardy publishes *Far from the Madding Crowd* as a serial, 1874.

◆ The first exhibition of impressionist paintings is held in Paris, 1874.

◆ Lewis Miller and John Heyl Vincent establish the Chautauqua movement in upstate New York, 1874.

◆ Richard Wagner completes his "Ring" cycle, the *Ring of the Nibelung*, 1874.

◆ Leo Tolstoy publishes *Anna Karenina*, 1875.

◆ George Bizet composes *Carmen*, 1875.

◆ Mary Baker Eddy publishes *Science and Health, with Key to the Scriptures*, 1875.

◆ On May 17, 1875, the first Kentucky Derby is run.

◆ Pytor Tchaikovsky composes the ballet *Swan Lake*, 1875–1876.

◆ August Renoir paints *Le Bal au Moulin de la Galette*, 1876.

◆ A Centennial Exposition is held in Philadelphia, 1876.

◆ Mark Twain publishes *The Adventures of Tom Sawyer*, 1876.

◆ Alexander Graham Bell patents the telephone, 1876.

◆ Thomas Edison establishes a research facility at Menlo Park, New Jersey, 1876.

◆ Queen Victoria is given the title "Empress of India," 1877.

FAST FACTS ABOUT ULYSSES S. GRANT

◆ Grant was a noted horseman and gained a reputation as a young man for his ability to break untrained horses.

◆ When Grant was first commissioned after graduating from West Point, he rode proudly into Cincinnati in his new uniform, only to be ridiculed by a small boy and imitated by a drunk. For the rest of his career, he avoided full dress uniforms, often wearing informal clothing with only shoulder straps to show his rank.

◆ Grant's best man and the two ushers at his wedding in 1848 would all, as officers of the Confederacy, surrender to him at Appomattox in 1865.

◆ Although Grant gained the reputation of being a hard drinker, he seems rather to have been a sporadic binge drinker with a low tolerance for alcohol. He drank when he was bored, depressed, or lonely; Julia's presence apparently kept him from the desire to drink. There is no record whatsoever of his being drunk or impaired during military crises or while president.

◆ As an unsuccessful farmer in 1857, Grant pawned his pocket watch to buy Christmas presents for his family.

◆ In 1858 Grant acquired a slave that had belonged to his father-in-law; in early 1859, Grant set the man free.

◆ In December 1862 Grant issued General Orders No. 11, expelling all Jews residing within his district of command, purportedly in an attempt to suppress the trade between Northerners and the Confederacy. The order was revoked after protests were made to the federal government.

◆ When Grant went to the White House to meet Lincoln and receive command of the Union forces in 1864, there were so many people wanting to see him that he had to stand on a chair.

◆ On April 14, 1865, President Lincoln invited General and Mrs. Grant to accompany him and Mrs. Lincoln to the theater that night, but Grant declined because he wished to visit his children. He thereby avoided assassination, as he had been included in the plot formed by John Wilkes Booth and his accomplices.

◆ In 1866 Grant was given the rank of General of the Armies of the United States; he was the first to bear that title since George Washington.

◆ At his first inauguration, Grant refused to ride in the carriage with the outgoing president, Andrew Johnson, who then decided not to attend the inauguration.

◆ Grant's first inaugural parade featured eight military divisions, at that time the largest such group to march in an inaugural parade.

◆ In 1883 Grant was elected president of the National Rifle Association.

◆ Grant wrote his memoirs on the advice of Mark Twain; the book was so successful that it provided for his family for the rest of their lives.

◆ Grant's tomb is the largest mausoleum in North America.

Rutherford B. Hayes

Nickname: The Dark-Horse President, Rud, the Fraudulent President, Rutherford the Rover
Presidency: 19th president, 1877–1881
Party: Republican
Life dates: October 4, 1822–January 17, 1893 (70 years, 105 days)

EARLY LIFE AND EDUCATION

Rutherford Birchard Hayes was born on October 4, 1822, in Delaware, Ohio. At the time of his birth his father, Rutherford Hayes, Jr., a farmer with an interest in a whiskey distillery, had been dead for ten weeks. His mother was Sophia Birchard Hayes, who had moved with her husband from Vermont to Ohio in 1817. Rutherford was the youngest of five children, but by the time he was born his parents had already lost their first son, who died at birth, and a daughter, Sarah Sophia, who died at age four the year before Rutherford was born. When he was two, his nine-year-old brother, Lorenzo, went skating on a mill pond and drowned. Only Rutherford and his sister Fanny grew to maturity. Fanny and Rutherford became very close.

Sophia Hayes's brother, Sardis Birchard, lived with the family for a few years and became a guardian and surrogate father to young Rutherford and Fanny. Sardis, a banker and businessman, helped support the family and encouraged Rutherford's education, and later, his political career.

Rutherford, called "Rud" as a boy, was sickly in his youth, and his mother was inclined to protect him, having lost three of her children. He first attended a local school, then a Methodist seminary in Norwalk, Ohio. He left Ohio in 1837 to attend a private school run by Isaac Webb in Middletown, Connecticut.

In 1838 Rutherford entered Kenyon College in Gambier, Ohio, graduating in 1842 as the class valedictorian. While attending Kenyon, he began a diary that he kept throughout his life. He often spent vacations with his sister Fanny, who had married a jeweler and businessman named William A. Platt and had moved to Columbus, Ohio.

Hayes began reading law at the offices of Sparrow and Matthews in Columbus, but his uncle Sardis thought he should acquire a formal education in the law, and Hayes left for Harvard University in 1843. He graduated from the law school in 1845. While in Boston and later during his law career in Ohio, Hayes often attended public lectures. He heard and admired many of the well-known intellectuals and orators of his day, including John Quincy Adams, Henry Wadsworth Longfellow, Daniel Webster, Ralph Waldo Emerson, and Henry Ward Beecher.

"How strange a scene is this in which we are such shifting figures, pictures, shadows. The mystery of our existence— I have no faith in any attempted explanation of it. It is all dark, unfathomed profound."

Rutherford B. Hayes, diary entry, October 24, 1850, following the death of his cousin, Sarah Wasson

EARLY CAREER

Hayes was admitted to the Ohio bar and began practice in Lower Sandusky, Ohio, where his uncle Sardis lived. It was a small town and did not offer much in the way of a clientele. In 1847 he became ill and traveled for his health; he stayed with a friend in Texas. When he returned to Ohio, he moved to Cincinnati, settling there in 1849 and establishing a much more satisfactory law practice. He argued for the defendants in several well-publicized criminal trials, winning a good reputation for himself. He served as a volunteer attorney for the underground railroad, helping slaves to win their freedom. In December 1853 he formed a law partnership with Richard M. Corwine and William K. Rogers.

Hayes was fond of the company of several young women at this time, and his sister Fanny endeavored to play matchmaker—to no avail. In 1847 Hayes had met Lucy Ware Webb from Chillicothe. Lucy, a college graduate, attracted his attention. They met again in Cincinnati in 1850. In June 1851 he proposed, telling Lucy that he loved her; she responded "I must confess, I like you very well." They were married on December 30, 1852, at Lucy's home. The marriage produced eight children between 1853 and 1873, seven boys and one girl. Three of the boys died in infancy.

MILITARY AND POLITICAL CAREER

Hayes helped found the Republican Party in Ohio. From 1858 to 1861, he was the city solicitor of Cincinnati. In April 1861 he lost his bid for reelection as city solicitor, but by the end of the month he had responded to President Lincoln's call for military service volunteers. He joined the Twenty-third Ohio Volunteer Infantry and was given a major's commission. From 1861 to 1865, he served as an officer in the Union Army and was wounded five times, once seriously at the Battle of South Mountain in 1862. A gifted leader who remembered his military service with pride for the rest of his life, he finished the war with the elevated rank of major general. While still in the army, he was nominated for the US House of Representatives. Hayes declared his duty to the army and refused to campaign, but he was elected anyway.

"An officer fit for duty who at this crisis would abandon his post to electioneer for a seat in Congress ought to be scalped. You may be perfectly sure I shall do no such thing."

Colonel Rutherford B. Hayes in 1864, on being told he had been nominated for a seat in the US House of Representatives; he did not campaign but was elected

The war ended prior to the start of his term, and he was able to serve a full term as a US congressman, from 1865 to 1867, during which time he aligned himself with the Radical Republicans. He urged (unsuccessfully) that the Fourteenth Amendment provide that literacy tests be given to all voters, black and white. He also sponsored a bill that would provide funds for the expansion and modernization of the Library of Congress.

Resigning from Congress to run for governor of Ohio, Hayes won the election and served as governor from 1868 to 1872. (He would serve again as governor from 1876 to 1877.) With little actual power, Hayes concentrated on reforms in hospitals, assistance for the poor, prisons, and the school system—reforms that he would advocate throughout his life. He helped to found the Ohio Agricultural and Mechanical College, a land-grant agricultural college that later became Ohio State University. Hayes urged the ratification of the Fifteenth Amendment to the Constitution, which protected the voting rights of African Americans. As the wife of the governor, Lucy Hayes shared many of her husband's interests. She visited hospitals, mental institutions, and orphanages. She also helped to found an orphanage in Columbus.

"No person connected with me by blood or marriage will be appointed to office."

Rutherford B. Hayes, diary entry, March 24, 1877, reflecting on the charges of nepotism leveled against his predecessor, Ulysses S. Grant

---

After 1872 Hayes had retired to the estate he had inherited from his uncle, but was urged by the Republican Party to run for governor again in 1875. He urged a "sound money" policy, which would give paper money a single and stable standard of value, in opposition to the Democratic Party's advocacy of the greenback plan, which called for the printing of new paper money. In 1875 he defeated his opponent in the gubernatorial race, William Allen, and won a national reputation.

Having proven that he could win in close elections, Hayes was attractive to Republican Party organizers seeking a presidential candidate for 1876. He had not been tainted by any of the scandals of the Grant administration. A number of other candidates vied for the nomination, but on the seventh ballot, Hayes was chosen as his party's candidate. Hayes's opponent was Samuel Tilden, the governor of New York.

Until 2000, no presidential election in US history was as disputed as the election of 1876. At first it appeared that Tilden had won—and he did have a greater number of popular votes—but there were charges that the Democrats had stuffed ballot boxes and prevented blacks from voting in southern states. Three states—Louisiana, South Carolina, and Florida—submitted two sets of electoral votes. Congress selected a fifteen-member electoral commission, as follows: five members from the Senate, five members from the House, and five members from the Supreme Court. The commission had seven Democrats and seven Republicans (including James Garfield), as well as one independent member, Justice David Davis. Davis was disqualified after being elected a Democratic senator from Illinois, and his Republican replacement, Joseph Bradley, provided the vote needed to elect Hayes. By one electoral vote, Hayes became president, but he became tagged with the nickname "The Fraudulent President," and his opponents never stopped trying to have him removed from office during his presidency.

PRESIDENCY

Although he was charged with being favorable towards the southern states, Hayes followed through with a process that had begun under President Grant—that of withdrawing federal troops from southern states and ending Reconstruction. Hayes was later criticized for the troop withdrawal and for having trusted in southern promises to protect the voting rights of African Americans (in general, a misplaced trust). He was also criticized by his opponents when he appointed a Democratic southerner and former Confederate, David Key, as his postmaster general.

In July 1877 a railroad strike began in West Virginia, carried out by railroad workers after wages and the size of the workforce had been cut. The strike soon spread to Baltimore and Pittsburgh, and then to other cities. State militias were generally unable to impose order. They were given orders to fire into the crowds, but rarely acted on such orders; still, in some cities there were people who were inevitably killed in the chaos of the protests. Hayes dispatched federal troops at the request of the governor of West Virginia, and gradually, the federal troops sent from place to place imposed order without bloodshed. Despite the eventual defeat of the strikers, the incident gave added impetus to the labor movement and efforts to unionize workers.

> "We have got rid of the fetish of the divine right of kings, and that slavery is of divine origin and authority. But the divine right of property has taken its place. The tendency plainly is towards . . . 'a government of the rich, by the rich, and for the rich.'"
>
> Rutherford B. Hayes, diary entry, March 1, 1890

Hayes was interested in civil service reform and issued an executive order that forbade federal employees to take part in political work. Their rights to vote, of course, were protected, but active work on campaigns and in party organizations was forbidden. He urged that civil service appointments be made on the basis of examinations and merit, rather than political patronage. He also demonstrated his conviction that the president, and not Congress, had the right to make these appointments when he removed Chester A. Arthur, the port collector of the New York customhouse, and his subordinate, Alonzo B. Cornell, from office, owing to their involvement with New York Senator Roscoe Conkling's political machine, an organization of politicians who did favors for citizens in return for votes. Ironically, Arthur would later become president and also a proponent of civil service reform. Hayes appointed Theodore Roosevelt, father of the future president, as the new port collector, and he also nominated a replacement for Cornell, but under Conkling's influence, the two appointments were blocked by Congress. The following year, even though the election of 1878 had left both houses of Congress with a Democratic majority, Hayes announced the appointments of two other men, and the appointments were confirmed by Congress. It was a notable victory for Hayes and for presidential power.

Hayes vetoed a Chinese exclusion bill because he thought it violated the Burlingame Treaty of 1868, which permitted the free immigration of Chinese to America, but there was considerable opposition to Chinese immigration in the United States, particularly in California, where the supply of cheap Chinese labor was resented by the growing American population. Hayes subsequently dealt with the Chinese government so that the United States could regulate the number of Chinese laborers immigrating to the country.

In May 1878 Democrats in the House of Representatives set in motion an investigation of the election of 1876, which Hayes correctly interpreted as an attempt to overturn the election result and to replace him in the White House. However, the investigation's findings confirmed the original decision of the electoral commission.

Another victory for Hayes came with the resumption of the specie (mainly gold) backing of paper currency, which he had urged in opposition to the greenback faction, whose members wanted to greatly increase the number of greenbacks in currency. Hayes saw the latter proposition as inflationary, but his fiscally conservative policies helped to put the country on a sounder financial footing, and the overall economy improved.

Hayes used his veto powers repeatedly when the appropriations bill came before him in 1879, as it did not include funding for the monitoring of polls by the army, a necessary step for the protection of the voting rights of black voters in the South.

In December 1879 the renowned French builder of the Suez Canal, Ferdinand de Lesseps, visited the United States to discuss his hopes for building a similar canal in Central America. In March 1880 Hayes issued a special message to the Senate, in which he reiterated his conviction that any canal in Central America must be under the control of the United States.

Lucy Hayes was a temperance advocate who did not serve alcohol in the White House. Many admired her for this stand, as the movement was popular in America, but critics dubbed her "Lemonade Lucy." She was nonetheless a popular hostess and first lady, admired for her cheerful, even disposition and her lively intellect.

Post-Presidential Career

Hayes had announced that he would not try for a second term at the beginning of his presidency, and remained true to his word. Lucy and Rutherford Hayes retired to their estate, Spiegel Grove, in Fremont, Ohio. In retirement, Hayes worked for a number of liberal causes, including prison reform, aid to blacks, and public education. He also opposed the death penalty.

Lucy Hayes died on June 25, 1889, and was deeply missed by her husband. Their daughter, Fanny Hayes, became her father's companion until his death of a heart attack on January 17, 1893, at Spiegel Grove. President-elect Cleveland and the governor of Ohio, William McKinley, both attended his funeral. Despite the controversy that surrounded his election, Hayes has generally been viewed favorably by posterity, not only for his abilities as president but for his noble character.

Birthplace: Delaware, OH
Residency: Ohio
Religion: unaffiliated, but attended Methodist Church
Education: Kenyon College, Gambier, OH, graduated 1842; Harvard Law School, graduated 1845
Place of Death: Spiegel Grove, Fremont, OH
Burial Site: Spiegel Grove State Park, Fremont, OH
Dates in Office: March 4, 1877–March 3, 1881 (4 years)
Age at Inauguration: 54 years, 151 days

FAMILY

Father: Rutherford Hayes (1787–1822)
Mother: Sophia Birchard Hayes (1792–1866)
Siblings: Rutherford was the fifth of five children; his siblings were an infant boy (1814; died at birth); Lorenzo Hayes (1815–1825); Sarah Sophia Hayes (1817–1821); Fanny Arabella Hayes (1820–1856).
Wife: Lucy Ware Webb (1831–1889), married on December 30, 1852, in Cincinnati, OH
Children: Birchard ("Birch") Austin Hayes (1853–1926); James Webb Cook Hayes (1856–1934); Rutherford ("Ruddy") Platt Hayes (1858–1927); Joseph Thompson Hayes (1861–1863); George Crook Hayes (1864–1866); Frances ("Fanny") Hayes (1867–1950); Scott Russell Hayes (1871–1923); Manning Force Hayes (1873–1874)

CAREER

Private: lawyer
Political: Member of the US House of Representatives (1865–1867); governor of Ohio (1868–1872; 1876–1877); president of the United States (1877–1881)
Military: during the Civil War, appointed by the governor of Ohio as a brevet major of a volunteer regiment, the Twenty-third Ohio Infantry (June 1861); appointed a judge advocate (September 1861); promoted to lieutenant colonel (October 1861); fought at Pearisburg, where he was slightly wounded (May 10, 1862); fought at South Mountain, where he was seriously wounded (September 14, 1862); promoted to colonel (October 1862); fought at Cloyd's Mountain (May 9, 1864), Winchester (September 19, 1864), Fishers Hill (September 21–22, 1864), and Cedar Creek (October 18, 1864); promoted to brigadier general of volunteers (November 1864) and brevetted major general of volunteers (March 1865)
Selected Works: *Diary and Letters of Rutherford Birchard Hayes* (Columbus, OH: The Ohio State Archaeological and Historical Society, 1922–1926); *Hayes: The Diary of a President, 1875–1881*, ed. by T. Harry Williams (New York: D. McKay Company, 1964); *Rutherford B. Hayes, 1822–1893, Chronology, Documents, Bibliographical Aids*, ed.

by Arthur Bishop (Dobbs Ferry, NY: Oceana Publications, 1969); *The Rutherford B. Hayes Papers*, in microfilm (Fremont, OH: Rutherford B. Hayes Presidential Center)

PRESIDENCY

Nomination: At the Republican Party's convention in Cincinnati in June of 1876, other contenders were James G. Blaine, Roscoe Conkling, Benjamin H. Bristow, and Oliver P. Morton. Hayes won the nomination on the seventh ballot; Representative William A. Wheeler of New York was chosen as the vice presidential candidate.

Election: elected president on November 7, 1876 [Although Tilden won the greater number of popular votes, there were twenty disputed electoral college votes that were decided by an electoral commission appointed by Congress. The election was not decided until the week before the inauguration; by a vote of eight to seven, the commission gave the disputed votes to Hayes.]

Opponent: Samuel J. Tilden, NY, Democratic Party

Vote Totals: Hayes, 4,036,572 popular, 185 electoral; Tilden, 4,284,020 popular, 184 electoral

Inauguration: March 5, 1877 [Note: The inauguration was on Monday, March 5, because March 4 was a Sunday, but Hayes took the oath of office at the White House on Sunday and again at the Capitol on Monday, thus avoiding a day in which there would have been no president.]

Vice President: William A. Wheeler, NY (1877–1881)

CABINET

Secretary of State: William M. Evarts, NY (1877–1881)

Secretary of the Treasury: John Sherman, OH (1877–1881)

Secretary of War: George W. McCrary, IA (1877–1879); Alexander Ramsey, MN (1879–1881)

Attorney General: Charles Devens, MA (1877–1881)

Postmaster General: David M. Key, TN (1877–1880); Horace Maynard, TN (1880–1881)

Secretary of the Navy: Richard W. Thompson, IN (1877–1880); Nathan Goff, Jr., WV (1881)

Secretary of the Interior: Carl Schurz, MO (1877–1881)

CONGRESS

45th Congress (1877–1879); Speaker of the House: Samuel J. Randall (PA, Democrat)

46th Congress (1879–1881); Speaker of the House: Samuel J. Randall (PA, Democrat)

SUPREME COURT APPOINTEES

John Marshall Harlan, KY; Associate Justice (1877–1911)

William Burnham Woods, GA; Associate Justice (1881–1887)

MAJOR EVENTS OF THE HAYES ADMINISTRATION

◆ The Compromise of 1877 is an agreement arranged by Republican and Democratic politicians whereby the South agrees to accept Hayes as president in return for concessions, including the removal of federal troops from southern states, the appointment of at least one southern Democrat to Hayes's cabinet, and the construction of a transcontinental railroad in the South.

◆ Federal troops withdraw from southern states, ending Reconstruction, 1877.

◆ The Desert Land Act of 1877 offers 640 acres of land at $.25 an acre to anyone who will settle the land and irrigate it within three years of settlement.

◆ In 1877 Hayes appoints Frederick Douglass as marshal of Washington, DC.

◆ In 1877 Chief Joseph leads the Nez Percé tribe in a running battle against US army forces over 1,600 miles of northwestern United States territory. When finally defeated, the Nez Percé were removed to a reservation in Native American Territory.

◆ Hayes sends troops to the Mexican border in June 1877 in an attempt to control the bandits operating there; Mexican President

Diaz sends troops to the border in protest against US incursions, but both sides decide to seek a peaceful settlement.

◆ In June 1877 Hayes issues an Executive Order forbidding federal employees from political involvement in an effort to end civil service corruption.

◆ Railroad workers strike and clash with federal troops, 1877.

◆ In September 1877 Hayes replaces the Collector of the Port of New York, Chester A. Arthur, and two other port employees, because of their involvement with New York Senator Roscoe Conkling's political machine. When Congress reconvenes, his appointments are blocked.

◆ A treaty is signed between the United States and Samoa, January 1878, allowing the United States to establish a naval station at Pago Pago and promising US military protection if Samoa is attacked.

◆ The Bland-Allison Silver Purchase Act passes over Hayes's veto, February 1878. The act provides for the free coinage of silver.

◆ The Timber and Stone Act of 1878 provides for the sale of western land deemed unfit for farming but fit for timbering and mining in 160-acre parcels at $2.50 per acre.

◆ Hayes repeatedly vetoes appropriations bills, 1879.

◆ A treaty between the United States and China, 1880, gives the United States authority to limit but not prohibit Chinese immigration and gives Chinese in the United States protection as citizens of a country enjoying most favored nation status.

MAJOR US AND WORLD EVENTS, 1877–1881

◆ Russia declares war on the Ottoman Empire, 1877.

◆ Porfirio Diaz becomes president of Mexico and retains power until 1911.

◆ The first Westminster Dog Show is held in Gilmore's Garden (later renamed Madison Square Garden), 1877; more than a thousand dogs compete.

◆ Henry Ossian Flipper becomes the first African American to graduate from the US military academy at West Point, 1877.

◆ The first Wimbledon lawn tennis championships are held, July 1877.

◆ Franz Schubert's *Second Symphony in B* premieres, October 1877.

◆ Johannes Brahms's *Second Symphony in D* premieres, December 1877.

◆ Thomas Edison patents a "talking machine"—a phonograph—in 1878.

◆ Greece declares war on Turkey, 1878.

◆ Gilbert and Sullivan's *H.M.S. Pinafore* premieres, 1878.

◆ The American Bar Association is founded, 1878.

◆ The artificial sweetener saccharin is discovered by Constantine Fahlberg, 1879.

◆ Henry James publishes *Daisy Miller*, 1879.

◆ Henrik Ibsen's *A Doll's House* is first produced, 1879.

◆ The Anglo-Zulu War, 1879, ends the Zulu nation; the British split formerly united Zulu lands among many subject chiefs.

◆ In 1879 Thomas Edison invents the first practical incandescent light bulb.

◆ Women lawyers are authorized by Congress to practice before the US Supreme Court, 1879.

◆ Frank Woolworth opens his first 5 and 10 cent store, April 1879.

◆ Gilbert and Sullivan's *The Pirates of Penzance* premieres, 1879.

◆ The cornerstone is laid for Iolani Palace in Hawaii, 1879.

◆ Fyodor Dostoevsky publishes *The Brothers Karamazov*, 1879–1880.

◆ August Rodin's sculpture *The Thinker* is cast, 1880.

◆ Pyotr Tchaikovsky composes the *1812 Overture*, 1880.

◆ Jacques Offenbach's *Les Contes d'Hoffman* (*Tales of Hoffman*) premieres, February 1880.

◆ The 1880 census gives the US population as 50 million.

◆ Cleopatra's Needle, an Egyptian obelisk, is erected in Central Park, 1881; its twin had been erected in London in 1879.

FAST FACTS ABOUT
RUTHERFORD B. HAYES

◆ Hayes was the first president to graduate from a formal law school.

◆ Hayes became president by a margin of one electoral vote.

◆ During the Civil War, future president William McKinley served under Hayes and was appointed as his quartermaster.

◆ Of the five future presidents who served in the Civil War, Hayes was the only one to be wounded.

◆ Hayes was the first president to visit the West Coast, which he did in 1880.

◆ During Hayes's presidency, the First Family usually spent evenings singing gospel hymns; they were often joined by the vice president and some cabinet members.

◆ When Hayes had the house at Spiegel Grove built, he said he wanted "a verandah with a house attached."

◆ Lucy Hayes was the first first lady to have a college degree; she graduated from Wesleyan Female College in Cincinnati, Ohio, in 1850.

◆ Lucy Hayes was a temperance advocate (although it was her husband who decided they should not serve alcohol in the White House) and gained the nickname "Lemonade Lucy" as a result.

◆ Lucy Hayes had greenhouses built at the White House because she loved to garden.

◆ During the Hayes presidency, the first telephone was installed in the White House— by Alexander Graham Bell.

◆ Lucy and Rutherford Hayes held the first Easter egg hunt on the White House lawn in 1877.

◆ For their 25th wedding anniversary, Lucy and Rutherford renewed their wedding vows at the White House and held a grand entertainment for the event.

James A. Garfield

Nickname: none
Presidency: 20th president, 1881
Party: Republican
Life dates: November 19, 1831–September 19, 1881 (49 years, 304 days)

EARLY LIFE AND EDUCATION

James Abram Garfield was born on November 19, 1831, in a log cabin in Orange, a village in Cuyahoga County, Ohio, to Eliza Ballou Garfield and Abraham (called Abram) Garfield, both of whom could trace their heritage back to seventeenth-century settlers in America. Eliza and Abram had moved to Ohio from New England in 1830. Although his parents had five children, at the time of James's birth, he was the youngest of four; he had two sisters and a brother (another brother had died, at age three, before James was born). In 1833 two years after James's birth, Abram Garfield died of pneumonia. Eliza sold some land and retained thirty acres, and the family, though poor, survived and stayed together, with Eliza working as a seamstress to supplement the income from the farm.

It was hoped that James, the youngest (and a recognizably intelligent child), would receive an education. He attended local schools, but when he was seventeen he wanted to leave home and become a sailor. He fell in with a cousin who was a canal-boat captain and who offered him a job driving the horses along the tow path next to the Ohio Canal. James held this job for only about six weeks, although the episode was later seized upon by biographers (and often overstated) as evidence of his humble start in life. But in October 1848 James fell ill with a fever and returned home to be nursed back to health by his mother. The experience apparently made him more amenable to the idea of continuing his education, and he enrolled in Geauga Academy in Chester, Ohio, in March 1849.

Following in his parents' footsteps, James converted to the Disciples of Christ, and was baptized by immersion in March 1850. He greatly admired the leader of the Disciples, Alexander Campbell. The sect believed in adult baptism and accepted the Bible as the only revelation of divine will. Campbell was the founder of Bethany College in Bethany, Virginia, which James briefly considered attending.

In the fall of 1851, James entered the Western Reserve Eclectic Institute in Hiram, Ohio, to continue his education. After the first term, he spent part of his time teaching elementary students, while continuing his own studies and reading classic literature. He also became accustomed to speaking publicly as a volunteer preacher for the Disciples of Christ.

At around that same time, James began courting a young woman, but a short time later came to realize that he did not love her and did not wish to marry her. He wrote to her explaining that he wished to discontinue the relationship. The woman's family, however, was very angry about his behavior, having considered the two to be engaged. Shortly thereafter, Garfield visited Bethany College, with hopes of continuing his education there, but he found Bethany to be disappointing and he disagreed with the regional population's widespread acceptance of slavery. He returned to Hiram and began to renew his acquaintance with Lucretia (nicknamed "Crete") Rudolph, with whom he had studied at Geauga Academy. Garfield was wary after his earlier romantic experience and decided to wait before entering into a formal engagement.

> **"The chief duty of government is to keep the peace and stand out of the sunshine of the people."**
>
> James Garfield, December 14, 1869

In 1854 he left Hiram for Williams College in Williamstown, Massachusetts. Garfield was influenced by the president of Williams, Mark Hopkins, who held the chair position for moral and intellectual philosophy and also served as the pastor of the college church. In addition to classics, Garfield studied mechanics, astronomy, political economy, chemistry, German, philosophy, logic, theology, and metaphysics. When he graduated in 1856, he was second in his class.

EARLY CAREER

After finishing his studies at Williams, Garfield returned to Hiram to teach at the Eclectic Institute; he also resumed preaching. After he had been home for about a year, Garfield was offered the presidency of the Institute in 1857, and served in that capacity until 1861. He also studied law during this period and was admitted to the Ohio bar in 1861.

In 1858 Garfield finally made up his mind to become engaged to Lucretia Rudolph. They were married in Hiram, on November 11, 1858. Their first child, a daughter named Eliza, was born in 1860. In 1859 Garfield was elected to the Ohio state legislature. While in the legislature, he spoke out against slavery, as the great national crisis gathered momentum and the nation was hurtling toward Lincoln's election and the outbreak of the Civil War. Garfield campaigned for Lincoln and argued against secession. After Fort Sumter had been fired on by Confederate troops, he was convinced that the North must fight.

MILITARY EXPERIENCE

In 1861 Garfield helped to organize the Forty-second Ohio Infantry. He was promoted from lieutenant colonel to full colonel almost immediately. He drilled his regiment thoroughly and was placed under the command of General Don Carlos Buell in Kentucky, who rewarded him with the command of a brigade.

> **"Remember that the genius of success is still the genius of labor. If hard work is not another name for talent, is the best possible substitute for it."**
>
> James Garfield, speech at Hiram, Ohio, June 14, 1867

At the Battle of Middle Creek on January 10, 1862, Garfield's forces, although greatly outnumbered and outgunned (having no cannon, compared to the enemy's twelve), held the Confederate troops until reinforcements arrived; they then defeated the Confederates, thus gaining control of eastern Kentucky. Garfield was promoted to brigadier general; his success, which was in contrast to the many early losses of the Union troops, made him famous. He fought at Shiloh and took part in rebuilding railroad bridges and fortifications. After becoming ill in 1862, he spent two months at home recovering. In June 1862 he was placed in charge of a court martial.

"The sin of slavery is one of which it may be said that without the shedding of blood there is no remission."

James Garfield, diary entry,
June 8, 1861

Garfield was asked by friends if he would object to being nominated for the US House of Representatives. He said that he would not, and was elected to that legislative body in the fall of 1862. Returning to active military duty in February 1863, he became chief of staff to Major General William S. Rosecrans. He fought at the Battle of Chickamauga in September 1863, and demonstrated bravery under fire that led to his promotion to major general. He then resigned in December 1863 to take up his duties in the US House of Representatives.

Lucretia and James did not initially enjoy a close relationship. He wondered whether he had made a mistake in marrying, and she noted that they spent very little time together. But shared troubles, such as his illness in 1862, during which she nursed him, and the death of their daughter Eliza at age three in 1863, brought them closer together.

POLITICAL CAREER

Joining the Radical Republicans in Congress, Garfield was respected for his expertise in military matters. He also served on the Ways and Means Committee. Garfield supported a return to the use of specie for government payments, having conducted a study of financial and economic matters and becoming convinced that payments in specie, as well as the payment of all war debts, were necessary for the country. When a new committee on banking and currency was created, he became its chairman.

An opponent of President Andrew Johnson on the subject of Reconstruction, he voted for his impeachment when Johnson was tried in Congress. Garfield supported Ulysses S. Grant for president in 1868 and 1872. In 1872 Garfield was implicated in the Crédit Mobilier scandal, though there was little evidence to connect him to it. A stock dividend of $329 was the tainted profit he was accused of making; the number was later used to taunt him during the presidential election of 1880.

In the disputed presidential election of 1876, Garfield was one of the members of the election commission that had been chosen to decide the election outcome. (Rutherford B. Hayes was declared the winner.) While President Hayes was at odds with the Democratic-dominated Congress over the appropriations bill in 1879, Garfield objected to the amendments being proposed by Democrats that would limit funds for the monitoring of elections by federal troops. He argued that these amendments were an attack on the Constitution because they would interfere with free elections.

In January 1880 Garfield was elected to the US Senate by the Ohio legislature.

There was a considerable movement within the 1880 Republican national convention held in Chicago to put Ulysses S. Grant forward to run for a third term in office. The faction in favor of this, headed by the powerful New York Senator Roscoe Conkling, was known as the Stalwarts. But there were others adamantly opposed to the idea of a third term for Grant. Candidates for the nomination included Treasury Secretary John Sherman of Ohio, the brother of General William Tecumseh Sherman, and Senator James Blaine of Maine, the Speaker of the House. After five days and many ballots, no one candidate had a majority. On the sixth day, Garfield received sixteen votes (from Wisconsin) on the thirty-fourth ballot. Garfield was chosen on the thirty-sixth ballot as the candidate—over his protests, as he had promised his support to Sherman. To appease the Stalwarts, Chester A. Arthur of New York, who belonged to Conkling's political circle, was selected as the vice-presidential candidate.

PRESIDENCY

Garfield continued to engage in the struggle for power with New York Senator Roscoe Conkling begun by President Hayes. Garfield's cabinet nominations were sent to the Senate for confirmation, leading to a Democratic filibuster. Conkling was incensed that Garfield had nominated Thomas James of New York for the position of postmaster general, believing that a more important cabinet post, such as secretary of the treasury, should be given to a prominent New Yorker. In addition, Garfield nominated William H. Robertson for the position of collector of the port of New York. The result of the Senate filibuster in May 1881 was that even the Republicans, who objected to some of the nominations, agreed to let the confirmation process wait until sessions of Congress resumed in December. Garfield countered by withdrawing all the names he had placed in nomination except that of Robertson, which secured the approval of the Republicans in the Senate. Conkling resigned from the Senate and took with him the junior senator from New York, Thomas C. Platt, in protest.

"The business of the country is like the level of the ocean, from which all measurements are made of heights and depths."

James Garfield, speech to the House of Representatives, January 7, 1870

On July 2, 1881, with the economy improving and the exercise of executive power becoming easier for Garfield, he was shot while waiting for a train in Washington's Baltimore and Potomac train station. The gunman was Charles Guiteau, a mentally disturbed man who had sought the ambassadorship to France and been denied; he apparently thought God had commanded him to murder Garfield. One bullet grazed Garfield's arm and another lodged in his torso. Garfield was taken to the White House, where several doctors tried (unsuccessfully) to locate the bullet, and in so doing generated a much larger wound and a serious infection. At times he seemed to improve, but he suffered from the summer heat and was moved to Elberon, New Jersey, where he would be able to take advantage of the sea breezes. Garfield subsequently suffered a massive heart attack and finally died in Elberon, on September 19, 1881.

Like Lincoln before him, Garfield lay in state in the Capitol's rotunda before being placed on a train that would make its way to Cleveland, Ohio, past thousands of mourning citizens, to be buried at Lakeview Cemetery.

On June 30, 1882, Guiteau was hanged for assassinating the president.

Lucretia Garfield outlived her husband by thirty-six years. She lived quietly in Mentor, Ohio, in the family home of "Lawnfield," and eventually built a house in Pasadena, California, where she died on March 14, 1918.

Birthplace: Orange Township, Cuyahoga County, OH
Residency: Ohio
Religion: Disciples of Christ
Education: Western Reserve Eclectic Institute (now Hiram College); Williams College, Williamstown, MA, graduated 1856
Place of Death: Elberon, NJ
Burial Site: Lake View Cemetery, Cleveland, OH
Dates in Office: March 4, 1881–September 19, 1881 (199 days)
Age at Inauguration: 49 years, 105 days

FAMILY

Father: Abraham (Abram) Garfield (1799–1833)
Mother: Eliza Ballou Garfield (1801–1888)
Siblings: James was the fifth of five children; his siblings were Mehitable ("Hitty") Garfield (1821–? [but married in 1837]); Thomas Garfield (1822–1910); Mary Garfield (1824–1884); and James Ballou Garfield (1826–1829).
Wife: Lucretia Rudolph Garfield (1832–1918), married November 11, 1858, at Hiram, OH
Children: Eliza Arabella Garfield (1860–1863); Harry Augustus Garfield (1863–1942); James

Rudolph Garfield (1865–1950); Mary Garfield (1867–1947); Irvin McDowell Garfield (1870–1951); Abram Garfield (1872–1958); Edward Garfield (1874–1876)

CAREER
Private: teacher, ordained minister, college president, lawyer
Political: Member of the OH Senate (1859–1861); member of the US House of Representatives, where he acted as chair of the Banking and Currency Committee, the Military Affairs Committee, and the Appropriations Committee, and as a member of the Ways and Means Committee (1863–1880); member of the US Senate (1880); president of the United States of America (1881)
Military: Civil War: helped to organize the Forty-second Ohio Infantry (1861); promoted from lieutenant to lieutenant colonel; defeated Confederates at the Battle of Middle Creek (January 1862), thus gaining control of eastern Kentucky; promoted to major general; fought at the Battle of Chickamauga (September 1863); appointed chief of staff to Major General William S. Rosecrans; resigned in December of 1863
Selected Works: *Crete and James: Personal Letters of Lucretia and James Garfield*, ed. by John Shaw (East Lansing: Michigan State University Press, 1994); *The Diary of James A. Garfield*, ed. with an introduction by Harry James Brown and Frederick D. Williams (East Lansing: Michigan State University, 1967–1981); *The Wild Life of the Army: Civil War Letters of James A. Garfield*, ed. with an introduction by Frederick D. Williams (East Lansing: Michigan State University Press, 1964); *The Works of James Abram Garfield*, ed. by Burke A. Hinsdale (Freeport, NY: Books for Libraries Press, 1970)

PRESIDENCY
Nomination: At the Republican convention in Chicago, Illinois, in June 1880, Garfield supported and spoke in favor of John Sherman of Ohio, one of the leading candidates at the start of the convention; other candidates were former President Grant, who wished to run for a third term, and James Blaine of Maine. The

convention was deadlocked for thirty-three ballots; Garfield had received a couple of votes on each ballot as a mark of respect, but Wisconsin threw its support to Garfield on the thirty-fourth ballot and he was then nominated on the thirty-sixth ballot. Chester A. Arthur of New York was nominated as the vice-presidential candidate.
Election: elected president on November 2, 1880
Opponent: Winfield S. Hancock, NY, Democrat
Vote Totals: 1880: Garfield, 4,453,295 popular, 214 electoral; Hancock, 4,414,082 popular, 155 electoral
Inauguration: March 4, 1881
Vice President: Chester Alan Arthur, NY (1881)

CABINET
Secretary of State: James G. Blaine, ME (1881)
Secretary of the Treasury: William Windom, MN (1881)
Secretary of War: Robert Todd Lincoln, IL (1881)
Attorney General: Isaac Wayne MacVeagh, PA (1881)
Postmaster General: Thomas L. James, NY (1881)
Secretary of the Navy: William H. Hunt, LA (1881)
Secretary of the Interior: Samuel J. Kirkwood, IA (1881)

CONGRESS
Although a special session of the Senate was called for the 47th Congress (1881–1883), the House did not meet during Garfield's term of office [Speaker of the House: J. Warren Keifer (OH, Republican)].

SUPREME COURT APPOINTEES
Stanley Matthews, OH; Associate Justice (1881–1889)

MAJOR EVENTS OF THE GARFIELD ADMINISTRATION
◆ Garfield removes the collector of the port of New York, E. A. Merritt, and submits W. H. Robertson to the Senate as his candidate,

signaling a continuation of the struggle between the presidency and Conkling over federal appointments.

❖ In May 1881 Frederick Douglass is appointed the recorder of deeds for Washington, DC.

❖ A letter is published exposing the Star Route frauds, a scheme to defraud the US Post Office; it attempts unsuccessfully to implicate Garfield.

❖ Prompted by Garfield's secretary of state, James Blaine, the United States attempts to improve its relations with the countries of Latin America.

❖ On July 2, 1881, the president is shot in a Washington train station by Charles Guiteau, a mentally disturbed man who had unsuccessfully sought to be appointed to office.

❖ Chief Sitting Bull surrenders to federal troops, July 1881.

❖ On September 19, 1881, President Garfield dies.

MAJOR US AND WORLD EVENTS, 1881

❖ In 1881 P. T. Barnum goes into partnership with James A. Bailey and James Hutchinson, creating "P. T. Barnum's Greatest Show on Earth, and the Great London Circus, Sanger's Royal British Menagerie, and the Great International Allied Shows United," the precursor of "Ringling Brothers and Barnum & Bailey's Circus."

❖ In March 1881 the Boers and the British sign a peace treaty, ending the first Boer War.

❖ In April 1881 French troops occupy Algeria and Tunisia.

❖ Clara Barton founds the American Red Cross on May 21, 1881.

❖ Tuskegee Normal and Industrial Institute is founded by Booker T. Washington, July 4, 1881, in Tuskegee, AL.

❖ The first US men's single tennis

championships are held in Newport, RI, at the end of August and beginning of September 1881.

FAST FACTS ABOUT
JAMES ABRAM GARFIELD

❖ Garfield was born in a log cabin.

❖ Garfield briefly worked on a canal boat, a fact later used by campaign biographers to great effect.

❖ Garfield was an ordained minister of the Disciples of Christ.

❖ During a seven-year period, Garfield was the president of a college, a state senator, a major general in the Union army, and a member of the US House of Representatives.

❖ Garfield was the first left-handed president.

❖ Lucretia Randolph was in Garfield's Greek class; they began to correspond about classical languages and gradually grew more intimate.

❖ Lucretia Garfield was somewhat ahead of her time; in a college essay she asked whether it was equitable for a woman teacher to be paid less than a male teacher if she teaches as well as he does.

❖ At the parade for Garfield's inauguration and at the inaugural ball, John Philip Sousa led the Marine Corps band. The inaugural ball was held at the National Museum of the Smithsonian Institution (the building is now the Arts and Industries Building).

❖ Before shooting Garfield, his assassin Charles Guiteau reportedly visited the Washington, DC, jail to make sure it met with his approval. He had a cab waiting to take him to the jail after the shooting, hoping to avoid being set on by an angry mob.

❖ Garfield might well have lived after the shooting had his doctors practiced sterilization.

Chester Alan Arthur

Nickname: The Gentleman Boss, Elegant Arthur, Chet, Prince Arthur
Presidency: 21st president, 1881–1885
Party: Republican
Life dates: October 5, 1829–November 18, 1886 (57 years, 44 days)
[Note: Arthur's birth date is often given as 1830, but this is incorrect—
Arthur made himself a year younger when he was in his forties.]

EARLY LIFE AND EDUCATION

Chester Alan Arthur was born October 5, 1829, in Fairfield, Vermont, the fifth child and first son of Malvina Stone Arthur and William Arthur. William Arthur was a Baptist minister, having become ordained the year before Chester was born. The family moved frequently from church to church, and moved to New York state in 1835, where William helped to found the New York Anti-Slavery Society.

Chester, called "Chet," probably received his earliest education from his father. He then attended an academy in Union Village, New York. When the family moved to Schenectady, he attended the Lyceum there in preparation for college.

Chester entered Union College, in Schenectady, New York, as a sophomore at age fifteen. He was a fair student and was genial and well-liked. He studied the Latin and Greek classics, and was introduced to such authors as Livy, Horace, Cicero, Herodotus, Homer, and Thucydides. He taught school during his winter vacations and after he graduated from Union College in 1848, at which time he began to study law at the State and National Law School. In 1851 Chester became the principal of a small academy

whose classes met in the basement of a church in North Pownal, Vermont. Three years later, James Garfield also taught at this little school.

In November 1852 Chester became the principal of the academy at Cohoes, New York. (He continued to study law.) One of his sisters, Malvina, was also a teacher there.

EARLY CAREER

Arthur was allowed to read law at the law offices of Culver and Parker, a New York City law firm. He was admitted to the New York bar in May 1854, and shortly thereafter was made a partner in Culver and Parker. Two of the cases in which he was involved were centered on the civil rights of African Americans.

One case was known as the Lemmon Slave Case; it concerned slaves who belonged to a Virginia slaveholder named Jonathan Lemmon, who had brought the slaves to New York state from Virginia (and planned to transport them from New York to Texas). A New York State Superior Court judge, Elijah Paine, was asked to issue a writ of habeas corpus, as New York state law forbade the holding of any person in bondage. The writ was issued and the slaves were declared free by virtue of their having been brought into a free state. Southerners were up in arms over this decision, while Northern abolitionists were elated. The case went to the US Supreme Court, where Judge Paine's decision was upheld. During the New York state proceedings, Arthur assisted in the case and made trips to Albany, New York, the state capital, to urge the governor and the legislature to support the decision.

As regards the other of these cases, Arthur was a principal attorney. In 1855 Lizzie Jennings, an African-American woman, was forcibly put off a streetcar (a horse-drawn carriage) that had been designated "whites only," in New York City, after she refused to leave the car. With Arthur as her attorney, Lizzie Jennings brought suit against the Third Avenue Railway Company, the operators of the service, and won. Arthur asked for $500 in damages, but Lizzie was awarded only $250, plus court expenses. Thus did Arthur make a significant contribution to the desegregation of New York City public transportation.

At around this time Arthur began his political career as a member of the Whig Party and supported Henry Clay, but he joined the new Republican Party and supported John C. Frémont for president in 1856.

Arthur lived in a boarding house in New York City. Another boarder at the house was a young medical student named Dabney Herndon. Dabney introduced Arthur to his cousin, Ellen ("Nell") Lewis Herndon, when she and her mother traveled to New York to visit him. Ellen was a pretty, young woman with an excellent singing voice. The Herndons were a well-connected Virginia family; Ellen's father was Commander William Lewis Herndon, a career naval officer who had won fame as an explorer of the Amazon River. While Arthur was on a trip to the western United States in 1857, Commander Herndon died in a gale at sea, as he heroically helped the women and children aboard the ship to safety before going down with the ship.

Arthur returned east to comfort Ellen and to help her widowed mother manage her business affairs. He traveled to Virginia to meet the rest of the family, and although of much humbler background than the Herndons, the tall, attractive, well-educated young attorney won approval as Ellen's fiancé. The two were married on October 25, 1859, in New York City.

> ## "Madam, I may be President of the United States, but my private life is nobody's damn business."
>
> Chester Alan Arthur, speaking to a temperance reformer

Their first child, a son named William Lewis Herndon Arthur, after Ellen's father, was born in 1860 and died only three years later. A boy, also named Chester Alan Arthur, was born in 1864, and a girl, named Ellen Herndon Arthur, was born in 1871.

As a young couple, the Arthurs settled in New York City. At the outbreak of the Civil War in 1861, Arthur, who had joined the New York state militia a few years earlier, was appointed to the important post of Quartermaster General of the State of New York, responsible for the quartering (lodging) and provisioning of New York's troops. He was given the rank of brigadier general. His new position caused some tension with Ellen's family, whose sympathies were wholly Confederate.

In 1863 Arthur returned to his law practice when a new Democratic governor was elected in New York and such patronage positions as Quartermaster General were filled by members of the Democratic party.

POLITICAL CAREER

Arthur's law career was successful and made him financially secure. He maintained his interest in Republican politics, becoming a supporter of US Senator Roscoe Conkling, the head of New York's Republican machine. Through Conkling's influence, President Ulysses S. Grant appointed Arthur to the post of Collector of the Port of New York in 1871. This position was an important and profitable one, as the collector oversaw the busiest port in the United States and collected its duties and fines. He also, in keeping with the political patronage system of the era, placed members of his party in government jobs and collected a portion of their salaries for use by the party. Arthur was regarded as efficient and hardworking in his position, but his ties to Conkling and his compliance with the system that had integrated the collector's post with the Republican party machinery led to his being targeted by President Rutherford B. Hayes, who was determined to dismantle the system.

In 1878 Hayes sought the resignation of Arthur and several subordinates and put forth his own candidates for the offices. Conkling saw this as a call to battle and fought Hayes while Congress was in session. When the session ended, Hayes suspended Arthur and the others, effectively removing them from office. Conkling and Arthur began touting former President Grant as a candidate to replace Hayes in office in the 1880 presidential election.

In January 1880 Ellen Arthur sang at a benefit concert, and she is believed to have contracted illness at the event. Within several days she was critically ill. She developed pneumonia and had lost consciousness by the time Arthur returned home from Albany; she died on January 12, 1880. Arthur was still grief-stricken when he went to the Republican nominating convention in Chicago in June of that year as part of the so-called "Stalwart" faction of the Republican Party, headed by Conkling, which supported former President Grant's bid for a third term. When Garfield was nominated by the Half-Breeds, the faction opposed to the Stalwarts, as a compromise candidate, Arthur was chosen as the vice-presidential candidate—as a concession to the Stalwart faction.

Garfield and Arthur were elected, but Arthur did not play a large part in Garfield's presidency. He was at his home in New York when Garfield died, and it was there that he took the presidential oath of office on September 19, 1881. He repeated the oath two days later in the vice-president's office in the Capitol.

PRESIDENCY

Many people were appalled that Arthur had succeeded to the presidency—having little respect for him in the wake of his dismissal from the New York port collector position. Three months into his presidency, Secretary of State James Blaine resigned because of his political differences with Arthur.

"Men may die, but the fabrics of our free institutions remain unshaken. No higher or more assuring proof could exist of the strength and permanence of popular government than the fact that though the chosen of the people be struck down, his constitutional successor is peacefully installed without shock or strain except the sorrow which mourns bereavement."

Chester Alan Arthur, on becoming president after President Garfield's death, September 22, 1881

Arthur, however, surprised his critics by distancing himself from Conkling and his former Republican Party associates. In August 1882 Arthur vetoed the Rivers and Harbors Act, a bill that appropriated millions of dollars for special-interest projects and deliberately inflated their budgets; it was passed over his veto, but the public took notice of his somewhat surprising stance. He signed the Pendleton Act, passed in January 1883, which established a bipartisan Civil Service Commission and, in due course, made the apportionment of some government positions contingent on competitive written examinations and protected employees against removal from office for political reasons.

Arthur also urged the prosecution of those connected with the "Star Route" scandal, in which vast sums of tax monies were appropriated for postal services that were never delivered. But in spite of the efforts of Arthur and others, no convictions were handed down.

Arthur repeatedly exercised his veto power, though the laws in question were often passed by Congress over his veto. He vetoed the First Chinese Exclusion law in 1882, arguing that it contravened existing treaty provisions with the Chinese; however, it was passed over his veto. International relations were generally good under Arthur; he also recognized Korea as a nation and received its ambassadors. In 1884 the United States and Mexico negotiated a treaty on their shared border.

Arthur signed, in 1882, a bill for the construction of steel ships and a new steel navy; he had urged the appropriations as the US navy had become obsolete in the years after the Civil War.

Arthur also urged a reduction of tariffs. Drawing on the findings of a commission he set up to investigate the issue of tariffs, Arthur recommended a tariff reduction of 20 to 25 percent. Congress instead passed the so-called "Mongrel Tariff" in 1883, reducing many tariffs only slightly. The high tariffs became a political cause embraced by the Democrats; in this area, as in many others, Arthur proved to be at odds with his own party.

As president, Arthur took pleasure in dressing well and living well. He undertook the refurbishing of the White House with Louis Comfort Tiffany as the design consultant, and socialized with elegant, cultured people. He was an epicure who entertained lavishly in the White House. His younger sister, Mary Arthur McElroy, assumed the duties of White House hostess during the socially active winter seasons. Arthur continued to struggle over the loss of Ellen, however; he kept her portrait in the White House and had fresh flowers placed beside it each day. He also donated a church window in her honor to the St. John's Episcopal Church, across from the White House, where she had sung in the choir as a girl, and asked that the church remain lit at night so that he could see the window from his private quarters in the White House.

> **"No man ever entered the presidency so profoundly and widely distrusted, and no one ever retired . . . more generally respected."**
>
> Alexander K. McClure, publisher, about President Arthur

Arthur was diagnosed with Bright's disease, a kidney disorder, after his first year in the White House. He kept the diagnosis a secret, however, and kept himself in the running for the nomination for presidential candidate in the 1884 election so as not to impart an appearance of weakness. He was not nominated, having alienated many of his former supporters—but, paradoxically, also having gained the respect of many Americans.

POST-PRESIDENTIAL CAREER

Arthur retired to New York City, where he died on November 18, 1886. He was buried beside Ellen in Albany, New York. Although nearly forgotten by modern Americans, he is generally regarded by historians with respect for having governed honestly and effectively.

Birthplace: Fairfield, VT
Residency: New York
Religion: Episcopalian
Education: Union College, Schenectady, NY, graduated 1848
Place of Death: New York City, NY
Burial Site: Rural Cemetery, Albany, NY
Dates in Office: September 19, 1881–March 3, 1885 (3 years, 166 days)
Age at Inauguration: 51 years, 350 days

FAMILY

Father: William Arthur (1796–1875)
Mother: Malvina Stone Arthur (1802–1869)

Siblings: Chester was the fifth of nine children; his siblings were Regina Arthur (1822–1910); Jane Arthur (1824–1842); Almeda Arthur (1826–1899); Ann Eliza Arthur (1828–1915); Malvina Arthur (1832–1920); William Arthur (1834–1915); George Arthur (1836–1838); Mary Arthur (1829–1917).

Wife: Ellen ("Nell") Lewis Herndon Arthur (1837–1880); married on October 25, 1859, in New York City, NY

Children: William Lewis Herndon Arthur (1860–1863); Chester Alan Arthur (1864–1937); Ellen Herndon Arthur (1871–1915)

CAREER

Private: teacher, school principal, lawyer

Political: Collector of the Port of New York (1871–1878); vice president under Garfield (1881); president of the United States (1881–1885)

Military: Quartermaster General for New York state (1862–1863)

Selected Works: *Chester A. Arthur Papers,* microfilm archives (Washington, DC: Library of Congress); *James A. Garfield, 1831–1881: Chester A. Arthur, 1830–1886; Chronology, Documents, Bibliographical Aids,* ed. by Howard B. Furer (Dobbs Ferry, NY: Oceana Publications, 1970)

PRESIDENCY

Nomination: 1880: At the Republican Party convention in Chicago in June of 1880, Arthur was chosen as the vice-presidential candidate with James Garfield as the presidential candidate.

Election: n/a

Opponent: n/a

Vote Totals: n/a

Inauguration: none; Arthur took the oath of office at his home in New York City on September 20, 1881, and then again in the Vice President's Office in the US Capitol on September 21, 1881.

Vice President: none

CABINET

Secretary of State: James G. Blaine, ME (1881); Frederick T. Frelinghuysen, NJ (1881–1885)

Secretary of the Treasury: William Windom, MN (1881); Charles J. Folger, NY (1881–1884);

Walter Q. Gresham, IN (1884); Hugh McCulloch, IN (1884–1885)

Secretary of War: Robert Todd Lincoln, IL (1881–1885)

Attorney General: Isaac Wayne McVeagh, PA (1881); Benjamin H. Brewster, PA (1882–1885)

Postmaster General: Thomas L. James, NY (1881–1882); Timothy O. Howe, WI (1882–1883); Walter Q. Gresham, IN (1883–1884); Frank Hatton, IA (1884–1885)

Secretary of the Navy: William H. Hunt, LA (1881–1882); William E. Chandler, NH (1882–1885)

Secretary of the Interior: Samuel J. Kirkwood, IA (1881–1882); Henry M. Teller, CO (1882–1885)

CONGRESS

47th Congress (1881–1883); Speaker of the House: J. Warren Keifer (OH, Republican)

48th Congress (1883–1885); Speaker of the House: John G. Carlisle (KY, Democrat)

SUPREME COURT APPOINTEES

Samuel Blatchford, NY; Associate Justice (1882–1893)

Horace Gray, MA; Associate Justice (1882–1902)

MAJOR EVENTS OF THE ARTHUR ADMINISTRATION

◆ Secretary of State James Blaine resigns because of political differences with Arthur, December 15, 1881.

◆ A bill passed in February 1882 mandating the use of the census to determine US congressional representation results in an increase in the membership of the House of Representatives, to 325 members.

◆ In March 1882 the Senate ratifies the Geneva Convention of 1864 that set standards for the care of the wounded during war and the neutrality of medical personnel.

◆ In March 1882 the Edmunds Act makes "unlawful cohabitation," an offense easier to prove than polygamy, the basis for denying the vote to those found guilty of it; the law prohibits cohabitants and polygamists from voting and is directed against Utah Mormons practicing polygamy.

◆ Arthur vetoes the First Chinese Exclusion law in 1882; the law prohibits immigration to the United States by paupers, lunatics, and criminals, as well as suspends Chinese immigration. A revised version is passed, which bans Chinese immigration for ten years (this provision would later be regularly renewed).

◆ Arthur vetoes the Carriage of Passengers at Sea Act in July 1882; the act prescribes space allocations for cabin and steerage passengers and requires masters of emigrant ships to restrict steerage passengers to the decks assigned to them.

◆ In August 1882 Arthur vetoes the Rivers and Harbors Act, which provides for pork barrel expenditures to improve rivers and harbors; it is passed over his veto.

◆ A bill in 1882 appoints a commission to study tariffs; the commission recommends lowering tariffs. The Tariff Act of 1883, dubbed the "Mongrel Tariff Act," lowers some tariffs and raises others, but is unpopular in the South and West.

◆ The Pendleton Act, passed in January 1883, establishes a bipartisan Civil Service Commission, making some government positions dependent on competitive written examinations and protecting employees against termination of their employment for political reasons.

◆ Arthur signs a bill for the construction of a new steel navy, 1883.

◆ Congress repeals the 1862 requirement that US government officeholders take an oath pledging that they have never engaged in any illegal or disloyal activity (the oath was designed to keep former high-ranking Confederates out of political office).

◆ The US Bureau of Labor is created within the Department of the Interior (a separate Department of Labor will be created in 1913).

◆ On July 4, 1884, France presents the United States with the Statue of Liberty in Paris (she arrives in the United States in 1885 and is unveiled in October 1886).

◆ An act is passed in February of 1885 prohibiting the fencing of government lands in the west.

◆ Arthur dedicates the Washington Monument on February 21, 1885.

◆ In February 1885 Congress passes the Contract Labor Law (also called the Foran Act), which prohibits companies from importing labor from other countries to lower wages, break strikes, etc.

MAJOR US AND WORLD EVENTS, 1881–1885

◆ On October 22, 1881, the Boston Symphony Orchestra gives its first concert.

◆ On October 26, 1881, the gunfight at the OK Corral occurs between Virgil Earp (the town marshal of Tombstone, Arizona, where the fight takes place), Morgan Earp, Wyatt Earp, and Doc Holliday, on one side, and Ike and Billy Clanton, Billy "The Kid" Claiborne, and Tom and Frank McLaury on the other.

◆ On November 15, 1881, the American Federation of Labor (AFL) is founded.

◆ John L. Sullivan, the bare-knuckle boxing champion, knocks out Paddy Ryan on February 7, 1882.

◆ In March 1882 Robert Koch publishes his work on the tuberculosis bacillus.

◆ On May 20, 1882, the Triple Alliance is formed between Germany, Italy, and Austria-Hungary, with each promising to aid either of the others if attacked.

◆ On April 3, 1882, Jesse James is shot and killed by Robert Ford, whom he had recruited to help him to perform a bank robbery.

◆ In July 1882 Richard Wagner's opera *Parsifal* is first performed in Bayreuth, Germany.

◆ The Knights of Columbus are founded in New Haven, Connecticut, in 1882.

◆ The Brooklyn Bridge is completed in 1883; it is opened with President Arthur and New York governor Grover Cleveland in attendance.

◆ On August 26, 1883, the Krakatoa Volcano in Indonesia erupts; the massive eruption causes huge tsunamis that kill more than 30,000 people.

◆ Mark Twain publishes *Life on the Mississippi*, 1883.

◆ Robert Louis Stevenson publishes *Treasure Island*, 1883.

◆ Friedrich Nietzsche publishes *Also Sprach Zarathustra*, 1883.

◆ The Orient Express makes its first run, on June 5, 1883, from Paris to Varna Port on the Black Sea (it will run to Constantinople [Istanbul] when the rail line is completed in 1889).

◆ Standard time is adopted by US and Canadian railroads in 1883, and by many nations at an international conference in 1884.

◆ Construction begins, in Chicago, on the world's first skyscraper, 1884.

◆ The first volume of the *Oxford English Dictionary* is published, 1884.

◆ On January 26, 1885, Charles George Gordon, Governor-General of the Sudan, dies at Khartoum, where he had been under siege, since March 1884, while attempting to evacuate British-sponsored Egyptian troops. The siege was led by Muhammad Ahmad (called "the mahdi," the title of a legendary leader of Islam).

FAST FACTS ABOUT CHESTER ALAN ARTHUR

◆ Political opponents circulated the falsehoods that Arthur was born in Ireland or Canada, which would have made him ineligible for the presidency.

◆ Arthur taught at the North Pownal Academy in Vermont; three years after he left, James A. Garfield was hired to teach penmanship at the academy.

◆ As an attorney, Arthur represented Lizzie Jennings, a black woman who refused to get off a whites-only New York City streetcar and was subsequently forced off. She sued the streetcar company and, with Arthur's representation, won $250. The company later issued orders to its drivers to admit African Americans on all of its buses.

◆ Ellen Arthur died before her husband became president. In her memory, Arthur donated a stained glass window to St. John's Episcopal Church, across from the White House, where she had sung in the choir as a girl. The window was placed so that Arthur could see it from his private quarters.

◆ Arthur's younger sister, Mary Arthur McElroy, served as White House hostess during her brother's presidency.

◆ Arthur was famous for his elegant clothing and manners; among his belongings was a dark green carriage, drawn by matched bay horses, stocked with monogrammed lap robes for passengers. He reportedly had eighty pairs of trousers in his wardrobe.

◆ Arthur's middle name, Alan, was pronounced "Ah-LAN," not "AL-un."

◆ In August 1882, just under a year into his presidency, Arthur was diagnosed with Bright's disease, a kidney ailment.

◆ Arthur knew starting in 1882 that he was suffering from a fatal kidney disorder, but kept the fact a secret, even when seeking the presidential nomination in 1884 (he was not nominated). He died in 1886.

Grover Cleveland

Nickname: Big Steve, Uncle Jumbo, the Guardian President, the Veto Mayor, the Veto Governor
Presidency: 22nd president, 1885–1889
Party: Democratic
Life dates: March 18, 1837–June 24, 1908 (71 years, 98 days)

EARLY LIFE AND EDUCATION

Stephen Grover Cleveland was born on March 18, 1837, in Caldwell, New Jersey, the fifth of nine children of Ann Neal Cleveland and Richard Falley Cleveland. Richard Cleveland was a Yale graduate and a Presbyterian minister who named his third son Stephen Grover after an elderly minister he admired. When the boy was four years old, the family moved to Fayetteville, New York, near Syracuse. "Big Steve," as he was sometimes called, attended the Fayetteville Academy; but before long he had dropped his first name entirely and began to use his middle name.

In 1851 the family moved to Clinton, New York, so that the elder Cleveland could take a less demanding position as a pastor, as his health was failing. Grover studied at the Clinton Academy and looked forward to admission to Hamilton College. However, he first had to earn some money. He worked as a store clerk in Fayetteville for two years before returning to Clinton, at which time his father moved again, to Holland Patent, New York, where he died three weeks later. Grover had no choice but to work to help support his family; he joined his brother as a teacher at the New York Institute for the Blind in New York City.

After one year at the New York Institute for the Blind, Cleveland decided that the law might be a good career for him and headed west to Cleveland, Ohio, hoping to begin his law studies there. However, fate, so to speak, intervened. On his way west he stopped to visit an aunt in Buffalo, New York. She urged him to stay in Buffalo, and in that city he became an assistant to her husband, Lewis F. Allen, a cattle breeder, for whom he registered pedigrees of cattle. Through the family's connections, he soon found a place, clerking and studying law, in the law firm of Rogers, Bowen, and Rogers.

EARLY CAREER

Cleveland was admitted to the New York bar in 1859 and remained with Rogers, Bowen, and Rogers until 1862. During the Civil War, two of Cleveland's brothers served in the Union army, but Cleveland himself, as the main support of his family, paid for a substitute to fulfill his military obligation—a permitted practice at the time. In 1863 he accepted an appointment to become the assistant district attorney of Erie County, New York. After a few years he ran for the position of district attorney, but, as a Democrat, was defeated in the largely Republican county. He had become increasingly active in politics, attending city and state conventions as a delegate.

In 1869 he formed a law firm, Laning, Cleveland, and Folsom, with Alfred P. Laning and Oscar Folsom. Cleveland's friendship with Oscar Folsom and the members of Folsom's family was lifelong. In 1870 Cleveland was elected sheriff of Erie County, earning a good living and establishing many political contacts, also serving as the public executioner and having to supervise the unpleasant task of hanging condemned murderers. After his three-year term, he returned to private practice and formed a firm with Lyman K. Bass and Wilson S. Bissell. Bass left the firm because of ill health and was replaced by George J. Sicard.

In 1874 Cleveland had a relationship with a woman named Maria Halpin, who subsequently bore a child she claimed was Cleveland's. It was later alleged that the child, named Oscar Folsom Cleveland, may have been fathered by Cleveland, by Oscar Folsom, Cleveland's former law partner, or by someone else. Halpin, who was said to be emotionally disturbed, eventually suffered a breakdown and was institutionalized. Cleveland paid for the child's care until the child was adopted, after which Cleveland never saw him again.

POLITICAL CAREER

Cleveland's growing reputation as a lawyer led to his being selected as a candidate for mayor of Buffalo in 1881. He won election and set about to prove himself a reform politician, as he worked hard to put in place cost-effective municipal services, and without reliance on partisan politics. He unhesitatingly used his veto powers on bills he deemed fiscally irresponsible or as catering to special interests, and he thereby created a political model, which he would remain faithful to in his later political positions. He was so successful as mayor that, in 1882, he was nominated for the position of governor of New York. He won the election. Cleveland, a calm and methodical man, confidently took on the new responsibilities that were thrust upon him by the governorship. However, as

governor, he missed the support and encouragement of his mother, who died in July 1882.

As governor, Cleveland continued down his path of reform and using the power of veto, which put him at odds with the Democratic Party machine, embodied by Tammany Hall in New York and led by "Honest" John Kelly. He repeatedly vetoed bills that gave special privileges to towns, cities, or groups of people—even turning down the bill that would have provided funds for the city of Fayetteville, New York, his boyhood home, to enable the purchase of a steam fire engine. He approved legislation that transferred the power of appointment to some political offices from the New York City Board of Aldermen to the mayor of New York City, and supported legislation that gave veterans preference in the hiring for public works projects. He also signed legislation that established a bureau of labor statistics.

> "The lesson should be constantly enforced that though the people support the Government, Government should not support the people."
>
> Grover Cleveland, in vetoing a farm relief bill, 1887

Cleveland, a bachelor and accustomed to a bachelor's life, lived simply in the executive mansion in Albany, New York. He worked long, hard hours; his amusements consisted of occasional fishing trips, playing poker on Sunday evenings, and convivial eating and drinking. A tall, large man, Cleveland enjoyed plain food and would later complain about French cooking in the White House.

Cleveland's performance as governor contributed to an enhanced political reputation and talk among members of the Democratic Party that he would make a good candidate for the presidency. At the convention in Chicago, in July

1884, Cleveland was nominated on the fourth ballot. The delegates chose Thomas Hendricks of Indiana as his running mate, in hopes of securing that state's electoral votes; it was assumed that Cleveland would be able to carry his home state of New York and the Democratic southern states.

The Republican candidate was James Blaine of Maine. In the course of the campaign, rumors of the child Cleveland may have fathered were publicized by his opponents. In a surprising move, Cleveland instructed the handlers of his campaign to "tell the truth." He acknowledged fatherhood, which diffused much of the campaign's rancor and negativity. Still, newspapers printed cartoons that bore the caption "Ma, Ma, where's my Pa? Going to the White House! Ha Ha Ha!"—highlighting the Maria Halpin affair and motivating Cleveland's opponents to contrast Cleveland's admitted affair with James Blaine's reportedly spotless personal life. However, Cleveland's supporters responded, "We are told that Mr. Blaine has been delinquent in office but blameless in public life, while Mr. Cleveland has been a model of official integrity but culpable in personal relations. We should therefore elect Mr. Cleveland to the public office for which he is so well qualified to fill, and remand Mr. Blaine to the private station which he is admirably fitted to adorn."

The voting was in accordance with the Democratic Party's hopes—Cleveland carried the southern states, New York, and Indiana, as well as New Jersey and Connecticut, and became the first Democratic president since James Buchanan. An important factor in his victory was the support of the Mugwumps, Republicans who supported reform and deserted Blaine to campaign for Cleveland.

PRESIDENCY

In his first term as president, Cleveland continued to uphold the legacy of his prior executive actions. He appointed officials, including his cabinet members, on the basis of merit and used the veto often. He vetoed many bills intended to grant pensions to Civil War veterans and vetoed a bill that would have distributed seed grain to western farmers enduring a drought. He signed the Interstate Commerce Act in 1887, which created the Interstate Commerce Commission, and the Dawes Act of 1887, which authorized the apportioning of land to individual Native Americans rather than to entire tribes. He supported the expansion and modernization of the Navy.

> "He mocks the people who propose that the Government shall protect the rich and that they in turn will care for the laboring poor."
>
> Grover Cleveland, fourth annual message to Congress, December 3, 1888

Cleveland scored a clear victory when he called for an investigation into government practices whereby millions of acres of land in the western United States had been granted to the railroads, and forced the railroads to return 81 million acres to the government. He was also firm in his refusal to recognize congressional power as detailed in the Tenure of Office Act of 1867, which required the president to obtain the consent of the Senate before removing from office those government officers who had been appointed by Congress. This act was repealed in 1887.

Cleveland continued to advocate a "hardmoney" approach to the economy; that is, he believed that currency should be redeemable for gold. He also believed in reducing the high protective tariffs in place at the time, but had limited success in convincing Congress to do so, despite his having devoted his entire State of the Union message in 1887 to the issue.

At the beginning of Cleveland's term, his sister Rose Elizabeth Cleveland acted as the White House hostess. She was not quite right for the job, as it happened, as she was bored by social life and mostly interested in scholarly pursuits. Because Cleveland was a bachelor, his private affairs attracted some attention from the press, which speculated that he might be courting Emma Folsom, the widow of his former law partner, Oscar Folsom. Cleveland had remained close to the Folsom family through the years. He had bought Oscar's infant daughter Frances—whom he would eventually marry, (nicknamed Frank or, by the press after their marriage, Frankie)—her first baby carriage. After Oscar Folsom's death, Cleveland gave advice to the Folsoms on the subject of their financial affairs—and of Frank's education (she became a graduate of Wells College in Aurora, New York). Soon after his inauguration, Emma and Frank visited him in the White House. Romance blossomed between Cleveland and the younger Folsom, and Frank accompanied Cleveland on a trip to Europe. She was already engaged to the president, although this information was not given to the press. On June 2, 1886, Cleveland married Frances Folsom in a private ceremony at the White House. He was the only president to marry at the White House. Young and beautiful, Frances became an extremely popular First Lady. Her clothing and hairstyle were copied, her image was used regularly in advertising, and reporters dogged the First Family relentlessly. Frances Cleveland held two public receptions a week at the White House, making it a point to hold one on Saturday so that working women could attend.

Cleveland lost some of his popularity in the course of his first term as president—in part because he was less of a reformer than the Mugwumps desired and was not, all things considered, a charismatic president; in his bid for reelection in 1888, despite his winning the popular vote, he was defeated in the electoral college by Benjamin Harrison, the grandson of former president William Henry Harrison. On leaving the White House, Frances Cleveland confidently told the staff that she and her husband would return in four years.

[Note: For Cleveland's second presidency and later life, please see the entry for Grover Cleveland as the 24th president on page 187.]

Birthplace: Caldwell, NJ
Residency: New York
Religion: Presbyterian
Education: did not attend college
Place of Death: Princeton, NJ
Burial Site: Princeton Cemetery, Princeton, NJ
Dates in Office: March 4, 1885–March 3, 1889 (4 years) [Note: This is Cleveland's first term; see also the entry for the 24th presidency, Cleveland's second term.]
Age at Inauguration: 47 years, 351 days

FAMILY
Father: Richard Falley Cleveland (1804–1853)
Mother: Ann (or Anne) Neal Cleveland (1806–1882)
Siblings: Stephen Grover Cleveland was the fifth of nine children; his siblings were Anna Neal Cleveland (1830–1909); William Neal Cleveland (1832–1906); Mary Allen Cleveland (1833–1914); Richard Cecil Cleveland (1835–1872); Margaret Louise Falley Cleveland (1838–1932); Lewis Frederick Cleveland (1841–1872); Susan Sophia Cleveland (1843–1938); Rose Elizabeth Cleveland (1846–1918)
Wife: Frances Folsom Cleveland (1864–1947); married June 2, 1886, in the Blue Room of the White House, Washington, DC
Children: Ruth Cleveland (1891–1904); Esther Cleveland (1893–1980); Marion Cleveland (1895–1977); Richard Folsom Cleveland (1897–1974); Francis Grover Cleveland (1903–1995)

CAREER
Private: lawyer
Political: assistant district attorney (1863–1865); sheriff of Erie County, NY (1870–1873); mayor of Buffalo, NY (1881–1882); governor of NY (1883–1884); president of the United States (1885–1889; 1893–1897)
Military: none [Note: During the Civil War, Cleveland purchased a substitute to serve for him in the Union Army, a lawful procedure at the time.]
Selected Works: *Fishing and Shooting Sketches*, illustrated by Henry S. Watson (New York:

Abercrombie & Fitch, 1966); *Grover Cleveland, 1837–1908; Chronology, Documents, Bibliographical Aids*, ed. by Robert I. Vexler (Dobbs Ferry, NY: Oceana Publications, 1968); *Letters of Grover Cleveland, 1850–1908*, selected and ed. by Allan Nevins (New York: Da Capo Press, 1970); *Presidential Problems* (Freeport, NY: Books for Libraries Press, 1971)

PRESIDENCY

Nomination: 1884: The Democratic convention was held in Chicago, July 8–11, 1884; despite some opposition from Tammany Hall, Cleveland was nominated on the fourth ballot, and Thomas Hendricks of Indiana was nominated for vice president.

1888: The Democratic convention was held in St. Louis, MO, June 5–7, 1888, and Cleveland was unanimously selected as the presidential candidate on the first ballot; Allan G. Thurman of Ohio was selected as the vice presidential candidate.

[Note: For the 1892 election, please see the entry for the 24th president.]

Election: 1884: elected president on November 4, 1884

1888: defeated by Benjamin Harrison on November 6, 1888

Opponent: 1884: James G. Blaine, ME, Republican; Benjamin F. Butler, MA, Anti-Monopolist and Greenback; John St. John, KS, Prohibition; Anson J. Streeter, IL, Union Labor

1888: Benjamin Harrison, OH, Republican; Clinton B. Fisk, NJ, Prohibition; Anson J. Streeter, IL, Union Labor

Vote Totals: 1884: Cleveland, 4,874,621 popular, 219 electoral; Blaine, 4,848,936 popular, 182 electoral; Butler, 175,096 popular, 0 electoral; St. John, 147,482 popular, 0 electoral; Streeter, 150,369 popular, 0 electoral

1888: Harrison, 5,447,129 popular, 233 electoral; Cleveland, 5,537,857 popular, 168 electoral; Fisk, 249,506 popular, 0 electoral; Streeter, 146,935 popular, 0 electoral

Inauguration: March 4, 1885

Vice President: Thomas A. Hendricks, IN (1885–1889)

CABINET

Secretary of State: Thomas F. Bayard, DE (1885–1889)

Secretary of the Treasury: Daniel Manning, NY (1885–1887); Charles S. Fairchild, NY (1887–1889)

Secretary of War: William C. Endicott, MA (1885–1889)

Attorney General: Augustus H. Garland, AR (1885–1889)

Postmaster General: William F. Vilas, WI (1885–1888); Donald M. Dickinson, MI (1888–1889)

Secretary of the Navy: William C. Whitney, NY (1885–1889)

Secretary of Agriculture: Norman J. Coleman, MO (1889)

Secretary of the Interior: Lucius Q. C. Lamar, MA (1885–1888); William F. Vilas, WI (1888–1889)

CONGRESS

49th Congress (1885–1887); Speaker of the House: John G. Carlisle (KY, Democrat)

50th Congress (1887–1889); Speaker of the House: John G. Carlisle (KY, Democrat)

SUPREME COURT APPOINTEES

Lucius Quintus C. Lamar, MS; Associate Justice (1888–1893)

Melville Weston Fuller, IL; Chief Justice (1888–1910)

MAJOR EVENTS OF THE CLEVELAND ADMINISTRATION

❖ On May 4, 1886, a labor strike for an eight-hour workday escalates into the Haymarket Riot, during which a bomb is thrown into a crowd at Haymarket Square in Chicago. Twelve people, including a number of police officers, are killed and seven activists are later sentenced to death (four are hanged), despite the lack of substantial evidence linking them to the crime. Three men are eventually pardoned.

❖ In the Presidential Succession Act of 1886, the plan of succession was altered from that established in 1792 with the removal of the president pro tempore of the Senate and the speaker of the House of Representatives from the line of succession, and their replacement by the cabinet members—in the order their departments were created.

◆ On September 4, 1886, Geronimo surrenders to the US Army in Arizona after a decade of evading capture.

◆ In 1886 the Supreme Court decides, in *Wabash, St. Louis & Pacific Railroad Company v. Illinois,* to limit the power of states to regulate interstate rates for railroads.

◆ The Interstate Commerce Act, in 1887, creates the Interstate Commerce Commission.

◆ In 1887 Cleveland devotes his entire annual message to Congress to a single topic, which no other president has ever done. He argues against the high tariff. However, the Mills bill, passed in July 1888, provides for only slight reductions in tariff rates.

◆ The Edmunds-Tucker Act of 1887 (upheld by the Supreme Court in 1890) seizes the property of the Mormon Church that is not used exclusively for worship, requires loyalty oaths for voter eligibility, disenfranchises women, and declares wives to be competent witnesses against their husbands in polygamy trials.

◆ In 1887 the US Congress repeals the Tenure in Office Act of 1867, which had required that the president obtain the consent of the Senate before he could remove from their positions any government officers who had received prior approval from the Congress.

◆ On February 8, 1889, Congress passes a bill creating the Department of Agriculture, as a cabinet level department, out of the Bureau of Agriculture established by Abraham Lincoln.

◆ The Dawes Act, 1887, authorizes the executive branch of the US government to survey Indian tribal land and divide it into allotments for individual Indians.

◆ On October 1, 1888, Cleveland signs the Scott Act, permanently banning Chinese laborers from immigrating to or returning to the United States.

MAJOR US AND WORLD EVENTS, 1885–1889

◆ On March 14, 1885, Gilbert and Sullivan's *The Mikado* is first staged.

◆ Sir Richard Burton publishes a translation of the *Arabian Nights,* also called *A Thousand and One Nights,* 1885–1888.

◆ In July 1885 Louis Pasteur administers the first rabies vaccine to a nine-year-old boy.

◆ On January 29, 1886, Karl Benz is granted a patent on the "Patent Motorwagen," recognized as the first gasoline-powered automobile.

◆ In 1886 Dr. John Stith Pemberton develops a cola drink that will be named Coca-Cola.

◆ Auguste Rodin exhibits his sculpture *The Kiss,* 1886.

◆ On October 28, 1886, the Statue of Liberty is dedicated before thousands of spectators.

◆ British Prime Minister William Gladstone proposes a Home Rule bill in Parliament to establish a separate Irish legislature, but the bill is defeated, 1886.

◆ The American Federation of Labor (AFL) is created, 1886, from the Federation of Organized Trades and Labor Unions, which had been formed in 1881.

◆ Robert Louis Stevenson publishes two of his best-known novels, *The Strange Case of Dr. Jekyll and Mr. Hyde,* 1886, and *Kidnapped,* 1887.

◆ Queen Victoria of Great Britain celebrates her Golden Jubilee on June 20 and 21, 1887, marking fifty years of her reign.

◆ Arthur Conan Doyle publishes *A Study in Scarlet,* the first Sherlock Holmes mystery, 1888 (the story is first published serially in a magazine in 1887).

◆ In June 1888 Kaiser Wilhelm II becomes the German emperor.

◆ In 1888 George Eastman introduces the first Kodak camera for amateur photographers; film for 100 pictures is preloaded in the camera; after pictures are taken, the entire camera is returned to the company for developing.

◆ William Burroughs receives a patent for his adding machine, 1888.

◆ The National Geographic Society is founded in January 1888 and publishes the first *National*

Geographic magazine before the end of the year.

◆ Nikolai Rimsky-Korsakov composes *Scheherazade*, 1888.

◆ During the period August through November of 1888, five women are murdered in London by a killer nicknamed Jack the Ripper.

◆ On January 30, 1889, the Archduke Rudolf of Austria and his mistress, the Baroness Marie Vetsera, are found dead, purportedly by suicide. Although evidence throws doubt on this theory, no other satisfactory explanation surfaces.

FAST FACTS ABOUT GROVER CLEVELAND

◆ Cleveland was the only president to serve two nonconsecutive terms.

◆ An avid fisherman, Cleveland published a book about fishing and shooting.

◆ On June 2, 1886, Cleveland married Frances Folsom in a private ceremony at the White House. (He is the only president to be married at the White House.) His twenty-one-year-old bride, Frances, was a beautiful and popular First Lady.

◆ At Cleveland's wedding, the wedding march was played by the US Marine Band, with John Philip Sousa conducting.

◆ Esther Cleveland, Grover and Frances Cleveland's daughter, was born in the White House in 1893 and was the first child of a president to be born there.

◆ Cleveland vetoed more bills in his two terms of office than all previous presidents combined.

◆ Cleveland left Washington in 1893 because of illness; he, with his doctors, privately boarded a boat anchored in the East River in New York, and there a cancerous growth was removed from his mouth. He was fitted with a prosthetic piece to replace the part of his jaw that had been removed and returned to work five weeks later. The public never knew.

◆ Cleveland's second vice president, Adlai Stevenson, was the grandfather of the Adlai Stevenson who was the governor of Illinois and the Democratic candidate for president in 1952 and 1956.

◆ Vice President Stevenson, when asked whether President Cleveland had ever consulted him about such matters as what to say in a speech, replied wryly, "Not yet, but there are still a few weeks of my term remaining."

◆ Cleveland's sister Rose Elizabeth Cleveland assumed the duties of White House hostess for the first two years of her brother's first term of office, although she was more interested in scholarly pursuits than in social duties. She admitted that she relieved the boredom of greeting guests in receiving lines at the White House by conjugating Greek verbs to herself at the same time.

◆ Although the legend persists that the Baby Ruth candy bar was named for Grover and Frances Cleveland's daughter Ruth Cleveland, the claim is doubtful: Ruth Cleveland died in 1904 and the candy bar did not appear until 1920. The candy bar's manufacturer, in making the assertion that the candy bar had been named for the daughter of President Cleveland, may have been trying to avoid paying Babe Ruth, famous as a baseball player for the New York Yankees, for the use of his name.

◆ As a sheriff in Buffalo, NY, Cleveland acted as public executioner and personally hanged two men convicted of murder.

◆ After retiring from his second term of office, Cleveland became a trustee of Princeton University, in which position he helped to block a proposal made by the president of the university, Woodrow Wilson, to set up undergraduate residence halls similar to those at British universities.

◆ One of Cleveland's ancestors, Aaron Cleveland, was a member of the Connecticut legislature and had introduced the first bill in an American legislature calling for the abolition of slavery.

◆ In 1913 Frances Folsom Cleveland became the first presidential widow to remarry; she married Thomas J. Preston, Jr., a professor of archaeology at Princeton University.

Benjamin Harrison

Nickname: Kid Gloves Harrison, Little Ben, The Centennial President, The Pious Moonlight Dude
Presidency: 23rd president, 1889–1893
Party: Republican
Life dates: August 20, 1833–March 13, 1901 (67 years, 205 days)

EARLY LIFE AND EDUCATION

Benjamin Harrison was born in North Bend, Ohio, on August 20, 1833, the second child and second son of the ten children of Elizabeth Ramsey Irwin Harrison and John Scott Harrison. John Scott Harrison also had two daughters from a prior marriage (there had also been a son, who died at age two). Benjamin was born into a family with a distinguished political tradition; his great-grandfather, Benjamin Harrison, was a signer of the Declaration of Independence; his grandfather, William Henry Harrison, was the ninth president of the United States; and his father, a successful farmer, was elected to the US House of Representatives (from Ohio) when Benjamin was twenty.

Young Benjamin was tutored at home. He then attended a preparatory school, the Farmers' College in Cincinnati, for two years. He went on to study at Miami University in Oxford, Ohio, and graduated fourth in his class in 1852. As a young man about five foot, six inches tall, Benjamin was reserved and serious. He was introduced to and attracted to lively Caroline Lavinia Scott (called Carrie). She was the daughter of a Presbyterian minister, professor, and founder of the Oxford Female Institute, from which she graduated. Caroline loved music and dancing (although her Presbyterian father disapproved of the latter), and developed her artistic abilities by learning to paint china. She also briefly taught music.

The couple were married on October 20, 1853. They had two children, Russell Benjamin Harrison, born in 1854, and Mary Scott Harrison, born in 1858; an unnamed infant died at birth, in 1861.

EARLY CAREER

Harrison read law at the law offices of Storer and Gwynne in Cincinnati, then moved with his bride to Indianapolis in 1854. He earned a reputation as a first-rate lawyer and went into partnership with William Wallace, son of a former Indiana governor, in 1855. While endeavoring to build his law practice, Harrison earned money as a court crier. He joined the newly formed Republican Party, campaigning for John C. Frémont, the party's presidential candidate in 1856.

In 1857 he was elected to the position of Indianapolis city attorney. He became the secretary of the Republican State Central Committee, and campaigned for Abraham Lincoln in the presidential election of 1860. He was elected to the post of State Reporter for the Indiana Supreme Court: he reported on the court's decisions (and augmented his income by doing so).

———

"If I were to select a watchword that I would have every young man write above his door and on his heart, it would be that good word 'Fidelity.' I know of no better. The man who meets every obligation to the family, to society, to the State, to his country, and his God, to the very best measure of his strength and ability, cannot fail of that assurance and quietness that comes of a good conscience, and will seldom fail of the approval of his fellow-men, and will never fail of the reward which is promised to his faithfulness."

Benjamin Harrison, in a speech given at the Phi Delta fraternity, Knox College, Galesburg, IL, October 8, 1890

———

MILITARY SERVICE

After the Civil War broke out, Harrison, at the request of the Indiana governor, joined the Seventieth Indiana Infantry Regiment, in 1862, with the rank of second lieutenant. He became the regiment's drillmaster. He was promoted to the rank of colonel, and first served under General Don Carlos Buell in Kentucky, where the Seventieth Indiana had been stationed. At the beginning of 1864, Harrison was given command of his brigade and placed under General Joseph Hooker. He fought in General William Tecumseh

Sherman's Atlanta campaign, which originated at Chattanooga, Tennessee, and ended in Atlanta, Georgia. He was rewarded for his achievements in the campaign and, recommended for promotion by General Hooker, was promoted to the rank of brigadier general. Harrison returned to Indiana to recruit new soldiers, then fought at Nashville, Tennessee, before rejoining his brigade for the march through the Carolinas and Virginia. Harrison was proud of his service, but he did not glorify war and deplored its violence.

After taking part in the review of troops in Washington at the end of the war, he left the service and returned to his law practice and the duties of reporter for the Indiana Supreme Court. In 1875 he built a house in Indianapolis, where he lived with his family for the rest of his life (excepting the years spent in Washington).

POLITICAL CAREER

Harrison became a successful lawyer and won fame for his skills as an orator. He retained his interest in Republican politics and worked for Ulysses S. Grant's presidential campaigns in 1868 and 1872. He himself harbored political ambition, and hoped for nomination to run for governor of Indiana in 1872, though he was not nominated. He refused to accept nomination for the governor's job in 1876, but when the Republican Party's candidate had to withdraw, Harrison accepted the nomination. Having only a short time to campaign, he was defeated.

Harrison was appointed as a member of the Mississippi River Commission in 1879 by President Rutherford B. Hayes. The commission was charged with carrying out surveys of the river, improving its navigation, promoting its commerce, and protecting the banks of the river.

When President Hayes declined to run again in 1880, Harrison supported James Garfield's candidacy. He turned down the offer of a cabinet position from Garfield, having been elected to the US Senate in 1880. He served in the Senate from 1881 to 1887. As a Senator, he supported a high tariff, a strong US Navy, and civil service reform. The Indiana state legislature had become predominantly Democratic during his term in the Senate, however, and he was not reelected in 1886.

Harrison's national reputation and the support of James Blaine of Maine made it possible for him to win the presidential nomination on the eighth ballot at the Republican convention in 1888. New Yorker Levi Morton was chosen as the vice-presidential candidate. Harrison and leading members of the Republican Party believed that the major issue of the day was the tariff. The Democrats favored free trade or a low tariff, while the Republicans argued for a high tariff—as a protection for American business.

Harrison conducted what was called a "front-porch campaign," giving speeches to those who came to Indianapolis. He was elected to the presidency in 1888 with 233 electoral votes to Cleveland's 168, although Cleveland had won more popular votes.

PRESIDENCY

Harrison was inaugurated one hundred years after the inauguration of George Washington—hence the epithet "the Centennial President." He began his term with a Republican Congress in place, and a number of bills designed to correct or improve domestic economic conditions were passed. The Sherman Silver Purchase Act of 1890 and the McKinley Tariff of 1890 were passed as a result of compromise agreements among Congressmen representing western and southern interests. Western interests and small farmers urged the passage of the Sherman Silver Purchase Act, which required the government to buy 4.5 million ounces of silver each month—virtually all of the silver produced by western mines. Currency could be redeemed for either gold or silver, but as the market price of silver had dropped, there was a run on gold. The McKinley Tariff placed high tariffs on imports and drove the price of many goods up, but protected goods manufactured in the United States.

The Dependent Pension Act provided pensions for any disabled veteran, whether the veteran had incurred the disability during wartime or not. It also extended benefits to dependents of veterans and led to the disbursement of millions of dollars to Civil War veterans and their families.

Harrison supported civil service reform and appointed Theodore Roosevelt as the Civil Service Commissioner, on May 7, 1889. Roosevelt served in that capacity for four years; he was able to bring a strong spirit of reform to the civil service and was witness to a transition: from an era in which civil service jobs were political spoils to one in which such jobs were awarded on the basis of examination results and merit.

> **"The purity of the ballot box, the wise provisions and careful guardianship that shall always make the expression of the will of the people fair, pure and true, is the essential thing in American life."**
>
> Benjamin Harrison, in a speech given at Salt Lake City, Utah, May 9, 1891

Harrison was also a strong supporter of increasing US naval strength. He advocated a two-ocean navy and the acquisition of overseas naval bases to serve the expanded navy. Congress approved funds in 1890 for the building of three steel battleships, and additional funds in 1892 for another, even larger ship, the *Iowa*, which would see service in the Spanish-American War in 1898.

Under Harrison's presidency and by virtue of the diplomacy of Secretary of State James Blaine, a number of potential diplomatic standoffs were averted. One such standoff in the making was the developing tension between the United States and Chile, which began with the seizure by the United States of a ship that belonged to Chilean anti-government rebels engaged in running arms from San Diego, California, to the rebel forces in Valparaiso, Chile. The rebels were ultimately victorious, and the new Chilean government naturally viewed the United States with suspicion. Two American sailors were killed in a fight in Valparaiso; Harrison vehemently denounced the incident as an unprovoked attack. With the only voice in the cabinet that did not support war between the United States and Chile belonging to Secretary of State James Blaine, an ultimatum was sent to Chile. Chile agreed to pay an indemnity, and the tensions abated.

"To the law we bow with reverence. It is the one king that commands our allegiance. We will change our king when his rule is oppressive."

Benjamin Harrison, speech at Indianapolis, IN, July 12, 1888

The first Pan-American Conference took place in Washington, DC, in 1889, and led to improved relations between the United States and the nations of Latin America. On another diplomatic front, the United States agreed, with Great Britain and Germany, to protectorate status for Samoa—the role of protector to be shared by the three nations. In addition, Harrison hoped to annex Hawaii, but the Congress, under Democratic control after the midterm elections in 1890, refused to approve the proposed annexation.

Harrison's wife Caroline had not been pleased about moving into the White House when her husband was elected to the presidency. She found the living quarters cramped and proposed extending the White House: she drew up elaborate plans for a new west wing, for use as office space, and a new east wing, which would serve as an art gallery. Congress refused to fund the plans, however; she instead turned to reconfiguring and refurbishing the White House. In designing her own White House china, she became inspired enough to begin collecting White House china used during previous administrations. Her work became the basis for the collection seen today in the China Room of the White House.

Harrison was nominated by his party for a second term. During the campaign for reelection, Caroline Harrison was diagnosed with tuberculosis; she died in the White House on October 25, 1892.

Against a backdrop of labor troubles, strikes, and a worsening economy provoking disenchantment among voters, Harrison lost the election in 1892 to the former president, Grover Cleveland.

POST-PRESIDENTIAL CAREER

Harrison returned to Indiana and resumed the practice of law; in his late career he argued a case before the Supreme Court. In 1898 and 1899, he represented Venezuela in an arbitration with Great Britain over a boundary dispute between Venezuela and British Guiana. He also became a popular lecturer.

Harrison remarried in 1896. He married a thirty-seven-year-old widow, Mary Scott Lord Dimmick, a niece of Caroline Harrison who had served as her secretary. His children did not attend the wedding. Mary gave birth to a daughter, Elizabeth, in 1897.

Harrison died in Indianapolis, Indiana, on March 31, 1901, at age sixty-seven. He was buried at Crown Hill Cemetery in Indianapolis.

Birthplace: North Bend, OH
Residency: Indiana
Religion: Presbyterian
Education: Miami University, Oxford, OH; graduated 1852
Place of Death: Indianapolis, IN
Burial Site: Crown Hill Cemetery, Indianapolis, IN
Dates in Office: March 4, 1889–March 3, 1893 (4 years)
Age at Inauguration: 55 years, 196 days

FAMILY

Father: John Scott Harrison (1804–1878) [Note: John Scott Harrison was the son of President William Henry Harrison.]
Mother: Elizabeth Ramsey Irwin Harrison (1810–1850)
Siblings: Benjamin was the second of ten children; his siblings were Archibald Irwin

Harrison (1832–1870); Mary Jane Harrison (1835–1867); Anna Symmes Harrison (1837–1838); John Irwin Harrison (b. 1839, died the same year); Carter Bassett Harrison (1840–1905); Anna Symmes Harrison (1842–1926); John Scott Harrison (1844–1926); James Findlay Harrison (1847–1848); James Irwin Harrison (1849–1850). Benjamin also had two half-sisters and a half-brother from his father's first marriage, to Lucretia Knapp Johnson (1804–1830); they were Elizabeth Short Harrison (1825–1904); William Henry Harrison (1827–1829); Sarah Lucretia Harrison (1829–?; but lived to maturity and was married).

Wife: Caroline Lavinia Scott Harrison (1832–1892), married October 20, 1853, in Oxford, OH; Mary Scott Lord Dimmick Harrison (1858–1948), married April 6, 1896, in New York City, NY

Children: with Caroline Lavinia Scott Harrison: Russell Benjamin Harrison (1854–1936); Mary Scott Harrison (1858–1930); an unnamed infant (b. 1861, died at birth); with Mary Scott Lord Dimmick Harrison: Elizabeth Harrison (1897–1955)

CAREER

Private: lawyer, Indiana State Supreme Court reporter

Political: member of the US Senate (1881–1887)

Military: Harrison raised and drilled the 70th Indiana Volunteer Regiment (1862); fought under General Sherman in the Atlanta campaign; fought in the Battles of Resaca (May 13–15, 1864), Golgotha (June 16, 1864), Dallas/New Hope Church (May 26–June 1, 1864), and Peachtree Creek (July 20, 1864); was promoted to brigadier general, for bravery; commanded a brigade at the Battle of Nashville (December 15–16, 1864).

Selected Works: *Benjamin Harrison, 1833–1901; Chronology, Documents, Bibliographical Aids*, ed. by Harry J. Sievers (Dobbs Ferry, NY: Oceana Publications, 1969); *The Correspondence Between Benjamin Harrison and James G. Blaine, 1882–1893*, collected and edited by Albert T. Volwiler (Philadelphia: The American Philosophical Society, 1940); *The Papers of Benjamin Harrison*, microfilm archive (Washington, DC: Library of Congress); *Speeches of Benjamin Harrison,*

Twenty-Third President of the United States, compiled by Charles Hedges (Port Washington, NY: Kennikat Press, 1971); *This Country of Ours*, 2nd ed. (New York: Charles Scribner, 1897); *Views of an Ex-President* (Indianapolis, The Bowen-Merrill Company, 1901)

PRESIDENCY

Nomination: 1888: The Republican convention, held in Chicago, June 19–25, 1888, nominated Benjamin Harrison on the eighth ballot; Levi P. Morton of NY was chosen as the vice-presidential candidate.

1892: The Republican convention, held in Minneapolis, Minnesota, June 7–10, 1892, nominated President Harrison for reelection on the first ballot; Whitelaw Reid of New York was chosen as the vice-presidential candidate.

Election: 1888: elected president on November 6, 1888

1892: defeated by Grover Cleveland, November 8, 1892

Opponent: 1888: Grover Cleveland, NY, Democrat; Clinton Fisk, NJ, Prohibition; Alson Streeter, IL, Union Labor

1892: Grover Cleveland, NY, Democrat; James Weaver, IA, Populist; John Bidwell, CA, Prohibition

Vote Totals: 1888: Harrison, 5,443,892 popular, 233 electoral; Cleveland, 5,534,488 popular, 168 electoral; Fisk, 249,819 popular, 0 electoral; Streeter, 146,602 popular, 0 electoral

1892: Cleveland, 5,559,898 popular, 277 electoral; Harrison, 5,190,819 popular, 145 electoral; Weaver, 1,026,595 popular, 22 electoral; Bidwell, 270,879 popular, 0 electoral

Inauguration: March 4, 1889

Vice President: Levi P. Morton, NY (1889–1893)

CABINET

Secretary of State: James G. Blaine, ME (1889–1892); John W. Foster, IN (1892–1893)

Secretary of the Treasury: William Windom, MN (1889–1891); Charles Foster, OH (1891–1893)

Secretary of War: Redfield Proctor, VT (1889–1891); Stephen B. Elkins, WV (1891–1893)

Attorney General: William H. Miller, IN (1889–1893)
Postmaster General: John Wanamaker, PA (1889–1893)
Secretary of the Navy: Benjamin F. Tracy, NY (1889–1893)
Secretary of Agriculture: Jeremiah M. Rusk, WI (1889–1893)
Secretary of the Interior: John W. Noble, MO (1889–1893)

CONGRESS
51st Congress (1889–1891); Speaker of the House: Thomas B. Reed (ME, Republican)
52nd Congress (1891–1893); Speaker of the House: Charles F. Crisp (GA, Democrat)

SUPREME COURT APPOINTEES
David Josiah Brewer, KS; Associate Justice (1890–1910)
Henry Billings Brown, MI; Associate Justice (1891–1906)
George Shiras, Jr., PA; Associate Justice (1892–1903)
Howell Edmunds Jackson, TN; Associate Justice (1893–1895)

MAJOR EVENTS OF THE HARRISON ADMINISTRATION
◆ The Joint Conference on Samoan Affairs is held in Berlin, 1889; Great Britain, Germany, and the United States evaluate their respective spheres of influence with regard to Samoa, and establish Samoan neutrality and independence.
◆ Harrison appoints Theodore Roosevelt as the US Civil Service Commissioner, May 7, 1889.
◆ The first Pan-American Conference is convened in Washington, DC, in 1889, reflecting Secretary of State James Blaine's interest in the improvement of relations with Latin America.
◆ North Dakota becomes a state, November 2, 1889.
◆ South Dakota becomes a state, November 2, 1889.
◆ Montana becomes a state, November 8, 1889.
◆ Washington becomes a state, November 11, 1889.
◆ The Oklahoma Territory is opened to homesteaders, April 1889.
◆ The Dependent and Disability Pensions Act, 1890, grants pensions to veterans, including those who were disabled by nonmilitary causes, and increases compensation to the dependents of veterans.
◆ Idaho becomes a state, July 3, 1890.
◆ Wyoming becomes a state, July 10, 1890.
◆ The Sherman Antitrust Act, 1890, prohibits the establishment of monopolies.
◆ The Sherman Silver Purchase Act, 1890, includes an agreement by the US government to purchase 4.5 million ounces of silver each month and to redeem US Treasury notes in either silver or gold. The price of silver drops, so notes are redeemed for gold rather than silver, leading to a run on gold.
◆ The McKinley Tariff of 1890 raises the tariff, and therefore the prices, on many goods.
◆ In September 1890 an Anti-Lottery Bill is passed.
◆ The US Army massacres Sioux Indians at Wounded Knee, South Dakota, on December 29, 1890.
◆ Nine circuit courts of appeal are created, 1891.
◆ In 1892 workers in both the steel and the silver industries strike. The strike by steel workers in Homestead, PA, leads to a battle between the strikers at Carnegie Steel and Pinkerton detectives sent to break the strike; three Pinkertons and seven steel workers are killed. The strike lasts from July to November and ends the power of the union at Carnegie Steel.
◆ On October 25, 1892, First Lady Caroline Harrison dies of tuberculosis.
◆ Cherokee land in Indian Territory is opened to white settlement, 1892.
◆ Americans in Hawaii under Stanford Dole depose Queen Liliuokalani, January 17, 1893, and Harrison asks the Senate to give consent to a proposed annexation of Hawaii (it refuses).

MAJOR US AND WORLD EVENTS, 1889–1893

◆ The Eiffel Tower opens in Paris, March 31, 1889.

◆ The Johnstown Flood in Johnstown, PA, leaves more than 2,000 dead, May 31, 1889.

◆ On July 8, 1889, the first *Wall Street Journal* is published.

◆ The French cabaret Moulin Rouge opens in Paris, 1889.

◆ Gustav Mahler's *Symphony No. 1 ("Titan")* premieres, November 20, 1889.

◆ Mark Twain publishes *A Connecticut Yankee in King Arthur's Court*, 1889.

◆ Vincent Van Gogh paints "The Starry Night" in June 1889.

◆ An early form of the jukebox that uses phonograph cylinders is mass-produced, 1889.

◆ Sir Arthur Conan Doyle's first Sherlock Holmes story, *A Study in Scarlet*, is written (1886), published in Great Britain (1887), and published in the United States (1890).

◆ Conan Doyle's *The Sign of the Four* is published, 1890.

◆ Nellie Bly (the pseudonym of newspaper reporter Elizabeth Cochrane) breaks the fictitious record of Jules Verne's characters in *Around the World in 80 Days* by completing the journey, in 72 days, on January 25, 1890.

◆ The United Mine Workers of America is founded, 1890.

◆ The 1890 census shows a US population of nearly 63 million people.

◆ Alexander Borodin's opera *Prince Igor* premieres, 1890.

◆ Henrik Ibsen's *Hedda Gabler* premieres, 1890.

◆ Cecil John Rhodes becomes prime minister of Cape Colony in southern Africa, 1890.

◆ The first volume of Emily Dickinson's poetry is published posthumously, 1890.

◆ William James publishes *The Principles of Psychology*, 1890.

◆ Nikola Tesla invents the Tesla coil, an induction coil that produces high-frequency alternating currents, 1891.

◆ On May 5, 1891, Carnegie Hall opens with a concert conducted by Peter Ilyich Tchaikovsky.

◆ In March 1891 a mob breaks open a jail in New Orleans and hangs eleven of the nineteen Italian-Americans who had been accused of, and cleared in, the murder of a police chief. The incident popularizes the word "mafia" in America.

◆ Thomas Hardy publishes *Tess of the d'Urbervilles*, 1891.

◆ James Dewar invents the Dewar flask—also called a vacuum flask or bottle and later trademarked as a Thermos flask—which keeps liquids hot or cold, 1892.

◆ On January 1, 1892, Ellis Island opens for the reception of immigrants to the United States.

◆ Oscar Wilde's play *Lady Windermere's Fan* opens, February 1892.

◆ The University of Chicago, founded by John D. Rockefeller, begins classes, 1892.

◆ Ruggero Leoncavallo's opera *Il Pagliacci* premieres, May 21, 1892.

◆ Giuseppe Verdi's opera *Falstaff* premieres, February 9, 1893.

FAST FACTS ABOUT BENJAMIN HARRISON

◆ Harrison is the only president who was the grandson of a president, William Henry Harrison.

◆ A campaign song for the Republicans in 1888 contained the lyric "Grandfather's hat fits Ben," a reference to William Henry Harrison's presidency.

◆ Harrison's father, John Harrison, was a member of the US House of Representatives from 1853 to 1857.

◆ Harrison's great-grandfather, Benjamin Harrison, was one of the signers of the Declaration of Independence.

◆ Harrison is the only president to be preceded and succeeded by the same president.

◆ Harrison won a majority of electoral votes in 1888, but President Cleveland won a majority of popular votes.

◆ More new states (six) entered the Union during Harrison's term than during that of any other president.

◆ Harrison's youthful nickname, "the pious moonlight dude," came into being as a result of the many evenings he spent courting his first wife.

◆ Electric lights were installed in the White House during Harrison's term.

◆ Harrison had a reserved personality and was criticized for being cold; his staff called him "the human iceberg," and opponents described his handshake as being like "a wet petunia."

◆ Caroline Harrison started the tradition of a White House Christmas tree.

◆ As First Lady, Caroline Harrison established the White House's collection of china and designed her own china pattern.

◆ Caroline Harrison and other prominent women helped raise money for the Johns Hopkins Medical School, but only on the condition that women would be admitted.

◆ In 1890 Caroline Harrison was one of the founders of (and the first president general of) the national chapter of the Daughters of the American Revolution.

◆ Four years after Caroline Harrison's death, Benjamin Harrison married Mary Scott Lord Dimmick, Caroline's niece, twenty-five years his junior.

Grover Cleveland

Presidency: 24th president, 1893–1897
Party: Democratic
[Note: See biographical information in the entry for Grover Cleveland as the 22nd president. Only information specific to his second term is presented here.]

GROVER CLEVELAND

[Note: For Cleveland's early life, education, career, and first presidency, please see the entry for Grover Cleveland as the 22nd president on page 172.]

BETWEEN TWO TERMS

At the end of his first term as president, Cleveland returned to private life—and a position as a lawyer with a Wall Street firm. The Clevelands' first child, Ruth, was born in 1891. There would be four more children: Esther, born in 1893, who was the first child of a president born in the White House; Marion, born in 1895; followed by the two boys, Richard, born in 1897, and Francis, born in 1903. Cleveland purchased a home near Bourne, on Cape Cod, in Massachusetts.

Cleveland was not pleased with the direction in which national events had been heading under Benjamin Harrison. Harrison had, for example, signed a bill that gave every Union veteran a pension (the type of bill Cleveland would have vetoed immediately) and supported a high tariff. Cleveland was quite willing to become his party's candidate again in 1892, and at the Democratic convention in Chicago, he was se-

lected on the first ballot. Adlai E. Stevenson of Illinois was selected as his running mate.

Benjamin Harrison did little campaigning for the 1892 presidential election, as his wife had become ill and died in October 1892. Out of respect for the Harrisons, Cleveland also refrained from campaigning. But victory went to Cleveland; he was elected by a narrow margin in the popular vote, but by a wide margin of electoral votes: 277 to Harrison's 145. Just as Frances Cleveland had predicted, the Clevelands returned to the White House.

SECOND PRESIDENCY

One of the first problems faced by Cleveland as he entered his second term was the Panic of 1893, which triggered an economic depression. The run on gold that had been prompted by the Sherman Silver Purchase Act of 1890 had contributed to the problem, which then escalated with the failure of the Philadelphia and Reading Railroad, the National Cordage Company, the Erie Railroad, the Northern Pacific Railroad, and the Union Pacific Railroad. Silver prices dropped when India, the world's second largest consumer of silver, stopped coining silver, and many American silver mines closed. The US economy remained depressed for about three years, with thousands of businesses failing and high unemployment. President Cleveland, who believed in allowing economic cycles to play out naturally, without federal intervention, continued to support the gold standard, and in fact the ability of the government to support the gold standard gradually improved after a few years. Cleveland also supported the repeal of the Sherman Silver Purchase Act in November 1893.

Cleveland authorized the use of federal troops to put down rioting strikers during the Pullman workers' strike of 1894, in Chicago. The action alienated workers and caused some to express fears that the president was becoming a tyrant.

In June 1893 a cancerous tumor was removed from Cleveland's jaw. Because Cleveland worried that the news of his illness might add to the public's existing high anxiety over a troubled economy, the operation was performed in secret on a friend's yacht as it sailed in the East River and Long Island Sound, near New York City. Part of his jaw was replaced with a rubber prosthetic piece, but as the insertion of the prosthesis was via the inside of his mouth, the resulting disfigurement was virtually nil. He recuperated during the summer of 1893, and in August he addressed the Congress.

With respect to international affairs, Cleveland tried to keep the United States out of foreign entanglements. He resisted efforts by some in Congress who proposed the annexation of Hawaii. When the United States was asked to arbitrate in the dispute between Venezuela and Great Britain over the border between Venezuela and British Guiana, Cleveland again sent warships—to enforce the Monroe Doctrine, and to underscore that Central and South America were to be considered as part of US spheres of influence.

Cleveland also tried to prevent United States involvement in the revolt of Cuba against Spain in 1895. The American public, however, was sympathetic to the Cuban desire for self-rule—a sympathy that would become manifest during the Spanish-American War a few years later.

POST-PRESIDENTIAL CAREER

After leaving office, the Cleveland family settled in Princeton, New Jersey, in a home they called "Westland." Cleveland lectured, wrote articles for magazines, and served as a trustee of Princeton University. He became a member of the board of the Equitable Life Assurance Society and helped to reorganize the company; he subsequently accepted a position as head of the Association of Life Insurance Presidents. The Cleveland family was devastated when, in 1904, the eldest daughter Ruth died from diphtheria. On June 24, 1908, Grover Cleveland succumbed to a heart attack at his Princeton home, with his wife by his side.

Frances Cleveland continued to live in Princeton and became the first presidential widow to remarry when she wed Thomas Preston, Jr., a professor of archaeology at Princeton, in 1913. She donated her time to humanitarian work during World War I and remained active in the alumni association of her alma mater, Wells College. She died on October 29, 1947; her second husband lived until 1955.

Cleveland's legacy is a mixed one. Some pundits and historians rate him as a near-great president—this based mainly on his having reclaimed much of the executive power that had become diminished over the years at the hands of powerful Congresses, starting in Abraham Lincoln's day. However, Cleveland was not a president who proposed new legislation or attempted to articulate a vision for the future. He did not react vigorously to the general suffering caused by the economic depression of his second term, and his penchant for vetoing legislation that he thought was partisan often made him appear to be unfeeling toward those in real need. Nevertheless, he was and is esteemed for his honesty, his hard work, and his opposition to political favoritism in appointments—and he enjoyed the advantage of Frances Cleveland, an unusually and unprecedentedly popular First Lady.

Dates in Office: March 4, 1893–March 3, 1897 (4 years)
Age at Inauguration: 55 years, 351 days

PRESIDENCY

Nomination: 1892: At the Democratic convention, held in Chicago, June 21–23, 1892, Cleveland was nominated on the first ballot. Adlai Ewing Stevenson of Illinois was selected as the vice-presidential candidate.

Election: elected president on November 8, 1892

Opponent: Benjamin Harrison, IN, Republican; James Weaver, IA, Populist; John Bidwell, CA, Prohibition

Vote Totals: Cleveland, 5,553,898 popular, 277 electoral; Harrison, 5,190,819 popular, 145 electoral; Weaver, 1,026,595 popular, 22 electoral; Bidwell, 270,879 popular, 0 electoral

Inauguration: March 4, 1893

Vice President: Adlai E. Stevenson, IL (1893–1897)

CABINET

Secretary of State: Walter Q. Gresham, IL (1893–1895); Richard Olney, MA (1895–1897)

Secretary of the Treasury: John G. Carlisle, KY (1893–1897)

Secretary of War: Daniel S. Lamont, NY (1893–1897)

Attorney General: Richard Olney, MA (1893–1895); Judson Harmon, OH (1895–1897)

Postmaster General: Wilson S. Bissell, NY (1893–1895); William L. Wilson, WV (1895–1897)

Secretary of the Navy: Hilary A. Herbert, AL (1893–1897)

Secretary of Agriculture: Julius S. Morton, NE (1893–1897)

Secretary of the Interior: Hoke Smith, GA (1893–1896); David R. Francis, MO (1896–1897)

CONGRESS:

53rd Congress (1893–1895); Speaker of the House: Charles F. Crisp (GA, Democrat)

54th Congress (1895–1897); Speaker of the House: Thomas B. Reed (ME, Republican)

SUPREME COURT APPOINTEES

Edward Douglass White, LA; Associate Justice (1894–1910) [Note: White was named Chief Justice by President Taft and served in that capacity from 1910 to 1921.]

Rufus Wheeler Peckham, NY; Associate Justice (1896–1909)

MAJOR EVENTS OF THE SECOND CLEVELAND ADMINISTRATION

❖ The Panic of 1893 sets off a depression after a run on gold and the failure of railroads, banks, and many businesses. Unemployment hits about 18 percent.

❖ A cancerous tumor is removed from Cleveland's jaw in June 1893, without the public's knowledge.

❖ The Sherman Silver Purchase Act is repealed, November 1893.

❖ Jacob Sechler Coxey of Ohio leads "Coxey's Army," about 500 unemployed people, in a march on Washington, DC, in 1894; the march is intended to urge Congress to increase the amount of money in circulation and spend the money on public works to combat unemployment. While unsuccessful, the march does publicize the plight of the unemployed.

❖ A strike by Pullman railroad workers in 1894, led by labor leader Eugene Debs, provokes a federal injunction against the strike on the grounds that the US mails had been disrupted by the break in train service. Cleveland supports sending federal troops to Chicago to maintain order in the face of union protests.

❖ Americans in Hawaii, led by businessman Stanford Dole and aided by US marines, overthrow the monarchy of Queen Liliuokalani, 1893. The United States recognizes a new Hawaiian republic in 1894.

❖ In *Pollock v. Farmers' Loan and Trust Co.*, in 1895, the Supreme Court declares an income tax imposed by the Wilson-Gorman Tariff unconstitutional.

❖ In *Debs v. the United States*, 1895, the Supreme Court affirms the use of injunctions to break strikes by upholding the arrest of Eugene V. Debs.

❖ In *United States v. E. C. Knight Co.*, 1895, the Supreme Court rules that the Sherman Antitrust Act is constitutional but does not apply to manufacturing firms—in this case, the E. C. Knight Company, which controls about 98 percent of US sugar refining.

◆ The United States declares its neutrality in the conflict between Cuba and Spain, 1895.
◆ In response to a longstanding dispute between Venezuela and Great Britain over the border between Venezuela and British-owned British Guiana, Cleveland's secretary of state, Richard Olney, asserts the Monroe Doctrine, which calls for the disputing parties to submit to arbitration. While rejecting the Monroe Doctrine, the contending parties nonetheless agree to arbitration by an American boundary commission. Former President Benjamin Harrison represents Venezuela in the dispute.
◆ Utah becomes a state, January 4, 1896.
◆ The Supreme Court in 1896, in *Plessy v. Ferguson,* hands down the decision that sets the precedent for "separate but equal" facilities for whites and African Americans.
◆ At the Democratic convention, on July 9, 1896, William Jennings Bryan makes the "Cross of Gold" speech in opposition to the gold standard.
◆ Cleveland vetoes a bill that would ban illiterate immigrants from the United States, 1897.

MAJOR US AND WORLD EVENTS, 1893–1897
◆ From May 1 to October 31, 1893, the World's Columbian Exposition in Chicago draws about 27 million visitors.
◆ On June 20, 1893, Lizzie Borden is found innocent of the murders of her father and stepmother.
◆ In December 1893 Antonin Dvorak's *Symphony No. 9 in E Minor,* called "From the New World," premieres in New York City.
◆ The first Stanley Cup is won in 1893 by the Montreal Amateur Athletic Association hockey club.
◆ Edvard Munch paints *The Scream,* 1893.
◆ Thomas Edison makes two short films whose subject is his assistant Fred Ott: *Fred Ott Holding a Bird* and *The Edison Kinetoscopic Record of a Sneeze* (also called *Fred Ott's Sneeze*), 1894.

◆ In 1894 Congress makes Labor Day a national holiday.
◆ Shibasaburo Kitasato discovers the infectious agent of bubonic plague, 1894.
◆ On October 15, 1894, French artillery officer Alfred Dreyfus is arrested in France on suspicion of treason.
◆ On October 20, 1894, Czar Alexander III of Russia dies; his son Nicholas II becomes czar and is crowned on May 14, 1896.
◆ Amateur astronomer Percival Lowell establishes the Lowell Observatory in Flagstaff, Arizona, 1894.
◆ Anthony Hope publishes *The Prisoner of Zenda,* 1894.
◆ Rudyard Kipling publishes *The Jungle Book,* 1894.
◆ From August 1894 to April 1895, Japan and China engage in the first Sino-Japanese War over control of Korea; Japan defeats China and forces it to sign the Treaty of Shimonoseki (also called the Treaty of Maguan).
◆ In 1895 Josef Breuer and Sigmund Freud publish *Studies in Hysteria,* in which they discuss the "talking cure" and the basic ideas of psychoanalysis.
◆ H. G. Wells publishes *The Time Machine,* 1895.
◆ Oscar Wilde's *The Importance of Being Earnest* opens, 1895.
◆ Stephen Crane publishes *The Red Badge of Courage,* 1895.
◆ In November 1895 Wilhelm Conrad Röntgen discovers X rays.
◆ By way of the Treaty of Addis Ababa in 1896, Italy recognizes the independence of Ethiopia.
◆ Giacomo Puccini's opera *La Bohème* is first produced in Turin, 1896.
◆ The first modern Olympics are held in 1896 in Athens, Greece; 14 countries and 245 athletes participate.
◆ George Carmack discovers gold in the Klondike on August 16, 1896 (the news reaches the United States in July 1897).
[Note: For "Fast Facts" about Grover Cleveland, please see the entry for the 22nd president.]

William McKinley

Nickname: The Idol of Ohio
Presidency: 25th president, 1897–1901
Party: Republican
Life dates: January 29, 1843–September 14, 1901 (58 years, 228 days)

EARLY LIFE AND EDUCATION

William McKinley was born to Nancy Campbell Allison McKinley and William McKinley on January 29, 1843, in Niles, Ohio. He was the seventh of nine children. His forebears were Scottish-Irish immigrants who had settled in Pennsylvania before moving to Ohio. Both his grandfather and his father were ironmongers. William attended local schools until the age of nine, when, in 1852, the McKinley family moved to Poland, Ohio, primarily so that the McKinley children could attend the Poland Academy. William showed an early interest in public speaking and became the president of the school's first debating club.

He graduated from the academy in 1860 and briefly attended Allegheny College in Meadville, Pennsylvania; however his studies were cut short by illness. He also suffered from depression during this period. Around the time he was making a recovery, his father suffered business losses. For financial reasons, William was not able to return to college. He worked for a time in an Ohio post office and as a teacher, until April 1861, at which point war broke out; William was quick to answer the call for volunteers.

CIVIL WAR

At the age of eighteen, McKinley enlisted as a private in the Poland Guards—part of the 23rd Regiment of Ohio Volunteer Infantry that was commanded by Rutherford B. Hayes. McKinley was made quartermaster clerk in November 1861 and promoted to quartermaster sergeant in April 1862. He fought at the Battle of Antietam, on September 17, 1862, and, although advised to retreat, carried food to his men through enemy fire. He was promoted to the rank of lieutenant in November 1862, and was made brigade quartermaster in January 1863. He again rode through enemy fire, at the Battle of Kernstown, on July 24, 1864, and was promoted to the rank of captain. He fought at the Battle of Berryville, September 3–4, 1864, in which the horse on which he was riding was shot; he was promoted to brevet major, his rank at the time of his military discharge at the end of the war.

Like many of the men who later rose to political prominence, McKinley was proud of his Civil War service and retained strong ties to the men with whom he had served. He continued to be called "Major" throughout his career, preferring that to other titles.

EARLY CAREER

After he returned to Poland, McKinley began to read law with Judge Charles Glidden in Youngstown, Ohio. He spent one term at the Albany School of Law in Albany, New York. In 1867 he was admitted to the Ohio bar, and during that same year he campaigned for his former military commander, Rutherford B. Hayes, who was running for governor of Ohio. In 1868 he campaigned for Ulysses S. Grant for president.

"A liberal education is the prize of individual industry. It is the greatest blessing that a man or woman can enjoy, when supported by virtue, morality, and noble aims."

William McKinley, in a speech given in Philadelphia, February 22, 1898

McKinley moved to Canton, Ohio, to set up his law practice, which quickly grew, and he was elected as county prosecutor in 1869 (he failed to win reelection to the post in 1871). By that time he had met Ida Saxton, the daughter of a banker in Canton. She was considered a belle, and McKinley fell in love with her and proposed. They were married on January 25, 1871, in Canton. Their first child, a daughter named Kate, was born on Christmas Day of that same year. In 1873, pregnant with her second child and experiencing difficulties with that pregnancy, Ida received word that her mother had died; the multiple shocks to her system (including a difficult labor and delivery) considerably weakened her. During the post partum period, she suffered from depression and, for the first time in her life, seizures. She was diagnosed with epilepsy and had seizures for the rest of her married life. The second child, a daughter, also named Ida, lived only five months. Two years later, in 1875, Kate died.

McKinley remained devoted to Ida throughout their marriage. He would sit by her side and, when there was a seizure, he would throw his handkerchief over her face, both to hide its contortions from others and because the darkness helped to soothe her.

POLITICAL CAREER

In 1877 McKinley was elected to the US House of Representatives. He served until 1891, except for a brief hiatus during 1884 and 1885 when he was forced to give up his seat in Congress (his opponent had successfully contested the results of his most recent election). He regained his seat in 1885. He was a member of the influential Ways and Means Committee and became its chair in 1889. He championed civil service reform and bimetallism (using both gold and silver as the basis for currency). He became an expert on tariffs, and in 1890 sponsored the McKinley Tariff, a bill that raised protective tariffs. McKinley believed that the legislation was necessary for the protection of American business, but he eventually became convinced that, apropos of trade between the United States and other countries, reciprocal trade agreements were necessary.

McKinley's activities as a member of Congress attracted the attention of Marcus ("Mark") Hanna, a wealthy industrialist with interests in coal, railroads, and banking. McKinley faced many challenges in his runs for the Congress, as the Democratic Party in Ohio repeatedly redrew the districts to its own advantage. When gerrymandering in Ohio brought about McKinley's loss of his seat in Congress in 1890, McKinley, supported by Mark Hanna, was able to win election to the governorship of Ohio, in 1891 and again in 1893. McKinley served as governor until 1896, and as governor tried to ease the growing differences between management and labor groups in the state. He urged the adoption of a system of arbitration for the settlement of labor disputes; yet, despite his actions on behalf of his state's workers, he called in the National Guard in 1894 to thwart the threats of violence that were coming from striking Ohio mine workers.

McKinley faced personal financial difficulties in 1893 when, after cosigning bank notes for a friend, the friend slid into bankruptcy, leaving McKinley responsible for a $130,000 debt. Hanna raised the money via the solicitation of donations from his personal friends. Rather unexpectedly, McKinley garnered a modicum of sympathetic understanding from the general public, as many people were facing personal financial crises during the depression that followed the Panic of 1893.

McKinley had been mentioned as a possible presidential candidate as early as the 1888 presidential election, and when his term as governor was concluded, in 1896, he started to actively pursue the nomination. Mark Hanna helped to solidify McKinley's base of support in Ohio (including among prominent, wealthy Republicans in the state). Hanna raised money for the campaign after McKinley received the nomination—on the first ballot at the 1896 convention, held in St. Louis, Missouri.

The Democratic candidate was William Jennings Bryan, who opposed the gold standard and the protective tariff, which the Republicans argued would help to restore US prosperity. Bryan argued for the unrestricted coinage of silver as a way of increasing the supply of money. Both parties and both candidates were supporting the Cubans in their struggle against Spain. McKinley ran a "front-porch" campaign: he spoke to supporters from the porch of his home in Canton (as more than a thousand campaign workers spoke in support of him across the nation). Bryan, famous for his oratorical skill, traveled extensively during his campaign. But McKinley scored a resounding victory over his opponent, by a margin of 600,000 popular votes, and received 271 electoral votes to Bryan's 176.

PRESIDENCY

Within a few weeks of his inauguration, McKinley called a special session of Congress to discuss revision of the tariff laws. The result was the Dingley Tariff of 1897, which mandated large increases in tariffs, but also contained provisions for reciprocal trade treaties with other nations.

McKinley accepted the idea of international bimetallism and advocated for an international treaty whereby a number of countries would agree to use both silver and gold as the basis of their currencies. However, talks with Great Britain and France on the subject of international bimetallism did not lead to agreement, and McKinley eventually became convinced that the gold standard was the best policy for the United States. In 1900 the Gold Standard Act was passed; it recognized gold as the standard for US currency and set a minimum amount of gold (worth $150 million) as the amount the Treasury Department was required to hold in reserve.

"The mission of the United States is one of benevolent assimilation."

William McKinley, in a letter, December 21, 1898

The most momentous event of McKinley's presidency, the Spanish-American War, grew out of political unrest in Cuba. Spain refused to grant independence to Cuba, and rumors of cruelties being perpetrated against the Cubans were rampant in the United States (in part owing to the sensationalized, "yellow journalism" news stories that appeared regularly in the newspapers of William Randolph Hearst and described the "atrocities" that the "cruel Spanish" were inflicting on the Cubans). McKinley urged the Cubans and the Spanish to resolve their dispute among themselves, and there was some progress made. But Spain continued to refuse to grant independence to the Cubans. The United States, wishing to make a show of its friendly relations with Spain—or as a show of strength, sent the US battleship *Maine* to Havana, where its captain met cordially with members of the Spanish government for several weeks, and saw no sign of the Cuban rebels. On

February 15, 1898, the *Maine* was blown up in Havana Harbor; 266 Americans were killed. It was never found out who or what was responsible for the tragedy. However, US newspapers proclaimed that the explosion was a despicable act of sabotage by the Spaniards. Many newspapers, led by Hearst's New York *Journal*, made "Remember the *Maine*! To hell with Spain!" a rallying cry for war.

In April 1898 McKinley, not inclined toward war, sent a message to Congress in which he advocated for "neutral intervention": the United States should intervene in Cuba, without taking sides, in order to end the dispute, protect the Cuban people, and protect American citizens in Cuba. However, Congress soon responded by passing resolutions that led to a declaration of war with Spain.

As volunteers rushed to join the army, the Pacific fleet, under the command of Admiral George Dewey, in Hong Kong at the time of the declaration of war, headed toward the Philippines and the Spanish fleet stationed there. On May 1, 1898, the American fleet soundly defeated the Spanish squadron in Manila Bay.

Meanwhile, military supplies and facilities for transporting soldiers to Cuba were woefully in arrears for the quarter of a million men who had volunteered to go to Cuba to fight. Enthusiastic private citizens who could afford to do so outfitted soldiers ready to go to war. Theodore Roosevelt, the Assistant Secretary of the Navy, resigned his position and assembled a group of sportsmen and cowboys from the western United States who called themselves the Rocky Mountain Riders; they would become better known as the Rough Riders. Joining other volunteers in Tampa, Florida, the Rough Riders set off for Cuba and soon found themselves slogging through jungle in one hundred-degree heat. The Spanish forces occupied the San Juan hills near Santiago, Cuba. The Rough Riders, the Ninth Cavalry, an African-American regiment, and thousands of other regular and volunteer troops led the successful attack on the hills. The Spanish troops surrendered.

While US forces held the Spanish army at bay, the Spanish navy attacked the US ships that were blocking Santiago harbor. It was a hopeless foray; four US battleships and a large fleet of smaller ships crushed the Spanish squadron, sinking most of it. As a final blow, a US force quickly took possession of Spanish-held Puerto Rico. Spain agreed to peace talks.

"I have already transmitted to Congress the report of the naval court of inquiry on the destruction of the battle ship *Maine* in the harbor of Havana during the night of the fifteenth of February. The destruction of that noble vessel has filled the national heart with inexpressible horror. Two hundred and fifty-eight brave sailors and marines and two officers of our Navy, reposing in the fancied security of a friendly harbor, have been hurled to death, grief and want brought to their homes, and sorrow to the nation."

William McKinley, in a message to Congress, April 11, 1898

The Treaty of Paris was signed in Paris in December 1898. It placed Guam and Puerto Rico under US control; the United States agreed to pay Spain twenty million US dollars for possession of the Philippines. Cuba was granted its independence, although the United States imposed restrictions on the new nation: the United States was to oversee the transition to a new government in Cuba and restricted Cuba from forming alliances with other countries.

McKinley appointed William Howard Taft to become the chief civil administrator in the Philippines, and to oversee its transition to a new government. But the US army in the Philippines was met with a guerrilla insurgency there. Following on the heels of the speedy and popularly supported Spanish-American War, the Philippine-American War became a bloody and protracted struggle. It ended, for the most part, by 1902, but there continued to be pockets of resistance to US rule, and it was not until after World War II that the Philippines would become independent.

"My wife, be careful, Cortelyou, how you tell her—oh, be careful!"

William McKinley, speaking to his secretary George Cortelyou shortly after being shot, September 6, 1901

The United States's desire to create spheres of influence in Asia became greatly increased as a result of its acquisition of the Philippines; it prompted the Open Door Policy, whereby the United States encouraged the European powers to trade freely with China and to respect its territorial integrity. When the Boxer Rebellion broke out in China in 1900, the United States joined forces with Japan and a number of European countries in putting down the rebellion and in exacting a huge indemnity from China.

Vice President Hobart died in 1899; McKinley accepted Theodore Roosevelt, who was riding a wave of postwar popularity, as his running mate for the 1900 presidential election. Facing William Jennings Bryan once again, McKinley again was the victor, winning by a plurality of nearly one million popular votes.

In 1901 McKinley traveled to Buffalo, New York, to attend the Pan-American Exposition. On September 6 he was shot by anarchist Leon Czolgosz and died eight days later, on September 14, 1901.

Ida McKinley returned to Canton, Ohio, and lived quietly. In Canton she experienced a remission of her symptoms until the time of her death in the spring of 1907.

McKinley is often described as the first modern president. He is regarded as a president who wielded the executive power of the federal government very ably. However reluctant he may have been to involve the United States in the Cuban conflict, his willingness to prosecute the war aggressively helped to establish the United States as a world power. Esteemed even by his political opponents for his tender devotion to his wife, he was also admired for his ability to attain his political goals without making enemies. Some historians have charged that he was unduly influenced by others—most notably Mark Hanna—but the greater part of the evidence is that McKinley led and Hanna followed. Historically, McKinley has been much overshadowed by the larger-than-life persona of his successor, Theodore Roosevelt.

Birthplace: Niles, OH
Residency: Ohio
Religion: Methodist
Education: Allegheny College, Meadville, PA, (McKinley entered in 1860; left because of illness); Albany Law School, Albany, New York (one term)
Place of Death: Buffalo, NY
Burial Site: McKinley National Memorial and Museum, Canton, OH
Dates in Office: March 4, 1897–September 14, 1901 (4 years, 194 days)
Age at Inauguration: 54 years, 34 days

FAMILY
Father: William McKinley (1807–1892)
Mother: Nancy Campbell Allison McKinley (1809–1897)
Siblings: William was the seventh of nine children; his siblings were David Allison McKinley (1829–1892); Annie McKinley (1831–1889); James Rose McKinley (1833–1889); Mary McKinley (1835–1868); Helen McKinley (1839–1924); Sarah Elizabeth McKinley (1840–1931);

Abbie Celia McKinley (1845–1846); Abner Osborn McKinley (1847–1904).

Wife: Ida Saxton McKinley (1847–1907), married on January 25, 1871

Children: Katherine ("Katie") McKinley (1871–1875); Ida McKinley (born in 1873; died at five months)

CAREER

Private: lawyer

Political: member of the US House of Representatives (1877–1891); governor of Ohio (1892–1896); president of the United States (1897–1901)

Military: McKinley enlisted as a private in the Poland, Ohio Guards at the beginning of the Civil War, and was made quartermaster clerk (November 1861); was promoted to quartermaster sergeant (April 1862); was promoted to lieutenant (November 1862); was made brigade quartermaster (January 1863); rode through enemy fire at the Battle of Kernstown (July 24, 1864); was promoted to captain; fought at the Battle of Berryville (September 3–4, 1864), in which the horse he was riding was shot; was promoted to brevet major; served until the end of the war.

Selected Works: *The Last Speech of William McKinley, President of the United States, Delivered at Buffalo, New York, September 5, 1901* (Cambridge: Cambridge University Press, 1901); *Papers of William McKinley,* archival manuscript collection (Washington, DC: Library of Congress); *Speeches and Addresses of William McKinley, from March 1, 1897 to May 30, 1900* (New York: Doubleday & McClure Co., 1900); *The Tariff: A Review of the Tariff Legislation of the United States from 1812 to 1896* (New York: G.P. Putnam's Sons, 1904)

PRESIDENCY

Nomination: 1896: The Republican convention was held in St. Louis, MO, June 16–18, 1896. McKinley was nominated on the first ballot; Garret A. Hobart of NJ was chosen as the vice-presidential candidate.

1900: The Republican convention was held in Philadelphia, PA, June 19–21, 1900; McKinley was nominated on the first ballot; Theodore Roosevelt of NY was chosen as the vice-presidential candidate.

Election: 1896: elected president on November 3, 1896

1900: reelected president on November 6, 1900

Opponent: 1896: William Jennings Bryan, NE, Democratic; John Palmer, IL, National Democrat; Joshua Levering, MD, Prohibition; Charles Matchett, NY, Socialist Labor

1900: William Jennings Bryan, NE, Democratic; John Woolley, IL, Prohibition; Eugene V. Debs, IN, Socialist; Wharton Barker, PA, Populist; Joseph Maloney, MA, Socialist Labor

Vote Totals: 1896: McKinley, 7,112,138 popular, 271 electoral; Bryan, 6,508,172 popular, 176 electoral; Palmer, 133,730 popular, 0 electoral; Levering, 125,088 popular, 0 electoral; Matchett, 36,359 popular, 0 electoral

1900: McKinley, 7,228,864 popular, 292 electoral; Bryan, 6,371,932 popular, 155 electoral; Woolley, 210,864 popular, 0 electoral; Debs, 87,945 popular, 0 electoral; Barker, 50,989 popular, 0 electoral; Maloney, 40,943 popular, 0 electoral

Inauguration: 1896: March 4, 1897

1900: March 4, 1901

Vice President: Garret Hobart, NJ (1897–1899 [died in office]); Theodore Roosevelt, NY (1901)

CABINET

Secretary of State: John Sherman, OH (1897–1898); William R. Day, OH (1898); John M. Hay, DC (1898–1901)

Secretary of the Treasury: Lyman J. Gage, IL (1897–1901)

Secretary of War: Russell A. Alger, MI (1897–1899); Elihu Root, NY (1899–1901)

Attorney General: Joseph McKenna, CA (1897–1898); John W. Griggs, NJ (1898–1901); Philander C. Knox, PA (1901)

Postmaster General: James A. Gary, MD (1897–1898); Charles Emory Smith, PA (1898–1901)

Secretary of the Navy: John D. Long, MA (1897–1901)

Secretary of Agriculture: James Wilson, IA (1897–1901)
Secretary of the Interior: Cornelius N. Bliss, NY (1897–1899); Ethan Hitchcock, MO (1899–1901)

CONGRESS
55th Congress (1897–1899); Speaker of the House: Thomas B. Reed (ME, Republican)
56th Congress (1899–1901); Speaker of the House: David B. Henderson (IA, Republican)

SUPREME COURT APPOINTEES
Joseph McKenna, CA; Associate Justice (1898–1925)

MAJOR EVENTS OF THE McKINLEY ADMINISTRATION
◆ The Dingley Tariff of 1897 raises tariffs by more than 50 percent, on average.
◆ A strike by coal miners in Pennsylvania leads to violence in Lattimer, PA, where nineteen unarmed strikers are killed by a sheriff and his deputies on September 10, 1897.
◆ In the Maximum Freight Rate Case, 1897, the Supreme Court rules that the Interstate Commerce Commission (ICC) can initiate legal action to revise rates for the shipment of commodities by railroad if the ICC deems the rate unfair, but that the ICC cannot establish rates. The case reflects the dissatisfaction of shippers over the railroads' general rate increases.
◆ In 1898 McKinley appoints members of the US Industrial Commission, which is charged with investigating railroad rates, the impact of immigration on labor markets, and industrial concentration. Its report helps to launch the trust-busting efforts of Theodore Roosevelt during his tenure as president.
◆ The US battleship *Maine* is blown up by a mine and sunk in Havana harbor, February 15, 1898.
◆ In April 1898 McKinley urges "neutral intervention" in Cuba, stating that the United States has a duty to bring peace to Cuba without favoring either Cuba or Spain, to provide relief to the inhabitants of Cuba, and to protect American citizens in Cuba.

◆ The Volunteer Army Act passes on April 22, 1898, and provides for a volunteer army in time of war; McKinley immediately calls for 125,000 volunteers.
◆ The Spanish-American War begins in April 1898.
◆ On May 1, 1898, Commodore George Dewey and the US fleet in the Pacific defeat the Spanish fleet in Manila Bay; the battle begins with Dewey instructing, "You may fire when you are ready, Gridley."
◆ In June US troops land in Cuba and on July 1, 1898, successfully attack the San Juan hills. Both San Juan Hill and Kettle Hill are taken by Theodore Roosevelt's Rough Riders and 8,000 other troops, including regulars, volunteers, and African-American troops.
◆ The Spanish fleet attempts to leave Santiago harbor in Cuba, July 3, 1898, but is completely destroyed by the US fleet, three times its strength, under Admiral Schley.
◆ The United States annexes Hawaii, July 7–8, 1898.
◆ In July 1898 US troops occupy Puerto Rico.
◆ The United States and Spain sign an armistice in August 1898 and conclude the Treaty of Paris in December 1898. The United States gains Puerto Rico, Guam, and the Philippines from Spain; Cuba is given independence, but with restrictions imposed by the United States, including a prohibition against its making alliances with other countries.
◆ The Erdman Arbitration Act, June 1898, authorizes government mediation in disputes between interstate railroad carriers and their workers; it also prohibits discrimination against or the blacklisting of union labor.
◆ The War Revenue Act, June 1898, provides for taxes on inheritances, tobacco, telephone service, tea, liquor, and amusements.
◆ In September 1898 McKinley appoints the Dodge Commission to investigate the War Department in the wake of complaints about the supplies and rations given to the troops during the war, and the methods used to combat the diseases to which the troops were prey.

◆ Following McKinley's lead, in 1899 Secretary of State John Hay pursues an Open Door Policy for China; he seeks a treaty with other nations whereby China will not be put under the sphere of influence of any single nation, each nation may trade with China, and each nation will respect China's territory.

◆ On November 21, 1899, Vice President Garret Hobart dies in Paterson, NJ.

◆ In April 1900 McKinley appoints William Howard Taft to the Second Philippine Commission, charging him with the formation of a civilian government in the Philippines.

◆ The Gold Standard Act, 1900, establishes gold as the only specie for which currency can be redeemed; it also mandates that the Treasury maintain $150 million in gold reserves and sets the price of gold at $20.67 per ounce.

◆ Two Hay-Pauncefote Treaties are concluded; the first, signed in February 1900, provides for the building of the Panama Canal but restricts US authority; the second, signed in November 1901, does not restrict US authority and is ratified by Congress.

◆ The United States agrees with The Netherlands in December 1900 to purchase the Dutch West Indies, which become the US Virgin Islands when the transaction is completed in 1917.

◆ McKinley is reelected on November 6, 1900, with Theodore Roosevelt of NY as his vice president.

◆ The Platt Amendment is passed, March 1, 1901; it is part of the Army Appropriation Act of 1901. The amendment provides that Cuba will allow US intervention in the event of incursion by a foreign power against the independence of Cuba; it also provides that the US will be allowed to purchase or lease Cuban territory for coaling or naval stations.

◆ McKinley is shot by Leon Czolgosz, September 6, 1901, at the Buffalo Pan-American Exposition.

◆ McKinley dies of his wounds on September 14, 1901, eight days after being shot.

MAJOR US AND WORLD EVENTS, 1897–1901

◆ On April 19, 1897, the first Boston Marathon is run; the winner, John J. McDermott, finishes in 2 hours, 55 minutes, 10 seconds.

◆ On April 27, 1897, Grant's Tomb is dedicated.

◆ Edmund Rostand publishes the play *Cyrano de Bergerac*, 1897.

◆ Bram Stoker publishes *Dracula*, 1897.

◆ H. G. Wells publishes *The Invisible Man*, 1897.

◆ On May 14, 1897, John Philip Sousa's "Stars and Stripes Forever" is first performed, in Philadelphia, PA.

◆ On June 12, 1897, a massive earthquake strikes Assam, India, killing more than 1,500 people.

◆ The first ship carrying gold from Alaska arrives in San Francisco on July 15, 1897; on July 17 another ship arrives in Seattle. The Klondike gold rush begins.

◆ On August 29, 1897, the first Zionist Congress meets in Basel, Switzerland; it is led by Theodor Herzl.

◆ On September 1, 1897, the first section of Boston's subway system opens.

◆ In September 1897 the first issue of *McCall's* magazine is published.

◆ The *New York Sun* runs an editorial, on September 21, 1897, which answers the question posed in a letter from a little girl, replying, "Yes, Virginia, there is a Santa Claus."

◆ Ransom E. Olds founds the Olds Motor Vehicle Company, 1897.

◆ In 1897 the *Katzenjammer Kids* comic strip, created by Rudolph Dirks, debuts in the *American Humorist*, the Sunday supplement of the *New York Journal*.

◆ Sir Joseph John Thomson, an English physicist, in a lecture given on April 30, 1897, announces his discovery of the electron, the first subatomic particle discovered.

◆ In 1898 Guglielmo Marconi achieves the first wireless transmission of sound signals, from Northern Ireland to Rathlin Island, off the coast of Ireland.

◆ Horatio Kitchener (Earl Kitchener of Khartoum) leads combined British and Egyptian forces in the Battle of Omdurman on September 2, 1898, defeating the forces of Muhammed Ahmad, a religious leader known as the Mahdi.

◆ In 1898 artist Frederick Remington, in Cuba to depict the rebellion against Spain, asks his boss, newspaper magnate William Randolph Hearst, to recall him because there is no war. Hearst replies, "You furnish the pictures, I'll furnish the war."

◆ H. G. Wells publishes *The War of the Worlds*, 1898.

◆ In 1898 Oscar Wilde publishes *The Ballad of Reading Gaol*, a description of his imprisonment in England.

◆ In 1897–1898 Sir Ronald Ross discovers that malaria is transmitted by the Anopheles mosquito.

◆ The Boer War (also called the South African War) between Great Britain and the Boers (Dutch settlers in South Africa) begins in 1899; the war continues until 1902, ending with British victory and the inclusion of South Africa in the British Empire.

◆ Sigmund Freud publishes *The Interpretation of Dreams*, 1899.

◆ The trademarked name Aspirin is first used by the Bayer Company, 1899.

◆ Kate Chopin publishes *The Awakening*, 1899.

◆ Educator John Dewey publishes *The School and Society*, 1899.

◆ Edward Elgar's *Enigma Variations* premieres in London, June 19, 1899.

◆ German mathematician David Hilbert lays the basis for modern geometry with the publication of *Grundlagen der Geometrie* (*Foundations of Geometry*), 1899.

◆ The Boxer Rebellion of 1900 pits the Boxers, Chinese revolutionaries, against foreigners (and, at first, the ruling Manchu [Qing] Dynasty, to which the Boxers are later reconciled); the Boxers are defeated by combined Japanese, US, and European forces.

◆ On January 14, 1900, Giacomo Puccini's *Tosca* premieres in Rome.

◆ The American League of Professional Baseball Clubs is organized, 1900.

◆ British archaeologist Sir Arthur Evans unearths the palace of Knossos on Crete, 1900.

◆ The *Exposition Universelle,* a world's fair, is held in Paris, 1900, and introduces the Art Deco style.

◆ On June 1, 1900, Carry Nation, a temperance advocate, attacks three saloons operating illegally, in Kiowa, Kansas.

◆ On July 29, 1900, King Umberto I of Italy is assassinated by anarchist Gaetano Bresci.

◆ On September 8, 1900, a category 4 hurricane hits Galveston, Texas; many ignore warnings of the impending storm, which leaves more than 8,000 dead in its wake.

◆ Theodore Dreiser publishes *Sister Carrie*, 1900.

◆ Joseph Conrad publishes *Lord Jim*, 1900.

◆ L. Frank Baum publishes *The Wonderful Wizard of Oz*, 1900.

◆ In 1900 German physicist Max Planck formulates Planck's radiation law, from which he deduces the existence of discrete packets of energy, called quanta, and launches quantum physics as a field of study.

◆ The 1900 census shows a US population of 76.2 million people.

◆ The first Davis Cup tennis match is held between the United States and Great Britain in Brookline, MA, 1900; the US teams wins.

◆ On January 10, 1901, the first major oil gusher in Texas erupts, in the Spindletop oil field in Beaumont, Texas.

◆ On January 22, 1901, Queen Victoria of Great Britain dies and is succeeded by her son, King Edward VII.

◆ The colonies in Australia are federated under an act of the British Parliament and Australia establishes its own parliament in Melbourne, 1901.

◆ Pablo Picasso exhibits his work for the first time in June 1901.

◆ Rudyard Kipling publishes *Kim*, 1901.

FAST FACTS ABOUT WILLIAM McKINLEY

◆ During the Civil War, McKinley served under Rutherford B. Hayes in the Twenty-third Ohio

Infantry regiment; McKinley was Hayes's quartermaster.

◆ McKinley was the last president who had served in the Civil War.

◆ McKinley's first presidential campaign, costing an estimated $3.5 million, was the most expensive to date; he spent twenty times the money his opponent, William Jennings Bryan, spent.

◆ McKinley adopted the practice of wearing a red carnation in his lapel; in 1904 the red carnation was made the official state flower of Ohio.

◆ McKinley's 1896 campaign was the first to widely distribute campaign buttons and memorabilia.

◆ McKinley's first inauguration, in 1897, was recorded by both the gramophone and the motion picture camera, both invented by Thomas Edison.

◆ McKinley was the first president to ride in an automobile, in 1899.

◆ McKinley enjoyed good relations with the press; space was set aside for reporters on the second floor of the White House and they were given daily briefings by the president's secretaries.

◆ McKinley was devoted to his wife, Ida, an invalid. When he was governor and residing in temporary quarters adjacent to the Ohio Capitol building, he waved to her window from his office daily at three o'clock, so she would know he was thinking of her.

◆ McKinley made extensive use of the telephone to stay in touch with his political allies, his subordinates, and even with army commanders during the Spanish-American War.

◆ Even when president, McKinley preferred being addressed as "Major" over any other title; he claimed that he had earned that title, but was not so sure about any other.

◆ After being shot, McKinley urged that his assassin not be harmed by the crowd.

◆ Although doctors could not find the bullet lodged in McKinley's body, they were reluctant to use the X-ray machine, developed by Thomas Edison and shown at the Pan-American Exposition, because they did not know what effects it might have on the president.

Theodore Roosevelt

Nickname: TR, Teddy, Tedie, Teedie, Thee, The Trust-Buster,
Bull Moose
Presidency: 26th president, 1901–1909
Party: Republican
Life dates: October 27, 1858–January 6, 1919 (60 years, 71 days)

EARLY LIFE AND EDUCATION

Theodore Roosevelt, Jr., was born in New York City on October 27, 1858, to Martha Bulloch Roosevelt and Theodore Roosevelt. The Roosevelt family had settled in New York in the mid-seventeenth century; one of Theodore's forebears had been a member of the New York Senate in the late eighteenth century and had urged adoption of the fledgling US Constitution. Theodore's paternal grandfather, Cornelius Van Schaack Roosevelt, acquired a substantial fortune in land speculation, and the senior Theodore Roosevelt was a philanthropist who supported many New York charities. He was a founding member of the New York Orthopedic Hospital, the American Museum of Natural History, and the Metropolitan Museum of Art.

Theodore had an older sister, Anna ("Bamie" or "Bye"), and younger siblings: a brother, Elliott ("Ellie"), and a sister, Corinne ("Conie"). He himself was called "Teedie" or "Thee" by his family, and disliked "Teddy" as a nickname.

His mother's family was long established in Georgia, and during the Civil War her sympathies were entirely with the Confederacy, for which some of her relatives were fighting. Two

of her brothers served on the *CSS Alabama* (of the Confederate States Navy) before it was sunk; they were rescued and lived in England after the war. Young Theodore watched in 1865 as President Lincoln's funeral procession passed through Union Square in New York City.

As a boy, Theodore was nearsighted, frail, and suffered from asthma attacks. He was told by his father that he needed to "make his body," and a gymnasium was installed in their home, where Theodore lifted weights and exercised vigorously. The children were tutored at home, sometimes by their father. The family traveled in Europe from May 1869 until March 1870, and again in 1872, at which time they also visited the Holy Land. Theodore, Elliott, and Corinne also spent five months in Dresden, Germany, studying the German language. Theodore developed a strong interest in natural science, collecting specimens and learning to distinguish birds by their songs.

One of his friends from childhood and adolescence was Edith Carow, whom he dated before he entered Harvard in 1876. At Harvard, he plunged enthusiastically into his studies and into various athletic pursuits (including riding and boxing), as well as extracurricular activities such as the Rifle Club, the Natural History Club, and the elite Porcellian Club. In February 1878 his father died of stomach cancer.

By 1878 Roosevelt's friendship with Carow had considerably faded. In October 1878 he met Alice Hathaway Lee, a young woman from a prominent Boston family, the daughter of a banker. He fell in love immediately and pursued her ardently, although she refused his first proposal. Eventually she relented and agreed to marry him. In June 1880 he graduated from Harvard, magna cum laude and a member of Phi Beta Kappa; in October he entered Columbia Law School and married Hathaway Lee. They settled in New York City. In 1882 they sailed to Europe and spent time in London, Paris, and Venice. When they visited the Alps, Theodore climbed the Matterhorn.

> "When he goes to a wedding, he wants to be the bride, and when he goes to a funeral, he wants to be the corpse."
>
> Remark about Theodore Roosevelt's affinity for being in the spotlight, made by a relative at the wedding of Eleanor and Franklin Roosevelt, March 17, 1905

While studying at Columbia Law School, Roosevelt learned that his interest in the law was less solid than he had thought and was becoming eclipsed by other interests. He dropped out of law school to pursue those interests.

EARLY CAREER

In November 1881 Roosevelt was elected to the first of three terms in the New York State Assembly. He became an outspoken, independent advocate of reform. He favored a union-sponsored measure to regulate conditions for factory workers, pushed for legislation

to ease conditions in New York City housing tenements, and also sought tougher penalties for men who abused their wives and children. As a young state legislator, he published his first book (in 1882), *The Naval War of 1812*, a book he had begun as an undergraduate at Harvard. It became a standard reference on the subject, was read on both sides of the Atlantic, and for years was required reading at the US Naval Academy.

In 1883 Roosevelt went bison hunting in the Badlands of Dakota, and thus began Roosevelt's lifelong love affair with the American West. In November 1883 he was reelected to the state assembly. He was working in Albany on February 12, 1884, when his daughter, Alice Lee Roosevelt, was born in New York City. He returned immediately to the city when he received a telegram asking him to do so, only to find that both his wife and his mother were dying. Both women died on February 14. He then made a decision to leave his infant daughter in the care of his sister Bamie, and he returned to the Badlands. In the West he enjoyed not only hunting, but also ranching, the natural beauty of the land, being able to hold his own with cowboys and ranch hands, and (on one occasion) acting as a deputy sheriff and undertaking to track down lawbreakers. In 1885 he published *Hunting Trips of a Ranchman*, an account of his experiences in the West.

Roosevelt returned to New York from the Dakota Territory and renewed his friendship with Edith Kermit Carow; they became engaged. In 1886 he ran as the Republican candidate for mayor of New York City, but was defeated. He married Edith on December 2, 1886, at St. George's Church, Hanover Square, in London, England, where she had been living. In March 1887 the couple, along with Roosevelt's daughter Alice, took up residence at Sagamore Hill, Roosevelt's brand new home in Oyster Bay, on Long Island, New York. Edith raised Alice, as well as her own four sons and a daughter (Theodore, Kermit, Ethel, Archibald, and Quentin).

Roosevelt continued to write; in 1887 and 1888 he published biographies of two US politi-

Colonel Theodore Roosevelt and his Rough Riders atop a hill following the Battle of San Juan in July, 1898.

cal figures, Gouverneur Morris and Thomas Hart Benton, among other books.

FURTHER POLITICAL CAREER

In 1889 Roosevelt was appointed as the US Civil Service Commissioner by President Benjamin Harrison, and kept in that position by Grover Cleveland when Cleveland defeated Harrison in 1892. Roosevelt brought to the office his astounding fund of energy and his reforming spirit; he embraced the ethic whereby civil service posts were filled on the basis of ability, rather than as reward for political support, and the number of civil service positions filled on the basis of examination results doubled under his tenure as Civil Service Commissioner. Roosevelt's individualism annoyed Republican party bosses, but he acquired a well-deserved reputation for getting things done.

In 1895 Roosevelt was appointed to the Board of Police Commissioners of New York City. The Board was riddled with corruption. Roosevelt tackled the problem with grit and enthusiasm; he removed from office those who took bribes and insisted on a strict enforcement of the laws. He formulated a police training program and was a zealous opponent of the patronage system and the use of social connection (rather than merit) as a basis for promotion within the police force.

In April 1897 Roosevelt was appointed the Assistant Secretary of the Navy by President William McKinley. He brought his usual administrative efficiency to the job, as well as a firm conviction that the navy ought to be expanded in size and power. He also urged war with Spain, despite the fact that President McKinley was opposed to it. On February 15, 1898, the US battleship *Maine* was destroyed by a mysterious explosion in Havana harbor, and the resulting outcry from the American public made the impending war almost inevitable.

THE SPANISH-AMERICAN WAR

In May 1898 Roosevelt resigned from his position as Assistant Secretary of the Navy and recruited the first US Volunteer Cavalry Regiment from among his friends, which included fellow Ivy League sportsmen and rough-hewn western cowboys. Colonel Leonard Wood, a professional soldier, became the unit's commander; Roosevelt was given the rank of lieutenant colonel. The unit that came to be known as the "Rough Riders" traveled to Tampa, Florida, the staging point prior to shipment to Cuba. The Rough Riders landed in Cuba on June 22, 1898. After an inordinately difficult march carried out in the heat of the Cuban summer, they arrived at a point outside Santiago, a city held by the Spanish forces, who were encamped on the adjacent San Juan Hills.

> **"I wish to preach, not the doctrine of ignoble ease, but the doctrine of the strenuous life."**
>
> Theodore Roosevelt, in a speech given in Chicago, April 10, 1899

The Rough Riders—who, despite their name, were mostly on foot (though Roosevelt had a horse)—along with 8,000 other troops charged up Kettle Hill and San Juan Hill on July 1, 1898. Roosevelt later recounted that he killed an enemy soldier with his bare hands in the assault. After capturing the hills, the American forces also took over Santiago; after a naval battle in which the Spanish fleet in Cuba was destroyed, the war was effectively over.

Following a custom of the time, Roosevelt, while in Cuba, was accompanied by a newspaperman, and word of his exploits reached US newspapers even prior to his return to the United States. On August 15 the Rough Riders landed at Montauk, on Long Island, and three months later, on November 8, 1898, Roosevelt was elected the governor of New York. As governor, he worked to better the lives of laborers; he gave state employees an eight-hour workday (in part, to set an example). He spurred the passage of legislation that made racial segregation in public schools illegal. He led the conservationist movement. Although liberal in many of his views and a supporter of pro-labor measures, he did not hesitate to call out the National Guard to suppress a strike. He also pushed for a franchise tax on corporations.

Roosevelt persisted in his reform efforts and his fight against political corruption. After Vice President Garret Hobart died in office in 1899, during McKinley's first term, Roosevelt was suddenly the obvious choice for the number two spot, and he became McKinley's running mate in the 1900 presidential election. Allegedly, Republican Party bosses in New York did what they could to get Roosevelt nominated in order to get rid of him; they knew that the vice president's job would afford him little scope for his reform efforts.

McKinley conducted a front-porch campaign (he delivered a series of speeches from the front porch of his home in Canton, Ohio), while Roosevelt toured the country giving speeches. The two were elected on November 6, 1900. The Roosevelts went to Washington in March 1901. In September, McKinley was assassinated while attending an exposition in Buffalo, New York, and Roosevelt was the president.

PRESIDENCY

Only forty-two years old when he became the president, Roosevelt plunged with his customary vigor into making the office his own, which he did so successfully that he had little trouble in becoming elected to the presidency in his own right in 1904. As the president, he started out by asking Congress to limit the power of trusts and asked the Justice Department to launch a law suit against Northern Securities for its violation of the Sherman Anti-Trust Act; in March 1904, the company was ordered to break up into parts. More than forty anti-trust suits were filed during his presidency.

Roosevelt was not only interested in breaking up monopolies; he also wished to regulate big business. He fought for the strengthening of the Interstate Commerce Commission and the passage of the Hepburn Railway Act of 1906 (which enabled the commission to better regulate the practices of the railroad companies). He ordered an investigation of the meat-packing industry; the investigation led to the passage of the Meat Inspection Act and the Pure Food and Drug Act. The Department of Commerce and Labor was created in 1903. When the mining industry was faced with a five-months-long strike by members of United Mine Workers, he became the first president to intervene in a management-labor dispute: he summoned the leaders of both parties to the White House and virtually forced the opposing parties to come to an agreement. His aggressive intervention in the dispute was in keeping with his sponsorship of (in his own words) "the Square Deal" to which all Americans were entitled.

"Yes, Haven, most of us enjoy preaching, and I've got such a bully pulpit!"

Theodore Roosevelt during his first term as president, describing the advantage of the presidency in response to his friend George Haven Putnam, who had accused him of preaching.

One area in which Roosevelt's actions had far-reaching implications was the nascent conservationist movement. Roosevelt was the first conservation president. In part stemming from his earliest experience in the Dakotas, he was convinced of the need to protect environmental treasures and resources and to preserve them for future generations. He advocated the Reclamation (or Newlands) Act, which provided that funds derived from the sale of public lands in the western United States would be used to build dams and initiate irrigation projects in the region. In May 1902 he authorized the creation of Crater Lake National Park in Oregon—one of five national parks he created. In March 1903 he established Pelican Island, Florida, as the first federally protected wildlife refuge; he went on to create fifty-one federal bird reservations in all. In February 1905 he signed the act that established the National Forest Service, and he was responsible for the designation of 150 national forests.

With respect to foreign affairs, Roosevelt expanded the influence of the United States, not only in Latin America, but also in Asia; the United States's acquisition of the Philippines (after the Spanish-American War) had greatly multiplied US ties to the region. In December 1902 Venezuela was in debt to the German nation; there were reports that Germany was on the cusp of sending armed forces to Venezuela to collect the debt. Roosevelt warned that the United States would send its ships to Venezuela if Germany attempted to use military force to collect its debt. Foreign creditors were also threatening to intervene in the affairs of the Dominican Republic; the United States took control of its customs collections and distributed the monies collected among US creditors, creditors of other nations, and the Dominican government.

Roosevelt was determined to build a canal in Panama in order to open up a direct route between the Atlantic and Pacific oceans. Panama was at that time part of the republic of Colombia, and the Colombian government was not entirely receptive to US plans to build in Panama. Roosevelt gave tacit approval to the antigovernment rebels in Panama and even sent a warship to Panama to show support. Panama gained its independence in late 1903, and an agreement between the United States and the new Panamanian government was reached in 1904; it allowed the United States to build the canal.

Roosevelt set up negotiations between Russian and Japanese diplomats to end the Russo-Japanese War; he invited the diplomats to his home in Oyster Bay. Negotiations continued at a naval base in Portsmouth, New Hampshire. His efforts led to the Treaty of Portsmouth, signed in August 1905. In December 1906 Roosevelt became the first American to receive a

Nobel prize: he was awarded the Nobel Peace prize in recognition of his work in the negotiations that led to the Treaty of Portsmouth.

"There is a homely old adage which runs: 'Speak softly and carry a big stick; you will go far.'"

Theodore Roosevelt, in a speech given in Chicago, April 2, 1903. There are other occasions on which Roosevelt used these words, which have become an American proverb.

Long an advocate of a strong navy, Roosevelt, in December 1907, ordered what came to be called the "Great White Fleet" (US Navy ships that had received a coat of white paint) on an around-the-world goodwill cruise. His plan was to showcase the naval might of the United States. The fleet returned to the United States on February 22, 1909.

"The Brownsville incident" was perhaps the low point of the Roosevelt presidency. In August 1906 Roosevelt ordered the dishonorable discharges of three companies of African-American soldiers who had been accused of inciting a riot in Brownsville, Texas. Fourteen of the men were later allowed to reenlist. Subsequent investigation of the incident has suggested that the soldiers were framed by a local racist conspiracy.

The Roosevelt offspring almost ran amok in the White House; they ran through the halls, played with water pistols, and took care of a variety of animals. Edith Roosevelt indulged her children's high spirits, but at the same time exercised a steadying influence over them—and over her husband. She guarded the family's privacy, ran the household efficiently, and was well-liked by the White House staff. Her relationship with her stepdaughter Alice Lee Roosevelt, however, was not always smooth. Alice was a lively and sometimes outrageous girl. When she was told by her parents that she could not smoke

under their roof, she promptly went up to the roof of the White House to smoke. She wore makeup and drove her automobile too fast; when other women were wearing feather boas around their necks, she got a real boa constrictor and wore it to an event. But, all things considered, she was extremely popular. Songs were written about her. Her favorite color, a shade of blue-gray, became known as "Alice Blue." On February 17, 1906, Alice wed Nicholas Longworth, a US congressman from Ohio, at the White House. She became an outspoken fixture of the social scene in Washington. Her famous motto—embroidered on a pillow and displayed in her home—was: "If you haven't got anything nice to say, come and sit by me."

In the latter part of Roosevelt's second term, he faced increased resistance from Congress (with respect to the more progressive parts of his agenda), and in October 1907 the stock market crashed. Despite these challenges, he remained extremely popular and was urged to run for a third term. He declined, handpicking William Howard Taft, who had been his Secretary of War, as his successor. Taft was duly nominated and elected president in 1908.

POST-PRESIDENTIAL CAREER

Roosevelt left the country after the 1908 election, in part to allow Taft to come into his own as president. Roosevelt spent a year on safari in Africa; the trip was sponsored by the Smithsonian Institution and the National Geographic Society. He wrote several accounts of his big-game hunting in Africa. One of those accounts became the book *African Game Trails*, which was published in 1910.

At around the time Roosevelt returned to the United States, he recognized that his relations with Taft were becoming strained, and as Taft's presidency evolved, Roosevelt, along with many Republicans, became convinced that Taft, with his more conservative political agenda, was dismantling many of the reforms that Roosevelt had spawned. While on a speaking tour of the western United States, Roosevelt delivered a speech on August 31, 1910, in which he urged a "New Nationalism," a progressive agenda that included conservationism, trust-busting, the protection of workers, and the creation of social programs to aid the poor and protect children and women.

Roosevelt traveled again to Europe and represented the United States at the funeral of King Edward VII in Great Britain. He then returned to New York. In 1912 he announced his candidacy for president. He won almost every primary election; however, the delegates to the Republican convention voted to nominate Taft. Roosevelt and his supporters left the convention and formed the National Progressive ("Bull Moose") Party, with Roosevelt as its candidate.

In October 1912, on his way to give a campaign speech in Milwaukee, Roosevelt was shot by saloonkeeper John N. Schrank, an unbalanced man who claimed he opposed third terms. Wounded in the chest, Roosevelt insisted on giving his speech anyway—for an hour and a half—and only then did he allow himself to be taken for medical treatment. The split between Taft and Roosevelt enabled the Democrats to triumph in the 1912 election; Woodrow Wilson became president.

In 1914 Roosevelt traveled to South America for a lecture tour and an exploration of Brazil's River of Doubt. He became gravely ill and nearly died on the trip. He returned to New York and continued to write; not long after his return to the United States he published *Through the Brazilian Wilderness* and, in 1915, *America and the World War*.

In 1917 the United States entered the World War. Roosevelt asked President Wilson if he could organize a volunteer troop, but Wilson turned him down. Roosevelt's sons, Theodore, Archibald, Kermit, and Quentin, all enlisted in the war. Roosevelt toured the country and urged Americans to buy war bonds. In 1918 his youngest son Quentin, serving as a fighter pilot in France, was shot down and killed.

On January 6, 1919, a little more than two months after his sixtieth birthday, Roosevelt died of an embolism. He was buried at Young's Memorial Cemetery in Oyster Bay. Edith Roosevelt lived to be eighty-seven, and, during her middle (and autumnal) years, spent her time traveling, reading, and enjoying her family; she died on September 30, 1948.

Birthplace: New York, NY
Residency: New York
Religion: Dutch Reformed
Education: Harvard University, graduated 1880; Columbia University Law School (did not graduate)
Place of Death: Sagamore, Oyster Bay, NY
Burial Site: Young's Memorial Cemetery, Oyster Bay, NY
Dates in Office: September 14, 1901–March 3, 1909 (7 years, 171 days)
Age at Inauguration: 42 years, 322 days

FAMILY
Father: Theodore Roosevelt (1831–1878)
Mother: Martha Bulloch Roosevelt (1834–1884)
Siblings: Theodore was the second of four children; his siblings were Anna ("Bamie" or "Bye") Roosevelt (1855–1931); Elliott ("Ellie" or "Nell") Roosevelt (1860–1894); Corinne ("Conie" or "Pussie") Roosevelt (1861–1933).
Wife: Alice Hathaway Lee Roosevelt (1861–1884), married October 27, 1880, in Brookline, MA; Edith Kermit Carow Roosevelt (1861–1948), married December 2, 1886, in London, England
Children: with Alice Roosevelt: Alice Longworth Roosevelt (1884–1980); with Edith Roosevelt: Theodore Roosevelt (1887–1944); Kermit Roosevelt (1889–1943); Ethel Roosevelt (1891–1977); Archibald Roosevelt (1894–1979); Quentin Roosevelt (1897–1918)

CAREER
Private: writer, rancher
Political: member of the NY state legislature (1882–1884); member of the US Civil Service Commission (1889–1895); president of the New York Police Board (1895–1897); assistant secretary of the Navy (1897–1898); governor of New York state (1898–1900); vice president under McKinley (1901); president of the United States (1901–1909)
Military: Roosevelt, given the rank of colonel, was the commander of the Rough Riders cavalry unit in the Spanish-American War (1898); took a

leading part in the storming of Kettle and San Juan Hills in the battle for Santiago, Cuba; was recommended for the Medal of Honor (awarded posthumously in 2001).

Selected Works: Theodore Roosevelt was a prolific writer and published more than three dozen books in his lifetime. A selection of these, as well as of later collections, follows: *African Game Trails: An Account of the African Wanderings of an American Hunter-Naturalist*, intro. by H. W. Brands and illus. by Kermit Roosevelt and others (New York: Cooper Square Press, 2001); *American Ideals, and Other Essays, Social and Political* (New York: AMS Press, 1969); *A Book-Lover's Holidays in the Open* (Birmingham, AL: Palladium Press, 1999); *The Boyhood Diary of Theodore Roosevelt, 1869–1870: Early Travels of the 26th President*, ed. by Shelley Swanson Sateren (Mankato, MN: Blue Earth Books, 2001); *Forgotten Tales and Vanished Trails*, ed. and compiled with an introduction and notes by Jim Casada (Birmingham, AL: Palladium Press, 2001); *Good Hunting: In Pursuit of Big Game in the West* (Birmingham, AL: Palladium Press, 2000); *Gouverneur Morris*, with an intro. by Mary-Jo Kline (New York: Chelsea House, 1980); *Letters*, selected and ed. by Elting E. Morison (Cambridge: Harvard University Press, 1951–1954); *Letters and Speeches* (New York: Library of America, 2004); *The Naval War of 1812*, new intro. by H. W. Brands (New York: Da Capo Press, 1999); *Ranch Life and the Hunting-Trail*, illus. by Frederic Remington (Birmingham, AL: Palladium Press, 1999); *The Rough Riders; and, An Autobiography* (New York: Library of America, 2004); *The Selected Letters of Theodore Roosevelt*, ed. by H. W. Brands (New York: Cooper Square Press, 2001); *Thomas H. Benton* (New York: AMS Press, 1972); *The Winning of the West* (Lincoln: University of Nebraska Press, 1995).

PRESIDENCY

Nomination: 1904: At the Republican convention in Chicago, held June 21–23, 1904, Roosevelt was nominated unanimously on the first ballot; Charles Fairbanks of IN was chosen as the vice-presidential candidate.

Election: 1904: reelected president on November 8, 1904 (after succeeding to presidency on the death of President McKinley in 1901)

Opponent: 1904: Alton B. Parker, NY, Democrat; Eugene V. Debs, IN, Socialist; Silas Swallow, PA, Prohibition; Thomas Watson, GA, Populist

Vote Totals: 1904: Roosevelt, 7,630,457 popular, 336 electoral; Parker, 5,083,880 popular, 140 electoral; Debs, 402,810 popular, 0 electoral; Swallow, 259,102 popular, 0 electoral; Watson, 114,070 popular, 0 electoral

Inauguration: 1904: March 4, 1905

Vice President: Charles Warren Fairbanks, IN (1905–1909)

CABINET

Secretary of State: John Hay, DC (1901–1905); Elihu Root, NY (1905–1909); Robert Bacon, NY (1909)

Secretary of the Treasury: Lyman J. Gage, IL (1901–1902); Leslie M. Shaw, IA (1902–1907); George B. Cortelyou, NY (1907–1909)

Secretary of War: Elihu Root, NY (1901–1904); William H. Taft, OH (1904–1908); Luke Wright, TN (1908–1909)

Attorney General: Philander C. Knox, PA (1901–1904); William H. Moody, MA (1904–1906); Charles J. Bonaparte, MD (1906–1909)

Postmaster General: Charles Emory Smith, PA (1901–1902); Henry C. Payne, WI (1902–1904); Robert J. Wynne, PA (1904–1905); George C. Cortelyou, NY (1905–1907); George von Lengerke Meyer, MA (1907–1909)

Secretary of the Navy: John D. Long, MA (1901–1902); William H. Moody, MA (1902–1904); Paul Morton, IL (1904–1905); Charles J. Bonaparte, MD (1905–1906); Victor H. Metcalf, CA (1906–1908); Truman H. Newberry, MI (1908–1909)

Secretary of Agriculture: James Wilson, IA (1901–1909)

Secretary of the Interior: Ethan A. Hitchcock, MO (1901–1907); James R. Garfield, OH (1907–1909)

Secretary of Commerce and Labor: George B. Cortelyou, NY (1903–1904); Victor H. Metcalf, CA (1904–1906); Oscar S. Straus, NY (1906–1909)

CONGRESS:

57th Congress (1901–1903); Speaker of the House: David B. Henderson (IA, Republican)
58th Congress (1903–1905); Speaker of the House: Joseph G. Cannon (IL, Republican)
59th Congress (1905–1907); Speaker of the House: Joseph G. Cannon (IL, Republican)
60th Congress (1907–1909); Speaker of the House: Joseph G. Cannon (IL, Republican)

SUPREME COURT APPOINTEES

Oliver Wendell Holmes, MA; Associate Justice (1902–1932)
William Rufus Day, OH; Associate Justice (1903–1922)
William Henry Moody, MA; Associate Justice (1906–1910)

MAJOR EVENTS OF THE ROOSEVELT ADMINISTRATION

◆ On December 3, 1901, Roosevelt addresses Congress and asks it to limit the power of trusts.

◆ In November 1901 the United States and Great Britain agree, under the Hay-Pauncefote Treaty, that the United States will have control of the proposed Panama Canal.

◆ In 1902 Roosevelt instructs his attorney general, Philander Knox, to file suits pursuant to the Sherman Anti-Trust Act of 1890; Knox files against J. P. Morgan's Northern Securities Company and John D. Rockefeller's Standard Oil Company.

◆ The Newlands Reclamation Act of 1902 sets aside money from the sale of public lands in the western United States for the irrigation of arid lands in the region; the United States Reclamation Service is created within the United States Geological Survey to administer the project.

◆ In late 1902 British and German ships blockade Venezuelan ports to force Venezuela to pay its outstanding debts; through Roosevelt's efforts, the matter is submitted to the Permanent Court of Arbitration in the Hague.

◆ In a 1902 strike by the United Mine Workers, Roosevelt becomes the first president to mediate in a labor dispute when he invites representatives of the workers and the mine owners to the White House and forces a compromise.

◆ The Hay-Bunau-Varilla Treaty of 1903 provides for the construction of a canal across the Isthmus of Panama and guarantees that the United States will protect the independence of the Republic of Panama (which had recently revolted against Colombian control and received the support of the US navy).

◆ The United States concludes a treaty with Cuba in February 1903 that provides for the sale or lease of Cuban lands to the United States for coaling and naval stations.

◆ In 1903 the Department of Commerce and Labor is created; they will become separate departments in 1913.

◆ The Supreme Court rules, in *Champion v. Ames*, February 1903, that the police power of the federal government is superior to that of the states.

◆ In May 1904 Roosevelt dispatches warships to Tangiers, Algeria, demanding the release of Ion Perdicaris, initially believed to be a naturalized American citizen but actually a Greek citizen, who had been captured by a Moroccan chieftain named Raisuli. Secretary of State John Hay sends a telegram to the Moroccan government demanding "Perdicaris alive or Raisuli dead," and Perdicaris is released.

◆ On November 8, 1904, Roosevelt is elected, defeating Democratic candidate Alton B. Parker.

◆ In a message given to Congress on December 6, 1904, Roosevelt puts forth the Roosevelt Corollary to the Monroe Doctrine, which states that the United States is justified in intervening in the affairs of countries of the Western Hemisphere for the purpose of ending chronic unrest or wrongdoing.

◆ In December 1904 the United States joins more than twenty other countries in signing the Convention for the Exemption of Hospital Ships, in Time of War, from the Payment of All Duties and Taxes Imposed for the Benefit of the State—an agreement not to charge port duties to Red Cross hospital ships during war time.

◆ On February 1, 1905, Congress establishes the National Forest Service, building on the existing Bureau of Forestry.

◆ In February 1905 the US government assumes responsibility for the debt of the Dominican Republic when it takes over the collection of the country's custom duties and the distribution of monies to its debtors and to the Dominican government. In April 1905 the General Customs Receivership is established so that the United States can administer the finances of the Dominican Republic.

◆ In *Lochner v. New York*, 1905, the Supreme Court strikes down New York's maximum-hour labor law, arguing that it interferes with the right of employers and employees to make a contract.

◆ The Treaty of Portsmouth is signed, September 5, 1905, in Portsmouth, NH. It ends the Russo-Japanese War. Roosevelt plays a significant diplomatic role.

◆ The Algeciras Conference, supported by Roosevelt, is held in Algeciras, Spain, in 1906 at the urging of the German Kaiser Wilhelm II (who wished to put forward German claims to land in North Africa, and particularly in Morocco). The conference confirms that an "open door" policy is to be recognized by all powers participating in the conference, which reflects the already prevailing notion that Africa is a land available for colonization; it recognizes French and Spanish interests in Morocco by giving them supervisory powers over the Moroccan police.

◆ The Hepburn Act, 1906, increases the power of the Interstate Commerce Commission over the railroads.

◆ The Pure Food and Drug Act, 1906, forbids the manufacture, sale, or transportation of adulterated or misbranded or poisonous or deleterious food, drugs, medicines, and liquors.

◆ The Meat Inspection Act, 1906, provides that animals must be inspected before and after slaughter and establishes standards of cleanliness for slaughterhouses and meat processing plants.

◆ Under the authority of the Platt Amendment, Secretary of War William Howard Taft is assigned to serve as provisional governor of Cuba, 1906.

◆ In 1906 Roosevelt is awarded the Nobel Peace Prize for his work on the Treaty of Portsmouth.

◆ On February 24, 1907, the United States and Japan conclude a "Gentleman's Agreement" in which Japan agrees to deny passports to Japanese wishing to immigrate to the United States in return for the United States's pledge to rescind the segregation of Japanese children in San Francisco schools, which had begun in May 1906.

◆ At the Second Hague Conference in 1907, the United States advocates the establishment of a world court, though the desire of each country to appoint its own judges makes the idea unworkable; more successful is the establishment of guidelines for the use of arbitration in the resolution of disputes between countries.

◆ In March 1907 Roosevelt orders troops to Honduras because of disturbances in that country, including an invasion of the country by Nicaragua.

◆ The Panic of 1907 follows stock market crashes in March and October, and spurs bank failures across the country; the pumping of $35 million in federal funds into the economy—and the actions of J. P. Morgan and a handful of bank executives organized by Morgan—help to stem the panic.

◆ Oklahoma becomes a state, November 16, 1907.

◆ From December 16, 1907, to February 22, 1909, the "Great White Fleet" of the US Navy (so named because the ships had been painted white) travels around the world, visiting many ports and showcasing US naval power.

◆ In May 1908 Congress passes a child labor law for the District of Columbia.

◆ In June 1908 Roosevelt establishes the National Conservation Commission.

◆ In January 1909 the United States and Austria-Hungary agreed to use the Court of Arbitration at The Hague to resolve any disputes between them.

◆ From 1901 to 1909 Roosevelt establishes 150 national forests, 51 federal bird reservations, 4 national game preserves, 5 national parks (doubling their number), and 18 national monuments, including Devils Tower (WY), the Petrified Forest (AZ), Chaco Canyon (NM),

Muir Woods (CA), the Grand Canyon (AZ), and Mount Olympus (WA).

MAJOR US AND WORLD EVENTS, 1901–1909

◆ On October 29, 1901, President McKinley's assassin, Leon Czolgosz, is electrocuted.

◆ The first Nobel prizes are awarded, 1901.

◆ Guglielmo Marconi, in Newfoundland, Canada, receives a radio signal that has been transmitted from Cornwall, England, and thus the first transatlantic radio transmission is achieved, on December 12, 1901.

◆ In 1901 Austrian physician Karl Landsteiner publishes his findings of three main blood groups (a fourth is identified in 1902); cross-matching prior to blood transfusion begins in 1907.

◆ On January 1, 1902, the first football game associated with the Tournament of Roses parade is played in Pasadena, CA; the University of Michigan defeats Stanford University so soundly that the next Tournament of Roses football game will not take place until 1916; the games later take the name "Rose Bowl" from the stadium built in 1923.

◆ On January 28, 1902, Andrew Carnegie founds the Carnegie Institution, an organization dedicated to scientific discovery.

◆ The Boer War in South Africa ends in 1902 with a British victory. Among the participants in the war were Mohandas K. Gandhi, who served as a stretcher-bearer; Arthur Conan Doyle, who ran a field hospital; Rudyard Kipling, who wrote for an army newspaper; and Winston Churchill, a British soldier.

◆ On May 8, 1902, Mount Pelée in Martinique erupts, killing more than 30,000 people.

◆ In 1902 Marie and Pierre Curie isolate two new chemical elements, which they name polonium and radium.

◆ Filmmaker Georges Méliès creates Le Voyage dans la Lune (A Trip to the Moon), 1902.

◆ Joseph Conrad publishes Heart of Darkness, 1902.

◆ Thomas Mann publishes Buddenbrooks, 1902.

◆ Beatrix Potter publishes The Tale of Peter Rabbit, 1902.

◆ Owen Wister publishes The Virginian, 1902.

◆ Claude Debussy's Pelléas et Mélisande premieres in Paris, April 30, 1902.

◆ Enrico Caruso joins the Metropolitan Opera Company and makes recordings for the Victor Talking Machine Company, 1903.

◆ On February 11, 1903, Anton Bruckner's Ninth Symphony premieres in Vienna, Austria.

◆ In February 1903 the first "teddy bear" is introduced in America, purportedly getting its name from a story of Teddy Roosevelt's having refused to shoot a captive bear while on a hunting trip.

◆ King Alexander I and Queen Drago of Serbia are assassinated during a Serbian army revolt, 1903.

◆ At a medical conference in 1903, Ivan Pavlov reads a paper on "The Experimental Psychology and Psychopathology of Animals," in which he defines conditioned reflexes and notes both physiological and psychological elements of such reflexes.

◆ The first Tour de France bicycle race is held, 1903; Maurice Garin is the winner.

◆ The Russian Social Democratic Labor Party splits into two groups, the Bolsheviks and the Mensheviks.

◆ Jack London publishes The Call of the Wild in installments in the Saturday Evening Post, 1903.

◆ Samuel Butler publishes The Way of All Flesh, 1903.

◆ The Pittsburgh Pirates and the Boston Americans play the first World Series, a best-of-nine series that is over after eight games—Boston winning five games and Pittsburgh three. Boston's pitching staff includes Cy Young.

◆ W. E. B. Du Bois publishes The Souls of Black Folk, 1903.

◆ On December 17, 1903, Orville and Wilbur Wright sustain the flight of a powered heavier-than-air craft at Kitty Hawk, NC. The flight lasts for 12 seconds; the craft travels 120 feet.

◆ The Russo-Japanese War begins, 1904.

◆ Longacre Square in New York is renamed Times Square when the New York Times moves its headquarters there, 1904.

◆ The Louisiana Purchase Exposition, a world's fair, runs in St. Louis, MO, from April 30 to December 1, 1904.

◆ In 1904 Great Britain and France sign the *Entente Cordiale,* according to which France agrees to respect British interests in Egypt and Britain agrees to respect French interests in Morocco; both agree to free passage through the Suez Canal.

◆ The New York City subway begins operation, 1904.

◆ Anton Chekhov's *The Cherry Orchard* is published, 1904.

◆ Henry James publishes *The Golden Bowl,* 1904.

◆ Giacomo Puccini's *Madame Butterfly* debuts in Milan, 1904.

◆ Igor Stravinsky composes the *Piano Sonata in F Sharp Minor,* 1904.

◆ Gustav Mahler's *Symphony No. 5* premieres in Cologne, Germany, 1904.

◆ The Russian Revolution of 1905 takes place; it includes Bloody Sunday (January 9), on which unarmed demonstrators are shot, and the publication of the October Manifesto, in which Tsar Nicholas II promises the Russian people a constitution and a duma (a legislature).

◆ Norway separates from its union with Sweden, 1905.

◆ Edith Wharton publishes *The House of Mirth,* 1905.

◆ Jack London publishes *White Fang,* 1905.

◆ The Baroness Orczy publishes *The Scarlet Pimpernel,* 1905.

◆ In 1905 Albert Einstein publishes papers in which he puts forth his theory of relativity and the law of the conservation of mass and energy ($E = mc^2$).

◆ Claude Debussy's *La Mer* and *Clair de Lune* premiere, 1905.

◆ Franz Lehár's *The Merry Widow* premieres, December 28, 1905.

◆ Industrial Workers of the World (IWW) is formed, 1905.

◆ Upton Sinclair's *The Jungle,* an exposé of the Chicago meat-packing industry, is serialized in 1905 and published in book form in 1906, leading to the passage of the Pure Food and

Drugs Act in 1906 and to an increase in investigative journalism, dubbed "muckracking" by President Theodore Roosevelt.

◆ On April 6, 1906, Mount Vesuvius, in Vesuvius, Italy (near Naples), erupts.

◆ On April 18, 1906, an earthquake devastates San Francisco, killing about 6,000 people.

◆ Henry Adams publishes *The Education of Henry Adams,* 1906.

◆ The first Montessori School is opened by Maria Montessori in Rome, Italy, 1907.

◆ Sidney Olcott makes the first film version of *Ben-Hur,* 1907.

◆ Robert Baden-Powell creates his first scout camp for boys, in England in 1907, and publishes *Scouting for Boys* in 1908, beginning the Boy Scout movement.

◆ The *Triple Entente* forms between Great Britain, France, and Russia, 1907.

◆ Louis B. Mayer opens his first movie theater, in Haverhill, MA, 1907.

◆ In 1908 Henry Ford introduces the Model T automobile.

◆ Bulgaria declares its independence from the Ottoman Empire, 1908.

◆ The "Young Turk" Revolution of 1908 deposes Sultan Abdülhamid of the Ottoman Empire.

◆ Lucy Maud Montgomery publishes *Anne of Green Gables,* 1908.

◆ E. M. Forster publishes *A Room with a View,* 1908.

◆ Kenneth Grahame publishes *The Wind in the Willows,* 1908.

◆ Sergei Rachmaninoff's *Symphony No. 2* premieres, January 26, 1908.

◆ On February 12, 1909, the National Association for the Advancement of Colored People (NAACP) is formed.

FAST FACTS ABOUT THEODORE ROOSEVELT

◆ Roosevelt disliked the nickname "Teddy"; his family called him "Teedie" or "Thee."

◆ The Rough Riders included polo players, football players, and cowboys.

◆ Theodore Roosevelt made the nickname "White House" official in September 1901.

❖ Roosevelt's first wife, Alice Lee Roosevelt, and his mother, Martha Bulloch Roosevelt, died on the same day (February 14, 1884) and in the same house. Reportedly, he never mentioned his wife's name after her death.

❖ Theodore Roosevelt's brother Elliott was the father of Eleanor Roosevelt; Franklin D. Roosevelt was a distant cousin of Theodore Roosevelt.

❖ On February 17, 1906, Roosevelt's daughter Alice Roosevelt married Nicholas Longworth, a congressman from Ohio who would become Speaker of the House, in the East Room of the White House.

❖ Alice Roosevelt was dubbed "Princess Alice" by the press; the name alluded to her wild behavior (she wore makeup, smoked, drove fast, and once draped a boa constrictor around her neck for shock value) and helped to make her a celebrity. President Roosevelt once said publicly that he could either run the country or control Alice, but that he could not do both. In her later years, she became known as "the other Washington monument."

❖ The Apache Chief Geronimo attended Roosevelt's inauguration in 1905.

❖ At the time of his inauguration, Roosevelt was the youngest president the United States had ever had.

❖ On January 15, 1904, cellist Pablo Casals played at the White House for President Theodore Roosevelt; he would play again at the White House on November 13, 1961, for President John F. Kennedy.

❖ During a boxing match that took place in the White House, Roosevelt received a blow that left him blind in his left eye.

❖ Roosevelt was the first American to win a Nobel prize; he was awarded the Nobel Peace prize in 1906 for his contributions to the Treaty of Portsmouth, which ended the Russo-Japanese War.

❖ Roosevelt wrote more than forty books; their genres included autobiographical stories, hunting and wilderness guides, biography, history, and political essays.

❖ When Roosevelt invited Booker T. Washington, the African-American founder of

the Tuskegee Institute, to dine at the White House, a storm of protest was raised.

❖ Roosevelt was the first president to travel outside the United States during his presidency; he and Mrs. Roosevelt traveled to Panama in November 1906.

❖ At a 1912 speech he gave in New York City while running for president as the candidate of the National Progressive Party, Roosevelt declared "The principles for which we stand are the principles of fair play and a square deal for every man and woman in the United States."

❖ Roosevelt enjoyed the Maxwell House brand coffee (named for the Maxwell House Hotel in Nashville, TN) he was served at the Hermitage, Andrew Jackson's home in Nashville. He said it was "good to the last drop!" and his words were later used as an advertising slogan by General Foods, when it bought the brand.

❖ In 1910, after he had left the presidency, Roosevelt accepted an invitation to be a passenger in an airplane during a demonstration flight and flew in the plane for approximately four minutes.

❖ On October 14, 1912, while running for president as the National Progressive (Bull Moose) Party's candidate, Roosevelt was shot in the chest while he was on his way to deliver a campaign speech. He insisted it was nothing, and went on to speak for an hour and a half. When the speech was concluded, he was rushed to the hospital. Wilson and Taft, the other candidates, suspended their campaigns until he had recovered.

❖ Roosevelt's face is carved into Mount Rushmore, along with Washington's, Jefferson's, and Lincoln's.

❖ Roosevelt and his son, Theodore Roosevelt, Jr., were both Congressional Medal of Honor winners. The father was given the award posthumously for his actions during the Spanish-American War, and the son received his award, also posthumously, for his bravery in World War II, in which he was among the first to storm the beaches at Normandy on June 6, 1944.

William Howard Taft

Nickname: Big Bill, Peaceful Bill
Presidency: 27th president, 1909–1913
Party: Republican
Life dates: September 15, 1857–March 8, 1930 (72 years, 174 days)

EARLY LIFE AND EDUCATION

William Howard Taft was born on September 15, 1857, in Cincinnati, Ohio. He was the son of Louisa Maria Torrey Taft and Alphonso Taft and the second of their five children. His father also had two sons from an earlier marriage. Alphonso Taft was a lawyer and a civic leader in Cincinnati. He was a member of the boards of trustees of several railroad companies, companies that had contributed greatly to the wealth and prosperity of Cincinnati. He was a judge of the Superior Court of Cincinnati. He ran for the US House of Representatives and for governor of Ohio, but was defeated in both elections. In 1876 he served for a brief time as President Ulysses S. Grant's Secretary of War, and then as Grant's attorney general, a position in which he served until the end of Grant's term in 1877. Alphonso Taft served as the US ambassador to Austria-Hungary from 1882 to 1884, and then as the ambassador to Russia. Louisa Taft was an active, independent woman; she organized book clubs, an art association, and a kindergarten. She had high expectations for her children.

Despite his having been overweight as a child, William liked sports and played baseball. He attended Woodward High School, a private high school in Cincinnati, before going—as his father had hoped—to Yale. He was graduated from Yale second in his class in 1878, and returned to Cincinnati to study law at the Cincinnati Law School, from which he was graduated in 1880. He was admitted to the Ohio bar in 1880.

EARLY CAREER

Taft's first public office position came about primarily via his family connections; he became an assistant prosecuting attorney for Hamilton County, Ohio, in 1881. In 1885 Taft became the assistant county solicitor in Hamilton County.

Taft had met Helen ("Nellie") Herron at a sledding party in 1879, when she was eighteen. The year before she had visited the White House with her parents, who were close friends of President and Mrs. Hayes. During that visit, an ambition to become the First Lady was planted in her. Nellie became a graduate of Ohio's Miami University; she became a schoolteacher and even established, with her friends, a literary salon. Taft, as a young man, attended the salon and was captivated by her intellect as well as her independent spirit. Nellie believed that he would have the kind of career she hoped for in a husband, and they were married on June 19, 1886. They had two sons, Robert and Charles, and a daughter, Helen.

"Next to the right of liberty, the right of property is the most important individual right guaranteed by the Constitution and the one which, united with that of personal liberty, has contributed more to the growth of civilization than any other institution established by the human race."

William Howard Taft, *Popular Government*, 1913

Taft was appointed a judge of the Ohio Superior Court in 1887—to fill out the unfinished term of a departing judge—and in the following year he was elected to a full term as a superior court judge in his own right. His principal ambition, from very early on in his career, was appointment to the US Supreme Court, and he urged Ohio Governor Joseph Foraker to ask President Benjamin Harrison to make the appointment. Because of Taft's youth—he was still in his early thirties—Harrison thought him not an ideal candidate for the Supreme Court, and appointed him instead as solicitor general of the United States in 1890.

FURTHER CAREER

A year later, in 1891, Taft was appointed a judge of the Sixth US Circuit Court of Appeals, based in Cincinnati. Nellie had enjoyed their brief time in Washington during her husband's stint as solicitor general, but Taft had been less than happy in that position and disliked the public speaking it entailed; he opted to go with the Ohio circuit court judgeship. Taft spent eight

years as an Ohio circuit court judge; during this period (from 1896 to 1900) he was also a professor of law and dean at the University of Cincinnati Law School.

Among the friends Taft made during his time in Washington was Theodore Roosevelt. Taft petitioned President William McKinley (like Taft, an Ohioan) to obtain Roosevelt's appointment as Assistant Secretary of the Navy. McKinley appointed Roosevelt to the position in 1897. In 1900 McKinley asked Taft to go to the Philippine Islands, which had recently become a US protectorate, and to set up a civil government there. A civil commission was established, and Taft was asked to become its president. With Nellie's urging and McKinley's promise to consider him for the US Supreme Court in the event of a vacancy, he agreed to go.

When he arrived in the Philippines, Taft found a country still embroiled in armed conflict. Filipino nationalists, led by Emilio Aguinaldo, were resisting US rule, and the US soldiers were fighting to put down the rebellion. The US attempt to crush the rebellion was especially bloody and brutal—and Taft was deeply disturbed by it. He immediately clashed with the US military governor, General Arthur MacArthur (whose son Douglas MacArthur would become the Supreme Commander of the Allied Powers in the Pacific during World War II), who was not eager to turn the embattled country over to a civilian. Following the capture of Aguinaldo, Taft managed to obtain MacArthur's removal from the Philippines, and he hunkered down to draft a constitution (very similar to the US Constitution) for the country.

The new governance structure called for a civil governor, a post to which Taft was appointed. In the Philippines Taft created a judicial system, improved the economy, built schools and roads, and arranged for the United States to buy land from the Roman Catholic Church, which was then sold to Filipinos at low interest rates. He was committed to (and even passionate toward) his work in the Philippines; he even turned down two offers of Supreme Court appointments from Theodore Roosevelt, who had become president when McKinley was assassinated.

The Tafts lived very well in the Philippines; they resided in a large house with many servants. Taft was generally very popular with the Filipinos, who, having just endured martial rule under MacArthur, were grateful for Taft's even-handedness, his acknowledged desire to treat the people fairly and provide them with good governance.

Roosevelt appreciated Taft's work in the Philippines and showed his appreciation by making Taft his Secretary of War in 1904. Roosevelt also made him his confidant. Taft was aware of his knowledge deficit with respect to military affairs, but Roosevelt believed that his own expertise in this department would suffice for the both of them. He steered Taft toward projects that would make good use of his administrative and juridical abilities. Not only did Taft continue to supervise affairs in the Philippines, in 1906 he functioned as the provisional governor of Cuba.

Taft was asked to oversee the construction of the Panama Canal. Roosevelt sent him around the world on diplomatic missions. In 1907 Taft was sent to Japan to improve the strained relations between Japan and the United States, due in part to a San Francisco law that had mandated the segregation of Asian children in San Francisco schools (it was later rescinded). Roosevelt and Taft had become close friends, and Roosevelt expressed his confidence in Taft openly and often.

When Roosevelt declared that he would not run for president in 1908, many expected that Taft, whom Roosevelt had more or less chosen as his successor, would seek the nomination. Taft wasn't sure that he wanted to run for president, but Roosevelt and Mrs. Taft convinced him to do so. He was easily nominated at the Republican convention, and Roosevelt and Mrs. Taft became workers in his campaign. They spurred him on, and helped him to write his speeches.

Taft was elected president: he won 321 electoral votes to William Jennings Bryan's 162, and he won the popular vote by a margin of more than a million votes.

PRESIDENCY

Mrs. Taft's delight in being the First Lady was considerably diluted when she suffered a stroke in May 1909. She had made a near-recovery after one year, yet it continued to be rough going for her—to be perpetually hampered by the after-effects of her illness. She formalized the atmosphere of the White House, insisted that footmen dress in livery outfits, and arranged for White House dinners to be followed by musical or theatrical entertainment. Her most memorable achievement as First Lady, though, was her supervision of the planting of 3,000 Japanese cherry trees along the Potomac River.

> "The putting into force of laws which shall secure the conservation of our resources, as far as they may be within the jurisdiction of the Federal Government, including the more important work of savings and restoring our forests and the great improvement of waterways, are all proper government functions which must involve large expenditure if properly performed."
>
> William Howard Taft, inaugural address, March 4, 1909

Most of Taft's supporters expected him, as the president, to carry on with Roosevelt's progressive agenda. Many Republicans (unsurprisingly) believed that Roosevelt had gone quite far enough in making progressive changes; they welcomed the more conservative Taft. One sign of an impending departure from the Roosevelt legacy was Taft's selection of his (somewhat more conservative) cabinet members; he appointed Philander Knox, the former attorney general, as his Secretary of State; George Wickersham, a corporate attorney, as Attorney General; and Charles Nagel, another corporate attorney, as Secretary of Commerce and Labor.

Taft won popularity as a trust-buster, and proved to be a more efficient trust-buster than Roosevelt himself. His handling of the tariff problem, however, did not enhance his popularity. Taft supported and signed the Payne-Aldrich Tariff Act of 1909, a compromise bill that raised some tariffs, lowered others, and pleased almost no-one. Taft asked Congress to pursue a constitutional amendment that would allow the federal government to collect income taxes. The power of the Interstate Commerce Commission was expanded during the Taft years: the commission was granted greater control of the railroads and, for the first time, the power to regulate the communications companies, such as the telephone and telegraph companies.

Taft was much less interested in conservation matters than Roosevelt had been. One of the most difficult episodes of his presidency—and an incident that inflicted great damage on his friendship with Roosevelt—was the Pinchot-Ballinger Controversy of 1909. Gifford Pinchot, a friend of Roosevelt, was the Chief Forester of the Forestry Service (then part of the Department of Agriculture). He helped to develop the concepts of the national forest, the responsible management of forests, and the renewable resource. He also increased the sizes of the national forests by giving public lands reserve status. Richard Ballinger, whom Taft had appointed as the Secretary of the Interior, believed that Pinchot's actions were illegal. Meanwhile, Louis Glavis, chief of the Field Division of the Department of Interior, charged that Ballinger had conspired to defraud the US government of Alaskan coal fields by opening them up to private mining interests and pushing through land claims for his former clients—claims to lands, moreover, that Roosevelt had protected from development before Ballinger opened them up. Pinchot backed Glavis in his accusations against Ballinger, which, by implication, accused the Taft administration.

Both Taft and the Congress conducted investigations that concluded that Ballinger had not acted improperly, and in early 1910 Taft dismissed Pinchot and Glavis for their insubordination (for their having criticized Ballinger, and, indirectly, Taft). However, a great deal of public opinion was on the side of Pinchot and concurred with his accusations that Taft and Ballinger were betraying Roosevelt's conservation legacy.

As part of Taft's foreign policy, which was given the name of "Dollar Diplomacy," he strove to expand US trade with other countries by making investments in those countries and, in some instances, providing financial aid to them. However, he was not reluctant to use military force to further American interests when he deemed that such force was necessary; he sent US warships to Nicaragua in 1912 to support its antigovernment rebels and to protect US citizens there—after five hundred of the antigovernment rebels, including two US advisors (or, as the Nicaraguan government claimed, US mercenaries), were killed by the forces of Nicaraguan president and dictator José Santos Zelaya. Along similar lines, Taft was ready to send troops to Mexico to protect US interests there, but Congress objected, and the assembled troops did not go to Mexico.

Roosevelt had spent the first year of Taft's presidency in Africa (and, in so doing, had removed his larger-than-life presence from the American scene). But when he returned to the United States, he was appalled at the direction in which the Taft administration seemed to be moving, and he resolved to run for a third term as president in 1912. Although he won most of the primaries, the Republican Convention delegates, who were part of the Republican Party machinery, were loyal to Taft and nominated him. Roosevelt and his supporters left the convention and formed the National Progressive ("Bull Moose") Party. Roosevelt was named as the party's presidential candidate. With the opposing side essentially split in two, Democrat Woodrow Wilson won the election of 1912, and Taft received fewer popular votes than any incumbent president seeking reelection had ever received.

SUPREME COURT SERVICE

Taft accepted a position as a professor of law at the Yale University Law School after he left the presidency. He wrote several books about law and government; Mrs. Taft wrote her memoirs. In 1921 President Warren G. Harding appointed Taft as Chief Justice of the Supreme Court, fulfilling Taft's greatest ambition. Once claiming that he forgot that he had ever been president, Taft brought the full range of his administrative gifts to the job. He reduced the Court's backlog of cases and, with the help of Congress, gave Supreme Court justices more control over the selection of cases for hearing by the Court.

Taft served as Chief Justice until just before his death. He retired on February 3, 1930, and died a month later, on March 8, 1930, in Washington, DC. He was buried at Arlington National Cemetery.

"I don't remember that I ever was president."

William Howard Taft as Chief Justice of the Supreme Court

Helen Taft maintained her involvement with the Girl Scouts, the Colonial Dames, and assorted cultural activities. She died in Washington, DC, on May 22, 1943, and was buried at Arlington National Cemetery next to her husband.

The political tradition goes deep in the Taft family. The president's son Robert Alphonso Taft served in both houses of Congress and gave his name to the Taft-Hartley Act of 1947 (also known as the Labor-Management Relations Act). Taft's grandson, also named Robert, served in both houses of Congress. Taft's great-grandson Robert Alphonso Taft II became governor of Ohio in 1999.

Birthplace: Cincinnati, OH
Residency: Ohio
Religion: Unitarian
Education: Yale University, graduated 1878; University of Cincinnati Law School, graduated 1880
Place of Death: Washington, DC
Burial Site: Arlington National Cemetery, Arlington, VA
Dates in Office: March 4, 1909–March 3, 1913 (4 years)
Age at Inauguration: 51 years, 170 days

FAMILY

Father: Alphonso Taft (1810–1891)
Mother: Louisa Maria Torrey Taft (1827–1907)
Siblings: William was the second of five children; his siblings were Samuel Davenport Taft (b. 1855, died the same year); Henry Waters Taft (1859–1945); Horace Dunn Taft (1861–1943); Frances ("Fanny") Louise Taft (1865–1950); he also had two half-brothers from his father's first marriage to Fanny Phelps Taft (1823–1852): they were Charles Phelps Taft (1843–1929) and Peter Rawson Taft (1845–1889).
Wife: Helen ("Nellie") Herron Taft (1861–1943), married June 19, 1886, in Cincinnati, OH
Children: Robert Alphonso Taft (1889–1953); Helen Herron Taft (1891–1966); Charles Phelps Taft (1897–1983)

CAREER

Private: lawyer, reporter, college professor, dean of the University of Cincinnati Law School
Political: judge in the Ohio Superior Court (1887–1890); US solicitor general (1890–1892); US circuit court judge (1892–1900); governor-general of the Philippines (1901–1904); Secretary of War under Theodore Roosevelt (1904–1908); president of the United States (1909–1913); Chief Justice of the US Supreme Court (1921–1930)
Military: none
Selected Works: *The Collected Works of William Howard Taft*, ed. by David H. Burton (Athens: Ohio University Press, 2001–2003); *Four Aspects of Civic Duty, and Present Day Problems*, ed. with commentary by David H.

Burton and A. E. Campbell (Athens: Ohio University Press, 2001); *Liberty Under Law and Selected Supreme Court Opinions*, ed. with commentary by Francis Graham Lee (Athens: Ohio University Press, 2004); *Our Chief Magistrate and His Powers*, with a foreword, introduction, and notes by H. Jefferson Powell (Durham, NC: Carolina Academic Press, 2002); *Political Issues and Outlooks: Speeches Delivered Between August 1908 and February 1909*, ed. with commentary by David H. Burton (Athens: Ohio University Press, 2001); *Popular Government and the Anti-Trust Act and the Supreme Court*, ed. with commentary by David Potash and Donald F. Anderson (Athens: Ohio University Press, 2003); *Taft Papers on League of Nations*, ed. with commentary by Frank X. Gerrity (Athens: Ohio University Press, 2003); *William Howard Taft, 1857–1930: Chronology, Documents, Bibliographic Aids*, ed. by Gilbert J. Black (Dobbs Ferry, NY: Oceana Publications, 1970)

PRESIDENCY

Nomination: 1908: The Republican convention was held in Chicago, June 16–19, 1908. Taft was nominated on the first ballot as Roosevelt's chosen successor; James S. Sherman of NY was selected as the vice-presidential candidate.

1912: The Republican convention was held in Chicago, June 8–22, 1912. Roosevelt, who had not wanted to run in 1908, was running again. The party power brokers wanted to nominate Taft again, despite the fact that Roosevelt had won most of the primaries. Roosevelt and his supporters left the convention and formed the National Progressive (Bull Moose) Party; the remaining Republicans nominated Taft. James Sherman, the vice president during Taft's first term, was nominated again as running mate, but died at the end of October; the party then selected Nicholas M. Butler of NY, the president of Columbia University, as Taft's running mate.

Election: 1908: elected president on November 3, 1908

1912: defeated by Woodrow Wilson on November 5, 1912

Opponent: 1908: William Jennings Bryan, NE, Democrat

1912: Woodrow Wilson, NJ, Democrat; Theodore Roosevelt, NY, Progressive (Bull Moose)

Vote Totals: 1908: Taft, 7,676,320 popular, 321 electoral; Bryan, 6,412,294 popular, 162 electoral

1912: Wilson, 6,296,547 popular, 435 electoral; T. Roosevelt, 4,118,571 popular, 88 electoral; Taft, 3,486,720 popular, 8 electoral

Inauguration: March 4, 1909

Vice President: James S. Sherman, NY (1909–1912)

CABINET

Secretary of State: Philander C. Knox, PA (1909–1913)

Secretary of the Treasury: Franklin MacVeagh, IL (1909–1913)

Secretary of War: Jacob M. Dickinson, TN (1909–1911); Henry L. Stimson, NY (1911–1913)

Attorney General: George W. Wickersham, NY (1909–1913)

Postmaster General: Frank H. Hitchcock, MA (1909–1913)

Secretary of the Navy: George von Lengerke Meyer, MA (1909–1913)

Secretary of Agriculture: James Wilson, IA (1909–1913)

Secretary of the Interior: Richard A. Ballinger, WA (1909–1911); Walter L. Fisher, IL (1911–1913)

Secretary of Commerce and Labor: Charles Nagel, MO (1909–1913)

CONGRESS

61st Congress (1909–1911); Speaker of the House: Joseph G. Cannon (IL, Republican)

62nd Congress (1911–1913); Speaker of the House: James Beauchamp Clark (MO, Democrat)

SUPREME COURT APPOINTEES

Edward Douglass White, LA; Chief Justice (1910–1921) [Note: White was originally named to the Court as an associate justice by President Cleveland and served from 1894 to 1910.]

Horace Harmon Lurton, TN; Associate Justice (1910–1914)

Charles Evans Hughes, NY; Associate Justice (1910–1916)

Willis Van Devanter, WY; Associate Justice (1911–1937)

Joseph Rucker Lamar, GA; Associate Justice (1911–1916)

Mahlon Pitney, NJ; Associate Justice (1912–1922)

MAJOR EVENTS OF THE TAFT ADMINISTRATION

◆ Taft signs the Payne-Aldrich Tariff Act, August 6, 1909, a compromise bill that lowers the tariff on some goods and raises it on others.

◆ The Pinchot-Ballinger Controversy of 1909, in which US Chief Forester Gifford Pinchot accuses Secretary of the Interior James Ballinger of misconduct in environmental affairs, leads to the dismissal of Pinchot by Taft and provokes a split in the Republican Party in 1912—between Taft supporters and those who, supporting Roosevelt, form the National Progressive (Bull Moose) Party.

◆ On May 17, 1909, First Lady Helen Taft suffers a stroke.

◆ Taft delivers a message to Congress, June 16, 1909, in which he urges a tax on the income of corporations and a constitutional amendment that will allow for a personal income tax.

◆ The Congress passes the 16th Amendment to the Constitution, allowing for the levy of a personal income tax, on July 12, 1909; the Amendment is ratified on February 3, 1913.

◆ US warships are sent to Nicaragua to protect US citizens and interests in that nation during the political unrest there that includes the execution of 500 revolutionaries.

◆ The Mann-Elkins Act, 1910, extends the jurisdiction of the Interstate Commerce Commission to include communications companies—telephone, telegraph, and cable companies.

◆ Taft signs the Postal Savings Bank Act on June 25, 1910; it allows some banks to pay interest on small savings accounts.

◆ On June 25, 1910, Congress passes the Mann Act, which prohibits the transportation of women across state lines for immoral purposes.

◆ In 1911 Congress passes a law that sets the number of members of the House of Representatives at 435; the law takes effect in 1913.

◆ In August 1911 Taft signs general arbitration treaties with France and with England, which expanded the countries' policies of arbitration during times of international disputes.

◆ New Mexico becomes a state, January 6, 1912.

◆ Arizona becomes a state, February 14, 1912.

◆ On May 13, 1912, the 17th Amendment to the Constitution, which provides for the direct election of US Senators, is passed by Congress; it is ratified on April 8, 1913.

◆ In 1912 Taft signs the bill that establishes the Children's Bureau, charged with studying and reporting on the welfare of children.

◆ On August 24, 1912, Taft signs the Panama Canal Act, which exempts US ships sailing from one US port to another via the canal from paying the toll; many believe this act violates the provisions of the Hay-Pauncefote Treaty.

◆ In September 1912 US Marines are sent to Santo Domingo in the Dominican Republic to keep the peace among warring factions in the wake of its two regime changes in two years.

◆ On October 30, 1912, Vice President John Sherman dies.

◆ On November 5, 1912, Taft loses his bid for reelection to Woodrow Wilson.

◆ Taft vetoes a bill that calls for the literacy test as a requirement for those wishing to immigrate to the United States, February 1913.

◆ On February 18, 1913, a coup d'état in Mexico deposes President Madero and makes General Victoriano Huerta president; Taft refuses to involve the United States.

◆ On March 1, 1913, Congress passes the Webb-Kenyon Act, which prohibits the shipment of liquor into "dry" states (those that do not allow the sale and consumption of alcohol).

◆ On the evening of March 3, 1913, the night before Wilson's inauguration, a suffragette parade, organized by Alice Paul and Lucy Burns, takes place in Washington, DC.

MAJOR US AND WORLD EVENTS, 1909–1913

◆ On April 9, 1909, US explorer Robert Peary and five companions reach the North Pole; they are the first men to do so. (Later, a claim is made that they missed the North Pole by several miles.)

◆ From June 1, 1909, until October 16, 1909, the Alaska-Pacific-Yukon Exposition, a world's fair, is held in Seattle, WA, on the grounds of the University of Washington.

◆ In August 1909 astronomer H. Knox Shaw photographs Halley's Comet.

◆ On November 10, 1909, a US federal court rules that Standard Oil is a monopoly under the Sherman Anti-Trust Act.

◆ February 8, 1910, William D. Boyce launches the Boy Scouts of America after a trip to England during which a Boy Scout guided him to his destination through fog and then refused to take a tip. (The Boy Scout explained that Scouts did not accept tips for good turns.) Impressed, Boyce then met with Boy Scout founder Lord Robert Baden-Powell to discuss his plan to start a similar organization in the United States.

◆ The 1910 census shows a US population of 92.2 million people.

◆ In 1910 German scientist Paul Ehrlich announces that he has found a cure for syphilis.

◆ The National Collegiate Athletic Association (NCAA) is formed from the Intercollegiate Athletic Association of the United States (IAAUS), 1910.

◆ The opera Der Rosenkavalier, by Richard Strauss, premieres, 1910.

◆ In 1910 Dr. Leo Baekeland launches the General Bakelite Corporation after obtaining a patent for the new plastic he has developed.

◆ In 1910 the Union of South Africa is formed from Cape Colony, Natal Colony, the South African Republic, and the Orange Free State.

◆ On August 22, 1910, Korea is annexed by Japan.

◆ In November 1910 the Mexican Revolution gets underway, as Francisco Madera tries to overthrow the government of President Porfirio Díaz.

◆ E. M. Forster publishes Howard's End, 1910.

◆ Gustav Mahler's Symphony No. 8 premieres in Munich, September 12, 1910.

◆ Victor Herbert's Naughty Marietta premieres on Broadway, November 7, 1910.

◆ On March 25, 1911, a fire at the Triangle Shirtwaist Company in lower Manhattan kills 146 workers, all of them girls and young women. The tragedy leads to the passage of fire safety laws, including laws that stipulate that public exit doors must open outward and must not be locked during operating hours.

◆ On October 10, 1911, the Wuchang Uprising in China overthrows the Qing (Manchu) Dynasty, making way for the establishment of the Republic of China and the presidency of Sun Yat-sen.

◆ Edith Wharton publishes Ethan Frome, 1911.

◆ Frances Hodgson Burnett publishes The Secret Garden, 1911.

◆ On May 24, 1911, Edward Elgar's Symphony No. 2 premieres in London.

◆ In 1911 Dutch physicist Heike Kamerlingh Onnes discovers superconductivity—the near total absence of electrical resistance in some materials when they are cooled to temperatures approaching absolute zero.

◆ On May 15, 1911, the Supreme Court orders John D. Rockefeller's Standard Oil Company to break up, because it is considered a monopoly.

◆ The first Indianapolis 500 race is held on May 30, 1911; Ray Harroun, who has an average speed of 74.59 miles per hour, wins the race.

◆ On December 14, 1911, Norwegian explorer Roald Amundsen and four companions reach the South Pole; they are the first men to do so.

◆ Juliette Gordon Low establishes the Girl Scouts, holding its first meeting in Savannah, GA, on March 12, 1912.

◆ On the night of April 14–15, 1912, the Titanic sinks in the North Sea

◆ On July 30, 1912, Emperor Mutsuhito of Japan dies and is succeeded by his son,

Emperor Yoshihito; this marks the transition from the Meiji Era to the Taisho Era.

◆ In October 1912 Montenegro declares war on Turkey; the conflict becomes the First Balkan War, which ends in December 1912.

◆ On October 14, 1912, Theodore Roosevelt is shot on his way to deliver a campaign speech; he gives the speech (it lasts an hour and a half) before consenting to go to a hospital for treatment.

◆ Thomas Mann publishes *Death in Venice*, 1912.

◆ Zane Grey publishes *Riders of the Purple Sage*, 1912.

◆ Carl Jung publishes *The Theory of Psychoanalysis*, 1912.

◆ On April 12, 1912, Fenway Park in Boston opens.

◆ February 1, 1913, Grand Central Station opens, in New York City.

◆ On February 17, 1913, the International Exhibition of Modern Art (the Armory Show) opens in New York City, displaying works by Degas, Delacroix, Renoir, Monet, Van Gogh, Brancusi, Matisse, Dufy, Braque, Gauguin, and many others.

FAST FACTS ABOUT WILLIAM HOWARD TAFT

◆ Taft twice turned down Supreme Court positions he ardently desired, partly because he wanted to complete the job he had started as the chief civil administrator of the Philippines, and partly because his wife wanted him to become president instead.

◆ Taft was a large man, standing over six feet tall and weighing more than 300 pounds.

◆ Helen Taft was the first First Lady to accompany her husband to the reviewing stand at his inauguration.

◆ The Oval Office was built in the center of the West Wing of the White House in 1909 for President Taft.

◆ Taft's Latin America policy was dubbed "Dollar Diplomacy"; it referred to the precept that the holding out of financial incentives to other nations and other entities would further US goals more effectively than armed forces.

◆ Helen Taft oversaw the planting of 3,000 Japanese cherry trees in Washington, DC, and, with the wife of the Japanese ambassador, planted the first two trees.

◆ Relations between Taft and Roosevelt deteriorated after Taft became the president.

◆ Taft received only 23 percent of the popular vote in his bid for reelection, the lowest percentage of any incumbent president who has sought reelection.

◆ Taft was the only president to serve as the Chief Justice of the Supreme Court.

◆ Taft launched the presidential tradition of throwing the first baseball pitch of the season at a major league game, on April 14, 1910. The game was between the Washington Senators and the Philadelphia Athletics.

◆ Taft argued for the need for Congress to appropriate money for a separate Supreme Court Building; it did so in 1929. The building was completed in 1935, after Taft's death; during his tenure as Chief Justice, the Court met in the Old Senate Chamber of the Capitol.

◆ Taft was the first president to be an avid golfer.

◆ Taft is one of two presidents buried in Arlington National Cemetery; the other is John Fitzgerald Kennedy.

◆ Helen Taft was the first First Lady to donate her inaugural gown to the Smithsonian Institution.

Woodrow Wilson

Nickname: The Schoolmaster in Politics, Tommy
Presidency: 28th president, 1913–1921
Party: Democrat
Life dates: December 28, 1856–February 3, 1924 (67 years, 36 days)

EARLY LIFE AND EDUCATION

Thomas Woodrow Wilson was born December 28, 1856, in Staunton, Virginia. He was the third child of Jessie Janet Woodrow Wilson and Joseph Ruggles Wilson. He had two older sisters, Marion and Annie, and a younger brother, Joseph. His father was educated at the Princeton Theological Seminary and ordained as a Presbyterian minister. Soon after Thomas's birth, the family moved to Augusta, Georgia, where Joseph Wilson was both a church pastor and a teacher at the Augusta Female Seminary (later Mary Baldwin College). In part because of the Civil War's disruption of civilian lives, the future president and his siblings were educated mostly at home. Joseph and Jessie Wilson took great care to provide their children with a well-rounded education. Young Thomas may have suffered from dyslexia; he did not read until he was ten years old.

Thomas lived through the Civil War as a Southerner; his father supported the Confederacy and, during one summer, served as a chaplain to Confederate troops. In 1865, when Thomas was eight, he watched as Jefferson Davis, the former president of the Confederacy, was being paraded, in chains, through the streets of Augusta and en route to a Union prison.

In 1870 Joseph Wilson was offered a professorship at the Columbia Theological Seminary, in Columbia, South Carolina, and the family moved to Columbia. In 1874, the Wilsons moved to Wilmington, North Carolina.

Thomas Woodrow Wilson was known as Tommy until his college days, at which time he started to become known as Woodrow. In 1873 he entered Davidson College in North Carolina, but was forced to leave after one year because of illness (which may have been partly, or mostly, homesickness). He studied again with his father at home, for about a year, and then enrolled at the College of New Jersey (later known as Princeton University) in 1875; he graduated in 1879. At Princeton he studied history and politics; he took part in literary and debating clubs (he organized the Liberal Debating Society), and played baseball.

He then attended the University of Virginia's law school for a time, but left in the winter of 1880 for a variety of reasons that included ill health and an episode of depression that had been triggered by a rejection (he was rejected by a cousin to whom he had proposed marriage). At the University of Virginia he had been made aware that he didn't really like the law: he saw clearly that he had some interest in its conceptual aspect; far less in its practical aspect. He continued to study law at home, however, and was admitted to the Georgia bar in 1882.

EARLY CAREER

Wilson started up a law practice in Atlanta with Edward Renick, a former classmate at the University of Virginia. He practiced law—not very successfully—for only a year before deciding to leave the profession, having realized that his passion was politics.

During his year of law practice, his mother had asked him to take care of family business in Rome, Georgia. In Rome he met Ellen Axson, in April 1883. She was the daughter of a Presbyterian minister and had graduated from the Rome Female College. Wilson later remembered that his first thought, on meeting Ellen, was: "What splendid, laughing eyes!" Ellen Axson had a strong interest in art and studied art in New York City in 1884 after she had accepted Wilson's proposal of marriage.

> "The history of liberty is a history of resistance. The history of liberty is a history of the limitation of governmental power, not the increase of it."
>
> Woodrow Wilson, speech at the New York Press Club, September 9, 1912

Wilson had decided that he did not wish to marry until he had completed yet another educational endeavor: he had enrolled in Johns Hopkins University for postgraduate studies in history and political theory. He was awarded the Ph.D. degree from Johns Hopkins in 1885. His doctoral dissertation, *Congressional Govern-*

ment, became a classic text in the field of US government studies.

After graduation he accepted a teaching position at Bryn Mawr College in Bryn Mawr, Pennsylvania. Very shortly thereafter he and Ellen were married, in Savannah, Georgia, in 1885. Margaret, the first of their three daughters, was born in 1886; Jessie was born in 1887; and Eleanor, in 1889.

Wilson was not entirely happy at Bryn Mawr. For one thing, he had come to the conclusion that a career of teaching women might be an impediment to the fulfillment of his political goals. He accepted a teaching position at Wesleyan University in Middletown, Connecticut, in 1888, and there coached the football team as well. He was happier at Wesleyan, but happier still when Princeton University offered him a professorship of jurisprudence and political economy, which he accepted, in 1890. He was a popular professor at Princeton; during his time there he was the author of many erudite works and solidified a growing national reputation as an educator and scholar.

In 1902 Wilson became the president of Princeton University. He was the first Princeton president who had not previously been a clergyman. He reorganized the curriculum and instituted a preceptorial system similar to that used in British universities, wherein young scholars were hired as preceptors—as tutors, advisors, and assistants to senior professors—to help bridge the gap between students and faculty. Not all of Wilson's ideas for the school were embraced, however. He tried, unsuccessfully, to abolish the eating clubs that functioned as exclusive social clubs and hoped to replace them with "a quadrangle system" that would have placed students in residential halls, built around quadrangles (courtyards), with their own dining rooms and faculty advisors. An even bigger dispute occurred when a new graduate school facility was scheduled to be constructed; Wilson wanted it built near the center of the undergraduate campus to promote the exchange of ideas between graduate and undergraduate students. The dean of the graduate school, Andrew West, wanted it to be built at a site that was several miles away from the undergraduate campus. West prevailed when an alumnus left money to the university on the condition that it be used to implement the West plan. Wilson did not accept defeat easily and ended friendships with those who disagreed with him.

In 1906 Wilson suffered a stroke and lost sight in one eye. His doctors advised him to take it easy for a while. Wilson, for the most part, ignored his doctors' advise. It was around the time he became president of Princeton University that he first attracted the attention of Colonel George Harvey, a former journalist, former managing editor at *Harper's Weekly*, and New Jersey Democratic Party boss who also happened to be quite wealthy.

POLITICAL CAREER

With Harvey's backing, Wilson became the candidate of the Democratic Party in the race for governor of New Jersey in 1909 and was elected in 1910. He served as governor until 1912, and during that time became known for a series of progressive reforms, including the improvement of working conditions, the establishment of a workers' compensation program, the regulation of public utilities, and election reform in the state. He made changes to the state's public school system and supported antitrust legislation.

With his reputation as a progressive politician firmly established, Wilson sought the Democratic Party's nomination for president in 1912. He won the nomination after a protracted contest—and not until the forty-sixth ballot. His Republican opponents included the incumbent president, William Howard Taft, and former president Theodore Roosevelt, who had withdrawn his support from Taft. Roosevelt believed that Taft had betrayed the progressive agenda that Roosevelt had done so much to advance during his presidency. Despite his having won in many of the Republican primary elections, Roosevelt was not able to secure the nomination from the party that Taft controlled. Roosevelt and his supporters subsequently formed the Progressive ("Bull Moose") Party.

The Republican split between Taft support-ers and Roosevelt supporters gave Wilson the victory. Although he received only 42 percent of the popular vote, he received 435 of the 531 electoral votes.

PRESIDENCY

Wilson had campaigned on a "New Freedom" platform that called for banking reform, tariff reduction, and stronger antitrust legislation. As president, he lost no time in pursuing these reforms. He decided to take his case for tariff reform directly to Congress. He spoke before a joint session of Congress (in contrast to a long tradition whereby presidents communicated with Congress only via written messages). The Underwood Tariff Act passed in Congress in October 1913; it lowered tariffs from about 40 percent to about 26 percent, on average, and provided for an income tax intended to offset the loss of funds that the tariff reduction would give rise to.

> **"Conservatism is the policy of 'make no change and consult your grandmother when in doubt.'"**
>
> Woodrow Wilson, *Philosophy*, 1918

Banking reform came in the form of the Federal Reserve Act of 1913 (sometimes called the Owen-Glass Act or Glass-Owen Act). The legislation, which had been supported by Wilson, called for a system of federal reserve banks that would include twelve regional banks and a board of governors, the latter to have its headquarters in Washington, DC.

Wilson turned to strengthening the Sherman Antitrust Act of 1890 and the nation's antitrust laws. He and progressive members of Congress proposed legislation that became the Clayton Antitrust Act of 1914. It clarified and/or added to the prior antitrust laws and prohibited a wide range of unfair business practices. Wilson proposed the establishment of several new federal government commissions to monitor industry. The Federal Trade Commission Act of 1914 established the Federal Trade Commission, set up to enforce federal antitrust and consumer protection laws. The new Federal Trade Commission was given the power to issue "cease and desist" orders to businesses engaged in illegal activity.

"If you think too much about being reelected, it is very difficult to be worth reelecting."

Woodrow Wilson, speech in Philadelphia, PA, October 25, 1913

There were limits to Wilson's progressive sympathies, however. He endorsed segregation in federal government offices and in federal government lunchrooms and restrooms, and he refused to support the women's suffrage movement. And although he was positively pro-labor and pro-union, when a long-standing strike by miners in Colorado provoked violent confrontation between strikers and strike breakers, the Colorado governor (with Wilson's consent) sent in National Guard troops. The presence of the troops triggered the Ludlow Massacre, in which National Guard members opened fire with machine guns on the striking miners. The miners returned fire.

Wilson's domestic policy actions were very suddenly eclipsed by the world events of the summer of 1914. On June 28, 1914, the Archduke Franz Ferdinand of Austria was assassinated by a Serbian anarchist in Sarajevo, Serbia. Austria-Hungary declared war on Serbia; the declaration of war set in motion a series of catastrophic events that very quickly plunged most of Europe and, eventually, other parts of the world into a catastrophic and unprecedentedly destructive war, the "Great War," later World War I. Wilson echoed the sentiments and wishes of US citizens when he declared that the United States would remain neutral.

On the eve of this calamitous war, on August 6, 1914, Ellen Axson Wilson died of Bright's Disease, a kidney disorder. Wilson was devastated by her death. He had for many years relied heavily on his wife for emotional support and companionship. He turned to his daughters for solace; however, two of his daughters were married and the third was ensconced in a career. At a time when he appeared to be at his lowest point, he met Edith Galt.

Edith Bolling Galt, a widow of some means who had operated her husband's jewelry store business after his death and later sold the business, was introduced to Wilson when she visited her friend Helen Bone, a cousin of the president's, at the White House. The president, somewhat improbably, fell in love with Galt and urged her to marry him, over the objections of some of his political advisors, who feared that—because not a great deal of time had passed since the death of his first wife—there might be political fallout from such an action. On December 18, 1915, he married Edith Galt at her home in Washington, DC.

In the wake of the Spanish-American War at the end of the nineteenth century, the United States had not only won a clear victory in the war, but had also won territorial concessions. Several US presidents (Wilson's immediate predecessors) had not been shy about showcasing US military might in Latin America nor about flexing US political and military muscle in the region. Wilson, however, wanted to atone for what, in his view, had been acts of aggression and political and military blunders. At the time of the 1914 opening of the Panama Canal, he persuaded Congress to repeal the 1912 Panama Canal Act, which exempted many US ships from paying the required toll for passage through the canal. Yet, despite his personal loathing of imperialism, Wilson sent troops to invade and occupy Nicaragua, Haiti, the Dominican Republic, and Mexico during times of unrest in those places. In the end (in part owing to prevailing political winds) he resorted to the same kinds of military actions in the region that his predecessors had.

Meanwhile, German submarine attacks on

merchant and passenger ships had rendered US citizens somewhat less likely to crave US neutrality vis-à-vis the European war. Anti-German feeling in the United States was much exacerbated by the sinking of the British ocean liner *Lusitania*, on May 7, 1915. The ship had been destroyed by a German submarine.

Wilson was reelected in 1916 with the campaign slogan "He kept us out of war"—something he tried in earnest to do. Wilson hoped to act as a mediator among the European powers, and urged them to accept "peace without victory," as peace was in the world's best interest. German attacks on merchant ships, including those of neutral countries, continued. Wilson terminated US diplomatic relationships with Germany. Wilson and the American people were stunned and outraged when it was revealed that British intelligence personnel had intercepted and decoded what became known as the Zimmerman Telegram, which was turned over to the United States in late February 1917. In it, German Foreign Secretary Arthur Zimmerman had asked the Mexican government to declare war on the United States if the United States declared war on Germany. It further stated that unrestrained submarine warfare would be resumed.

On April 6, 1917, the United States declared war on Germany. The United States's transition from a nation of isolationist temperament to a nation at war almost turned the country upside-down. Wilson first wanted to prepare the military. A draft was inaugurated: four million men were drafted and, of those, two million were sent to Europe. Wilson promoted the sale of war bonds as a way of financing the war. He was concerned that antiwar sentiment would inflict great damage on the war effort so he created the Committee on Public Information, essentially a ministry of propaganda; its purpose was to convince all US citizens that the declaration of war by the United States had been the right thing to do. At Wilson's urging, Congress passed the Espionage Act and the Sedition Act, which outlawed draft-dodging and prohibited US citizens from speaking out against the war or the US government.

Weary British and French troops who had endured years of horror (and of their compatriots being slaughtered) were buttressed by the influx of American soldiers. Although the American soldiers were inexperienced, the sheer weight of their numbers helped to turn the tide and to force a German retreat. The armistice that ended the war was signed on November 11, 1918.

> **"That a peasant may become king does not render the kingdom democratic."**
>
> Woodrow Wilson, 1910

In January 1918 Wilson made a speech to Congress in which he detailed his "Fourteen Points" plan; it described the fourteen elements Wilson believed to be essential to a lasting peace. Those points included freedom of the seas, armament reductions, and a restoration of territory and sovereignty to various European nations, including Belgium, France, Italy, Serbia, and Turkey. His final point called for the establishment of "a general association of nations" in order to "afford mutual guarantees of political independence and territorial integrity." That association of nations would be called the League of Nations. Wilson himself traveled to Paris to attend the peace conference and to present his plan. The conference produced the Treaty of Versailles.

Wilson returned to the United States. Although the Treaty of Versailles fell short of his ideal and was more punishing of the Germans than he thought wise, Wilson submitted it to Congress for its ratification. Wilson embarked on a speaking tour in September 1919 to urge American support for the treaty and for the League of Nations. On October 28, 1919, in Pueblo, Colorado, Wilson suffered a massive stroke. He was thereafter confined to his bedroom in the White House (and for the remainder of his presidency) and rarely saw anyone other than his doctors and his wife. Edith Wilson carried written inquiries to her husband and emerged with his responses. To what degree she made policy decisions remains an open question. She had been a part of her husband's political life since their marriage and knew his position on most questions.

In 1920 Congress refused to ratify the Treaty of Versailles and refused to join the League of Nations. The Republican majority in Congress reflected the prevailing desire of US citizens for isolation and essentially blamed Wilson for the nation's involvement in the war. The United States concluded a separate treaty with Germany and never joined the League of Nations.

POST-PRESIDENTIAL CAREER

Wilson left the highest office in the land a bitter and deeply disappointed man. He and Mrs. Wilson retired to a home in Washington, DC, where Edith continued to supervise every detail of his care. Ironically, in December 1920 Wilson was awarded the 1919 Nobel Peace Prize, in recognition of his role as a founder of the League of Nations.

Wilson died on February 3, 1924; Edith Wilson lived until December 28, 1961. She wrote a book, *My Memoirs*, that was published in 1938. She maintained her interest in politics for the rest of her life. She attended President John F. Kennedy's inauguration in her last months of life.

Despite his disappointment and disillusionment at the time of his retirement, Wilson was a powerful and effective president who had wielded considerable influence in the Congress and in the nation. His ideas for a League of Nations were more effectively realized after World War II at the founding of the United Nations, headquartered in the United States in part as a tribute to him.

Birthplace: Staunton, VA
Residency: New Jersey
Religion: Presbyterian
Education: Davidson College, Davidson, NC, 1873, left because of poor health; College of New

Jersey (later Princeton University), graduated 1879; University of Virginia Law School, 1880, left because of poor health; Johns Hopkins University, Baltimore, MD, graduated with a Ph.D. in history and political science, 1886
Place of Death: Washington, DC
Burial Site: Washington National Cathedral, Washington, DC
Dates in Office: March 4, 1913–March 3, 1921 (8 years)
Age at Inauguration: 56 years, 65 days

FAMILY

Father: Joseph Ruggles Wilson (1822–1903)
Mother: Janet ("Jessie") Woodrow Wilson (1826–1888)
Siblings: Woodrow was the third of four children; his siblings were Marion Williamson Wilson (1850–1890); Annie Josephson Wilson (1853–1916); Joseph Ruggles Wilson (1867–1927).
Wife: Ellen Louise Axson Wilson (1860–1914), married June 24, 1885, in Savannah, GA; Edith Bolling Galt Wilson (1872–1961), married December 18, 1915, in Washington, DC
Children: by Ellen Louise Axson Wilson: Margaret Woodrow Wilson (1886–1944); Jessie Woodrow Wilson (1887–1933); Eleanor Randolph Wilson (1889–1967)

CAREER

Private: lawyer, history instructor at Bryn Mawr College (1885–1888), professor of jurisprudence and political economy at Princeton University (1890–1902), president of Princeton University (1902–1910)
Political: governor of New Jersey (1911–1913); president of the United States (1913–1921)
Military: none
Selected Works: *Congressional Government: A Study in American Politics*, intro. by Walter Lippmann (Baltimore: Johns Hopkins University Press, 1981); *Constitutional Government in the United States*, intro. by Sidney A. Pearson, Jr. (New Brunswick, NJ: Transaction Publishers, 2002); *George Washington* (Birmingham, AL: Palladium Press, 2001); *A History of the American People; The Hoover-Wilson Wartime*

Correspondence, ed. and with commentaries by Francis William O'Brien (Ames: Iowa State University Press, 1974); *The Papers of Woodrow Wilson*, ed. by Arthur S. Link et al. (Princeton, NJ: Princeton University Press, 1966–1994); *The Public Papers of Woodrow Wilson*, ed. by Ray Stannard Baker and William E. Dodd (New York: Harper, 1925–1927); *A President in Love: The Courtship Letters of Woodrow Wilson and Edith Bolling Galt*, ed. by Edwin Tribble (Boston: Houghton Mifflin, 1981); *The Priceless Gift: The Love Letters of Woodrow Wilson and Ellen Axson Wilson*, ed. by Eleanor Wilson McAdoo (Westport, CT: Greenwood Press, 1975); *The State: Elements of Historical and Practical Politics*, ed. with introductions by Richard M. Pious (Farmington, NY: Dabor Social Science Publications, 1978); *Two Peacemakers in Paris: The Hoover-Wilson Post-Armistice Letters, 1918–1920*, ed. and with commentaries by Francis William O'Brien (College Station: Texas A&M University Press, 1978); *Woodrow Wilson, 1856–1924: Chronology, Documents, Bibliographical Aids*, ed. by Robert I. Vexler (Dobbs Ferry, NY: Oceana Publications, 1969); *Woodrow Wilson's Case for the League of Nations*, compiled with his approval by Hamilton Foley (Port Washington, NY: Kennikat Press, 1967)

PRESIDENCY

Nomination: 1912: At the Democratic Convention in Baltimore, Maryland, held at the end of June and early July, Wilson was nominated on the forty-sixth ballot.

1916: Wilson was renominated, with only one vote in opposition, at the Democratic Convention in Baltimore, Maryland, in mid-June of 1916.

Election: 1912: elected president on November 5, 1912

1916: elected president on November 7, 1916

Opponent: 1912: William Howard Taft, OH, Republican; Theodore Roosevelt, NY, Progressive ("Bull Moose"); Eugene V. Debs, IN, Socialist

1916: Charles Evans Hughes, NY, Republican; Allan L. Benson, NY, Socialist

Vote Totals: 1912: Wilson, 6,296,184 popular, 435 electoral; Taft, 3,486,242 popular, 8 electoral;

Roosevelt, 4,122,721 popular, 88 electoral; Debs, 901,551 popular, 0 electoral

1916: Wilson, 9,126,868 popular, 277 electoral; Hughes, 8,548,728 popular, 254 electoral; Benson, 590,524 popular, 0 electoral

Inauguration: 1912: March 4, 1913

1916: March 5, 1917 [Note: March 4, 1917, was a Sunday, so Wilson took the oath of office in the President's Room at the Capitol, and then took it again on March 5, when he delivered his inaugural address to the public.]

Vice President: Thomas R. Marshall, IN (1913–1921)

CABINET

Secretary of State: William Jennings Bryan, NE (1913–1915); Robert Lansing, NY (1915–1920); Bainbridge Colby, NY (1920–1921)

Secretary of the Treasury: William G. McAdoo, NY (1913–1918); Carter Glass, VA (1918–1920); David F. Houston, MO (1920–1921)

Secretary of War: Lindley Miller Garrison, NJ (1913–1916); Newton D. Baker, OH (1916–1921)

Attorney General: James Clark McReynolds, TN (1913–1914); Thomas Watt Gregory, TX (1914–1919); Alexander Mitchell Palmer, PA (1919–1921)

Postmaster General: Albert S. Burleson, TX (1913–1921)

Secretary of the Navy: Josephus Daniels, NC (1913–1921)

Secretary of Agriculture: David Franklin Houston, MO (1913–1920); Edwin Thomas Meredith, IA (1920–1921)

Secretary of the Interior: Franklin K. Lane, CA (1913–1920); John Barton Payne, IL (1920–1921)

Secretary of Labor: William B. Wilson, PA (1913–1921)

Secretary of Commerce: William C. Redfield, NY (1913–1919); Joshua W. Alexander, MO (1919–1921)

CONGRESS

63rd Congress (1913–1915); Speaker of the House: James Beauchamp Clark (MO, Democrat)

64th Congress (1915–1917); Speaker of the House: James Beauchamp Clark (MO, Democrat)

65th Congress (1917–1919); Speaker of the House: James Beauchamp Clark (MO, Democrat)

66th Congress (1919–1921); Speaker of the House: Frederick H. Gillett (MA, Republican)

SUPREME COURT APPOINTEES

James Clark McReynolds, TN; Associate Justice (1914–1941)

Louis Dembitz Brandeis, MA; Associate Justice (1916–1936)

John Hessin Clarke, OH; Associate Justice (1916–1922)

MAJOR EVENTS OF THE WILSON ADMINISTRATION

◆ On March 4, 1913, Congress divides the Department of Labor and Commerce into two separate departments.

◆ In April 1913 Wilson addresses a joint session of Congress to ask for tariff reform.

◆ In May 1913 the United States officially recognizes the new Republic of China.

◆ In August 1913 the United States refuses to recognize the government of President Victoriano Huerta of Mexico, who had seized power from President Francisco Madero in a coup d'état. Madero, who died four days after the coup, was alleged to have been shot and killed by a member of Huerta's army as he tried to escape to safety.

◆ The Underwood-Simmons Tariff Act, 1913, removes tariffs from many items and lowers the overall rate to about 26 percent; it also provides for a progressive income tax, meaning high income earners are required to pay taxes at higher rates.

◆ In 1913 the first Form 1040 appears.

◆ The Federal Reserve Act of 1913 (also called the Owen-Glass Act or Glass-Owen Act) provides for a system of federal reserve banks, with twelve regional reserve banks and a board of governors in Washington, DC.

◆ The 17th Amendment to the Constitution, which provides for the direct election of US Senators, is ratified in 1913.

◆ In Mexico in April 1914 soldiers in Huerta's army detain several US Marines, then release

them; the US government demands a formal apology. When Huerta refuses to apologize, Wilson orders US warships to Tampico Bay.

◆ Wilson asks Congress to approve the use of force against Mexico; Congress complies, in April 1914.

◆ On April 21, 1914, US forces seize the customs house in Veracruz, Mexico, and demand an apology from President Huerta for the detention of US Marines earlier in the month.

◆ Wilson agrees to accept arbitration in the dispute with Mexico, but President Huerta is forced to resign in July 1914; he goes into exile.

◆ In 1914 and 1915, Wilson sends Edward Mandell House to meet with British, French, and German leaders as part of an unsuccessful attempt to mediate an end to the European war (called "the Great War" and, eventually, World War I).

◆ The Federal Trade Commission Act in 1914 creates the Federal Trade Commission, empowered to issue "cease and desist" orders to corporations found to be acting illegally.

◆ On August 6, 1914, First Lady Ellen Axson Wilson dies at the White House of Bright's disease (a kidney disorder).

◆ The Clayton Antitrust Act, October 1914, prohibits price fixing, discriminatory rebates and discounts, the ownership of competing companies for the purpose of limiting competition, and interlocking directorates (the same person acting as a director for competing companies); it also limits the use of injunctions against labor unions, as well as recognizes boycotts, strikes, and picketing as legal actions.

◆ In 1914 Wilson signs a bill making Mother's Day a national holiday.

◆ The Smith-Lever Act of 1914 gives money to land-grant colleges (established by the Morrill Act of 1862) for education and research in agriculture, home economics, and rural energy.

◆ On January 28, 1915, Wilson signs into law the "Act to Create the Coast Guard."

◆ On May 7, 1915, the British ocean liner *Lusitania* is sunk by a German U-boat; 1,198 people are killed, including 128 Americans.

◆ Apprehensive toward internal strife in Haiti

that has been triggered by the assassination of its president, the United States sends troops to Haiti in July 1915, beginning an occupation that will last until 1934.

❖ On December 18, 1915, Wilson marries Edith Bolling Galt at her home in Washington, DC.

❖ Wilson sends US Marines to the Dominican Republic in 1916 after repeated upheavals and coups have failed to create a stable government; the US occupation lasts until 1924.

❖ In 1916 US troops led by General John Pershing are sent to Mexico in pursuit of Pancho Villa and other Mexican guerrillas who have conducted a raid on US territory, but the US troops fail to capture Pancho Villa.

❖ After a German submarine torpedoes the British steamer *Sussex* in March 1916, the United States demands that Germany end its practice of torpedoing civilian ships; Germany makes the "*Sussex* Pledge" and agrees not to sink passenger ships.

❖ The National Defense Act of 1916 gives the name "National Guard" to the state militias and designates them the reserve force of the US Army.

❖ The Federal Farm Loan Act of 1916 establishes twelve regional banks that are to provide funds to local farm associations, from which farmers will be able to obtain loans.

❖ On August 25, 1916, the National Park Service is established by act of Congress.

❖ The Adamson Act of 1916 orders an eight-hour workday and overtime wages for railroad workers.

❖ In November 1916 Wilson is reelected; he defeats Charles Evans Hughes of NY. His campaign slogan is "He kept us out of war."

❖ In January 1917 Wilson urges European powers to accept "Peace without Victory," in hopes that a nonpunitive settlement of the European war will prevent future conflicts.

❖ On January 17, 1917, the United States purchases the Danish West Indies, which become the US Virgin Islands (St. Thomas, St. John, St. Croix, and many smaller islands).

❖ On February 24, 1917, the so-called Zimmerman Telegram, intercepted by British

intelligence officers, is turned over to the United States government. The telegram, sent from German Foreign Secretary Arthur Zimmerman to the German ambassador to Mexico, states that Germany is planning to resume unrestricted submarine warfare and asks the ambassador to seek a Mexican alliance with Germany against the United States. Reportage of the telegram on March 1 increases support among US citizens for US involvement in the war.

❖ The United States severs diplomatic relations with Germany, February 3, 1917.

❖ On April 6, 1917, the United States declares war on Germany.

❖ Wilson creates the Committee on Public Information (CPI) in April 1917; its purpose is to influence public opinion in favor of the war effort.

❖ The Immigration Act of 1917 bars the immigration of a wide variety of people, including those who are insane, alcoholics, beggars, vagrants, those with tuberculosis, felons, polygamists, anarchists, and the illiterate.

❖ In May 1917 the War Industries Board is formed under the leadership of Bernard Baruch; its purpose is to persuade industries to increase their efficiency for the sake of the war effort.

❖ In June 1917 General John J. Pershing and the American Expeditionary Force arrive in France.

❖ Liberty Loan Bonds are widely sold to help finance the war, 1917–1918.

❖ The Selective Service Act of 1917 requires all men between the ages of 21 and 30 to register for military service.

❖ The Espionage Act of 1917 establishes punishments of a $10,000 fine or up to twenty years' imprisonment for a variety of offenses, including obstruction of the sale of war bonds or the recruitment of troops, and attempts to incite military personnel to insubordination or mutiny.

❖ In 1917 and 1918, the Food Administration, under Herbert Hoover, encourages "Meatless Mondays" and "Wheatless Wednesdays" as a way of conserving needed food supplies.

◆ To help feed the people of Europe, where millions of farmers have become soldiers and crops have been destroyed by war, Americans till "War Gardens" in 1917 and 1918, and "Victory Gardens" after the war.

◆ Wilson, in a speech to Congress, details his "Fourteen Points" plan, January 8, 1918.

◆ In March 1918 Congress establishes daylight savings time.

◆ In France, US troops fight at Cantigny in May 1918 and at Chateau-Thierry and Belleau Wood in June 1918.

◆ US troops take part in the Meuse-Argonne offense of late September 1918 and sustain appalling casualties, but the sheer numbers of US troops and Allied troops help to break the German lines.

◆ From March 1918 until the spring of 1919, an epidemic of influenza (also called the Spanish influenza) sweeps the world; in the United States, more than half a million people die.

◆ The Sedition Act of 1918 extends the prohibitions of the Espionage Act of 1917 to include disloyal or abusive speech about the army, the flag, or the government.

◆ On November 11, 1918, an armistice is signed between the Allied and German governments in the Forest of Compiègne in France.

◆ The 18th Amendment to the Constitution, which prohibits the consumption of alcohol, is passed by Congress on December 18, 1917, and is ratified on January 16, 1919.

◆ Wilson leads the American peace mission to Paris; he leaves the United States on December 4, 1918.

◆ The Paris Peace Conference opens, on January 18, 1919.

◆ On February 14, 1919, Wilson speaks before the Paris Peace Conference and submits his plan for an association of nations, to be called the League of Nations.

◆ The Treaty of Versailles is signed, June 1919.

◆ Wilson submits the Treaty of Versailles to Congress and in September 1919 embarks on a nationwide speaking tour to drum up support for the Treaty of Versailles and the League of Nations.

◆ On October 2, 1919, Wilson suffers a massive stroke and is thereafter confined to the White House.

◆ On October 28, 1919, Congress passes the Volstead Act, which provides for the enforcement of the 18th Amendment (Prohibition), over Wilson's veto.

◆ In 1919 the Supreme Court upholds the right of the government to restrict civil liberties in times of "clear and present danger," thus upholding the Espionage Act.

◆ The 19th Amendment to the Constitution, which grants women the right to vote, is passed by Congress on June 4, 1919; it is ratified on August 18, 1920.

◆ On January 15, 1920, Prohibition begins.

◆ In January 1920 the Senate votes against the United States becoming a member of the League of Nations.

◆ On March 19, 1920, Congress refuses to ratify the Treaty of Versailles.

◆ In May 1920 Wilson vetoes the congressional resolution that calls for an end to the war with Germany.

◆ In November 1920 Wilson wins the Nobel Peace prize for his role as founder of the League of Nations.

MAJOR US AND WORLD EVENTS, 1913–1921

◆ In March 1913 President Francisco Madero of Mexico, King George I of Greece, and Chinese nationalist Sung Chiao-jen are assassinated.

◆ *The Rite of Spring*, a ballet with music by Igor Stravinsky, premieres in Paris on May 29, 1913.

◆ D. H. Lawrence publishes *Sons and Lovers*, 1913.

◆ Willa Cather publishes *O Pioneers!*, 1913.

◆ Alfred North Whitehead and Bertrand Russell publish *Principia Mathematica*, 1913.

◆ George Bernard Shaw publishes *Pygmalion*, 1913.

◆ Edgar Rice Burroughs publishes *Tarzan of the Apes*, 1913.

◆ In 1913 Danish physicist Niels Bohr publishes three papers detailing his theory of atomic structure.

◆ James Joyce publishes *Dubliners*, 1914.

◆ On June 28, 1914, Archduke Franz Ferdinand of Austria is assassinated in Sarajevo, Serbia.

◆ World War I develops: On July 28, 1914, Austria-Hungary declares war on Serbia. Russia then comes to the aid of Serbia, so Germany declares war on Russia, and then on Russia's ally, France; Germany invades Belgium and Great Britain declares war on Germany for violating Belgium's neutrality; by the end of August, Japan declares war on Germany.

◆ The Panama Canal opens for traffic on August 15, 1914; the first ship through is a US ship, the *Ancon*.

◆ On September 18, 1914, the Irish Home Rule bill passes in the British Parliament, although it is not implemented until after World War I.

◆ Robert Frost's *North of Boston*, which includes the poems "Mending Wall" and "The Death of the Hired Man," is published in Great Britain in 1914 and a year later in the United States.

◆ Between September 5 and 12, 1914, the First Battle of the Marne is fought outside of Paris, France. At a horrific cost in lives, the German advance is halted by the French and British forces, and both sides settle into trench warfare for the next three years.

◆ The New York Stock Exchange closes in July 1914 and reopens in November to sell war bonds.

◆ In October and November of 1914, Russia, Great Britain, and France declare war on the Ottoman Empire (Turkey).

◆ On February 8, 1915, D. W. Griffith's *Birth of a Nation* premieres; the film is hailed for its demonstration of cinematic skill but also disparaged for its racist bias.

◆ In 1915 Alfred Wegener publishes *The Origin of Continents and Oceans*, which puts forth his theory of continental drift.

◆ In February 1915 British, Australian, and New Zealand forces mount their attack on Turkish forces stationed at Gallipoli, near Constantinople; after a year's deadlock and half a million casualties for both sides, the attacking forces are withdrawn.

◆ In 1915 the Germans begin using poison gas on the battlefield.

◆ Franz Kafka publishes *The Metamorphosis*, 1915.

◆ T. S. Eliot publishes *The Love Song of J. Alfred Prufrock*, 1915.

◆ D. H. Lawrence publishes *The Rainbow*, 1915.

◆ In 1915 Nevada passes a law making divorce obtainable after a residence there of six months.

◆ In the 1916 elections, Montana's Jeannette Rankin becomes the first woman elected to the US Congress.

◆ On July 6, 1916, the famous lithograph of Uncle Sam proclaiming "I want you!", the work of illustrator James Montgomery Flagg, is published on the cover of *Leslie's Weekly*.

◆ From February to July in 1916, German forces assault the French town of Verdun and the surrounding area, while French counterattacks under General Pétain hold the Germans back; the area changes hands repeatedly until the Germans retreat in order to concentrate on the Battle of the Somme.

◆ During the first two weeks of July in 1916, British and French forces attack German positions in northeastern France, in the First Battle of the Somme. There are more than a million casualties among all combatants, and only about five miles of ground are gained.

◆ D. W. Griffith's *Intolerance* premieres, 1916.

◆ In January 1917 the British intercept the Zimmerman Telegram and decode it, then obtain an encoded copy from an Allied agent in Mexico (so that the Germans will not realize their code has been broken) and deliver it to the United States.

◆ In February 1917 Russia's Czar Nicholas II is overthrown and a provisional government is formed from the Russian *Duma* (parliament).

◆ From late July to November in 1917, the British attack German forces in the Third Battle of Ypres (Battle of Passchendaele) in Belgium; after nearly 600,000 casualties from among the two armies, the British gain about five miles of territory but fail to reach the Belgian coast and the German submarine base that had been the original target.

◆ On June 17, 1917, the British royal family changes its surname from Saxe-Coburg-Gotha to Windsor to distance itself from its German connections.

◆ In the 1917 October Revolution in Russia, the Bolshevik Party creates a government based on the Soviets (elected councils); it is initially socialist, but becomes communist.

◆ On November 2, 1917, the Balfour Declaration, issued by the British government, calls for the establishment of a Jewish homeland in Palestine.

◆ On March 3, 1918, the Treaty of Brest-Litovsk between Germany, Austria, and Soviet Russia entails a separate peace with Russia and excludes Russia's allies (Great Britain, France, and the United States); the treaty is later annulled by the treaties that end the war.

◆ In March 1918 Moscow replaces Petrograd as the capital of the Soviet Union.

◆ From March 21 to April 5, 1918, during the Second Battle of the Somme, a German offensive causes British troops to retreat, but the Allies reinforce the line and stop the German advance near Amiens, France.

◆ From July 15 to July 18, 1918, the Second Battle of the Marne is fought. It is the last major German offensive of the war. The German soldiers are met with unexpectedly strong Allied resistance; as the German offensive halts, the Allied offensive begins, and within a few days the Allies cross the Marne.

◆ On July 16, 1918, Czar Nicholas II of Russia, the Empress Alexandra, and at least three of their daughters (as confirmed by decades-later DNA analysis) are executed by Bolsheviks at Ekaterinburg.

◆ On October 30, 1918, an armistice is signed at Mudros (Mondros) on the Aegean isle of Lemnos between the Ottoman Empire and the Entente Delegation (Great Britain, France, and Russia).

◆ In September 1918 British forces occupy Palestine.

◆ On November 9, 1918, Kaiser Wilhelm II of Germany abdicates.

◆ On November 11, 1918, an armistice is signed near Compiègne, France, ending World War I.

◆ On November 11, 1918, Emperor Charles I of Austria abdicates.

◆ From March through November of 1918, an outbreak of Spanish influenza (flu) in the United States takes more than half a million lives.

◆ Booth Tarkington publishes *The Magnificent Ambersons*, 1918.

◆ Willa Cather publishes *My Ántonia*, 1918.

◆ Popular recordings in 1918 include those by Al Jolson, Enrico Caruso, and the Original Dixieland Jazz Band.

◆ In 1918 Marie Stopes publishes *Married Love*, arguing for equality between marriage partners; the book is banned in the United States.

◆ In January 1919 the first meeting of the Dáil, one of the two Houses of the Oireachtas (the Irish parliament), takes place in Dublin.

◆ On February 5, 1919, United Artists is formed by Charlie Chaplin, Douglas Fairbanks, Sr., Mary Pickford, and D. W. Griffith.

◆ Notable films of 1919 include D. W. Griffith's *Broken Blossoms*, with Lillian Gish, and Robert Wiene's *The Cabinet of Dr. Caligari*.

◆ On August 11, 1919, the Constitution of the German Federation, known as the Weimar Constitution, becomes law.

◆ In November 1919 Nancy, Lady Astor, an American-born resident of Great Britain, is elected to Parliament and becomes the first woman to take a seat in the House of Commons.

◆ Hermann Hesse publishes *Demian*, 1919.

◆ H. L. Mencken publishes *The American Language*, 1919.

◆ Sherwood Anderson publishes *Winesburg, Ohio*, 1919.

◆ W. Somerset Maugham publishes *The Moon and Sixpence*, 1919.

◆ Popular recordings in 1919 include those by Al Jolson and Eddie Cantor, and recordings of songs by composer Irving Berlin.

◆ On January 10, 1920, the League of Nations meets for the first time and ratifies the Treaty of Versailles.

◆ The 1920 census shows a US population of 106 million people.

◆ The League of Women Voters is founded in 1920 by Carrie Chapman Catt and other leaders of the suffrage movement.

◆ In May 1920 Thomas Masaryk becomes president of Czechoslovakia.

◆ Notable films of 1920 include *Dr. Jekyll and Mr. Hyde*, with John Barrymore; *Pollyanna*, with Mary Pickford; *Way Down East*, with Lillian Gish; and *The Mark of Zorro*, with Douglas Fairbanks, Sr.

◆ F. Scott Fitzgerald publishes *This Side of Paradise*, 1920.

◆ Sinclair Lewis publishes *Main Street*, 1920.

◆ D. H. Lawrence publishes *Women in Love*, 1920.

◆ Edith Wharton publishes *The Age of Innocence*, 1920.

◆ H. G. Wells publishes *The Outline of History*, 1920.

◆ Detective Hercule Poirot debuts in Agatha Christie's *The Mysterious Affair at Styles*, 1920.

◆ Gustav Holst's *The Planets* premieres, November 15, 1920.

◆ Gabriel Fauré's *Masques et Bergamasques* premieres, 1920.

◆ In January 1920 the Boston Red Sox sell Babe Ruth to the New York Yankees, giving rise to the so-called "Curse of the Bambino"—a proposed explanation for the failure of the Red Sox to win another World Series thereafter.

◆ In April 1920 Italian immigrants Nicola Sacco and Bartolomea Vanzetti are arrested for murder in South Braintree, Massachusetts.

◆ In 1920 members of the Chicago White Sox, including Shoeless Joe Jackson and seven others, are banned from baseball after being accused of throwing the 1919 World Series in return for payoffs from gamblers.

◆ The National Football League is founded in Canton, OH, in 1920, with Jim Thorpe as its first president.

◆ In 1920 the Negro National Baseball League is founded in Kansas City by Rube Foster.

◆ On February 21, 1921, Rex Ingram's *The Four Horsemen of the Apocalypse* premieres; the film stars Rudolph Valentino.

FAST FACTS ABOUT WOODROW WILSON

◆ Wilson may have been dyslexic; he did not learn to read until he was ten years old.

◆ Wilson was the first president to hold a Ph.D. degree earned in the traditional way (as opposed to its being an honorary distinction).

◆ Not only was Wilson the son of a Presbyterian minister: his mother was the daughter of a Presbyterian minister and so was his first wife.

◆ Wilson was the first president from the South since before the Civil War.

◆ Wilson signed the orders that made Mother's Day a national holiday.

◆ Wilson appointed Louis Brandeis to the Supreme Court in 1916; Brandeis was the first Jewish member of the Supreme Court.

◆ Wilson was the first president to cross the Atlantic Ocean while president.

◆ During World War I, Wilson gave his permission to sheep owners to have their sheep graze on the White House lawn; their wool was used by the Red Cross in the war effort.

◆ Wilson is the only US president buried in the National Cathedral and the only president buried within the District of Columbia.

◆ Wilson's uncle, James Woodrow, was a professor at the Columbia Theological Seminary who was tried before the General Assembly of the Southern Presbyterian Church for teaching the theories of Charles Darwin.

◆ Ellen Wilson was interested in art; in 1905 she began spending summers with the artists' colony in Old Lyme, Connecticut, a seat of American impressionist painting. She entered her own landscapes in juried shows under a pseudonym and won prizes.

◆ Edith Wilson survived her husband by 37 years; she died on his birthday in 1961.

Warren Gamaliel Harding

Nickname: none
Presidency: 29th president, 1921–1923
Party: Republican
Life dates: November 2, 1865–August 2, 1923 (57 years, 273 days)

EARLY LIFE AND EDUCATION

Warren Gamaliel Harding was born on November 2, 1865, in Blooming Grove, Ohio. He was the first of eight children of Phoebe Elizabeth Dickerson Harding and George Tryon Harding. George Harding was a farmer who studied homeopathic medicine and became a doctor after he had moved his family to Caledonia, Ohio; at the same time Phoebe Harding also studied homeopathic medicine and became a midwife.

George Harding purchased an ownership interest in a local newspaper, the *Caledonia Argus*, and made his eldest son a printer's apprentice. Warren had learned to read at an early age and was interested in oratory; his interest in language suddenly veered toward the printing trade and he learned to set type. He did well in his studies, too, in local schools, and in 1879, at the age of fourteen, he entered the Ohio Central College in Iberia, Ohio. He graduated in 1882.

EARLY CAREER

The Harding family had moved to Marion, Ohio, and Warren joined them there. He taught grammar school for a term, tried reading law but found it dull, sold casualty insurance, and

participated in a village band. His earnings from his multiple pursuits enabled him to buy a share of the *Marion Daily Star* newspaper (for $300) and he become a publisher; he soon bought out the two friends who were his partners. He also started up another paper, the *Weekly Star,* which was more overtly political than the *Daily Star,* and its editorials reflected Harding's support for the Republican Party.

Harding was the editorial voice of his two newspapers. He supported public service projects in Marion, such as the introduction of streetcars and electric street lights. His papers were critical of Amos Kling—banker, landlord, and one of the wealthiest and most influential men in town. Kling developed an animosity toward Harding that was not in any way mollified when Harding began courting his daughter, Florence ("Flossie") Mable Kling De Wolfe. Florence herself was not on good terms with her father; she had rebelled against him in 1880 by eloping with Henry De Wolfe, a local man. Their marriage produced a son, Marshall. De Wolfe, who suffered from alcoholism, deserted his wife and young son in 1882. Florence returned to Marion and, faced with the necessity of making her own living and taking care of her son, agreed to let her father raise Marshall. She divorced De Wolfe in 1886.

Florence supported herself by teaching piano. One of her pupils was Warren Harding's sister. It is alleged that Florence, five years Harding's senior, pursued him. Florence's father objected to Harding for a multitude of reasons, which included the existence of a rumor that the Harding family was of partial African-American lineage. It was the kind of rumor that, in another era (prior to the Civil War), often became attached to white individuals and/or families with strong abolitionist sentiments (which the Hardings had once displayed).

Over Amos Kling's objections, Florence and Warren Harding were married on July 8, 1891. Florence went to work in her husband's newspaper business. She worked as the circulation manager, managed advertising and home delivery, and generally brought efficiency and order to the running of the paper. Harding remained completely in control of the editorial side. Harding nicknamed his ambitious wife "The Duchess."

Harding did not enjoy a robust constitution. He had a heart condition and apparently suffered from fatigue and bouts of depression. He checked into the Battle Creek Sanitarium of Dr. J. H. Kellogg, in Battle Creek, Michigan, several times between 1889 and 1901. During these periods of absence his wife assumed an even greater role in the management of his business.

POLITICAL CAREER

A prominent local citizen, Harding was elected to the Ohio Senate in 1898 and served there until 1903. He was generally well-liked and became known for his willingness to have a drink or to take part in a poker game. He also became known for his oratorical skills and his party loyalty, and for the fact that he was not apt to take the initiative in sponsoring legislation. In 1903 he was elected the Lieutenant Governor of Ohio; he served in that post from 1904 to 1905.

Harding had a rocky relationship with Mrs. Harding; they argued often and he sometimes traveled without her. In 1904 she became seriously ill with nephritis, a condition that left her weak and even adversely affected her appearance. At the time of her illness, Harding helped to effect a reconciliation between his wife and her father, who had gradually come to accept Harding. Harding was a handsome, charming man; stories of his extramarital affairs swirled about him during his entire political career. In 1905 he began an affair with Carrie Fulton Phillips, the wife of his longtime friend James Phillips, which lasted about fifteen years.

> "America's present need is not heroics but healing; not nostrums but normalcy; not revolution but restoration."
>
> Warren G. Harding, speech in Boston, MA, June 1920

Harding ran for governor of Ohio in 1910, but was defeated. In 1910 the Republican Party was split between its conservatives (who supported President Taft) and its progressives (who supported Theodore Roosevelt). Although Harding was a compromise candidate, he had run against a popular incumbent and was soundly defeated. Two years later, at the Republican National Convention in 1912, Harding gave the speech that renominated William Howard Taft for president. Taft subsequently lost the election to Woodrow Wilson.

Harding was elected a US senator from Ohio in 1914. He had become a Republican Party stalwart, but his Senate career was not particularly distinguished. He supported President Wilson's decision to go to war but opposed the League of Nations.

In 1920 Harding was chosen as the Republican candidate for president; he was again the compromise candidate. He ran a "front-porch" campaign and adopted the slogan "Back to Normalcy," designed to appeal to a war-weary population, many of whom desired a retreat from the progressive politics of Theodore Roosevelt and Woodrow Wilson.

Harding's opponent was James M. Cox, the governor of Ohio. Harding and running mate Calvin Coolidge were elected on November 2, 1920, by considerable margins; they received 60 percent of the popular vote. It was the first presidential election in which women could vote.

PRESIDENCY

Harding's cabinet was a strange mixture of men of talent and ability (such as Secretary of State Charles Evans Hughes, Secretary of the Treasury Andrew Mellon, and Secretary of Commerce Herbert Hoover) and men of dubious talent and ability (notably, Secretary of the Interior Albert Fall and Attorney General Harry Daugherty).

Early in Harding's term, his administration did score a victory of sorts as it hosted the Naval Arms Limitation talks (the Washington Conference), which it had called together and which kicked off in November 1921. The United States hosted representatives of Great Britain, France, Italy, and Japan, all of whom agreed to limit the size (tonnage) of their ships and to refrain from building new ships for a time. Other nations represented at the conference agreed to respect Chinese territorial integrity. The former Allied powers also agreed not to use poison gas in wartime and to submit disputes among themselves to arbitration. Japan agreed to return the Kiaochow territory (which it had seized in 1914) to China.

Harding's domestic policy agenda included his strong support for the Emergency Tariff Act of 1921, which increased the tariffs on imported agricultural goods, and which was reinforced by the Fordney-McCumber Tariff Act of 1922, which raised tariff rates generally. The Fordney-McCumber Tariff Act and a number of similar laws were intended to protect US farmers from inexpensive imports. Harding (successfully) fought for the passage of budget legislation, which called for the creation of a Bureau of the Budget and required the president to submit a budget proposal to Congress annually. He supported the 1921 Emergency Quota Act; it established national quotas for immigrants. The passage of the legislation had been driven primarily by the widespread fear among American laborers that their jobs were being taken by immigrants.

Florence Harding blossomed into a welcoming White House hostess who even helped to plan her husband's poker games (at which the Hardings served alcohol in defiance of Prohibition). Late in the autumn of 1922, she became acutely ill with Bright's disease, a kidney disease. She eventually recovered, however, and returned to her public duties as First Lady. She interested herself in the welfare of veterans and frequently visited sick veterans at the Walter Reed Hospital. She opened the White House to public tours and often joined the tours herself.

> **"I don't know what to do or where to turn in this taxation matter. Somewhere there must be a book that tells all about it, where I could go to straighten it out in my mind. But I don't know where the book is, and maybe I couldn't read it if I found it."**
>
> Warren G. Harding, 1923

In March 1921 Harding had appointed Albert Fall as Secretary of the Interior. In the autumn of 1921, Fall covertly agreed to lease part of the federal oil and gas reserves at Teapot Dome, Wyoming; Buena Vista, California; and Elk Hills, California, to two of his friends in the oil business—Harry F. Sinclair of Mammoth Oil Corporation, who was granted the Teapot Dome leases, and Edward L. Doheny of the Pan-American Petroleum and Transport Company, who was granted the California leases. Congress had designated the reserves for use by the US Navy and had placed them under the control of Edwin Denby, the Secretary of the Navy. Denby signed the lease agreements. When reports of these deals were published in the *Wall Street Journal*, Harding stated publicly that he had known of and approved Fall's actions, though it is unlikely that he knew the full details of just how wrongful they were at the time. There was no evidence that Harding had profited personally in any way. The scandal quickly became known as the "Teapot Dome" affair. Congress ordered the cancellation of the leases, and the Supreme Court ruled that the leases themselves and Harding's transfer of authority to Fall had been illegal.

A Senate investigation was called for by Senator Robert La Follette of Wisconsin and others, but Senate hearings on the leases did not begin until after Harding's death (in 1923). At the end of January 1924, Albert Fall and Edwin Denby were forced to resign from office, though Denby was eventually cleared of all charges. After separate trials, Fall and Sinclair each served short prison sentences.

"I have no trouble with my enemies. I can take care of my enemies in a fight. But my friends, my goddamned friends, they're the ones who keep me walking the floor at nights!"

attributed to Warren G. Harding by journalist William Allen White, 1923

However, in early 1923, rumors of malfeasance within the Harding administration were gathering momentum, and Harding saw much of his popularity slipping away. In addition to the Teapot Dome scandal, it was being reported that Charles R. Forbes, the man Harding had appointed to head the Veterans' Bureau, had participated in a range of criminal activities (he was later convicted of fraud and bribery). Harding attempted to recapture public favor by undertaking a "Voyage of Understanding" tour of the United States. He left Washington in June 1923 for a trip that was to include Canada and Alaska. On August 2, 1923, Harding died in San Francisco, apparently of a heart attack (although the initial diagnosis was that he had been felled by food poisoning). Florence Harding refused to allow an autopsy.

Although it is generally agreed that Harding did not profit from the illegal actions of his appointees, his reputation as a leader was irrevocably damaged by the many scandals associated with his administration, especially as much of the information about them did not surface until after his death. Until it was supplanted by "Watergate," "Teapot Dome" remained the catchphrase for presidential scandal.

Harding's personal life came under unwelcome scrutiny after his death as well. In 1927 Nan Britton published an autobiographical account, *The President's Daughter*. The much younger Nan wrote about her affair with the president, described a rendezvous and tryst in the White House (in a closet next to the Oval Office), and claimed that Harding was the father of her illegitimate daughter Elizabeth. Nan maintained that the Harding family had refused to pay child support and that she had written the book to make money to support her daughter. When it was favorably reviewed by H. L. Mencken, no fan of Harding, the book did sell well. Harding partisans pointed out that Harding had believed himself to be sterile and had often lamented his having no children.

Florence Harding returned to Marion, Ohio, where she lived for another sixteen months before finally succumbing to the kidney disease she had suffered from for many years.

Harding's reputation suffered greatly in the years after his death, although much of what was written or rumored has since been discounted. He was tainted by the scandals of his administration, even though he had not been directly involved in them. Harding was a very popular president, but subsequent evaluations of the US presidencies have consistently ranked Harding as one of the worst, and even the worst, president.

Birthplace: Blooming Grove, OH
Residency: Ohio
Religion: Baptist
Education: Ohio Central College, Iberia, OH; graduated 1882
Place of Death: San Francisco, CA
Burial Site: Harding Memorial, Marion, OH
Dates in Office: March 4, 1921–August 2, 1923 (2 years, 151 days)
Age at Inauguration: 55 years, 122 days

FAMILY
Father: George Tryon Harding (1843–1928)
Mother: Phoebe Elizabeth Dickerson Harding (1843–1910)
Siblings: Warren was the eldest of eight children; his siblings were Charity Malvina Harding (1867–1951); Mary Clarissa Harding (1868–1913); Eleanor Priscilla Harding (1872–1878); Charles Alexander Harding (1874–1878); Abigail Victoria Harding (1875–1935); George Tryon Harding (1878–1934); Phoebe Caroline Harding (1879–1951).
Wife: Florence ("Fossie") Mabel Kling De Wolfe Harding (1860–1924), married July 8, 1891, in Marion, OH [Note: Florence Harding had been married in 1880 to Henry De Wolfe; they divorced in 1885 and had one son, Marshall Eugene De Wolfe (1880–1915).]
Children: After Harding's death, Nan Britton, in a book entitled *The President's Daughter,* claimed that Harding was the father of her daughter, Elizabeth Ann Britton, born in 1919.

CAREER
Private: teacher, reporter, publisher
Political: member of the Ohio state legislature (1899–1903); lieutenant governor of Ohio (1903–1905); member of the US Senate (1915–1921); president of the United States (1921–1923)
Military: none
Selected Works: *Our Common Country: Mutual Good Will in America,* ed. by Warren G. Harding III, intro. by Robert H. Ferrell (Columbia: University of Missouri Press, 2003); *Papers of Warren G. Harding, 1908–1923* (originals held by Ohio Historical Society, Columbus, OH; microfilm collection held by Library of Congress);

Speeches and Addresses of Warren G. Harding, President of the United States, reported and compiled by James W. Murphy, official reporter, US Senate (Washington, DC, 1923); *Warren G. Harding, 1865–1923: Chronology, Documents, Bibliographical Aids,* ed. by Philip R. Moran (Dobbs Ferry, NY: Oceana Publications, 1970)

PRESIDENCY
Nomination: 1920: With no clear favorite going into the Republican convention in Chicago, June 9–12, 1920, Harding was nominated on the tenth ballot. Calvin Coolidge of Massachusetts was chosen as the vice-presidential candidate.
Election: elected president on November 2, 1920
Opponent: James M. Cox, OH, Democratic; Eugene V. Debs, IN, Socialist; P. P. Christensen, UT, Farmer; Aaron S. Watkins, OH, Prohibition
Vote Totals: Harding, 16,147,885 popular, 404 electoral; Cox, 9,141,535 popular, 127 electoral; Debs, 913,937 popular, 0 electoral; Christensen, 265,462 popular, 0 electoral; Watkins, 188,948 popular, 0 electoral
Inauguration: March 4, 1921
Vice President: Calvin Coolidge, MA (1921–1923)

CABINET
Secretary of State: Charles Evans Hughes, NY (1921–1923)
Secretary of the Treasury: Andrew William Mellon, PA (1921–1923)
Secretary of War: John Wingate Weeks, MA (1921–1923)
Attorney General: Harry M. Daugherty, OH (1921–1923)
Postmaster General: William Harrison Hays, IN (1921–1922); Hubert Work, CO (1922–1923); Harry Stewart New, IN (1923)
Secretary of the Navy: Edwin Denby, MI (1921–1923)
Secretary of Agriculture: Henry Cantwell Wallace, IA (1921–1923)
Secretary of the Interior: Albert Bacon Fall, NM (1921–1923); Hubert Work, CO (1923)
Secretary of Labor: James John Davis, PA (1921–1923)

Secretary of Commerce: Herbert Clark Hoover, CA (1921–1923)

CONGRESS:
67th Congress (1921–1923); Speaker of the House: Frederick H. Gillett (MA, Republican)

SUPREME COURT APPOINTEES
William Howard Taft, CT; Chief Justice (1921–1930)
George Sutherland, UT; Associate Justice (1922–1938)
Pierce Butler, MN; Associate Justice (1923–1939)
Edward Terry Sanford, TN; Associate Justice (1923–1930)

MAJOR EVENTS OF THE HARDING ADMINISTRATION
◆ The Emergency Tariff Act of 1921 increases tariffs on imported agricultural goods.
◆ In the Thompson-Urrutia Treaty, ratified in Congress in April 1921, the United States agrees to pay Colombia $25 million in reparation for its loss of Panama.
◆ On May 19, 1921, Congress passes the Emergency Quota Act, which restricts immigration to the United States from any foreign country to three percent of the number of people from that country living in the United States at the time of the 1910 census.
◆ On November 11, 1921, Harding dedicates the Tomb of the Unknowns (also known as the Tomb of the Unknown Soldier) in Arlington National Cemetery.
◆ In 1921 Harding transfers control of the Teapot Dome, WY, and Elk Hill, CA, oil reserves from the Department of the Navy to the Department of the Interior, headed by Secretary Albert Fall.
◆ The Budget and Accounting Act of 1921 provides that an annual budget will be submitted to Congress by the president, creates the Bureau of the Budget, and establishes the General Accounting Office.
◆ Harding appoints former President William Howard Taft as chief justice of the Supreme Court, 1921.
◆ The Federal Highway Act of 1921 allots matching federal funds for the construction of state highways, to be provided by a gasoline tax.
◆ The International Conference on Naval Limitation, known as the Washington Conference, 1921–1922, is intended to curb the naval arms race; the United States, Great Britain, France, Italy, and Japan all agree to limit the size (tonnage) of their ships and to refrain from building new ships for a time. Other nations in attendance agree to respect Chinese territorial integrity.
◆ On April 10, 1921, Congress passes the Sheppard-Towner Maternity and Infancy Protection Act, which provides federal monies for state child welfare programs and other related programs; one of its goals is the reduction of infant mortality. The Act expires in 1929.
◆ On June 1, 1921, a race riot in Tulsa, OK, kills 85 people.
◆ In February 1922 the Capper-Volstead Act (also known as the Cooperative Marketing Act) exempts agricultural cooperatives from antitrust laws.
◆ On May 30, 1922, the Lincoln Memorial is dedicated.
◆ The Federal Narcotics Control Board is established in 1922; it is empowered to curb the importation into the United States of non-medicinal narcotics.
◆ The White House Police Force is established in 1922 at Harding's request; it later becomes part of the Secret Service.
◆ The Fordney-McCumber Tariff of 1922 raises tariff rates.
◆ The Cable Act of 1922 stipulates that an American woman who marries a non-American man does not lose her citizenship, and that a non-American woman who marries an American man does not automatically become a citizen, but must go through the process of naturalization.
◆ The head of the Veterans' Bureau, Charles Forbes, resigns his post on January 29, 1923, and flees to Europe; it is later discovered that he has defrauded the US government of millions of dollars.

◆ On March 4, 1923, Harding signs the Agricultural Credits Act, which provides for the establishment of regional banks to provide loans to farm cooperative associations, from which farmers will then be able to borrow.

◆ The Hardings leave on a "Voyage of Understanding" trip through the American West in June 1923.

◆ On August 2, 1923, Harding dies in San Francisco, CA, of a heart attack or cerebral hemorrhage.

◆ After Harding's death, the Teapot Dome Scandal continues to unfold, eventually leading to a prison term for former Secretary of the Interior Albert Fall.

MAJOR US AND WORLD EVENTS, 1921–1923

◆ In March 1921 Marie Stopes opens a birth-control clinic in London, England.

◆ In March 1921 the Polish-Soviet War ends with the Treaty of Riga, which gives Poland parts of Belorussia and Ukraine.

◆ On July 14, 1921, Italian anarchists Nicola Sacco and Bartolomeo Vanzetti are convicted of murder in Massachusetts.

◆ In the fall of 1921 Atlantic City, NJ, hosts the first Miss America contest, which is won by 16-year-old Margaret Gorman of Washington, DC.

◆ Noteworthy films of 1921 include *The Kid*, with Charlie Chaplin; D. W. Griffith's *Orphans of the Storm*, with Lillian and Dorothy Gish; and *The Sheik*, with Rudolph Valentino.

◆ Booth Tarkington publishes *Alice Adams*, 1921.

◆ Sergei Prokofiev composes *The Love for Three Oranges*, 1921.

◆ King Tut's (Tutankhamun's) tomb is discovered in Egypt's Valley of the Kings in November 1922 by Howard Carter and his patron, Lord Carnarvon.

◆ In 1922 Canadian physiologist Frederick Banting, with the assistance of Charles Best and others, discovers insulin.

◆ In March 1922 Mohandas (Mahatma) K. Gandhi is imprisoned in India for civil disobedience.

◆ James Joyce's *Ulysses* is published, 1922.

◆ F. W. Murnau's vampire film, *Nosferatu*, premieres, 1922.

◆ The *Reader's Digest* is first published, 1922.

◆ The British Broadcasting Company (BBC) begins radio broadcasting in 1922.

◆ F. Scott Fitzgerald publishes *Tales of the Jazz Age* and *The Beautiful and the Damned*, 1922.

◆ T. S. Eliot publishes *The Waste Land*, 1922.

◆ Hermann Hesse publishes *Siddhartha*, 1922.

◆ On August 22, 1922, Irish revolutionary leader Michael Collins is assassinated.

◆ In October 1922 Benito Mussolini becomes prime minister of Italy.

◆ On December 30, 1922, Vladimir Lenin proclaims the formation of the Union of Soviet Socialist Republics (USSR).

◆ On March 3, 1923, Henry Booth Luce introduces *Time* magazine.

◆ On April 26, 1923, Prince Albert marries Lady Elizabeth Bowes-Lyon; they will become King George VI and Queen (Consort) Elizabeth, the parents of Queen Elizabeth II of Great Britain.

◆ A. A. Milne publishes *The House at Pooh Corner*, 1923.

◆ P. G. Wodehouse publishes *The Inimitable Jeeves*, 1923.

◆ Popular music recordings of 1923 include recordings by Jelly Roll Morton, Eddie Cantor, Bessie Smith, and Louis Armstrong.

FAST FACTS ABOUT WARREN G. HARDING

◆ Al Jolson campaigned for Harding and wrote the campaign song, "Harding, You're the Man for Us."

◆ The vice-presidential candidate who ran with James Cox, Harding's opponent in the 1920 election, was the Assistant Secretary of the Navy, Franklin D. Roosevelt.

◆ Eugene V. Debs, another of Harding's opponents in the 1920 election, ran for president while serving a ten-year prison sentence, having been convicted under the Espionage Act for his opposition to World War I. (Harding, after winning the election, commuted Debs's sentence and had him released from prison in 1921.)

◆ Harding was the first sitting US senator to be elected president.

◆ On February 8, 1922, Harding had the first radio installed in the White House.

◆ Harding was the first president heard on the radio, on June 14, 1922, when he dedicated the Francis Scott Key Memorial in Baltimore, MD.

◆ Harding's was the first election in which the results were announced by radio.

◆ Harding was the first president to travel to his inauguration by automobile.

◆ Harding was the first president to visit both Canada and Alaska.

◆ The 1920 election was the first in which women had the right to vote.

◆ Harding hosted poker games twice-weekly at the White House and called the men who played his "poker cabinet."

◆ Despite the fact that Prohibition made the manufacture, transportation, or sale of alcohol illegal, Harding served liquor at the White House during his presidency.

◆ Florence Harding kept a little red book in which she listed the names of persons she thought had been rude to her or her husband.

◆ Harding referred to his wife as "the Duchess."

◆ Harding's favorite breakfast was waffles smothered in chipped beef and gravy.

◆ After Harding's death, a story circulated that Florence Harding had poisoned her husband, either to spare him from the coming scandal or because she was tired of his philandering. (There is no evidence for this version of his death.)

Calvin Coolidge

Nickname: Cal, Silent Cal
Presidency: 30th president, 1923–1929
Party: Republican
Life dates: July 4, 1872–January 5, 1933 (60 years, 185 days)

EARLY LIFE AND EDUCATION

John Calvin Coolidge was born on July 4, 1872, in Plymouth Notch, Vermont. His parents were Victoria Josephine Moor Coolidge and Colonel John Coolidge. He was named John, after his father, but he generally went by the name of Calvin as a way to distinguish father from son. His father ran the Plymouth Notch post office and general store; the family lived in an attached cottage. One of his grandfathers lived on adjacent farm property. Calvin was one of two children. His younger sister, Abigail ("Abbie"), was born in 1875. When Calvin was four, the family moved into a house that was just across the street. Cooldige Sr. also farmed, founded the Plymouth Cheese Factory in 1890, acted as a deputy sheriff, was a deacon of the church, and was elected to the state legislature.

In 1885, when Calvin was twelve, his mother, Victoria Coolidge, died of consumption (tuberculosis); in 1890, Calvin's sister Abbie died, at age fourteen, from appendicitis. His father married again in 1891. Calvin's stepmother, Carrie Brown Coolidge, had been a schoolteacher. The relationship between Calvin and his stepmother was a good one.

Calvin attended the Black River Academy in Ludlow, Vermont, and graduated in 1890. He then attended the St. Johnsbury Academy (also in Vermont) for a single term in 1891 to prepare for college. Calvin entered Amherst College in Amherst, Massachusetts, in the fall of 1891, from which institution he was graduated cum laude in 1895. At college he was quite shy yet developed a reputation for being a wit, and he became a member of the Phi Gamma Delta fraternity during his senior year. He was asked to give the Grove Oration, a humorous address, at the graduation ceremonies. In it he referred to the town of Amherst as "largely made up of beautiful scenery and a kindly regard for a college man's money."

Calvin Coolidge, as a young man, was attracted to the law and took a position as a law clerk with the firm of Hammond and Field in Northampton, Massachusetts, as part of which he began to read the law. He was admitted to the Massachusetts bar in 1897.

EARLY CAREER

Coolidge set up his own law practice in 1898 and right away plunged into Republican Party politics. He was soon appointed to the position of city councilman in Northampton. He was the vice president of the Nonatuck Savings Bank for about one year, from 1898 to 1899.

Members of the city council of Northampton elected Coolidge to the post of city solicitor for the city of Northampton, a position he held from 1900 to 1902. He was not reelected in 1902, but in 1903 he became the clerk of courts for Hampshire County, Massachusetts, and served in that capacity until 1904. He acted as chairman of the Hampshire County Republican Committee in 1904.

In 1904 Coolidge met Grace Goodhue, a teacher at the Clarke School for the Deaf. They belonged to the same church, attended the same social events, and shared many of the same interests. Coolidge was shy and Grace was outgoing, but the two were quite taken with each other from the beginning and were married, on October 4, 1905, at Grace's father's home. The next year their first son, John, named after Coolidge's father, was born. In 1908 a second son, Calvin Coolidge, Jr., was born. The family lived in one-half of a duplex house in Northampton.

MASSACHUSETTS POLITICIAN

As a married man, Coolidge continued to go forward in his political career. He was a candidate in the election for the Northampton Board of Education in 1905, but lost. In 1906 he was elected to the Massachusetts House of Representatives and served in that capacity from 1907 to 1908. He was the mayor of Northampton from 1910 to 1911. In 1911 he was elected to the Massachusetts state senate, in which legislative body he quickly emerged as a Republican leader. He was a state senator from 1912 to 1915, and served as the senate's president from 1914 to 1915. After becoming president of the state senate, he delivered an address, known as the "Have Faith in Massachusetts" speech, in which he praised the value of hard work, and noted: "History reveals no civilized people among whom there were not a highly educated class, and large aggregations of wealth. . . ."

Coolidge was lieutenant-governor of Massachusetts from 1916 to 1918. He was elected the governor of the state in 1918, and served as gov-

ernor until 1921. Coolidge, who had acquired a reputation for being hardworking and honest, generally supported business interests. He also supported various kinds of labor legislation, including legislation that strove to limit the working hours of women and children. As Massachusetts governor, Coolidge rose to national prominence during the 1919 Boston police strike. He responded to the strike by calling out the state militia, and declared in a telegram to Samuel Gompers, president of the American Federation of Labor: "There is no right to strike against the public safety by anybody, anywhere, any time." Coolidge stated that the right of the police to form a union had never been granted and that their action had therefore been unlawful.

Coolidge supported President Woodrow Wilson's decision to go to war and the war effort; he urged that party politics be put aside in favor of national unity. He advocated popular support for the war effort and cooperation with the national government, stating: "The only hope of a short war is to prepare for a long one." He also supported the position that only an unconditional surrender on the part of Germany would constitute an end to war.

> "It is a great advantage to a president and a major source of safety to the country, for him to know that he is not a great man."
>
> Calvin Coolidge, *Autobiography*, 1929

At the Republican National Convention in 1920, Coolidge won the nomination for vice president and so joined Warren G. Harding on the ticket. The two candidates received 16.1 million (popular) votes; the Democratic ticket, consisting of James Cox of Ohio and Franklin D. Roosevelt of New York, pulled in 9.1 million votes. Harding received 404 electoral votes to Cox's 127. Many saw the election as a repudiation of Woodrow Wilson's progressive government and of the involvement of the United States in European affairs.

Coolidge served as vice president under Harding from 1921 to 1923. Harding was gregarious and popular, whereas Coolidge was taciturn and little noticed as vice president. On August 2, 1923, President Harding died in San Francisco. Coolidge received the news in Vermont, where he was visiting his father. The senior Coolidge, a justice of the peace and a notary, administered the oath of office to his son, at 2:47 in the morning, in the sitting room of his home.

PRESIDENCY

In his first State of the Union address, Coolidge outlined several legislative proposals, including a federal tax cut of 25 percent. He also supported the consolidation of the railroad companies and the proposed increases in their rates. He favored federal spending on highway programs, and also supported the new Bureau of the Budget.

In the early days of his presidency the scandals of the Harding administration were coming to light, really for the first time. Coolidge appointed a bipartisan council to investigate allegations of wrongdoing by members of the Harding administration. Above all there was the Teapot Dome scandal, in which government officials, most notably Secretary of the Interior Albert Fall, were alleged to have accepted bribes in return for leasing oil reserves belonging to the federal government to private companies. Calvin was served well by his reputation for honesty as he endeavored to punish those who had committed crimes and to restore confidence in the presidency.

At the Republican National Convention in Cleveland in 1924, Coolidge was nominated for the presidency. His Democratic opponent was John W. Davis of West Virginia, a lawyer who had served as an ambassador to Great Britain. Davis was a compromise candidate for the Democrats. Another opponent was Senator Robert LaFollette of Wisconsin, the Progressive Party candidate. Coolidge used the slogan "Keep Cool with Coolidge," which alluded to the general

sense of peace and prosperity that prevailed in the country in the summer of 1924. Coolidge won the election handily, with 54 percent of the popular vote, versus almost 30 percent for Davis and about 16 percent for LaFollette. But the victory was an empty one for Coolidge. Approximately one month after the national convention, Calvin Coolidge, Jr., his sixteen-year-old son, died of blood poisoning, which he contracted when a blister on his foot (that appeared after a tennis game) became infected. "When he went the power and the glory of the Presidency went with him," Coolidge wrote in his autobiography. It was a reference to the magnitude of his personal bereavement in the aftermath of his son's death.

"I favor the policy of economy, not because I wish to save money, but because I wish to save people. The men and women of this country who toil are the ones who bear the cost of the government. Every dollar that we carelessly waste means that their life will be so much the more meager."

Calvin Coolidge, his inaugural address, March 4, 1925

An advocate of tax cuts, Coolidge opposed congressional legislation that, in his view, was going to spend money unnecessarily. He twice vetoed farm relief bills that would have provided for the government purchase of surplus crops. He shared the opinion of his Secretary of the Treasury, Andrew Mellon, that America prospered if American business prospered. Coolidge's most famous statement ("the business of America is business") is actually a misquotation. What he said (to the American

Society of Newspaper Editors) was: "The chief business of the American people is business."

"You lose."

Calvin Coolidge to a woman who told him she had bet she could get at least three words out of him, 1922

Coolidge spoke for the majority of Americans in opposing US membership in the League of Nations. It was his vice president, Charles Dawes, who gave his name to the Dawes Plan, which was to help Germany to settle its massive war reparations debt to the former Allied nations in the wake of the first World War. The Dawes Plan provided for payments to the Allied nations to begin at 1 billion marks (in the first year) and to increase gradually, until reaching 2.4 billion marks (by the fourth year). The plan was criticized by some for failing to set a total amount of reparations due, but it worked well enough for a while, until the end of the decade, at which time it became apparent that Germany could not continue to meet its annual payments. The Dawes Plan was replaced by the Young Plan in 1929.

Somewhat paradoxically (for a president famous for his taciturnity and his reserved nature), Coolidge held frequent press briefings and made use of the relatively new medium of radio to talk to the nation. Mrs. Coolidge, who was, on the other hand, warm and gregarious, was forbidden by her husband to drive an automobile, wear trousers, dance, or speak to the press. Grace Coolidge also indulged her taste for decorating and remodeled parts of the White House. She assembled a panel of experts to restore rooms in the White House to the original federal style, and was also responsible for the construction of a "sky parlor," a sunroom on the White House's third floor.

In 1928 Coolidge declined to run for another term as president, although—given his popularity at the time—it is likely that he would have been reelected had he chosen to run.

POST-PRESIDENTIAL CAREER

Upon leaving the presidency, Coolidge returned to Massachusetts. In May 1930 the Coolidge family moved to "the Beeches," a large house in Northampton, where Coolidge wrote his autobiography. At the end of his life, he was a trustee of Amherst College, and he was president of the American Antiquarian Society from 1930 to 1932. He died on January 5, 1933, at the Beeches, and was buried in Vermont.

Mrs. Coolidge continued to work with the hearing-impaired and kept in touch with members of her college sorority, Pi Beta Phi. She was a lifelong fan of baseball and followed the Boston Red Sox with enthusiasm. She died in Northampton, Massachusetts, on July 8, 1957, and was buried next to her husband in Plymouth Notch Cemetery in Plymouth, Vermont.

Birthplace: Plymouth Notch, VT
Residency: Massachusetts
Religion: Congregationalist
Education: Amherst College, Amherst, MA; graduated 1895
Place of Death: Northampton, MA
Burial Site: Plymouth Notch Cemetery, Plymouth, VT
Dates in Office: August 3, 1923–March 3, 1929 (5 years, 214 days)
Age at Inauguration: 51 years, 30 days

FAMILY
Father: John Calvin Coolidge (1845–1926)
Mother: Victoria Josephine Moor Coolidge (1846–1885)
Siblings: Abigail ("Abbie") Coolidge (1875–1890)
Wife: Grace Anna Goodhue Coolidge (1879–1957), married on October 4, 1905, in Burlington, VT
Children: John Coolidge (1906–2000); Calvin Coolidge (1908–1924)

CAREER
Private: lawyer
Political: member of the city council of Northampton, MA (1899); city solicitor for the city of Northampton (1900–1901); clerk of the

courts in Northampton (1904); member of the Massachusetts House of Representatives (1907–1908); mayor of Northampton (1910–1911); member of the Massachusetts Senate (1912–1915); lieutenant governor of Massachusetts (1916–1918); governor of Massachusetts (1919–1921); vice president under Harding (1921–1923); president of the United States (1923–1929)

Military: none

Selected Works: *America's Need for Education and Other Educational Addresses* (Boston: Houghton Mifflin Company, 1925); *The Autobiography of Calvin Coolidge* (Rutland, VT: Academy Books, [1984], 1929); *Calvin Coolidge, 1872–1933; Chronology, Documents, Bibliographical Aids,* ed. by Philip R. Moran (Dobbs Ferry, NY: Oceana Publications, 1970); *Have Faith in Massachusetts!* (Boston: Houghton Mifflin Company, 1919); *The Papers of Calvin Coolidge,* archival microfilm (Washington, DC: Library of Congress); *The Personal Files of President Calvin Coolidge,* archival microfilm (Northampton, MA: Forbes Library, 1986); *The Price of Freedom: Speeches and Addresses* (New York: C. Scribner's Sons, 1924); *The Quotable Calvin Coolidge: Sensible Words for a New Century,* compiled and ed. by Peter Hannaford (Bennington, VT: Images from the Past, 2001); *The Talkative President: The Off-the-Record Press Conferences of Calvin Coolidge,* ed. by Robert H. Ferrell and Howard H. Quint (New York: Garland Publishing, 1979)

PRESIDENCY

Nomination: 1924: The Republican convention met in Cleveland, OH, June 10–12, 1924, and nominated incumbent Calvin Coolidge without opposition; Charles Dawes of Illinois was selected as the vice-presidential candidate.

Election: 1924: elected president on November 4, 1924 (Coolidge succeeded to the presidency on the death of Warren G. Harding in 1923)

Opponent: John W. Davis, WV, Democratic; Robert M. LaFollette, WI, Progressive

Vote Totals: Coolidge, 15,723,789 popular, 382 electoral; Davis, 8,386,242 popular, 136 electoral; LaFollette, 4,831,706 popular, 13 electoral

Inauguration: March 4, 1925

Vice President: Charles Gates Dawes, IL (1925–1929)

CABINET

Secretary of State: Charles Evans Hughes, NY (1923–1925); Frank B. Kellogg, MN (1925–1929)

Secretary of the Treasury: Andrew W. Mellon, PA (1923–1929)

Secretary of War: John W. Weeks, MA (1923–1925); Dwight F. Davis, MO (1925–1929)

Attorney General: Harry M. Daugherty, OH (1923–1924); Harlan F. Stone, NY (1924–1925); John G. Sargent, VT (1925–1929)

Postmaster General: Harry S. New, IN (1923–1929)

Secretary of the Navy: Edwin Denby, MI (1923–1924); Curtis D. Wilbur, CA (1924–1929)

Secretary of Agriculture: Henry C. Wallace, IA (1923–1924); Howard M. Gore, WV (1924–1925); William M. Jardine, KS (1925–1929)

Secretary of the Interior: Hubert Work, CO (1923–1928); Roy O. West, IL (1929)

Secretary of Labor: James J. Davis, IN (1923–1929)

Secretary of Commerce: Herbert C. Hoover, CA (1923–1928); William F. Whiting, MA (1928–1929)

CONGRESS

68th Congress (1923–1925); Speaker of the House: Frederick H. Gillett (MA, Republican)

69th Congress (1925–1927); Speaker of the House: Nicholas Longworth (OH, Republican)

70th Congress (1927–1929); Speaker of the House: Nicholas Longworth (OH, Republican)

SUPREME COURT APPOINTEES:

Harlan Fiske Stone, NY; Associate Justice (1925–1941) [Note: Stone was named Chief Justice by President Franklin D. Roosevelt and served in that capacity from 1941 to 1946.]

MAJOR EVENTS OF THE COOLIDGE ADMINISTRATION

◆ The Foreign Service Act passes in May 1924 and merges the consular service with the diplomatic corps, making the Foreign Service part of the State Department. The law also provides for written examinations for foreign service positions, promotions based on merit, and the rotation of postings.

◆ On June 2, 1924, Coolidge signs the Indian Citizenship Act, which grants citizenship to Native Americans.

◆ On July 7, 1924, Calvin Coolidge, Jr., dies of blood poisoning after his blistered toe becomes infected following a tennis game.

◆ On November 4, 1924, Coolidge wins the presidential election against John W. Davis of WV.

◆ The Dawes Plan, which provides for gradually increasing reparations payments to the former Allied nations from Germany and for the removal of French and Belgian troops from the Ruhr region of Germany, is signed in August 1924.

◆ The Immigration Act of 1924 puts a cap on the total numbers of immigrants entering the United States and defines a formula that restricts immigration from Italy and southern Europe, as well as prohibits immigration from Japan.

◆ In May 1924 Coolidge vetoes a bill that will give bonus certificates to World War I veterans, but the bill is passed over his veto.

◆ A pact between the United States, on the one side, and Nicaragua, Guatemala, and El Salvador, on the other, is signed in May 1924. The latter parties agree to stop giving aid to insurgents in Honduras.

◆ The Judges' Bill of 1925 reduces the caseload of the US Supreme Court by its diversion of appeals cases to the federal appeals courts; it reserves the Supreme Court for consideration of cases that require an interpretation of the Constitution.

◆ The Air Mail Act of 1925, also called the Kelly Act, authorizes the postmaster general to contract for domestic airmail service with private carriers.

◆ The Revenue Acts of 1926 and 1928 cut income, inheritance, and excise taxes.

◆ In May 1926 Congress passes the Air Commerce Act, which gives the government the primary responsibility for establishing air routes, licensing pilots, and enforcing safety rules.

◆ In May 1926 US Marines are sent to Nicaragua to quell a revolt, launching a military presence that will last until 1933.

◆ In July 1926 Congress passes the US Army Air Corps Act, which creates the Air Corps out of the existing Air Service, specifying that it be part of the Army rather than a separate service, and creates an additional assistant secretary of war position for the furtherance of military aeronautics.

◆ The Radio Act of 1927 creates the Federal Radio Commission, which is given responsibility for the granting of licenses to radio stations.

◆ The McNary-Haugen Farm Bill, which provides for the government purchase of agricultural surpluses, is introduced in 1924, 1926, and 1927, and is twice vetoed by Coolidge.

◆ In March 1927 the Supreme Court rules in *Nixon v. Herndon* that a Texas law that prohibits African Americans from voting in primaries is unconstitutional.

◆ A meeting held in Geneva in the summer of 1927 between the United States, Great Britain, and Japan fails to achieve hoped-for naval arms limitations and convinces the United States to resume expansion of its navy (funding is approved by Congress in early 1929).

◆ On August 10, 1927, Coolidge speaks at the dedication of Mount Rushmore, after which sculptor Gutzon Borglum begins the drilling for the project that will continue until 1941.

◆ The Jones-White Act, also known as the Merchant Marine Act, is passed in May 1928 and is intended to encourage private shipbuilding in the United States.

◆ The Kellogg-Briand Pact, also called the Pact of Paris, is signed on August 27, 1928, by fifteen nations that agree to renounce "recourse to war for the solution to international controversies."

MAJOR US AND WORLD EVENTS, 1923–1929

◆ On November 8, 1923, in what is commonly referred to as the Beer Hall Putsch, Adolf Hitler and his followers attempt to overthrow the

Weimar government of Germany. The putsch fails and Hitler is tried for treason, but he is given a lenient sentence and wins great popular support.

❖ As part of the Second International Judicial Police Conference, which takes place in Vienna, Austria, in 1923, Interpol is founded.

❖ On January 21, 1924, Vladimir Lenin dies and Joseph Stalin begins to assume power in the Soviet Union.

❖ On May 10, 1924, J. Edgar Hoover is appointed Director of the Federal Bureau of Investigation.

❖ On November 4, 1924, Nellie Tayloe Ross of Wyoming becomes the first woman to be elected governor of a state.

❖ On Thanksgiving Day (November 27) in 1924, Macy's Department Store in New York City holds a parade it calls the "Christmas Day Parade." It will be known more accurately in future years as the "Thanksgiving Day Parade."

❖ In 1924 Richard Loeb and Nathan Leopold, two wealthy young men from Chicago, kidnap and murder Bobby Franks; during the subsequent trial, Clarence Darrow argues passionately against the death penalty. Loeb and Leopold are sentenced to life in prison.

❖ Notable films of 1924 include Erich von Stroheim's *Greed* and Raoul Walsh's *The Thief of Bagdad*.

❖ Herman Melville publishes *Billy Budd*, 1924.

❖ Thomas Mann publishes *The Magic Mountain*, 1924.

❖ Edna Ferber publishes *So Big*, 1924.

❖ E. M. Forster publishes *A Passage to India*, 1924.

❖ Popular music hits of 1924 include Al Jolson's "California, Here I Come" and the Paul Whiteman Orchestra's recording of George Gershwin's "Rhapsody in Blue."

❖ In 1924 astronomer Edwin Hubble announces the existence of galaxies beyond the Milky Way.

❖ The Geneva Protocol is entered into in 1925; it reinforces the prohibition against the use of poisonous gases in war and adds a prohibition against bacteriological weapons. The United States is a signatory.

❖ John Scopes, a Tennessee high school science teacher, is arrested for teaching evolution. The resulting trial, in July 1925, pits Clarence Darrow as his attorney against William Jennings Bryan, who represents the state of Tennessee. Though Scopes is found guilty and fined, the case focuses attention on the differences between those who accept the science of evolution and religious fundamentalists who deny it in favor of creationism.

❖ In December 1925 Colonel Billy Mitchell, a decorated airman, is court-martialed for insubordination after he has accused senior officers of the Army and Navy of incompetence; he continues to insist, however, that the United States should establish a separate air force.

❖ Theodore Dreiser publishes *An American Tragedy*, 1925.

❖ F. Scott Fitzgerald publishes *The Great Gatsby*, 1925.

❖ Sinclair Lewis publishes *Arrowsmith,* 1925.

❖ Adolf Hitler publishes the first volume of *Mein Kampf* ("My Struggle") in 1925 and the second volume in 1927.

❖ Franz Kafka publishes *The Trial*, 1925.

❖ Popular music hits of 1925 include Marian Anderson's "Nobody Knows the Trouble I've Seen," Ben Bernie's "Sweet Georgia Brown," and Paul Whiteman's "Charleston."

❖ Notable films of 1925 include *Ben-Hur* with Ramon Novarro, Harold Lloyd's *The Freshman*, Charlie Chaplin's *Gold Rush*, and *The Phantom of the Opera* with Lon Chaney.

❖ Sergei Prokofiev's *Symphony No. 2* is first performed in Paris, 1925.

❖ The musical *No, No, Nanette* opens in both London and New York, 1925.

❖ On March 16, 1926, Robert Goddard launches his first viable rocket, dubbed "Nell," from a field in Massachusetts; it rises 41 feet into the air.

❖ On April 6, 1926, Irishwoman Violet Gibson fails in her attempt to assassinate Italian dictator Benito Mussolini but wounds him in the nose.

❖ In April 1926 army officer Reza Khan is crowned Reza Shah Pahlevi of Iran.

◆ In December 1926, after her husband asks for a divorce, author Agatha Christie disappears for 11 days and is later found at a hotel, registered under the name of the woman her husband wishes to marry.

◆ In 1926, with the support of the philanthropist John D. Rockefeller, the restoration of Colonial Williamsburg begins.

◆ A. A. Milne publishes *Winnie the Pooh*, 1926.

◆ Ernest Hemingway publishes *The Sun Also Rises*, 1926.

◆ Georgette Heyer publishes *These Old Shades*, 1926.

◆ Franz Kafka publishes *The Castle*, 1926.

◆ Henry W. Fowler publishes *Fowler's Modern English Usage*, 1926.

◆ Popular music hits of 1926 include Al Jolson's "When the Red, Red Robin Comes Bob-Bob-Bobbin' Along," Louis Armstrong's "Muskrat Ramble," and Gertrude Lawrence's "Do, Do, Do."

◆ Notable films of 1926 include F. W. Murnau's *Faust*, *The Son of the Sheik* with Rudolph Valentino, and *The Scarlet Letter* with Lillian Gish.

◆ In the greatest natural disaster in US history, the Mississippi River floods in the spring of 1927, killing thousands and leaving nearly a million people homeless.

◆ On May 21, 1927, Charles A. Lindbergh lands at Le Bourget Field near Paris after completing the first solo transatlantic flight, having left Long Island, New York, 33 hours and 32 minutes earlier.

◆ On August 23, 1927, Nicola Sacco and Bartolomeo Vanzetti are executed after they are tried for robbery and a double murder. During the trial their political beliefs (they were anarchists) bring them to national attention.

◆ On September 7, 1927, Philo T. Farnsworth transmits the first electronic television signal, which is received by his brother-in-law viewing a vacuum tube television display in the next room.

◆ In October 1927 *The Jazz Singer*, one of the first "talkies," or movies with sound, is released; it stars Al Jolson. The movie is a hit and popularizes sound pictures.

◆ Other notable films of 1927 include Fritz Lang's *Metropolis*, Buster Keaton's *The General*, *Seventh Heaven* with Janet Gaynor, and *Wings* with Clara Bow and Buddy Rogers.

◆ In 1927 the first Ryder Cup golf tournament is held in Worcester, Massachusetts. The United States defeats Great Britain.

◆ In 1927 Babe Ruth hits 60 home runs during the 154-game season, a record that will stand until it is broken by Roger Maris in 1961 in an expanded 162-game season.

◆ In 1927 Eliot Ness joins the Treasury Department and is assigned to the Bureau of Prohibition in Chicago, where he assembles a team that becomes known as the "Untouchables," for their resistance to corruption.

◆ Popular music hits of 1927 includes Ben Bernie's "Ain't She Sweet?", Gertrude Lawrence's "Someone to Watch Over Me," and Bix Beiderbecke's "In a Mist."

◆ Thornton Wilder publishes *The Bridge of San Luis Rey*, 1927.

◆ Willa Cather publishes *Death Comes for the Archbishop*, 1927.

◆ Hermann Hesse publishes *Steppenwolf*, 1927.

◆ Nan Britton publishes *The President's Daughter* in 1927, about her affair with President Harding and about the illegitimate daughter who is, she alleges, the result of their affair.

◆ Virginia Woolf publishes *To the Lighthouse*, 1927.

◆ In 1928 Sir Alexander Fleming observes mold on a staphylococcus culture that has somehow produced a bacteria-free area around itself; he names the active ingredient penicillin.

◆ On June 17, 1928, Amelia Earhart becomes the first woman to fly across the Atlantic Ocean.

◆ On July 16, 1928, President Alvaro Obregon of Mexico is assassinated by Leon Toral, a Roman Catholic extremist who had objected to Obregon's anticlericism.

◆ Aldous Huxley publishes *Point Counter Point*, 1928.

◆ D. H. Lawrence publishes *Lady Chatterley's Lover*, 1928.

◆ Dorothy L. Sayers publishes *Lord Peter Views the Body*, 1928.

◆ Margaret Mead publishes *Coming of Age in Samoa*, 1928.

◆ Popular music hits of 1928 include Paul Robeson's "Ol' Man River," Helen Kane's "I Wanna Be Loved by You," Duke Ellington's "Black and Tan Fantasy," Fanny Brice's "My Man," and Ben Bernie's "Let's Misbehave."

◆ In 1928 Mickey Mouse becomes a star in *Steamboat Willie*, his third film appearance.

◆ Notable films of 1928 include *The Singing Fool* with Al Jolson, *West of Zanzibar* with Lon Chaney and Lionel Barrymore, *The Circus* with Charlie Chaplin, and *The Mysterious Lady* with Greta Garbo.

◆ In August 1928 Ahmet Zogu becomes King Zog I of Albania.

◆ In October 1928 Haile Selassie becomes king of Abyssinia.

◆ On November 28, 1928, Maurice Ravel's *Bolero* premieres in Paris.

◆ Arnold Schoenberg's *Variations for Orchestra* is first performed in Berlin, 1928.

◆ On February 14, 1929, seven gangsters are killed in Chicago in what is dubbed the "St. Valentine's Day Massacre"; the killings are assumed to be masterminded by Al Capone, but no convictions result.

FAST FACTS ABOUT CALVIN COOLIDGE

◆ In 1891 Coolidge listened to the address of President Benjamin Harrison at the centennial celebration of Vermont's statehood.

◆ As a college senior, Coolidge wrote an essay entitled "The Principles Fought for in the American Revolution" and won first prize (a medal) in a national contest sponsored by the Sons of the American Revolution.

◆ Coolidge's grandfather believed that farming was the only respectable occupation, so he deeded forty acres to Calvin for life. Calvin was aware that he could neither sell the land nor

lose it to creditors, and that it had been assumed that he would have to cultivate it.

◆ As a boy, Coolidge was so shy that he dreaded having to meet the adults who came to his home to visit his parents.

◆ After President Harding died in 1923, Coolidge was administered the oath of office by his father, a justice of the peace and a notary; when he won the presidency in 1924, the oath of office was administered by Chief Justice William Howard Taft.

◆ Coolidge's campaign slogan was "Keep Cool with Coolidge."

◆ Coolidge was the first president to deliver a radio address from the White House and the first whose State of the Union address (in 1923) was broadcast on the radio.

◆ Alice Roosevelt, the daughter of Theodore Roosevelt, said of Coolidge that he looked as though he had been "weaned on a pickle."

◆ Coolidge forbade his wife to talk to reporters, wear trousers, drive a car, or fly in an airplane. Grace Coolidge nevertheless became extremely popular with the press and the American people.

◆ Coolidge was photographed in a variety of unusual outfits: a full Indian headdress, a cowboy outfit, and the smock he wore when he worked on the family farm.

◆ Despite the fact that Coolidge was famously taciturn, he and Grace Coolidge entertained often in the White House and seldom dined alone.

◆ Coolidge slept a lot compared to most presidents: seven or eight hours a night, and two or three hours for his afternoon nap.

◆ Among the various performers invited to the White House during the Coolidge years were Sergei Rachmaninoff, Al Jolson, John Barrymore, Douglas Fairbanks, Sr., and Mary Pickford.

◆ Coolidge liked to spend evenings at the White House sitting in a rocking chair on the front porch and smoking cigars.

Herbert Clark Hoover

Nickname: Bert, Chief, the Great Engineer, the Great Humanitarian
Presidency: 31st president, 1929–1933
Party: Republican
Life dates: August 10, 1874–October 20, 1964 (90 years, 71 days)

EARLY LIFE AND EDUCATION

Herbert Clark Hoover was born on August 10, 1874, in West Branch, Iowa. His parents were Hulda Minthorn Hoover and Jesse Hoover. His father was a blacksmith who also owned a store that sold farm tools and machinery. Before her marriage, his mother had been a teacher. Herbert (or Bert, as he was called) had an older brother, Theodore, and a younger sister, Mary. The family lived in the two-room cottage in which Bert was born, but in 1879 they moved to a larger home nearby. The Hoovers were members of a Quaker community that stressed the values of hard work, peace, compromise, charity, and temperance.

In 1880 Jesse Hoover died of heart failure after contracting pneumonia. Hulda Hoover worked as a seamstress and attended Quaker meetings in West Branch, and sometimes traveled to speak at other Quaker meetings. In 1884 Hulda, upon returning from one of her travels, came down with a cold that worsened and became pneumonia; she died from pneumonia and typhoid fever. The three Hoover children went to live with relatives. Bert first went to live with an uncle who lived near West Branch, but in 1885 he went to live with his uncle Henry

John Minthorn in Newberg, Oregon. His uncle was a doctor who lived on a farm, and Bert did chores on the farm. He attended the Friends Pacific Academy in Newberg. When his uncle moved to Salem, Oregon, and established a real estate office in Salem, Bert worked as a clerk for him. He also attended school at night and took classes in bookkeeping, typing, and math.

Bert became acquainted with several mining engineers while working in the real estate office and was intrigued by their descriptions of their occupational pursuits. His family wanted him to attend a Quaker college, but he had already decided to become an engineer. His ambition was to attend Stanford University, a newly-formed university, in Palo Alto, California. He entered Stanford as part of its first class in 1891 and graduated in 1895 with a degree in geology.

At Stanford, Hoover managed the baseball and football teams. He was the class treasurer during his junior and senior years. As treasurer he set up an efficient bookkeeping system and eliminated the class debt. He also organized a laundry service and a newspaper delivery service. He spent summers working for the US Geological Survey. And he worked for Dr. John C. Banner, who presided over the department of geology. During his senior year, he was introduced to a new female student who was studying geology, Lou Henry. Whereas Bert was shy, Lou was outgoing and friendly. They soon discovered that they had been born within one hundred miles of each other in Iowa. Lou's family had moved to California for the sake of her mother's health, and Lou had spent a portion of her formative years hiking, fishing, and camping with her father. She had earned a teaching degree but was attracted to the study of geology because of her love of the outdoors, a quality that Bert admired.

Mining Engineer

After graduating from Stanford, Hoover worked for a while in a gold mine in California, and then, unable to find an engineering position, he took a job as a typist in mining expert Louis Janin's engineering office. Janin sent Hoover to work in mines in New Mexico and Colorado, and in 1897 recommended him for a position with the British mining firm of Bewick, Moreing and Company. They sent him to work in the gold mining fields of Australia. Hoover traveled the hot, dusty lands of western Australia and evaluated mines for his employer. When he was offered the chance to go to China, to serve jointly as a representative of Bewick, Moreing and Company and as an engineer for the Chinese government, he cabled a proposal of marriage to Lou Henry, who accepted. He returned to Monterey, California, and he and Lou were married on February 10, 1899; the couple left for China the next day.

Hoover's initial work efforts in China were often frustrated by the Chinese government bureaucracy, but this became a secondary consideration in June 1900 when the Hoovers found themselves caught up in the Boxer Rebellion, an uprising of a peasant group, the "Righteous and Harmonious Fists," against Western commercial and political influence in China. The Boxers also wanted to execute any Chinese associated with Christianity. The Hoovers became trapped in the city of Tientsin with other foreigners and some Chinese (many of them Christian) who had taken refuge there and were protected only by a small international force. Lou Hoover nursed the wounded, while Bert helped organize food distribution and firefighting efforts. The rebellion was over by August 1900 and the Hoovers were able to get out of China. They spent some time in England and then returned to China.

Hoover was successful in managing his firm's interests in China, and in 1901 was offered a partnership in Bewick, Moreing and Company. His new position sent him around the world many times, and in his travels he was frequently joined not only by Lou but also by the couple's son, Herbert Hoover, Jr., born in London in 1903, and their second son, Allan, born in London in 1907. During these years, Hoover also embarked on a program of self-education and began to read widely.

In 1909 Hoover left the firm of Bewick, Moreing and set up his own international consulting firm, both an engineering consulting firm and a financial consulting firm; it speculated in mining ventures and offered its consultants' expertise in mining operations and finances to other mining companies. He lectured on mining at Columbia University and Stanford University in 1909 and published his lectures under the title of *Principles of Mining*, which became a standard mining textbook. He and Lou translated into English *De Re Metallica*, a sixteenth-century mining text written in medieval Latin; the translation was published in 1912. That same year, Hoover became a member of the Board of Trustees of Stanford University. He had by then amassed a considerable personal fortune and was worth several million dollars.

Public Career

Hoover had for some time wanted to immerse himself in some form of public service. In 1913 Hoover was appointed by President Wilson as a special representative and promoter of the Panama-Pacific Exposition, which was to celebrate the opening of the Panama Canal and was to be held in San Francisco. The exposition was also intended to attract businesses to the Pacific coast of the United States. Hoover's job was to persuade foreign governments to provide exhibits for the exposition. He was attempting to interest Great Britain and Germany in contributing to the exposition when the project went into sudden eclipse because of the outbreak of war in Europe in 1914. Hoover soon turned his efforts to helping the many US citizens who had been stranded in Europe by the outbreak of war. He became the head of the Committee of American Residents in London for Assistance to American Travelers. Hoover and the committee helped more than 120,000 US citizens to obtain passage on ships back to United States; the committee also made loans to the stranded Americans and helped them to obtain food and lodging while they waited for transportation.

And then an even more pressing need came to Hoover's attention: as a result of the German invasion of Belgium, millions of Belgians were on the verge of starvation. Belgium was a nation that imported much of its food, and the British were blockading the ports of the European continent to prevent supplies from reaching the Germans. Hoover became the chairman of the Commission for Relief in Belgium and arranged for food, clothing, and funds to be collected and then distributed in Belgium, under an agreement whereby both the British and German governments would treat the commission as a neutral organization.

As a result of Hoover's successes in food distribution in Europe, President Wilson asked him, in 1917, to become the US Food Administrator; it was the year in which the United States entered the war. The Hoover family took up residence in Washington, DC. Food producers in the United States needed to feed not only the country's own citizens, but also US troops and their allies. Hoover called on the American people to observe "meatless Mondays" and "wheatless Wednesdays." He urged Americans to plant their own gardens; these "war gardens" were the precursors of the "victory gardens" of World War II. During this time, Hoover also began collecting documents that traced the history of the war and sending them to Stanford University, where they would eventually become part of the Hoover War Library (now part of the Hoover Institution).

During the war, great damage was inflicted on to the farmlands of Europe, to such an extent that even after the war, both the Allied countries and the defeated Germany needed further assistance. Hoover continued to work for food relief after the war and was named the director of the American Relief Administration, which contributed to the feeding of 350 million people in more than twenty countries. Meanwhile, Lou Hoover was caught up in her own humanitarian work. She assisted young women who had moved to Washington to do war work to obtain meals and housing. She also at this time became involved with the Girl Scouts—a natural choice for her, given her enthusiasm for outdoor activities. In 1922 she became the national president of the Girl Scouts.

> **"Twenty million people are starving. Whatever their politics, they shall be fed!"**
>
> Herbert Hoover, when questioned about his efforts to provide famine relief to Bolshevik Russia in 1921

Coming to the end of his work in Europe, Hoover planned to return to engineering. Lou Hoover began overseeing the construction of a house in California that would overlook the Stanford campus; it would be the Hoover family's first permanent home. They were not settled there for long, however, before Hoover was asked to become the Secretary of Commerce under President Warren G. Harding. In 1921 the Hoovers returned to Washington. When Harding died in office, in 1923, Hoover was asked to remain in his cabinet position by President Calvin Coolidge.

As Secretary of Commerce, Hoover had jurisdiction over the relatively new areas of regulation of the radio broadcasting and commercial aviation industries. He supported trade associations and the right of workers to form collective bargaining units. Hoover drew on his engineering experience as the overseer of the Bureau of Standards, which worked toward the standardization of measurements and tools used across many different industries. His goal was to make the economy more stable and less vulnerable to the fluctuations of markets and conditions.

While Secretary of Commerce, Hoover united several existing child welfare organizations and formed the American Child Health Association in 1923, and as its president realized improvements in the areas of child nutrition, the pasteurization of milk, infant mortality, vaccinations, and the eradication of child labor. In 1924 Hoover became the chairman of the Street and Highway Safety Commission and pushed for a uniform motor vehicle code in the United States.

> "We in America today are nearer to the final triumph over poverty than ever before in the history of any land."
>
> Herbert Hoover, in his acceptance speech for the Republican Party nomination for the presidency, 1928

Beginning with his time as the US Food Administrator, Hoover had become well known and popular in the United States. He came to the aid of those in crisis once again in 1927, when the Mississippi overflowed its banks, in what was, at that time, the worst flooding in US history. Hoover, merging his organizational and humanitarian instincts yet one more time, directed the relief effort. In the following year Calvin Coolidge declined to run again for president, and Hoover—at the height of his popularity in 1928—agreed to be the Republican Party's candidate.

Nominated on the first ballot at the 1928 Republican National Convention, and joined on the ticket by the Senate majority leader, Charles Curtis of Kansas, Hoover faced off against Alfred Smith of New York, the Democratic candidate. Smith was a Roman Catholic who favored ending Prohibition, both of which worked against him, even among members of his own party. Hoover defeated Smith, and became the president of the United States in what was his first attempt to win elective office. As the president-elect, he embarked on a one-month goodwill tour of South America.

PRESIDENCY

Hoover entered office with every expectation that his record of great achievement would be upheld. He hoped to study the problems facing the country and then to solve them using his (by-this-time legendary) efficiency and organizational acumen. He also hoped to inspire the American people with his philosophy of individual initiative and volunteerism.

Hoover immediately weighed in on two national debates: aid to farmers and tariff reform (which was also tied to the needs of famers). He called together a special session of Congress, which passed the Agricultural Marketing Act in June 1929; it created the Federal Farm Board. The Federal Farm Board was granted a revolving fund of $500 million for the purpose of making loans to farm cooperatives. The tariff bill that was finally passed in 1930, the Hawley-Smoot Tariff Act, had begun as a proposal for fairly modest increases in agricultural tariffs, but the original bill underwent so many changes during the congressional arguments that it finally increased tariff rates for both agricultural and manufactured goods to the highest they had ever been. Hoover also advocated and worked toward a number of progressive reforms. He favored conservation efforts, labor legislation, arms limitations, education and health care for Native Americans, and prison reform.

His presidency would forever be defined, however, by the calamitous stock market crash of October 1929 and the Great Depression that followed on its heels. The Depression had many causes (some of which are still being debated).

In addition there were effects of the Depression that, in circular fashion, contributed to its worsening, and cause and effect became blurred. Among the factors that led to the Depression were the excessive speculation in the stock market during the 1920s, the unequal distribution of wealth, the overproduction of manufactured goods, the spate of bank failures, growing unemployment, and the decline in international trade that was a consequence of the Hawley-Smoot Tariff. Drought and dust storms in the early 1930s also served to worsen the nation's economic woes.

Hoover responded by summoning business leaders to the White House and exacting pledges from them that they would maintain jobs and salary levels. He urged labor leaders to steer clear of calls for strikes. However, he opposed direct federal assistance to those in need because it contradicted his philosophy of helping people to help themselves, and he stressed, as he always had, the importance of voluntary action and cooperative activity. He regarded "the dole" as contrary to the ideals of the American people.

In 1931 Hoover urged a moratorium on the collection and payment of debts owed to or by European countries, believing that improvement of economic conditions in Europe would be followed by similar improvement in the United States. He also supported the formation, in early 1932, of the Reconstruction Finance Corporation, which was to provide loans to banks, railroads, farm associations, and large insurance companies. The Emergency Relief and Construction Act, passed in July 1932 over Hoover's veto, provided funds for public works as part of an effort to create jobs. The Revenue Act, also passed in 1932, raised personal income tax rates.

Hoover's presidency was marked by a surprising failure of public relations. As the Secretary of Commerce, Hoover had been a regular source of information for reporters, but as president, he was—or appeared to be—less open and available. His opposition to direct federal aid for the hurting American people was seen as callous and uncaring. As the Depression worsened, Hoover was blamed for some of its horrors. Americans were critical of the lavish entertainments that were given at the White House, even though the Hoovers paid for them with personal funds (in fact Hoover had his entire presidential salary donated to charity).

"I know, but I had a better year than Hoover."

Babe Ruth, referring to his salary of $80,000, which was $5,000 more than the president's salary, 1930

Against a president thus beleaguered by circumstance and (arguably) his own personal biases, the Democrats in 1932 were putting forward the warm, charismatic Franklin Roosevelt as their presidential candidate. Hoover ran for reelection but was soundly defeated by Roosevelt; he left the White House in early 1933 frustrated, saddened, and far less popular than when he had entered it. It is sadly ironic that Hoover, "the Great Engineer" and "the Great Humanitarian," was judged to be ineffective and even impotent in the face of a calamitous economic depression and great suffering among the American people, and left behind a tarnished presidential legacy.

POST-PRESIDENTIAL CAREER

The Hoovers settled into their home in California that overlooked Stanford University for a time, and Hoover worked toward the establishment of the library that would bear his name at Stanford. He also traveled a great deal.

Hoover was critical of Franklin Roosevelt and his New Deal legislation. Given his conservative stance and lingering unpopularity with those who blamed him for the Depression, Hoover remained out of favor with his own party throughout much of the 1930s.

Hoover continued to do humanitarian work. He became chairman of the Boys' Club of America in 1936 and spearheaded the movement to establish about five hundred additional clubs in the United States. In 1939 Hoover helped to raise funds for war relief in Poland, Finland, and Belgium. He opposed US involvement in the Second World War until after the attack on Pearl Harbor in 1941. In 1944 Lou Henry Hoover died of a heart attack in New York City, where the Hoovers had been living.

"Here are the documents which record the suffering, the self-denial, the heroic deeds of men. Surely from these records there can be help to mankind in its confusions and perplexities, and its yearnings for peace."

Herbert Hoover, June 20, 1941, at the dedication of the Hoover Tower at Stanford, a repository for the archives of the Hoover Institution Library

---

In 1946 postwar famine threatened Europe and other parts of the world, and President Harry Truman called on Hoover to make surveys of world famine and to head the Famine Emergency Commission. In 1947 Truman asked Hoover to improve the efficiency of the federal government and federal agencies. He became the chairman of the Commission on the Organization of the Executive Branch of the Government, called the first Hoover Commission. In 1953 Hoover headed the Second Hoover Commission at the request of President Dwight D. Eisenhower. But Hoover opposed the dropping of the atom bomb on Japanese cities, opposed many of the government's Cold War policies, and opposed the "red scare," or hunt for Communists, in the United States. He continued to urge diplomacy and moral argument, rather than force, as the correct approach in international affairs.

In 1958 Hoover, then in his eighties, served as a US representative to the World's Fair in Brussels, Belgium. In 1962 Hoover was present at the dedication of the Hoover Presidential Library and Museum in West Branch, Iowa. He died at the age of ninety in 1964 in New York City and was buried in West Branch, Iowa.

Birthplace: West Branch, IA
Residency: California
Religion: Quaker (Society of Friends)
Education: Stanford University, Stanford, CA, graduated 1895
Place of Death: New York, NY
Burial Site: Herbert Hoover National Historic Site, West Branch, IA
Dates in Office: March 4, 1929–March 3, 1933 (4 years)
Age at Inauguration: 54 years, 206 days

FAMILY
Father: Jesse Clark Hoover (1847–1880)
Mother: Hulda Randall Minthorn Hoover (1848–1883)
Siblings: Herbert was the second of three children; his siblings were Theodore Jesse Hoover (1871–1955) and Mary (May) Hoover (1876–1953).
Wife: Lou Henry Hoover (1874–1944), married February 10, 1899, in Monterey, CA
Children: Herbert Charles Hoover (1903–1969) and Allan Henry Hoover (1907–1993)

CAREER

PRIVATE: MINING ENGINEER
Political: head of the Commission for Relief in Belgium (1915–1919); US Food Administrator (1917–1918); director of the American Relief Administration (1919–1920); Secretary of Commerce (1921–1928); chairman of the Street and Highway Safety Commission (1924); president of the United States (1929–1933); chairman of the first Hoover Commission (1947); chairman of the second Hoover Commission (1953)
Military: none

Selected Works: *American Individualism; The Challenge to Liberty* (West Branch, IA: Herbert Hoover Presidential Library Association, 1989); *A Boyhood in Iowa* (Council Bluffs, IA: Yellow Barn Press, 1986); *Georgius Agricola De re metallica*, tr. from the Latin ed. of 1556, intro., annotations, and appendices by Herbert Clark Hoover and Lou Henry Hoover (London: The Mining Magazine, 1912); *Herbert Hoover, 1874–1964; Chronology, Documents, Bibliographical Aids*, ed. by Arnold S. Rice (Dobbs Ferry, NY: Oceana Publications, 1971); *The Hoover Commission Report on Organization of the Executive Branch of the Government, 1947–1949* (New York: McGraw-Hill, 1949); *The Hoover-Wilson Wartime Correspondence, September 24, 1915, to November 11, 1918*, ed. and with commentaries by Francis William O'Brien (Ames: Iowa State University Press, 1974); *The Memoirs of Herbert Hoover* (New York: Garland Publishing, 1979); *The Ordeal of Woodrow Wilson*, with a new intro. by Mark Hatfield (Baltimore, MD: Johns Hopkins University Press, 1992); *Papers of Herbert Hoover*, archival microfilm (Washington, DC: Library of Congress); *Principles of Mining: Valuation, Organization, and Administration; Copper, Gold, Lead, Silver, Tin, and Zinc* (New York, Hill Publishing Company, 1909); *The State Papers and Other Public Writings of Herbert Hoover*, collected and ed. by William Starr Myers (Garden City, NY: Doubleday, Doran & Company, 1934); *Two Peacemakers in Paris: The Hoover-Wilson Post-Armistice Letters, 1918–1920*, ed. and with commentaries by Francis William O'Brien (College Station: Texas A&M University Press, 1978)

PRESIDENCY

Nomination: 1928: The Republican convention was held in Kansas City, from June 12 to 15, 1928; Hoover, as a popular member of the Coolidge administration, was chosen on the first ballot. Charles Curtis of Kansas was chosen as the vice-presidential candidate.

1932: The Republican convention was held in Chicago, from June 14 to 16, 1932; Hoover and Curtis were renominated without opposition.

Election: 1928: elected president on November 6, 1928

1932: defeated by Franklin D. Roosevelt on November 8, 1932

Opponent: 1928: Alfred Smith, NY, Democratic; Norman Thomas, NY, Socialist

1932: Franklin D. Roosevelt, NY, Democratic; Norman Thomas, NY, Socialist; William Foster, IL, Communist

Vote Totals: 1928: Hoover, 21,427,123 popular, 444 electoral; Smith, 15,015,464 popular, 87 electoral; Thomas, 267,478 popular, 0 electoral

1932: Roosevelt, 22,821,857 popular, 472 electoral; Hoover, 15,761,586 popular, 59 electoral; Thomas, 884,885 popular, 0 electoral; Foster, 103,311 popular, 0 electoral

Inauguration: March 4, 1929

Vice President: Charles Curtis, KS (1929–1933)

CABINET

Secretary of State: Henry Lewis Stimson, NY (1929–1933)

Secretary of the Treasury: Andrew W. Mellon, PA (1929–1932); Ogden L. Mills, NY (1932–1933)

Secretary of War: James W. Good, IA (1929); Patrick J. Hurley, OK (1929–1933)

Attorney General: William DeWitt Mitchell, MN (1929–1933)

Postmaster General: Walter F. Brown, OH (1929–1933)

Secretary of the Navy: Charles F. Adams, MA (1929–1933)

Secretary of Agriculture: Arthur M. Hyde, MO (1929–1933)

Secretary of the Interior: Ray L. Wilbur, CA (1929–1933)

Secretary of Labor: James J. Davis, IN (1929–1930); William N. Doak, VA (1930–1933)

Secretary of Commerce: Robert P. Lamont, IL (1929–1932); Roy D. Chapin, MI (1932–1933)

CONGRESS:

71st Congress (1929–1931); Speaker of the House: Nicholas Longworth (OH, Republican)
72nd Congress (1931–1933); Speaker of the House: John N. Garner (TX, Democrat)

SUPREME COURT APPOINTEES

Charles Evans Hughes, NY; Chief Justice (1930–1941)

Owen Josephus Roberts, PA; Associate Justice (1930–1945)

Benjamin Nathan Cardozo, NY; Associate Justice (1932–1938)

MAJOR EVENTS OF THE HOOVER ADMINISTRATION

◆ The Agricultural Marketing Act of 1929 creates the Federal Farm Board, which can make loans to farmers or buy their surplus crops.

◆ The Immigration Act (Johnson-Reed Act) of 1929 amends the Immigration Act of 1924; it tightens the restrictions against immigration from many nations by allotting to each national group a percentage of the overall number of immigrants being allowed to enter the United States.

◆ On October 24, 1929, "Black Thursday," the overly inflated stock market crashes, sending the share price of many stocks plummeting and ushering in the Great Depression. On October 29, 1929, "Black Tuesday," a record number of stocks are sold at low prices, which intensifies the continuing downward spiral of stock prices.

◆ The Hawley-Smoot (or Smoot-Hawley) Tariff, 1930, raises the tariffs on many imported items, both agricultural and manufactured; it is the highest US tariff ever. Other countries retaliate by raising their tariffs, and the negative effect on trade worsens the Depression.

◆ On July 3, 1930, the Veterans Administration Act, which establishes the Veterans Administration, is signed by Hoover.

◆ In July 1930 the United States ratifies the provisions of the agreement reached at the London Naval Conference, which has just set ratios for the numbers of ships and submarines that the United States, Great Britain, and Japan can build.

◆ On March 3, 1931, "The Star-Spangled Banner" is officially adopted as the national anthem.

◆ In December 1931 Congress passes a one-year moratorium on the collection of debts owed to the United States in return for an agreement by European countries not to collect debts owed to them by the United States.

◆ On January 7, 1932, Secretary of State Henry L. Stimson sends letters to the heads of state of Japan and China that announce the Stimson Doctrine, according to which the United States refuses to recognize the government of Manchukuo, the Japanese-controlled area of Manchuria in China.

◆ The Federal Home Loan Bank Act, passed in 1932, establishes twelve federal home loan banks for the purpose of making federal funds available for home mortgages.

◆ The 1932 Reconstruction Finance Act establishes the Reconstruction Finance Corporation, which is to provide loans to banks, railroads and other industries, agricultural credit agencies, and individual states for public works and unemployment relief.

◆ On July 28, 1932, Hoover orders the eviction of the Bonus Army, approximately 10,000 veterans who are encamped along the Anacostia River after having marched to Washington to seek immediate cash for bonus certificates not payable until 1945. General Douglas Macarthur (Army Chief of Staff), in command of the federal troops used to disperse the protestors and aided by Major Dwight Eisenhower and Major George Patton, complies with Hoover's orders.

◆ On November 7, 1932, the Supreme Court rules in *Powell v. Alabama* that due process was violated in the case of nine young black men who were accused of raping two white women in Scottsboro, Alabama. Three separate trials were held and decided in one day—with all nine defendants sentenced to death. The attorneys appointed to represent the nine men had not consulted with their clients before the day of the trial.

◆ The Revenue Act of 1932 raises income, estate, and corporate taxes.

◆ The 20th Amendment to the Constitution, which shortens the period between elections and the swearing in of elected officials (changing swearing-in dates from March to January), is passed by Congress on March 2, 1932, and ratified on January 23, 1933.

◆ The 21st Amendment to the Constitution, repealing the prohibition of alcohol enacted by the 18th Amendment, is passed by Congress on February 20, 1933, and ratified on December 5, 1933.

MAJOR US AND WORLD EVENTS, 1929–1933

◆ On May 16, 1929, in the first Academy Awards ceremony, awards are given to Janet Gaynor, for best actress; Emil Jannings, for best actor; *Wings* and *Sunrise,* as the two best films; and a special award is given to Charlie Chaplin, for *The Circus.*

◆ On April 15, 1929, the Birth Control Clinical Research Center established by Margaret Sanger in New York City is raided by the police, who arrest staff members and seize patients' records; the case is dismissed a month later because the raid is considered a violation of the right of physicians to practice medicine.

◆ On November 18, 1929, an earthquake off the coast of Newfoundland measures 7.2 on the Richter scale.

◆ In 1929 Ernest O. Lawrence invents the cyclotron, a particle accelerator that enables scientists to "smash" atomic nuclei, at the University of California at Berkeley.

◆ Notable films of 1929 include Luis Buñuel's *Un Chien Andalou (An Andalusian Dog), The Broadway Melody* with Charles King and Anita Page, the Marx Brothers' *Coconuts, The Kiss* with Greta Garbo, and *The Virginian* with Gary Cooper.

◆ Sinclair Lewis publishes *Dodsworth,* 1929.

◆ Thomas Wolfe publishes *Look Homeward, Angel,* 1929.

◆ Erich Maria Remarque publishes *All Quiet on the Western Front,* 1929.

◆ Ernest Hemingway publishes *A Farewell to Arms,* 1929.

◆ William Faulkner publishes *The Sound and the Fury,* 1929.

◆ Virginia Woolf publishes *A Room of One's Own,* 1929.

◆ Popular songs of 1929 include Eddie Cantor's "Makin' Whoopee," Bob Haring's "Pagan Love Song," Ethel Waters's "Am I Blue?," and Maurice Chevalier's "Louise."

◆ The planet Pluto is discovered by astronomer Clyde Tombaugh, 1930.

◆ In May 1930 the arrest of Mohandas Gandhi provokes another wave of widespread civil disobedience among Indian citizens, who are protesting the longstanding British colonial rule of India.

◆ Construction of the Hoover Dam (on the Colorado River) begins, September 1930.

◆ On November 14, 1930, Japanese Prime Minister Yuko Hamaguchi is shot by a right-wing radical and dies approximately nine months later.

◆ The 1930 census shows a US population of 123.2 million people.

◆ Uruguay wins the first World Cup for soccer, 1930.

◆ John Dos Passos publishes *The 42nd Parallel,* 1930.

◆ Dashiell Hammett publishes *The Maltese Falcon,* 1930.

◆ William Faulkner publishes *As I Lay Dying,* 1930.

◆ Carolyn Keene publishes *The Secret of the Old Clock* in 1930; it is the first mystery in the Nancy Drew mystery series.

◆ Popular songs of 1930 include Al Jolson's "To My Mammy," Harry Richman's "Puttin' on the Ritz," and the Ben Selvin Orchestra's "Happy Days Are Here Again."

◆ Notable films of 1930 include Lewis Milestone's *All Quiet on the Western Front, Anna Christie* with Greta Garbo, the Marx Brothers' *Animal Crackers,* and *Little Caesar* with Edward G. Robinson.

◆ In 1931 the state of Nevada legalizes gambling, which reinforces an earlier decision made by the Nevada legislature in 1869. Nevada also, in 1931, shortens the residency requirement for divorce, making Reno, Nevada, in particular a popular destination for those seeking a divorce.

◆ Mathematician Kurt Gödel publishes his "incompleteness theorem" in 1931, which posits that within any mathematical system, there are true statements that cannot be proved with the axioms of that system; thus, any system of mathematics is incomplete.

◆ Al Capone is sent to prison for income tax invasion, 1931.

◆ On May 1, 1931, the Empire State Building opens in New York City.

◆ The murder of Salvatore Maranzano, *capo di tutti capi* ("boss of all the bosses"), on September 10, 1931, ends the so-called Castellammare War between rival organized crime factions in New York City.

◆ On December 9, 1931, Spain adopts a republican constitution and abolishes its monarchy.

◆ Popular music hits of 1931 include Cab Calloway's "Minnie the Moocher," Duke Ellington's "Mood Indigo," and Bing Crosby's "Star Dust."

◆ The *Symphony No. 3 in E Flat Major* by Dmitri Shostakovich is first performed in November 1931.

◆ Notable films of 1931 include *Frankenstein* with Boris Karloff, *Dracula* with Bela Lugosi, Charlie Chaplin's *City Lights*, *The Champ* with Wallace Beery, and *The Public Enemy* with James Cagney.

◆ Pearl S. Buck publishes *The Good Earth*, 1931.

◆ Dashiell Hammett publishes *The Glass Key*, 1931.

◆ In February 1932 a "General Conference for the Limitation and Reduction of Armaments" is convened in Geneva, Switzerland.

◆ On March 1, 1932, the son of Anne Morrow Lindbergh and Charles Lindbergh is kidnapped; his body is discovered in May 1932.

◆ On March 19, 1932, the Sydney Harbor Bridge officially opens.

◆ On May 6, 1932, French President Paul Doumer is assassinated by Paul Gorguloff, a Russian immigrant. On May 10, 1932, Albert Lebrun becomes president of France.

◆ On May 15, 1932, Prime Minister Inukai Tsuyoshi of Japan is assassinated during an attempted coup by Japanese naval officers.

◆ Amelia Earhart flies solo across the Atlantic Ocean, becoming the first woman to do so; she lands in England on May 21, 1932.

◆ On September 18, 1932, the Kingdom of Saudi Arabia is proclaimed by Ibn Saud (King Abdul Aziz bin Abdul Rahman Al Saud).

◆ In 1932 Sir John Douglas Cockcroft and Ernest Thomas Sinton Walton split the atom, using artificially accelerated particles to produce a nuclear reaction.

◆ In February 1932 Sir James Chadwick describes his discovery of the neutron in an article in *Nature* magazine.

◆ In game three of baseball's World Series between the New York Yankees and the Chicago Cubs, Babe Ruth hits his famous "called shot": he points at the center field bleachers and then propels the ball to the spot at which he had pointed.

◆ In both the 1932 summer Olympics in Los Angeles, California, and the 1932 winter Olympics at Lake Placid, New York, the United States wins the most medals.

◆ On November 8, 1932, CBS becomes the first television network to air coverage of a presidential election.

◆ William Faulkner publishes *Light in August*, 1932.

◆ Aldous Huxley publishes *Brave New World*, 1932.

◆ Erskine Caldwell publishes *Tobacco Road*, 1932.

◆ Popular music hits of 1932 include Fred Astaire's "Night and Day," Rudy Vallee's "Brother, Can You Spare a Dime?" and Louis Armstrong's "All of Me."

◆ Notable films of 1932 include *Tarzan, the Ape Man* with Johnny Weismuller and Maureen O'Sullivan, *Shanghai Express* with Marlene Dietrich, *Red Dust* with Clark Gable and Jean Harlow, *I Am a Fugitive from a Chain Gang* with Paul Muni, the Marx Brothers' *Horse Feathers*, *Dr. Jekyll and Mr. Hyde* with Fredric March, and *Grand Hotel* with Greta Garbo, John Barrymore, Joan Crawford, and Lionel Barrymore.

◆ On January 30, 1933, Paul von Hindenburg, president of the Weimar Republic of Germany, appoints Adolf Hitler chancellor of the cabinet.

◆ In February and March of 1933 Japan creates the supposedly independent state of "Manchuko" (or "Manchukuo") out of the province of Manchuria in China.

◆ On February 17, 1933, the first issue of *Newsweek* is published, at ten cents a copy. The magazine in no time has a circulation of 50,000.

FAST FACTS ABOUT HERBERT HOOVER

◆ Hoover was the first president born west of the Mississippi River.

◆ Hoover was a member of the first class to graduate from Stanford University.

◆ By the age of ten, Hoover was an orphan.

◆ Throughout his career, even when he was Secretary of Commerce or president, Hoover was called "Chief" by staff members; the title derived from his positions as the chief engineer of various mining operations.

◆ During the Boxer Rebellion in China, Hoover risked his life to rescue Chinese children from the murderous Boxer rebels.

◆ At the beginning of World War I, Hoover headed a committee that helped more than 120,000 US citizens stranded in Europe to return to the United States.

◆ Although Hoover is associated with the phrase "a chicken in every pot, a car in every garage (or backyard)," he never made such a campaign promise. These words were used in an advertisement created by the Republican National Committee that claimed such prosperity existed in the United States because of the actions and policies of the Coolidge and Hoover administrations, meaning that a vote for Hoover would be a vote to continue the happy status quo.

◆ A self-made millionaire, Hoover refused his salary as president.

◆ Hoover was the first president to have a telephone on his desk.

◆ Hoover, a lifelong baseball fan, advocated giving batters four strikes instead of three because he thought that good pitching was boring to watch.

◆ Lou Henry Hoover was the first woman to major in geology at Stanford University.

◆ Both Lou and Herbert Hoover knew several languages; they would speak Mandarin if they wished to avoid being understood by the White House staff.

◆ Lou Henry Hoover was active in the Girl Scouts and the National Amateur Athletic Federation; she had hiked and camped with her father during her formative years, and was an advocate of exercise and outdoor activities for girls.

◆ The Hoovers entertained lavishly while they lived in the White House; they used their own money, but were criticized for their entertainments at a time when many Americans were enduring the hardships of the Depression.

◆ Both President Truman (in 1947) and President Eisenhower (in 1953) put Hoover in charge of commissions appointed to reorganize the federal government.

◆ Hoover lived longer after his presidency (31 years) than any other president thus far.

Franklin Delano Roosevelt

Nickname: FDR
Presidency: 32nd president, 1933–1945
Party: Democratic
Life dates: January 30, 1882–April 12, 1945 (63 years, 72 days)

EARLY LIFE AND EDUCATION

On January 30, 1882, Franklin Delano Roosevelt was born on his family's estate of Springwood in Hyde Park, New York, located north of New York City on the Hudson River. His father was James Roosevelt, a wealthy member of a Dutch family that had come to America in the 1640s. His mother was Sara Delano Roosevelt, James's second, much younger wife, who was the daughter of a wealthy merchant who made his fortune in the tea and opium trade in China and who had grown up on an estate called Algonac, farther up the Hudson River, near Newburgh, New York. During his first marriage James Roosevelt had had a son, James "Rosy" Roosevelt, who was already grown by the time Franklin was born. Franklin thus grew up as if he had been an only child. During his childhood he was surrounded by nurses and governesses and the tender solicitude of his family, but he had little contact with other children and with those less fortunate.

Sara Roosevelt devoted herself to her son and his education. Franklin was tutored at home, but his education also included frequent trips to Europe and summer vacations at the family's summer house on Campobello Island, in the Bay of Fundy off the coast of New Brunswick, Canada (the island is also accessible from the northeastern shores of Maine). He developed a keen interest in natural history and the outdoors, enjoyed sailing, and also became an avid stamp collector, a hobby he pursued throughout his life.

In 1896, at the age of fourteen, Franklin entered the Groton School in Massachusetts. The headmaster, Endicott Peabody, had attempted to model the school after English boarding schools and espoused religious observance and physical activity as well as academics. He also urged the students to consider public service professions, such as politics. Franklin was not outstanding in either athletics or academics, but he did fit comfortably into the world of Groton, with its population of young men of similar social standing.

From Groton it was a natural step to enroll at Harvard University, where Franklin was, again, less than eminent in pursuits academic and athletic. His grades continued to be average, but Franklin entered into a number of extracurricular activities, most notably the college newspaper, *The Crimson*. He became its editor in chief during his junior year. He received his bachelor's degree on June 24, 1903. He failed, however, to win admission to the most exclusive of Harvard's social clubs, the Porcellian, a disappointment made worse by the fact that his distant cousin Theodore Roosevelt (who had become president while Franklin was at Harvard) had been so honored.

> "Let me assert my firm belief that the only thing we have to fear is fear itself."
>
> Franklin D. Roosevelt, speech, July 2, 1932

During Franklin's freshman year at Harvard, his father died from heart disease; soon afterward Sara Roosevelt took an apartment in Boston to be near her son. That son, tall, slender, aristocratic, and set apart by the affability and charm that would only increase in later years and put him in good stead as a politician, led an active social life in Boston. He was equally at home in New York social circles when he enrolled at the Columbia University Law School in 1905.

In 1902, while Franklin was still at Harvard, he renewed his acquaintance with Eleanor Roosevelt, his fifth cousin once removed (with whom he had spent some time during childhood). Christened Anna Eleanor Roosevelt, she was the daughter of Anna Hall Roosevelt, a beautiful woman who had grown up on her family's estate, "Tivoli," on the Hudson River, and Elliott Roosevelt, Theodore Roosevelt's younger brother. Eleanor's childhood was almost devoid of the warmth and security that defined Franklin's; her mother, who made no secret of her disappointment in her plain little daughter and called her "Granny" (because of her serious demeanor), died when Eleanor was eight. Elliott Roosevelt, whom Eleanor adored, was an alcoholic who sometimes behaved unpredictably, to the point of his sometimes exhibiting violence. When Eleanor was ten, he died. Eleanor was already living with her maternal grandmother, Mary Ludlow Hall, at this point and stayed with her until 1899, at which time she was enrolled at the Allenswood School, near London, England. At Allenswood Eleanor gained a measure of self-confidence; she was a good student and popular with the other girls.

In 1902 Eleanor returned from England and made her debut. She was tall and slender and possessed of good manners and a knack for putting others at ease in conversation. She joined the Junior League of the City of New York in 1903 and taught a calisthenics class to young women who lived on the Lower East Side of Manhattan; it was the start of her lifelong involvement in social causes. Franklin pursued her quietly and in 1903 they became engaged. Sara Roosevelt was opposed to the engagement and spirited her son away on a five-week Caribbean cruise early in 1904, and at the same time asked the pair to conceal their engagement and wait for a year. Eventually, however, she bowed to her son's wishes, and Franklin and Eleanor were married on March 17, 1905, at the New York City home of one of Eleanor's relatives. The bride's uncle, President Theodore Roosevelt, gave her away.

EARLY CAREER

After a honeymoon trip to Europe, Eleanor and Franklin moved into a home in New York City that Sara had rented and furnished for them. Roosevelt resumed his studies at Columbia, but dropped out without graduating after he passed the New York state bar examination in 1907. He entered the Wall Street law firm of Carter, Ledyard, and Milburn, but his legal career was short-lived. From the beginning, Roosevelt was more interested in politics than in the practice of the law.

Eleanor and Franklin became parents when their daughter Anna was born in 1906, followed by James, born in 1907; Franklin, Jr., in 1909; and Elliott, in 1910. Franklin, Jr., died of influenza in the first year of his life. Another child, also named Franklin, Jr., was born in 1914, and their youngest child, John, was born in 1916. In 1908 the Roosevelts moved into a new townhouse that Sara Roosevelt had built for them. Actually it was one of a pair of adjacent and adjoining townhouses (which sported interconnecting doors). Sara lived in the other. She was a domineering and constant presence. She visited frequently, imposed her will on the young couple, and was inclined to spoil the Roosevelt children.

In 1910, when Democratic leaders in Dutchess County (where Hyde Park is located) approached Roosevelt and asked him to run for the New York state senate, he seized the opportunity. Although Theodore Roosevelt was a Republican, the members of Franklin's family tended to be Democrats. He waged a vigorous campaign and—against all expectations—won. He took his seat in Albany. Eleanor moved the family to Albany, where she found, for the first time, a modicum of independence from her mother-in-law.

During his first term in office, Roosevelt strove to address the concerns of his constituents, many of whom were farmers, and to take on the power of Tammany Hall, New York City's Democratic Party machine. Roosevelt, as the leader of a small group of Democratic legislators, challenged the party's top candidate for the US Senate, who had been handpicked by Tammany Hall. After several months another candidate was selected.

Roosevelt supported progressive reform efforts in New York state and campaigned for Woodrow Wilson for president in 1912. Roosevelt was reelected to the state senate in 1912, and it was around this time that he attracted the attentions of journalist Louis McHenry Howe, who became Roosevelt's most trusted political advisor and strategist. Roosevelt did not complete his second term in the state legislature. In March 1913 he was appointed the Assistant Secretary of the Navy by the incoming President Wilson, primarily as a reward for his having worked on Wilson's campaign; the Roosevelt family was on its way to Washington, DC. Roosevelt was doubly happy at the appointment, given his lifelong interest in sailing and ships and the auspi-

cious fact that Theodore Roosevelt had held the same position early in his political career.

Secretary of the Navy Josephus Daniels, despite basic differences with Roosevelt, gave him latitude in his position and in time came to hold Roosevelt in his esteem and affection. Roosevelt was brash and cocky at times; he once told Eleanor that he thought that he could do a better job of managing the Navy than his boss. Roosevelt and Daniels found themselves at odds over the potential involvement of the United States in the Great War. Roosevelt thought that it was almost inevitable that the United States would join Great Britain and France against Germany, but Daniels was an isolationist who wanted to keep the United States out of the war. Roosevelt worked hard to increase the strength and readiness of the United States Navy so that they would be prepared in the eventuality of US participation in the conflict.

As the United States entered the war, Roosevelt argued for an aggressive prosecution of the war. Eleanor volunteered at the Red Cross canteen in Washington and recruited women to knit clothing for soldiers; she also visited the war wounded at the US Naval Hospital. In 1918 Roosevelt traveled to Europe on an army inspection call and returned to the United States with double pneumonia. While supervising her husband's care during his illness, Eleanor discovered love letters that had been written by Lucy Mercer, her personal secretary, to her husband. She confronted him with the letters and offered to divorce him, something that Roosevelt did not want. Not only did Roosevelt have his children and political career to consider (divorce would have brought an end to his political aspirations); Sara Roosevelt weighed in on the matter and threatened to cut him off financially if he did not agree to stop seeing Mercer. Eleanor and Franklin remained married. However, the personal distress that Eleanor suffered as a result of her discovery changed the nature of their marriage forever, and she became more independent as a result.

In 1920 Roosevelt was nominated to be the running mate of Democratic presidential candidate James N. Cox of Ohio, but the two candidates were defeated by Calvin Coolidge and Charles Gates Dawes. The American people were turning away from the progressive policies of Woodrow Wilson; some were angry at his decision to take the country to war.

POLIO AND RETURN TO POLITICS

In the wake of his defeat in the 1920 election, Roosevelt was considering a return to his former life as a lawyer in New York City. Then tragedy struck. In August 1921, while vacationing at Campobello, Roosevelt was stricken with polio (poliomyelitis) and his legs became permanently paralyzed. Although he was told he would never walk again, Roosevelt fought valiantly to regain the use of his legs; eventually he was able to walk again, with the use of leg braces and a cane.

During the next several years, Roosevelt concentrated on his physical recovery. He endured an arduous rehabilitation process that included exercises and spending time in warm-climate places such as Florida and Georgia. He found those places to be especially alluring when he realized that he had more movement in his legs at the end of swimming in warm water. In 1927 he spent a large part of his fortune in purchasing and rehabilitating a vacation spa in Warm Springs, Georgia, which became the Warm Springs Foundation, a treatment center for polio victims. He also built a "cottage" for himself in Warm Springs and returned to it on a regular basis for the rest of his life. Meanwhile, Eleanor's political life underwent expansion; she strove to keep the Roosevelt name in the public eye and ear and worked to recruit women—who had been granted the vote in 1920—into the ranks of the Democratic Party in New York.

Sara Roosevelt wanted her son to retire to Hyde Park and live in retirement as a country gentleman. It was not what he wanted. Eleanor, along with Louis Howe, supported Roosevelt's desire to return to the political arena and helped him to do so. At the 1924 and 1928 Democratic National Conventions, Roosevelt made the nominating speech for Governor Al Smith of New York. (Smith was defeated in his bid for the presidency both times.) In 1928 Roosevelt decisively

reentered politics when he agreed to run for governor of New York. On November 4, 1928, he won the election, and was reelected, by a landslide, in 1930, when the country was already mired in a catastrophic economic depression.

> "Once I prophesied that this generation of Americans had a rendezvous with destiny. That prophecy now comes true. To us much is given; more is expected. This generation will nobly save or mainly lose the last best hope of earth. The way is plain, peaceful, generous, just.
>
> Franklin D. Roosevelt, message to Congress, January 4, 1939

As governor of New York, Roosevelt, facing the Great Depression, focused on combating the state's economic woes. He supported a number of relief measures, such as tax breaks for farmers, old-age pensions, and state aid for electric power generation. His popularity as governor gave him a strong standing as he went into the 1932 Democratic National Convention; he was vying with Al Smith, who hoped to run again, and Speaker of the House John Nance Garner of Texas. In the course of the convention Garner was promised the vice-presidential spot in exchange for the release of his own delegates and their transfer of support to Roosevelt. The transfer of delegates secured the nomination for Roosevelt on the fourth ballot. Roosevelt flew to Chicago to accept the nomination, in part to promote the idea that he was healthy and vigorous (despite the fact that he was paraplegic).

Given Hoover's unpopularity, few were surprised when Roosevelt won the election by a landslide, on November 8, 1932. He had received nearly 23 million votes to Hoover's nearly 16 million, and 472 electoral votes to Hoover's

59. In addition, the Democrats had won comfortable majorities in both the Senate and the House of Representatives.

In February 1933, in Miami, Florida, an attempt was made to assassinate Roosevelt (while he was still the president-elect). The gunman missed, and instead killed Anton Cermak, the mayor of Chicago, who died three weeks later.

PRESIDENCY

Roosevelt was inaugurated on March 4, 1933, and so began the "One Hundred Days," the first three months of his presidency, during which time he introduced into Congress and pushed hard for the passage of an unprecedented volume of legislation. The new legislation was to lay the foundations for his "New Deal" program, his plan for coming to the aid of a people in dire straits. Roosevelt himself ordered all banks to close (with the idea that they would remain closed until they were determined to be financially stable by boards of examiners). The closure of banks was intended to prevent another public run on banks (in which depositors demanded to remove all their money from the banks) and to stave off panic. He then called together a special session of Congress, to take place on the very same day, March 9, 1933. In that session Congress gave Roosevelt virtually everything he wanted. Both the House and the Senate passed new banking legislation in a matter of hours. Roosevelt signed the bills into law, also on the same day.

The legislation passed during the One Hundred Days was far-reaching and signified a dramatic change in the degree to which the federal government was involved in the lives of US citizens. The legislation ushered in a multitude of new federal agencies; they all became known by their initials (e.g., CCC, WPA, NRA), and the New Deal agencies were sometimes referred to, collectively, as "Alphabet Soup." Agencies that regulated agricultural prices, distributed money to the needy, and gave public works employment to young unemployed men (building roads, bridges, and hospitals; planting trees to prevent soil erosion; constructing dams and waterways to prevent flooding and provide irrigation; bring-

ing electric power to rural regions) were all quickly brought into being by the legislation of the One Hundred Days. Roosevelt also, during the One Hundred Days, inaugurated his series of radio addresses, known as "fireside chats," in which he strove to restore confidence in government and instill calm in an anxious populace.

> **"The test of our progress is not whether we add more to the abundance of those who have much; it is whether we provide enough for those who have too little."**
>
> Franklin D. Roosevelt, second inaugural address, January 20, 1937

Improvements were slow in the making, however, and in 1935 Roosevelt put the New Deal on an even more liberal footing and pushed for legislation that introduced Social Security, legitimized labor unions and allowed them to organize and engage in collective bargaining, and expanded the scope of public works employment. Roosevelt was easily reelected to a second term in 1936. But in his second inaugural address, which he gave in January 1937, he made the sobering assessment: "I see one-third of the nation ill-housed, ill-clad, and ill-nourished."

The New Deal had met with significant opposition from the Supreme Court; in fact the Court, dominated by conservatives, had struck down a number of New Deal programs. In the way of response, Roosevelt submitted a plan for judicial reform to Congress. He proposed increasing the number of justices from nine to fifteen, which would have enabled him to appoint new justices and to create a new majority in the Court. The proposal came to be known as an attempt to "pack" the court, and it failed.

Roosevelt was also determined to improve US relations with the nations of Latin America.

He had said in 1933: "In the field of world policy I would dedicate this nation to the policy of the good neighbor." It became known as the "Good Neighbor" policy; it was a policy of cooperation and nonintervention that had originally been elaborated by President Hoover. During most of the 1930s, Americans were strongly isolationist, and had come to regard their country's entry into World War I as a grave mistake. Roosevelt, on the other had, despite a series of Neutrality Acts passed by Congress in the late 1930s, saw dangers accumulating and felt it was necessary for the United States to come to the aid of those who were opposing the rising Nazi and fascist empires. When Great Britain declared war on Germany after its invasion of Poland in September 1939, Roosevelt tried to balance the US neutrality stance against what he believed was a great need to assist Great Britain in its hour of peril. He persuaded the Congress to pass the Lend-Lease Act in March 1941. The Lend-Lease Act gave Roosevelt the power to sell, transfer, exchange, and/or lend war materiel to Great Britain (and eventually many other countries) to help it to defend itself against the Axis powers, in return for whatever compensation the president deemed acceptable.

Breaking with the two-term tradition that had been followed by presidents since its establishment by George Washington, Roosevelt ran for a third term and was reelected, on November 5, 1940. The vice president during the first two terms, John Nance Garner, disagreed with Roosevelt's decision to run for a third term, and he was replaced on the ticket by Henry A. Wallace, the Secretary of Commerce.

Roosevelt had campaigned in 1940 with the promise that he would not send "our boys" to fight in a foreign war. But on December 7, 1941, Japanese planes bombed the US naval installation at Pearl Harbor in Hawaii, and there was immediate consensus that the United States had no choice but to go to war. The United States had placed an embargo on trade with Japan, one of the Axis powers (the others were Germany and Italy); Japan responded with the surprise attack. US military strategists had been predicting that Japan would attack British or Dutch possessions in the Pacific and had not anticipated a direct attack on Hawaii, as it was far from Japan and would have been difficult for Japanese planes to approach without their being detected. The day after the bombing of Pearl Harbor, the United States declared war on Japan, and within a few days Japan's allies, Italy and Germany, declared war on the United States.

"Yesterday, December 7, 1941— a date that will live in infamy— the United States of America was suddenly and deliberately attacked by naval and air forces of the Empire of Japan."

Franklin D. Roosevelt, radio address, December 8, 1941

In early 1942, with the country mobilizing for war and attempting to expand its agricultural and manufacturing outputs to support the military effort, the Depression became a thing of the past, although it continued to haunt many Americans who had endured it.

Believing that the greatest threat—by far— was coming from Germany, Roosevelt concentrated on the war in Europe. The United States and its British and Free French allies (as well as the Soviet Union, which had been attacked by Germany in mid-1941) made plans to attack Axis positions in North Africa first, and then Italy, to be followed by the launching of a massive invasion of France's Normandy coast. The Normandy invasion was planned for June 1944. Known as "D-Day," the invasion took place on June 6.

Roosevelt was elected to an unprecedented fourth term of office, on November 7, 1944. Vice President Henry A. Wallace, thought by many to have become too liberal, was replaced by Senator Harry S. Truman of Missouri, who brought a base of Southern support to the ticket.

President Franklin D. Roosevelt with Prime Minister Winston Churchill (left) and Marshal Joseph Stalin (right) at the Yalta Conference in February, 1945.

With the end of the war in Europe in sight (but with the war in the Pacific against Japan increasing in its intensity), Roosevelt continued to meet with Churchill, Stalin, and other leaders to discuss the continuing war against Japan, as well as to make post-war plans. The Allied leaders agreed to the joint occupation of Germany after the war and outlined plans for the organization of the United Nations. At one of these meetings, in the Russian city of Yalta in January 1945, it was apparent that Roosevelt was not in good health. After he returned to Washington, he left for a vacation in Warm Springs, Georgia, in April 1945. He was joined in Warm Springs by Lucy Mercer (who had become Mrs. Rutherford and was living quietly in South Carolina). They were by this time simply old friends, old friends who very much enjoyed one another's company.

On April 12, in his cottage at Warm Springs, Roosevelt—in good spirits over the impending German surrender and the conclusion of the European war—sat for an artist who was painting his portrait and chatted gaily with Mrs. Rutherford. Very suddenly he began to complain of a headache and collapsed in his chair. He died the same day, on April 12, 1945, at Warm Springs, Georgia, of a cerebral hemorrhage. A funeral train carried his body back to Washington. He was buried in Hyde Park, New York.

Eleanor was appointed by President Truman as a US delegate to the United Nations in 1945. She was appointed again as a delegate to the United Nations by President John F. Kennedy in 1961. Eleanor had always been energetic and had worked tirelessly throughout her husband's political career—writing newspaper columns, making speeches, and traveling around the country. She had written countless memos to her husband in which she put forth her ideas and urged him to do more for the social causes she championed: assistance for the poorest Americans, African-American civil rights, and women's rights. She had once described herself as his "spur," and noted that he might have been happier with someone less critical than she. She died in New York City on November 10, 1962.

Few presidents have faced crises of the same magnitude as those confronted by Roosevelt during his presidency. Both the Depression and World War II were enormous challenges to the nation, and the United States was fundamentally reshaped by the leadership of Franklin D. Roosevelt. He expanded the power of the president and the role played by the federal government in the lives of Americans in ways that prior generations of Americans would have never even imagined. His presidency was a substantial turning point in the political, social, and cultural fortunes of the United States.

Birthplace: Hyde Park, Dutchess County, NY
Residency: New York
Religion: Episcopalian
Education: Harvard College, graduated 1903; Columbia Law School, 1905–1907, did not graduate (though he did pass the NY bar exam)
Place of Death: Warm Springs, GA
Burial Site: Hyde Park, Dutchess County, NY
Dates in Office: March 4, 1933–April 12, 1945 (12 years, 39 days)
Age at Inauguration: 51 years, 33 days

FAMILY

Father: James Roosevelt (1828–1900)
Mother: Sara Delano Roosevelt (1854–1941)
Siblings: Franklin had a half-brother, James ("Rosy") Roosevelt (1854–1927), from his father's first marriage to Rebecca B. Howland (1831–1876)
Wife: (Anna) Eleanor Roosevelt (1884–1962), married March 17, 1905, in New York City [Note: Roosevelt married a distant cousin, so Eleanor's birth name and married name were both Roosevelt.]
Children: Anna Eleanor Roosevelt (1906–1975); James ("Jimmy") Roosevelt (1907–1991); Franklin Delano Roosevelt, Jr. (1909; died when

eight months old); Elliott Roosevelt (1910–1990); Franklin Delano Roosevelt, Jr. (1914–1988); John Aspinwall Roosevelt (1916–1981)

CAREER

Private: lawyer
Political: New York state senator (1910–1913); Assistant Secretary of the Navy (1913–1919); governor of New York (1929–1932); president of the United States (1933–1945)
Military: none
Selected Works: *Churchill and Roosevelt: The Complete Correspondence*, ed. with commentary by Warren F. Kimball (Princeton, NJ: Princeton University Press, 1984); *Complete Presidential Press Conferences of Franklin D. Roosevelt*, introduction by Jonathan Daniels (New York: Da Capo Press, 1972); *The Essential Franklin Delano Roosevelt*, ed. with an introduction by John Gabriel Hunt (New York; Gramercy Books, 1995); *F.D.R., His Personal Letters*, foreword by Eleanor Roosevelt, ed. by Elliott Roosevelt (New York: Duell, Sloan, and Pearce, 1947–1950); *Fireside Chats* (New York: Penguin Books, 1995); *Franklin D. Roosevelt and Foreign Affairs*, ed. by Edgar B. Nixon (Cambridge, MA: Belknap Press of Harvard University Press, 1969); *Great Speeches: Franklin Delano Roosevelt*, ed. by John Grafton (Mineola, NY: Dover Publications, 1999); *Looking Forward* (New York: Da Capo Press, 1973); *On Our Way* (New York: Da Capo Press, 1973); *President Franklin D. Roosevelt's Office Files, 1933–1945*, microfilm, project coordinator Robert E. Lester (Bethesda, MD: University Publications of America, 1990–1994); *The Public Papers and Addresses of Franklin D. Roosevelt*, compiled by Samuel I. Rosenman (New York: Russell & Russell, 1969); *Roosevelt and Frankfurter: Their Correspondence, 1928–1945*, annotated by Max Freedman (Boston: Little, Brown, 1968); *Wartime Correspondence Between President Roosevelt and Pope Pius XII*, with an introduction and notes by Myron C. Taylor (New York: Da Capo Press, 1975)

PRESIDENCY

Nomination: 1932: At the Democratic convention, held in Chicago, June 27–July 2,

1932, Roosevelt was selected as the presidential candidate on the fourth ballot; John Nance Garner of Texas was chosen as the vice-presidential candidate (Garner, another presidential hopeful, was promised the vice presidency in exchange for his release of his delegates, who would then go over to Roosevelt).

1936: At the Democratic convention, held in Philadelphia, June 23–27, 1936, Roosevelt and Garner were nominated for a second term with no opposition.

1940: The Democratic convention was held in Chicago, July 15–18, 1940; breaking with a two-term tradition established by George Washington, Roosevelt agreed to run for a third term and was nominated on the first ballot. Roosevelt's new choice for vice president, Henry Wallace of Iowa, was nominated in spite of initial opposition.

1944: The Democratic convention was held in Chicago, July 19–21, 1944; because of the US involvement in World War II, Roosevelt was renominated without opposition. Vice President Henry Wallace had alienated many Democrats and was replaced with Harry Truman of Missouri as the vice-presidential candidate.

Election: 1932: elected president on November 8, 1932

1936: reelected president on November 3, 1936

1940: reelected president on November 5, 1940

1944: reelected president on November 7, 1944

Opponent: 1932: Herbert Hoover, IA, Republican; Norman Thomas, NY, Socialist; William Foster, IL, Communist

1936: Alfred Landon, KS, Republican; William Lemke, ND, Union

1940: Wendell Wilkie, IN, Republican

1944: Thomas Dewey, NY, Republican

Vote Totals: 1932: Roosevelt, 22,809,638 popular, 472 electoral; Hoover, 15,758,901 popular, 59 electoral; Thomas, 881,951 popular, 0 electoral; Foster 103,311 popular, 0 electoral

1936: Roosevelt, 27,752,869 popular, 523 electoral; Landon, 16,674,665 popular, 8 electoral; Lemke, 882,479 popular, 0 electoral

1940: Roosevelt, 27,307,819 popular, 449 electoral; Wilke, 22,321,018 popular, 82 electoral

1944: Roosevelt, 25,606,585 popular, 432 electoral; Dewey, 22,014,745 popular, 99 electoral

Inauguration: 1932: March 4, 1933

1936: January 20, 1937

1940: January 20, 1941

1944: January 20, 1945

Vice President: John Nance Garner (1933–1941); Henry A. Wallace (1941–1945); Harry S. Truman (1945)

CABINET

Secretary of State: Cordell Hull, TN (1933–1944); Edward R. Stettinius, Jr., VA (1944–1945)

Secretary of the Treasury: William H. Woodin, NY (1933); Henry Morgenthau, Jr., NY (1934–1945)

Secretary of War: George H. Dern, UT (1933–1936); Harry H. Woodring, KS (1936–1940); Henry L. Stimson, NY (1940–1945)

Attorney General: Homer S. Cummings, CT (1933–1939); Frank Murphy, MI (1939–1940); Robert H. Jackson, NY (1940–1941); Francis B. Biddle, PA (1941–1945)

Postmaster General: James A. Farley, NY (1933–1940); Frank C. Walker, PA (1940–1945)

Secretary of the Navy: Claude A. Swanson, VA (1933–1939); Charles Edison, NJ (1940); Frank Knox, IL (1940–1944); James V. Forrestal, NY (1944–1945)

Secretary of Agriculture: Henry A. Wallace, IA (1933–1940); Claude R. Wickard, IN (1940–1945)

Secretary of the Interior: Harold L. Ickes, IL (1933–1945)

Secretary of Labor: Frances Perkins, NY (1933–1945)

Secretary of Commerce: Daniel C. Roper, SC (1933–1938); Harry L. Hopkins, NY (1938–1940); Jesse H. Jones, TX (1940–1945); Henry A. Wallace, IA (1945)

CONGRESS:

73rd Congress (1933–1935); Speaker of the House: Henry T. Rainey (IL, Democrat)

74th Congress (1935–1937); Speaker of the House: Joseph W. Byrns (TN, Democrat) [Note: Byrns died on June 4, 1936]; William B. Bankhead (AL, Democrat)

75th Congress (1937–1939); Speaker of the House: William B. Bankhead (AL, Democrat)
76th Congress (1939–1941); Speaker of the House: William B. Bankhead (AL, Democrat) [Note: Bankhead died on September 15, 1940]; Sam Rayburn (TX, Democrat)
77th Congress (1941–1943); Speaker of the House: Sam Rayburn (TX, Democrat)
78th Congress (1943–1945); Speaker of the House: Sam Rayburn (TX, Democrat)

SUPREME COURT APPOINTEES
Harlan Fiske Stone, NY; Chief Justice (1941–1946) [Note: Stone was originally named to the Court as an associate justice by President Coolidge and served from 1925 to 1941.]
Hugo Lafayette Black, AL; Associate Justice (1937–1971)
Stanley Forman Reed, KY; Associate Justice (1938–1957)
Felix Frankfurter, MA; Associate Justice (1939–1962)
William Orville Douglas, CT; Associate Justice (1939–1975)
Frank Murphy, MI; Associate Justice (1940–1949)
James Francis Byrnes, SC; Associate Justice (1941–1942)
Robert Houghwout Jackson, NY; Associate Justice (1941–1954)
Wiley Blount Rutledge, IA; Associate Justice (1943–1949)

MAJOR EVENTS OF THE ROOSEVELT ADMINISTRATION
◆ The 21st Amendment to the Constitution, repealing the prohibition of alcohol enacted by the 18th Amendment, is passed by Congress on February 20, 1933, and is ratified on December 5, 1933.
◆ The first three months of the new Roosevelt administration are referred to as the "First One Hundred Days," during which a large volume of legislation implementing the "New Deal" is passed.
◆ Frances Perkins is named the Secretary of Labor and becomes the first woman cabinet member, March 4, 1933.

◆ Roosevelt orders that all the nation's banks be closed from March 5 to March 13, 1933. The Emergency Banking Act is passed by Congress on March 9; it authorizes the reopening of banks after they have been found to be financially stable by examiners. Under the act, the United States ends its reliance (in May 1933) on the gold standard; citizens are required to surrender gold coins, bullion, and certificates to the government in exchange for paper money.
◆ On March 12, 1933, Roosevelt gives his first "fireside chat" radio broadcast.
◆ The Beer-Wine Revenue Act passes March 22, 1933, legalizing beer and wine and requiring them to be taxed.
◆ On March 31, 1933, the Civilian Conservation Corps (CCC), a New Deal program, is created by Congress. It is to hire unemployed single young men, between the ages of eighteen and twenty-five, to work on conservation projects in rural areas.
◆ The Federal Emergency Relief Act is passed on May 12, 1933; it creates the Federal Emergency Relief Administration (FERA) and gives federal monies to individual states for distribution to the poor and unemployed.
◆ On May 18, 1933, the Tennessee Valley Authority (TVA) is created by the federal government to promote the economic development of the Tennessee River basin; the TVA is responsible for the building of dams and reservoirs and the generation of electric power in the area.
◆ The Federal Securities Act, signed on May 27, 1933, regulates the public offering and sale of securities and provides for the establishment of the Securities and Exchange Commission (SEC), which will oversee securities markets.
◆ The Agricultural Adjustment Act of 1933 creates the Agricultural Adjustment Administration (AAA); it is part of an effort to stabilize farm income by controlling production and making loans to farmers.
◆ The National Industrial Recovery Act (NIRA), passed on June 16, 1933, creates the Federal Emergency Relief Administration (FERA) and the National Recovery

Administration (NRA), which will be responsible for the regulation of industry and the establishment of codes of fair competition.

◆ The Banking Act of 1933 (also called the Glass-Steagall Act) establishes the Federal Deposit Insurance Corporation (FDIC).

◆ On November 8, 1933, the Civil Works Administration (CWA) is set up and organized to provide work for tens of thousands of unemployed building schools, hospitals, bridges, and roads. It is intended as a short-term program, designed to carry the nation through a difficult winter. In May 1934 a severe dust storm in the western United States strips millions of tons of soil from the land; this is one of many storms of the mid-1930s that turns the area into a "Dust Bowl."

◆ The Gold Reserve Act, passed on January 30, 1934, orders that all gold privately held be surrendered to the US Treasury.

◆ The Civil Works Emergency Relief Act, passed on February 15, 1934, provides additional funding for civil works employment programs.

◆ On June 6, 1934, Roosevelt appoints Joseph P. Kennedy as the first SEC chairman.

◆ On June 19, 1934, the Federal Communications Commission (FCC) is created to regulate interstate and international communications. It is charged with overseeing all forms of wired and wireless communications and the bringing of communications services to rural areas.

◆ The Federal Credit Union Act of 1934 establishes federal credit unions in which members can safely deposit their money and from which they can obtain low-interest loans.

◆ The Emergency Relief Appropriations Act of 1935 creates the Works Progress Administration (WPA), which puts millions of unemployed Americans to work building roads, bridges, airports, and public buildings; the WPA also includes the Federal Arts Project, the Federal Writers' Project, and the Federal Theatre Project, which provide employment for artists and writers.

◆ The National Youth Administration is created in June 1935 to provide employment for students and those young people no longer in school but too young to obtain employment via WPA agencies.

◆ The National Labor Relations Act (Wagner Act) is passed on July 5, 1935, creating the National Labor Relations Board (NLRB) and guaranteeing workers the right to join unions.

◆ The Social Security Act of 1935 creates the Social Security Administration (SSA) and provides for a payroll tax to fund retirement, disability, and death benefits for American workers.

◆ On August 23, 1935, the Banking Act is passed, changing the structure of the Federal Reserve System.

◆ On August 30, 1935, the Revenue Act (Wealth Tax Act) is passed; it increases the tax rate on incomes of greater than $50,000 as well as estate taxes on larger estates. It also increases the corporate tax—except on small corporations, for which the rate is reduced.

◆ A Neutrality Act is passed by Congress in August 1935 (in the wake of Italy's attack on Ethiopia in May 1935) and allows the president to declare an embargo on arms shipments to the belligerents in foreign wars.

◆ The Soil Conservation Act, 1935, creates the Soil Conservation Service, a federal agency that will provide farmers with equipment, seed, seedlings, and planning assistance as part of an effort to reduce soil erosion.

◆ The National Industrial Recovery Act is declared unconstitutional by the Supreme Court, in *Schecter Poultry Corporation v. United States*, 1935, on the basis that the federal government is not empowered to regulate trade within a state.

◆ On September 9, 1935, Roosevelt attends the dedication of the Boulder Dam (originally called the Hoover Dam) on the Colorado River. (Its original name is reinstated in 1947.)

◆ A new Neutrality Act is passed by Congress in February 1936; it prohibits the United States from extending loans or credit to belligerents in foreign wars. (It amends the Neutrality Act of 1935.)

◆ The Rural Electrification Act creates the Rural Electrification Administration (REA) and appropriates federal funds for bringing electricity and telephone service to rural areas, 1936.

◆ The Walsh-Healey Act of 1936 mandates overtime pay for hours in excess of 8 hours per day or 40 hours per week, a minimum wage, and child labor standards for companies receiving government contracts.

◆ On November 3, 1936, Roosevelt is elected to his second term of office; he defeats Alfred M. Landon of Kansas.

◆ In January 1937 the 20th Amendment to the Constitution, ratified in 1933, takes effect, and the date of the presidential inauguration is changed from March 4 to January 20, to lessen the "lame duck" period during which the outgoing president remains in office.

◆ In January 1937 workers belonging to United Automobile Workers strike at the General Motors plant in Flint, Michigan.

◆ The Bankhead-Jones Farm Tenant Act, passed by Congress on July 22, 1937, creates the Farm Security Administration, which will make low-interest loans to tenant farmers and establish work camps for migrant farm workers.

◆ In May 1937 the Supreme Court affirms the constitutionality of both the old age benefit provisions and the unemployment compensation provisions of the Social Security Act.

◆ On September 1, 1937, the US Housing Authority (USHA) comes into being as part of the US Housing Act (the Wagner-Steagall Act); it will administer low-interest loans to communities for low-cost public housing.

◆ Another Neutrality Act (prompted by the outbreak of the Spanish Civil War in July 1936) is passed in 1937 and extends the prohibitions against providing arms or loans to belligerents in foreign wars to include participants in civil wars.

◆ Roosevelt proposes to increase the numbers of judges in all federal courts and to increase the number of Supreme Court justices to fifteen; his plan is criticized as an attempt at "court-packing" and fails, 1937.

◆ On January 2, 1938, Roosevelt establishes the March of Dimes.

◆ In May 1938 the House of Representatives forms the Committee to Investigate Un-American Activities; it is initially set up as a temporary committee and will investigate pro-Nazi and pro-fascist activities in the United States.

◆ On June 23, 1938, the Civil Aeronautics Authority is established.

◆ The Fair Labor Standards Act (FLSA), known as the Fair Wage and Hour Law, is passed on June 25, 1938; it establishes the first national minimum wage and mandates overtime pay.

◆ The Agricultural Adjustment Act of 1938 empowers the Agricultural Adjustment Administration to store surplus produce in years of high yield and to release the surplus in years of low yield.

◆ In 1939 Roosevelt closes US ports to the ships and submarines of all belligerent nations.

◆ On August 2, 1939, Albert Einstein writes a letter to Roosevelt in which he states that "[I]t may be possible to set up a nuclear chain reaction in a large mass of uranium." He goes on to say that such a chain reaction would liberate vast amounts of energy, and that "[t]his new phenomenon would also lead to the construction of bombs."

◆ A Neutrality Act is passed in November 1939 and allows a belligerent in a foreign war to purchase American arms if the foreign nation pays cash and transports the arms in its own ships.

◆ On May 25, 1940, Roosevelt establishes the Office for Emergency Management by executive order; the office will help to coordinate the efforts of relief agencies and of a number of federal agencies that have been established in response to the European war.

◆ The Alien Registration Act (also called the Smith Act), passes on June 29, 1940, and makes it illegal for anyone in the United States to "aid, abet, or advocate the overthrow of the government"; the act also requires all alien residents of the United States (over fourteen years of age) to register with the government and to file statements of their occupations and political beliefs.

◆ On July 1, 1940, Congress passes the Selective Training and Service Act, which institutes the first peacetime draft in US history.

❖ On November 5, 1940, Roosevelt is elected to his third term in office; he defeats Wendell Wilkie of Indiana.

❖ In a radio address given on December 29, 1940, Roosevelt calls on US industries and US workers to help to supply the United Kingdom with war materials, and says the United States should serve as the "arsenal of democracy."

❖ In a speech delivered before Congress on January 6, 1941 (later known as the "Four Freedoms" speech), Roosevelt notes that Americans "look forward to a world founded upon four essential human freedoms: the freedom of speech and expression," "the freedom of every person to worship God in his own way," "freedom from want," and "freedom from fear."

❖ In March 1941 Congress passes the Lend-Lease Act, which allows the United States to send war materials and necessities such as food to Great Britain and other nations in return for cash payments or "any other direct or indirect benefit which the President deems satisfactory."

❖ On March 19, 1941, Roosevelt establishes, by executive order, the National Defense Mediation Board for the settlement of labor disputes in defense industries.

❖ On June 28, 1941, the Office of Scientific Research and Development is established for physics research and the research development of nuclear fission.

❖ In June 1941 Roosevelt issues Executive Order 8802; it forbids employment discrimination on the part of companies that hold government contracts.

❖ The Office of Price Administration (OPA) is created in 1941 to curb inflation; after the outbreak of the war, the OPA will oversee the rationing of meat, sugar, shoes, rubber, gasoline, and other commodities.

❖ The Fair Employment Practices Committee (FEPC) is established in 1941 to investigate discrimination in employment in the defense industry.

❖ The Atlantic Charter is issued, on August 14, 1941, by Roosevelt and Churchill; it outlines common principles and goals of the United States and the United Kingdom, such as the freedom of all people to choose their own government, freedom of the seas, and disarmament. Much of the charter is later reflected in the charter of the United Nations.

❖ On November 26, 1941, Roosevelt signs the bill establishing the fourth Thursday in November as Thanksgiving Day, a national holiday.

❖ In November 1941 the US ambassador to Japan, Joseph Grew, informs the US State Department that the Japanese are contemplating an attack on Pearl Harbor; his warning is ignored.

❖ On December 7, 1941, in what is seen as a surprise attack, Japanese planes taking off from aircraft carriers bomb the US fleet at Pearl Harbor in Hawaii; the attack sinks five of the eight battleships there, damages other ships and US combat planes, and kills more than 2,400 Americans. Roosevelt, addressing the nation, calls it "a day that will live in infamy."

❖ On December 8, 1941, the United States declares war on Japan.

❖ On December 11, 1941, Germany and Italy declare war on the United States.

❖ US, British, and Canadian government officers meet at the Arcadia Conference, which takes place in Washington, DC, in late December 1941; it includes a meeting between Roosevelt and Churchill.

❖ On December 19, 1941, the Office of Censorship is established to monitor international communications, including mail communications, cables, newspapers, magazines, radio, and films.

❖ On January 12, 1942, Roosevelt establishes the National War Labor Board (NWLB) by executive order; it will set policy favorable to the creation of a strong wartime labor workforce.

❖ In a letter written January 15, 1942, Roosevelt asks the baseball commissioner to keep baseball going during the war, reasoning that people would be working longer and harder and were going to need recreation.

❖ On January 20, 1942, Congress decrees that daylight savings time will be inaugurated immediately throughout the United States; the law remains in effect until the end of September 1945.

◆ The Emergency Price Control Act is signed by Roosevelt on January 30, 1942, and establishes an Office of Price Administration that can freeze prices and rents.

◆ On February 19, 1942, Roosevelt signs Executive Order 9066; it enables the Secretary of War to define geographical areas from which "any and all persons may be excluded," which leads to the detention and internment of Japanese-Americans.

◆ The Bataan Peninsula in the Philippines falls to the Japanese on April 9, 1942; 70,000 US and Filipino prisoners are force-marched on a 63-mile march through the jungle. It becomes known as the Bataan Death March. As many as 10,000 prisoners die from starvation, exhaustion, and the bayonet wounds they have received from Japanese soldiers.

◆ On April 18, 1942, US planes bomb Tokyo, in a mission led by Lieutenant Colonel James ("Jimmy") Doolittle.

◆ The Stabilization Act of 1942 is passed by Congress on October 2, 1942, and freezes wages, prices, and salaries to the levels of September 15, 1942.

◆ In the Battle of the Coral Sea, May 4–8, 1942, the Allies block the Japanese plan to invade Port Moresby in New Guinea, although at the cost of three US ships—a destroyer, a fleet carrier, and an oiler.

◆ In May 1942 the Philippines surrender to Japan.

◆ On May 15, 1942, Roosevelt signs the bill that creates the Women's Auxiliary Army Corps (WAAC); women are used primarily in clerical and communications jobs.

◆ On May 30, 1942, the British launch a one thousand bomber raid on Cologne.

◆ The Office of War Information (OWI) is created on June 13, 1942; it will consolidate several federal information offices. The OWI will create a photographic record of the domestic war effort, release war news, and launch a propaganda campaign abroad.

◆ The Revenue Act of 1942 increases income tax and allows deductions for medical expenses and some investments.

◆ The Battle of Midway, June 4, 1942, is a turning point in the war in the Pacific. The Americans intercept Japanese intelligence, which enables the US Pacific Fleet to surprise the Japanese fleet and sink four Japanese carriers. (One US carrier is lost.)

◆ From August 1942 through February 1943, various battles at Guadalcanal (one of the Solomon Islands in the South Pacific) and in the seas around the island result in a US victory over the Japanese, from whom the Americans seize control of the Guadalcanal airfield.

◆ On October 23, 1942, British forces under Generals Harold Alexander and Bernard Montgomery defeat German General Erwin Rommel and the *Deutsches Afrika Korps* at El Alamein in Egypt, which turns back the German advance in North Africa and enables the Allies to retain control of the Suez Canal.

◆ In early November 1942 Operation Torch, the Allied invasion of French North Africa, is launched with Dwight D. Eisenhower in command.

◆ In January 1943 the Casablanca Conference brings together Roosevelt, Churchill, and General Charles de Gaulle; the participants agree to call for unconditional surrender from the Axis powers.

◆ British troops capture Tripoli, Libya, January 23, 1943.

◆ From the summer of 1942 to early February 1943, the Germans attempt to capture Stalingrad in the Soviet Union, with estimated losses of 800,000 Axis soldiers and more than a million Soviet soldiers. On January 31, 1943, German Field Marshal Friedrich Paulus surrenders to the Soviet Union, which deals an enormous blow to the German war effort.

◆ From April 19 to May 16, 1943, Polish Jews in the Warsaw ghetto resist their deportations by the Nazis to the Treblinka extermination camp; against overwhelming odds, the Jews resist for nearly a month before the Nazis prevail.

◆ On April 13, 1943, the 200th anniversary of Thomas Jefferson's birth, Roosevelt dedicates the Jefferson Memorial.

◆ From July 5 to August 23, 1943, the Battle of Kursk takes place in western Russia; the Germans attack a bulge in the front lines of the Soviet defenses, but their tanks meet stiff resistance. It is the largest tank battle (more than 6,000 tanks take part) in history and helps the Soviets take the offensive.

◆ Sicily is invaded by the Allies on July 10, 1943.

◆ On July 22, 1943, US forces under General Patton take Palermo in Sicily; on August 17, 1943, British forces under General Montgomery take Messina.

◆ On July 25, 1943, Italian King Victor Emmanuel has Mussolini arrested and Marshal Pietro Bagdoglio, the Army Chief of Staff, is made the head of a new government. Bagdoglio begins negotiations with the Allies for peace.

◆ From August 11 to 24, 1943, Roosevelt and Churchill meet at the Quebec Conference to discuss plans for the invasions of mainland Italy and of France.

◆ On September 3, 1943, the Allies land on the mainland of Italy; on September 8 Italy surrenders to the Allies, although the Germans are still in possession of much of the Italian peninsula.

◆ On October 13, 1943, Italy declares war on Germany.

◆ Roosevelt, Churchill, and Stalin meet in Tehran, Iran, November 28 to December 1, 1943, and Stalin agrees that the Soviets will fight an offensive against the Nazis on the eastern front to coincide with the planned Allied invasion of Nazi-occupied France on the western front.

◆ Because of China's status as an ally of the United States during the war, on December 17, 1943, Roosevelt signs an act repealing the Chinese Exclusion Acts. The new act sets quotas for Chinese immigration.

◆ On December 24, 1943, Roosevelt appoints General Dwight D. Eisenhower as supreme commander of the Allied troops who are in

preparation for "Operation Overlord," the planned Allied invasion of France.

◆ In January 1944 American troops land at Anzio, just south of Naples and less than forty miles from Rome, in Italy. Surrounded and penned in by the Germans for several months, the Allies break free in May and advance toward Rome.

◆ In January 1944 Russian troops cross into Poland.

◆ In April 1944 the Supreme Court rules, in *Smith v. Allwright*, that a whites-only Democratic primary in Texas is unconstitutional.

◆ In May 1944 Monte Cassino, Italy, falls to the Allies, which helps to break the Germans' Gustav Line (a defensive line).

◆ On June 4, 1944, Rome is taken by American forces.

◆ On June 6, 1944 (known as D-Day), 156,000 Allies commanded by General Dwight D. Eisenhower storm the beaches of Normandy in France.

◆ On June 15–16, 1944, the Battle of the Philippine Sea is fought as US troops take the Mariana Islands; US fighter pilots destroy more than 400 Japanese fighter planes, which virtually annihilates Japanese air power.

◆ On June 22, 1944, Roosevelt signs the Servicemen's Readjustment Act (later known as the GI Bill of Rights), which will provide veterans with funds for education, housing, unemployment pay, and assistance in finding jobs.

◆ From July 1 to 22, 1944, delegates from forty-four nations meet at the Bretton Woods Conference in New Hampshire and establish the International Bank for Reconstruction and Development (later known as the World Bank) and the International Money Fund (IMF).

◆ In August 1944 the Allies land in southern France.

◆ From August 21 to October 7, 1944, representatives of the United Kingdom, China, the Soviet Union, and the United States meet at the Dumbarton Oaks Conference in Washington, DC, to discuss the formation after the war of the United Nations.

◆ On August 25, 1944, Paris is liberated by Allied troops, led by a division of the Free French forces; the German forces in Paris surrender.

◆ From September 11 to 16, 1944, at the second Quebec Conference (the Octagon Conference), Roosevelt and Churchill decide to advance against Germany on two fronts.

◆ In September 1944 in "Operation Market Garden," thousands of Allied paratroopers are dropped behind German lines to secure bridges in Holland and thus provide avenues for the Allies to advance into Germany; the paratroopers succeed initially but meet stiff resistance at Arnhem, and Operation Market Garden ultimately fails.

◆ From October 23 to 26, 1944, the Battle of Leyte Gulf is fought; it begins with a US assault on the Philippine island of Leyte and includes several naval battles that take place in the surrounding seas; the US losses are six ships, compared with Japanese losses of twenty-eight ships.

◆ On November 7, 1944, Roosevelt is elected to his fourth term in office; he defeats Thomas Dewey of New York.

◆ From late 1944 through the first half of 1945, US planes (mostly B-29s) bomb Japan, initially with little effect but eventually causing great devastation.

◆ From December 16, 1944, to January 16, 1945, the Battle of the Bulge (also called the Ardennes offensive or the Battle of the Ardennes), representing the last German offensive on the western front, is fought; the German army tries unsuccessfully to push the Allies, who are approaching Germany, back into southern Belgium.

◆ In January 1945 US troops land on the main Philippine island of Luzon; they reach Manila on February 2, 1945.

◆ On January 26, 1945, Soviet troops liberate Auschwitz, the largest of the Nazi concentration camps, where it is estimated that between 1 million and 1.5 million people were killed.

◆ From February 4 to 11, 1945, Roosevelt, Churchill, and Stalin come together for the Yalta Conference, in the city of Yalta (on the Black Sea), to discuss the final attack on Germany and spheres of influence in post-war Europe.

◆ The United States fire-bombs the city of Dresden, Germany, on February 8, 1945, killing about 45,000 people.

◆ On February 13–14, 1945, the Allies further bomb the city of Dresden, virtually destroying the city.

◆ On February 19, 1945, US forces land on Iwo Jima and finally secure the island by March 16, which frees up the island for use as an air base by US fighter planes.

◆ In March 1945 Allied forces reach the Rhine River and, at the end of the month, cross it and advance into Germany and toward Berlin.

◆ On April 1, 1945, US forces land on Okinawa.

◆ The Battle of Berlin begins, April 16, 1945, with an attack on the city by the Soviet army; the city surrenders on May 2, 1945, after Hitler's suicide on April 30, 1945.

◆ In April 1945 at the San Francisco Conference, representatives from forty-six countries meet to establish a charter for the United Nations.

◆ Roosevelt dies at Warm Springs, Georgia, on April 12, 1945.

MAJOR US AND WORLD EVENTS, 1933–1945

◆ In February 1933, after Roosevelt was elected but prior to his inauguration, Giuseppe Zangara attempts to assassinate Roosevelt during a public appearance in Miami but misses and instead kills Anton Cermak, the mayor of Chicago. Zangara, later executed, is thought to be either insane from the pain of an untreated ulcer or a hit man backed by the Chicago mob.

◆ On March 23, 1933, the Enabling Act is passed by the German Reichstag; it removes legislative powers from the Reichstag and transfers them to the cabinet. The cabinet is headed by the chancellor, Adolf Hitler, who thus becomes dictator.

◆ Japan (in March 1933) and Germany (in October 1933) leave the League of Nations.

◆ In May 1933 Mohandas K. Gandhi endures a three-week hunger strike in protest against the treatment of the "untouchables," the lowest caste in Indian society.

◆ A world's fair, dubbed the Century of Progress International Exhibition, is held in Chicago, Illinois, from May 27 to November 12, 1933, and from May 26 to October 31, 1934.

◆ Settling a dispute between Denmark and Norway, the International Court at The Hague determines that Greenland belongs to Denmark.

◆ On July 22, 1933, Wiley Post completes the first solo flight around the world, which has lasted 7 days and 19 hours.

◆ In July 1933 all political parties other than the Nazi Party become illegal in Germany.

◆ Gertrude Stein publishes *The Autobiography of Alice B. Toklas*, 1933.

◆ Dashiell Hammett publishes *The Thin Man*, 1933.

◆ In 1933 Erle Stanley Gardner publishes *The Case of the Velvet Claws* and *The Case of the Sulky Girl*, the first two Perry Mason mysteries.

◆ Sergei Prokofiev composes *Peter and the Wolf*, 1933.

◆ Igor Stravinsky composes *Persephone*, 1933.

◆ Popular music hits of 1933 include Eddy Duchin's "Night and Day," Ethel Waters's "Stormy Weather," and Bing Crosby's "Shadow Waltz."

◆ Notable films of 1933 include Laurel and Hardy's *Sons of the Desert*, *Queen Christina* with Greta Garbo, *Little Women* with Katharine Hepburn, *King Kong* with Fay Wray, *The Invisible Man* with Claude Rains, the Marx Brothers' *Duck Soup*, *42nd Street* with Ruby Keeler, and *Dinner at Eight* with Billie Burke, Lionel Barrymore, John Barrymore, Marie Dressler, Jean Harlow, and Wallace Beery.

◆ On May 23, 1934, Clyde Barrow and Bonnie Parker, believed to be guilty of automobile theft, bank robbery, kidnapping, and murder, are shot and killed by police officers near Sailes, Louisiana.

◆ On May 28, 1934, five children are born to Olivia and Elzire Dionne in Ontario, Canada; the five babies become known as the Dionne Quintuplets.

◆ On June 29, 1934, the "Night of the Long Knives" sets off a political purge, during which Hitler and members of his inner circle arrest and execute political opponents, including Ernst Röhm, the head of the Sturmabteilung (SA), a paramilitary group that protected the Nazis (but was feared to be plotting against Hitler).

◆ On July 22, 1934, gangster John Dillinger is fatally shot by police while leaving the Biograph movie theater in Chicago.

◆ On August 2, 1934, President Paul von Hindenburg of Germany dies; Adolf Hitler becomes the Führer and Chancellor of Germany, doing away with the title of president.

◆ On August 13, 1934, Al Capp's "L'il Abner" comic strip debuts.

◆ From October 15, 1934, to October 1935, the Chinese Communist Army, fleeing Chiang Kai-shek's Nationalist forces, endures a year-long, 6,000-mile trek called the "Long March"; the Communists lose nearly 90 percent of their 85,000 strong army on the march.

◆ On November 27, 1934, gangster Lester M. Gillis, better known as "Baby Face Nelson," is fatally wounded in a gun battle with FBI agents near Barrington, Illinois; two FBI agents are killed as well.

◆ At the end of December 1934 Japan announces that it will withdraw from the Washington Naval Treaty of 1922 and the London Naval Treaty of 1930 when they expire in 1936; Japan plans to build its Yamato-class battleships.

◆ In 1934 a former burlesque hall, the Apollo Theater in New York City, opens with "Jazz à la Carte," marking the beginning of the theater's existence as the premier venue for African-American talent.

◆ Robert Graves publishes *I, Claudius*, 1934.

◆ Henry Miller publishes *Tropic of Cancer*, 1934.

◆ F. Scott Fitzgerald publishes *Tender Is the Night*, 1934.

◆ James M. Cain publishes *The Postman Always Rings Twice*, 1934.

◆ Agatha Christie publishes *Murder on the Orient Express*, 1934.

◆ Evelyn Waugh publishes *A Handful of Dust*, 1934.

◆ Popular music hits of 1934 include Bing Crosby's "Love in Bloom," the Paul Whiteman Orchestra's "Smoke Gets in Your Eyes" and "You're the Top," and Benny Goodman's "Moon Glow."

◆ Notable films of 1934 include *The Thin Man* with William Powell and Myrna Loy, *The Scarlet Pimpernel* with Leslie Howard, *Of Human Bondage* with Leslie Howard and Bette Davis, *It's a Gift* with W. C. Fields, *It Happened One Night* with Clark Gable and Claudette Colbert, *The Gay Divorcee* with Fred Astaire and Ginger Rogers, and *Cleopatra* with Claudette Colbert.

◆ In March 1935 Hitler announces that Germany is rearming in defiance of the Treaty of Versailles that had ended the war of 1914–1918; other European nations protest but take no action.

◆ On September 8, 1935, Senator Huey "Kingfish" Long of Louisiana is assassinated, presumably by Dr. Carl Austin Weiss, the son-in-law of one of Long's political enemies. Weiss is immediately shot and killed by Long's bodyguards.

◆ In October 1935 Italy under Mussolini invades Ethiopia; the Italians drop gas bombs on the Ethiopian people.

◆ In 1935 Reza Shah Pahlavi asks that his country be referred to as Iran, not Persia.

◆ In 1935 Parker Brothers introduces its new board game, Monopoly.

◆ Charles F. Richter and Beno Gutenberg of the California Institute of Technology develop the Richter Scale for measuring the magnitude of earthquakes, 1935.

◆ In 1935 architect Frank Lloyd Wright designs Fallingwater, a home near Pittsburgh, Pennsylvania, for the family of Edgar J. Kaufmann.

◆ On May 25, 1935, Babe Ruth hits his record 714th home run in his final season of baseball.

◆ John O'Hara publishes *Butterfield 8*, 1935.

◆ James T. Farrell publishes *Studs Lonigan: A Trilogy*, 1935.

◆ Laura Ingalls Wilder publishes *Little House on the Prairie*, 1935.

◆ George Gershwin's *Porgy and Bess* is first performed, 1935.

◆ Popular music hits of 1935 include the Dorsey Brothers Orchestra's "I'm Always Chasing Shadows," Louis Prima's "The Lady in Red," and Guy Lombardo and His Royal Canadians' "Red Sails in the Sunset."

◆ Notable films of 1935 include *Alice Adams* with Katharine Hepburn, James Whale's *Bride of Frankenstein* with Elsa Lanchester and Boris Karloff, *Captain Blood* with Errol Flynn and Olivia de Havilland, *David Copperfield* with Freddie Bartholomew and W. C. Fields, *The Littlest Rebel* with Shirley Temple, Alfred Hitchcock's *The 39 Steps*, *A Tale of Two Cities* with Ronald Colman, and *Mutiny on the Bounty* with Clark Gable and Charles Laughton.

◆ On January 20, 1936, King George V of the United Kingdom dies, and his son, Edward VIII, becomes king.

◆ In January 1936 the Baseball Hall of Fame chooses its first honorees: Ty Cobb, Babe Ruth, Honus Wagner, Christy Mathewson, and Walter Johnson.

◆ On March 7, 1936, Adolf Hitler announces that Germany is repudiating the portion of the Treaty of Versailles that had established the Rhineland area of Germany as a demilitarized zone and that German troops will occupy the supposed demilitarized zone.

◆ In May 1936 Italy formalizes its conquest of Ethiopia by annexing the country.

◆ A military uprising on July 17, 1936, begins the Spanish Civil War, which pits the ruling Republican Party against the Nationalist Party led by General Francisco Franco.

◆ On October 25, 1936, the Axis agreement of Germany and Italy is announced.

◆ Beginning on November 18, 1936, the United Automobile Workers (UAW) launches a series of sit-down strikes against General Motors (GM), which eventually shuts down seventeen GM plants before an agreement is reached in early 1937.

◆ In November 1936 the Bay Bridge between San Francisco and Oakland, California, opens.

◆ On November 23, 1936, Henry Luce publishes the first issue of *Life* magazine, with a cover photograph of Fort Peck Dam by Margaret Bourke-White.

◆ On November 25, 1936, the Anti-Communist Pact of Germany and Japan (against the Soviet Union) is announced.

◆ On December 11, 1936, King Edward VIII of the United Kingdom abdicates the throne in order to marry Wallis Simpson, an American divorcee; Edward's brother becomes King George VI.

◆ Margaret Mitchell publishes *Gone with the Wind*, 1936.

◆ Ayn Rand publishes *We the Living*, 1936.

◆ William Faulkner publishes *Absalom, Absalom!*, 1936.

◆ British mathematician Alan Turing publishes his paper "On Computable Numbers," 1936.

◆ John Maynard Keynes publishes *General Theory of Employment, Interest, and Money*, 1936.

◆ Popular music hits of 1936 include Bing Crosby's "Pennies from Heaven," Tommy Dorsey's "Alone," Fred Astaire's "The Way You Look Tonight," and Benny Goodman's "The Glory of Love."

◆ Notable films of 1936 include *Camille* with Greta Garbo, *The Great Ziegfeld* with William Powell, Charlie Chaplin's *Modern Times*, Frank Capra's *Mr. Deeds Goes to Town* with Gary Cooper, *My Man Godfrey* with William Powell and Carole Lombard, *The Petrified Forest* with Humphrey Bogart, *Rose Marie* with Nelson Eddy and Jeanette MacDonald, and *San Francisco* with Clark Gable, Jeanette MacDonald, and Spencer Tracy.

◆ In 1936 German filmmaker Leni Riefenstahl makes the Nazi propaganda films *Triumph of the Will* and *Olympia*; they are hailed as critical successes but later denounced as the propaganda pieces that they are.

◆ The Second Sino-Japanese War (1937–1945) begins in 1937 when Chinese military forces rebel against Japan's occupation of eastern China.

◆ On May 6, 1937, the German airship *Hindenburg* bursts into flames as it is attempting to moor at Lakehurst, New Jersey, after a flight from Frankfurt, Germany; of the ninety-seven passengers and crew aboard, thirty-six people die.

◆ On May 27, 1937, the Golden Gate Bridge between San Francisco and Marin County, California, opens.

◆ On July 3, 1937, while attempting an around-the-world flight, pilot Amelia Earhart and her navigator Fred Noonan vanish.

◆ The British Broadcasting Corporation (BBC) televises both the coronation of King George VI and the Wimbledon tennis matches in 1937.

◆ Agatha Christie publishes *Death on the Nile*, 1937.

◆ J. R. R. Tolkien publishes *The Hobbit*, 1937.

◆ John Steinbeck publishes *Of Mice and Men*, 1937.

◆ Isaak Dinesen publishes *Out of Africa*, 1937.

◆ Zora Neale Hurston publishes *Their Eyes Were Watching God*, 1937.

◆ Popular music hits of 1937 include Benny Goodman's "Goodnight, My Love," Bing Crosby's "Sweet Leilani," Guy Lombardo's "September in the Rain," and Tommy Dorsey's "Once in a While."

◆ Notable films of 1937 include Walt Disney's *Snow White and the Seven Dwarfs*, *The Prisoner of Zenda* with Ronald Colman, *Captains Courageous* with Freddie Bartholomew, *The Good Earth* with Paul Muni and Luise Rainer, Frank Capra's *Lost Horizon* with Ronald Colman and Jane Wyatt, *Nothing Sacred* with Carole Lombard, *Stage Door* with Katharine Hepburn, *Stella Dallas* with Barbara Stanwyck, Laurel and Hardy's *Way Out West*, the Marx Brother's *A Day at the Races*, and *Dead End* with Humphrey Bogart and the Dead End Kids.

◆ An exhibit of surrealistic art is held in Paris from January 17 to February 24, 1938, and includes works by Salvador Dali, Marcel Duchamp, Marc Chagall, Rene Magritte, Man Ray, and others.

◆ Adolf Hitler announces the Anschluss (annexation) of Austria by Germany, March 13, 1938.

◆ On June 22, 1938, boxer Joe Louis defeats Max Schmeling, who had defeated Louis in 1936, with a knockout in the first round.

◆ On September 30, 1938, British Prime Minister Neville Chamberlain, French Prime Minister Édouard Deladier, and German Chancellor Adolf Hitler sign the Munich Pact, which recognizes Germany's claim to the Sudetenland, an area under Czechoslovakian rule.

◆ Germany marches into the Sudetenland on October 1, 1938; on October 5 Czech president Edvard Benes resigns.

◆ On October 27, 1938, E. I. du Pont de Nemours, Inc., announces the invention of nylon, the first synthetic fiber.

◆ On October 30, 1938, Orson Welles, in a radio broadcast, reads from *The War of the Worlds*, a story by H. G. Wells; the reading resembles a news broadcast, and thousands of listeners are convinced that the United States is being invaded by Martians.

◆ On November 1, 1938, Seabiscuit beats War Admiral in a match race between the two champion race horses; the race is broadcast on radio.

◆ The night of November 9–10, 1938, during which thousands of Jewish-owned businesses in Germany are looted and destroyed by the Nazis, becomes known as "Kristallnacht" (the "night of broken glass").

◆ In 1938 American tennis player Don Budge becomes the first man to win the Grand Slam of tennis (he wins the Australian Open, the French Open, the Championships at Wimbledon, and the US Open).

◆ On June 1, 1938, the first *Superman* comic book, written by Jerry Siegel and with illustrations by Joseph Schuster, is published by Action Comics.

◆ Thornton Wilder's play *Our Town* opens on Broadway, 1938.

◆ Elizabeth Bowen publishes *The Death of the Heart*, 1938.

◆ Graham Greene publishes *Brighton Rock*, 1938.

◆ Eric Knight publishes *Lassie, Come Home*, 1938.

◆ Daphne du Maurier publishes *Rebecca*, 1938.

◆ Marjorie Kinnan Rawlings publishes *The Yearling*, 1938.

◆ Popular music hits of 1938 include Artie Shaw's "Begin the Beguine," Ella Fitzgerald and Chick Webb's "A-Tisket, A-Tasket," Benny Goodman's "Don't Be That Way," and Bing Crosby's "I've Got a Pocketful of Dreams."

◆ Notable films of 1938 include *Algiers* with Charles Boyer, *The Adventures of Robin Hood* with Errol Flynn and Olivia de Havilland, *Bringing Up Baby* with Cary Grant and Katharine Hepburn, *Jezebel* with Bette Davis and Henry Fonda, Alfred Hitchcock's *The Lady Vanishes*, *Pygmalion* with Leslie Howard and Wendy Hiller, Frank Capra's *You Can't Take It with You* with Jean Arthur and James Stewart, *Holiday* with Cary Grant and Katharine Hepburn, and *Boys Town* with Spencer Tracy.

◆ Germany begins occupying the rest of Czechoslovakia in March 1939.

◆ Franco and the Nationalists take Madrid March 28, 1939, which ends the Spanish Civil War.

◆ Italy invades Albania, April 7, 1939.

◆ Hungary leaves the League of Nations in April 1939, and Spain leaves in May 1939.

◆ On May 22, 1939, the Pact of Steel, an agreement between Germany and Italy that strengthens their existing alliance, is announced.

◆ On June 12, 1939, the Baseball Hall of Fame opens in Cooperstown, New York.

◆ In August 1939 Hitler and Stalin enter into a secret agreement whereby Germany will be free to invade Poland without fear of interference from the Soviet Union; effectively, the Soviet Union will take eastern Poland, Finland, and the Baltic states, while Germany will take western Poland.

◆ On September 1, 1939, German troops march into Poland.

◆ The United Kingdom, France, and Australia declare war on Germany, September 3, 1939.

◆ In mid-September 1939 the United States declares its neutrality, while Canada and South Africa declare war on Germany.

◆ On September 27, 1939, Warsaw surrenders; Germany completes its annexation of western Poland by early October.

◆ Georg Elsner attempts to assassinate Hitler on November 8, 1939, by planting a bomb at the Bürgerbräukeller in Munich; the bomb detonates thirteen minutes after Hitler leaves and kills eight people.

◆ On November 30, 1939, the Soviet Union invades Finland.

◆ The Battle for the Atlantic begins in 1939 and lasts throughout the war, as German U-boats attempt to keep supplies from reaching the United Kingdom.

◆ In 1939 theoretical physicist J. Robert Oppenheimer, with Hartland Snyder, publishes an article about what will later be called black holes; with George M. Volkoff, he publishes an article about neutron stars.

◆ John Steinbeck publishes *The Grapes of Wrath*, 1939.

◆ Raymond Chandler publishes *The Big Sleep*, 1939.

◆ James Joyce publishes *Finnegan's Wake*, 1939.

◆ Katherine Anne Porter publishes *Pale Horse, Pale Rider*, 1939.

◆ Nathanael West publishes *The Day of the Locust*, 1939.

◆ Bob Kane creates the comic *Batman* for DC Comics, 1939.

◆ Popular music hits of 1939 include Judy Garland's "Over the Rainbow," Will Glahe's "Beer Barrel Polka," Larry Clinton's "Deep Purple," and Glenn Miller's "Stairway to the Stars."

◆ Notable films of 1939 include *Gone with the Wind* with Vivien Leigh and Clark Gable, *The Hunchback of Notre Dame* with Charles Laughton, Ernst Lubitsch's *Ninotchka* with Greta Garbo, John Ford's *Stagecoach* with John Wayne, *Wuthering Heights* with Merle Oberon and Laurence Olivier, Frank Capra's *Mr. Smith Goes to Washington* with James Stewart, *Dark Victory* with Bette Davis, *Destry Rides Again* with James Stewart and Marlene Dietrich, *Goodbye, Mr. Chips* with Robert Donat, and *The Wizard of Oz* with Judy Garland, Ray Bolger, Jack Haley, and Bert Lahr.

◆ The war between Finland and the Soviet Union ends on March 12, 1940; in the armistice the Soviet Union dictates harsh terms to Finland.

◆ On March 18, 1940, Hitler and Mussolini hold a meeting (one of three) at Brenner Pass, between Austria and Italy, to discuss their alliance.

◆ On April 9, 1940, Germany invades Norway. Norwegian army officer Vidkun Quisling declares himself head of the government; his name later becomes a synonym for "traitor" and as such he is executed after the war.

◆ On May 10, 1940, Germany invades the Netherlands, Belgium, and Luxembourg.

◆ On May 13, 1940, Germany begins the invasion of France.

◆ At the end of May 1940 Belgium surrenders to Germany.

◆ In May and June 1940 more than 300,000 British, French, and Belgian troops, in danger of being overrun by German forces, are evacuated from Dunkirk, France, to the United Kingdom.

◆ On June 10, 1940, Italy declares war on France and the United Kingdom; Canada declares war on Italy; Norway surrenders to Germany.

◆ The Germans march into Paris on June 13, 1940; France surrenders to Germany on June 22.

◆ In June 1940 hundreds of Polish prisoners are among the first sent to the Auschwitz concentration camp.

◆ From July to September 1940 German planes bomb Great Britain in the Battle for Britain; 57 consecutive nights of bombing begin over London on September 10, in what is called "the Blitz."

◆ A new French government that will cooperate with the Germans is established in Vichy, France, in July 1940.

◆ In August 1940 Lithuania, Latvia, and Estonia are made part of the Soviet Union.

◆ On August 20, 1940, exiled Russian revolutionary Leon Trotsky is assassinated in Mexico City, Mexico, by Ramón Mercader.

◆ Four young French boys, hiking in the woods in the south of France, discover caves at Lascaux whose walls are adorned with prehistoric paintings, mostly of animals, from about 15,000 years BCE.

❖ On September 27, 1940, the Tripartite Pact between Germany, Italy, and Japan is announced.

❖ On October 28, 1940, Italy invades Greece.

❖ On the night of November 11–12, 1940, in the Battle of Taranto, the British Royal Navy carries out the first air strike launched from an aircraft carrier in history against the Italian fleet anchored in the harbor of Taranto; it destroys the Italian ships in the harbor and thus secures supply lines to British troops in North Africa.

❖ In November 1940 Germany bombs the English city of Coventry and the British bomb the German city of Hamburg, resulting in great destruction in each city.

❖ Hungary, Romania, and Slovakia join the Axis powers in November 1940.

❖ On December 8, 1940, British forces attack Italian forces in Egypt.

❖ The 1940 census shows a US population of 132.2 million people.

❖ In February 1940 Frank Sinatra debuts as a singer with the Tommy Dorsey Band.

❖ Richard Wright publishes *Native Son*, 1940.

❖ Dr. Seuss (Theodore Seuss Geisel) publishes *Horton Hatches an Egg*, 1940.

❖ Raymond Chandler publishes *Farewell, My Lovely*, 1940.

❖ Ernest Hemingway publishes *For Whom the Bell Tolls*, 1940.

❖ Carson McCullers publishes *The Heart Is a Lonely Hunter*, 1940.

❖ Sergei Rachmaninoff composes *Symphonic Dances*, 1940.

❖ Dmitri Shostakovich's *Piano Quintet* is premiered, 1940.

❖ Popular music hits of 1940 include Glenn Miller's "In the Mood" and "Tuxedo Junction," Bing Crosby's "Only Forever," and Tommy Dorsey's "I'll Never Smile Again" (with Frank Sinatra on vocals).

❖ Notable films of 1940 include Walt Disney's *Fantasia*, Alfred Hitchcock's *Foreign Correspondent* with Joel McCrea, *The Bank Dick* with W. C. Fields, Howard Hawks's *His Girl Friday* with Cary Grant and Rosalind Russell, *The Letter* with Bette Davis, *The Mark of Zorro* with Douglas Fairbanks, Jr., George Cukor's *The Philadelphia Story* with Katharine Hepburn and Cary Grant, Walt Disney's *Pinocchio*, Alfred Hitchcock's *Rebecca* with Joan Fontaine and Laurence Olivier, *The Thief of Bagdad* with Sabu, *The Shop Around the Corner* with James Stewart and Margaret Sullavan, John Ford's *The Grapes of Wrath* with Henry Fonda, and Charlie Chaplin's *The Great Dictator*.

❖ On January 21 and 22, 1941, Australian and British troops capture Tobruk, Libya, from Italian forces.

❖ On February 12, 1941, German Field Marshal Erwin Rommel arrives in North Africa as the commander of the *Deutsches Afrika Korps;* his military brilliance will earn him the nickname "Desert Fox."

❖ Bulgaria joins the Axis powers, March 1, 1941.

❖ The Battle of Matapan, March 27–March 29, 1941, results in a British naval victory over Italian naval forces that have assembled off Cape Matapan, at the southern tip of Greece.

❖ On April 6, 1941, German forces invade Greece and Yugoslavia.

❖ In mid-April 1941 Yugoslavia and Greece fall to the Axis powers.

❖ Nazi Party leader Rudolf Hess parachutes into Scotland on May 10, 1941, and claims to want to negotiate a peace agreement with the British government; he is arrested and held as a prisoner of war by the British throughout the war.

❖ On May 20, 1941, Germans troops invade Crete.

❖ On May 24, 1941, the German battleship *Bismarck* sinks the British battle cruiser *Hood*; three days later, the *Bismarck* is sunk by British aircraft and ships that have pursued it.

❖ In May 1941 Bob Hope performs his first USO show for American soldiers in California and makes his first USO tour in 1942.

❖ In May 1941 the British Royal Navy takes possession of an Enigma cryptography machine (found on a captured German submarine) that is later used to break the code of German naval vessels.

❖ On June 22, 1941, in what is called "Operation Barbarossa," the German Army invades the Soviet Union; Germany commits more than three million men to the campaign but has underestimated the USSR's strength, and the German troops are unprepared for the devastating Russian winter, which arrives early that year and is even colder than usual.

◆ At the end of July 1941 Hitler asks his political heir, Hermann Göring, to begin carrying out the "final solution," the plan to exterminate European Jews.

◆ In September 1941 German troops begin the siege of Leningrad in the Soviet Union.

◆ By the end of November 1941 German troops are near Moscow, but continue to meet with fierce resistance from Soviet troops and to take a beating from the Russian winter.

◆ A. J. Cronin publishes *The Keys of the Kingdom*, 1941.

◆ James M. Cain publishes *Mildred Pierce*, 1941.

◆ Budd Schulberg publishes *What Makes Sammy Run?*, 1941.

◆ C. S. Lewis publishes *The Screwtape Letters*, 1941.

◆ Eudora Welty publishes *A Curtain of Green*, 1941.

◆ W. Somerset Maugham publishes *Up at the Villa*, 1941.

◆ The FCC issues licenses to ten television stations and commercial television gets underway in 1941; one of the first nationally syndicated shows is the game show *Truth or Consequences*.

◆ Popular music hits of 1941 include Glenn Miller's "Chattanooga Choo-Choo," the Andrews Sisters' "Boogie Woogie Bugle Boy," and Jimmy Dorsey's "Maria Elena."

◆ Notable films of 1941 include Orson Welles's *Citizen Kane*, Preston Sturges's *Sullivan's Travels* with Joel McCrea, Frank Capra's *Meet John Doe* with Gary Cooper, John Huston's *The Maltese Falcon* with Humphrey Bogart and Mary Astor, John Ford's *How Green Was My Valley* with Roddy McDowall, Walt Disney's *Dumbo*, Preston Sturges's *The Lady Eve* with Barbara Stanwyck and Henry Fonda, William Wyler's *The Little Foxes* with Bette Davis, *The Wolf Man* with Lon Chaney, Jr., and

Alfred Hitchcock's *Suspicion* with Cary Grant and Joan Fontaine.

◆ In January 1942 Japan declares war on the Netherlands; Japan invades Burma; and Thailand declares war on the United States and the United Kingdom.

◆ On February 15, 1942, Singapore surrenders to the Japanese.

◆ In late February and early March 1942 Japanese naval forces defeat a combined force of US, British, Dutch, and Australian ships in the Battle of the Java Sea. The Japanese victory allows them to continue taking Pacific territories.

◆ In March 1942 Japanese forces capture Rangoon, Burma; Java; and the Andaman Islands (situated between India and Burma).

◆ In August 1942 the civil disobedience movement in India in opposition to British colonial rule gathers strength; Mohandas K. Gandhi is arrested by the British.

◆ On August 19, 1942, an Allied force (5,000 Canadians and 1,100 British Commandos and US Rangers) attack German positions at Dieppe, France; nearly half the force is killed or captured, but the raid later provides valuable information for D-Day planning.

◆ On August 22, 1942, Brazil joins the Allies and declares war on Germany and Italy.

◆ In November 1942 Germany invades Vichy France.

◆ In December 1942 scientists working under the direction of Enrico Fermi generate a controlled fission chain reaction at the University of Chicago, one of the sites of the "Manhattan Project," which aims to create an atomic weapon.

◆ Elliot Paul publishes *The Last Time I Saw Paris*, 1942.

◆ Albert Camus publishes *L'Étranger* (*The Stranger*), 1942.

◆ Marjorie Kinnan Rawlings publishes *Cross Creek*, 1942.

◆ Daphne du Maurier publishes *Frenchman's Creek*, 1942.

◆ Popular music hits of 1942 include Bing Crosby's "White Christmas," the Andrews Sisters' "Don't Sit Under the Apple Tree," and Glenn Miller's "Kalamazoo."

◆ Notable films of 1942 include Michael Curtiz's *Casablanca* with Humphrey Bogart and Ingrid Bergman, Orson Welles's *The Magnificent Ambersons* with Joseph Cotten, *Now, Voyager* with Bette Davis, Preston Sturgis's *Palm Beach Story* with Claudette Colbert and Joel McCrea, George Stevens's *Woman of the Year* with Katharine Hepburn and Spencer Tracy, Walt Disney's *Bambi*, Jacques Tourneur's *Cat People* with Simone Simon, *King's Row* with Robert Cummings and Ronald Reagan, William Wyler's *Mrs. Miniver* with Greer Garson, *Yankee Doodle Dandy* with James Cagney, and *The Pride of the Yankees* with Gary Cooper.

◆ On January 15, 1943, the Pentagon building in Washington, DC, is completed.

◆ In June 1943 the US government contracts with the University of Pennsylvania to build a calculating machine that will make ballistic trajectory calculations; that machine will become the ENIAC (Electronic Numerical Integrator And Computer) computer, in the autumn of 1945.

◆ In October 1943 Italy joins the Allies and declares war on Germany.

◆ Robert Graves publishes *Claudius the God*, 1943.

◆ Antoine de Saint-Exupery publishes *Le Petit Prince* (*The Little Prince*), 1943.

◆ Jean-Paul Sartre publishes *Being and Nothingness*, 1943.

◆ Betty Smith publishes *A Tree Grows in Brooklyn*, 1943.

◆ Ayn Rand publishes *The Fountainhead*, 1943.

◆ Rodgers and Hammerstein's *Oklahoma!* opens, 1943.

◆ Popular music hits of 1943 include Dinah Shore's "You'd Be So Nice to Come Home To," the Ink Spots's "Don't Get Around Much Anymore," Rudy Vallee's "As Time Goes By," and the Mills Brothers's "Paper Doll."

◆ Notable films of 1943 include *For Whom the Bell Tolls* with Gary Cooper and Ingrid Bergman, William Wellman's *The Ox-Bow Incident* with Henry Fonda and Harry Morgan, *Bataan* with Robert Taylor, *The Song of Bernadette* with Jennifer Jones, *Phantom of the Opera* with Claude Rains, Alfred Hitchcock's *Shadow of a Doubt* with Joseph Cotten and Teresa Wright, and *Watch on the Rhine* with Paul Lukas and Bette Davis.

◆ In June 1944 Iceland gains its independence from Denmark.

◆ On July 20, 1944, high-ranking Nazi officers attempt to kill Hitler by leaving a bomb in a conference room; although the bomb explodes, Hitler survives and the unsuccessful conspirators are either killed by the Nazis or, like General Erwin Rommel, made to commit suicide.

◆ On August 4, 1944, Anne Frank, a Jewish girl who will become famous for the diary she has kept while living in hiding, is discovered with her family in their hiding place in Amsterdam; the family is taken to concentration camps, and Anne dies at the Bergen-Belsen camp in Germany.

◆ Physicist Erwin Schrödinger publishes *What Is Life?*, 1944.

◆ Astrid Lindgren publishes *Pippi Longstocking*, 1944.

◆ W. Somerset Maugham publishes *The Razor's Edge*, 1944.

◆ John Hersey publishes *A Bell for Adano*, 1944.

◆ Harry Brown publishes *A Walk in the Sun*, 1944.

◆ Howard Fast publishes *Freedom Road*, 1944.

◆ Kathleen Winsor publishes *Forever Amber*, 1944.

◆ Popular music hits of 1944 include Bing Crosby's "Swinging on a Star" and "I Love You," Harry James's "I'll Get By," Judy Garland's "The Trolley Song," and the Andrews Sisters's "Shoo-Shoo Baby."

◆ Notable films of 1944 include Billy Wilder's *Double Indemnity* with Fred MacMurray and Barbara Stanwyck, Frank Capra's *Arsenic and Old Lace* with Cary Grant, Leo McCarey's *Going My Way* with Bing Crosby, Howard Hawks's *To Have and Have Not* with Humphrey Bogart and Lauren Bacall, Vincente Minnelli's *Meet Me in St. Louis* with Judy Garland, Otto Preminger's *Laura* with Gene Tierney and Dana Andrews, Alfred Hitchcock's *Lifeboat* with Tallulah

Bankhead, *Jane Eyre* with Joan Fontaine, and George Cukor's *Gaslight* with Ingrid Bergman and Charles Boyer.

❖ In January 1945 Soviet troops liberate the Auschwitz and Birkenau concentration camps.

❖ A photograph of American Marines raising an American flag on Iwo Jima is taken, on February 23, 1945, by Associated Press photographer Joe Rosenthal; Rosenthal is later awarded the Pulitzer Prize for this picture.

❖ On March 22, 1945, the Arab League is formed in Cairo, Egypt. The founding members are Egypt, Syria, Lebanon, Iraq, Jordan (then Transjordan), Yemen, and Saudi Arabia.

❖ On April 10, 1945, the Allies liberate the Buchenwald concentration camp in Germany.

FAST FACTS ABOUT FRANKLIN DELANO ROOSEVELT

❖ One of the major issues of the 1932 Democratic convention was the repeal of Prohibition; the delegates, after much discussion, decided to add a plank that favors repeal to the party's platform.

❖ Roosevelt ran as the vice-presidential candidate in 1920 on a ticket with James Cox of Ohio, but they were defeated.

❖ Roosevelt is the only president to serve more than two terms of office; he was elected to four terms, but died only three months into his fourth term.

❖ Roosevelt's dog, Fala, was a Scottish terrier who was his constant companion; as a puppy, Fala was fed so much by members of the White House staff that he became sick, and Roosevelt thereafter ordered that no one but himself should feed Fala. A statue of Fala is included in the Roosevelt Memorial in Washington, DC.

❖ Endicott Peabody, the headmaster at the Groton School when Roosevelt was a student there, was an Episcopal priest and later officiated at the wedding of Eleanor and Franklin.

❖ Franklin Roosevelt was a fifth cousin to President Theodore Roosevelt; Eleanor Roosevelt was Theodore Roosevelt's niece.

❖ In 1933, for the first time, all of the members of the Electoral College were invited to see Roosevelt take the oath of office.

❖ Roosevelt was the first president to ride in an airplane while president, in 1943.

❖ Roosevelt was the first president to appear on television, on April 30, 1939, when he was televised at the opening ceremonies of the New York World's Fair.

❖ Prior to his first run for the presidency, Roosevelt consulted a group of college professors for their advice; this group was dubbed the "Brain Trust."

❖ By a tacit agreement (one that would be unthinkable today), the press refrained from photographing Roosevelt in his wheelchair or mentioning his paralysis, so that few Americans were aware of the extent of the president's disability.

❖ Roosevelt was an avid stamp collector; as president, he took part in designing some US postage stamps and approved all of the new stamps.

❖ In 1932 Roosevelt became the first Democrat to attend a national nominating convention and accept the presidential nomination in person.

❖ Roosevelt was the first president to leave the United States to visit a foreign war zone (while the president).

❖ The Roosevelt Memorial in Washington, DC, includes six waterfalls and nine sculptures, including one of FDR seated in a wheelchair with his dog, Fala, by his side, and one of Eleanor Roosevelt, the only instance in which a First Lady is so honored at the site of a presidential memorial.

Harry S. Truman

Nickname: Give 'Em Hell Harry
Presidency: 33rd president, 1945–1953
Party: Democratic
Life dates: May 8, 1884–December 26, 1972 (88 years, 232 days)

EARLY LIFE AND EDUCATION

Harry S. Truman was born on May 8, 1884, in Lamar, Missouri, to Martha ("Mattie") Ellen Young Truman and John Anderson Truman. A son of the Trumans had been stillborn in 1882; Harry was the eldest surviving child, and was followed by another boy, John Vivian Truman (called Vivian), and a girl, Mary Jane. Harry explained in later years that the "S" in his name was a compromise, intended to stand for either "Solomon" or "Shipp" (his grandfathers were Solomon Young and Anderson Shipp Truman). Harry himself put a period after the letter, but because it is not, strictly speaking, an abbreviation, some have argued that it should not have a period.

The Trumans moved to a farm located near Hendersonville, Missouri, shortly after Harry's birth, and in 1887 moved to Grandfather Young's farm. In 1890 the family moved into Independence, Missouri, and John Truman embarked on a second career as a stock trader. That same year, Harry, whose vision was poor, received his first pair of eyeglasses. Harry attended the Sunday School at the First Presbyterian Church (though the Trumans were Baptists, his mother had found the Presbyterian Church more welcoming) and there met five-year-old Elizabeth Wallace, a blonde, blue-eyed girl called Bess or Bessie. He was smitten by her even at the age of five, but was so shy that he did not speak to her until years later. Bess was an athletic girl and her family was well-off; Harry believed himself to be unworthy of her, but the Sunday School experience touched off a devotion that would last a lifetime.

In 1894 Harry and Vivian both fell ill with diphtheria. Harry was ill for many months. Already an enthusiastic reader, he turned even more to books. His mother, whose protective instinct had become sharpened by Harry's long convalescence, cautioned him to avoid rough play and encouraged his reading. When the Truman family moved to another home in 1895 and acquired a piano, Harry was encouraged to play. He took lessons, practiced for two hours every day, and dreamed of a career as a concert pianist. In 1900 he and his music teacher attended a concert of the Polish pianist and composer Ignace Paderewski. His teacher even managed to introduce him to Paderewski—at the time the world's most famous pianist. Eventually, however, Harry decided that he did not possess the talent to make a career as a pianist.

He retained his love for music throughout his life and often played the piano (even as president of the United States) to amuse others.

In 1901 Harry and Bess graduated from high school. Bess enrolled in Miss Barstow's Finishing School for Girls in Kansas City. Shortly after she returned home in 1903, her father committed suicide. David Wallace had been a handsome, charming man with personal demons and a drinking problem. Bess, her three younger brothers, her mother, and her grandmother left Independence for a year. The Wallace family retreated from view for a while and members of the family staunchly refused to discuss the suicide.

Harry had hoped to be appointed to West Point, but he was rejected because of his poor eyesight. At about the same time, his father's business failed; John Truman had gambled on wheat futures and lost. The family moved to Kansas City for a time; John Truman worked as a night watchman and Harry took a job in the mailroom of the Kansas City *Star* newspaper.

EARLY CAREER

Harry's next job was as a timekeeper for the L. J. Smith Company, a railroad construction firm that was doing work for the Santa Fe Railroad. The job, which lasted for six months, toughened him; for a while he lived in hobo camps along the Missouri River where the Santa Fe ran.

In 1903 Truman took a job as a bank clerk in Kansas City. In 1905, he became a bookkeeper at another bank and joined the Missouri National Guard. He entered the National Guard as a private but was soon promoted to the rank of corporal. When the Truman family moved again, to a farm, he remained in Kansas City and took a room at a boardinghouse. At the same boardinghouse was Arthur Eisenhower, the elder brother of Dwight D. Eisenhower.

But in 1906, by which time the Trumans were settled in at Grandfather Young's farm in Grandview, Missouri, Harry's father and brother Vivian asked him to return to the family fold and to help them run the farm. He became a farmer working under his father's direction. In 1910 Harry renewed his acquaintance with Bess Wal-

lace and began courting her. He wrote her frequent letters and went into Independence whenever he could, escorting her to concerts and the theater or having dinner at the Wallace home (the Wallaces were living with Bess's maternal grandmother). Harry proposed to Bess in 1911; when she turned him down, he wrote her a letter thanking her for doing it in such a friendly fashion and confessing that he had never really expected her to say yes. In 1913 she agreed to become secretly engaged; her mother did not approve of Harry and felt strongly that he was her daughter's social inferior.

"There's been a lot of talk lately about the burdens of the presidency. Decisions that the president has to make often affect the lives of tens of millions of people around the world, but that does not mean that they should take longer to make. Some men can make decisions and some cannot. Some men fret and delay under criticism. I used to have a saying that applies here, and I note that some people have picked it up, 'If you can't stand the heat, get out of the kitchen.'"

Harry S. Truman in his autobiography, *Mr. Citizen*, published in 1960

In 1914 Harry's father died. Being in possession of a bit more autonomy following his father's death, Truman invested in a zinc mine and then tried selling oil leases, but these endeavors were not successful, and he still worried about the farm. With war looming, Truman enlisted in the army in August 1916 (he even memorized the eye chart in order to pass the eye test). The United States entered the war in April of 1917. Truman received special training in artillery at Camp Doniphan in Oklahoma. In 1918 he received a captain's commission and shipped out to France. He was given command of Battery D, the 129th Field Artillery regiment. The men of Battery D were known for their rowdiness and had shown little respect for authority under previous commanders. But Truman forced his men to buckle under and demoted troublemakers to a lower rank. He explained to the noncommissioned officers: "I didn't come over here to get along with you. You've got to get along with me." Truman's toughness, coupled with his genuine concern for his men and his natural friendliness, won him their respect. In September 1918 Truman saw action for the first time in the Vosges Mountains. His regiment was part of the Argonnes campaign and continued hammering against German positions in France until just before the armistice on November 11, 1918.

"Right now, I'm where I want to be—in command of this battery. I'd rather be here than president of the United States."

Harry S. Truman in 1918, during World War I, while on active duty in France in command of the 129th Field Artillery for the Missouri National Guard

---

Truman was discharged in May 1919. He returned home and he and Bess were finally married on June 28, 1919, in Independence. Truman and an army friend opened a haberdashery (a men's clothing store) in Kansas City, Missouri, but the business failed in 1922. Truman refused to file bankruptcy and paid off his share of the firm's debts over the next fifteen years.

POLITICAL CAREER

Truman's interest in politics was lifelong; as a teenager, he and his father had attended the 1900 Democratic National Convention in Kansas City, at which William Jennings Bryan was nominated to run against President McKinley. A few years later, Truman had the opportunity to hear President Theodore Roosevelt speak from the back of a railroad car.

One of Truman's friends from the 129th Artillery regiment was Jim Pendergast, whose uncle was Tom J. Pendergast, the Democratic Party leader of Jackson County, Missouri. The elder Pendergast was a man of somewhat mixed reputation, and he was looking for a clean-cut candidate to run for judge of the eastern district county court of Jackson County. Truman fit the bill and Tom Pendergast endorsed Truman. Truman was elected in 1923 and served until 1925. The position was primarily administrative in nature, and his responsibilities included managing the county's property and finances. At the same time, he attended the Kansas City School of Law at night. In 1924 Bess and Harry's only child, Margaret, was born.

In 1924 Truman failed to win reelection to the county court judgeship, but in 1926 he was elected presiding judge of Jackson County Court and served in that capacity until 1934. Although he made some concessions to the Pendergast political machine, Truman gained a reputation for personal honesty. In 1934, with the support of the Pendergast organization, Truman ran for the US Senate and defeated the incumbent, Roscoe C. Patterson.

Truman was a loyal Democratic supporter of President Franklin D. Roosevelt and New Deal legislation. Although his congressional peers initially viewed him with some suspicion because of his connection to the Pendergast machine, Truman's hard work and honesty soon won him the friendship of many of those peers. Throughout his career he also maintained ties with his former army comrades and was an active member of veterans organizations as well as of the Masons, which he had joined as a young farmer. (In 1940 he became a Grand Master of the Masonic Order.)

As a senator, Truman was instrumental in drafting several bills related to transportation issues, including the Civil Aeronautics Act of 1938, which created the Civil Aeronautics Board and the Civil Aeronautics Administration; it was also responsible for issuing air carrier route certificates, regulating airline fares, and investigating aircraft accidents. He was a member of the subcommittee on railroads of the Interstate Commerce Committee and, in that capacity, led the Senate investigation (with Senator Burton Kendall Wheeler of Montana) into US railroad finances. That investigation led to the Transportation Act of 1940 (also called the Wheeler-Truman Act), which mandated an expanded regulation of the railroads by the Interstate Commerce Commission.

Truman was reelected to the Senate in 1940. That summer the mortgage on the family farm in Grandview was foreclosed, and Truman's mother and sister moved to Independence. Friends of the family bought the farm (and sold it back to the Truman family a few years later).

In 1941, as the United States was gearing up for some kind of participation in the European war, Truman was appointed as the head of the Special Senate Committee to investigate defense spending (the Truman Committee), which exposed corruption and cost overruns in defense industries and saved the federal government billions of dollars. During the war years the Truman Committee produced a great number of detailed reports on the nation's defense programs. The work of Truman and the committee garnered national attention for Truman. Truman's solid reputation placed him in good stead when, in 1944, Roosevelt planned to replace Vice President Henry A. Wallace. Wallace was seen as too liberal and, as a result of a trip he had made to the Soviet Union and China, possibly pro-Communist. It was believed that Wallace would be a handicap in the 1944 election, particular among southern Democrats. Truman was regarded as having more appeal for mainstream voters. Roosevelt indicated that Truman would be an acceptable candidate, and Truman was chosen as Roosevelt's running mate despite his repeated assertions that he did not want the nomination.

On January 20, 1945, Truman became vice president and served in that post for eighty-three days. Upon Roosevelt's death, on April 12, 1945, Truman was sworn in as president.

PRESIDENCY

A few weeks after Truman assumed the presidency, on May 7, 1945, Germany surrendered. At the end of June he spoke at the United Nations founding conference meeting in San Francisco for the drafting of the United Nations charter, and in July he attended the Potsdam Conference in Germany. Truman met with Churchill and Stalin at Potsdam to discuss the post-war fate of Germany. (Churchill was replaced by his successor Clement Attlee midway through the conference.)

> **"You members of this Conference are to be the architects of the better world. In your hands rests our future. By your labors at this Conference, we shall know if suffering humanity is to achieve a just and lasting peace."**
>
> Harry S. Truman, address to the United Nations Conference on International Organization, April 25, 1945

Truman was informed of the existence of the atomic bomb after he became the president. Throughout the summer of 1945 Japan had been refusing the Allies' demand for unconditional surrender. On August 6, 1945, Truman announced the dropping of the first atomic bomb on Hiroshima; the second atomic bomb was dropped on Nagasaki three days later. The use of the bomb and its horrifying consequences shocked the world. The decision to drop the bomb was made after the US military estimated that as many as half a million US soldiers would be lost if a land invasion of Japan were to become necessary. On August 14, 1945, Truman announced the end of the war with Japan.

With the war ended, Truman turned to the problem of returning the nation to a peacetime economy. On September 6, 1946, Truman, a New Deal Democrat through and through, announced his twenty-one point legislative program, in which he laid out his vision for a postwar America. His twenty-one policy points included a minimum wage, improved benefits for war veterans, expansions in Social Security benefits, and housing subsidies.

But also during the post-war period, Truman faced the burgeoning threat of Soviet expansion in eastern Europe. On March 12, 1947, Truman addressed Congress and requested the appropriation of funds for Greece and Turkey, whose governments were being threatened by Communist-led insurgencies. Truman feared the expansion of Communism, and his passionate belief in the principle of helping governments in crisis to resist Communism became known as the Truman doctrine.

It was the start of the Cold War. The Marshall Plan, formally known as the European Recovery Program, which was a plan devised by Secretary of State George Marshall to use the resources of the United States to stimulate the recoveries of devastated European nations (and to help those nations to resist Communism), had also been motivated in part by anti-Communist fervor. In Germany the Soviet Union tried to cut off Berlin from the rest of Germany and to prevent persons and supplies coming from the United States, France, and the United Kingdom to enter the city, which was situated in the sector of Germany controlled by the Soviet Union in the aftermath of the war. Truman responded by ordering the Berlin airlift, a daily operation in which supplies were flown into the city of Berlin that continued for more than a year, until September 1949.

Both the Democrats and the Republicans sounded out General Dwight D. Eisenhower, a great hero of the recent war, about running for president in 1948, but he wasn't interested. The Democrats nominated Truman, with Senator Alben W. Barkley of Kentucky as his running mate. Truman's nomination was not without controversy; conservative Southerners had been angered by Truman's support for civil rights. A large number of Southern state delegates to the Democratic National Convention walked out of the convention and formed the States' Rights ("Dixiecrat") Party. The new party nominated South Carolina's Strom Thurmond for president. The Republicans nominated Thomas E. Dewey, the governor of New York. Truman gave an impassioned speech at the convention and waged an exhaustive "whistle-stop" campaign tour. Despite expectations that he would lose, Truman was victorious.

In 1949 Truman signed the National Security Act Amendment, which established a unified Department of Defense, and on August 24, 1949, Truman announced that the North Atlantic Treaty (which had been signed by the representatives of twelve nations in Washington on April 4) had gone into effect. It was this treaty that brought the North American Treaty Organization (NATO) into existence.

At the end of World War II, Korea, having been liberated from Japanese occupation, was divided at the 38th parallel into Soviet and US zones of occupation. The country remained divided in the post-war era. In 1948 two governments were established: that of North Korea (the Democratic People's Republic of Korea), under Kim Il-Sung, a Communist regime; and that of South Korea (the Republic of Korea), under Syngman Rhee, which was on good terms with western European nations and the United States. When North Korea, supported by the Soviet Union and China, invaded South Korea in June 1950, the United Nations called for the military defense of South Korea. The United Nations passed a resolution that called on all United Nations members to provide what military assistance they could to help South Korea to resist its invaders, a resolution that would undoubtedly have been vetoed by the Soviet Union had they not been boycotting the UN's Security Council because of the United Nation's failure to admit the People's Republic of

China. The bulk of the men that made up the United Nations-sponsored intervention force were US troops under General Douglas MacArthur.

To get around the necessity of asking Congress to declare war, Truman called the US military intervention in Korea a "police action." Truman was criticized because the Congress had never declared war on Korea; when the war dragged on, it was often referred to as "Truman's War." The United Nations (primarily US) forces initially took heavy losses, but as they were reinforced and as US bombing support was provided, they began to push the North Koreans back beyond the 38th parallel. MacArthur's bold strategy in landing amphibious troops north of the enemy lines at Inchon gave the US forces an advantage, but the advantage was lost when United Nations and South Korean forces were met by Chinese forces who had joined the North Koreans and were launching repeated southward offensives.

MacArthur had assured Truman that the Chinese would not come into the war. The mistake was, in Turman's view, forgivable, but some of MacArthur's subsequent actions (in early 1951) were less so. After having been ordered by the president not to issue public statements about war policy, MacArthur publicly criticized Truman for his strategy (which centered on simply driving back the invaders of South Korea) and put forth his own strategy, essentially a more aggressive pursuit of the war that included an extension of the war into mainland China (with help from the Nationalist Chinese). When Truman sent MacArthur his proposed peace initiative, which ratified the existing boundary between North and South Korea (the 38th parallel) and did not include the reunification of Korea, MacArthur went public with his own proposal, in which he threatened the Communist Chinese and offered to meet with enemy commanders to discuss ending the war. Truman relieved MacArthur of his command on April 11, 1951. MacArthur, a war hero, was immensely popular in the United States at that time, and Truman was criticized for his decision. But a majority of Americans was also not in favor of extending the war into China. An armistice (a temporary suspension of hostilities) was signed by the United Nations Command and North Korea on July 27, 1953, at which time Truman was no longer the president. No peace treaty was ever signed, and in theory the war has never been ended. The division between North and South Korea continues to the present day.

"I've said many a time that I think the Un-American Activities Committee in the House of Representatives was the most un-American thing in America!"

Harry S. Truman, in a speech given at Columbia University, April 29, 1959

Truman's popularity suffered as a result of his clash with MacArthur. At the same time Senator Joseph McCarthy, whom Truman loathed and who even accused the Truman administration of participation in a Communist conspiracy, contributed to this growing discontent with Truman and his administration. The American people were moving further and further to the right politically. On March 29, 1952, Truman announced that he would not run for a third term.

During a renovation of the White House that began in 1948 and lasted until 1952 the Truman family lived across the street in the Blair House, normally the vice president's residence. During her husband's presidency, Bess Truman fulfilled her duties as First Lady responsibly, if unenthusiastically. She had no desire to emulate her predecessor, Eleanor Roosevelt, and did not make statements to the press. A confidant and advisor to her husband, Bess disliked the idea of a public role for herself and resented the degree to which her family's privacy was compromised by the presidency.

POST-PRESIDENTIAL CAREER

In early 1953 the Trumans returned to Independence. Truman worked on the plans for the Truman Library, traveled, and wrote his memoirs. He supported the candidacy of John F. Kennedy in 1960 and attended the Kennedy inauguration in 1961. Margaret Truman married and became the mother of four sons.

Harry died on December 26, 1972, and was buried at the Truman Library in Independence. Bess died on October 18, 1982, and was buried beside him.

Birthplace: Lamar, MO
Residency: Missouri
Religion: Baptist
Education: University of Kansas City Law School (1923–1925; did not graduate)
Place of Death: Kansas City, MO
Burial Site: Truman Library, Independence, MO
Dates in Office: April 12, 1945–January 20, 1953 (7 years, 283 days)
Age at Inauguration: 60 years, 339 days

FAMILY

Father: John Anderson Truman (1851–1914)
Mother: Martha Ellen Young Truman (1852–1947)
Siblings: Harry was the second-born but eldest surviving child of four; his siblings were a stillborn child (1882); John Vivian Truman (1886–1965); Mary Jane Truman (1889–1978)
Wife: Elizabeth ("Bess") Virginia Wallace Truman (1885–1982), married on June 28, 1919, in Independence, MO
Children: Margaret (Mary) Truman (1924–)

CAREER

Private: timekeeper for a railroad construction crew, bank clerk, farmer, part-owner of an oil company, part-owner of a haberdashery (men's clothing store)
Political: judge, the eastern district county court of Jackson County, Missouri (1923–1925); presiding judge of Jackson County (1926–1934); member of the US Senate (1935–1945); US vice president under Roosevelt (1945); president of the United States (1945–1953)

Military: Truman enlisted as a private in the Missouri National Guard (1905), was promoted to corporal, left the National Guard in 1911; reenlisted in 1916 as a first lieutenant eight months before the United States entered World War I; was sent to France in command of Battery D of the 129th Field Artillery, was promoted to captain (1918); was discharged as a major (1919), but remained in the reserves until 1945, when he retired as a colonel.

Selected Works: *The Autobiography of Harry S. Truman*, ed. by Robert H. Ferrell (Columbia: University of Missouri Press, 2002); *Dear Bess: The Letters from Harry to Bess Truman, 1910–1959*, ed. by Robert H. Ferrell (Columbia: University of Missouri Press, 1998); *Defending the West: The Truman-Churchill Correspondence, 1945–1960*, ed. with an introduction by G. W. Sand (Westport, CT: Praeger Publishers, 2004); *Eleanor and Harry: The Correspondence of Eleanor Roosevelt and Harry S. Truman*, ed. and with commentary by Steve Neal, foreword by Gloria Steinem (New York: Scribner, 2002); *Harry S. Truman, 1884–1972: Chronology, Documents, Bibliographical Aids*, ed. by Howard B. Furer (Dobbs Ferry, NY: Oceana Publications, 1970); *Letters Home*, ed. by Monte M. Poen (Columbia: University of Missouri Press, 2003); *Memoirs of Harry S. Truman* (New York: Da Capo Press, 1986–1987); *Miracle of '48: Harry Truman's Major Campaign Speeches and Selected Whistle-Stops*, ed. by Steve Neal, foreword by Robert V. Remini (Carbondale: Southern Illinois University Press, 2003); *Mr. Citizen* (New York: Geis Associates, 1960); *Off the Record: The Private Papers of Harry S. Truman*, ed. by Robert H. Ferrell (Columbia: University of Missouri Press, 1997); *Talking with Harry: Candid Conversations with President Harry S. Truman*, ed. and with commentary by Ralph E. Weber (Wilmington, DE: SR Books, 2001); *Where the Buck Stops: The Personal and Private Writings of Harry S. Truman*, ed. by Margaret Truman (New York: Warner Books, 1989)

PRESIDENCY

Nomination: 1948: The Democratic Convention was held July 12 to 14, 1948, in

Philadelphia; Truman was nominated on the first ballot, with Alben R. Barkley of Kentucky selected as the vice-presidential candidate.

Election: elected president on November 2, 1948
Opponent: Thomas Dewey, NY, Republican; Strom Thurmond, SC, States' Rights Democratic Party (Dixiecrats)
Vote Totals: Truman, 24,179,347 popular, 303 electoral; Dewey, 21,991,292 popular, 189 electoral; Thurmond, 1,175,930 popular, 39 electoral
Inauguration: January 29, 1949
Vice President: Alben R. Barkley, KY (1949–1953)

CABINET

Secretary of State: Edward R. Stettinius, Jr., VA (1944–1945); James Byrnes, (1945–1947); George C. Marshall, (1947–1949); Dean G. Acheson, (1949–1953)
Secretary of the Treasury: Henry Morgenthau, Jr., NY (1945); Frederick M. Vinson, (1945–1946); John W. Snyder, (1946–1953)
Secretary of War: Henry L. Stimson, NY (1945); Robert B. Patterson, NY (1945–1947); Kenneth C. Royall, NC (1947) [Note: Secretary of War ceased to be a cabinet position when the Department of War was combined with the Department of the Navy to form the Department of Defense in 1947.]
Secretary of Defense: James Forrestal, (1947–1949); Louis Johnson, (1949–1950); George C. Marshall, (1950–1951); Robert Lovett, (1951–1953)
Attorney General: Francis B. Biddle, PA (1945); Thomas C. Clark, (1945–1949); J. Howard McGrath, (1949–1952); James P. McGranery, (1952–1953)
Postmaster General: Frank C. Walker, PA (1945); Robert E. Hannegan, (1945–1947); Jesse M. Donaldson, (1947–1953)
Secretary of the Navy: James Forrestal, NY (1945–1947) [Note: Secretary of the Navy ceased to be a cabinet position when the Department of the Navy was combined with the Department of War to form the Department of Defense in 1947.]
Secretary of Agriculture: Claude R. Wickard, IN (1945); Clinton P. Anderson, (1945–1948); Charles F. Brannan, (1948–1953)

Secretary of the Interior: Harold L. Ickes, IL (1945–1946); Julius A. Krug, (1946–1949); Oscar L. Chapman, (1949–1953)
Secretary of Labor: Frances Perkins, NY (1945); Lewis B. Schwellenbach, (1945–1948); Maurice J. Tobin, (1948–1953)
Secretary of Commerce: Henry A. Wallace, IA (1945–1946); William Averell Harriman, (1946–1948); Charles Sawyer, (1948–1953)

CONGRESS:

79th Congress (1945–1947); Speaker of the House: Sam Rayburn (TX, Democrat)
80th Congress (1947–1949); Speaker of the House: Joseph W. Martin, Jr. (MA, Republican)
81st Congress (1949–1951); Speaker of the House: Sam Rayburn (TX, Democrat)
82nd Congress (1951–1953); Speaker of the House: Sam Rayburn (TX, Democrat)

SUPREME COURT APPOINTEES

Harold Hitz Burton, OH; Associate Justice (1945–1958)

Fred Moore Vinson, KY; Chief Justice (1946–1953)

Tom Campbell Clark, TX; Associate Justice (1949–1967)

Sherman Minton, IN; Associate Justice (1949–1956)

MAJOR EVENTS OF THE TRUMAN ADMINISTRATION

◆ On April 12, 1945, President Franklin D. Roosevelt dies in Warm Springs, Georgia, and Truman becomes president.

◆ US troops meet Soviet troops at Torgau on the Elbe River on April 26, 1945, cutting Germany in two.

◆ On May 7, 1945, Germany surrenders; May 8 is declared V-E (Victory in Europe) Day.

◆ On June 26, 1945, the charter for the United Nations is signed in San Francisco; fifty-one countries are the original members.

◆ From July 17 until August 2, 1945, Truman, Stalin, and Churchill (replaced on July 28 by his successor Clement Attlee) attend the Potsdam Conference, held in Potsdam, Germany; the leaders discuss plans for post-war Germany and there is an agreement to call for Japan's unconditional surrender.

◆ At the end of July 1945, Japan rejects the Potsdam Conference demand for unconditional surrender.

◆ On July 30, 1945, a Japanese submarine torpedoes and sinks the USS Indianapolis; only 316 of 1,199 crew members survive.

◆ The first atomic bomb ever to be used as a weapon of war, nicknamed "Little Boy," is dropped by the Enola Gay, a US aircraft, on Hiroshima, Japan, August 6, 1945.

◆ The second atomic bomb, nicknamed "Fat Man," is dropped by the United States on Nagasaki, Japan, August 9, 1945.

◆ Japan surrenders on August 14, 1945 (because of the difference in time zones it is August 15 in Japan), and the day is commemorated in the United States as V-J (Victory in Japan) Day.

◆ Representatives of Japan sign the surrender papers aboard the USS Missouri, on September 2, 1945.

◆ In August and September 1945 Korea declares its independence from Japan. Japanese troops surrender to US troops occupying southern Korea (soon to become the Republic of South Korea) and Soviet troops occupying northern Korea (to become the Democratic People's Republic of Korea).

◆ In September 1945 Truman presents his "21 Point Plan" to Congress, which calls for civil rights legislation, expansions in Social Security, employment programs, increased unemployment compensation, an increased minimum wage, and housing subsidies. His program is dubbed the "Fair Deal," but few of his proposals are acted on by Congress.

◆ The Employment Act of 1946 pledges the federal government to use its resources to promote maximum employment.

◆ In September 1946 Secretary of Commerce Henry Wallace, in a speech given in New York City, criticizes the Truman administration's foreign policy, which Wallace sees as excessively aggressive, and argues in favor of conciliation toward the Soviet Union. Truman demands and receives Wallace's resignation.

◆ In late 1946 Truman appoints the President's Committee on Civil Rights (PCCR), which studies segregation; the PCCR's report is cited by Truman in his repeated appeals for civil rights legislation.

◆ The Truman Doctrine is announced on March 12, 1947, and pledges US support for governments resisting Communism and for "free peoples who are resisting attempted subjugation by armed minorities or by outside pressures." The doctrine is signed into law on May 22, 1947. The new law authorizes $400 million in aid to Greece, whose government is being challenged by a Communist-led insurgency, and Turkey, which seeks aid for modernization.

◆ The 22nd Amendment to the Constitution, which limits presidents to two terms in office, is passed by Congress on March 21, 1947 (and ratified on February 27, 1951).

◆ Truman signs Executive Order 9835 on March 22, 1947, which authorizes a panel of federal government employees to search out any "infiltration of disloyal persons" into the federal government.

◆ On June 5, 1947, Secretary of State George C. Marshall gives a speech at Harvard University in which he denounces Communism and outlines a plan for European economic recovery (which comes to be known as the Marshall Plan). The plan calls for the provision of economic aid to the countries of western Europe with the express goal of enabling them to resist Communism.

◆ On June 23, 1947, Congress passes the Labor-Management Relations Act (Taft-Hartley Act) over Truman's veto. The act narrows the rights of labor unions that had been granted under the Wagner Act of 1935 and establishes a requirement that labor union officers must swear under oath that they are not supporters of the Communist Party.

◆ Truman signs the Presidential Succession Act on July 18, 1947; the act restores the original 1792 provisions for presidential succession (which had been changed in 1886). The 1947 act provides that the order of succession of the president is as follows: the vice president; the president pro tempore of the Senate; the Speaker of the House of Representatives; the cabinet officers in the order of the establishment of the departments.

◆ On July 26, 1947, Truman signs the National Security Act, which establishes the National Security Council (NSC), the Central Intelligence Agency (CIA), the Department of Defense (formed from the Department of War and Department of the Navy), and a new Department of the Air Force.

◆ On October 5, 1947, Truman delivers the first presidential address to be televised from the White House; he speaks about the world food crisis and urges US citizens to conserve food in order to help meet the needs of people in parts of the world in which there are food shortages.

◆ On April 3, 1948, Truman signs the Economic Recovery Act of 1948, which inaugurates the Economic Recovery Program (also known as the Marshall Plan), proposed by Secretary of State George C. Marshall. The act also authorizes the formation of the Economic Cooperation Administration (ECA), which will be responsible for distributing billions of dollars in aid to European countries over the next several years.

◆ On June 24, 1948, the Soviet Union begins the Berlin blockade; it denies the United Kingdom, France, and the United States their access rights to their respective sectors of the city of Berlin, which lies within Russian-occupied East Germany.

◆ On June 26, 1948, Truman announces the Berlin airlift, a daily delivery of supplies to Berlin in defiance of the Soviet blockade; the airlift continues until May 12, 1949, when the Soviets lift the blockade.

◆ On July 20, 1948, Truman announces the second peacetime military draft (the first was instituted by Roosevelt in 1940).

◆ Executive Order 9981, issued by Truman on July 26, 1948, establishes "equality of treatment and opportunity" in the US armed forces for all persons without regard to "race, color, religion, or national origin"; it orders the desegregation of the armed services.

◆ On November 2, 1948, Truman surprises many by defeating Thomas E. Dewey in the presidential election.

◆ On March 28, 1949, Secretary of Defense James Forrestal, suffering from depression, resigns his position. He falls to his death from a window of the Bethesda Naval Hospital in May, his death presumably a suicide.

◆ The North Atlantic Treaty, signed on April 4, 1949, creates the North Atlantic Treaty Organization (NATO). Signatories include the United States, Canada, Belgium, Luxembourg, the Netherlands, and the United Kingdom.

◆ On July 15, 1949, Truman signs the Housing Act, which makes "a decent home and suitable living environment for every American family" a goal of the federal government and provides federal funding for low-cost housing projects.

◆ In January 1950 Senator (Carey) Estes Kefauver of Tennessee asks for a Senate investigation into organized crime; the request leads to the establishment of the Special Committee on Organized Crime in Interstate Commerce (the "Kefauver Committee"), of which he becomes chairman.

◆ Alger Hiss, a former official of the US State Department, is convicted of perjury, on January 21, 1950, for his having denied passing classified papers to Whittaker Chambers, a journalist and Communist Party member who spied for the Soviet Union in the years before World War II.

◆ At the end of January 1950, Truman announces US plans to develop the hydrogen bomb, an atomic bomb hundreds of times more powerful than the atomic bombs used during World War II.

◆ On February 9, 1950, Senator Joseph McCarthy of Wisconsin gives a public speech in which he claims to be in possession of the names of 205 State Department employees who are members of the Communist Party; although he subsequently fails to release a single name, he becomes nationally famous and will spend the next four years attempting to prove the Communist affiliations of various members of government, the military, and the entertainment industry.

❖ In April 1950 the National Security Council (NSC) presents a report (NSC-68) to Truman that assesses the threat to national security posed by the Soviet Union and its atomic capability.

❖ The Senate passes the Internal Security Act (also called the McCarran Act) over Truman's veto on September 23, 1950; the act requires Communist organizations to register with the Attorney General and allows the detention of "individuals deemed likely to engage in espionage or sabotage" during an "internal security emergency."

❖ In May 1950 the Kefauver Committee launches fifteen months of hearings into organized crime; it calls more than 800 witnesses and the hearings captivate a national television audience.

❖ On June 25, 1950, North Korea invades South Korea.

❖ On June 26 and 27, 1950, the United Nations Security Council passes a resolution that calls for North Korea to halt its invasion and then for all member nations to provide military assistance to the South Koreans.

❖ On June 28, 1950, North Korean troops capture Seoul.

❖ From September 15 to 28, 1950, in what becomes known as the Battle of Inchon, US Marines under General Douglas MacArthur land at Inchon in South Korea and launch an offensive against the invading North Korean People's Army; MacArthur lands troops behind enemy lines and the US forces retake Seoul.

❖ In September 1950 Truman signs the Revenue Act of 1950, which raises personal income and corporation taxes; the increases are an attempt to pay for the Korean War.

❖ In October 1950 Truman travels to Wake Island to meet with General McArthur, who assures him that the Chinese will not come to the aid of the North Koreans in the war.

❖ In October 1950 South Korean and UN troops cross the 38th parallel into North Korea. By the end of October, the deployment of Chinese troops and Soviet air support has turned the tide in favor of the North Koreans.

❖ Truman signs the Puerto Rican Commonwealth Bill in October 1950; the bill allows Puerto Rico to write its own constitution.

❖ Two Puerto Rican nationalists, Griselio Torresola and Oscar Collazo, try to assassinate Truman on November 1, 1950, in Washington, DC. In the gun battle outside Blair House, where the president is staying during White House renovations, Collazo and one of the White House policemen, Leslie Coffelt, are killed. Torresola is later sentenced to life imprisonment and is released in 1979.

❖ In December 1950 Truman declares a state of emergency in response to the increased involvement of the People's Republic of China in the Korean War. He imposes wage and price controls (a power he is granted by the state of emergency).

❖ On January 5, 1951, Chinese and North Korean troops capture Seoul.

❖ Truman recalls MacArthur on April 11, 1951, and replaces him with General Matthew B. Ridgway as Supreme Commander of the United Nations forces in Korea. He makes General James A. Van Fleet commander of the US Eighth Army.

❖ On September 1, 1951, a security pact is signed in San Francisco between Australia, New Zealand, and the United States—the Australia, New Zealand, United States Security Treaty (ANZUS or ANZUS Treaty).

❖ On September 8, 1951, a peace treaty is signed in San Francisco between Japan and forty-seven Allied nations; Japan renounces any claim to Korea or any part of China and the Allies agree to end the post-war occupation of Japan.

❖ On October 31, 1951, Congress passes the Mutual Security Act, which establishes the Mutual Security Agency. It is a foreign aid agency and in effect replaces the Marshall Plan.

❖ On March 20, 1952, the Senate ratifies the peace treaty with Japan.

❖ In March 1952 Truman announces that he will not run for reelection; in July, Adlai Stevenson is chosen as the Democratic nominee.

❖ In April 1952 Truman issues an executive order that directs the Secretary of Commerce to seize and operate most of the nation's steel mills in order to forestall a threatened strike. The steel companies sue the federal government on the grounds that the executive branch of the federal government has no right to issue such an order and that that privilege is reserved to Congress. The Supreme Court concurs, in *Youngstown Sheet & Tube Co. v. Sawyer,* a decision regarded by many as an appropriate restoration of the balance of powers that had become compromised by the growth of the power of that executive branch.

◆ In June 1952 Congress passes over Truman's veto the Immigration and Nationality Act (the McCarran-Walter Act), which repeals blanket prohibitions against immigration into the United States that have been based solely on race, while it imposes more selective immigration quotas that are based on race and nationality (with a bias in favor of allowing more Europeans than Asians to enter the country).

◆ On July 25, 1952, Puerto Rico's constitution is proclaimed.

◆ On November 1, 1952, the first hydrogen bomb is detonated by the United States on a small island, Enewetak, in the Marshall Islands of the Pacific. The bomb is estimated to be hundreds of times more powerful than the atomic bomb that destroyed Hiroshima, Japan. The bomb is made possible by the work of physicists Edward Teller and Stanislaw Marcin Ulam.

MAJOR US AND WORLD EVENTS, 1945–1953

◆ On April 28, 1945, Italian dictator Benito Mussolini and his mistress, Claretta Petacci, are shot and killed, then hung upside down in Milan, where crowds jeer at them.

◆ On April 29, 1945, Adolf Hitler marries his mistress, Eva Braun.

◆ On April 30, 1945, Adolf Hitler and Eva Braun commit suicide in Hitler's bunker underneath the Reich Chancellery in Berlin.

◆ On May 1, 1945, Hitler's successor, Joseph Goebbels, and his wife commit suicide; they first murder their six children.

◆ Throughout May 1945 the Allies liberate Nazi concentration camps, including Mauthausen, where future Nazi hunter Simon Wiesenthal is among those liberated.

◆ On May 23, 1945, former Gestapo leader Heinrich Himmler commits suicide while being held by the British.

◆ In July 1945 the Allies agree to govern Germany via the establishment of four occupation zones: France, the United Kingdom, the Soviet Union, and the United States will each oversee a section.

◆ On July 16, 1945, the first nuclear explosion is detonated near Alamogordo, New Mexico.

◆ Colonel Juan Perón takes over the government of Argentina in October of 1945; he also marries Eva (Evita) Duarte, his mistress, who helps him rally support for his rule.

◆ On October 18, 1945, the war crimes trials of high-ranking Nazis begin in Nuremberg, Germany; the trials last until 1949.

◆ On October 23, 1945, Jackie Robinson is signed to play for the Montreal Royals, a farm team for the Brooklyn Dodgers.

◆ On October 24, 1945, Vidkun Quisling, a Norwegian politician and wartime collaborator with the Nazis, is executed in Norway.

◆ Yugoslavia is declared a republic by the Communist-led Constitutional Assembly, and Marshal Tito becomes its president, November 29, 1945.

◆ In November 1945 US poet Ezra Pound, who had been indicted for treason against the United States for his pro-fascist radio broadcasts in Italy during the war, is flown back to the United States and, after being jailed, is committed to a hospital ward for the criminally insane.

◆ Evelyn Waugh publishes *Brideshead Revisited,* 1945.

◆ George Orwell publishes *Animal Farm,* 1945.

◆ Richard Wright publishes *Black Boy,* 1945.

◆ John Steinbeck publishes *Cannery Row,* 1945.

◆ Norman Mailer publishes *The Naked and the Dead,* 1945.

◆ Nancy Mitford publishes *The Pursuit of Love,* 1945.

- E. B. White publishes *Stuart Little*, 1945.
- Colette publishes *Gigi*, 1945.
- Jean-Paul Sartre publishes *The Age of Reason*, 1945.
- In November 1945 *Ebony* magazine makes its debut.
- Popular music hits of 1945 include Johnny Mercer's "Ac-Cent-Tchu-Ate the Positive" and "On the Atchison, Topeka, and Santa Fe," Les Brown and Doris Day's "Sentimental Journey," and Perry Como's "Till the End of Time."
- Notable films of 1945 include *National Velvet* with Elizabeth Taylor, Michael Curtiz's *Mildred Pierce* with Joan Crawford, Alfred Hitchcock's *Spellbound* with Ingrid Bergman and Gregory Peck, Elia Kazan's *A Tree Grows in Brooklyn* with Dorothy McGuire, Leo McCarey's *The Bells of St. Mary's* with Ingrid Bergman and Bing Crosby, and Billy Wilder's *The Lost Weekend* with Ray Milland.
- Albania is declared a republic by Enver Hoxha, who also declares himself prime minister, January 11, 1946.
- On February 1, 1946, Trygve Lie of Norway is elected the first Secretary General of the United Nations.
- In February 1946 the rule of Juan Perón in Argentina is formalized when he wins the presidential election.
- On March 2, 1946, Ho Chi Minh becomes president of North Vietnam.
- Winston Churchill makes a speech, on March 5, 1946, at Westminster College, Fulton, Missouri, in which he refers to an "iron curtain" that divides the Soviet Union and its sphere of influence from the democratic countries of Europe.
- On April 1, 1946, Singapore becomes a crown colony of the United Kingdom.
- Italians vote to abolish the monarchy and establish a republic in June 1946.
- On July 22, 1946, a bomb planted by the Irgun, an underground Jewish paramilitary organization in Palestine, explodes in the King David Hotel in Jerusalem, killing ninety-one people, including British soldiers and administrators, as well as Jewish and Arab civilians.
- After having been found guilty in the Nuremberg war crimes trials, Nazi leader Hermann Göring poisons himself on October 15, 1946, just before he was to have been executed.
- On December 11, 1946, the United Nations Children's Fund (UNICEF) is founded.
- In late 1946 tensions between the French colonial authorities in Vietnam and Ho Chi Minh, who is leading a resistance movement against the French, escalate into the First Indochina War, which continues until 1954.
- In 1946 Tupperware brand products are introduced by inventor Earl Tupper; the first home parties are held in 1948.
- W. Somerset Maugham publishes *Then and Now*, 1946.
- Robert Penn Warren publishes *All the King's Men*, 1946.
- Eugene O'Neill publishes *The Iceman Cometh*, 1946.
- Paramhansa Yogananda publishes *The Autobiography of a Yogi*, 1946.
- Popular music hits of 1946 include Dinah Shore's "Come Rain or Come Shine," Frankie Lane's "On the Sunny Side of the Street," Frank Sinatra's "That Old Black Magic," and Bing Crosby's "When Irish Eyes Are Smiling."
- Irving Berlin's *Annie Get Your Gun* has its Broadway premiere, 1946.
- Jerome Kern and Oscar Hammerstein II's *Show Boat* begins a Broadway revival, 1946.
- Notable films of 1946 include William Wyler's *The Best Years of Our Lives* with Dana Andrews, Fredric March, and Harold Russell, Howard Hawks's *The Big Sleep* with Humphrey Bogart and Lauren Bacall, Alfred Hitchcock's *Notorious* with Cary Grant and Ingrid Bergman, David Lean's *Brief Encounter* with Celia Johnson and Trevor Howard, Frank Capra's *It's a Wonderful Life* with James Stewart, *The Postman Always Rings Twice* with Lana Turner and John Garfield, and John Ford's *My Darling Clementine* with Henry Fonda.
- Dr. Edwin Land demonstrates the first "instant camera," the Polaroid "Land" Camera, before a meeting of the Optical Society of America on February 21, 1947.

◆ On April 15, 1947, Jackie Robinson, playing for the Brooklyn Dodgers, becomes the first African-American player in Major League baseball.

◆ On April 28, 1947, Thor Heyerdahl and five companions sail westward from Peru on a balsa-wood raft named *Kon-Tiki;* they travel nearly 5,000 miles in 101 days, to Raroia Island, near Tahiti, in the South Pacific. Heyerdahl demonstrates the practicality of his theory that prehistoric people from the continent of South America could have settled the Polynesian islands.

◆ Gangster Benjamin "Bugsy" Siegel is found dead in his Beverly Hills, California, home on June 29, 1947; he is believed to have been shot by Meyer Lansky's henchmen in retaliation for Siegel's having stolen money from funds provided by Lansky for the construction of the Flamingo Hotel and Casino in Las Vegas, Nevada, a project Siegel managed for Lansky.

◆ On the evening of July 2, 1947, residents of Roswell, New Mexico, report seeing a flash or streak of light in the sky and hearing an explosion. There is some speculation afterward that an alien spacecraft crash-landed and that the US government is covering up the truth about the event.

◆ On July 19, 1947, Burma's acting prime minister Aung San and six of his Councillors are assassinated in the Burmese Council Chamber in Rangoon.

◆ In August 1947 India becomes independent of Great Britain and part of the new nation is partitioned off to become the separate nation of Pakistan; millions of Hindus migrate from Pakistan into India and millions of Muslims migrate from India into Pakistan. Jawaharlal Nehru becomes prime minister of India; Muhammed Ali Jinnah becomes governor-general of Pakistan.

◆ On October 14, 1947, Air Force test pilot Captain Charles ("Chuck") Yeager flies the experimental X-1 aircraft and attains speeds faster than the speed of sound, the first time such a feat is accomplished.

◆ Toward the end of 1947 tensions between India and Pakistan, arising from the disputed possession of Kashmir and economic differences, escalate into an undeclared war; there are repeated bloody clashes between Hindus and Muslims fleeing one country for the other.

◆ US aviation innovator Howard Hughes pilots the first and only flight (just over a mile) of the H-4 or *Hercules* aircraft, nicknamed the "Spruce Goose," an eight-engine wooden aircraft that is the largest ever built, November 2, 1947.

◆ Princess Elizabeth of the United Kingdom marries Philip Mountbatten, prince of Greece and Denmark, at Westminster Abbey in London, November 20, 1947.

◆ On November 24, 1947, the Hollywood Ten, a group of US screenwriters and directors, are cited for contempt of Congress for refusing to cooperate with the House Un-American Activities Committee (HUAC) and blacklisted by the major Hollywood studios the next day. The ten, who refuse to answer questions put to them by the committee, include Ring Lardner, Jr., Dalton Trumbo, and John Howard Larson.

◆ On November 29, 1947, the UN General Assembly votes to divide British-ruled Palestine into two states, one Arab and one Jewish.

◆ Albert Camus publishes *La Peste* (*The Plague*), 1947.

◆ James Michener publishes *Tales of the South Pacific*, 1947.

◆ Margaret Wise Brown publishes *Goodnight Moon*, 1947.

◆ Mickey Spillane publishes *I, the Jury*, 1947.

◆ Ralph Ellison publishes *The Invisible Man*, 1947.

◆ *Meet the Press* has its television premiere, 1947.

◆ *The Howdy Doody Show* debuts on television, 1947.

◆ *A Streetcar Named Desire*, by Tennessee Williams, debuts on Broadway, 1947.

◆ *Brigadoon*, with book and lyrics by Alan Jay Lerner and music by Frederick Loewe, debuts on Broadway, 1947.

◆ Popular music hits of 1947 include Peggy Lee's "Golden Earrings," Jo Stafford's "In the Still of the Night," Frank Sinatra's "Night and Day," and Arthur Godfrey's "Too Fat Polka."

❖ Notable films of 1947 include Michael Powell's *Black Narcissus* with Deborah Kerr, *The Bishop's Wife* with Cary Grant and Loretta Young, Elia Kazan's *Gentleman's Agreement* with Gregory Peck, Jacques Tourneur's *Out of the Past* with Robert Mitchum, *Miracle on 34th Street* with Maureen O'Hara and Edmund Gwenn, Joseph Mankiewicz's *The Ghost and Mrs. Muir* with Gene Tierney, and Michael Curtiz's *Life with Father* with William Powell.

❖ Burma becomes independent from the United Kingdom, January 4, 1948.

❖ On January 30, 1948, Mohandas Gandhi is assassinated in New Delhi, India, by a Hindu fanatic.

❖ Ceylon (later Sri Lanka) gains its independence from the United Kingdom (but remains a member of the British Commonwealth of Nations), February 4, 1948.

❖ On April 7, 1948, the United Nations establishes the World Health Organization (WHO).

❖ Colombian presidential candidate Jorge Eliécer Gaitán is assassinated on April 9, 1948; the assassination sparks a riot in Bogatá and ten years of violence in Colombia.

❖ The state of Israel is proclaimed on May 14, 1948; it is immediately invaded by the armies of Syria, Lebanon, Transjordan, Egypt, Saudi Arabia, and Iraq. Chaim Weizmann becomes Israel's first president and David Ben-Gurion becomes the first prime minister.

❖ In June 1948 Chinese Communists in Malaya murder three British rubber planters, triggering a campaign of murder and terror. The ensuing fight against the Communists waged by the British is dubbed the "Malayan Emergency" by the British and lasts until 1960.

❖ The national political conventions are televised for the first time in 1948 (the Republican Convention in June and the Democratic Convention in July).

❖ In early September 1948 Queen Wilhelmina of the Netherlands abdicates and her daughter, Juliana, becomes queen.

❖ On September 17, 1948, UN mediator Count Folke Bernadotte of Sweden is assassinated in Jerusalem, presumably by Jewish extremists who have rejected his proposed solution to the territorial disputes between Palestinians and the new state of Israel.

❖ On December 28, 1948, Prime Minister Mahmud Fahmi Nokrashi of Egypt is assassinated by a member of the Muslim Brotherhood, an Islamic political and terrorist organization.

❖ The *Texaco Star Theater*, which later becomes the *Milton Berle Show*, premieres in 1948; Milton Berle becomes so popular that he is known as "Mr. Television."

❖ *The Toast of the Town*, which later becomes the *Ed Sullivan Show*, premieres in 1948. Sullivan's first show includes the television debut of a young comedy team, Dean Martin and Jerry Lewis.

❖ Sir Winston Churchill publishes the first volume of *The Second World War*, 1948.

❖ Norman Mailer publishes *The Naked and the Dead*, 1948.

❖ Alan Paton publishes *Cry, the Beloved Country*, 1948.

❖ Graham Greene publishes *The Heart of the Matter*, 1948.

❖ Alfred Kinsey publishes *Sexual Behavior in the Human Male*, 1948.

❖ Popular music hits of 1948 include Dinah Shore's "Buttons and Bows," Vaughn Monroe's "Red Roses for a Blue Lady," Art Mooney's "I'm Looking Over a Four-Leaf Clover," and Peggy Lee's "Mañana (Is Soon Enough for Me)."

❖ Notable films of 1948 include Laurence Olivier's *Hamlet*, George Stevens's *I Remember Mama* with Irene Dunne, John Huston's *Key Largo* with Humphrey Bogart, Lauren Bacall, and Edward G. Robinson, Howard Hawks's *Red River* with John Wayne and Montgomery Clift, John Huston's *The Treasure of the Sierra Madre* with Humphrey Bogart, Preston Sturges's *Unfaithfully Yours* with Rex Harrison, and Orson Welles's *The Lady from Shanghai* with Rita Hayworth.

❖ On February 4, 1949, Shah Mohammed Riza Pahlevi is wounded in an assassination attempt in Teheran, Iran.

◆ The Republic of Ireland formalizes its withdrawal from the British Commonwealth in April 1949.

◆ The Federal Republic of Germany (becoming known as "West Germany") is formed in May 1949; Konrad Adenauer is elected chancellor in August.

◆ The German Democratic Republic ("East Germany") is formed in the area of Germany that had been occupied by the Soviet Union, October 1949, with Otto Grotewohl as premier.

◆ On August 29, 1949, the Soviet Union detonates its first atomic bomb in Kazakhstan.

◆ On October 1, 1949, Chairman Mao Zedong proclaims the People's Republic of China.

◆ Coming under pressure from Indonesian president Sukarno (who had proclaimed Indonesia's independence in 1945), the Dutch agree to sovereignty for Indonesia, December 27, 1949.

◆ Field Marshal Phibun Songgram becomes the leader of Siam in 1949 and changes the name of the country to Thailand.

◆ The Prohibition of Mixed Marriages Act is passed in South Africa in 1949 and signals the beginning of the policy of apartheid ("apartness").

◆ The first Bollingen Prize for poetry, established by Paul Mellon and administered through the Yale University Library, is awarded to Ezra Pound in 1949.

◆ Nevil Shute publishes A Town Like Alice, 1949.

◆ George Orwell publishes 1984, 1949.

◆ George R. Stewart publishes Earth Abides, 1949.

◆ Shirley Jackson publishes The Lottery, 1949.

◆ Nancy Mitford publishes Love in a Cold Climate, 1949.

◆ Simone de Beauvoir publishes The Second Sex, 1949.

◆ Richard Rodgers and Oscar Hammerstein II's South Pacific debuts on Broadway, 1949.

◆ The Lone Ranger premieres on television, 1949.

◆ The Academy of Television Arts and Sciences presents its annual awards for the first time in 1949; the original name for the award is the "Immy," later changed to the "Emmy."

◆ Popular music hits of 1949 include Frankie Laine's "Georgia on My Mind," the Weavers's "Goodnight Irene," and Perry Como's "Some Enchanted Evening."

◆ Notable films of 1949 include George Cukor's Adam's Rib with Katharine Hepburn and Spencer Tracy, William Wyler's The Heiress with Olivia de Havilland, John Ford's She Wore a Yellow Ribbon with John Wayne, Carol Reed's The Third Man with Orson Welles and Joseph Cotten, Robert Hamer's Kind Hearts and Coronets with Alec Guinness, and Robert Rossen's All the King's Men with Broderick Crawford.

◆ In 1949 and 1950 Chinese Nationalists under Chiang Kai-shek retreat to the island of Taiwan (called Formosa by the Portuguese), as Communists under Mao Zedong consolidate their rule in mainland China.

◆ On January 17, 1950, masked men commit armed robbery of the Brink's Company offices in Boston, Massachusetts, stealing more than $1.2 million in cash and another $1.5 million in securities. In 1956, eight men are tried and found guilty for their part in the robbery; another man confesses. Most of the money is not recovered.

◆ German (and later British) scientist Klaus Fuchs, who had been involved in the Manhattan Project and the head of a British atomic research facility, is convicted in Great Britain of supplying atomic secrets to the Soviet Union, on March 1, 1950; he subsequently serves nine years of a fourteen-year prison sentence.

◆ In 1950 French foreign minister Robert Schuman presents the "Schuman Plan," which proposes that French and German coal and steel production be pooled and placed under a common authority; it leads, in 1952, to the European Coal and Steel Community and eventually to the European Union.

◆ North Korea invades South Korea, June 25, 1950.

◆ On July 5, 1950, the Knesset (the Israeli parliament) passes the "Law of Return," which grants every Jew the right to emigrate to Israel; the only exceptions are criminals, those who would endanger the security of the state, or those who would pose a threat to the public health.

❖ American swimmer Florence Chadwick swims across the English Channel, from France to England, and breaks Gertrude Ederle's record in October 1950; in September 1951 she crosses the English Channel again, this time from England to France, and so becomes the first woman to have swum the English Channel both ways.

❖ In October 1950 Chinese troops invade Tibet.

❖ In 1950 South Africa passes a number of laws that expand the enforcement of apartheid, including a Population Registration Act, which requires that all inhabitants of South Africa be classified in accordance with their "racial characteristics," and a Group Areas Act, which creates separate areas for the races to live and do business in.

❖ The 1950 census shows a US population of 151.3 million people.

❖ On October 2, 1950, Charles M. Schultz's *Peanuts* comic strip debuts in seven newspapers.

❖ Thor Heyerdahl publishes *Kon-Tiki*, 1950.

❖ Ray Bradbury publishes *The Martian Chronicles*, 1950.

❖ C. S. Lewis publishes *The Lion, the Witch, and the Wardrobe*, 1950.

❖ Isaac Asimov publishes *I, Robot*, 1950.

❖ Mervyn Peake publishes *Gormenghast*, 1950.

❖ Television debuts of 1950 include *What's My Line?*, *The Jack Benny Show*, *Truth or Consequences*, and *The George Burns and Gracie Allen Show*.

❖ *Guys and Dolls*, with book by Abe Burrows and Jo Swerling and music and lyrics by Frank Loesser, debuts on Broadway, 1950.

❖ *Carousel*, with music by Richard Rodgers and Oscar Hammerstein II, debuts in London, 1950.

❖ Popular music hits of 1950 include Nat King Cole's "Mona Lisa," Patti Page's "The Tennessee Waltz," and the "Third Man Theme" (from the 1949 film *The Third Man*), with separate versions recorded by Guy Lombardo and Anton Karas.

❖ Notable films of 1950 include Joseph Mankiewicz's *All About Eve* with Bette Davis, John Huston's *The Asphalt Jungle* with Sterling Hayden, Henry Koster's *Harvey* with James Stewart, Billy Wilder's *Sunset Boulevard* with William Holden and Gloria Swanson, Vincente Minnelli's *Father of the Bride* with Spencer Tracy and Elizabeth Taylor, Walt Disney's *Cinderella*, and George Cukor's *Born Yesterday* with Judy Holliday and William Holden.

❖ On March 6, 1951, the trial of Ethel and Julius Rosenberg for conspiracy to commit espionage begins; the Rosenbergs are charged with passing secrets on the design of the atomic bomb to the Soviet Union. They are convicted (in 1951) and executed in 1953.

❖ In March 1951 the first UNIVAC (Universal Automatic Computer) is delivered to the Census Bureau; it features a stored memory, a keyboard, and magnetic tape.

❖ On July 16 and 17, 1951, King Leopold III of Belgium abdicates and his son Baudouin becomes king.

❖ King Abdullah of Jordan is assassinated by a Palestinian nationalist on July 20, 1951; his son Talal is king briefly before Talal's son Hussein becomes king in 1953.

❖ On October 16, 1951, the first president of Pakistan, Liaquat Ali Khan, is assassinated by a fanatical army officer, Saad Akbar, at Rawalpindi, in Pakistan.

❖ King Idris I of Libya proclaims the independence of the United Kingdom of Libya on December 24, 1951. (Italy had relinquished all claims to Libya in 1947.)

❖ The first Pan American Games, held in Buenos Aires, Argentina, open on February 25, 1951.

❖ J. D. Salinger publishes *Catcher in the Rye*, 1951.

❖ Herman Wouk publishes *The Caine Mutiny*, 1951.

❖ James Jones publishes *From Here to Eternity*, 1951.

❖ Isaac Asimov publishes *Foundation*, 1951.

❖ Ray Bradbury publishes *The Illustrated Man*, 1951.

◆ Daphne du Maurier publishes *My Cousin Rachel*, 1951.

◆ Television premieres of 1951 include *I Love Lucy*, *Search for Tomorrow*, *Love of Life*, *Dragnet*, and the *Roy Rogers Show*.

◆ Richard Rodgers and Oscar Hammerstein II's *The King and I* debuts on Broadway, 1951.

◆ Popular music hits of 1951 include Frankie Laine's "Get Happy," Perry Como's "Hello, Young Lovers," Doris Day's "Lullaby of Broadway," Nat King Cole's "Red Sails in the Sunset," and "Cry," recorded by Johnnie Ray, backed up by The Four Lads.

◆ Notable films of 1951 include Elia Kazan's *A Streetcar Named Desire* with Marlon Brando and Vivien Leigh, Alfred Hitchcock's *Strangers on a Train* with Farley Granger and Robert Walker, Vincente Minnelli's *An American in Paris* with Gene Kelly and Leslie Caron, John Huston's *African Queen* with Humphrey Bogart and Katharine Hepburn, Walt Disney's *Alice in Wonderland*, and George Stevens's *A Place in the Sun* with Montgomery Clift and Elizabeth Taylor.

◆ On February 6, 1952, King George VI of the United Kingdom dies and his daughter, Princess Elizabeth, becomes Queen Elizabeth II (her coronation is held on June 2, 1953).

◆ King Farouk of Egypt is overthrown in a military coup d'état led by Gamal Abdel Nasser in July of 1952.

◆ In October 1952 the British colonial rulers of Kenya declare a state of emergency in response to the Mau Mau uprising against British rule. The Mau Mau are a militant group of Kenyan nationalists that includes Jomo Kenyatta. Imprisoned because of his Mau Mau affiliation from 1952 to 1959, Kenyatta becomes prime minister of Kenya in 1963.

◆ King Talal of Jordan is declared unfit to rule (because of mental illness) by the Jordanian parliament in 1952; his son Hussein becomes king in 1953.

◆ Medical advances in 1952 include the first open-heart surgery and the first sexual reassignment ("sex-change") operation.

◆ Samuel Beckett publishes the play *Waiting for Godot*, 1952 (first performed in early 1953).

◆ Ralph Ellison publishes *Invisible Man*, 1952.

◆ E. B. White publishes *Charlotte's Web*, 1952.

◆ Edna Ferber publishes *Giant*, 1952.

◆ John Steinbeck publishes *East of Eden*, 1952.

◆ Ernest Hemingway publishes *The Old Man and the Sea*, 1952.

◆ In February 1952 Sam Phillips launches Sun Records in Memphis, Tennessee.

◆ Charlie Chaplin travels to London in 1952 for the premiere of his film *Limelight* and, at the behest of Senator Joseph McCarthy, is denied a visa for return to the United States because of Chaplin's supposed Communist sympathies.

◆ On November 25, 1952, *The Mousetrap*, a play by Agatha Christie, opens in London and begins the longest run in theater history.

◆ Television shows premiering in 1952 include *The Adventures of Ozzie and Harriet*, *The Today Show*, *American Bandstand*, *The Guiding Light*, and *The Honeymooners*.

◆ Popular music hits of 1952 include Eddie Fisher's "Lady of Spain," Louis Armstrong's "A Kiss to Build a Dream On," Rosemary Clooney's "Tenderly," and Jimmy Boyd's "I Saw Mommy Kissing Santa Claus."

◆ Notable films of 1952 include Cecil B. DeMille's *The Greatest Show on Earth* with Charlton Heston and Betty Hutton, John Ford's *The Quiet Man* with John Wayne and Maureen O'Hara, Stanley Donen and Gene Kelly's *Singin' in the Rain* with Gene Kelly and Debbie Reynolds, George Cukor's *Pat and Mike* with Spencer Tracy and Katharine Hepburn, and Fred Zinnemann's *High Noon* with Gary Cooper and Grace Kelly.

FAST FACTS ABOUT HARRY TRUMAN

◆ Truman first met his future wife, Bess Wallace, in a Sunday school class, when they were both children.

◆ Truman was a skilled pianist, but he quit taking lessons when he was fifteen years old because he believed he was not talented enough to become a professional musician. His favorite composers included Beethoven, Mozart, Debussy, Chopin, Gershwin, and Johann Strauss, Jr.

❖ As a young piano student in 1900, Truman was taken by his teacher, Mrs. White, to attend a concert given by the great Polish pianist and composer Ignace Paderewski; he was introduced to Paderewski, under whom Mrs. White had studied.

❖ When Truman first wore his National Guard uniform to his grandmother's home, she said it reminded her of the Civil War uniforms of the Union soldiers; because of the unpleasant memories this evoked for her, he never again wore the uniform to her house.

❖ Truman worked in Kansas City after he graduated from high school; he lived in a boardinghouse, another of whose residents was Arthur Eisenhower, an older brother of Dwight D. Eisenhower.

❖ Truman's eyesight was so bad that he memorized the eye chart so that he could pass the eye test for entrance to the army.

❖ Truman was once named one of the ten best-dressed US senators.

❖ The 1948 Republican and Democratic National Conventions were the first presidential nominating conventions to be televised.

❖ On the night of the 1948 presidential election, Truman's opponent, Governor Thomas Dewey, went to bed thinking he had won the election and woke up the next morning to find that Truman had won. He likened his feeling upon making this discovery to waking up in a sealed coffin with a lily in his hand. "If I'm alive, what am I doing here?" he asked himself, "and if I'm dead, why do I have to go to the bathroom?"

❖ In a famous photograph taken the morning after the election, Truman triumphantly holds up a newspaper that bears the erroneous headline, "Dewey Wins!"

❖ Truman was the first president to have a television in the White House.

❖ Truman sometimes referred to his wife as "the Boss" and his daughter Margaret as "the Boss's Boss."

❖ "The buck stops here" plaque that sat on Truman's desk was a gift from a friend, Fred Canfil, who had seen one like it in an office within an Oklahoma federal reformatory.

❖ On July 30, 1965, in a ceremony at the Truman Library, President Lyndon B. Johnson signed the bill that created Medicare. Harry and Bess Truman received the first two Medicare registration cards.

❖ Since 1980 Margaret Truman has written more than a dozen murder mysteries set in Washington, DC.

Dwight D. Eisenhower

Nickname: Ike
Presidency: 34th president, 1953–1961
Party: Republican
Life dates: October 14, 1890–March 28, 1969 (79 years, 168 days)

EARLY LIFE AND EDUCATION

David Dwight Eisenhower was born on October 14, 1890, in Denison, Texas. He was the third of seven sons of David Jacob and Ida Elizabeth Stover Eisenhower, members of a Mennonite sect called the River Brethren, who believed in pacifism and plain dress and practiced avoidance of tobacco and alcohol. When David was a young boy, his mother inverted his birth name to Dwight David because she did not want to see her son called "Dave" or "Davy." Dwight's father, David Eisenhower, came from a prosperous farming family in Abilene, Kansas. He had studied engineering in college, but after marrying Ida in 1885, decided to go into business with a partner, operating a general store to support his new family. The store failed and David reluctantly moved to Texas to work for the Missouri, Kansas, and Texas Railroad. As soon as he had established a home there, Ida and their two sons, Arthur and Edgar, joined him in Denison, where Dwight was born. When David's brother-in-law arranged a better-paying job for him as an engineer, the family returned to Abilene, Kansas, in 1891. Four more sons were born; one died in infancy, but the Eisenhowers reared six healthy, active boys. When Dwight started school, his classmates had trouble pronouncing his last name and arrived at "Ike," a shortened version that became his nickname.

The Eisenhowers had little money but the family was resourceful, hardworking, and close-knit. They grew much of their own food and kept chickens and milk cows. Ike, like all his brothers, helped with chores around the home, including cooking and mending, but also spent as much time as he could reading about history. He also enjoyed sports, especially baseball and football, as well as playing poker, fishing, and camping.

When Ike graduated from Abilene High School in 1909, he wanted to continue his education but did not have the money to do so. He worked at the Belle Springs Creamery in Abilene for the next two years. A friend who was interested in securing an appointment to the US Naval Academy at Annapolis inspired Ike to apply to the academy as well, but after earning a high score on the entrance exam, he found that he was too old to be admitted. He had also taken the test for the US Military Academy at West Point, however, and received an appointment that allowed him to enter on June 14, 1911. His mother, mindful of the River Brethren's pacifism, cried when he left for West Point, but she and her husband, who both believed in allowing their sons to make their own choices, accepted his decision.

> "I have found out in later years [that] we were very poor, but the glory of America is that we didn't know it then."
>
> Dwight D. Eisenhower, on his childhood, as quoted in *Time*, June 16, 1952

At West Point, Ike was a good though not outstanding student. He played football, but injured his knee during a game. Before it healed completely, he injured it again dismounting from a horse after cavalry exercises. He was quite depressed about the end of his football career, but rebounded to support the team, first as a cheerleader and then as coach for the junior varsity team.

Eisenhower was honest, open, and likable, but broke the rules on occasion and received many demerits for minor infractions ranging from tardiness to not saluting properly. During his education at West Point, he also demonstrated characteristics that would stand him in good stead throughout his career: Eisenhower had the ability to convince others to work together, and he could get along with difficult personalities.

Eisenhower graduated June 12, 1915, in a class later known as "the class that the stars fell on," in recognition of the many West Pointers from that year who became generals. One of Eisenhower's classmates and closest friends was Omar Bradley; he and Eisenhower would later both become five-star generals.

EARLY CAREER

Although there was a chance that Eisenhower's knee injury would prevent his receiving a commission, he was duly commissioned a second lieutenant. He asked to be posted to the Philippines, but was sent instead to Fort Sam Houston in San Antonio, Texas, where the violent activity of Mexican revolutionary Pancho Villa, including a raid on the U.S. town of Columbus, New Mexico, was causing some concern. Eisenhower trained National Guardsmen, who were called to service to help police the American-Mexican border. In October 1915 he was introduced to the Doud family from Denver, Colorado, who were spending the winter in San Antonio. Ike was immediately smitten with the petite, blue-eyed, eighteen-year-old Mary (called "Mamie") Geneva Doud. Mamie's father, John Doud, had been a successful meatpacker and had retired when Mamie was seven. Mamie was the second of his four daughters; she enjoyed a very comfortable upbringing and had completed her education with a year of finishing school. Pretty and vivacious, she was popular with many young men, but Ike was persistent and won the affection of her family. By the end of the year, they were engaged, although her father cautioned that life as a military wife would be difficult.

Ike married Mamie in her family's Denver home on July 1, 1916, the same day he received word that he had been promoted to first lieutenant. Mamie then faced the realities of life as an army wife: shabby quarters and Ike's frequent absences on duty. He is reported to have bluntly told her that his country came first and she came second. He was briefly posted to Fort Oglethorpe, Georgia, and Fort Leavenworth, Kansas. With the entry of the United States into World War I in April 1917, Eisenhower was promoted to captain in May of that year. He requested combat duty but was told that he was better suited to serve as an instructor. Meanwhile, Mamie gave birth to their first child, a son named Doud Dwight Eisenhower, nicknamed "Icky," on September 24, 1917, in San Antonio.

Eisenhower was assigned to the Tank Corps in February 1918, serving at Camp Meade, Maryland, and subsequently at camps in Pennsylvania, New Jersey, and Georgia. Many of his superiors did not believe tanks would prove particularly useful in warfare, but after the war ended, Eisenhower met an officer who shared his enthusiasm for the potential uses of tanks in battle, Colonel George S. Patton. Eisenhower and Patton became fast friends and endlessly discussed ways to use tanks to create a military advantage, conducting sometimes dangerous experiments and formulating theories that flew in the face of accepted army tactics. After the two published their theories, they were reprimanded by their commanding officers.

In 1919 Eisenhower acted as an observer of the Transcontinental Motor Truck Trip, an army convoy designed to test motorized transport over long distances. From Illinois to California, virtually no paved roads existed; Ike noted in his report that the sandy desert roads in the Southwest made the transport of heavy vehicles particularly difficult. The lack of a unified highway system in the United States deeply concerned Ike, and he would later address this problem when he became president. In July 1920 Eisenhower was promoted to major.

Perhaps the most difficult moment in Eisenhower's life came in late 1920, when three-year-old Icky contracted scarlet fever. After weeks of illness, the boy died on January 2, 1921. Mamie and Ike rarely talked about their loss, but every year on Icky's birthday, Ike sent Mamie a dozen yellow roses in remembrance of their first-born son.

A year later the Eisenhowers found themselves at Camp Gaillard in the Panama Canal Zone, where Ike, at General Fox Conner's request, had been assigned as Conner's executive officer. Mamie found the hot, humid, mildewed, and bug-ridden Canal Zone another trying military post, but Eisenhower had found a mentor in Conner, whom he described as "the ablest man I ever knew." Conner soon had Eisenhower reading about great military leaders and campaigns, and the pair spent many hours discussing what Eisenhower had learned, reviewing tactics and battles from such conflicts as the American Revolution, the Napoleonic Wars, and the Civil War.

Mamie returned to Denver before the birth of their second son, John Sheldon Doud, on Au-

gust 3, 1922. She later returned to the Canal Zone, but was relieved when Ike was assigned to Camp Meade in Maryland, although Ike was less pleased to discover that his job would be coaching the football team. With Conner's help, Ike gained admittance to the prestigious Command and General Staff School at Fort Leavenworth, Kansas, the training ground for the army's leaders. Eisenhower entered the school on August 19, 1925, and graduated first in a class of 245 on June 18, 1926.

Eisenhower served next as a battalion commander at Fort Benning, Georgia, from August 1926 until January 1927, when he was assigned to the American Battle Monuments Commission, directed by General John J. Pershing. After George Washington, Pershing's title of General of the Armies made him the U.S. military's second highest-ranking officer of all time. In 1927 Eisenhower, then stationed in Washington, DC, wrote a guidebook to World War I battlefields in Europe. For the next year Ike attended the army's War College, a postgraduate course for leaders; he again graduated first in his class. Then he, Mamie, and John headed for Europe: Eisenhower was assigned to visit the battlefields of France before revising the guidebook he had written.

In the fall of 1929, the family headed back to Washington, where Ike served as executive officer to General George V. Moseley, the Assistant Secretary of War. It was in this position that Eisenhower took part in the government's attempt to disperse the so-called Bonus Army, thousands of World War I veterans (often accompanied by their families) who had marched on Washington and camped out there, pleading for the government to pay bonuses that had been granted in 1924 but were not payable until 1945. The growing poverty of the Depression had been the catalyst behind this call for immediate payment, and the Bonus Army camped on the Anacostia Flats across the Anacostia River from Washington while awaiting the decision of Congress. The Senate voted against paying the bonuses, and President Herbert Hoover ordered that the Bonus Army be dispersed. General Douglas MacArthur, as Army Chief of Staff, led infantry, cavalry, and tanks against the veterans. He was assisted by Eisenhower and Patton. Ignoring Hoover's orders to cease and desist, MacArthur crossed the river and led his troops into the main camp of the protesting veterans; the camp was burned and many veterans and their families were injured (in fact, two babies died in the ensuing melee). Eisenhower later described the scene as "pitiful."

"Oh, yes, I studied dramatics under him for 12 years."

Dwight D. Eisenhower, on being asked whether he knew General Douglas MacArthur, as quoted by journalist Quentin Reynolds

---

Eisenhower was next assigned, in February 1933, as chief military aide to MacArthur. When MacArthur was sent to the Philippines in 1935 as military advisor to the newly elected president of the Philippines, Manuel Quezon, he asked Eisenhower to assume the post of assistant military advisor. Eisenhower initially resisted, as he disliked MacArthur and often disagreed with his policies, but MacArthur made the request an order. Eisenhower served in the Philippines from September 1935 to December 1939; he was promoted to lieutenant colonel on July 1, 1936. He was also awarded the Distinguished Service Star of the Philippines.

Between the years of 1940 and 1941, Eisenhower served at Fort Ord, California; Fort Lewis, Washington; and Fort Sam Houston. Eisenhower, entering his fifties, assumed that before long he would retire with the rank of lieutenant colonel, but as US entry into World War II began to seem more likely, he hoped to have, at long last, the opportunity for a field command.

WORLD WAR II

When the United States declared war against the Axis powers on December 8, 1941, it was a matter of days before Eisenhower was sum-

moned to Washington to join the General Staff in the War Plans Division (later called the Operations Division). General George C. Marshall, the Army Chief of Staff, asked Eisenhower for his advice on the war in the Pacific, and Ike recommended that the United States concentrate on the war in Europe while fighting a defensive war in the Pacific, saving the Philippines if possible. He noted the importance of Australia as an ally and a base of operations in the region. In February 1942 Eisenhower was made chief of the War Plans Division and in March temporarily promoted to major general.

Increasing responsibilities followed at a dizzying pace for a man who had been relatively unknown before the war. Eisenhower planned for the invasion of Europe and traveled to London to coordinate the efforts of the various Allied nations. General Marshall named him commanding general of the European Theater in June 1942, paying tribute to not only his knowledge of military strategy, his hard work, and his organizational skills, but also his ability to work with many different people, most of whom found him accessible and forthcoming. He contributed to the US building of strong relationships with Allied leaders, including Prime Minister Winston Churchill of Great Britain.

Eisenhower commanded the Allied forces for Operation Torch, the invasion of North Africa in November 1942. He came under heavy criticism for his decision to work with the French General Jean-François Darlan, who had been part of the pro-Nazi Vichy government of France. But Eisenhower gambled that Darlan's influence would weigh with the French troops already in North Africa, and, as hoped, Darlan was able to win their support for the Allies when the invasion came. In mid-1943 Eisenhower directed the invasion of Sicily and then the Italian mainland; Rome was liberated in June 1944. Eisenhower, temporarily promoted to four-star general in February 1943, was subsequently given a permanent promotion to major general in August 1943.

Throughout 1943 and early 1944, Eisenhower was occupied with the planning for the invasion of Nazi-held France. He was appointed supreme

General Dwight D. Eisenhower meeting American paratroopers in England, 1944.

commander of the Allied Expeditionary Forces in December 1943, commanding the largest multinational force in history. After waiting anxiously for stormy weather conditions to improve, Eisenhower gave the command for the D-Day invasion of Normandy to commence on June 6, 1944. In one day more than 150,000 amphibious troops stormed the beaches of Normandy. Eventually, more than a million Allied soldiers fought on the Western front, liberating Paris in August 1944. Eisenhower managed to control and direct such egotistic personalities as George C. Patton and the British General Bernard Montgomery; he also was able to make good use of his long-standing friendship with Omar Bradley.

Eisenhower was criticized by some for allowing the Russians to reach Berlin first, but, as always, he took military and political considerations into account before making a decision. At the Yalta Conference in 1945 before

the war's official end, President Franklin D. Roosevelt and Churchill had promised Soviet leader Joseph Stalin a central role in the invasion of Germany, in part because of Russia's heavy wartime casualties and in part to ensure Soviet participation in any possible invasion of Japan. Like Roosevelt and Churchill, Eisenhower was adamant that the Allies maintain good post-war relations with the Soviet Union. After the German surrender on May 7, 1945, Eisenhower was appointed the military governor of the US zone in Germany.

During the war, Eisenhower was separated from Mamie for long periods of time, including the day of their son John's graduation from West Point, coincidentally occurring on June 6, 1944. While he was away, Ike and Mamie exchanged many letters, including some in which Ike denied rumors linking him romantically with Kay Summersby, an Irish volunteer in the British Motor Transport Corps who had been assigned as his driver during a visit to London. Evidence to support the supposed affair is slight. Summersby wrote a book in 1948, *Ike Was My Boss*, that did not mention an affair; a second book, *Past Forgetting: My Love Affair with Dwight D. Eisenhower*, was only published after her death and alleges an emotional intimacy and stolen kisses, but no sexual relationship. Eisenhower's aides agreed that her friendship was invaluable to Ike during the stressful D-Day planning stages; the two frequently had dinner together and played bridge.

In late 1945 Eisenhower became the army chief of staff and served for two years in this capacity, retiring from the army in February 1948. He accepted a position as president of Columbia University and wrote his memoirs, *Crusade in Europe*, in 1948. The book became an instant best-seller and, for the first time in his life, Ike attained some financial wealth.

POLITICAL CAREER

Eisenhower's preeminence as America's military hero prompted President Harry S. Truman to offer him the position of supreme allied Commander of the North American Treaty Organization (NATO) in 1950, an appointment that Eisenhower accepted. Truman was also influenced by the high esteem with which most of Europe's leaders continued to regard the former general. Both major political parties courted Eisenhower during this period as a possible presidential candidate, and as the election of 1952 neared, Ike himself feared that US membership in NATO would be threatened by the election of any of the active Republican and Democratic candidates. Declaring himself a Republican, Eisenhower sought, and won, that party's nomination as its presidential candidate, selecting Senator Richard M. Nixon of California as his vice-presidential running mate. As a distinguished World War II hero, Eisenhower was a popular candidate from the start. He campaigned energetically, both in person and on television, and won an impressive victory over Democrat Governor Adlai Stevenson of Illinois, capturing 442 electoral votes to Stevenson's 89.

PRESIDENCY

One of Eisenhower's first actions as president was to visit Korea to secure an armistice in the war there. Foreign affairs occupied him a great deal; he felt more comfortable addressing them than domestic issues, although he also worked hard to educate himself in that arena. Eisenhower was assisted by a very able Secretary of State, John Foster Dulles. Together they crafted the Southeast Asian Treaty Organization

"Every gun that is made, every warship launched, every rocket fired signifies, in the final sense, a theft from those who hunger and are not fed, those who are cold and are not clothed. This world in arms is not spending money alone. It is spending the sweat of its laborers, the genius of its scientists, the hopes of its children. . . . This is not a way of life at all, in any true sense. Under the cloud of threatening war, it is humanity hanging from a cross of iron."

Dwight D. Eisenhower, in an address dubbed the "Chance for Peace" speech, given before the American Society of Newspaper Editors, Washington, D.C., April 16, 1953

(SEATO) in 1954, in response to the threat of Communist domination in the area. Later, during Eisenhower's second term, in 1957, he articulated his position regarding the fight against Communism in the Eisenhower Doctrine, which announced US military support for the countries of the Middle East if they were threatened by Communism.

In domestic affairs, Eisenhower took a fairly low-key approach, attempting to balance the budget, end price controls, and help the economy to flourish by downsizing the military, thus lowering congressional expenditures on it. Eisenhower avoided direct confrontation with Senator Joseph McCarthy and McCarthy's attempt to uncover Communist subversives within the government and elsewhere. Privately, Eisenhower disliked McCarthy and his approach; his insistence that McCarthy's hearings about possible Communists serving in the armed forces be televised in 1954 led to many Americans becoming disenchanted with McCarthy's tactics.

On September 23, 1955, Eisenhower suffered a heart attack. After a nearly two-month hospital stay, he recuperated at the farm he and Mamie had bought in Gettysburg, Pennsylvania. Eisenhower recovered sufficiently to mount a reelection campaign in 1956, defeating Stevenson once again, this time by 457 electoral votes to 73.

During his second term, Eisenhower addressed the shortcomings he had observed back in 1919 during the Transcontinental Motor Truck Trip and created a lasting legacy with the Federal Aid Highway Act of 1956, which established the interstate highway system in the United States. As a result of the act, more than 40,000 miles of roads were built.

Another important development during Eisenhower's second term was the Soviet Union's launch of the *Sputnik* satellite on October 4, 1957. The United States responded by creating the National Aeronautics and Space Administration (NASA) in 1958, the same year that it successfully launched the *Explorer I* satellite.

A more complex issue facing Eisenhower was civil rights. Although not outspoken on the subject, he supported the Supreme Court's decision in banning segregation in schools. When the governor of Arkansas attempted to block the integration of schools in Little Rock in 1957, Eisenhower sent 101st Airborne troops to protect the black students who were enrolling there. Eisenhower also subsequently signed the Civil Rights Act of 1957, which created a commission to examine instances of black citizens being prevented from voting.

"In the councils of government, we must guard against the acquisition of unwarranted influence, whether sought or unsought, by the military-industrial complex."

Dwight D. Eisenhower, in his farewell address to the nation, January 17, 1961

Although Eisenhower continued to pursue peaceful coexistence with the Soviet Union, relations became seriously strained in 1960 when the Soviets shot down an American U-2 spy plane. The United States initially tried to deny the incident, but did suffer some embarrassment when the Soviets revealed that they had captured the pilot. A proposed summit in Paris to discuss nuclear disarmament was cancelled by the Soviets because of this incident. Before leaving office in 1961, Eisenhower called for the necessity of maintaining the United States as a strong military power, but warned against long and costly military ventures that might be detrimental to its future.

POST-PRESIDENTIAL CAREER

In 1961 Eisenhower and Mamie, both extremely popular with the American people, retired to their farm in Gettysburg, their first permanent home since the start of Ike's military career. In his retirement, Ike loved to play golf, go fishing, play cards, and devote time to his hobby, painting. He also wrote several books chronicling his presidential career and postpresidential life. The Eisenhowers spent their winters in Palm Desert, California. They were pleased when Eisenhower's vice president, Richard Nixon, was elected president in

1968, and when Nixon's daughter Julie married their grandson, David Eisenhower, the same year.

After a series of debilitating heart attacks, Eisenhower died on March 28, 1969, at the Walter Reed Army Hospital in Washington, DC. He was buried in the Place of Meditation, a chapel at the Eisenhower Center in Abilene, Kansas, as was Mamie when she died in 1979.

Eisenhower's popularity has never been in doubt, but the evaluation of his performance as president has grown increasingly favorable as time goes by. His military experience made him comfortable in delegating responsibility, while still exerting enormous control over his staff. Widely respected for his personal integrity, he sought consensus from others but ultimately made his own decisions and was guided by his own principles.

Birthplace: Denison, TX
Residency: Kansas
Religion: Presbyterian
Education: US Military Academy, West Point, NY, graduated 1915
Place of Death: Washington, DC
Burial Site: Eisenhower Center, Abilene, KS
Dates in Office: January 20, 1953–January 20, 1961 (8 years)
Age at Inauguration: 62 years, 98 days

FAMILY

Father: David Jacob Eisenhower (1863–1942)
Mother: Ida Elizabeth Stover Eisenhower (1862–1946)
Siblings: Dwight was the third of seven sons; his brothers were Arthur Bradford Eisenhower (1886–1958); Edgar Newton Eisenhower (1889–1971); Roy Jacob Eisenhower (1892–1942); Paul Dawson Eisenhower (1894–1895); Earl Dewey Eisenhower (1898–1968); Milton Stover Eisenhower (1899–1985)
Wife: Mary ("Mamie") Geneva Doud Eisenhower (1896–1979), married on July 1, 1916, in Denver, CO
Children: Doud Dwight ("Icky") Eisenhower (1917–1921); John Sheldon Doud Eisenhower (1922–)

CAREER

Private: president of Columbia University (1948–1953)
Political: president of the United States (1953–1961)
Military: Eisenhower graduated from the US Military Academy at West Point in 1915 (ranked 61st of 164 graduates), commissioned a second lieutenant and stationed at Fort Sam Houston, San Antonio, TX; promoted to captain (1917); during World War I, served as instructor at Fort Oglethorpe, GA, at Fort Leavenworth, KS, and at Camp Colt in Gettysburg, PA, a tank training center; received Distinguished Service Medal; promoted to major (August 1920); sent to Camp Meade, MD; assigned to 20th Infantry Brigade in the Panama Canal Zone (1922–1924) under the command of General Fox Conner; attended Army Command and General Staff School at Fort Leavenworth, KS, and graduated in 1926 (ranked 1st of 275 graduates); served at Fort Benning, GA (1926); graduated from the Army War College (June 1928); served in France as a member of the Battle Monuments Commission; served in the Washington, DC, Office of the Assistant Secretary of War (1929); became aide to Army Chief of Staff General Douglas MacArthur (1933–1939), accompanying MacArthur to the Philippines; promoted to lieutenant colonel (1936); promoted to full colonel (March 1941); named commander of 3rd Army (June 1941); appointed by General George C. Marshall to War Plans Division in Washington, DC, and tasked with planning for an Allied invasion of Europe; promoted to brigadier general (September 1941); promoted to major general (March 1942); named by General Marshall as commander of US troops in Europe (June 1942); promoted to lieutenant general (July 1942); placed in charge of Operation Torch, the Allied invasion of North Africa (November 1942–May 1943); promoted to full general (February 1943); directed invasion of Italy (July 1943–June 1944); appointed supreme commander of Allied Expeditionary Forces (December 1943); planned Operation Overlord, the Normandy invasion (June 6, 1944); named five-star general, General of the Army (December 1944); named Army

Chief of Staff (1945); left active duty (May 1948); named supreme commander of the North American Treaty Organization (NATO) after the outbreak of the Korean War (1950); retired from the US Army in June 1952 to pursue presidency.
Selected Works: *At Ease: Stories I Tell to Friends* (Blue Ridge Summit, PA: TAB Books, 1988); *The Churchill-Eisenhower Correspondence, 1953–1955*, ed. by Peter G. Boyle (Chapel Hill: University of North Carolina Press, 1990); *Crusade in Europe* (Baltimore: Johns Hopkins University Press, 1997); *Dear General: Eisenhower's Wartime Letters to Marshall*, ed. by Joseph Patrick Hobbs (Baltimore: Johns Hopkins University Press, 1999); *The Diaries of Dwight D. Eisenhower, 1953–1969*, microfilm, ed. by Robert Lester (Frederick, MD: University Publications of America, 1987); *Dwight D. Eisenhower, 1890–1969: Chronology, Documents, Bibliographical Aids*, ed. by Robert I. Vexler (Dobbs Ferry, NY: Oceana Publications, 1970); *Eden-Eisenhower Correspondence, 1955–1957*, ed. by Peter G. Boyle (Chapel Hill: University of North Carolina Press, 2005); *Eisenhower: The Prewar Diaries and Selected Papers, 1905–1941*, ed. by Daniel D. Holt (Baltimore: Johns Hopkins University Press, 1998); *Letters to Mamie*, ed. and with commentary by John S. D. Eisenhower (Garden City, NY: Doubleday, 1978); *The Macmillan-Eisenhower Correspondence, 1957–1969*, ed. by E. Bruce Geelhoed and Anthony O. Edmonds (Houndmills, Basingstoke, Hampshire, New York: Palgrave Macmillan, 2004); *Minutes and Documents of the Cabinet Meetings of President Eisenhower, 1953–1961*, microfilm (Washington, DC: University Publications of America, 1980); *The Papers of Dwight David Eisenhower*, ed. by Alfred D. Chandler, Jr. (Baltimore: Johns Hopkins Press, 1970–c. 2001); *President Dwight D. Eisenhower's Office Files, 1953–1961*, microfilm (Bethesda, MD: University Publications of America, 1990); *Report by the Supreme Commander to the Combined Chiefs of Staff on the Operations in Europe of the Allied Expeditionary Force, 6 June 1944 to 8 May 1945* (Washington, DC: Center of Military History, US Army, 1994); *The White House Years* (Garden City, NY: Doubleday, 1963–1965)

PRESIDENCY

Nomination: 1952: Both parties had approached Eisenhower about running for president; once he declared himself to be a Republican, he was nominated on the first ballot at the Republican convention, held July 7–11, 1952, in Chicago, IL. Richard M. Nixon of CA was selected as the vice-presidential candidate.

1956: Eisenhower was nominated on the first ballot at the Republican convention, held August 20–23, 1956, in San Francisco, CA; Nixon was again selected for the vice-presidential slot.
Election: 1952: elected president on November 4, 1952

1956: elected president on November 6, 1956
Opponent: 1952: Adlai Stevenson, IL, Democrat

1956: Adlai Stevenson, IL, Democrat
Vote Totals: 1952: Eisenhower, 33,778,963 popular, 442 electoral; Stevenson, 27,314,992 popular, 89 electoral

1956: Eisenhower, 35,581,003 popular, 457 electoral; Stevenson, 25,738,765 popular, 73 electoral
Inauguration: 1952: January 20, 1953

1956: January 21, 1957 [Note: January 20, 1957, was a Sunday, so the inauguration was held on January 21.]
Vice President: Richard M. Nixon, CA (1953–1961)

CABINET

Secretary of State: John Foster Dulles, NY (1953–1959); Christian A. Herter, MA (1959–1961)
Secretary of the Treasury: George M. Humphrey, MI (1953–1957); Robert B. Anderson, TX (1957–1961)
Secretary of Defense: Charles E. Wilson, MI (1953–1957); Neil H. McElroy, OH (1957–1959); Thomas S. Gates, Jr., PA (1959–1961)
Attorney General: Herbert Brownell, Jr., NY (1953–1957); William P. Rogers, NY (1957–1961)
Postmaster General: Arthur E. Summerfield, MI (1953–1961)
Secretary of Agriculture: Ezra Taft Benson, ID (1953–1961)
Secretary of the Interior: Douglas McKay, OR (1953–1956); Frederick A. Seaton, NE (1956–1961)

Secretary of Labor: Martin P. Durkin, IL (1953); James P. Mitchell, NJ (1953–1961)
Secretary of Commerce: Sinclair Weeks, MA (1953–1958); Frederick H. Mueller, MI (1959–1961)
Secretary of Health, Education, and Welfare: Oveta Culp Hobby, TX (1953–1955); Marion B. Folsom, NY (1955–1958); Arthur S. Flemming, OH (1958–1961) [Note: This new department was created under Eisenhower, and made effective on April 11, 1953.]

CONGRESS

83rd Congress (1953–1955); Speaker of the House: Joseph W. Martin, Jr. (MA, Republican)
84th Congress (1955–1957); Speaker of the House: Sam Rayburn (TX, Democrat)
85th Congress (1957–1959); Speaker of the House: Sam Rayburn (TX, Democrat)
86th Congress (1959–1961); Speaker of the House: Sam Rayburn (TX, Democrat)

SUPREME COURT APPOINTEES

Earl Warren, CA; Chief Justice (1953–1969)
John Marshall Harlan, NY; Associate Justice (1955–1971)
William J. Brennan, Jr., NJ; Associate Justice (1956–1990)
Charles Evans Whittaker, MO; Associate Justice (1957–1962)
Potter Stewart, OH; Associate Justice (1958–1981)

MAJOR EVENTS OF THE EISENHOWER ADMINISTRATION

◆ The Department of Health, Education, and Welfare (HEW) comes into existence, April 11, 1953.
◆ Eisenhower signs the Submerged Lands Act on May 22, 1953, which grants coastal states the title to lands and the natural resources they contain below the waters, for up to three miles from the coastline of the state.
◆ On July 26, 1953, the United States and North Korea sign an armistice ending the Korean War.
◆ In August 1953 the Central Intelligence Agency (CIA) helps oust Prime Minister

Mohammed Mossadegh in Iran, consolidating the authority of Mohammed Reza Pahlavi as the shah.
◆ On September 30, 1953, Eisenhower appoints Earl Warren as chief justice of the Supreme Court of the United States.
◆ Eisenhower approves a secret document (National Security Council Paper 162/2) that argues for maintaining and expanding the supply of nuclear weapons held by the United States in late October, 1953.
◆ December 8, 1953, Eisenhower proposes the peaceful development of atomic power in a speech at the United Nations.
◆ On January 21, 1954, the USS Nautilus, the first nuclear submarine, is launched from Groton, Connecticut, and christened by Mamie Eisenhower.
◆ At the Berlin Conference in late January 1954, representatives of the United Kingdom, France, the United States, and the Soviet Union meet and discuss an end to the Korean War, the conflict between the French and Vietnamese, and the occupation of Germany.
◆ The United States tests a hydrogen bomb approximately a thousand times more powerful than the nuclear bomb dropped on Hiroshima; the hydrogen bomb is exploded on Bikini Atoll in the Marshall Islands on March 1, 1954.
◆ On April 1, 1954, Eisenhower signs a bill creating the United States Air Force Academy; the site chosen for the school is near Colorado Springs, Colorado.
◆ At an April 7, 1954 news conference, Eisenhower refers to the "domino theory" in discussing the rise of Communism in Southeast Asia. The theory posits that if one country in Indochina (an area including Vietnam, Laos, and Cambodia) falls to Communism, another country (e.g., Burma or Thailand) will likely follow it, thus inducing the surrounding nations to fall like a line of dominoes.
◆ From April through June 1954, television airs the hearings of the Committee on Government Operations, at which committee chairman, Senator Joseph McCarthy, questions suspected Communists in the US Army. McCarthy's

abrasive style and inability to produce compelling evidence supporting his claims cause the public to lose confidence in him.

◆ From April through July 1954, the first of a series of conferences is held in Geneva, Switzerland, to discuss ending the conflicts in Korea and Indochina. France and Vietnam reach the so-called Geneva Accords, an agreement calling for a cease-fire between their opposing forces in Vietnam and the division of that country into two military zones, one held by Ho Chi Minh's pro-Communist forces in the north, and the other, an anti-Communist, US-supported south, led by Ngo Dinh Diem.

◆ On May 13, 1954, the United States and Canada sign the St. Lawrence Seaway Act, allowing the United States to participate with Canada in seaway construction.

◆ On May 17, 1954, in *Brown v. the Board of Education of Topeka, Kansas*, the Supreme Court rules that segregated schools are unconstitutional.

◆ Jacobo Arbenz Guzmán, president of Guatemala, is forced to resign on June 27, 1954, by an army of exiles supported by the CIA, working to protect the interests of US firms with extensive holdings in Guatemalan agriculture (especially bananas).

◆ On December 2, 1954, the Senate censures Senator Joseph McCarthy for his conduct, specifically citing him for contempt against the committee formed to study charges against him for questionable financial affairs in 1952, and for unethical abuses of power in the Senate.

◆ The Southeast Asia Treaty Organization (SEATO), an alliance of France, Australia, the United States, Great Britain, Pakistan, Thailand, New Zealand, and the Philippines, is formed in 1954 to combat Communism in Southeast Asia.

◆ As conflict intensifies between Taiwan and Communist China, the United States signs a mutual defense pact with Taiwan in late 1954 and, in early 1955, Eisenhower announces that the United States would use atomic weapons in the event of a war with China.

◆ A second Geneva Conference (known as the Summit Conference) is held in July 1955 and brings together Eisenhower, Nikolai Bulganin, and Nikita Khrushchev of the Soviet Union, Anthony Eden of Great Britain, and Edgar Faure of France to discuss European issues, including the reunification of Germany and disarmament.

◆ At the Summit Conference in 1955, Eisenhower proposes an "open skies" agreement whereby the United States and the Soviet Union would be free to fly over each other's territory without fear of attack; the Soviet Union rejects his proposal.

◆ In July 1955 Senate Majority Leader Lyndon B. Johnson suffers a heart attack.

◆ On September 24, 1955, Eisenhower suffers a heart attack in Denver, Colorado; he is hospitalized but slowly recovers, quelling doubts about his fitness to run for a second term.

◆ On November 25, 1955, the Interstate Commerce Commission bans segregation on interstate buses and trains.

◆ Rosa Parks is arrested on December 1, 1955, for refusing to give her seat on a Montgomery, Alabama, bus to a white man, as required by local segregation laws. Her action and subsequent arrest trigger a bus boycott in Montgomery (led by Dr. Martin Luther King, Jr.) that lasts until December 1956, when the Supreme Court upholds a lower court's ruling that Montgomery's segregation law is unconstitutional.

◆ The Presidential Libraries Act, 1955, formalizes the precedent set by Franklin D. Roosevelt, the construction of presidential libraries through private funds but their maintenance by the federal government.

◆ After trying to convince Richard Nixon to take a cabinet post rather than seek reelection as vice president, Eisenhower announces in April 1956 that Nixon will remain his running mate in the upcoming election.

◆ In June 1956 Eisenhower signs into law a bill adding the words "under God" to the Pledge of Allegiance.

◆ At the end of July 1956 Eisenhower signs a joint resolution of Congress that authorizes "In God We Trust" as the national motto of the United States.

◆ In late July 1956 President Gamal Abdal Nasser of Egypt nationalizes the Suez Canal, angering Great Britain and France, who then support Israel in its attack on and occupation of the Sinai Peninsula. Britain and France withdraw in the face of UN criticism and threats of Soviet intervention; Nasser emerges as an Arab leader.

◆ The Federal Aid Highway Act of 1956 standardizes the interstate highway system of the United States.

◆ The Social Security Act of 1956 amends Social Security to include disability insurance.

◆ On November 6, 1956, Eisenhower redefeats Adlai Stevenson, Democrat from Illinois, for the presidency.

◆ On January 5, 1957, Eisenhower proposes the "Eisenhower Doctrine," a policy formulated by Secretary of State John Foster Dulles that urges US support, both military and economic, for countries in the Middle East threatened by Communist aggression; the policy is approved by Congress.

◆ On February 14, 1957, the Southern Christian Leadership Conference (SCLC) is formed by Dr. Martin Luther King, Jr., Ralph David Abernathy, Fred Shutterworth, and Bayard Rustin to coordinate the efforts of, and provide assistance to, local organizations working for African-American equality.

◆ In July 1957 the US Surgeon General reports that a link exists between cigarette smoking and lung cancer.

◆ The governor of Arkansas calls up the Arkansas National Guard on September 4, 1957, to prevent black students from enrolling at Little Rock High School. The Guard is then placed under federal command by Eisenhower, who also dispatched 1,000 members of the 101st Airborne division to protect the enrolling black students.

◆ The Civil Rights Act of 1957 is signed by Eisenhower on September 9; the act creates a commission on civil rights to investigate possible instances of black citizens being denied the right to vote.

◆ Vice President Richard M. Nixon visits Caracas, Venezuela, in May 1958. His limousine is kicked and pelted with stones by a mob of anti-American demonstrators.

◆ At the end of May 1958 unknown soldiers from World War II and the Korean War are interred at the Tomb of the Unknowns at Arlington National Cemetery, joining an unknown soldier from World War I who had been buried there in 1921.

◆ In July 1958, in response to a request from Lebanese President Chamille Chamoun, who feared the pan-Arab movement that had just overthrown the Iraqi monarchy, the United States dispatches troops to Beirut, Lebanon, to protect the existing government.

◆ Eisenhower signs, on July 29, 1958, the National Aeronautics and Space Act, creating the National Aeronautics and Space Agency (NASA), a civilian agency formed for "research into problems of flight within and outside the earth's atmosphere."

◆ In September 1958 Eisenhower signs the National Defense Education Act (NDEA), which provides aid to education at all levels. The act is designed primarily to improve education in science and math, as the United States is concerned about being outstripped by other nations (especially the Soviet Union).

◆ Eisenhower's assistant Sherman Adams (with a position akin to chief of staff) resigns in September 1958 amid allegations he has accepted personal gifts (a Vicuna coat, among other items) in return for White House favors.

◆ In October 1958 the United States, United Kingdom, and Soviet Union meet at a conference in Geneva to discuss nuclear disarmament.

◆ In April and May 1959 Eisenhower writes to Khrushchev, suggesting a partial ban on nuclear testing.

◆ On April 25, 1959, the St. Lawrence Seaway, linking the Great Lakes with the Atlantic Ocean, opens to shipping. Official opening ceremonies on June 26, 1959, are attended by Eisenhower and Queen Elizabeth II (representing Canada).

◆ In July 1959 Nixon, on a trip to Moscow, debates Khrushchev about the merits of capitalism versus communism. The dialogue is dubbed the "kitchen debate" because one exchange between the two men takes place next to an exhibit of Westernized model kitchens at the American National Exhibition in Moscow.

◆ In September 1959 Eisenhower signs the Labor Management and Report Act (also called the Landrum-Griffin Act), which provides for the regulation of labor unions and their funds in the wake of charges of improper financial arrangements between employers and labor officials.

◆ From September 25 to 27, 1959, Khrushchev visits Eisenhower at Camp David; tensions between the two superpowers ease somewhat and the two leaders discuss a possible future summit.

◆ The Antarctic Treaty, signed December 1, 1959, by the United States, the Soviet Union, Argentina, Australia, Japan, New Zealand, Norway, France, South Africa, Belgium, Chile, and the United Kingdom, declares Antarctica free of military activity, nuclear tests, radioactive waste disposal, and territorial disputes; the treaty also promotes international scientific cooperation in Antarctica.

◆ Alaska becomes a state, January 3, 1959.

◆ Hawaii becomes a state, August 21, 1959.

◆ In March 1960 Eisenhower authorizes CIA training of Cuban expatriates for a possible invasion of Cuba.

◆ On May 1, 1960, a US reconnaissance plane (a U-2) is shot down over the Soviet Union and its pilot, Francis Gary Powers, is captured. Powers is convicted of espionage by the Soviets and sentenced to hard labor; after nearly two years, he is traded for Soviet spy Rudolf Ivanovich Abel, who had been convicted in 1957 of espionage in the United States.

◆ On May 17, 1960, Soviet leader Nikita Khrushchev demands an apology from Eisenhower for US spy plane activity over the Soviet Union; Eisenhower refuses and plans for a summit between the two nations in Paris are abruptly cancelled.

◆ Congress amends the Federal Communications Act in 1960 to outlaw "payola," the practice of paying radio stations or disc jockeys to play a specific record on the air. Although the practice had been widespread for decades, the 1960 investigation into payola specifically targeted rock and roll.

◆ In 1960 the Food and Drug Administration (FDA) approves the first oral contraceptive or birth control pill (with the trade name of Enovid).

◆ The Supreme Court rules in a key civil rights case, *Boynton v. Virginia*, that segregation in the restaurants of bus terminals serving interstate travelers is prohibited.

◆ Eisenhower announces the severing of diplomatic relations with Cuba on January 3, 1961.

MAJOR US AND WORLD EVENTS, 1953–1961

◆ In March 1953 Joseph Stalin dies and Georgy Malenkov succeeds him as premier of the Soviet Union.

◆ On April 2, 1953, James Watson and Francis Crick publish "Molecular Structure of Nucleic Acids: A Structure for Deoxyribose Nucleic Acid [DNA]" in *Nature* magazine, beginning a new era in genetic science.

◆ On April 7, 1953, Dag Hammarskjöld is elected secretary general of the United Nations.

◆ Sir Edmund Hillary, a New Zealand beekeeper and mountain climber, and Tenzing Norgay, a Nepalese guide and climber, reach the summit of Mount Everest on May 29, 1953.

◆ On June 2, 1953, Elizabeth II's coronation takes place at Westminster Abbey in the United Kingdom.

◆ On June 19, 1953, Julius and Ethel Rosenberg are executed in the United States after being convicted of conspiracy to commit espionage on behalf of the Soviet Union.

◆ Fidel Castro leads about 160 men in attacking the Moncada military barracks in Santiago de Cuba on July 26, 1953; this abortive attempt at a coup results in Castro's arrest and two-year imprisonment.

◆ Iranian Prime Minister Muhammed Mossadegh is overthrown by the shah, Mohammed Reza Pahlavi, and his supporters in August 1953; the shah and his followers receive help from US and British intelligence agencies (the CIA and MI-6).

◆ On August 12, 1953, the Soviet Union, utilizing the work of scientists Igor Tamm and Andrei Sakharov, detonates a hydrogen bomb.

◆ In November 1953 Cambodia becomes independent of France.

◆ Lavrenti Beria, formerly head of the Soviet secret police, is tried and executed for conspiracy in December 1953; his attempt to seize power had been thwarted by Georgy Malenkov, Vyacheslav Molotov, and Nikita Khrushchev.

◆ Maureen Connolly becomes the first woman to win the Grand Slam of tennis (Australian Open, French Open, Wimbledon, and US Open), 1953.

◆ Lloyd C. Douglas publishes *The Robe*, 1953.

◆ Ray Bradbury publishes *Fahrenheit 451*, 1953.

◆ Raymond Chandler publishes *The Long Goodbye*, 1953.

◆ James Baldwin publishes *Go Tell It on the Mountain*, 1953.

◆ Alfred Kinsey publishes *Sexual Behavior in the Human Female*, 1953.

◆ Ian Fleming publishes *Casino Royale*, the first novel featuring British agent James Bond, 1953.

◆ Elvis Presley visits Sun Records in Memphis, Tennessee, and makes a recording of "My Happiness" and "That's When Your Heartaches Begin" as a gift for his mother, 1953.

◆ Television series premiering in 1953 include *General Electric Theater*, *Candid Camera*, *Make Room for Daddy* (later called *The Danny Thomas Show*), *Romper Room*, and *Name That Tune*.

◆ Arthur Miller's *The Crucible* opens on Broadway, January 1953.

◆ Notable films of 1953 include Fred Zinnemann's *From Here to Eternity* with Burt Lancaster and Deborah Kerr, Henry Koster's *The Robe* with Richard Burton and Jean Simmons, George Stevens's *Shane* with Alan Ladd, Laszlo Benedek's *The Wild One* with Marlon Brando, Billy Wilder's *Stalag 17* with William Holden, William Wyler's *Roman Holiday* with Gregory Peck and Audrey Hepburn, and Fritz Lang's *The Big Heat* with Glenn Ford.

◆ On January 14, 1954, Hollywood star Marilyn Monroe and baseball legend Joe DiMaggio marry at City Hall in San Francisco; they divorce nine months later, in October 1954.

◆ In February 1954 Gamal Abdal Nasser, an army officer who had been instrumental in the 1952 military coup ousting Egypt's King Farouk, becomes president of Egypt.

◆ On May 6, 1954, British physician Roger Bannister becomes the first person to run a mile in less than 4 minutes (clocking in at 3 minutes, 59.4 seconds).

◆ K2, the second-highest mountain in the world, is scaled for the first time by two Italian climbers, Lino Lacedelli and Achille Compagnoni, on July 31, 1954.

◆ The first issue of *Sports Illustrated* is published August 16, 1954, with Eddie Mathews of the Milwaukee Braves on the cover.

◆ On October 18, 1954, the I.D.E.A. Company of Indianapolis, Indiana, announces the commercial availability of the first transistor radio, the Regency TR-1 (an earlier model had been developed at Texas Instruments in May 1954; transistors were developed in the late 1940s).

◆ In late October 1954 Algeria begins a revolution against French rule that lasts until Algerian independence on July 3, 1962.

◆ Kingsley Amis publishes *Lucky Jim*, 1954.

◆ William Golding publishes *The Lord of the Flies*, 1954.

◆ J. R. R. Tolkien publishes the first two volumes of *The Lord of the Rings* trilogy, 1954.

◆ James Michener publishes *Sayonara*, 1954.

◆ Isaac Asimov publishes *The Caves of Steel*, 1954.

◆ Elvis Presley, with Bill Black and Winfield "Scotty" Moore, records the first of his released singles, "That's All Right Mama" with "Blue Moon of Kentucky" on the flip side, in 1954.

◆ Other popular music hits of 1954 include Doris Day's "Secret Love," Jo Stafford's "Make Love to Me," Kitty Kallen's "Little Things Mean a Lot," and the Chordette's "Mr. Sandman."

◆ Richard Adler and Jerry Ross's *The Pajama Game* debuts on Broadway, 1954.

◆ Television series debuting in 1954 include *Captain Kangaroo*, *The Tonight Show* (with Steve Allen as host), and *Dragnet*.

◆ Notable films of 1954 include Alfred Hitchcock's *Dial M for Murder* with Grace Kelly and Ray Milland, Elia Kazan's *On the Waterfront* with Marlon Brando, Alfred Hitchcock's *Rear Window* with James Stewart and Grace Kelly, Billy Wilder's *Sabrina* with Humphrey Bogart and Audrey Hepburn, George Cukor's *A Star Is Born* with Judy Garland and James Mason, Edward Dmytryk's *The Caine Mutiny* with Humphrey Bogart, Federico Fellini's *La Strada* with Anthony Quinn and Giulietta Masina, and Akira Kurosawa's *The Seven Samurai* with Toshiro Mifune.

◆ Winston Churchill resigns as prime minister, April 5, 1955; Anthony Eden becomes the next prime minister of Great Britain.

◆ On April 12, 1955, Dr. Thomas Francis, Jr., holds a press conference at the University of Michigan to announce that trials of the polio vaccine developed by Dr. Jonas Salk have been successful.

◆ Physicist Albert Einstein dies on April 18, 1955, in Princeton, New Jersey.

◆ In May 1955, following the admission of West Germany to NATO, the Warsaw Pact for mutual defense is signed by the Soviet Union, Bulgaria, Romania, Albania, Hungary, Poland, East Germany, and Czechoslovakia.

◆ On July 17, 1955, Disneyland opens in Anaheim, California.

◆ On September 30, 1955, actor James Dean dies in an automobile accident in California.

◆ Tennessee Williams wins the Pulitzer Prize for *Cat on a Hot Tin Roof*, 1955.

◆ First publication of the *Guinness Book of World Records*, 1955.

◆ Françoise Sagan publishes *Bonjour Tristesse*, 1955.

◆ Vladimir Nabokov publishes *Lolita* (in Paris), 1955.

◆ J. R. R. Tolkien publishes the third volume of the *Lord of the Rings* trilogy, 1955.

◆ Graham Greene publishes *The Quiet American*, 1955.

◆ Patricia Highsmith publishes *The Talented Mr. Ripley*, 1955.

◆ Television series debuting in 1955 include *Gunsmoke*, *Captain Kangaroo*, *The Honeymooners*, *Alfred Hitchcock Presents*, the *Lawrence Welk Show*, *This Is Your Life*, *The $64,000 Question*, and *The Mickey Mouse Club*.

◆ Richard Adler and Jerry Ross's *Damn Yankees* debuts on Broadway, 1955.

◆ Popular music hits of 1955 include Carl Perkins's "Blue Suede Shoes," Bill Haley and the Comets' "Rock Around the Clock," the Four Aces' "Love Is a Many Splendored Thing," and Mitch Miller's "The Yellow Rose of Texas."

◆ Notable films of 1955 include Nicholas Ray's *Rebel Without a Cause* with James Dean, Sal Mineo, and Natalie Wood, Billy Wilder's *The Seven Year Itch* with Marilyn Monroe and Tom Ewell, Alfred Hitchcock's *To Catch a Thief* with Cary Grant and Grace Kelly, Delbert Mann's *Marty* with Ernest Borgnine, Walt Disney's *Lady and the Tramp*, Elia Kazan's *East of Eden* with James Dean, John Sturges's *Bad Day at Black Rock* with Spencer Tracy, John Ford and Mervyn LeRoy's *Mister Roberts* with Henry Fonda and Jack Lemmon, Joseph Mankiewicz's *Guys and Dolls* with Marlon Brando and Frank Sinatra, Henri-Georges Clouzot's *Diabolique* with Simone Signoret, and Fred Zinnemann's *Oklahoma!* with Gordon MacRae.

◆ In February 1956 Soviet leader Nikita Khrushchev popularizes the phrase "cult of personality" in decrying the adulation of Joseph Stalin.

◆ In March and April 1956 France and then Spain relinquish their protectorates over Morocco and the country becomes independent.

◆ Tunisia becomes independent from France, March 1956.

◆ On April 19, 1956, American actress Grace Kelly marries Prince Rainier of Monaco in a civil service followed by a nuptial mass the next day.

◆ Marilyn Monroe marries playwright Arthur Miller on June 29, 1956, in a civil ceremony and on July 1, 1956, in a Jewish religious ceremony, both near New York City; the couple divorces in 1961.

◆ On the night of July 25, 1956, south of Nantucket, the Italian luxury liner *Andrea Doria* is struck by the Swedish liner *Stockholm;* the *Andrea Doria* sinks. Forty-six of the *Andrea Doria*'s passengers and crew perish, as well as five crew members from the *Stockholm*.

◆ In the fall of 1956, following a revolution in Hungary, leader Imre Nagy announces that the East European country intends to withdraw from the Warsaw Pact. Soviet tanks and troops overrun the country, reinstating a Communist government, killing thousands, and forcing about 200,000 Hungarians to become refugees.

◆ In December 1956 Fidel Castro and a small band of armed supporters land in Cuba and begin several years of guerrilla warfare against the government of Fulgencio Batista.

◆ Rocky Marciano retires undefeated as the world heavyweight boxing champion, 1956.

◆ Albert Camus publishes *The Fall* (*La Chute*), 1956.

◆ Edwin O'Connor publishes *The Last Hurrah*, 1956.

◆ Philip K. Dick publishes *Minority Report*, 1956.

◆ Grace Metalious publishes *Peyton Place*, 1956.

◆ Television series debuting in 1956 include *The Edge of Night, As the World Turns, The Price Is Right, Name That Tune, The Nat King Cole Show, Playhouse 90, To Tell the Truth,* and *Twenty-One*.

◆ Elvis Presley releases "Heartbreak Hotel," "Don't Be Cruel," and "Love Me Tender," 1956.

◆ Other popular music hits of 1956 include The Platters' "The Great Pretender," Guy Mitchell's "Singing the Blues," Carl Perkins's "Blue Suede Shoes," Little Richard's "Long Tall Sally," and Chuck Berry's "Roll Over Beethoven."

◆ Alan Jay Lerner and Frederick Loewe's *My Fair Lady* debuts on Broadway, 1956.

◆ Notable films of 1956 include George Stevens's *Giant* with Elizabeth Taylor, Rock Hudson, and James Dean, John Ford's *The Searchers* with John Wayne and Natalie Wood, Cecil B. DeMille's *The Ten Commandments* with Charlton Heston, Anatole Litvak's *Anastasia* with Ingrid Bergman, Fred M. Wilcox's *Forbidden Planet* with Walter Pidgeon, William Wyler's *Friendly Persuasion* with Gary Cooper, Walter Lang's *The King and I* with Yul Brynner and Deborah Kerr, Albert Lamorisse's *The Red Balloon* (*La Ballon Rouge*), and Don Siegel's *Invasion of the Body Snatchers* with Kevin McCarthy.

◆ In 1957 Wham-O begins production of its Pluto Platters, a toy for which the name Frisbee is soon adopted, probably from the Frisbie Baking Company, whose pie plates had long been thrown and caught in the same way as the plastic Frisbee.

◆ On March 6, 1957, Ghana becomes the first sub-Saharan independent African nation; it is created from the former British colony of the Gold Coast and part of Togoland, which had been a UN trust territory under British administration.

◆ On March 25, 1957, the Treaty of Rome is signed by France, West Germany, Italy, Belgium, the Netherlands, and Luxembourg. The treaty creates the European Economic Community (Common Market) in 1958, which eventually expands to include the United Kingdom, Greece, Spain, Portugal, and other European nations. The organization is a precursor of the European Union (EU) formed in 1993.

◆ In April 1957 IBM releases FORTRAN (FORmula TRANslation) I, a compiled computer programming language widely adopted by the scientific community.

◆ In early 1957 copies of Allen Ginsberg's *Howl*, which had initially been printed in England, are seized by US customs officials on the grounds that the poem is obscene. Lawrence Ferlinghetti, a founder of San Francisco's City Lights Bookstore (the publisher of the poem), is acquitted in the subsequent obscenity trial when the poem is found to have redeeming social value.

◆ On August 31, 1957, the Federation of Malaya (later incorporated into Malaysia) becomes independent of the United Kingdom.

◆ *Sputnik I,* the first artificial satellite to orbit Earth, is launched on October 4, 1957, by the

Soviet Union. A second Sputnik is launched in November and carries Laika, a dog.

◆ In the fall of 1957 baseball's New York Giants announce their move to San Francisco, and baseball's Brooklyn Dodgers announce their move to Los Angeles.

◆ In 1957 American tennis player Althea Gibson becomes the first black player to win the singles event at Wimbledon (she also triumphs at the US Open in 1957).

◆ Jack Kerouac publishes *On the Road*, 1957.

◆ Ayn Rand publishes *Atlas Shrugged*, 1957.

◆ Neville Shute publishes *On the Beach*, 1957.

◆ John Cheever publishes *The Wapshot Chronicle*, 1957.

◆ Dr. Seuss (Theodore Seuss Geisel) publishes *The Cat in the Hat*, 1957.

◆ Eugene O'Neill publishes *Long Day's Journey into Night*, 1957.

◆ Television series debuting in 1957 include *Leave It to Beaver*, *Maverick*, *Perry Mason*, and *Wagon Train*.

◆ Stephen Sondheim and Leonard Bernstein's *West Side Story* debuts on Broadway, 1957.

◆ Meredith Willson's *The Music Man* debuts on Broadway, 1957.

◆ Popular music hits of 1957 include Fats Domino's "Blueberry Hill," the Everly Brothers' "Bye Bye Love," Johnny Mathis's "Chances Are," Nat King Cole's "When I Fall in Love," Buddy Holly's "Peggy Sue," "That'll Be the Day," and "Not Fade Away," and Elvis Presley's "Jailhouse Rock," "Loving You," "Teddy Bear," and "All Shook Up."

◆ Notable films of 1957 include David Lean's *The Bridge on the River Kwai* with William Holden and Alec Guinness, Richard Thorpe's *Jailhouse Rock* with Elvis Presley, Stanley Kubrick's *Paths of Glory* with Kirk Douglas, Sidney Lumet's *12 Angry Men* with Lee J. Cobb and Henry Fonda, Billy Wilder's *Witness for the Prosecution* with Marlene Dietrich and Tyrone Power, John Sturges's *Gunfight at the O.K. Corral* with Kirk Douglas and Burt Lancaster, Akira Kurosawa's *Throne of Blood* with Toshiro Mifune, Ingmar Bergman's *Wild Strawberries* with Bibi Andersson, Federico Fellini's *Nights of Cabiria* with Giulietta Masina, and Mark Robson's *Peyton Place* with Lana Turner.

◆ On January 1, 1958, Singapore becomes independent of British rule.

◆ In January 1958 the United States successfully launches a satellite, the *Explorer I*, and from its data, James Van Allen confirms the existence of a band of charged particles trapped in the earth's magnetic field (thereafter referred to as the Van Allen radiation belt).

◆ Egypt and Syria unite to form the United Arab Republic with Gamal Abdal Nasser as president, February 1958; the union lasts until September 1961.

◆ On March 27, 1958, Nikita Khrushchev becomes premier of the Soviet Union, replacing Nikolai Bulganin, whom Khrushchev had forced from office for supposed "anti-Party" activity.

◆ From April 17 to October 19, 1958, a world's fair (the so-called Expo '58) is held in Brussels, Belgium.

◆ On June 16, 1958, former Hungarian leader Imre Nagy is hanged for treason after failing in his attempts to resist the Soviet domination of Hungary.

◆ In July 1958 a military coup leads to the murder of Iraqi King Faisal II and the ascendancy of General Abdul Karim Qassim, who becomes the prime minister of the new Iraqi republic.

◆ In October 1958 Pope Pius XII dies and Angelo Giuseppe Roncalli, the cardinal chosen as the new pope, becomes Pope John XXIII.

◆ During late 1958 Guinea becomes independent of France; the French Sudan, Chad, Gabon, and the Republic of the Congo become autonomous republics within the French Community.

◆ Elvis Presley is drafted into the US Army and serves two years in Germany, from 1958 to 1960.

◆ Ian Fleming publishes *Dr. No*, 1958.

◆ Truman Capote publishes *Breakfast at Tiffany's*, 1958.

◆ John O'Hara publishes *From the Terrace*, 1958.

◆ Graham Greene publishes *Our Man in Havana*, 1958.

◆ Chinua Achebe publishes *Things Fall Apart*, 1958.

◆ T. H. White publishes *The Once and Future King*, 1958.

◆ William J. Lederer and Eugene Burdick publish *The Ugly American*, 1958.

◆ Poul Anderson publishes *The Enemy Stars*, 1958.

◆ Robert A. Heinlein publishes *Have Spacesuit—Will Travel*, 1958.

◆ Mary Renault publishes *The King Must Die*, 1958.

◆ Jan Potocki publishes *The Saragossa Manuscript*, 1958.

◆ Popular music hits of 1958 include the Everly Brothers' "All I Have to Do Is Dream," the Big Bopper's "Chantilly Lace," Jerry Lee Lewis' "Great Balls of Fire," Chuck Berry's "Johnny B. Goode," The Platters' "Smoke Gets in Your Eyes," and The Champs' "Tequila."

◆ Television series debuting in 1958 include *The Donna Reed Show*, *The Rifleman*, *Sea Hunt*, *Wanted: Dead or Alive*, and *77 Sunset Strip*.

◆ Notable films of 1958 include Richard Brooks's *Cat on a Hot Tin Roof* with Elizabeth Taylor and Paul Newman, Orson Welles's *Touch of Evil* with Charlton Heston and Janet Leigh, Alfred Hitchcock's *Vertigo* with James Stewart and Kim Novak, Vincente Minnelli's *Gigi* with Leslie Caron and Louis Jourdan, Jacques Tati's *Mon Oncle*, and Stanley Kramer's *The Defiant Ones* with Sidney Poitier and Tony Curtis.

◆ In January 1959 Fulgencio Batista flees Cuba; by the summer Fidel Castro, as premier, consolidates his power.

◆ On February 3, 1959, a plane crash near Clear Lake, Iowa, kills rock and roll musicians Buddy Holly, the Big Bopper (Jiles Perry Richardson, Jr.), and Ritchie Valens.

◆ On February 22, 1959, Lee Petty wins the first Daytona 500, although the judging committee announces three days later, after examining newsreel footage of the high-speed car race, that Petty and Johnny Beauchamp had crossed the finish line nearly simultaneously.

◆ In February 1959 Greece and Turkey reach an agreement in Zurich, Switzerland, declaring the independence of Cyprus.

◆ In March 1959 Tibetans rebel against the Chinese presence in Tibet; the rebellion is crushed, but the Dalai Lama (born Lhamo Thondup) and many of his followers go into exile.

◆ On June 3, 1959, Singapore becomes a self-governing crown colony of Great Britain.

◆ In August 1959 the *Explorer VI* satellite provides the first picture of Earth from space.

◆ In testimony before the House Committee on Interstate and Foreign Commerce on November 2, 1959, Charles Van Doren, an English professor and member of a noted academic family of poets and authors, admits that he was given answers and coached during his $138,000 winning streak on the television game show *Twenty-One*.

◆ The Guggenheim Museum, designed by Frank Lloyd Wright, opens in New York City, 1959.

◆ Ruth Handler, a co-founder of Mattel Corporation, introduces Barbie at the New York City Toy Fair in 1959.

◆ Ian Fleming publishes *Goldfinger*, 1959.

◆ Philip Roth publishes *Goodbye, Columbus*, 1959.

◆ James A. Michener publishes *Hawaii*, 1959.

◆ William S. Burroughs publishes *The Naked Lunch*, 1959.

◆ Allen Drury publishes *Advise and Consent*, 1959.

◆ Kurt Vonnegut publishes *The Sirens of Titan*, 1959.

◆ Mervyn Peake publishes *Titus Alone*, the third novel in the *Gormenghast* trilogy, 1959.

◆ Günter Grass publishes *The Tin Drum*, 1959.

◆ Robert A. Heinlein publishes *Starship Troopers*, 1959.

◆ Philip K. Dick publishes *Time Out of Joint*, 1959.

◆ Leon Uris publishes *Exodus*, 1959.

◆ Popular music hits of 1959 include Bobby Darin's "Dream Lover" and "Mack the Knife," The Flamingoes' "I Only Have Eyes for You," Ritchie Valens's "La Bamba," Johnny Mathis's

"Misty," The Platters' "Smoke Gets in Your Eyes," and Frankie Avalon's "Venus."

◆ Television series debuting in 1959 include *The Twilight Zone, Bonanza, Hawaiian Eye, The Many Loves of Dobie Gillis, Rawhide,* and *The Untouchables.*

◆ Richard Rodgers and Oscar Hammerstein II's *The Sound of Music* debuts on Broadway, 1959.

◆ Notable films of 1959 include William Wyler's *Ben Hur* with Charlton Heston, Alfred Hitchcock's *North by Northwest* with Cary Grant and Eva Marie Saint, Billy Wilder's *Some Like It Hot* with Marilyn Monroe, Tony Curtis, and Jack Lemmon, Joseph Mankiewicz's *Suddenly, Last Summer* with Montgomery Clift, Katharine Hepburn, and Elizabeth Taylor, Michael Gordon's *Pillow Talk* with Rock Hudson and Doris Day, Otto Preminger's *Anatomy of a Murder* with James Stewart, François Truffaut's *The 400 Blows,* and Fred Zinnemann's *The Nun's Story* with Audrey Hepburn.

◆ On February 1, 1960, four black college students in Greensboro, North Carolina, refuse to leave a lunch counter in a Woolworth's store after being refused service; their protest is the first of a series of peaceful sit-ins against segregation.

◆ In February 1960 Adolph Coors III, in line to become president of the Coors Brewing Company, is kidnapped and killed.

◆ Notorious Nazi Adolf Eichmann is captured in Argentina by Israeli agents in May 1960; two years later, after a well-publicized trial, he is hanged for war crimes.

◆ In June 1960 Mali and Senegal, formerly part of French West Africa, become independent; the Somali Republic is created from the former British Somaliland and Italian Somaliland, and the Republic of the Congo, formerly the Belgian Congo, becomes independent of Belgium.

◆ Sirimavo Bandaranaike is elected prime minister of Ceylon (now Sri Lanka) in 1960, thus becoming the first woman in the world to be elected head of state.

◆ In August 1960 the former French dependencies of Côte d'Ivoire, Chad, and Gabon become independent.

◆ The Organization of Petroleum Exporting Countries (OPEC) is formed in September 1960 by Saudi Arabia, Iran, Iraq, Kuwait, and Venezuela to control the pricing and production of oil.

◆ On October 1, 1960, Nigeria becomes independent of the United Kingdom.

◆ In October 1960 Soviet leader Nikita Khrushchev, during a general session of the United Nations, becomes angry at criticism of Soviet activity in Eastern Europe. Khrushchev famously takes off his shoe and bangs it on the desk.

◆ In November 1960 Mauritania becomes independent of France.

◆ The 1960 census shows a US population of 179.3 million people.

◆ William Shirer publishes *The Rise and Fall of the Third Reich,* 1960.

◆ Harper Lee publishes *To Kill a Mockingbird,* 1960.

◆ Brian Aldiss publishes *Galaxies Like Grains of Sand,* 1960.

◆ Joy Adamson publishes *Born Free,* 1960.

◆ Dr. Seuss (Theodore Seuss Geisel) publishes *Green Eggs and Ham,* 1960.

◆ Television series debuting in 1960 include *The Andy Griffith Show, Candid Camera, The Flintstones, My Three Sons,* and *Route 66.*

◆ Alan Jay Lerner and Frederick Loewe's *Camelot* debuts on Broadway, 1960.

◆ The Beatles, consisting of John Lennon, Paul McCartney, George Harrison, and Pete Best (who was later replaced by Ringo Starr), play a series of clubs in Hamburg, Germany, in August and September 1960.

◆ Popular music hits of 1960 include Roy Orbison's "Only the Lonely," Brian Hyland's "Itsy Bitsy Teenie Weenie Yellow Polka Dot Bikini," Ray Charles's "Georgia on My Mind," Elvis's "It's Now or Never" and "Are You Lonesome Tonight?", Mark Dinning's "Teen Angel," and Chubby Checker's "The Twist."

◆ The first star on the Hollywood "Walk of Fame" is awarded to Joanne Woodward, 1960.

◆ Notable films of 1960 include Stanley Kubrick's *Spartacus* with Kirk Douglas, Billy

Wilder's *The Apartment* with Jack Lemmon and Shirley MacLaine, Stanley Kramer's *Inherit the Wind* with Spencer Tracy, Alfred Hitchcock's *Psycho* with Anthony Perkins and Janet Leigh, Richard Brooks's *Elmer Gantry* with Burt Lancaster and Jean Simmons, Jean-Luc Goddard's *Breathless* with Jean-Luc Belmondo and Jean Seberg, Federico Fellini's *La Dolce Vita* with Marcello Mastroianni, and Ingmar Bergman's *The Virgin Spring* with Max von Sydow.

◆ On January 17, 1961, Patrice Lumumba, the first prime minister of the Congo, is assassinated.

FAST FACTS ABOUT DWIGHT DAVID EISENHOWER

◆ Eisenhower was the first president who was born in Texas.

◆ In the early 1900s Eisenhower's older brother Arthur and Harry S. Truman lived in the same Kansas City boarding house; Ike was still in high school at the time.

◆ Eisenhower's football career at West Point was ended by a knee injury sustained in a game against Tufts (and later aggravated while dismounting from horseback). During his days on the Army team Eisenhower played against the legendary Jim Thorpe, a member of the Carlisle (Pennsylvania) Indian School team, a fact which led to the popular myth that Eisenhower had injured his knee while attempting to tackle Thorpe.

◆ Eisenhower's West Point class is sometimes called the "class the stars fell on" because of the record number of generals it produced (some fifty-nine). One of Eisenhower's classmates was Omar N. Bradley, who, like Eisenhower, became a five-star general.

◆ While serving at Camp Meade, Maryland, Eisenhower met another young officer, George C. Patton, who enthusiastically pursued the development of tank tactics. Both believed that tanks would be essential to victory in the next war, a view neither shared nor encouraged by their superiors.

◆ While president, Eisenhower suffered a heart attack in 1955, and a slight stroke in 1957; he was also operated on for ileitis (also called Crohn's disease, an inflammation of the small intestine) in 1956.

◆ The Eisenhowers celebrated their 40th wedding anniversary in the White House and their 50th anniversary in 1966 after his presidency. They were the first presidential couple to celebrate a 50th wedding anniversary since Louisa and John Quincy Adams in 1847.

◆ Eisenhower was baptized, confirmed, and received his first communion in the National Presbyterian Church in Washington, DC, while he was president.

◆ The presidential retreat in Maryland that Franklin D. Roosevelt had called "Sharigri-La" was renamed "Camp David" by Eisenhower, in honor of his grandson.

◆ Eisenhower's grandson, David Eisenhower, married Julie Nixon, daughter of President Richard M. Nixon, in 1968 (after Nixon had been elected but before his inauguration).

◆ Eisenhower was the first president to hold a pilot's license; he received it in the Philippines in 1939.

John Fitzgerald Kennedy

Nickname: Jack; JFK
Presidency: 35th president, 1961–1963
Party: Democratic
Life dates: May 29, 1917–November 22, 1963 (46 years, 177 days)

EARLY LIFE AND EDUCATION

John Fitzgerald Kennedy was born on May 29, 1917, in Brookline, Massachusetts. He was the second son of Rose Fitzgerald Kennedy and Joseph Patrick Kennedy. His older brother was Joe Jr.; John, who was called Jack, was followed by five sisters (Rosemary; Kathleen, called Kick; Eunice; Patricia; and Jean) and two more brothers (Robert, called Bobby, and Edward, called Ted or Teddy).

Jack was born into a family that was prosperous and socially prominent among the Irish of Boston, and already had a history in politics. His father, Joe Kennedy, was the son of Patrick Joseph ("P. J.") Kennedy, a businessman and local politician. Jack's mother, Rose Fitzgerald Kennedy, was the daughter of the mayor of Boston, John "Honey Fitz" Fitzgerald, who had also served in the US House of Representatives. He was a charismatic presence in the life of his young grandchildren, and even after his political career had ended, continued to be popular with many Bostonians.

Rose Fitzgerald had married Joe Kennedy despite her father's initial objections. Marrying the mayor's daughter was but one step in Joe's ambitious plans to carve a place in the world for himself and his family. A bank president by the time he was twenty-five, he joined an investment firm the year of Jack's birth and soon made his first million. In 1927 the family moved to New York City and Joe went into the movie business. He achieved mixed success in the industry, but during this period had an infamous affair with movie star Gloria Swanson. Joe Kennedy was paradoxically devoted to his family and, at the same time, repeatedly unfaithful to Rose.

Kennedy found speculation in the stock market much more profitable than the movie business. He withdrew from the stock market before the crash in 1929, thus preserving a vast fortune, estimated at $100 million. Rumors also circulated that Joe made much of his money by bootlegging liquor during Prohibition (1920–1933).

Jack's early life was spent in the competitive, athletic, challenging family environment that Rose and Joe created. The children were expected to read newspapers and discuss current events at the dinner table. Rose also strongly emphasized the Roman Catholic faith as part of their heritage.

Within the context of the rough-and-tumble

lifestyle of the Kennedy clan, which regularly included touch football games, tennis matches, swimming, and sailing, Jack developed health problems at an early age. In February 1920, when he was not quite three years old, Jack contracted scarlet fever. He became seriously ill and was hospitalized for weeks. Within the next year, he also suffered from mumps and whooping cough.

> "My fellow Americans, ask not what your country can do for you; ask what you can do for your country."
>
> John F. Kennedy, inaugural address, January 20, 1961

Jack's formal education began at a public school in Brookline, Massachusetts. In the fall of 1924, he and Joe Jr. were enrolled at the Dexter School, a nearby private day school. The following summer, in 1925, the family began spending its summers in Hyannis Port on Cape Cod. Jack was briefly enrolled in the Canterbury Preparatory School in New Milford, Connecticut, but in 1931 he started high school by joining his brother Joe at Choate, a preparatory school in Wallingford, Connecticut. Jack was somewhat erratic as a student; he loved to play pranks and bend the rules. Like his older brother, he played football, but his health continued to be a concern. In May 1934 he experienced such severe abdominal pain that he was sent to the Mayo Clinic, where he was diagnosed with colitis (an inflammation of the lining of the colon).

Joe Sr. was a major contributor to the Democratic Party. He served as head of the Securities and Exchange Commission (SEC) from 1934 to 1935, and in 1938 President Franklin D. Roosevelt appointed him as ambassador to Great Britain. Most of the family accompanied him to England, but Joe Jr. and Jack were both students at Harvard by then. Jack received a leave of absence one semester in 1938 and spent six months in England, working as his father's secretary. The attractive, high-spirited family soon garnered the attention of the press and the British people. Rose, Rosemary, and Kathleen were presented at court and Kathleen, an attractive young woman with a sunny personality, was much sought after by eligible bachelors. However, Joe's performance as ambassador was less successful. He appeared accepting of the rise of fascism in Europe and, believing that Germany would win any war, counseled appeasement. Out of step with the times, he resigned at the end of 1940. His subsequent years were spent extending the family fortune and fostering the political careers of his sons.

Jack briefly attended the London School of Economics, followed by Princeton University, withdrawing from each school because of ill health. He then entered Harvard University in 1936, where he studied political science and graduated cum laude in 1940. His senior thesis, "Appeasement in Munich," addressed the rise of Nazi Germany and Great Britain's efforts to avoid war with Germany. He later expanded this thesis and published it in book form as *Why England Slept*. Jack studied at Stanford University for a term in 1940; he also traveled extensively, spending most of 1939 in Europe and then visiting Central and South America in the spring of 1941.

EARLY CAREER

Both Joe Jr. and Jack enlisted in the US Navy. Joe Jr. attended flight school. Jack, who initially had difficulty getting into the Navy because of his often poor health, was allowed to enlist in 1941 largely through his father's influence. Jack was sent to Washington, DC, to work in naval intelligence, but he almost immediately requested more active duty.

While in Washington, Jack met (through his sister Kathleen) a Danish-born journalist and married woman named Inga Arvad, with whom he began an affair. This marked the beginning of Kennedy's relentless womanizing that would characterize his behavior for the rest of his life. However, the affair with Arvad had ramifications beyond the sexual: She had interviewed high-ranking Nazis and socialized with them, and she was suspected (unfairly as it turned out) of being a German spy. J. Edgar Hoover, the director of the FBI, purportedly recorded conversations between Jack and Inga.

During this same period, the eldest of Jack's sisters, Rosemary, was at the center of one of the long string of tragedies that seemed to follow the family. Rosemary was mildly retarded. To cope with their daughter's limitations, Joe and Rose Kennedy hired special teachers for her, and Rosemary's siblings carefully included her in their activities, but as she matured, her behavior became harder to control. Some rumors exist that her naturally developing interest in men threatened to become an embarrassment to the family. Without telling Rose of his plans, Joe Kennedy arranged for Rosemary to undergo a prefrontal lobotomy, a then recently devised treatment for mental illness by severing some of the nerve connections in the front of the brain. While doctors had noted a lessening of anxiety and paranoia in some patients who had undergone prefrontal lobotomies, they also noticed a dullness and apathy in others. In Rosemary's case, the operation left her severely retarded. She was institutionalized and cared for by nuns for the next sixty-four years, until her death in 2005.

In March 1943 Jack was finally granted his request for active duty, placed in command of a PT (patrol torpedo) boat, the PT-109. The young lieutenant and his crew were assigned to duty in the Pacific near the North Solomon Islands. On the night of August 2, 1943, the boat was rammed by a Japanese destroyer and sunk. Although he himself was injured, Jack helped rescue the members of his crew, even towing one seriously burned sailor to safety by holding the strap of the man's life vest between his teeth. The crew reached an island and were rescued a week later. For his valiant efforts, Kennedy earned the Navy and Marine Corps Medal and the Purple Heart in 1944, and was discharged from duty on March 1, 1945. Before his discharge, however, Kennedy underwent his first back operation. He had been plagued by severe spinal pain since the late 1930s, and it would continue to afflict him for the rest of his life.

Yet another tragedy struck the family on August 12, 1944, when Joe Jr. volunteered to fly a dangerous and secret military mission. His Air Force plane, loaded with explosives and headed for a Nazi rocket base, exploded without warning over the English Channel. Joe and his copilot were instantly killed. The Kennedys were devastated by the loss of young Joe, especially Joe Sr., who had envisioned his oldest son as president someday.

Another loss soon followed. Jack's vivacious sister Kathleen had married an English peer, William Cavendish, the Marquess of Hartington (heir to the Duke of Devonshire), on May 6, 1944, giving her the title of the Marchioness of Hartington (Lady Hartington). Her parents had strongly disapproved of the marriage because Cavendish was not Roman Catholic. Only a few weeks after Joe's death, on September 9, 1944, Kathleen's husband was killed in action in Belgium. The young widow remained in England and a few years later fell in love again, this time with Peter Fitzwilliam. Her parents were once more disapproving: Fitzwilliam was married and awaiting a divorce. Kathleen and Peter hoped to sway her father and planned to travel to France, where Joe Sr. would soon be conducting some business. On May 13, 1948, Kathleen, Peter, and two pilots died in a plane over southern France.

Within four years, Jack had lost the two siblings closest to him, while his father lost the two children who were considered to be his favorite son and his favorite daughter. The force of Joe Kennedy's political ambitions now fell to Jack.

POLITICAL CAREER

After his discharge from the Navy, Jack Kennedy worked as a journalist in 1945 before returning to Massachusetts where, with the full support of his family, he embarked on a political career. Largely ignoring the existing Democratic Party machinery, Kennedy relied on his family, his friends from Harvard, and his Navy buddies to help him campaign. In 1946, at the age of twenty-nine, he was elected to the US House of

Representatives. He was reelected in 1948 and 1950.

In October 1947 Kennedy, while in London, was diagnosed with Addison's disease, an insufficiency of the adrenal glands, which regulate metabolism and the body's response to stress and inflammation. Returning from England, he was so ill that he received the last rites of the Catholic Church. He recovered but began taking corticosteroids on an almost daily basis; the fact of his disease was carefully kept from the public.

"I do not think it altogether inappropriate to introduce myself to this audience. I am the man who accompanied Jacqueline Kennedy to Paris, and I have enjoyed it."

John F. Kennedy, at a press luncheon in Paris, where his wife had proven wildly popular with the French people, June 2, 1961

In 1952 Kennedy decided to run for the US Senate. He faced a Republican incumbent, Henry Cabot Lodge, Jr., who belonged to an old, politically active Massachusetts family. Kennedy's father contributed money and advice; his brother Bobby, who had graduated from Harvard and the University of Virginia Law School, left his job with the Department of Justice to manage his campaign; his mother and sisters appeared at what became known as the "Kennedy teas." Held at hotels in cities throughout the state, the teas drew women by the thousands. Defying the expectations of some, Kennedy defeated Lodge; he was reelected in 1958.

As a young senator and eligible bachelor, Kennedy met Jacqueline Lee Bouvier, a soft-spoken young woman who had grown up in wealth and privilege and been chosen as debutante of the year in the winter of 1947–1948. After attend-

ing Vassar College and George Washington University, and spending a year in Paris studying at the Sorbonne, Jackie, as she was called, took a job at the *Washington Times-Herald* as an inquiring photographer. The two were married on September 12, 1953, in Newport, Rhode Island.

In 1955 Kennedy endured two more back operations. While recuperating, he wrote *Profiles in Courage*, a collection of short studies of American politicians who had defied public opinion to follow their conscience. The book received the Pulitzer Prize in history in 1957. In 1956 Kennedy was considered for the position of vice-presidential candidate when the Democratic Party renominated Adlai Stevenson as its presidential contender, but he lost out to Estes Kefauver. President Eisenhower was easily elected to a second term.

Kennedy and his wife suffered personal losses when Jackie's first pregnancy ended in a miscarriage and her second with a stillbirth. Finally, their daughter Caroline was born in 1957; John Jr. was born in November 25, 1960, just over two weeks after his father had been elected president. Kennedy had won most of the primaries, but just before the convention, Senate Majority Leader Lyndon B. Johnson announced his intention to seek the nomination. Kennedy, mindful of Johnson's strong base of support in the South, selected the Texan as his running mate. In his acceptance speech, Kennedy noted that "we stand today on the verge of a new frontier"; throughout the campaign and his presidency he used the term "new frontier" to symbolize the challenges and opportunities that faced America in the 1960s.

Kennedy ran against Republican candidate Richard M. Nixon, who had served as Eisenhower's vice president during both terms of office. In the first of four televised debates, Kennedy's easygoing charm resonated with audiences, while Nixon, recovering from the flu and having refused to wear makeup, looked ill and seemed uncomfortable. The debates focused mainly on the threat of Communism. Nixon repeatedly tried to focus on Kennedy's lack of experience; although many listeners decided that Nixon argued his points more cogently and won the debates on logic, those who watched them were convinced that Kennedy had triumphed.

During the campaign Nixon refused to make Kennedy's religion an issue, although many believed that a Roman Catholic could not—or should not—be elected. One fear was that a Catholic president would feel bound to follow any directive issued by the Holy See in Rome. Kennedy responded to this issue by publicly stating his support for the separation of church and state. In one of the closest elections in American history, Kennedy defeated Nixon to win the presidency.

PRESIDENCY

Kennedy's presidency was more often concerned with foreign affairs than domestic issues. The first event of importance was the Bay of Pigs invasion in April 1961. The plan, formulated under the Eisenhower administration before Kennedy was elected, called for the CIA to train Cuban exiles living in Florida for an invasion of Cuba, with the goal of overthrowing the government of Fidel Castro. Kennedy gave the go-ahead for the invasion, which was a complete fiasco. The entire invading force was either killed or captured.

A few months later, in June 1961, Kennedy met with the Soviet leader Nikita Khrushchev in Vienna. The two leaders discussed a variety of issues, but the main topic was Germany. Khrushchev asserted that Communism would "bury" the West. After the summit, Khrushchev ordered the construction of the Berlin Wall, which effectively prevented East Germans from moving to West Germany, which they had been doing in droves. In June 1963 Kennedy visited Berlin, declaring in a much heralded speech that "in the world of freedom, the proudest boast is 'Ich bin ein Berliner,'" thus contrasting the freedom of the citizens of West Berlin with the repression of those Germans subsisting behind the Berlin Wall.

In October 1962, under Kennedy's watch, the Cold War threatened to become a "hot" war, possibly even a nuclear war. Through its intelligence, the US government learned that the Soviet Union was shipping nuclear missiles to Cuba. With Cuba only 90 miles off the coast of Florida, this was perceived as a direct threat to America. Kennedy demanded that the missiles be removed and ordered a naval blockade of Cuba to prevent further deliveries. After a tense thirteen-day period, Khrushchev agreed to withdraw the missiles in return for an American promise not to invade Cuba, and war was averted.

"Let the word go forth from this time and place, to friend and foe alike, that the torch has been passed to a new generation of Americans, born in this century, tempered by war, disciplined by a hard and bitter peace, proud of our ancient heritage, and unwilling to witness or permit the slow undoing of those human rights to which this nation has always been committed, and to which we are committed today at home and around the world . . ."

John F. Kennedy, inaugural address, January 20, 1961

Few Americans realized the significance at the time of yet another attempt by the Kennedy administration to contain Communism. President Eisenhower had already provided military advisors to the government of South Vietnam, but Kennedy increased the US presence there significantly, and by the end of his presidency, about 16,000 Americans were in Vietnam. He never authorized the dispatching of combat troops, though. It wasn't until President Lyndon B. Johnson's presidency, when nearly half a million soldiers were actually dispatched there to fight the Viet Cong, which was allied with the Communists in the North.

Kennedy did make some positive advances on the international front, influencing the United Kingdom and the Soviet Union to also sign the Nuclear Test Ban Treaty in 1963. Although the treaty did not ban all nuclear tests, it did restrict them to underground tests, banning them from the atmosphere, under water, and in space.

"First, I believe that this nation should commit itself to achieving the goal, before this decade is out, of landing a man on the moon and returning him safely to earth."

John F. Kennedy, message to Congress, May 25, 1961

In domestic matters, one of Kennedy's enduring legacies was the Peace Corps, a volunteer agency created by executive order to send young Americans to developing countries in hopes of improving health, education, and living conditions there. Another significant area in which Kennedy provided inspiration was the space program, with him declaring in May 1961 that the United States would land a man on the moon before the end of the decade.

Soon after assuming office, Kennedy found himself caught in the middle of the most divisive domestic issue of the time: civil rights. He felt a certain obligation to many Southern Democrats who had helped ensure his election, but most were opposed to civil rights legislation. It was Kennedy's intention to only introduce such comprehensive legislation in a second term; in his first he concentrated on enforcing existing desegregation laws, several times using the Na-

tional Guard or troops from nationalized state guards to enforce the rights of African Americans to enroll at formerly all-white high schools and universities. African Americans, who had overwhelmingly supported Kennedy in the 1960 election, expressed disappointment that he would not do more legislatively. Amid rising racial tensions and shameful incidents in which peaceful civil rights protesters were attacked by police, he finally sent a civil rights bill to Congress in 1963; it was passed after his death. Kennedy's bill sought to eliminate all segregation in public facilities, ensure the right to vote for anyone who had completed a sixth-grade education, and end job discrimination.

During Kennedy's presidency, his family was a constant presence in the news and in his administration. He appointed his brother Bobby as the attorney general, a position in which Bobby aggressively pursued indictments of members of organized crime. Bobby also supported the efforts to enforce civil rights legislation and served as his brother's closest advisor. In 1962 younger brother Ted Kennedy was elected US Senator from Massachusetts, a position he has held for more than 40 years, serving as the principal architect of much of the Senate's socially progressive legislation.

Kennedy's beautiful and cultured wife, Jacqueline, was extremely popular worldwide. Her clothing and hairstyle were much imitated, and the results of her primary project as First Lady—the restoration of the White House to reflect the history of the presidents who had previously resided there—were presented to the American public in a televised tour of the completed rooms that she personally conducted. Jackie also believed that the White House should be a setting for the highest proponents of culture, so she frequently invited notable musicians, artists, and writers to display their talents there. The press and the public showed enthusiastic interest in the Kennedy's two young children, Caroline and John John (as he was called), who were on occasion photographed at play in the Oval Office as their father worked. The president and his wife, however, suffered a devastating personal loss in

President John F. Kennedy and Jacqueline Kennedy in Dallas, Texas, on November 22, 1963, the day of his assassination.

August 1963, when their premature son, Patrick Bouvier Kennedy, died two days after his birth.

On the whole, Kennedy was extremely popular both at home and abroad. The world reacted with stunned grief when he was assassinated by Lee Harvey Oswald in Dallas, Texas, on November 22, 1963, while riding in an open limousine. With the immediacy provided by television and intense press coverage, indelible images of the tragedy were created: Lyndon Johnson being sworn in as president aboard Air Force One, with Jackie standing next to him still attired in a blood-stained pink suit; the quarter of a million people who filed past Kennedy's coffin in the Capitol Rotunda; the somber funeral procession, led by a solitary, riderless black horse; "John John" saluting as his father's flag-draped coffin passed by, and the eternal flame lit at Kennedy's gravesite, in Arlington National Cemetery.

Although the Warren Commission, a government panel charged with investigating the as-

sassination, found that Oswald had acted alone in killing Kennedy, conspiracy theories abound, with many still believing that multiple gunmen had participated in the act. Other theories, of which there remain many, concern possible motives behind the assassination and implicate a scope of individuals and groups such as the mafia, the CIA, agents of Fidel Castro, and even Vice President Lyndon B. Johnson.

POST-PRESIDENCY

Bobby Kennedy resigned from his post as attorney general in 1964, and successfully ran for office, elected as a US senator from New York. In 1968 he mounted a campaign for the Democratic Party's 1968 presidential nomination and rapidly became the front-runner. However, in June 1964, he too was the victim of an assassin's bullet. In the basement of the Ambassador Hotel, in whose ballroom he had just delivered a victory speech after winning the California primary, he was assassinated by Sirhan Sirhan.

After leaving the White House, Jackie moved to New York City and focused her attention on raising her children. However, she was never free from the media's glare and, given the tragedies that continued to befall the family, she feared for the safety of her children. On October 20, 1968, Jackie married Aristotle Onassis, a wealthy Greek shipping magnate. On Onassis's privately owned island, Scorpios, Jackie and her children were finally able to escape constant attention from the media. The marriage was far from idyllic, however; Jackie took solace in extremely extravagant shopping sprees and Onassis soon reinitiated his longstanding affair with opera singer Maria Callas. Despite rumors of a possible divorce, Jackie became a widow for a second time when Onassis died in 1975.

> "For the great enemy of the truth is very often not the lie—deliberate, contrived, and dishonest—but the myth—persistent, persuasive, and unrealistic. Too often we hold fast to the clichés of our forebears. . . . We enjoy the comfort of opinions without the discomfort of thought."
>
> John F. Kennedy, Yale University commencement, June 11, 1962

Jackie returned to New York and worked as an acquiring editor, first at Viking Press, and then at Doubleday from 1978 to 1994. She died of a form of cancer of the lymphatic system on May 19, 1994, at the age of 64.

In yet another well-publicized family tragedy, John Kennedy Jr., his wife Carolyn Bessette Kennedy, and her sister Lauren Bessette died in 1999 when the small plane he was piloting crashed en route to Martha's Vineyard, Massachusetts, for cousin Rory Kennedy's wedding (daughter of Bobby).

John F. Kennedy's accomplishments as president were hampered by a largely uncooperative Congress; his potential leadership was also largely unrealized given the brevity of his presidency. Following his death, sensational revelations about his sexual escapades and his serious health issues (including the fact that he took an astonishing number of medications on a daily basis) were made public, yet he still remains an important symbol of youthful idealism and one of the country's most beloved presidents. Surrounded by young, intellectually gifted advisors, he spoke eloquently about his hopes for a better future. Despite the fact that three other families have each contributed two presidents to the nation (John Adams and his son John Quincy Adams; William Henry Harrison and his grandson Benjamin Harrison; George H. W. Bush and his son George W. Bush), the Kennedys are frequently spoken of as American's royal family or America's leading political dynasty, with JFK at its center.

Birthplace: Brookline, MA
Residency: Massachusetts
Religion: Roman Catholic
Education: Harvard University, graduated 1940
Place of Death: Dallas, TX
Burial Site: Arlington National Cemetery, Arlington, VA
Dates in Office: January 20, 1961–November 22, 1963 (2 years, 306 days)
Age at Inauguration: 43 years, 236 days

FAMILY

Father: Joseph Patrick Kennedy (1888–1969)
Mother: Rose Elizabeth Fitzgerald Kennedy (1890–1995)
Siblings: John F. Kennedy was the second of nine children; his siblings were Joseph Patrick Kennedy, Jr. (1915–1944); Rosemary Kennedy (1918–2005); Kathleen Kennedy (1920–1948); Eunice Mary Kennedy (1921–); Patricia Kennedy (1924–); Robert ("Bobby") Francis Kennedy (1925–1968); Jean Ann Kennedy (1928–); Edward ("Teddy") Moore Kennedy (1932–)

Wife: Jacqueline ("Jackie") Lee Bouvier Kennedy (1929–1994), married September 12, 1953, in Newport, RI [Note: Jacqueline Kennedy also married Aristotle Onassis in 1968; he died in 1975.]
Children: stillborn daughter (1956); Caroline Kennedy (1957–); John ("John-John") Fitzgerald Kennedy, Jr. (1960–1999); Patrick Bouvier Kennedy (1963)

CAREER
Private: none
Political: member of the US House of Representatives (1947–1953); member of the US Senate (1953–1961); president of the United States (1961–1963)
Military: entered US Navy as an ensign (September 1941); served in World War II; with the rank of lieutenant, became commander of a patrol torpedo boat, the PT-109, in the Pacific theater (March 1943); the boat sank after being rammed by a Japanese destroyer (August 3, 1943); although injured, Kennedy led the surviving members of his crew to safety; awarded Navy and Marine Corps Medal and Purple Heart; discharged on March 1, 1945.
Selected Works: *JFK Wants to Know: Memos from the President's Office, 1961–1963*, selected and ed. by Edward B. Claflin, preface by Pierre Salinger (New York: Morrow, 1991); *John F. Kennedy, 1917–1963, Chronology, Documents, Bibliographic Aids*, ed. by Ralph A. Stone (Dobbs Ferry, NY: Oceana Publications, 1971); *John F. Kennedy, Word for Word*, ed. by Maureen Harrison and Steve Gilbert (La Jolla, CA: Excellent Books, 1993); *The Kennedy Presidential Press Conferences*, intro. by David Halberstam (New York: E. M. Coleman Enterprises, 1978); *"Let the Word Go Forth": The Speeches, Statements, and Writings of John F. Kennedy*, selected and with an intro. by Theodore C. Sorensen (New York: Delacorte Press, 1988); *Papers of John F. Kennedy* (Boston, MA: John F. Kennedy Library, 1984); *Prelude to Leadership: The European Diary of John F. Kennedy, Summer 1945* (Washington, DC: Regnery Pub, 1995); *Profiles in Courage* (New York: HarperCollins,

2003); *Why England Slept* (Westport, CT: Greenwood Press, 1981)

PRESIDENCY
Nomination: 1960: The Democratic Convention was held in Los Angeles, CA, July 11–15; although Lyndon B. Johnson, the Senate majority leader, announced that he would seek the nomination, Kennedy, who had won most of the state primaries, secured it on the first ballot and then selected Johnson as his vice-presidential running mate.
Election: elected president on November 8, 1960
Opponent: Richard Milhous Nixon, CA, Republican
Vote Totals: Kennedy, 34,226,731 popular, 303 electoral; Nixon, 34,108,157 popular, 219 electoral
Inauguration: January 20, 1961
Vice President: Lyndon Baines Johnson, TX (1961–1963)

CABINET
Secretary of State: Dean Rusk, GA (1961–1963)
Secretary of the Treasury: C. Douglas Dillon, NJ (1961–1963)
Secretary of Defense: Robert S. McNamara, MI (1961–1963)
Attorney General: Robert F. Kennedy, MA (1961–1963)
Postmaster General: J. Edward Day, IL (1961–1963); John A. Gronouski, WI (1963)
Secretary of Agriculture: Orville Freeman, MN (1961–1963)
Secretary of the Interior: Stewart Udall, AZ (1961–1963)
Secretary of Labor: Arthur J. Goldberg, IL (1961–1962); W. Willard Wirtz, IL (1962–1963)
Secretary of Commerce: Luther H. Hodges, NC (1961–1963)
Secretary of Health, Education, and Welfare: Abraham Ribicoff, CT (1961–1962); Anthony J. Celebrezze, OH (1962–1963)

CONGRESS:
87th Congress (1961–1963); Speaker of the House: Sam Rayburn (TX, Democrat) [Note:

Rayburn died November 16, 1961]; John W. McCormack (MA, Democrat)

88th Congress (1963–1965); Speaker of the House: John W. McCormack (MA, Democrat)

SUPREME COURT APPOINTEES

Bryon Raymond White, CO; Associate Justice (1962–1993)

Arthur Joseph Goldberg, IL; Associate Justice (1962–1965)

MAJOR EVENTS OF THE KENNEDY ADMINISTRATION

❖ The 23rd Amendment, granting presidential electors to the District of Colombia, is passed by Congress on June 17, 1960, and ratified on March 29, 1961.

❖ As a presidential candidate, Kennedy promises the American people a "New Frontier" that will fight poverty and prejudice while seeking peace in the world.

❖ On March 1, 1961, Kennedy issues an executive order establishing the Peace Corps, a volunteer organization that sends its members, for a year or two, to developing nations, where they aid local residents in matters related to education, health, and agriculture.

❖ On April 17, 1961, the invasion of Cuba, at the Bay of Pigs, begins. Approximately 1,500 Cuban exiles trained and supported by the US government (specifically, by the CIA) attempt to invade Cuba to overthrow Fidel Castro, but the operation is a spectacular failure. Most of the invading force is captured; many are held for ransom, not returning to the United States until 1965.

❖ On May 5, 1961, under the US space program entitled Project Mercury, Alan B. Shepard becomes the first American to be launched into space, some three weeks after the Soviet Union launches the first man in space, Yuri Gagarin.

❖ In a speech to Congress on May 25, 1961, Kennedy announces that the United States will put a man on the moon before the end of the decade.

❖ In May 1961 a group of black and white civil rights workers attempt to ride buses in the South to test local compliance with Supreme Court-ordered desegregation. Called "Freedom Riders," the activists challenge previous custom, with whites taking their seats in the back of the bus and blacks riding up front. Despite some limited support from police under pressure from Attorney General Robert Kennedy, the Freedom Riders are physically attacked in some communities, and jailed in "protective custody" or for disturbing the peace in others.

❖ On June 4, 1961, Kennedy and Soviet Premier Nikita Khrushchev meet in Vienna to discuss Germany and other concerns, including nuclear arms and Laos. Little is accomplished, as the Soviet Union threatens to sign a treaty with East Germany, which would put at risk American, French, and British access rights to West Berlin. A possible armed conflict between the Soviets and the Americans in the months to come looms large.

❖ With Germans fleeing East Germany in droves for West Germany, the Berlin Wall is erected in August 1961, ostensibly closing off travel between the two countries.

❖ In August 1961 the Alliance for Progress charter is drawn up at a conference in Uruguay. It is hoped that the organization, funded jointly by the United States and Latin American countries, will help fight poverty, establish democratic governments, and battle Communism. The Alliance, in fact, results in few concrete accomplishments, and its organizing committee is later disbanded in 1973.

❖ In November 1961 a US naval force (of nearly 2,000 Marines) is dispatched to the Dominican Republic to force the replacement of President Rafael Trujillo, Jr. (son of the assassinated former ruler) with Joachim Balaguer, fully supported by the Kennedy administration.

❖ In January 1962 the United States participates in a world conference, hosted in Geneva, Switzerland, where the banning of nuclear tests is discussed. The United Kingdom and the Soviet Union also attend, but no agreement is reached.

◆ Kennedy officially halts trade between Cuba and the United States, February 7, 1962.

◆ On February 14, 1962, Jacqueline Kennedy leads the nation on a televised tour of the newly restored White House, demonstrating the restoration's meticulous attention to historical accuracy.

◆ Aboard the *Friendship 7* spacecraft, Mercury astronaut John Glenn becomes the first American to orbit the earth, February 20, 1962.

◆ On June 25, 1962, the Supreme Court decides, in *Engel v. Vitale*, that New York's so-called Regents' Prayer, a nondenominational morning prayer required by the state's Board of Regents, is unconstitutional, violating the separation of church and state.

◆ In July 1962 the United States learns that the Soviet Union is shipping ballistic missiles to Cuba; spy planes corroborate this in September and October. Kennedy orders a naval blockade of Cuba on October 23, 1962, to prevent further missile deliveries. For thirteen tense days, it appears that the United States and the Soviet Union may go to war, but communications between Kennedy and Khrushchev result, by October 28, in the Soviet agreement to withdraw the missiles from Cuba in exchange for a US promise not to invade Cuba. Tensions subside.

◆ On September 30, 1962, James H. Meredith, an Air Force veteran, becomes the first African American to attend the University of Mississippi. The Supreme Court orders the university to admit him, and US marshals accompany him everywhere on campus to enforce the order.

◆ On March 26, 1962, the Supreme Court rules in *Baker v. Carr* that courts can direct state governments to redraw district lines to ensure equal representation of voters. The case was prompted by Tennessee's use of outdated district lines giving rural voters disproportionate influence compared with urban voters in selecting state legislators.

◆ The 24th Amendment to the Constitution,

eliminating the poll tax, is passed by Congress on August 27, 1962, and ratified on January 23, 1964.

◆ In February 1963 the US-supported ruler of the Dominican Republic, Joachim Balaguer, is replaced by newly elected president Juan Bosch, whom the United States condemns as a Communist. With CIA support, the Dominican army stages a coup in September 1963.

◆ On March 18, 1963, the Supreme Court decides, in *Gideon v. Wainwright*, that it is a violation of the Sixth Amendment's guarantee of the right to counsel and the Fourteenth Amendment's right to due process to deny court-ordered representation to a defendant in a felony trial. The opinion further asserts that an indigent defendant cannot obtain a fair trial without legal representation.

◆ Kennedy delivers a radio and television address on the subject of civil rights, June 11, 1963, noting that the United States preaches freedom around the world but denies it to blacks at home. He asks Congress to enact legislation to ensure that any American, regardless of skin color, can be served in public facilities.

◆ NAACP organizer Medgar Evers is murdered outside his home in Mississippi, June 12, 1963.

◆ On June 26, 1963, Kennedy gives a public address in West Berlin, declaring "Ich bin ein Berliner" (which loosely translated means "I am a citizen of Berlin"), In his remarks, Kennedy celebrates the freedom of the West and decries the Berlin Wall as "the most obvious and vivid demonstration of the failures of the Communist system."

◆ Dr. Martin Luther King, Jr., delivers his stirring "I Have a Dream" speech at the Lincoln Memorial in Washington, DC, before a crowd of 250,000 civil rights demonstrators, on August 28, 1963.

◆ Four African-American girls are killed on September 15, 1963, when segregationists bomb the Sixteenth Street Baptist Church in Birmingham, Alabama.

◆ The Limited Test Ban Treaty passes in the US Senate, September 24, 1963. The treaty bans atomic testing in the atmosphere, underwater, and in space, but does not ban tests conducted underground.

◆ Ngo Dinh Diem, the corrupt president of South Vietnam, is assassinated on November 1, 1963, by Vietnamese generals acting with American support.

◆ On November 22, 1963, in Dallas, Texas, Lee Harvey Oswald shoots Kennedy from the Texas Book Depository along the presidential motorcade route; Texas Governor John B. Connally is wounded. Kennedy dies at Parkland Memorial Hospital in Dallas at 1:00 p.m.

◆ Immediately after Kennedy's death, his remains are transported to the presidential aircraft, Air Force One, standing by at Dallas's Love Field. Onboard, Vice President Lyndon B. Johnson is sworn in as president, with both Lady Bird Johnson and Jackie Kennedy at his side.

◆ Lee Harvey Oswald is shot and killed by Jack Ruby, a local nightclub owner, on November 24, 1963, in the basement of the Dallas jail from which Oswald is being moved.

MAJOR US AND WORLD EVENTS, 1961–1963

◆ Resistance to colonial rule in Angola leads to the outbreak of the Portuguese Colonial War on February 4, 1961.

◆ Russian astronaut Yuri Gagarin is the first human to be rocketed into orbital space on April 12, 1961.

◆ On April 25, 1961, Robert Noyce of Fairchild Semiconductor obtains the first patent for an integrated circuit (a computer chip); a patent application for a similar design is filed by Jack Kilby of Texas Instruments, but Noyce's application receives approval first.

◆ The United Kingdom grants Sierra Leone its independence on April 27, 1961.

◆ Rafael Trujillo, leader of the Dominican Republic, is assassinated, May 30, 1961.

◆ In June 1961 Iraq announces its intention to annex Kuwait, which, in turn, requests aid from the United Kingdom. British troops are dispatched to the region, but leave in October after Arab League troops replace them.

◆ En route to the Congo on a diplomatic mission, UN Secretary-General Dag Hammarskjöld dies in an air crash, September 18, 1961.

◆ On September 28, 1961, a military coup led by a group of Syrian army officers brings an end to the United Arab Republic, the union between Egypt and Syria.

◆ On November 12, 1961, the Russian city of Stalingrad is renamed Volgograd following Khrushchev's denunciations of Stalin's dictatorship.

◆ Fidel Castro announces that he is a Marxist on December 2, 1961, and that he will lead Cuba to embrace Communism.

◆ The East African republic of Tanganyika gains its independence from the British Commonwealth on December 9, 1961.

◆ On December 10, 1961, the Soviet Union and Albania sever diplomatic ties.

◆ In 1961 Roger Maris hits 61 home runs during the regular baseball season, breaking the 1927 record set by Babe Ruth.

◆ All of the members of the US figure-skating team, as well as officials and managers traveling with the team, are killed in a plane crash on February 15, 1961, while en route to the world figure-skating championships in Prague.

◆ Muriel Spark publishes *The Prime of Miss Jean Brodie*, 1961.

◆ Joseph Heller publishes *Catch-22*, 1961.

◆ Harold Robbins publishes *The Carpetbaggers*, 1961.

◆ Ian Fleming publishes *Thunderball*, 1961.

◆ Roald Dahl publishes *James and the Giant Peach*, 1961.

◆ Robert Heinlein publishes *Stranger in a Strange Land*, 1961.

◆ Polish author Stanislaw Lem publishes *Solaris*, 1961.

◆ Television series debuting in 1961 include *The Bullwinkle Show, The Avengers, The Dick Van Dyke Show, Hazel, The Jackie Gleason Show, Mister Ed, The Mike Douglas Show, Password*, and *Car 54, Where Are You?*

◆ Bob Merrill and Michael Stewart's *Carnival!* debuts on Broadway, 1961.

◆ Popular music hits of 1961 include Patsy Cline's "I Fall to Pieces" and "Crazy," Roy Orbison's "Crying," Del Shannon's "Runaway," The Miracles' "Shop Around," Ben E. King's "Stand by Me," Dion's "The Wanderer," Ray Charles's "Hit the Road, Jack," and Elvis Presley's "Surrender."

◆ Notable films of 1961 include Robert Rossen's *The Hustler* with Paul Newman, Robert Wise and Jerome Robbins's *West Side Story* with Natalie Wood, Blake Edwards's *Breakfast at Tiffany's* with Audrey Hepburn, Walt Disney's *101 Dalmations*, Daniel Petrie's *A Raisin in the Sun* with Sidney Poitier, David Swift's *The Parent Trap* with Hayley Mills, Stanley Kramer's *Judgment at Nuremberg* with Spencer Tracy, and John Huston's *The Misfits* with Clark Gable, Marilyn Monroe, and Montgomery Clift.

◆ On January 1, 1962, Western Samoa becomes independent of New Zealand.

◆ Cuba and the Soviet Union sign a trade agreement, January 9, 1962.

◆ On March 2, 1962, the Philadelphia Warriors' Wilt Chamberlain scores a record-breaking 100 points in a basketball game against the New York Knicks.

◆ On May 31, 1962, former Nazi Karl Adolf Eichmann is executed after being tried and convicted in Israel for his role in the Holocaust.

◆ Students for a Democratic Society (SDS) release their Port Huron Statement (so named because it is written, mainly by Tom Hayden, at Port Huron, Michigan), a manifesto of the "New Left," on June 15, 1962. The document details the dissatisfaction felt by many students with such problems as racial prejudice, the threat of nuclear war, the Cold War, and the lack of hope for a better future. It also urges political involvement, meaningful employment, and a role for universities as a starting point for change.

◆ After an accord is reached with France, a July 1962 referendum finds overwhelming support in Algeria for the country's independence from France.

◆ The launch of Telstar, one of the first communications satellites, on July 10, 1962, arouses public attention, with live television broadcasts between the United States and Europe.

◆ On August 5, 1962, actress Marilyn Monroe is found dead at her home in Los Angeles, California. Ruled an accidental overdose by the coroner, her death becomes the subject of numerous murder or suicide theories. Suspected culprits include the Kennedy family (presumably to hide the rumored affair between her and the president, and/or Robert Kennedy), the Mafia, Communists, and even Monroe's own psychiatrist.

◆ In the summer and fall of 1962 Jamaica, Rwanda, Burundi, Algeria, Uganda, and Trinidad and Tobago become independent nations.

◆ Boxer Sonny Liston knocks out Floyd Patterson to become the heavyweight champion of the world, September 25, 1962.

◆ On October 11, 1962, Pope John XXIII convenes the Second Vatican Council (also called Vatican II), which recommends sweeping reforms within the Roman Catholic Church, including greater lay participation in the liturgy, the use of vernacular language instead of Latin in the liturgy (in the United States, English), and various changes in the education and duties of the clergy and other religious. The Council continues its work until 1965 under the auspices of Pope John XXIII's successor, Pope Paul VI.

◆ U Thant of Burma becomes the new secretary-general of the United Nations, November 30, 1962.

◆ Leading men's golfers of 1962 include Arnold Palmer, Jack Nicklaus, and Gary Player.

◆ Australian Rod Laver wins the Grand Slam of tennis (the Australian Open, the French Open, Wimbledon, and the US Open) in 1962.

◆ Barbara Tuchman publishes *The Guns of August*, 1962.

◆ Ken Kesey publishes *One Flew Over the Cuckoo's Nest*, 1962.

◆ Vladimir Nabokov publishes *Pale Fire*, 1962.

◆ William Faulkner publishes *The Reivers*, 1962.

◆ Fletcher Knebel and Charles W. Bailey II publish *Seven Days in May*, 1962.

◆ Helen Gurley Brown publishes *Sex and the Single Girl*, 1962.

❖ Rachel Carson publishes *Silent Spring*, 1962.

❖ Madeleine L'Engle publishes *A Wrinkle in Time*, 1962.

❖ Anthony Burgess publishes *A Clockwork Orange*, 1962.

❖ Philip K. Dick publishes *The Man in the High Castle*, 1962.

❖ Dick Francis publishes *Dead Cert*, 1962.

❖ P. D. James publishes *Cover Her Face*, 1962.

❖ Television series debuting in 1962 include *The Alfred Hitchcock Hour*, *The Beverly Hillbillies*, *The French Chef* (with Julia Child), *The Jetsons*, *The Match Game*, *McHale's Navy*, *The Merv Griffin Show*, *The Saint*, *The Tonight Show* (with Johnny Carson), and *The Virginian*.

❖ Stephen Sondheim's *A Funny Thing Happened on the Way to the Forum* debuts on Broadway, 1962.

❖ The first single by the Beatles is released in 1962: "Love Me Do" with "P.S. I Love You" on the flip side.

❖ Other popular music hits of 1962 include Chubby Checker's "The Twist," Little Eva's "The Loco-Motion," Ray Charles's "I Can't Stop Loving You," Shelley Fabares's "Johnny Angel," and Roy Orbison's "Dream Baby."

❖ Notable films of 1962 include David Lean's *Lawrence of Arabia* with Peter O'Toole, Robert Mulligan's *To Kill a Mockingbird* with Gregory Peck, Blake Edwards's *Days of Wine and Roses* with Jack Lemmon and Lee Remick, Arthur Penn's *The Miracle Worker* with Anne Bancroft and Patty Duke, John Frankenheimer's *The Manchurian Candidate* with Frank Sinatra and Laurence Harvey, Stanley Kubrick's *Lolita* with James Mason and Sue Lyon, Terence Young's *Dr. No* with Sean Connery, François Truffaut's *Jules et Jim* with Jeanne Moreau, and J. Lee Thompson's *Cape Fear* with Robert Mitchum and Gregory Peck.

❖ With Great Britain having applied for admission to the European Union (EU) in 1961, Charles de Gaulle, president of France, vetoes its application as well as those of Ireland and Denmark in early 1963.

❖ France and Germany sign a treaty of cooperation on January 22, 1963.

❖ On March 21, 1963, California penal authorities end the use of Alcatraz Prison, situated on Alcatraz Island in San Francisco Bay, as a prison facility. Called "the Rock," Alcatraz was virtually inescapable and famed for its harsh conditions.

❖ On April 21, 1963, Michael E. DeBakey implants an artificial heart in a patient for the first time, at a Houston hospital. The plastic device functions and the patient lives for four days.

❖ The Organization of African Unity (OAU) is established in Ethiopia in May, 1963, with thirty-two founding member states. The organization's initial goals include an end to colonial status for African nations, settlement of boundary conflicts, an end to apartheid, economic development, and improved education.

❖ On June 3, 1963, Pope John XXIII dies; he is succeeded on June 21 by Cardinal Montini, who becomes Paul VI.

❖ The British Secretary of State for War, John Profumo, resigns on June 5, 1963, when the media exposes his attempts to conceal his affair with call girl Christine Keeler. The case causes a sensation when it is revealed that Keeler also had an affair with a Soviet attaché. Although suspicions of espionage proliferate, no evidence of this is found.

❖ On June 11, 1963, Thich Quang Duc, a Buddhist monk, sets himself on fire in Saigon to protest the policies of Ngo Dinh Diem's South Vietnamese government—specifically, the persecution of Buddhist monks ordered by Diem, a Roman Catholic.

❖ Soviet cosmonaut Valentina Tereshkova becomes the first woman in space, June 16, 1963, orbiting the earth 48 times in a flight that lasts a little over 70 hours.

❖ On June 17, 1963, the US Supreme Court rules that no locality may require recitation of the Lord's Prayer or Bible verses in public schools.

❖ On August 8, 1963, thieves in Great Britain make off with more than two million pounds from the robbery of the Glasgow-to-Euston train, in a heist dubbed the "Great Train Robbery." Twelve of the fifteen robbers are arrested, tried, and sentenced within the year.

◆ Dr. Martin Luther King, Jr. delivers his "I have a dream" speech on August 28, 1963.

◆ A Washington-to-Moscow "hot line" communications link opens, designed to reduce the risk of accidental war, on August 30, 1963.

◆ On September 16, 1963, at the suggestion of the British government, the Federation of Malaysia is formed from Malaya, Singapore, North Borneo (Sabah), and Sarawak, with the United Kingdom effectively ending its colonial rule of these areas.

FAST FACTS ABOUT JOHN FITZGERALD KENNEDY

◆ Kennedy's senior thesis at Harvard formed the basis for his book *Why England Slept*.

◆ Kennedy's book *Profiles in Courage*, which he wrote in 1955 while recuperating from back surgery, won the Pulitzer Prize in 1957.

◆ Although born to a wealthy family, Kennedy rarely carried cash and frequently borrowed from friends, usually without paying them back.

◆ Kennedy was the first Roman Catholic president.

◆ The presidential debates between Kennedy and the Republican nominee Nixon were the first to be televised.

◆ At age forty-three, Kennedy was the youngest man elected president, although not the youngest to serve (Theodore Roosevelt succeeded William McKinley after McKinley's assassination, about six weeks before Roosevelt's forty-third birthday).

◆ Former and future presidents at Kennedy's inauguration in 1961 included Harry S. Truman, Dwight D. Eisenhower, Lyndon B. Johnson, and Richard M. Nixon.

◆ Kennedy suffered from Addison's disease (a failure of the adrenal glands), for which he often took steroids. He also endured horrendous back pain; it has been reported that while Kennedy was president, he regularly received injections of painkillers.

◆ Kennedy was the first president to hold live news conferences for television.

◆ Kennedy refused the $50,000 expense account available to him as president and donated his $100,000 salary to charity.

◆ Cellist Pablo Casals played at the White House for President John F. Kennedy on November 13, 1961; he had previously performed there more than fifty years earlier, on January 15, 1904, for President Theodore Roosevelt.

◆ Kennedy collected scrimshaw, carved bone or ivory from a whale, an art practiced by Massachusetts seafarers (among others) for centuries. He also collected maritime art and ships' models.

◆ Kennedy enjoyed sailing and for his fifteenth birthday he received a sailboat from his parents.

◆ Because of his back problems, Kennedy often used a wooden rocking chair, the style of which came to be known as a "Kennedy rocker."

◆ Kennedy was the first president to appoint a sibling to a cabinet position; he named his brother, Robert F. Kennedy, as attorney general.

◆ During Kennedy's presidency, in 1962, his brother Edward ("Ted") Kennedy was elected US Senator from Massachusetts.

◆ Kennedy liked to smoke Petit Upmann cigars from Cuba. One night in 1961 he sent out his press secretary, Pierre Salinger, to buy at least a thousand Petit Upmanns. Salinger returned in the morning with 1,200 cigars, whereupon Kennedy signed an order banning Cuban imports into the United States.

◆ While living at the White House, the Kennedys had a country house built in Atoka, Virginia. Jackie called the home "Wexford," named after the county in Ireland from which Jack's family had emigrated.

◆ Much has been made of the seemingly amazing coincidences between the assassinations of Lincoln and Kennedy. Although there are some parallels (Lincoln was elected in 1860, Kennedy in 1960; both were succeeded by vice presidents named Johnson), some of the so-called parallels are inaccurate (for instance, Kennedy had a secretary named Lincoln, but there is no evidence to support Lincoln's having a secretary named Kennedy). Ultimately, "coincidence" is the operative word for any parallels between the two tragedies.

Lyndon B. Johnson

Nickname: LBJ; Landslide Lyndon
Presidency: 36th president, 1963–1969
Party: Democratic
Life dates: August 27, 1908–January 22, 1973 (64 years, 148 days)

EARLY LIFE AND EDUCATION

Lyndon Baines Johnson was born near Johnson City, Texas, on August 27, 1908, the eldest son of Samuel Ealy Johnson, Jr., and Rebekah Baines Johnson. Lyndon's father was a farmer and cattle speculator. His mother had been well educated, studying literature in college (though without earning a degree). She worked as a teacher of elocution and as a newspaper reporter, in which pursuit she met Sam Johnson, then serving as a state legislator. She placed a high value on education and was fiercely ambitious for Lyndon and his four younger siblings: Rebekah, Josefa, Sam, Jr., and Lucia.

Politics ran deep on both sides of the Johnson family. Lyndon's paternal grandfather, a Civil War veteran who served in the Confederate Army, helped to settle the Texas region and lent his name to Johnson City, Texas. His maternal grandfather had served as a Texas secretary of state and his maternal great-grandfather had been a noted Baptist minister and friend of Sam Houston, while a distant relative had once served as governor of Kentucky. The future president's father served five terms in the Texas state legislature. Rebekah Johnson found her married life poorer and harder than she had expected; she wanted her children, especially Lyndon, to make up for the disappointments suffered by her father and husband by achieving greatness.

In 1913 the Johnson family moved to Johnson City. In the 1920s, Sam Johnson and his family were hard hit by the agricultural depression, losing the family farm. After Lyndon graduated from high school in 1924 at the age of fifteen, he made his way to California, where he worked as an elevator operator, waited tables, washed dishes, and worked at other menial jobs. He returned to Texas a year later and spent several months working with a road construction crew. Agreeing with his mother that such a lifestyle honored neither himself nor his family, in 1927 Lyndon entered San Marcos College (now a branch of the Texas State University system), where he majored in history and prepared for a teaching career. He excelled on the debate team, worked on the college newspaper, and was active in campus politics, energetically organizing a group of students to challenge the athletes on campus, who had previously dominated student government. Lyndon worked a series of menial jobs until he became the assistant to the secretary of the college's president;

he also developed a close relationship with a popular professor at the college, demonstrating his ability to work his way into the power structure of an organization, an ability that would continue to be a hallmark of his style in future years. While still a student, Lyndon took a teaching job at an elementary school in Cotulla, Texas. Most of the students were poor Mexican-American children; Johnson was touched by their plight and worked relentlessly to develop activities that he thought would help them improve their lot in life.

EARLY CAREER

Before earning his B.S. in 1930, Johnson successfully managed the campaign for state legislature for Willy Hopkins, a young politician. After graduation, Johnson taught public speaking at Sam Houston High School in Houston. But in 1931, Hopkins recommended Johnson to a wealthy Texas congressman, Richard M. Kleberg, and Kleberg offered Johnson a job as his legislative secretary. Two weeks later, Johnson left for Washington, DC.

Johnson immediately began to immerse himself in national politics, using his boundless energy to meet and question people, read volumes of newspapers and legislative reports, and organize Kleberg's office while the congressman enjoyed the Washington social scene. Johnson met as many influential members of Congress as he could, becoming friends with Sam Rayburn, a fellow Texan and later Speaker of the House. Johnson also joined the Little Congress, a discussion group for legislative aides; he convinced others to join and was thus elected Speaker of the Little Congress, promising to revitalize the group and make it a force on Capitol Hill.

On a brief trip to Austin, Johnson met Claudia Alta Taylor, called "Lady Bird" from childhood, who had just graduated from the University of Texas with bachelor's degrees in both history and journalism. After meeting her at a party, Johnson asked her to breakfast the next morning and proposed by the end of the day. During the next several days, he spent every available minute with her, taking her to meet his mother and meeting her father in turn. After his return to Washington, he communicated with Lady Bird daily, and seven weeks later he traveled back to Texas to urge her again to marry him. A week later, on November 17, 1934, they were married in San Antonio.

FURTHER POLITICAL CAREER

In the spring of 1935, Johnson and Lady Bird returned to Texas, where he served for eighteen months as director of the National Youth Administration, an appointed position that allowed him to gain practical political experience and to widen his base of support in Texas precincts. When a congressional seat opened up in his district in early 1937, Johnson quickly threw his hat in the ring.

"I am a freeman, an American, a United States Senator, and a Democrat, in that order."

Lyndon B. Johnson, in the preface to his campaign biography, *The Lyndon Johnson Story*, 1964

On April 10, 1937, at the age of 28, Johnson was elected to the US House of Representatives. As a congressman, Johnson advocated public works, reclamation (the management of water, specifically via dams, power plants, and canals), public power programs, and other New Deal initiatives. During World War II, he served briefly in the Navy as a lieutenant commander, earning a Silver Star Medal for his service in the South Pacific, but he returned home after Roosevelt recalled all congressmen on active duty.

In 1941, Johnson (by then known as LBJ) made his first bid for a seat in the US Senate but lost in a special election to Governor W. Lee O'Daniel by a margin of less than 1,500 votes. He returned to the House of Representatives and continued to support Roosevelt. In 1942, Lady Bird purchased a struggling radio station in Austin with money she had inherited from her mother. Under Lady Bird's management, the station became a profitable and thriving business that grew to include other radio stations and several cable television stations. In 1944, Lady Bird and Lyndon had a daughter, Lynda Byrd Johnson, and in 1947, a second daughter, Luci Baines Johnson, was born. In 1949, the Johnsons purchased a ranch in the Texas hill country near where Lyndon had grown up.

"We can draw lessons from the past, but we cannot live in it."

Lyndon, B. Johnson, December 13, 1963

Johnson again campaigned for a Senate seat in 1948, running on a platform of "preparedness, peace, and progress" and urging stronger armed forces, a viable United Nations, and federal aid to Texas for soil conservation and rural electrification. After a contested Democratic primary runoff election, which he won by a mere 87 votes, Johnson was elected to the US Senate by a ratio of 2 to 1.

Johnson's rise in the Senate hierarchy was a rapid one. As a junior senator, he served on the Senate Armed Services Committee, headed the Senate Preparedness Investigating Subcommittee, which fought military inefficiency and waste, and supported the Korean War effort, despite his repeated—and politically strategic—attacks on Truman's conduct of the war. Johnson also denounced Truman's seizure of the steel mills as political "dictatorship." Acutely aware of his controversial win in 1948, Johnson worked hard to mend fences with affluent "Oil Texans" and a broad coalition of conservative Democrats and Republicans.

Again, Johnson's strategy paid off. In 1951 he was elected Senate minority whip. Two years later, in 1953, he was chosen as Senate minority leader. After the Democrats won control of Congress in the 1954 elections, Johnson, at the age of 46, was elected Senate majority leader. John-

son exhibited such a rare and "relentlessly overpowering persuasiveness" in marshalling bipartisan cooperation in Congress that presidential historian Louis Koenig described him as "one of the most illustrious floor leaders in Senate history."

In July of 1955, Johnson, who smoked incessantly, drank vast quantities of coffee and quite a bit of alcohol, and worked most of his waking hours, suffered a serious heart attack. He returned to his ranch in Texas to recuperate, wondering if his political career might be over. Coincidentally, President Eisenhower also suffered a heart attack in September of 1955 but recovered sufficiently to successfully seek reelection in 1956. Johnson returned to Washington to continue his pursuit of political power.

Johnson campaigned for the presidential nomination in 1960. Although he had considerable delegate support at the convention, the nomination went to John F. Kennedy, who quickly offered the vice-presidential nomination to Johnson. Most historians agree that Johnson's inclusion on the Democratic ticket was a determining factor in Kennedy's victory, with Kennedy needing Johnson to carry Texas and the South, which he did.

As vice president, Johnson headed the National Aeronautics and Space Council, the Peace Corps Advisory Council, the President's Committee on Equal Employment Opportunity, and served on the National Security Council and as a presidential emissary abroad. But, as many scholars and biographers have noted, the nature of the vice presidency was patently incompatible with Johnson's towering ambition and ego.

PRESIDENCY

The assassination of President Kennedy on November 22, 1963, elevated Johnson to the presidency. After being sworn in later that day aboard Air Force One, Johnson proved to be a masterful, reassuring leader in domestic affairs. Congress responded to Johnson's skillful leadership by enacting an $11 billion tax cut in January 1964 and by passing the sweeping Civil Rights Act in July 1964. That same year, Johnson also helped

Lyndon B. Johnson taking the presidential oath aboard Air Force One, following the assassination of President John F. Kennedy, November 22, 1963.

secure the passage of the Economic Opportunity Act, called for a "war against poverty," and outlined an ambitious program of social and economic reforms aimed at creating what he called the Great Society.

In the summer of 1964, the Republicans nominated Senator Barry M. Goldwater as their presidential nominee. An extreme conservative on domestic issues, Goldwater also advocated strong military action in Vietnam. Johnson, with Hubert H. Humphrey as his running mate, ran a low-key campaign and won a landslide election over Goldwater, who only carried his home state of Arizona and five other states in the Deep South.

Johnson's triumph in 1964 gave him a mandate for his Great Society initiatives. Congress cooperated by passing the Medicare program, which provided health services to the elderly, approving federal aid to elementary and secondary education, supplementing the war on poverty, and creating the Department of Housing and Urban Development (HUD). But perhaps Johnson's greatest legislative achievement was the passage of the Voting Rights Act of 1965.

Johnson's domestic achievements, however, were soon eclipsed by the nation's deepening involvement in the Vietnam War. As early as February 1965, US planes began to bomb North Vietnam. By the end of the year, Johnson had increased the number of troops in Vietnam to more than 180,000, and, by the end of 1968, the number had skyrocketed to more than 500,000.

Meanwhile, as the nation became entangled in the Vietnam conflict, racial tensions at home increased, triggering a series of violent race riots in Los Angeles, Detroit, Harlem, and other major American cities between 1965 and 1968. Racial violence, combined with the failure of some of Johnson's Great Society programs, resulted in Republican gains in the 1966 midterm elections, thus undermining Johnson's hopes for further congressional cooperation. But most historians agree that it was Johnson's ill-advised policy of military escalation in Vietnam that proved to be his undoing as president.

"A president's hardest task is not to do what is right, but to know what is right. Yet the presidency brings no special gift of prophecy or foresight. You take an oath, you step into an office, and you must then help guide a great democracy. . . . A president does not shape a new and personal vision of America. He collects it from the scattered hopes of the American past."

Lyndon B. Johnson, from his State of the Union address, January 4, 1965

It was also Johnson's misfortune to be president during one of the most tumultuous decades in US history. The serious convictions that fueled the civil rights movement, the women's movement, and the peace movement were accompanied by the burgeoning of rock music, "free love," easily available birth control, and illegal drug use, as young Americans seemed to be questioning the values of earlier generations.

The 1968 New Hampshire presidential primary, in which the anti-war candidate Eugene McCarthy made a strong showing, testified to Johnson's diminishing support. As the war dragged on, Johnson's closest advisors began calling for a de-escalation policy in Vietnam. Faced with mounting public and political opposition, Johnson made two surprise announcements on March 31, 1968: He would suspend bombing in most of North Vietnam in a peace effort and he would not accept his party's nomination for reelection.

Although Johnson suspended the bombing of North Vietnam on November 1, he failed to achieve any significant concessions in his peace efforts. And, in November 1968, Hubert Humphrey lost to the Republican presidential candidate, Richard M. Nixon, in a close election.

POST-PRESIDENTIAL CAREER
After Nixon was sworn in as president on January 20, 1969, Johnson returned with Lady Bird to his ranch in Texas. During his retirement, Johnson wrote his memoirs, entitled *The Vantage Point* (published in 1971), taught, and participated in a series of national symposia held at the Lyndon B. Johnson Library in Austin. Johnson died suddenly of a heart attack at his ranch on January 22, 1973. After his death, some hailed his patriotism, leadership, and courage, while others continued to question his policies and political motives. Most scholars agree, however, that Johnson was an extremely energetic, skillful, and ambitious politician, consummately talented in wielding power within Congress but less successful as the nation's chief executive.

Birthplace: near Johnson City, TX
Residency: Texas
Religion: Disciples of Christ
Education: Southwest Texas State Teachers College, graduated 1930; Georgetown Law School, attended briefly (in 1934)
Place of Death: near Stonewall, TX
Burial Site: Lyndon B. Johnson National Historical Park (LBJ Ranch), near Johnson City, TX
Dates in Office: November 22, 1963–January 20, 1969 (5 years, 59 days)
Age at Inauguration: 55 years, 87 days

FAMILY
Father: Sam Ealy Johnson, Jr. (1877–1937)
Mother: Rebekah Baines Johnson (1881–1958)
Siblings: Lyndon was the eldest of five children; his siblings were Rebekah Luruth Johnson (1910–1978); Josefa Hermine Johnson (1912–1961); Sam Houston Johnson (1914–1978); Lucia Huffman Johnson (1916–1997)

Wife: Claudia ("Lady Bird") Alta Taylor Johnson (1912–), married on November 17, 1934, in San Antonio, TX

Children: Lynda Bird Johnson (1944–); Luci Baines Johnson (1947–)

CAREER

Private: farm worker, elevator operator, janitor, road construction worker, teacher

Political: legislative secretary for US Representative Richard Kleberg (1931–1935); director of the National Youth Administration (1935–1937); member of the US House of Representatives (1937–1949); member of the US Senate (1949–1961); vice president under John F. Kennedy (1961–1963); president of the United States (1963–1969)

Military: Johnson was a lieutenant commander in the US Naval Reserve (1940); enlisted in the Navy (December 8, 1941) and served for one year before President Roosevelt recalled all members of Congress who had enlisted; awarded the Silver Star (1942).

Selected Works: *The Choices We Face* (New York: Bantam Books, 1969); *Daily Diary of President Johnson (1963–1969)*, microfilm, ed. by Paul Kesaris (Frederick, MD: University Publications of America, 1980); *The Johnson Presidential Press Conferences*, intro. by Doris Kearns Goodwin (New York: E. M. Coleman Enterprises, 1978); *Letters from the Hill Country: The Correspondence Between Rebekah and Lyndon Baines Johnson*, ed. by Philip R. Rulon (Austin, TX: Thorp Springs Press, 1982); *Lyndon B. Johnson, Chronology, Documents, Bibliographical Aids*, ed. by Howard B. Furer (Dobbs Ferry, NY: Oceana Publications, 1971); *Lyndon B. Johnson's Vietnam Papers: A Documentary Collection*, ed. by David M. Barrett (College Station, TX: Texas A&M University Press, 1997); *Reaching for Glory: Lyndon Johnson's Secret White House Tapes, 1964–1965*, ed. and with commentary by Michael Beschloss (New York: Simon & Schuster, 2001); *Taking Charge: The Johnson White House Tapes, 1963–1964*, ed. and with commentary by Michael Beschloss (New York: Simon & Schuster, 1997); *The Vantage Point: Perspectives of the Presidency, 1963–1969* (New York: Holt, Rinehart, and Winston, 1971)

PRESIDENCY

Nomination: 1964: the Democratic convention was held in Atlantic City, New Jersey, August 24–27, 1964. Johnson, the incumbent president since Kennedy's assassination, was nominated for reelection by acclaim, as was his choice for vice president, Senator Hubert Humphrey of Minnesota.

Election: elected president on November 3, 1964

Opponent: Barry M. Goldwater, AZ, Republican

Vote Totals: Johnson: 43,129,566 popular, 486 electoral; Goldwater: 27,178,188 popular, 52 electoral

Inauguration: January 20, 1965

Vice President: Hubert Humphrey, MN (1965–1969)

CABINET

Secretary of State: Dean Rusk, GA (1963–1969)

Secretary of the Treasury: C. Douglas Dillon, NJ (1963–1965); Henry H. Fowler, VA (1965–1968); Joseph Barr, IN (1968–1969)

Secretary of Defense: Robert S. McNamara, CA (1963–1968); Clark Clifford, MD (1968–1969)

Attorney General: Robert F. Kennedy, MA (1963–1965); Nicholas Katzenbach, NJ (1965–1967); Ramsey Clark, TX (1967–1969)

Postmaster General: John A. Gronouski, WI (1963–1965); Lawrence F. O'Brien, MA (1965–1968); W. Marvin Watson, TX (1968–1969)

Secretary of Agriculture: Orville Freeman, MN (1963–1969)

Secretary of the Interior: Stewart Udall, AZ (1963–1969)

Secretary of Labor: W. Willard Wirtz, IL (1963–1969)

Secretary of Commerce: Luther H. Hodges, NC (1963–1965); John T. Connor, NC (1965–1967); Alexander B. Trowbridge, NJ (1967–1968); Cyrus R. Smith, TX (1968–1969)

Secretary of Heath, Education, and Welfare: Anthony J. Celebrezze, OH (1963–1965); John W. Gardner, CA (1965–1968); Wilbur J. Cohen, WI (1968–1969)

Secretary of Housing and Urban Development: Robert C. Weaver, NY (1966–1969); Robert C. Wood, MO (1969) [Note: This department was created in 1965 by passage of the Housing and Urban Development Act.]
Secretary of Transportation: Alan S. Boyd, FL (1967–1969) [Note: This department was created by passage of the Transportation Act of 1966.]

CONGRESS

88th Congress (1963–1965); Speaker of the House: John W. McCormack (MA, Democrat)
89th Congress (1965–1967); Speaker of the House: John W. McCormack (MA, Democrat)
90th Congress (1967–1969); Speaker of the House: John W. McCormack (MA, Democrat)

SUPREME COURT APPOINTEES

Abe Fortas, TN; Associate Justice (1965–1969)
Thurgood Marshall, NY; Associate Justice (1967–1991)

MAJOR EVENTS OF THE JOHNSON ADMINISTRATION

◆ Johnson becomes the thirty-sixth president of the United States following the assassination of John F. Kennedy, on November 22, 1963, in Dallas, Texas.
◆ On November 24, 1963, presumed assassin Lee Harvey Oswald is shot and killed by Jack Ruby, a Dallas nightclub owner.
◆ On November 25, 1963, President John F. Kennedy is buried at Arlington National Cemetery.
◆ On November 29, 1963, Johnson issues an executive order establishing the Warren Commission (named for its chair, US Chief Justice Earl Warren) to investigate the Kennedy assassination. The commission's report, delivered in September of 1964, states that Lee Harvey Oswald acted alone in killing President Kennedy and wounding Texas Governor John Connally, that Oswald killed Texas patrolman J. D. Tippit, who tried to arrest Oswald several hours after the assassination, and that Jack Ruby acted alone in killing Oswald.
◆ In his State of the Union address on January 8, 1964, Johnson declares a "war on poverty" that leads to a number of laws designed to alleviate the problems of the poor.
◆ On January 9, 1964, three days of rioting began in the Panama Canal Zone, with more than 20 people killed and hundreds injured. The rioting is touched off by the refusal of Americans in the Canal Zone to fly the Panamanian flag alongside the US flag.
◆ The 24th Amendment to the Constitution, which eliminates the poll tax, is passed by Congress on August 27, 1962, and ratified on January 23, 1964.
◆ Johnson delivers a speech at the University of Michigan on May 22, 1964, in which he speaks of a "Great Society." In the speech, Johnson declares: "The Great Society rests on abundance and liberty for all. It demands an end to poverty and racial injustice, to which we are totally committed in our time. But that is just the beginning." The speech gives rise to one of the central themes of his presidency.
◆ On June 21, 1964, civil rights workers Michael Schwerner, Andrew Goodman, and James Earl Chaney are killed in Neshoba County, Mississippi, by members of the Ku Klux Klan. Known as the "Mississippi Burning" case, a trial held in October of 1967 results in the conviction of seven men for conspiracy to deprive the murder victims of their civil rights. Not until January of 2005 would an arrest on a murder charge be made.
◆ Johnson signs the Civil Rights Act of 1964, on July 2, 1964. The most sweeping civil rights legislation since Reconstruction, the Civil Rights Act of 1964 prohibits discrimination based on race, color, religion, or national origin. The law also provides the federal government with the powers to enforce desegregation, protect the right to vote, guarantee access to public accommodations, and withhold federal funds from "programs and activities" that are "administered in a discriminatory fashion."
◆ Racial riots erupt in Harlem on July 18, 1964, in protest of the shooting of a black youth by a white police officer and are followed by similar riots in Rochester, New York; Jersey City; Chicago; and Philadelphia.
◆ The US government announces that three

North Vietnamese gunboats had attacked a US destroyer, the *USS Maddox,* in the Gulf of Tonkin on August 2, 1964. It then announces that the attack has been followed (two days later) by a second North Vietnamese boat attack, on the *USS Maddox* and her escort, the *USS Turner Joy* (although it is discovered later that no such second attack had occurred, both the US sailors in the Gulf of Tonkin and US officials are convinced at the time that they were under attack). On August 7, Congress passes the Southeast Asia Resolution (also called the Gulf of Tonkin Resolution), which gives the president the power to take "all necessary measures to repel any armed attack against the forces of the United States and to prevent further aggression." Johnson signs the resolution on August 10, 1964.

◆ Johnson signs the Economic Opportunity Act on August 20, 1964; the act is designed to improve the lives of the poor and includes such programs as the Job Corps, community health centers, and VISTA (Volunteers In Service To America).

◆ On August 26, 1964, Johnson is nominated as the Democratic candidate for president of the United States at the Democratic National Convention in Atlantic City, New Jersey. Hubert Humphrey is nominated for vice president.

◆ Johnson defeats Republican candidate Barry Goldwater on November 3, 1964.

◆ Johnson delivers his inaugural address on January 20, 1965.

◆ In February of 1965, after eight Americans are killed in a surprise Viet Cong raid at Pleiku, South Vietnam, Johnson orders the bombing of North Vietnam.

◆ On March 3, 1965, Congress passes the Appalachian Regional Development Act, which authorizes $1.1 billion for the development of impoverished areas in eleven states.

◆ Johnson delivers his Johns Hopkins speech, on April 7, 1965, in which he announces that the United States is ready to begin discussions with North Vietnamese leaders on the subject of ending the Vietnam War.

◆ Johnson signs the Elementary and Secondary Education Bill in his hometown of Johnson,

Texas, on April 11, 1965. The bill provides funds to improve education for students from low-income families and funds the Head Start program and bilingual education.

◆ US Marines land in the Dominican Republic on April 28, 1965, where they have been sent to quell the ongoing war between leftist rebels in that country and the Dominican army.

◆ On June 7, 1965, the US Supreme Court decides in *Griswold v. Connecticut* that a Connecticut law prohibiting the sale of contraceptive devices violates the constitutional right to privacy; the Connecticut law is struck down.

◆ On July 28, 1965, Johnson announces that he has ordered that US military forces in Vietnam be increased from 75,000 men to 125,000.

◆ Johnson signs the Social Security Act of 1965 on July 30, 1965. The act establishes the Medicare and Medicaid programs.

◆ On August 6, 1965, Johnson signs the Voting Rights Act, which provides for federal review of any proposed changes to voter registration or voting practice so that discriminatory changes can be prevented; the act also outlaws literacy tests.

◆ Congress passes the Housing and Urban Development Act, which establishes the Department of Housing and Urban Development, on September 9, 1965. The department is charged with coordinating federal programs that provide low-income housing.

◆ Asserting that civil rights laws alone are not enough to remedy discrimination, President Johnson, on September 24, 1965, issues Executive Order 11246. The Order officially enforces affirmative action for the first time and requires government contractors to "take affirmative action" toward prospective minority employees in all aspects of hiring and employment.

◆ On October 3, 1965, Johnson signs the Immigration Bill on Liberty Island, New York; the act abolishes the restrictive national-origin quotas that had been in place since 1924, allowing immigrants to be admitted to the

United States based on their professions and skills rather than their nationalities.

❖ On October 8, 1965, Johnson undergoes gall bladder surgery.

❖ Johnson signs the Highway Beautification Act, on October 22, 1965; the act provides limitations on signs along the highway (particularly advertising billboards) and for the removal or screening of such sites as junkyards. Highway beautification is a particular interest of Lady Bird Johnson, who receives the pen with which the bill is signed.

❖ In January of 1966, Robert C. Weaver is appointed Secretary of the Department of Housing and Urban Development, becoming the first cabinet-level African American in the United States.

❖ On June 13, 1966, the Supreme Court rules in *Miranda v. Arizona* that statements made by prisoners under interrogation cannot be used as evidence unless minimum legal safeguards are in place, including the person in custody being informed of the right to silence (the right to avoid self-incrimination) and the right to counsel.

❖ Johnson signs the Freedom of Information Act (FOIA) into law on July 4, 1966; the law mandates that the government must provide information to citizens on request (within twenty working days) as long as doing so does not endanger national security.

❖ In September of 1966, Johnson signs the Transportation Act, which creates the Department of Transportation, a cabinet-level department that includes oversight of aviation, railroads, highways, and maritime traffic.

❖ On January 24, 1967, Johnson asks Congress for a record $112.9 billion to be used to wage war in Vietnam and to build the Great Society.

❖ The 25th Amendment to the US Constitution, which specifies the presidential line of succession in the event of presidential disability, is passed by Congress on July 6, 1965, and ratified on February 10, 1967.

❖ On June 12, 1967, the Supreme Court rules in *Loving v. Virginia* that the prohibition of interracial marriage is unconstitutional.

❖ Thurgood Marshall is sworn in as the first

black US Supreme Court justice, on October 2, 1967.

❖ Johnson signs the Air Quality Act, on November 21, 1967, authorizing the Department of Health, Education, and Welfare (HEW) to set federal air-quality standards.

❖ On January 23, 1968, North Korea seizes the US Navy ship *Pueblo*; it holds the 83 sailors onboard as spies. The United States protests that the ship was in international waters and begins a military buildup in the area while negotiating for the release of the sailors; 82 sailors are released on December 23, 1968, one sailor dies of wounds suffered during the capture of the ship.

❖ The Tet Offensive, a series of offensive strikes by the North Vietnamese Army, occurs throughout South Vietnam in January 1968; it marks a major turning point in the Vietnam War.

❖ The My Lai massacre takes place in Vietnam on March 16, 1968. It is a massacre by US soldiers of hundreds of unarmed Vietnamese civilians, mostly women and children. The event does not become public until late in 1969; in 1971, Lieutenant William Calley is convicted of murder for his part in the massacre. Calley serves a few days in prison before his release is ordered by President Richard M. Nixon; Calley serves a further several years under house arrest.

❖ On March 31, 1968, Johnson announces that he will not be a candidate for another term in office as president of the United States.

❖ On May 13, 1968, formal peace talks begin in Paris between the United States and North Vietnam.

❖ The General Agreement on Tariffs and Trade is signed on June 30, 1968.

❖ Johnson halts the bombing of North Vietnam, on October 31, 1968.

❖ Richard Nixon is elected president on November 5, 1968.

MAJOR US AND WORLD EVENTS, 1963–1969

❖ On December 12, 1963, Kenya becomes independent from the United Kingdom; Jomo Kenyatta becomes the first president of Kenya.

◆ The Pro Football Hall of Fame opens in Canton, Ohio, in September of 1963.

◆ John Cleland's 1749 novel, *Fanny Hill: The Memoirs of a Woman of Pleasure*, is published in the United States in 1963 and banned as obscene; the publisher files a court case in protest and the ban is lifted in December of 1966 by the US Supreme Court.

◆ Sylvia Plath publishes *The Bell Jar*, an autobiographical novel, in 1963, a month before her death by suicide.

◆ Kurt Vonnegut publishes *Cat's Cradle*, 1963.

◆ Mary McCarthy publishes *The Group*, 1963.

◆ John Le Carré publishes *The Spy Who Came In from the Cold*, 1963.

◆ Clifford D. Simak publishes *Way Station*, 1963.

◆ Eric Ambler publishes *The Light of Day*, 1963.

◆ Andre Norton publishes *Witch World*, 1963.

◆ Television series debuting in 1963 include *The Art Linkletter Show, Doctor Who, The Fugitive, General Hospital, Let's Make a Deal, Mutual of Omaha's Wild Kingdom, My Favorite Martian, The Outer Limits, The Patty Duke Show*, and *Petticoat Junction*.

◆ Popular music hits of 1963 include "Please Please Me," "I Want to Hold Your Hand," "Love Me Do," "From Me to You," and "She Loves You," by the Beatles; Lesley Gore's "It's My Party," The Drifters' "Up on the Roof," Jan and Dean's "Surf City," and Roy Orbison's "In Dreams."

◆ Notable films of 1963 include Tony Richardson's *Tom Jones* with Albert Finney and Susannah York, Martin Ritt's *Hud* with Paul Newman, Patricia Neal, and Melvyn Douglas, Stanley Donen's *Charade* with Cary Grant and Audrey Hepburn, Joseph L. Mankiewicz's *Cleopatra* with Richard Burton and Elizabeth Taylor, and Ralph Nelson's *Lilies of the Field* with Sidney Poitier.

◆ In January of 1964, the US Surgeon General issues a report linking cigarette smoking to lung disease.

◆ The Beatles begin their first tour of the United States in February of 1964, appearing on the *Ed Sullivan Show* on February 9, 1964.

◆ In early 1964, fighting breaks out between Greeks and Turks on the island of Cyprus; in March the UN Security Council agrees to send a multinational peacekeeping force to Cyprus.

◆ On March 13, 1964, Queens, New York, resident Catherine ("Kitty") Genovese is stabbed to death outside her home while thirty-eight witnesses fail to come to her aid or call the police. The killer is caught and sentenced, but the case becomes an indictment of the callous impersonality of modern urban life.

◆ IBM announces its System/360 family of mainframe computers on April 7, 1964; the family contains six compatible computers of different sizes and is an innovative and popular product that spawns many attempts to copy it.

◆ Nelson Mandela is sentenced to life imprisonment in a South African prison on June 12, 1964; he will not be released until 1990.

◆ On October 14, 1964, Nikita Khrushchev resigns as first secretary of the Communist Party and premier of the Soviet Union; the new first secretary is Leonid Brezhnev, who becomes the de facto leader, although Aleksei Kosygin becomes premier and Nikolai Podgorny becomes president.

◆ Dr. Martin Luther King, Jr., is awarded the Nobel Prize for Peace, December 10, 1964, for his leadership of the nonviolent effort to end discrimination in the United States.

◆ In 1964, the nations of Tanganyika and Zanzibar unite to form the new nation of Tanzania.

◆ In late 1964, the Free Speech Movement organization is formed at the University of California, Berkeley, to protest attempts by the Regents of the University to restrict the rights of students to hand out literature on political subjects (particularly in protest of racial discrimination). In December, more than a thousand students occupy Sproul Hall on the campus and are forcibly removed by hundreds of police officers; more than 700 students are arrested for trespassing and released the next day.

◆ Saul Bellow publishes *Herzog*, 1964.

◆ Roald Dahl publishes *Charlie and the Chocolate Factory*, 1964.

◆ Ernest Hemingway's *A Moveable Feast* is published posthumously in 1964.

◆ General Douglas MacArthur publishes *Reminiscences*, 1964.

◆ Martin Luther King, Jr., publishes *Why We Can't Wait*, 1964.

◆ Television series debuting in 1964 include *The Addams Family, Another World, Bewitched, Flipper, Gilligan's Island, Gomer Pyle U.S.M.C., Jeopardy!, The Munsters*, and *Peyton Place*.

◆ Jerry Bock and Sheldon Harnick's *Fiddler on the Roof* debuts on Broadway, 1964.

◆ Jerry Herman's *Hello, Dolly!* debuts on Broadway, 1964.

◆ Popular music hits of 1964 include the Beatles' "Can't Buy Me Love," "Twist and Shout," and "A Hard Day's Night," Roy Orbison's "Oh, Pretty Woman," The Drifters' "Under the Boardwalk," The Kinks' "You Really Got Me," and The Beach Boys' "Fun Fun Fun."

◆ Jerry Herman's *Hello, Dolly!* and Jerry Bock and Sheldon Harnick's *Fiddler on the Roof* debut on Broadway, 1964.

◆ Notable films of 1964 include George Cukor's *My Fair Lady* with Rex Harrison and Audrey Hepburn, Michael Cacoyannis's *Zorba the Greek* with Anthony Quinn, Alan Bates, and Irene Papas, Stanley Kubrick's *Dr. Strangelove: Or, How I Learned to Stop Worrying and Love the Bomb* with Peter Sellers and George C. Scott, Richard Lester's *A Hard Day's Night* with the Beatles, Blake Edwards's *A Shot in the Dark* with Peter Sellers, and Guy Hamilton's *Goldfinger* with Sean Connery.

◆ Martin Luther King, Jr., and 250 African Americans are arrested while marching for voter rights in Selma, Alabama, on February 2, 1965; on March 21–25, 1965, King leads a 50-mile march from Selma to Montgomery, Alabama, to protest in favor of African-American voting rights. The march attracts supporters from around the country and helps mobilize public opinion in favor of civil rights.

◆ Former Nation of Islam spokesman Malcolm X is shot to death before speaking at a rally in the Audubon Ballroom in Harlem, New York, February 21, 1965.

◆ On June 3, 1965, the Gemini IV spacecraft is launched; astronaut Edward H. White II becomes the first US astronaut to walk in space.

◆ On July 25, 1965, Bob Dylan unleashes a storm of controversy by playing electrically amplified music at the Newport Folk Festival.

◆ Race riots take place in the Watts section of Los Angeles during the six days of August 11–16, 1965. During this period 34 people die, more than 1,000 are injured, and nearly 4,000 are arrested, while fire damages total $175 million. The riot, touched off by the arrest of an inebriated black driver by white police officers, is considered to have deeper causes, including unemployment, discrimination, and substandard schools and housing in such inner-city black neighborhoods.

◆ On September 30, 1965, an attempted coup against President Sukarno of Indonesia takes place but is thwarted by General Suharto, under whose influence the Communist Party is outlawed and tens of thousands of Indonesian Communists are killed. By 1967 Suharto is appointed acting president, and in 1968 he becomes president in fact, with Sukarno being kept under house arrest.

◆ Beginning in the fall of 1965, Fidel Castro allows Cubans to immigrate to the United States; tens of thousands take advantage of the opportunity to do so by the end of the decade.

◆ On the night of November 9, 1965, a failure in the power grid causes a massive blackout throughout New England and New York, lasting approximately ten hours in most locations.

◆ On December 30, 1965, Ferdinand Marcos is inaugurated as president of the Philippines.

◆ Beginning late in 1965 in San Francisco and spreading throughout the country, "acid tests" are held, gatherings featuring psychedelic rock music, light shows, and the ingestion of LSD (lysergic acid diethylamide), a psychoactive drug.

◆ Mitch Leigh and Joe Lardon's *Man of La Mancha* debuts on Broadway, 1965.

◆ Ralph Nader publishes *Unsafe at Any Speed:*

The Designed-In Dangers of the American Automobile, 1965.

◆ Malcolm X and Alex Haley publish *The Autobiography of Malcolm X*, 1965.

◆ Margaret Forster publishes *Georgy Girl*, 1965.

◆ Arthur Hailey publishes *Hotel*, 1965.

◆ John Fowles publishes *The Magus*, 1965.

◆ James Michner publishes *The Source*, 1965.

◆ Bel Kaufman publishes *Up the Down Staircase*, 1965.

◆ Frank Herbert publishes *Dune*, 1965.

◆ Kurt Vonnegut, Jr., publishes *God Bless You, Mr. Rosewater*, 1965.

◆ Television series debuting in 1965 include *Days of Our Lives*, Green *Acres*, *Hogan's Heroes*, and *I Dream of Jeannie*.

◆ Popular music hits of 1965 include the Beatles' "Day Tripper," "Help!", "Ticket to Ride," and "Yesterday," Bob Dylan's "Like a Rolling Stone," Sonny and Cher's "I Got You Babe," Petula Clark's "Downtown," and Roger Miller's "King of the Road."

◆ Notable films of 1965 include Robert Wise's *The Sound of Music* with Julie Andrews, David Lean's *Doctor Zhivago* with Omar Sharif and Julie Christie, Martin Ritt's *The Spy Who Came in From the Cold* with Richard Burton, Richard Lester's *Help!* with the Beatles, and Sidney Lumet's *The Pawnbroker* with Rod Steiger.

◆ In January of 1966, Indira Gandhi becomes the prime minister of India. She is the daughter of India's first prime minister, Jawaharlal Nehru.

◆ In June of 1966, James Meredith (the first black student at the University of Mississippi in 1962, he graduated in 1964) organizes a "March Against Fear" from Memphis to Jackson, Mississippi, in protest against the violence being used against black protesters for civil rights. Meredith is shot by a sniper but the march is continued by Martin Luther King, Jr., Stokely Carmichael, and others; after recovering, Meredith rejoins the march just before it reaches Jackson.

◆ In July of 1966, Richard Speck brutally murders eight nurses in Chicago; he is arrested soon after and dies in prison in 1991.

◆ In August of 1966, Mao Zedong announces China's Cultural Revolution, a movement intended to revitalize Communism in China and correct the failures of the "Great Leap Forward." The movement fails to unify the country; production drops, schools are closed, and various factions attempt to solidify power in order to succeed Mao.

◆ In 1966, the National Organization for Women (NOW) is founded by a group of twenty-eight women, including Betty Friedan, who becomes the first president of NOW.

◆ Jacqueline Susann publishes *The Valley of the Dolls*, 1966.

◆ James Clavell publishes *Tai-Pan*, 1966.

◆ Bernard Malamud publishes *The Fixer*, 1966.

◆ Harold Robbins publishes *The Adventurers*, 1966.

◆ Jean Rhys publishes *Wide Sargossa Sea*, 1966.

◆ Thomas Pynchon publishes *The Crying of Lot 49*, 1966.

◆ Truman Capote publishes *In Cold Blood*, 1966.

◆ Brian W. Aldiss publishes *Man in His Time*, 1966.

◆ Robert A. Heinlein publishes *The Moon Is a Harsh Mistress*, 1966.

◆ Daniel Keyes publishes *Flowers for Algernon*, 1966.

◆ Television series debuting in 1966 include *Batman*, *Star Trek*, *That Girl*, and *The Newlywed Game*.

◆ Jerry Herman's *Mame* debuts on Broadway, 1966.

◆ Popular music hits of 1966 include Nancy Sinatra's "These Boots Are Made for Walkin'," the Beatles' "Yellow Submarine" and "Paperback Writer," Simon and Garfunkle's "Homeward Bound," Frank Sinatra's "Strangers in the Night," Sergeant Barry Sadler's "The Ballad of the Green Berets," and the Monkees' "Last Train to Clarksville."

◆ Notable films of 1966 include Michelanglo Antonioni's *Blow-Up* with David Hemmings, Vanessa Redgrave, and Sarah Miles, Philippe de Broca's *King of Hearts* with Alan Bates, Fred Zinneman's *A Man for All Seasons* with Paul Scofield and Robert Shaw, Robert Wise's *The*

Sand Pebbles with Steve McQueen, and Mike Nichols's *Who's Afraid of Virginia Woolf?* with Elizabeth Taylor, Richard Burton, George Segal, and Sandy Dennis.

◆ On January 27, 1967, three Apollo astronauts—Colonel Virgil I. Grissom, Colonel Edward White II, and Lieutenant Commander Roger B. Chaffee—are killed in a spacecraft fire during a simulated launch.

◆ *Biafra* secedes from Nigeria, on May 30, 1967.

◆ On June 5, 1967, Israeli and Arab forces clash; it is the start of a conflict that will become known as the Six Day War. The war ends with Israel occupying the Sinai Peninsula, the Golan Heights, the Gaza Strip, and the east bank of the Suez Canal.

◆ The People's Republic of China announces that it has detonated its first hydrogen bomb, on June 17, 1967.

◆ On July 23, 1967, a five-day riot begins in Detroit when police raid an after-hours club and arrest eighty-two people. Forty-three people are killed in the riot and more than a thousand are injured. Detroit citizens cite police brutality, lack of affordable housing, urban renewal projects that razed housing to create freeways, and lack of economic opportunity as factors leading to the riot.

◆ Dr. Christiaan N. Barnard and a team of South African surgeons perform the world's first successful human heart transplant, on December 3, 1967; the patient dies 18 days later.

◆ William Styron publishes *The Confessions of Nat Turner*, 1967.

◆ William Manchester publishes *Death of a President*, 1967.

◆ Ira Levin publishes *Rosemary's Baby*, 1967.

◆ Piers Anthony publishes *Chthon*, 1967.

◆ Chaim Potok publishes *The Chosen*, 1967.

◆ Mary Stewart publishes *The Gabriel Hounds*, 1967.

◆ Gabriel García Márquez publishes *One Hundred Years of Solitude*, 1967.

◆ Television series debuting in 1967 include *Love Is a Many Splendored Thing*, *Ironside*, *The Carol Burnett Show*, and *The Flying Nun*.

◆ Popular music hits of 1967 include the Monkees' "I'm a Believer," the Doors' "Light My Fire," Van Morrison's "Brown-Eyed Girl," Gladys Knight and the Pips' "I Heard It Through the Grapevine," the Beatles' "All You Need Is Love," Aretha Franklin's "Respect," and the Mamas and the Papas' "Words of Love."

◆ Notable films of 1967 include Norman Jewison's *In the Heat of the Night* with Rod Steiger and Sidney Poitier, Arthur Penn's *Bonnie and Clyde* with Faye Dunaway and Warren Beatty, Mike Nichols's *The Graduate* with Dustin Hoffman and Anne Bancroft, Stanley Kramer's *Guess Who's Coming to Dinner* with Spencer Tracy, Katharine Hepburn, Sidney Poitier, and Katharine Houghton, Stuart Rosenberg's *Cool Hand Luke* with Paul Newman, and Robert Aldrich's *The Dirty Dozen* with Lee Marvin, Ernest Borgnine, Charles Bronson, and Telly Savalas.

◆ Martin Luther King is killed in Memphis on April 4, 1968. James Earl Ray, indicted in King's murder, is captured in London on June 8. In 1969, Ray pleads guilty and is sentenced to 99 years in prison.

◆ Senator Robert F. Kennedy is shot by Sirhan Sirhan in the ballroom of a Los Angeles hotel after winning the California primary on June 5, 1968; he dies on June 6, 1968.

◆ Czechoslovakia is invaded by the Soviet Union on August 20, 1968.

◆ On October 11, 1968, Apollo 7, the first manned Apollo mission, is launched by NASA; the flight confirms that the command service module is operational and is another successful step toward the goal of landing a man on the moon.

◆ On October 20, 1968, former First Lady Jacqueline Kennedy marries Greek shipping magnate Aristotle Onassis on the Greek island of Skorpios.

◆ In December of 1968, Apollo 8 successfully orbits the moon.

◆ Ursula K. Le Guin publishes *A Wizard of Earthsea*, 1968.

◆ Peter Beagle publishes *The Last Unicorn*, 1968.

◆ Norman Mailer publishes *Armies of the Night*, 1968.

◆ Joan Didion publishes *Slouching Towards Bethlehem*, 1968.

◆ Arthur C. Clarke publishes *2001: A Space Odyssey*, 1968.

◆ Philip K. Dick publishes *Do Androids Dream of Electric Sheep?*, 1968.

◆ Alexander Key publishes *Escape to Witch Mountain*, 1968.

◆ Anne McCaffrey publishes *Dragonflight* and *Dragonrider*, 1968.

◆ Alexander Solzhenitsyn publishes *Cancer Ward*, 1968.

◆ John Updike publishes *Couples*, 1968.

◆ Gore Vidal publishes *Myra Breckinridge*, 1968.

◆ Television series debuting in 1968 include *Laugh-In*, *One Life to Live*, *The Doris Day Show*, *60 Minutes*, *Hawaii Five-O*, and *The Mod Squad*.

◆ In April of 1968, the musical *Hair* debuts on Broadway.

◆ Popular music hits of 1968 include the Doors' "Hello, I Love You," the Beatles' "Lady Madonna" and "Hey Jude," the Rolling Stones' "Jumpin' Jack Flash," Steppenwolf's "Born to Be Wild," and Otis Redding's "Sittin' on the Dock of the Bay."

◆ Notable films of 1968 include Peter Yates's *Bullitt* with Steve McQueen, Carol Reed's *Oliver!* with Mark Lester and Ron Moody, William Wyler's *Funny Girl* with Barbra Streisand and Omar Sharif, Anthony Harvey's *The Lion in Winter* with Katharine Hepburn and Peter O'Toole, Franklin J. Schaffner's *Planet of the Apes* with Charlton Heston and Roddy McDowell, Roman Polanski's *Rosemary's Baby* with Mia Farrow and John Cassavetes, Stanley Kubrick's *2001: A Space Odyssey* with Keir Dullea, George Dunning's *Yellow Submarine* with the Beatles, and Franco Zeffirelli's *Romeo and Juliet* with Leonard Whiting and Olivia Hussey.

FAST FACTS ABOUT LYNDON B. JOHNSON

◆ Johnson was the only president sworn into office by a woman; he took the oath of office from Judge Sarah T. Hughes of Texas on Air Force One at Love Field in Dallas.

◆ Johnson's mother was a Baptist, but he independently decided to become a member of the Disciples of Christ and was baptized as a teenager (in 1923) in the Pedernales River in Texas. His maternal great-grandfather, George Washington Baines, Sr., was a well-known Baptist preacher who was Sam Houston's pastor and the president of Baylor University (1861–1863).

◆ Johnson's nickname of "Landslide Lyndon" was originally given to him after a slim 87-vote victory in the Democratic primary in 1948 that led to his first term in the US Senate. The victory was challenged but upheld by the Supreme Court, despite evidence that both sides practiced election fraud. Ironically, Johnson did win a landslide victory over Arizona Senator Barry Goldwater in the 1964 presidential election.

◆ The term "Great Society" was defined in Johnson's 1965 State of the Union address and was thereafter used to refer to Johnson's domestic political agenda and domestic policies.

◆ Johnson nominated the first African-American member of the US Supreme Court, Thurgood Marshall.

◆ Lady Bird Johnson promoted the Head Start program for preschool children. She campaigned to beautify America, urging that billboards along highways be restricted and that flowers be planted along highways.

◆ Johnson's elder daughter, Lynda, married Charles Spittall Robb at the White House on December 9, 1967. His younger daughter, Luci, married Patrick Nugent on August 6, 1966. Luci was married while her father was in the White House, but the ceremony was held at the Church of the Immaculate Conception in Washington, DC.

◆ Johnson's son-in-law, Charles Robb, became governor of Virginia (1982–1986) and a US senator for Virginia (1989–2001).

◆ Him and Her, the best-known of President Johnson's dogs, were pedigreed beagles born on June 27, 1963. The President frequently played with the dogs and was often photographed with them. In 1964 President Johnson raised the ire of many when he lifted Him by his ears while greeting a group on the White House lawn.

◆ Lady Bird Johnson founded the National Wildflower Research Center in Austin, Texas, in 1982.

Richard M. Nixon

Nickname: Tricky Dick
Presidency: 37th president, 1969–1974
Party: Republican
Life dates: January 9, 1913–April 22, 1994 (81 years, 104 days)

EARLY LIFE AND EDUCATION

Richard Milhous Nixon was born on January 9, 1913, in Yorba Linda, California. Nixon's family was of modest means. His mother, Hannah Milhous, came from a devout Quaker family in Indiana. She met Francis Anthony Nixon while a student at Whittier College in California. Frank Nixon, originally from Ohio, had not graduated from high school. He worked a succession of odd jobs, including driving a trolley in Columbus where a case of frostbite inspired him to move to Southern California. The couple married in 1908, with Frank Nixon converting to his wife's faith. After trying to make a go of it in Yorba Linda, where Frank had attempted to establish a lemon-growing business, the Nixons settled in Whittier in 1922. In this small town, Frank ran a gas station and a small market.

Richard was one of five children, all boys. Donald was born in 1914 and Edward in 1930. Two of Richard's four brothers, Arthur, born in 1918, and Harold, born in 1909, died of tuberculosis. In Yorba Linda, young Richard himself nearly died twice, once almost bleeding to death from a head wound, and the second time while battling pneumonia.

In his memoirs, Nixon described his life in Whittier as "family, church, and school." As a boy, Richard was a diligent student who also worked long hours at his father's store. It was common for him to drive into Los Angeles in the morning before school to pick up vegetables or other supplies and then put in more time helping around the home when he returned from school, all before settling down to a night of study well into the wee hours. At Fullerton High School, Richard became a prize-winning debater. He subsequently transferred to Whittier High School and graduated first in his class in 1930.

Richard had won a partial scholarship to Harvard University, but due to his family's financial struggles as a result of the Depression, he could not afford to pay the remainder of the tuition. Unable to fulfill his boyhood dream of going to Harvard, Nixon attended Whittier College where he majored in history. Nixon was captain of the debate team; played football, for which he had the aptitude but not the size or the strength; and joined the drama club. Denied admittance to the elite Franklin Club, Nixon helped form the Orthogonians, a rival organization for students of lesser means like himself. He served as president of his freshman class and in his senior year ran for president of the student body. Candidate Nixon promised to promote dances with the school administration (at the time they were banned at the college), asserting that dances would help keep students on the Whittier campus, rather than forcing them to flee into Los Angeles for their recreation; he won the election. After graduating second in his class in 1934, Nixon received a scholarship to Duke University Law School, from which he graduated in 1937.

"What starts the process, really are the laughs and snubs and slights you get when you are a kid. Sometimes it's because you're poor or Irish or Jewish or ugly or simply that you are skinny. But if you are reasonably intelligent and if your anger is deep enough and strong enough, you learn that you can change those attitudes by excellence, personal gut performance, while those who have everything are sitting on their fat butts. . . ."

Richard M. Nixon to former aide Ken Clawson, several years after he resigned from the presidency

---

At Duke, Nixon lived in a farmhouse off campus that had no running water or electricity. Nixon was a studious young man (known as "Gloomy Gus" to some of his peers) who again graduated near the top of his class (he ranked third out of twenty-five students). Nixon was soon admitted to the California bar, in November 1937. In spite of his impressive accomplishments given somewhat difficult circumstances,

he received the first of many perceived snubs by the East Coast establishment when he applied to a number of prestigious New York City law firms. Nixon was turned down by all of them and had to settle for a position with Wingert and Bewley in his hometown of Whittier. He became responsible for collecting on the firm's bills and, on his own initiative, took on additional negligence and divorce cases, receiving a percentage of any settlement.

EARLY CAREER

On June 21, 1940, Nixon married Thelma Catherine Ryan, aged 28. Since birth she had been known as Pat because she was born on March 16, the day before St. Patrick's Day. Pat Nixon was born in Ely, Nevada, in 1912, the daughter of William Ryan and a German immigrant, Kate Halberstadt Ryan. William Ryan was employed in a copper mine when his daughter was born, but shortly afterward moved his family to Southern California where he worked on a truck farm. In 1925 Pat's mother died from cancer and thirteen-year-old Pat looked after her father and two brothers until Ryan died, a victim of silicosis, no doubt contracted during his years as a miner.

Pat Ryan was a high school teacher in Whittier when she first met Richard Nixon after they were both cast in *The Dark Tower*, a play being produced by the local theater group. The couple moved into an apartment in Whittier immediately after their marriage. Their first child Patricia ("Tricia") was born on February 21, 1946; Julie followed on July 5, 1948.

After two years of service with Wingert and Bewley, Nixon became junior partner in the firm of Bewley, Knoop and Nixon. Nixon tried to augment his modest salary with a business selling frozen orange juice. The enterprise, called the Citra-Frost Company, with Nixon as its president, failed. Nixon was appointed assistant city attorney of Whittier by his colleague Thomas Bewley, who was city attorney at the time.

After the United States entered World War II, Nixon found work in Washington, DC, with the tire-rationing department of the Office of Price Administration. He remained in the capital from January through June of 1942, but became disenchanted with the bureaucratic aspects of his job. Nixon set aside his Quaker pacifism and enlisted in the Navy, where he served until March 1946. After wedding Nixon, Pat had continued to work as a schoolteacher. While her husband was on naval duty, she found employment as a stenographer in San Francisco. She later worked in the Office of Price Administration as an economist.

> **"His able leadership, tireless efforts and devotion to duty were in keeping with the highest traditions of the United States Naval Service."**
>
> From a letter of commendation received by Richard M. Nixon from the US Naval Service, September 1944

Nixon was appointed a lieutenant junior grade in the US Naval Reserve on June 15, 1942. He completed his basic training at the Naval Training School, Quonset Point, Rhode Island. Nixon served at the Naval Reserve airbase in Ottumwa, Iowa, until May 1943 when he volunteered for duty at sea and was dispatched to the Pacific theater. Charged with running the South Pacific Air Transport Command, he prepared manifests and flight plans for cargo planes, their loading and unloading. Nixon was promoted to lieutenant on October 1, 1943, receiving a letter of commendation in the fall of the following year.

Returning to the US mainland, Lieutenant Nixon worked at the Fleet Air Wing in Alameda, California (from August to December 1944), at the Bureau of Aeronautics in Washington, DC, and as the bureau's Contracting Officer for Terminations in the Eastern District office in New York. He was released from active duty on March 10, 1946. Promoted to commander on June 1, 1953, Nixon officially retired from the Naval Reserve on June 1, 1966.

POLITICAL CAREER

In 1946, at the suggestion of local banker and family friend Herman Perry and the Whittier "Committee of 100," a group of businessmen from the surrounding environs, Nixon ran for a seat in California's 12th Congressional District, an area that included Whittier. During the campaign, Nixon attempted to portray his opponent, five-term incumbent, Democrat Jerry Voorhis, as a Communist sympathizer. Voorhis was never able to successfully counter Nixon's false claims, especially since he had been endorsed by a number of left-wing groups. Nixon handily won the election, securing some 65,500 votes to Voorhis's 50,000. He began his tenure in the House of Representatives on January 3, 1947, and was determined to make an impression from the start. He joined fourteen other Republicans in the Chowder and Marching Club that met every Wednesday. As a freshman, Nixon was a member of the House Education and Labor Committee and helped draft the Taft-Hartley Act of 1947 that attempted to "regulate away" much of the power of trade unions.

Representative Nixon's very public stance against Communism yielded him a place on the House Un-American Activities Committee (HUAC), established in 1937 to examine the alleged Communist infiltration of American life. When Nixon joined its ranks, HUAC was struggling to identify an issue that would resonate with the public. With Representative Karl E. Mundt of South Dakota, Nixon cosponsored anti-Communist legislation, the Mundt-Nixon bill, that prefigured the Internal Security Act of 1950 (also known as the McCarran Act, named after Senator Pat McCarran of Nevada).

It was, however, Nixon's role in the Alger Hiss case that brought him national attention. In August 1948 self-professed Communist Whittaker Chambers, former editor at *Time* magazine, accused Hiss of being a spy. Hiss, a graduate of Harvard Law School, had worked for President Franklin D. Roosevelt first at the Agricultural Adjustment Administration and then at the Yalta Conference; he had also served at the United Nations. He represented a brand of establishment New Deal Democrat that Nixon abhorred.

When HUAC subpoenaed Hiss and he took the witness stand, Nixon worked doggedly to prove that Chambers and Hiss knew each other, something which Hiss denied. Under Nixon's relentless cross-examination, Hiss finally admitted that he had known Chambers, although Chambers had gone by the name George Crosely in those encounters. Hiss continued to deny the charges of espionage, but in November 1948 the government produced rolls of microfilm of sensitive State Department documents from the mid-1930s, documents allegedly typed on Hiss's typewriter and stashed on Chambers's farm. Hiss was convicted of perjury and sentenced to five years in jail. As a result of his prominent role in the Hiss case, Richard Nixon became a national figure.

Nixon had been elected to a second term in the House, running unopposed. In 1950 he ran for the Senate against Helen Gahagan Douglas, another New Deal Democrat who felt the sting of Nixon's broad anti-Communist attack. Nixon dubbed Douglas the "Pink Lady" and tried to link her voting record in the House to a perceived pro-Communist agenda. The North Korean attack on South Korea, which occurred sometime between the primary and the election, helped Nixon's cause, which was then further strengthened when Communist China intervened in the conflict. Nixon's warnings against Communism suddenly seemed almost prophetic, and he won the election by 680,000 votes, capturing 59 percent of the vote. Nixon's campaign tactics, which included the printing of hundreds of thousands of anti-Douglas leaflets on pink paper, earned him the soubriquet "Tricky Dick" from the *Independent Review*, a Southern California newspaper. The name stuck with Nixon for the rest of his political career.

When he joined the US Senate in 1951, Nixon was only 38. He continued his vigorous anti-Communist campaign as a member of the Permanent Investigations Subcommittee run by Senator Joseph McCarthy of Wisconsin, whose dogged and indiscriminate attacks against supposed members of the Communist party gave

rise to the term "McCarthyism." Nixon was also a vocal critic of the Truman administration, particularly its conduct of the Korean War.

In 1952 Dwight D. Eisenhower selected Nixon as his vice-presidential running mate. Nixon was a good fit: His California roots would bring geographic balance to the ticket, he was young, and he had experience in the House and the Senate. In addition, Nixon was a compelling public speaker, whereas Eisenhower was not. Pat, who hated campaigning, tried to talk her husband out of accepting the offer, but Nixon was adamant. He wanted the job.

On the campaign trail, Eisenhower directed Nixon to continue his attacks on the Democrats. In his frequent public appearances, Nixon liked to describe himself and his wife as simple ordinary Americans. He drove a used car; he maintained mortgages on his house in Washington, DC, and the small home in Whittier where his parents lived. Nixon's character moved to the center stage of the campaign, however, when the media revealed that he had a secret $18,000 fund. Eisenhower ordered his running mate to clear his name on television, and Nixon was angered by Eisenhower's refusal to support him unconditionally.

On September 23 1952 Nixon appeared on prime-time TV for half an hour and admitted the existence of the fund. All the money would be spent on legitimate political expenses, he asserted, insisting that the fund was not illegal and that he and Pat did not have a lavish lifestyle, as was claimed. "Pat doesn't have a mink coat," he said. "But she does have a respectable Republican cloth coat." Appealing to Americans' fondness for animals (something which Franklin Roosevelt had once done to diffuse a potentially damaging situation), Nixon next acknowledged that he had accepted one gift, a little black-and-white cocker spaniel that arrived from Texas. His six-year-old daughter Tricia had named the dog Checkers. "And you know the kids love the dog and I just want to say this right now, that regardless of what they say about it, we're going to keep it." These famous remarks became known as the "Checkers speech." The largest television audience of all time, 58 million people, watched. An overwhelmingly positive response ensured that Eisenhower kept Nixon on the ticket.

In the November 4 election, Eisenhower defeated the Democratic candidate Adlai Stevenson by 33.8 million popular votes to 27.3 million. The electoral college vote was 442 to 89. As vice president, Nixon functioned as a member of the cabinet and the National Security Council, and met each week with the Republican leaders of Congress. In September 1955, after President Eisenhower suffered a heart attack, Nixon chaired the cabinet and did so on other occasions when Ike was incapacitated. While he held the post of vice president, Nixon traveled abroad frequently. During a visit to Caracas, Venezuela, in May 1958, Nixon's motorcade was attacked by an angry mob fueled by anti-American sentiments. Although the visit to Caracas was a diplomatic disaster, the incident, in fact, helped to strengthen Nixon's homeland popularity. In 1959 Nixon visited the Soviet Union, where he and Soviet leader Nikita Khrushchev had a famous exchange in a model General Electric kitchen at a trade fair. During what became known as the "kitchen debate," Nixon told Khrushchev, "Let's have far more communication and exchange in this very area that we speak of. We should hear you more on our televisions. You should hear us more on yours."

On November 6, 1956, the Eisenhower-Nixon ticket was reelected, defeating Stevenson again, by an even larger landslide. The popular vote was 35.6 to 25.8 million, the electoral college vote 457 to 73. The Republican Party did not hesitate to select Nixon as its presidential candidate four years later. With his running mate Henry Cabot Lodge of Massachusetts, Nixon ran against John F. Kennedy and Lyndon B. Johnson. The 1960 campaign featured the first televised presidential debate, in which Nixon came off poorly compared to the more charismatic Kennedy. Nixon's lead started to shrink, although the election itself was the closest of the twentieth century to that date. Kennedy received 34,227,096 popular votes to Nixon's 34,107,646 (303 electoral votes to 219).

After the defeat, Nixon spent the whole of 1961 writing *Six Crises*. In 1962 he ran for governor of California, but was defeated by the Democratic incumbent Edmund G. "Pat" Brown. Embittered by what he regarded as unfair treatment in the media, Nixon at a press conference the day after his defeat told reporters, "You won't have Nixon to kick around anymore, because, gentlemen, this is my last press conference."

Now ill at ease in California, Nixon moved his family to New York and joined a Wall Street law firm, Nixon, Mudge, Rose, Guthrie, and Alexander. Resisting entreaties to run for office in 1964, Nixon supported the candidacy of Barry Goldwater with a national speaking tour. In spite of Nixon's ringing endorsement, Goldwater was overwhelmingly defeated by Lyndon Johnson, whose 43 million votes easily trumped Goldwater's 27 million.

Nixon continued to campaign for Republican candidates and behind the scenes contemplated, and then launched, his return to politics. Ronald Reagan had gained prominence in Republican circles with a televised speech supporting Goldwater in 1964. Using the governorship of California that he had secured in 1966 as a base, Reagan campaigned hard for the 1968 nomination. Nixon, stressing a broad-based campaign, fended off Reagan and other candidates such as Governor Nelson Rockefeller of New York, winning the nomination on the first ballot at the convention in Miami Beach. In a surprise move, Nixon selected Spiro T. Agnew, the governor of Maryland, as his running mate.

In contrast to the Republicans, who united behind Nixon, the Democrats were in a state of chaos. With the Vietnam War proving increasingly unpopular, President Johnson found himself under attack from within his own party. Senator Eugene McCarthy of Minnesota, who opposed the Vietnam War, did well in the New Hampshire primary and shortly afterward Senator Robert F. Kennedy from New York, now espousing US withdrawal from Southeast Asia, threw his hat in the ring. With support daily eroding, Johnson decided to withdraw from the race. Only minutes after declaring victory in the California primary and poised to possibly become the Democratic candidate, Kennedy was assassinated, with his wife Ethel and supporters looking on. The Democratic Convention in Chicago later that summer was held amid anti-war protests and a violent police response. Johnson's vice president, Hubert H. Humphrey of Minnesota, who had entered the race after Johnson stepped down, won the nomination, naming Senator Edmund Muskie of Maine as his vice-presidential running mate.

Nixon started the campaign with a large lead. Without describing how he would achieve it, he promised a settlement to the war in Vietnam and campaigned on an otherwise vague platform that called for law and order, the formation of a volunteer army, and lower taxes and inflation. The strong third-party candidacy of former Governor George C. Wallace of Alabama affected the results for both parties, but actually took away more votes from Humphrey, weakened by party divisions over Vietnam, than Nixon.

When President Johnson announced that the United States would hold peace talks with North Vietnam and an end to the devastating bombing in the north, Humphrey's poll numbers improved. Nevertheless, Nixon held on to his edge, winning by 31,785,480 votes to Humphrey's 31,275,166 and Wallace's 9,906,473. The electoral college vote was 301 to 191 and 46. But Nixon's margin of victory in the popular vote was less than 1 percent, and only 43 percent of voters had pulled the lever for him. He also was the first twentieth-century president whose own party did not hold the majority in either the House or the Senate.

PRESIDENCY

On January 20, 1969, Richard Nixon was inaugurated as President of the United States on the East Portico of the US Capitol. On the domestic front, he faced an economy that was overheating with rising inflation and unemployment. Unemployment stood at 3.3 percent when he took office but reached 6 percent in 1970. Nixon countered with wage and price controls enacted in 1971. The economy seemed to rebounding by the 1972 election but slumped again in 1973,

when inflation reached 12 percent, fueled by the Arab oil boycott the same year.

Nixon worked to reform federal welfare programs. Supplemental Security Income provided an income to disabled Americans and payments under the Social Security, Medicare, and Medicaid programs were increased.

Nixon also promoted a large number of regulatory measures. The Occupational Safety and Health Administration (OSHA) was created in 1970 to combat workplace accidents. Numerous pieces of environmental legislation were passed under Nixon's watch, some over his strenuous objections. The Water Pollution Act of 1972 became law despite the president's veto and Nixon withheld much of the money earmarked under the Clean Air Act.

Both of Nixon's presidential terms were overshadowed by scandals. The most historic is commonly referred to as Watergate, the name of the Washington, DC, hotel that housed the headquarters of the Democratic National Committee (DNC), where five men hired by the Committee to Re-elect the President (known as CREEP or CRP) were arrested in the early morning hours of June 17, 1972. Nixon initially regarded Watergate as nothing more than a public relations problem, but as the crisis unraveled, it led inexorably to his resignation, the first of its kind in American presidential history.

"Watergate" is, in fact, an umbrella term for a number of events. In 1971 another group of covert operators known as "plumbers" burglarized the offices of a psychiatrist in search of privileged information that might discredit one of his patients, Daniel Ellsberg. Ellsberg, a government defense analyst, had leaked The Pentagon Papers, the exhaustively detailed study of the Vietnam War commissioned by former Secretary of Defense Robert S. McNamara, who had served during both the Kennedy and Johnson administrations. Nixon was desperate to plug any leaks—actual and potential—before the 1972 election (hence the term "plumbers"). Two of the "plumbers" had clear links to the government: E. Howard Hunt was a former CIA operative and G. Gordon Liddy an ex-FBI agent. The men Hunt, in turn, hired to commit both the Ellsberg and Watergate break-ins were Cuban expatriates involved in the ill-fated Bay of Pigs operation.

Primarily, though, Watergate refers to the CREEP-directed break-in at DNC headquarters (where the "plumbers" planned to install bugging devices) and the White House's circuitous efforts to conceal its role in the burglary with promises of clemency and payments to those involved. During this same time period the White House compiled an "enemies list" (for the most part it included the names of Democratic opponents and antiwar activists) against whom "dirty tricks" would be used. As part of his campaign against leaks, Nixon had started taping conversations in the White House, and in one such tape, he and aide H. R. Haldeman discussed how they might have the CIA pressure the FBI not to investigate the Watergate break-in. When the existence of the tape was revealed two years later, it ironically became the "smoking gun," the evidence that Nixon was aware of the cover-up.

> "He was a bold, innovative, high-risk President who had succeeded in bringing a majority of his countrymen with him on adventures into wholly new areas—most obviously, the opening to China, détente with the Soviets, and the beginnings of arms limitations."
>
> Nixon biographer Stephen Ambrose

Closely working with his National Security Adviser Henry Kissinger, Richard Nixon played an extremely proactive role in foreign affairs. When he became president, there were 540,000 US troops in Vietnam, and the United States maintained limited relations with the People's Re-

public of China and the Soviet Union. Nixon, the staunch anti-Communist, was able to reach out to both Communist powers, whose relations with each other were strained at best. Nixon supported Chinese admission to the United Nations in 1971, and his visit to China in February 1972 led to broader contacts between China and the United States.

Fear of too close a rapprochement between the United States and China caused the Soviet Union to make overtures to Washington. After Nixon traveled to Beijing, Soviet leader Leonid Brezhnev invited Nixon to Moscow, and Nixon thus became the first US president to visit the Soviet Union. The two superpowers signed a number of agreements, part of the process of "détente" that signaled a slow thaw in the Cold War between East and West. The Seabed Treaty of 1970 barred weapons of mass destruction on the ocean floor beyond the international twelve-mile limit. The Chemical Weapons Treaty of 1971 called for the removal of stockpiles of chemical and biological weapons, and the Strategic Arms Limitation Treaty (SALT) agreements froze ballistic missile deployment and, under the Anti-Ballistic Missile Treaty, limited the installation of weapons designed to counter nuclear attack to two sites per superpower.

In Vietnam, as he tried to engineer American withdrawal, Nixon pursued a policy of diplomatic negotiation augmented by periodic shows of force. After Kissinger's secret negotiations failed, the United States resumed bombing of North Vietnam in late 1969 and mined its harbors. Nixon next ordered the bombing of North Vietnamese supply routes in Cambodia, thereby extending American involvement into another country. American forces also attacked targets on the ground inside Cambodia, and in 1971 South Vietnamese forces, with US assistance, invaded Laos. Meanwhile, Nixon sought to publicly defend these actions by emphasizing the objective of "Vietnamization," the replacement of American troops with South Vietnamese forces coupled with the steady withdrawal of US forces.

Public protest over the war only increased, including demonstrations at Kent State and

Jackson State Universities that led to the shooting, and deaths, of several protesters and policemen. Nixon was eager for a resolution of America's role in Vietnam before the 1972 election. In a major offensive the North Vietnamese secured more territory until their advance was held back by US bombing. South Vietnamese leaders refused to agree to the North's retaining all the territory it had captured, a stipulation agreed to by both the United States and North Vietnam. Before November 2nd Kissinger assured the country that "peace was at hand," but what shape that peace would have was unclear.

Nixon received all but one of the votes cast for presidential nominees at the 1972 Republican Convention in Miami Beach (the other vote was cast for Representative Paul A. McCloskey of California). Nixon's Democratic opponent was Senator George S. McGovern of South Dakota. Though McGovern had won his party's nomination on the first ballot, he struggled to find a vice-presidential candidate; Senator Edward M. Kennedy of Massachusetts, Senator Abraham Ribicoff of Connecticut, and Governor Reubin Askew of Florida all turned him down, and his first choice, Senator Thomas F. Eagleton of Missouri, had to withdraw his name from nomination when the media revealed that he had years earlier received electric shock treatment for depression. Desperate to dispel the negative image these disclosures generated, McGovern turned to R. Sargent Shriver, the first director of the Peace Corps and former US ambassador to France (who was also the husband of Jean Kennedy).

On the campaign trail, McGovern called for an immediate withdrawal of US forces from Vietnam and charged that Watergate proved Nixon was running a corrupt administration. However, despite mounting problems within Nixon's administration, the Republicans were able to convince the electorate that McGovern was too liberal, a candidate not capable of the strong leadership that the turbulent times demanded. Nixon, again running with Spiro Agnew, achieved one of the greatest landslide victories in history, winning 61 percent of the vote to McGovern's 37.5 percent. The electoral college count was 520 to 17.

"When Richard Nixon left office, an agreement to end the war in Vietnam had been concluded, and the main lines of all subsequent policy were established: permanent dialogue with China; readiness without illusion to ease tensions with the Soviet Union; a peace process in the Middle East; the beginning, via the European Security Conference, of establishing human rights as an international issue; weakening Soviet hold on Eastern Europe. Richard Nixon's foreign policy goals were long range, and he pursued them without regard to domestic political consequences."

Henry Kissinger, in the eulogy he delivered at President Nixon's funeral, April 27, 1994

In January 1973, shortly after his second inauguration, the Paris Peace Accords signaled the end of US troop presence in Vietnam, the administration having persuaded South Vietnamese President Nguyen Van Thieu to accept the agreement. Nixon claimed that the United States had secured "peace with honor." However, fighting between North and South Vietnam resumed quickly, and Communist forces took control of the entire country after Saigon fell in April 1975.

WATERGATE AND NIXON'S RESIGNATION

Watergate returned to center stage when L. Patrick Gray, the nominee to replace J. Edgar Hoover as the director of the FBI, revealed that John W. Dean, White House legal counsel, had been present when the FBI questioned the Watergate "plumbers." In order to prevent Dean from having to testify before the Senate Watergate investigatory committee, Nixon claimed executive privilege. Dean, who was fired when Nixon aides H. R. Haldeman and John Erlichman resigned over their participation in the cover-up, eventually came clean, testifying to all that he knew of the sordid affair at the Watergate hearings, which commenced in May 1973.

In July, Archibald Cox, who had been appointed to the position of the Justice Department's special prosecutor in May, 1973, subpoenaed tapes of conversations in the White House. Nixon resisted and proposed a compromise in which John Stennis, a Democratic senator from Mississippi, would listen to the tapes and prepare summaries for Cox. In October, Cox refused the compromise and Nixon ordered Attorney General-designate Elliot Richardson to fire him. On October 20, Richardson refused and resigned in protest, along with his deputy, William Ruckelshaus, in an event that became known as the "Saturday Night Massacre." Three days later, under immense pressure, Nixon handed over the tapes. On November 21, a suspicious gap of nearly eighteen and a half minutes was discovered on a tape of the conversations that had taken place between Nixon and H. R. Haldeman just days after the Watergate break-in; Nixon's secretary Rose Mary Woods denied deliberately erasing the tapes.

In April, 1974, sixty-four White House tapes were subpoenaed for use in the trials against Nixon's former subordinates; the tapes were finally handed over in July after the Supreme Court, by a unanimous vote of 8-0, ordered Nixon to make them available. On May 9, 1974, impeachment hearings against Nixon began before the House Judiciary Committee. On July 27, the Judiciary Committee adopted the first Article of Impeachment by a vote of 27-11, charging Nixon with obstructing the investigation of the Watergate break-in. Two days later, the committee adopted the second Article of Impeachment, charging Nixon with misuse of power and violation of his oath of office. On July 30, the House Judiciary Committee adopted the third Article of Impeachment, this time charging Nixon with failure to comply with the House subpoenas.

On August 5, Nixon released conversation transcripts and three tapes, which eventually became known as the "Smoking Gun" due to their incriminating nature. The conversations on the tapes revealed that Nixon not only knew of the involvement of White House officials in the break-in, but he also ordered a cover-up of the Watergate break-in, and directed the FBI to abandon its investigation of the burglary. With this new insurmountable evidence at hand, the eleven Republicans on the Judiciary Committee who had voted against Nixon's impeachment announced that they would change their votes. Nixon soon realized that his support was swiftly diminishing, and on August 8, 1974, he resigned from the presidency, becoming the first American president to do so.

Numerous officials of the Nixon administration were prosecuted for their roles in the Watergate affair. Special counsel Charles W. Colson served seven months in prison for obstruction of justice. Dean served four months for obstruction of justice. Ehrlichman, who directed the activities of the "plumbers," served eighteen months for obstruction of justice, perjury, and conspiracy. Haldeman also served eighteen months. Hunt, who organized the Watergate and Ellsberg break-ins, was convicted of burglary, conspiracy, and wiretapping and spent thirty-three months in prison. Liddy was convicted for his role in the Watergate break-in; found guilty of conspiracy and contempt of court, he spent four years in jail. John Mitchell, former attorney general and head of CREEP, was convicted on charges of conspiracy, perjury, and obstruction of justice and served nineteen months. Lawyer Donald Segretti served four months for his role in campaign smear tactics against Nixon's opponents.

As an airplane carried Nixon back home to California, incoming President Gerald R. Ford

President Richard Nixon's final departure from the White House, August 9, 1974.

declared, "Our long national nightmare is over." Ford later granted Nixon a full pardon.

POST-PRESIDENTIAL CAREER

After his resignation, Nixon lived first in San Clemente, California, and then New York City, before settling in Saddle River, New Jersey. Nixon spent a great deal of time traveling. In 1985, during a single five-week fact-finding trip, he met with leaders in China, Japan, South Korea, Hong Kong, Singapore, Malaysia, Thailand, Burma, Pakistan, Turkey, and Great Britain.

On June, 22, 1993, Pat Nixon died of lung cancer, one day after the couple had celebrated their 53rd wedding anniversary. In April 1994 Nixon suffered a stroke and died in New York City on April 22, aged 81.

After a dignified funeral, with his body lying in state for one day at his presidential library in Yorba Linda, California, Nixon was buried beside his wife on the library grounds, on April 27. An estimated 50,000 people paid their respects to Nixon. Present at the services were then Pres-

ident Bill Clinton and First Lady Hillary Rodham Clinton, and four former presidents and their wives: George H. W. and Barbara Bush; Ronald and Nancy Reagan; Jimmy and Rosalynn Carter; and Gerald and Betty Ford. Eulogies were delivered by Henry Kissinger; then Senate Republican leader Robert Dole; then California Governor Pete Wilson; Clinton; and the Reverend Billy Graham.

Birthplace: Yorba Linda, CA
Residency: California
Religion: Quaker
Education: Whittier College, graduated 1934; Duke University Law School, graduated 1937
Place of Death: New York City
Burial Site: The Richard Nixon Library, Yorba Linda, CA
Dates in Office: January 20, 1969–August 9, 1974 (5 years, 201 days)
Age at Inauguration: 56 years, 11 days

FAMILY

Father: Francis "Frank" Anthony Nixon (1878–1956)
Mother: Hannah Milhous Nixon (1885–1967)
Siblings: Richard Nixon was the second of five brothers; his siblings were Harold; (Francis) Donald; Arthur; and Edward
Wife: Thelma Catherine "Pat" Ryan (1912–1993), married on June 21, 1940, in Riverside, CA
Children: Patricia ("Tricia") (1946–); Julie (1948–)

CAREER

Private: lawyer
Political: member of the US House of Representatives (1947–1950); member of the US Senate (1951–1953); US vice president under Eisenhower (1953–1961); president of the United States (1969–1974)
Military: entered the US Navy as an appointed lieutenant junior grade (June 1942); trained at the Naval Training School, Quonset Point, Rhode Island, before being stationed at the Naval Reserve Aviation Base in Ottumwa, Iowa (October 1942); assigned as Officer in Charge of the South Pacific Combat Air Transport

Command at Green Island, for which he received a Letter of Commendation, the American Campaign Medal, the Asiatic-Pacific Campaign Medal, and the World War II Victory Medal (May 1943); promoted to lieutenant (October 1943); assigned to Fleet Air Wing EIGHT (August 1944); served at the Bureau of Aeronautics, Navy Department, Washington, DC (December 1944); served in the Office of the Bureau of Aeronautics General Representative, New York (March 1945); promoted to lieutenant commander (October 1945); relieved of active duty (March 1946); retired in June of 1966

Selected Works: *In the Arena* (New York: Simon & Schuster, 1990); *Leaders* (New York: Random House Value, 1982); *1999: Victory Without War* (New York: Simon & Schuster, 1988); *No More Vietnams* (New York: Avon, 1995); *Real Peace* (New York: Little, Brown, 1984); *The Real War* (New York: Touchstone, 1990); *RN: The Memoirs of Richard Nixon* (New York: Touchstone, 1990); *Six Crises* (New York: Touchstone, 1990)

PRESIDENCY

Nomination: 1968: The Republican Convention was held in Miami Beach, FL, August 5–8, 1968; Nixon secured the nomination on the first ballot with 692 votes; Nelson Rockefeller received 277 votes, Ronald Reagan 182, and other candidates 182. Nixon selected Spiro T. Agnew as his vice-presidential running mate.

1972: The Republican Convention was held in Miami Beach, FL, August 21–23, 1972; Nixon and Agnew were renominated with Nixon receiving 1,347 votes (all but one vote). New Mexico's primary law required that the vote for Representative Paul N. McCloskey of California be counted and tallied in the official results as "other."

Election: 1968: elected president on November 5, 1968

1972: reelected president on November 7, 1972

Opponent: 1968: Hubert H. Humphrey, MN, Democrat; George C. Wallace, AL, American Independent

1972: George S. McGovern, SD, Democrat; John Hospers, CA, Libertarian

Vote Totals: 1968: Nixon, 31,785,480 popular, 301 electoral; Humphrey, 31,275,166 popular, 191 electoral; Wallace, 9,906,473 popular, 46 electoral

1972: Nixon, 47,165,234 popular, 520 electoral; McGovern, 29,168,110 popular, 17 electoral; Hospers, 2,691 popular, 1 electoral

Inauguration: 1968: January 20, 1969

1972: January 20, 1973

Vice President: Spiro T. Agnew, MD (1969–1973); Gerald R. Ford, MI (1973–1974)

CABINET

Secretary of State: William P. Rogers, MD (1969–1973); Henry A. Kissinger, MA (1973–1974)

Secretary of the Treasury: David M. Kennedy, IL (1969–1971); John B. Connally, TX (1971–1972); George P. Schultz, IL (1972–1974); William E. Simon, NJ (1974)

Secretary of Defense: Melvin R. Laird, WI (1969–1973); Elliot L. Richardson, MA (1973); James R. Schlesinger, VA (1973–1974)

Attorney General: John N. Mitchell, NY (1969–1972); Richard D. Kleindienst, AZ (1972–1973); Elliot L. Richardson, MA (1973); William B. Saxbe, OH (1973–1974)

Postmaster General: Winton M. Blount, AL (1969–1971) [Note: The Postmaster General ceased to be a cabinet position in 1971 when the department became the US Postal Service, a noncabinet agency.]

Secretary of Agriculture: Clifford M. Hardin, NE (1969–1971); Earl L. Butz, IN (1971–1974)

Secretary of the Interior: Walter J. Hickel, AK (1969–1970); Rogers C. B. Morton, MD (1971–1974)

Secretary of Labor: George P. Schultz, MN (1969–1970); James D. Hodgson, CA (1970–1973); Peter J. Brennan, NY (1973–1974)

Secretary of Commerce: Maurice H. Stans, NY (1969–1972); Peter G. Peterson, IL (1972–1973); Frederick B. Dent, SC (1973–1974)

Secretary of Health, Education, and Welfare: Robert H. Finch, CA (1969–1970); Elliot L. Richardson, MA (1970–1973); Caspar Weinberger, CA (1973–1974)

Secretary of Housing and Urban Development: George W. Romney, MI (1969–1973); James T. Lynn, OH (1973–1975)
Secretary of Transportation: John A. Volpe, MA (1969–1973); Claude Brinegar, CA (1973–1975)

CONGRESS
91st Congress (1969–1971); Speaker of the House: John W. McCormack (Democrat, MA)
92nd Congress (1971–1973); Speaker of the House: Carl B. Albert (Democrat, OK)
93rd Congress (1973–1975); Speaker of the House: Carl B. Albert (Democrat, OK)

SUPREME COURT APPOINTEES
Warren E. Burger, MN; Chief Justice (1969–1986)
Harry A. Blackmun, MN; Associate Justice (1970–1994)
Lewis F. Powell, VA; Associate Justice (1972–1987)
William H. Rehnquist, AZ; Associate Justice (1972–1986); Chief Justice (1986–)

MAJOR EVENTS OF THE NIXON ADMINISTRATION
❖ In March 1969 Nixon orders the secret bombing of Cambodia ("Operation Breakfast") to knock out North Vietnamese supply routes.
❖ In an address delivered to Congress, May 1969, Nixon announces reform of the military draft.
❖ On June 8, 1969, Nixon meets with President Nguyen Van Thieu of South Vietnam and announces the reduction of US forces in Vietnam, one aspect of his "Vietnamization" policy.
❖ During a press conference in Guam on July 25, 1969, Nixon describes what becomes popularly known as the "Nixon doctrine"—aid rather than troops for American allies in Asia.
❖ Nixon's nominee for associate justice of the Supreme Court, Clement F. Haynsworth, is rejected by the Senate, November 1969, due to ethics concerns.
❖ On November 24, 1969, Nixon signs the Nuclear Weapons Non-Proliferation Treaty; the United Kingdom and the Soviet Union are among the other 43 original parties to sign the treaty.

❖ January 1, 1970, Nixon signs the National Environmental Quality Policy Act requiring federal programs to measure their environmental impact.
❖ On April 8, 1970, the Senate rejects Nixon's nomination of G. Harrold Carswell, who had a history of supporting segregation, as Supreme Court associate justice.
❖ Nixon announces a plan to establish the Environmental Protection Agency (EPA) and the National Oceanic and Atmospheric Administration (NOAA), in addition to signing the Emergency Home Finance Act, which would allow for the development of a secondary mortgage market, thus expanding mortgages available to veterans and other groups, July 1970.
❖ On August 12, 1970, Nixon signs the Postal Reorganization Act, which effectively dismantles the office of the Postmaster General, effective 1971. In its place, a new government agency (no longer on the cabinet level) is established, the US Postal Service.
❖ On November 30, 1970, Nixon signs the Agricultural Act, which is designed to protect and improve farm income.
❖ On December 21, 1970, Elvis Presley entertains Nixon at the White House.
❖ Nixon signs the Clean Air Act on December 31, 1970, providing the Environmental Protection Agency the authority to create air pollution and emission standards for new factories and hazardous industrial pollutants.
❖ On February 11, 1971, an executive order establishes Columbus Day as a new federal holiday.
❖ Nixon begins clandestinely recording meetings in the Oval Office and Cabinet Room on February 16, 1971.
❖ On May 20, 1971, Nixon announces the Strategic Arms Limitation Talks (SALT) agreement with the Soviet Union. The treaty is later signed in 1972.
❖ In June 1971 Nixon ends the 21-year-old trade embargo on China, first initiated during the Korean War when political relations with China became strained.
❖ On June 13, 1971, the *New York Times* begins

its publication of *The Pentagon Papers*, a Defense Department in-depth study of the Vietnam War. The *Washington Post* follows suit.

❖ On July 12, 1971, Nixon signs the Emergency Employment Act to provide funding for the creation of jobs within the public sector.

❖ In August 1971, under the Economic Stabilization Act, wage and price controls are introduced, in addition to a new international economic system, resulting in the end of the gold standard.

❖ On September 3, 1971, White House "plumbers" burglarize a psychiatrist's office looking for information on one of his patients, Daniel Ellsberg, the former defense analyst who leaked *The Pentagon Papers*.

❖ Both Lewis F. Powell and William H. Rehnquist are confirmed as Supreme Court associate justices in December 1971.

❖ On January 7, 1972, Nixon announces that he will run for a second term.

❖ In February 1972 Nixon signs the Federal Election Campaign Act, which calls for more stringent disclosure requirements for federal candidates, political parties, and political action committees.

❖ During February 21–28, 1972, in an effort to create a more politically open relationship between the United States and China, Nixon becomes the first US president to visit China.

❖ Nixon signs the Equal Employment Opportunities Act, which will enforce affirmative action programs, on March 25, 1972.

❖ In May 1972 Nixon announces the mining of harbors in North Vietnam.

❖ On June 17, 1972, at 2:30 a.m., a night watchman arrests five men inside the headquarters of the Democratic National Committee (DNC) at the Watergate complex, Washington, DC. Two days later, the *Washington Post* reports that one of the men is a Republican Party security aide. John Mitchell, chairman of the Committee to Re-elect the President (CREEP) and former attorney general, denies any link between the Nixon campaign and the five men.

❖ On June 23, 1972, Nixon and White House Chief of Staff H. R. Haldeman discuss how the

CIA could be used to pressure the FBI into not delving too deeply into the Watergate scandal. Both describe the break-in as a national security issue. When the tape of this conversation is released in 1974, it becomes the "smoking gun" in the Senate's investigation of Nixon's role in the cover-up.

❖ In August 1972 media reports confirm that a $25,000 check made out to the Nixon reelection campaign has been traced to the bank account of a Watergate burglar.

❖ On August 23, 1972, Nixon accepts the presidential nomination at the Republican National Convention in Miami Beach.

❖ On October 10, 1972, a story by journalists Bob Woodward and Carl Bernstein runs in the *Washington Post* linking the Watergate break-in to illegal activities conducted on behalf of Nixon's reelection campaign.

❖ Nixon is reelected by a record landslide on November 7, 1972.

❖ The American bombing of North Vietnam comes to a halt on December 30, 1972.

❖ On January 15, 1973, Nixon orders a ceasefire in Vietnam.

❖ On January 20, 1973, Nixon is inaugurated for a second time.

❖ The Paris Peace Accords are signed on January 23, 1973, formally ending American military involvement in Vietnam.

❖ On January 30, 1973, James McCord and G. Gordon Liddy are convicted of conspiracy, burglary, and wiretapping for their part in the Watergate break-in. They are sentenced on March 23.

❖ On April 30, 1973, Nixon accepts the resignations of advisors H. R. Haldeman and John D. Erlichman, and Attorney General Richard Kleindienst. White House counsel John Dean is fired. Nixon goes on national television and accepts responsibility for the Watergate scandal while denying any personal involvement.

❖ The Senate votes to appoint a Watergate special prosecutor on May 1, 1973.

❖ On May 18, 1973, Senate Watergate hearings begin with former solicitor general Archibald Cox named as special prosecutor.

◆ Nixon signs a bill increasing Social Security benefits, July 11, 1973.

◆ On July 16, 1973, a former Nixon aide testifies before the Senate Select Watergate Committee about the secret tape-recording system at the White House. Nixon refuses to hand over any of his tape recordings to the committee.

◆ Representative Robert F. Drinan of Massachusetts introduces a motion calling for impeachment proceedings against President Nixon on July 31, 1973; the resolution is referred to the Judiciary Committee.

◆ Spiro T. Agnew resigns as vice president on October 10, 1973. Days later he is indicted for federal income tax evasion. House Minority Leader Gerald R. Ford is nominated to replace him and, after a thorough background investigation, becomes vice president on December 6.

◆ On October 20, 1973, in what is commonly known as the "Saturday night massacre," Attorney General Elliot Richardson and his deputy, William Ruckelshaus, resign after refusing to fire Watergate Special Prosecutor Archibald Cox. Cox is dismissed by acting Attorney General Robert Bork.

◆ The House votes to continue impeachment investigations on February 6, 1974.

◆ On March 6, 1974, Nixon vetoes the Energy Emergency Bill, which would have lowered domestic crude oil prices.

◆ Nixon signs the Fair Labor Standards Amendments on April 8, 1974. The amendments allow for the creation of a federal agency to insure and establish regulations for retirement pension plans, in addition to raising the minimum wage.

◆ Nixon announces that he will publish transcripts of forty-six taped conversations on April 29, 1974.

◆ On July 24, 1974, the Supreme Court rules that Nixon must hand over the subpoenaed tapes.

◆ The House Judiciary Committee votes to recommend three articles of impeachment against President Nixon, July 27–30, 1974.

◆ On August 8, 1974, Nixon announces his resignation on television. The next day, after a tearful farewell to his staff with his wife and daughters present, the First Family departs from the White House and travels to Andrews Air Force Base to fly to El Toro Marine Corps Air Station, California.

MAJOR US AND WORLD EVENTS, 1969–1974

◆ Riots break out in Prague on January 26, 1969, the day after student Jan Palach, who burned himself to death to protest the Soviet presence in Czechoslovakia, is buried.

◆ On March 2, 1969, the Anglo-French Concorde aircraft makes its maiden flight in Toulouse.

◆ Golda Meir is elected prime minister of Israel, March 7, 1969.

◆ On March 10, 1969, James Earl Ray is sentenced to 99 years in a Memphis prison for the murder of Dr. Martin Luther King, Jr.

◆ Harvard University students seize an administrative building in April 1969, to protest the war in Vietnam.

◆ After eleven years as the president of France, Charles de Gaulle resigns on April 28, 1969.

◆ Following a New York City police raid on the Stonewall Inn, a gay bar, a riot breaks out on nearby Sheridan Square in Greenwich Village, June 28, 1969. The violence continues for three nights. The event is regarded as the defining moment in the modern gay rights movement.

◆ The spacecraft *Apollo 11* lands on the moon on July 20, 1969. Neil Armstrong becomes the first human to set foot on the lunar surface.

◆ The Woodstock Festival takes place in upstate New York, August 15–17, 1969. Thousands overrun Max Yasgar's farm to attend the free concert.

◆ In October 1969 the US Supreme Court orders the immediate integration of all public and private schools..

◆ October 6, 1969, the "days of rage" commence when the Weathermen, a radical faction of the revolutionary student movement, destroy a statue honoring the police in Chicago's Haymarket Square. The Weathermen's actions are intended to protest the war in Vietnam and last through October 11.

◆ On November 19, 1969, the spacecraft *Apollo 12* lands on the moon.

◆ Jerzy Kosinski publishes *Steps*, 1969.

◆ Norman Mailer publishes *The Armies of the Night*, 1969.

◆ Television series debuting in 1969 include *Hee Haw*, *Where the Heart Is*, *Sesame Street*, *The Brady Bunch*, and *The Johnny Cash Show*.

◆ Popular music hits of 1969 include the Fifth Dimension's "Aquarius/Let the Sunshine In," Joe South's "Games People Play," Joni Mitchell's "Clouds," and Crosby, Stills & Nash's "Suite: Judy Blue Eyes."

◆ Notable films of 1969 include *Anne of the Thousand Days* with Genevieve Bujold and Richard Burton, *Butch Cassidy and the Sundance Kid* with Paul Newman and Robert Redford, *Hello, Dolly!* with Barbra Streisand, John Schlesinger's *Midnight Cowboy* with Dustin Hoffman and Jon Voight, and *The Prime of Miss Jean Brodie* with Maggie Smith.

◆ On January 16, 1970, Colonel Muammar Gaddafi takes control of Libya four months after a coup deposes King Idris.

◆ On April 14, 1970, an explosion on board the spacecraft *Apollo 13* puts astronauts James Lovell, Jack Swigert, and Fred Haise in imminent danger. The crew manages to safely bring back the damaged craft to Earth three days later.

◆ An antiwar demonstration at Kent State University leads to violence as National Guardsmen fire on a crowd of student protestors, killing four, on May 4, 1970. Ten days later, two students are killed when police open fire on demonstrators at Jackson State College in Mississippi.

◆ Jean Stafford publishes *Complete Stories of Jean Stafford*, 1970.

◆ Erik H. Erikson publishes *Ghandi's Truth*, 1970.

◆ Joyce Carol Oates publishes *Them*, 1970.

◆ Television series debuting in 1970 include *All My Children*, *Josie and the Pussycats*, *The Mary Tyler Moore Show*, *The Odd Couple*, and *The Partridge Family*.

◆ Popular music hits of 1970 include Simon and Garfunkel's "Bridge Over Troubled Water" and the Carpenters' "Close to You."

◆ Notable films of 1970 include *Five Easy Pieces* with Jack Nicholson, *Love Story* with Ryan O'Neal and Ali McGraw, Robert Altman's *M*A*S*H*, and *Patton* with George C. Scott.

◆ General Idi Amin seizes power in Uganda on January 25, 1971.

◆ On March 23, 1971, Congress passes the Twenty-sixth Amendment to the Constitution, which lowers the voting age from 21 to 18 years of age. The amendment is ratified on July 1, 1971.

◆ On March 29, 1971, Lieutenant William Calley is found guilty of the premeditated murder of twenty-two civilians in the Vietnamese village of My Lai in 1968. Testimony reveals that Calley had ordered his men to shoot everyone in the village, including old men, women, and children.

◆ Haitian ruler Francois "Papa Doc" Duvalier dies, April 22, 1971, after fourteen years in power.

◆ On September 8, 1971, prisoners take control of the maximum-security Attica Correctional Facility near Buffalo, New York, in protest over alleged dehumanizing conditions. Ten prison guards and twenty-nine inmates are killed five days later when Governor Nelson Rockefeller directs prison authorities to retake the facility.

◆ India and Pakistan go to war in November 1971, leading to the formation of the new nation of Bangladesh.

◆ Saul Bellow publishes *Mr. Sammler's Planet*, 1971.

◆ James McGregor Burns publishes *Roosevelt: Soldier of Freedom*, 1971.

◆ John Toland publishes *The Rising Sun*, 1971.

◆ Television series debuting in 1971 include *Masterpiece Theatre*, *Soul Train*, *All in the Family*, and *The Sonny and Cher Comedy Hour*.

◆ Andrew Lloyd Webber and Tim Rice's *Jesus Christ Superstar* debuts on Broadway, 1971.

◆ Popular music hits of 1971 include Carole King's "It's Too Late," Carole King and James Taylor's "You've Got a Friend," and Carly Simon's "One More Time."

◆ Notable films of 1971 include Stanley Kubrick's *A Clockwork Orange*, *The French Connection* with Gene Hackman, *The Last Picture Show* with Cybill Shepherd, Timothy Bottoms, and Jeff Bridges, and *Sunday, Bloody Sunday* with Peter Finch.

◆ On January 30, 1972, thirteen demonstrators are killed by British troops in Londonderry, Northern Ireland, on what becomes known as "Bloody Sunday."

◆ On May 15, 1972, Alabama Governor George C. Wallace is shot by Arthur Bremer while campaigning in the Democratic presidential primary in Laurel, MD. Wallace, who is paralyzed for the rest of his life as a result of his injuries, embodies Southern resistance to the civil rights movement.

◆ Three Japanese gunmen open fire at Lod Airport in Tel Aviv, killing twenty-six innocent bystanders, May 29, 1972. An investigaton reveals that the gunmen were recruited by the Popular Front for the Liberation of Palestine.

◆ On June 29, 1972, the Supreme Court declares the death penalty unconstitutional.

◆ Palestinian terrorists kill eleven Israeli athletes at the Munich Olympics on September 5, 1972.

◆ The last manned moon mission, Apollo 17, sets astronauts Eugene Cernan and Harrison Schmitt on the moon in December 1972.

◆ Joseph P. Lash publishes *Eleanor and Franklin*, 1972.

◆ Frank O'Hara publishes his *Collected Works*, 1972.

◆ Television series debuting in 1972 include *Sanford and Son*, *The Price Is Right*, *M*A*S*H*, *Kung Fu*, *The Bob Newhart Show*, and *The Waltons*.

◆ Jim Jacobs and Warren Casey's *Grease* debuts on Broadway, 1972.

◆ Popular music hits of 1972 include Roberta Flack's "The First Time Ever I Saw Your Face," Nilsson's "Without You," and Helen Reddy's "I Am Woman."

◆ Notable films of 1972 include Francis Ford Coppola's *The Godfather* with Marlon Brando, James Caan, Robert Duvall, and Al Pacino, *Deliverance* with Burt Reynolds and Jon Voight, and Bob Fosse's *Cabaret* with Liza Minnelli.

◆ On January 1, 1973, Great Britain, Denmark, and the Republic of Ireland join the European Economic Community (EEC).

◆ January 22, 1973, the Supreme Court rules in its landmark *Roe v. Wade* decision that the constitutional right to privacy includes "a woman's decision whether or not to terminate her pregnancy."

◆ Pablo Picasso dies on April 8, 1973, near Cannes, France, at the age of 91.

◆ On September 11, 1973, General Augusto Pinochet overthrows elected Chilean leader Salvador Allende and establishes a dictatorship.

◆ In October 1973 Egypt and Syria attack Israel during Yom Kippur, and Arab nations impose an oil embargo following Nixon's announcement of support for Israel. US and Soviet tensions over the conflict lead to the placement of US forces on DefCon Three, a defense readiness condition (based on a scale of 1–5) calling for an increase in readiness over "normal" condition. Henry Kissinger's "shuttle diplomacy" helps mediate a temporary resolution to the conflict.

◆ A military coup in Greece unseats self-appointed President George Papadopoulos on November 25, 1973.

◆ Spanish Prime Minister Admiral Luis Carrero Blanco is killed on December 20, 1973, by a car bomb explosion in Madrid. Basque separatists are blamed.

◆ Frances Fitzgerald publishes *Fire in the Lake*, 1973.

◆ Robert Coles publishes *Children of Crisis*, 1973.

◆ John Barth publishes *Chimera*, 1973.

◆ Television series debuting in 1973 include *Schoolhouse Rock!*, *The Young and the Restless*, *Kojak*, and *The Six Million Dollar Man*.

◆ Popular music hits of 1973 include Roberta Flack's "Killing Me Softly With His Song," and Stevie Wonder's "Superstition" and "You Are the Sunshine of My Life."

◆ Notable films of 1973 include George Lucas's *American Graffiti*, Ingmar Bergman's *Cries and Whispers*, Bernardo Bertolucci's *Last*

Tango in Paris with Marlon Brando, and *The Exorcist.*

◆ On February 8, 1974, three US astronauts return to earth after spending eighty-five days in the space station Skylab, thus setting a new endurance record.

◆ On February 14, 1974, Alexander Solzhenitsyn is charged with treason by Soviet authorities after being deported from the country and stripped of his citizenship.

FAST FACTS ABOUT RICHARD M. NIXON

◆ Nixon was nominated to the Republican presidential ticket a record five times.

◆ In 1968 Nixon's daughter, Julie, married Dwight David Eisenhower II, the son of President Eisenhower's son John.

◆ On November 14, 1969, Nixon became the first president to attend the launching of a man-operated space flight. The 10-day mission aboard the Apollo 12 was the second lunar landing.

◆ In October 1973 Nixon became the first president to nominate a vice president under the 25th Amendment.

◆ Nixon was the first US president to visit China while in office.

◆ Nixon is the only US president thus far to have served two terms as vice president, followed by two terms as president.

◆ Nixon became the third president against whom articles of impeachment were drawn up, the other two being Andrew Johnson and John Tyler. Of the three, Johnson was the only president to have been impeached, and subsequently tried by the Senate on those charges.

◆ Nixon was the first US president to resign from office.

◆ Nixon is the only president thus far to be pardoned by his successor for possible offenses against the United States.

◆ Nixon's nickname "Tricky Dick" derives from his early political career and his often devious campaign tactics, specifically those during his run for the Senate against Helen Gahagan Douglas, in which he suggested that Douglas's voting record reflected a pro-Communist agenda.

Gerald R. Ford

Nickname: Jerry
Presidency: 38th president, 1974–1977
Party: Republican
Life dates: July 14, 1913–

EARLY LIFE AND EDUCATION

Gerald R. Ford was born in Omaha, Nebraska, on July 14, 1913. Named Leslie Lynch King, Jr., at birth, he was the first and only child of Leslie Lynch King and Dorothy Ayer Gardener King. When young Leslie was less than one month old, his parents separated and his mother moved with her infant son to Grand Rapids, Michigan, where they lived with her parents. Dorothy King divorced Leslie King when their son was two years old.

Three years later, in 1916, Dorothy married Gerald Rudolf Ford, a well-respected Grand Rapids paint salesman. Although the boy's name was not legally changed until 1935, Dorothy and Gerald began calling her young son Gerald R. Ford, Jr., shortly after their marriage. In 1918 Gerald's younger half-brother Thomas was born, followed by Richard in 1924 and James in 1927. The Fords were generally regarded as a happy and close-knit Midwestern family.

As a child, Gerald was athletically gifted, a hard-working student, and extremely popular among his peers. He attended South High School in Grand Rapids, where he excelled academically, played on the varsity basketball, track, and football teams, and earned all-city and all-state football honors.

After graduating from high school, Ford attended the University of Michigan at Ann Arbor, where he majored in political science. Well respected by fellow students and his teachers, he was active in campus politics and a star linebacker on the university's national championship football team; he also diligently pursued his academic studies, although he was an average student, and worked part-time jobs to help with his expenses. Ford's remarkable athletic abilities, combined with his reputation for being a team player, earned him the offer of two lucrative professional football contracts during his senior year: from the Detroit Lions and the Green Bay Packers. He rejected both offers, if somewhat reluctantly, in favor of a position as an assistant football coach at Yale University, where he had applied to law school.

EARLY CAREER

Because of his full-time coaching duties for the football team, Ford was initially denied admission to Yale's law school. He was persistent, however, and the school eventually admitted him on a trial basis in 1939. Ford juggled coaching and his studies by taking classes part-time. In January 1941 he graduated from Yale Law School in the top third of his class and passed the Michigan bar exam that June. He returned from New Haven and set up a small legal practice in Grand Rapids with his longtime friend, Philip Buchen, who later became his chief White House Counsel. Although eager to begin his legal career, Ford, like most young men of the time, felt compelled to come to the defense of his country after the Japanese attack on Pearl Harbor, December 7, 1941; shortly after the United States's official entry into World War II, he enlisted in the US Naval Reserve. His initial duties were as an instructor at the Navy Preflight School in Chapel Hill, North Carolina. He was promoted to lieutenant and requested sea duty. In the early spring of 1943, Ford was assigned as a gunnery division officer on the *USS Monterey*, which took part in most of the major wartime operations in the South Pacific. As the war raged on, Ford was promoted to assistant navigator; in December of 1944, the *Monterey* was caught in a typhoon during which a fire started. The ship returned to the United States for repairs and Ford was again assigned as an instructor and sports coach. In October of 1945, he was promoted to lieutenant commander. After forty-seven months of active service, Ford was discharged in February of 1946.

POLITICAL CAREER

After the war, Ford returned to Grand Rapids and began practicing law with Butterfield, Keeney, and Amberg, a large, nationally prestigious law firm. But Ford soon grew bored with this pursuit and, encouraged by his politically active stepfather and a small coterie of family members, friends, and colleagues, decided to run, as a Republican, for a seat in the US House of Representatives. On November 2, 1948, at the age of 35, Ford was elected to Congress.

During the campaign, Ford courted Elizabeth ("Betty") Ann Bloomer Warren, a former model and dancer who had studied under Martha Graham, the legendary founder of modern dance technique, in New York City. Betty returned to Grand Rapids in 1941 and worked as a fashion coordinator at a department store, as well as teaching dance to handicapped children. Betty had been married to William Warren, a furniture salesman, but the couple divorced in 1947 after five years, and she met Gerald Ford soon after. On October 15, 1948, the couple married. Their first son, Michael Gerald, was born on March 14, 1950.

> ### "My fellow Americans, our long national nightmare is over."
>
> Gerald R. Ford, in his inaugural address, August 9, 1974

As a junior congressman, Ford worked hard, quickly earning the respect of his peers. In 1951 he was named to the House Appropriations Committee, and then rose to national prominence after becoming a ranking minority member of the Defense Appropriations Subcommittee in 1961. Ford's well-deserved reputation for fairness, honesty, diligence, and integrity led to his appointment, in 1963, to the Warren Commission, the body led by Supreme Court Chief Justice Earl Warren and charged with investigating the assassination of President John F. Kennedy. During this time, Ford and Elizabeth became the parents of three more children: John Gardner, born March 16, 1952; Steven Meigs, born May 19, 1956; and Susan Elizabeth, born July 6, 1957.

By 1965 Ford's influence in Congress was so great that he was named House minority leader. As the second most important congressional spokesman for the Republican Party, he sharply criticized the Johnson administration for its social spending programs, as well as its handling of American involvement in the Vietnam War. When Richard Nixon became president in 1968, Ford was one of his most outspoken and ardent supporters. After Spiro Agnew resigned from the office of vice president in 1973, pleading no contest to charges of federal income tax evasion, President Nixon selected Ford as his nominee for vice president.

Most historians concur that Nixon chose Ford because he needed a vice president who could work amicably and efficiently with all factions of Congress. And perhaps more important, Nixon had to select a nominee who would withstand the close scrutiny of the confirmation process without a hint of personal or political controversy. And Ford did not let Nixon down. On December 6, 1973, less than thirty days after his nomination, he was officially sworn in as vice president of the United States.

"I am acutely aware that you have not elected me as your President by your ballots. So I ask you to confirm me as your President with your prayers. And I hope that such prayers will also be the first of many."

Gerald R. Ford, from his inaugural speech, August 9, 1974

In the months that followed, the Watergate scandal, by then the center of national attention as the result of detailed published accounts in *The Washington Post* and reports by other media organizations, took its toll. After more than two years of such investigations and official inquiries by various governmental agencies, including the US Senate, the US House of Representatives, and the US Supreme Court, as well as a continuing stream of media coverage in newspapers and on television (the proceedings of the Senate investigation were televised), President Nixon resigned on August 9, 1974. That same day, Gerald R. Ford, at the age of 61, was sworn in as president of the United States; he took the oath of office in the East Room of the White House at virtually the same moment that Richard Nixon's resignation became effective.

PRESIDENCY

On September 8, 1974, in one of his first acts as chief executive, Ford granted Nixon a full pardon for his role in the Watergate affair, with the intention of sparing his predecessor any further embarrassment and moving the nation beyond the ordeal. His decision was met with significant public outrage; it eventually abated. Ford quickly nominated New York Governor Nelson A. Rockefeller to serve as vice president, and on December 19, 1974, Congress confirmed Rockefeller's appointment.

Soon after entering the White House, the Fords faced Betty's breast cancer. The First Lady underwent a mastectomy and chemotherapy. Naturally candid, she and her husband decided to make her medical condition public. American women took their cue from her and went to their doctors for examinations; she continued to be an advocate for women's health issues. She was equally candid with reporters in discussing her support for abortion rights and the Equal Rights Amendment (ERA), and her acceptance of the possibility that her unmarried daughter might engage in premarital sex. For the most part, her honesty made her very popular with the American people.

Ford hoped to restore public trust in the presidency, but he had inherited a fractured administration and a deeply troubled and divided nation. In addition, the new president had to deal with rising inflation and an increasingly sluggish economy, chronic energy shortages, and numerous foreign policy problems, including the country's continued presence in Vietnam, a source of growing dissension. In April 1975, following the collapse of President Nguyen Van Thieu's regime in South Vietnam, Ford ordered the evacuation of all American personnel remaining in that country. In other areas of international affairs, Ford, along with Secretary of State Henry Kissinger, worked hard to continue Nixon's policies of "détente," a relaxation of previously strained relations with the Soviet Union, and "shuttle diplomacy" (the use of an intermediary—in this case, Kissinger—to communicate between two opposing parties—

in this case, Israel and the Palestinians) in the Middle East. His diplomatic forays also included trips to Japan and China, strategic talks on the limitation of nuclear arms with Soviet leader Leonid Brezhnev, and US cosponsorship of the first international economic summit.

"This action closes a chapter in the American experience. I ask all Americans to close ranks, to avoid recrimination about the past, to look ahead to the many goals we share and to work together on the great tasks that remain to be accomplished."

Gerald R. Ford, in a speech explaining his decision to evacuate American personnel from South Vietnam, April 29, 1975

In January 1975 Ford established a commission, headed by Vice President Rockefeller, to investigate alleged abuses of power by the CIA, after disclosures implicating the agency in the Watergate scandal surfaced during the media investigations of 1973 and 1974. In its final report, the so-called Rockefeller Commission confirmed that unlawful acts had indeed been committed by the CIA, including the infiltration of dissident groups, mail tampering, testing of mind-altering drugs on unsuspecting citizens, and physical abuse and prolonged confinement of foreign defectors. In November 1975 Ford dismissed William E. Colby as CIA director, replacing him with George H. W. Bush.

The distrust of the intelligence community that led to the Rockefeller Commission also caused the Senate and the House to establish their own committees to investigate abuses by the CIA and FBI; the Senate's investigation was conducted by the Church Committee and the House's investigation was conducted by the Pike Committee. The various committees confirmed some suspicions about the invasion of citizens' privacy and interference in the affairs of other nations. The Senate established a Select Committee on Intelligence in 1976 and the House established a Permanent Select Committee on Intelligence in 1977 in response to these concerns.

During the month of September 1975, President Ford was the target of two assassination attempts; both attempts occurred during visits to California, and both assailants were women. On September 5, 1975, Lynette ("Squeaky") Alice Fromme, a follower of cult leader and convicted murderer Charles Manson, aimed a pistol at Ford as he moved through a crowd near the State Capitol in Sacramento. An alert Secret Service agent retrieved the weapon before it could be fired; the police subsequently determined that, although the gun was loaded, there was no bullet in the chamber. Approximately two weeks later, on September 22, Sara Jane Moore, apparently hoping to impress radical friends with whom she was no longer in a close relationship, fired a shot at Ford outside the St. Francis Hotel in San Francisco. The bullet missed him by five feet, wounding a taxi driver instead. Both women were sentenced to life imprisonment.

In the 1976 presidential primary season, Ford fought off a strong challenge by Ronald Reagan to garner the Republican nomination and named Senator Robert Dole of Kansas as his running mate. Capturing 240 electoral votes, Ford lost the national election by a narrow margin to former Georgia governor Jimmy Carter, who received 297 electoral votes.

POST-PRESIDENTIAL CAREER

After departing from the White House, Ford and his wife Betty moved to California, where they built a large home in Rancho Mirage. Ford's memoirs, *A Time to Heal: The Autobiography of Gerald R. Ford*, were published in 1979. In 1981 the Gerald R. Ford Library in Ann Arbor, Michigan, was officially dedicated, followed by the dedication of the Gerald R. Ford Museum in Grand Rapids, Michigan, in 1987.

Betty Ford had become addicted to painkillers prescribed for a pinched nerve and arthritis in the 1960s; she also became dependent on alcohol. In 1978, at the urging of her family, she entered a treatment program at the US Naval Hospital in Long Beach, California. In 1982, she cofounded the Betty Ford Center, a nonprofit residential treatment center.

Since leaving office, President Ford has continued to participate in the political process by speaking out on important issues, such as federal budget problems, federalism, and foreign affairs. As a result of his lifetime dedication to the American system of government, Ford has earned the reputation of being among the most honest, hard-working, and well-respected politicians of modern times.

Birthplace: Omaha, NE
Residency: California
Religion: Episcopalian
Education: University of Michigan, graduated 1935; Yale University Law School, graduated 1941
Place of Death: n/a
Burial Site: n/a
Dates in Office: August 9, 1974–January 20, 1977 (2 years, 164 days)
Age at Inauguration: 61 years, 26 days

FAMILY
Father: Leslie Lynch King (1881–1941) [Note: Gerald R. Ford was raised by his stepfather, Gerald Rudolf Ford (1890–1962), whom his mother married in 1916; she divorced King, his birth father, in 1914, having separated from him a few weeks after the birth of their only child.]
Mother: Dorothy Ayer Gardner King Ford (1892–1967)
Siblings: Gerald had three younger half-brothers, the children of his mother's second marriage to Gerald R. Ford, Sr.: Thomas Gardner Ford (1918–1995); Richard Addison Ford (1924–); James Francis Ford (1927–2001). He also had a half-brother and two half-sisters, the later children of his birth father, a man Ford saw only twice since his infancy: Marjorie B. King (1921–1993); Leslie ("Bud") Henry King (1923–1976); Patricia Jane King (1925–).

Wife: Elizabeth ("Betty") Ann Bloomer Warren (1918–), married on October 15, 1948, in Grand Rapids, MI
Children: Michael Gerald Ford (1950–); John ("Jack") Gardner Ford (1952–); Steven Meigs Ford (1956); Susan Elizabeth Ford (1957–)

CAREER
Private: lawyer
Political: member of the US House of Representatives (1949–1973); member of the Warren Commission (1963–1964); minority leader in House (1964–1973); US vice president under Nixon (1973–1974); president of the United States (1974–1977)
Military: Ford joined the US Naval Reserve in the spring of 1943, serving as a gunnery division officer on the USS *Monterey*, which actively participated in many of the major wartime operations in the South Pacific; later promoted to assistant navigator; discharged in April 1944 with the rank of lieutenant commander.
Selected Works: *Gerald R. Ford: Chronology, Documents, Bibliographic Aids*, ed. by George J. Lankevich (Dobbs Ferry, NY: Oceana Publications, 1977); *The Great Debates: Carter vs. Ford, 1976*, ed. by Sidney Kraus (Bloomington: Indiana University Press, 1979); *Humor and the Presidency* (New York: Arbor House, 1987); Selected Speeches [by] Gerald R. Ford, ed. by Michael V. Doyle (Arlington, VA: R. W. Beatty, 1973); *A Time to Heal: The Autobiography of Gerald R. Ford* (Norwalk, CT: Easton Press, 1987)

PRESIDENCY
Nomination: 1976: The Republican Convention was held in Kansas City, Missouri, August 16–19, 1976; Ford was nominated on the first ballot; Senator Robert Dole of Kansas was selected as the vice-presidential candidate.
Election: defeated on November 2, 1976
Opponent: Jimmy Carter, GA, Democratic
Vote Totals: 1976: Carter, 40,830,763 popular, 297 electoral; Ford, 39,147,793 popular, 240 electoral
Inauguration: not inaugurated; took oath of office following Richard Nixon's resignation on August 9, 1974, in the East Room of the White

House; the oath was administered by Chief Justice Warren Burger.

Vice President: Nelson A. Rockefeller, NY (1974–1977)

CABINET

Secretary of State: Henry A. Kissinger, MA (1974–1977)
Secretary of the Treasury: William E. Simon, NJ (1974–1977)
Secretary of Defense: James Schlesinger, NY (1974–1975); Donald Rumsfeld, IL (1975–1977)
Attorney General: William B. Saxbe, OH (1974–1975); Edward H. Levi, IL (1975–1977)
Secretary of Agriculture: Earl L. Butz, IN (1974–1976); John A. Knebel, OK (1976–1977)
Secretary of the Interior: Rogers C. B. Morton, Jr., MD (1974–1975); Stanley K. Hathaway, WY (1975); Thomas S. Kleppe, ND (1975–1977)
Secretary of Labor: Peter J. Brennan, NY (1974–1975); John T. Dunlop, MA (1975–1976); Willie J. Usery, GA (1976–1977)
Secretary of Commerce: Frederick B. Dent, IN (1974–1975); Rogers C. B. Morton, Jr., MD (1975–1976); Elliot L. Richardson, MA (1976–1977)
Secretary of Health, Education, and Welfare: Caspar W. Weinberger, CA (1974–1975); Forrest D. Matthews, AL (1975–1977)
Secretary of Housing and Urban Development: James T. Lynn, OH (1974–1975); Carla A. Hills, CA (1975–1977)
Secretary of Transportation: Claude S. Brinegar, CA (1974–1975); William T. Coleman, Jr., PA (1975–1977)

CONGRESS

93rd Congress (1973–1975); Speaker of the House: Carl B. Albert (OK, Democrat)
94th Congress (1975–1977); Speaker of the House: Carl B. Albert (OK, Democrat)

SUPREME COURT APPOINTEES

John Paul Stevens, IL; Associate Justice (1975–)

MAJOR EVENTS OF THE FORD ADMINISTRATION

❖ On August 9, 1974, Richard M. Nixon resigns as president of the United States and Gerald R. Ford is sworn in under the provisions of the 25th Amendment to the Constitution, which provides for presidential succession.

❖ Ford grants an unconditional pardon to former President Richard M. Nixon on September 8, 1974, for all "offenses against the United States" during his presidency. Ford's action is initially met with a storm of criticism, but the country soon seems willing to move on.

❖ In September of 1974, Ford announces a plan to grant limited clemency to Vietnam-era draft evaders and deserters in exchange for some other public service.

❖ The trial of five former Nixon aides (H. R. Haldeman, John Ehrlichman, John Mitchell, Robert Mardian, and Kenneth Parkinson) for their role in the Watergate break-in and cover-up begins on October 1, 1974; two other aides, Charles "Chuck" Colson and Gordon C. Strachan, had been indicted originally but the indictments were dropped—in Colson's case, when he pled guilty to breaking into the office of Daniel Ellsberg's psychiatrist (Ellsberg was the researcher who had turned the Pentagon Papers, which detailed US involvement in Vietnam, over to the *New York Times* newspaper).

❖ Ford gives a speech to Congress on October 8, 1974, in which he urges his "Whip Inflation Now," or "WIN" program, a far-reaching request for legislation relating to farming, energy supplies, additional unemployment, and increased taxes.

❖ In October of 1974, Ford signs an amendment to the Federal Election Campaign Act (FECA); the amendment creates the Federal Election Commission and specifies further limits on campaign contributions.

❖ On December 19, 1974, the Congress confirms New York Governor Nelson A. Rockefeller as vice president and he is sworn in that evening in the Senate chamber.

❖ On January 1, 1975, Ford signs the Privacy Act of 1974, which provides that the government will not have secret recordkeeping systems and that citizens will be able to find what information the government is keeping on them.

◆ On January 1, 1975, former senior White House officials John N. Mitchell, H. R. Haldeman, and John D. Erlichman are convicted of conspiracy, obstruction of justice, and perjury in the Watergate break-in and cover-up; Robert C. Mardian is convicted of conspiracy; and Kenneth W. Parkinson is acquitted.

◆ Ford establishes the US President's Commission on CIA Activities within the United States (also called "The Rockefeller Commission" because Vice President Rockefeller chairs the commission) on January 4, 1975. Its purpose is to investigate charges of illegal surveillance activity and abuses of power by the CIA.

◆ The US Senate establishes the Select Committee to Study Governmental Operations with Respect to Intelligence Activities (also called the "Church Committee" for its chair, Senator Frank Church) on January 27, 1975. The following month, on February 19, the House establishes its Select Committee on Intelligence, initially under the chairmanship of Representative Lucien Nedzi but then under Representative Otis G. Pike (and thus called the "Pike Committee"). The Church Committee focuses on suspected abuses by the CIA and the FBI, while the Pike Committee focuses on the CIA budget and the Agency's effectiveness in gathering intelligence.

◆ In March of 1975, Ford signs the Tax Reduction Act, which establishes the Earned Income Tax Credit (EITC).

◆ In April of 1975, the government of Cambodia under Lon Nol collapses and Communists (the party in Cambodia is known as the Khmer Rouge) force urban residents to leave the cities; private property, schools, newspapers, and religions are abolished. The following year, Pol Pot, the leader of the Khmer Rouge, becomes prime minister. By the end of the decade, when an invasion from Vietnam forces Pol Pot into hiding, between one and three million Cambodians are dead from starvation, forced labor, torture, and execution.

◆ President Nguyen Van Thieu of South Vietnam resigns on April 21, 1975. Six days later,

anarchy breaks out in Saigon as Communist forces draw closer to the city. As refugees frantically seek seats on the airlifts leaving Vietnam, Ford orders the immediate evacuation of any remaining Americans in the country. On April 30, 1975, the South Vietnamese government surrenders to the Viet Cong.

◆ The US merchant ship *Mayaguez* is seized by a Cambodian naval vessel on May 12, 1975. Two days later, US forces take back the ship. Although the entire crew onboard is saved, 15 US soldiers die in the recovery mission and another 23 die in a helicopter crash associated with the rescue attempt. An additional 50 soldiers are wounded and 3 declared missing.

◆ On June 9, 1975, Ford makes public the findings of the Rockefeller Commission, which confirm CIA abuses such as mail tampering, surveillance of dissident domestic groups, and the testing of mind-altering drugs on unsuspecting citizens, as well as information on the possible involvement of the CIA with the assassination of President Kennedy (which the Commission concludes is "farfetched speculation").

◆ On August 1, 1975, the Helsinki Accords are signed by the United States, Canada, and most of the countries of Europe. The signers agree to respect human rights, to cooperate in humanitarian, scientific, and economic areas, and to respect post-World War II national boundaries in Europe.

◆ Lynette "Squeaky" Fromme, a follower of imprisoned cult leader and murderer Charles Manson, attempts to shoot Ford on September 5, 1975, but is stopped by a Secret Service agent; she is convicted of the attempted assassination in November of 1975.

◆ On September 22, 1975, Sarah Jane Moore, a bookkeeper and sometime radical, tries to shoot Ford but after firing one wild shot is stopped by a bystander, Oliver Sipple.

◆ On November 29, 1975, a law is passed mandating free public education for handicapped children.

◆ In December of 1975, Ford signs the Energy Policy and Conservation Act, which establishes the Strategic Petroleum Reserve (an emergency supply of hundreds of millions of barrels of federally owned oil stored in underground caverns along the coast of the Gulf of Mexico).

◆ On January 29, 1976, the US House of Representatives votes to withhold public release of the findings of the Pike Committee. Although much of the report is eventually leaked to the press, it contains no shocking findings, although it recommends the formation of a standing congressional committee on intelligence.

◆ On April 26, 1976, the Church Committee releases its findings to the public. The report details domestic surveillance of US citizens and monitoring of private communications by both the CIA and the FBI, and CIA activities in foreign countries that include attempted assassination and tampering with elections.

◆ On May 28, 1976, Ford and Soviet leader Leonid Brezhnev sign the Treaty on Underground Nuclear Explosions for Peaceful Purposes (the so-called Peaceful Nuclear Explosions Treaty), which limits the size of underground nuclear explosions. The Treaty becomes effective in December of 1990.

◆ In September of 1976, Ford signs the Government in the Sunshine Act, which requires most federal agencies to hold meetings publicly (except where national security would be compromised). The Act eventually leads to televised coverage of many such meetings (including congressional proceedings) and on-line access to records about them.

◆ On November 2, 1976, Jimmy Carter narrowly defeats Ford in the presidential election.

◆ In November of 1976, nearly a hundred members of Congress are implicated in what becomes known as "Koreagate," an attempt by South Korea's intelligence community to purchase influence from US lawmakers.

MAJOR US AND WORLD EVENTS, 1974–1977

◆ On September 18, 1974, Hurricane Fifi hits Honduras, packing winds of more than 110 mph. Approximately 5,000 people are killed.

◆ The famed "Rumble in the Jungle" takes place October 30, 1974, in Kinshasa, Zaire, with boxer Muhammad Ali knocking out George Foreman in the eighth round.

◆ On November 20, 1974, the US Department of Justice files an antitrust suit against communications giant AT&T; the suit will lead to the breakup of the company in the early 1980s.

◆ The United States and West Germany launch *Helios 1* on December 10, 1974; the spacecraft later makes the closest recorded approach to the sun.

◆ On December 28, 1974, an earthquake occurs in Pakistan, with 5,200 people perishing in its wake.

◆ Carl Bernstein and Bob Woodward publish *All the President's Men*, a chronicle of their investigation of the Watergate scandal, in 1974.

◆ Erica Jong publishes *Fear of Flying*, 1974.

◆ Stephen King publishes *Carrie*, 1974.

◆ John Le Carré publishes *Tinker, Tailor, Soldier, Spy*, 1974.

◆ Studs Terkel publishes *Working*, 1974.

◆ Sidney Sheldon publishes *The Other Side of Midnight*, 1974.

◆ James Michener publishes *Centennial*, 1974.

◆ Ursula K. Le Guin publishes *The Dispossessed*, 1974.

◆ Gregory McDonald publishes *Fletch*, 1974.

◆ Television series debuting in 1974 include *Chico and the Man, Good Times, Happy Days, Kolchak: The Night Stalker, The Rockford Files*, and *The Six Million Dollar Man*.

◆ Popular music hits of 1974 include Olivia Newton-John's "I Honestly Love You," Barbra Streisand's "The Way We Were," and Paul McCartney and Wings' "Band on the Run."

◆ Notable films of 1974 include Mel Brooks's *Blazing Saddles* with Cleavon Little and Gene Wilder, Roman Polanski's *Chinatown* with Jack Nicholson and Faye Dunaway, Francis Ford Coppola's *The Godfather, Part II* with Al Pacino, Robert Duvall, Diane Keaton, and Robert De Niro, and Jack Clayton's *The Great Gatsby* with Robert Redford and Mia Farrow.

◆ The cover of *Popular Mechanics* magazine in January of 1975 features the Altair 8800, later considered by many to be the first personal computer. Available as a kit or already assembled, it features 256 bytes of RAM and toggle switches to operate and program it; it does not have a keyboard, monitor, or printer.

◆ On February 28, 1975, the first Lomé Convention is signed; the agreement covers economic cooperation between the European Economic Community (EEC) and many developing countries of Africa, the Caribbean, and the Pacific (ACP).

◆ On March 25, 1975, King Faisal of Saudi Arabia is assassinated by his nephew, Prince Faisal Ibu Musaed. Prince Musaed is considered mentally unbalanced and is executed by beheading in June of 1975.

◆ The Cambodian government surrenders to Communist rebel forces, April 16, 1975.

◆ In May 1975 the US unemployment rate hits 9.2 percent, the highest since 1941.

◆ In the summer of 1975, Mozambique, Cape Verde, and São Tomé and Príncipe become independent of Portugal, and the Comoros becomes independent of France.

◆ On July 17, 1975, a US Apollo spacecraft (the last of the Apollo craft) and a Soviet Soyuz spacecraft dock with each other in orbit; the astronauts and cosmonauts meet in the middle, shaking hands and exchanging gifts.

◆ White students riot in South Boston, Massachusetts, on October 24, 1975, in protest over the desegregation of public schools. The students boycott class and physically attack black students. Although the police manage to quell the violence, tensions again flare a month later when a Haitian boy is attacked by defiant white students.

◆ In November of 1975, Angola becomes independent of Portugal and Suriname becomes independent of the Netherlands.

◆ In 1975, Bill Gates and Paul Allen develop a BASIC computer language for the Altair 8800; the sale of this product marks the founding of Microsoft (originally, Micro Soft) Corporation.

◆ Agatha Christie publishes Curtain, 1975.

◆ James Clavell publishes Shogun, 1975.

◆ E. L. Doctorow publishes Ragtime, 1975.

◆ Milton Osborne publishes River Road to China, 1975.

◆ Joe Haldeman publishes The Forever War, 1975.

◆ Stephen King publishes Salem's Lot, 1975.

◆ P. D. James publishes The Black Tower, 1975.

◆ Jacob Bronowski publishes The Ascent of Man, 1975.

◆ Michael Crichton publishes The Great Train Robbery, 1975.

◆ Saul Bellow publishes Humboldt's Gift, 1975.

◆ Television series debuting in 1975 include Baretta, Barney Miller, Fawlty Towers, Good Morning America, The Jeffersons, One Day at a Time, Saturday Night Live, Starsky and Hutch, Wheel of Fortune, and Welcome Back, Kotter.

◆ Charlie Smalls's The Wiz debuts on Broadway, 1975.

◆ Edward Kelban and Marvin Hamlisch's A Chorus Line debuts on Broadway, 1975.

◆ Popular music hits of 1975 include Barry Manilow's "Mandy," the Average White Band's "Best of My Love," the Carpenters' "Please! Mr. Postman," and Linda Ronstadt's "You're No Good."

◆ Notable films of 1975 include Milos Forman's One Flew Over the Cuckoo's Nest with Jack Nicholson and Louise Fletcher, Stanley Kubrick's Barry Lyndon with Ryan O'Neal and Marisa Berenson, Robert Altman's Nashville with David Arkin and Ned Beatty, Sidney Lumet's Dog Day Afternoon with Al Pacino and John Cazale, Hal Ashby's Shampoo with Warren Beatty, Goldie Hawn, and Julie Christie, Terry Gilliam's and Terry Jones's Monty Python and the Holy Grail, John Sharman's The Rocky Horror Picture Show with Susan Sarandon, Barry Bostwick, and Tim Curry, Ken Russell's Tommy with Elton John, Ann-Margret, and Roger Daltry, and Steven Spielberg's Jaws with Roy Scheider and Richard Dreyfuss.

◆ On January 26, 1976, the first commercial flights of the Concorde take place: a British Airways flight from London to Bahrain and an Air France flight from Paris to Rio de Janeiro; each features the supersonic aircraft.

◆ The 12th Winter Olympic Games are held in Innsbruck, Austria, February 4–15, 1976. The games were originally slated to take place in Denver, Colorado, but the city is forced to withdraw after Colorado voters reject, by referendum, a $5 million bond to help finance the event.

◆ Khmer Rouge leader Pol Pot becomes prime minister of Cambodia on April 2, 1976, after Prince Norodom Sihanouk is forced into foreign exile.

◆ In May of 1976, doctors begin removing the respirator that has assisted coma victim Karen Ann Quinlan in breathing. The respirator is removed following a New Jersey Supreme Court decision in a case filed by her father. Surprisingly, she begins breathing on her own following the removal of the respirator and lives until June of 1985, although in a persistent vegetative state.

◆ On June 28, 1976, an Air France flight is forced by pro-Palestinian hijackers to land at Entebbe airport in Uganda. Passengers not carrying Israeli passports are released; the remaining passengers and crew are held in the airport. On July 4, 1976, a daring raid by Israeli commandos results in the rescue of most of the passengers; twenty Ugandan soldiers, all seven terrorists, three passengers, and the leader of the Israeli commandos are killed in the action.

◆ On July 3, 1976, the Supreme Court rules in *Gregg v. Georgia* that the death penalty is a constitutionally permissible form of punishment.

◆ The United States celebrates its Bicentennial with fireworks, the ringing of bells, and a gathering of ships in New York harbor, July 4, 1976.

◆ The Viking 1 landing module lands on Mars on July 20, 1976; Viking 2 lands on Mars on September 3, 1976. The Viking mission includes taking images of the surface of Mars and analyzing the surface and the atmosphere.

◆ In July 1976 the 21st Summer Olympic Games are held in Montreal, Canada. The events are mired in allegations of steroid use, with the East German women's swim team specifically targeted. Twenty-six African countries also boycott the Olympics to protest the International Olympic Committee's refusal to ban New Zealand from participating in the games. New Zealand's rugby team continues to compete against South Africa, banned from the Olympics since 1964 for its policy of apartheid.

◆ On September 9, 1976, China's leader, Mao Zedong, dies; a period of instability follows, with Hua Guofeng, Mao's chosen successor, surrendering power to Deng Xiaoping and his followers within a few years.

◆ On September 17, 1976, construction of the first space shuttle is completed; the shuttle is named the *Enterprise* after a write-in campaign by *Star Trek* fans.

◆ The 19-month civil war in Lebanon comes to an end in November 1976.

◆ Alex Haley publishes *Roots*, 1976.

◆ Jerzy Kosinski publishes *The Painted Bird*, 1976.

◆ Gail Sheehy publishes *Passages*, 1976.

◆ Gore Vidal publishes *1876*, 1976.

◆ Television series debuting in 1976 include *Alice, Charlie's Angels, Family Feud, The Gong Show, I, Claudius* (miniseries), *Laverne & Shirley, Mary Hartman, Mary Hartman, The Muppet Show, Quincy, Rich Man, Poor Man* (miniseries), and *Wonder Woman*.

◆ Popular music hits of 1976 include Stevie Wonder's "I Wish," George Benson's "This Masquerade," Chicago's "If You Leave Me Now," and "Afternoon Delight" by Starland Vocal Band.

◆ Notable films of 1976 include Sidney Lumet's *Network* with Faye Dunaway, William Holden, and Peter Finch, John G. Avildsen's *Rocky* with Sylvester Stallone and Talia Shire, Alan J. Pakula's *All the President's Men* with Dustin Hoffman and Robert Redford, Brian De Palma's *Carrie* with Sissy Spacek, Led Zeppelin's *The Song Remains the Same*, and Martin Scorsese's *Taxi Driver* with Robert De Niro and Jodie Foster.

◆ In January 1977 record shortages of electrical power and natural gas cause factories, offices, and schools on the eastern US seaboard to temporarily close.

FAST FACTS ABOUT GERALD R. FORD

◆ Ford was the first president whose parents had divorced; he only learned that Gerald R.

Ford, Sr., was not his biological father when he was thirteen years old.

❖ In the 1940s Ford briefly worked as a male fashion model for *Cosmopolitan* and *Look* magazines.

❖ In his youth Ford had received offers to play for two professional football teams, the Green Bay Packers and the Detroit Lions, but he declined both in favor of a coaching position at Yale, where he later attended law school.

❖ Ford served as a member of the Warren Commission that investigated the assassination of President John F. Kennedy.

❖ Ford was the first president to hold the posts of president and vice president without being elected to either; he was appointed to the vice presidency after scandal forced Nixon's first vice president, Spiro Agnew, to resign, and later became president following Nixon's historic resignation.

❖ Ford was the first president chosen under the 25th Amendment (which allows for a president to turn over power to the vice president), thus making him the first vice president to succeed to the presidency upon the resignation of the president.

❖ Ford was the first president to grant a pardon to a former president.

❖ Ford was the first president to visit Japan while in office.

❖ Ford was the first president to publicly disclose the results of his annual medical checkup. After a four-hour examination at Walter Reed Hospital in January 1975, he was given a clean bill of health.

❖ Ford's tendency toward occasional physical clumsiness was repeatedly lampooned by Chevy Chase on the television show *Saturday Night Live*.

❖ When Ford ran for the presidency in 1976, bumper stickers reading "Vote for Betty's Husband" reflected the popularity of the First Lady.

❖ As a young woman living in New York City, future first lady Betty Bloomer was chosen as a member of Martha Graham's auxiliary troupe and danced at Carnegie Hall.

❖ Betty Ford met and became friendly with former First Lady Bess Truman.

❖ Defeated by Jimmy Carter, the former governor of Georgia, in the 1976 election, Ford became the third president in the 20th century to be denied a second term.

James Earl Carter, Jr.

Nickname: Jimmy
Presidency: 39th president, 1977–1981
Party: Democratic
Life dates: October 1, 1924–

EARLY LIFE AND EDUCATION

James Earl Carter, Jr. was born on October 1, 1924 in Plains, Georgia, a small town 120 miles south of Atlanta. He was the first child of Bessie Lillian Gordy Carter and James Earl Carter, Sr., who had married a year earlier. James Jr., who was given the nickname Jimmy, was soon followed by two younger sisters and one younger brother: Gloria in 1926, Ruth in 1929, and Billy in 1937. While Carter ran a general store in Plains, the family lived in various apartments throughout the town, including one next door to Edgar Smith's family, which included Rosalynn Smith, Jimmy's future wife.

When Jimmy was four, the Carters moved to a farm in nearby Archery where Jimmy lived until he left for junior college. The family farm was lit with kerosene lamps, water came from a well, and there was an outdoor toilet. The family lived off of the farm's cash crops, consisting of peanuts and cotton. The land was worked by black tenant farmers whose children were Jimmy's closest friends in early childhood. Jimmy worked in the fields himself, assisting with the plowing and planting of crops. From the age of five he sold boiled peanuts on the street in Plains. As a boy, Jimmy spent most of the day playing outdoors on the farm, fishing and chasing animals. No stranger to physical activity, he broke both his arms and three ribs on different occasions.

Earl Carter concentrated his efforts on establishing a successful peanut business; however, he also served on the Sumter County Board of Education and was later elected to the Georgia state legislature in 1952. The Carter family attended Plains Baptist Church. Jimmy's mother worked as a nurse and would minister to the poor black families on the farm and its surrounding area. She also sold pecans from trees she owned on the family farm. She read constantly and encouraged her children to do the same. Carter counts *War and Peace* and James Agee's *Let Us Now Praise Famous Men*, works he read as a child, among his favorite books. Jimmy attended Plains High School, which had fewer than 300 students in eleven grades. He was an excellent student and member of the Future Farmers of America, a national organization offering an agricultural education; he also played on the school's basketball team. In 1941 he graduated as class valedictorian.

Jimmy's maternal uncle, Tom Gordy, made a career for himself in the navy. Jimmy was fascinated by his uncle's tales of foreign lands and world travel, and at an early age became determined to join the navy himself. He requested admissions information from the US Naval Academy before he had even entered high school.

"From the time I was five years old, I would always say that someday I would be going to Annapolis, and would become a naval officer.... With my parents' full backing, years before I graduated from high school, we sent off for some pamphlets to learn about the Naval Academy, and I adopted this as my exclusive goal in life."

Jimmy Carter in his memoir, *An Hour Before Daylight*, 2001

Securing admission to the US Naval Academy in Annapolis, Maryland, was an extremely competitive process, so to improve his chances, Jimmy studied for a year at the Georgia Institute of Technology in Atlanta before receiving his letter of acceptance from the academy in 1943. In 1945, while home on leave, Jimmy met Rosalynn Smith, by then a good friend of his sister Ruth. Rosalynn's father Edgar was a mechanic who had died when his daughter was thirteen. Her mother, Allie Murray Smith, was employed at the local post office and Rosalynn helped out by working in a beauty parlor. Like Jimmy, Rosalynn was valedictorian of her high school class.

Jimmy graduated from the US Naval Academy in June 1946 in the top 10 percent of his class. He and Rosalynn married a month later on July 7, 1946; Jimmy was twenty-one and Rosalynn seventeen. After their marriage, the couple moved to Norfolk, Virginia, where Jimmy reported for his first naval duty. In 1947, within a year of their union, John William Carter ("Jack") was born. He was followed by James Earl Carter III ("Chip") in 1950, Donnel Jeffrey Carter in 1952, and Amy Lynn Carter in 1968.

EARLY CAREER

Carter began his naval career as a radar officer and electronics instructor on the battleship *Wyoming*, which was being used as a training ship at the time. Carter continued his tour of duty on the *Mississippi*, where he served as a training and education officer, followed by submarine service in 1948, during which he attended the six-month submarine school in New London, Connecticut. Carter was next assigned to the *Pomfret* based in Pearl Harbor, where he was promoted to lieutenant junior grade on June 5, 1949. In 1951 he became engineering officer on the new submarine chaser *K-1*.

Carter next sought assignment to the fledgling nuclear submarine service being assembled by Captain Hyman Rickover, whom Carter later credited as the man—other than his father—who had the greatest influence on his life. On June 1, 1952, Carter was promoted to lieutenant. He was assigned to Schenectady, New York, where he studied nuclear physics at Union College, and later worked for a time at the US Atomic Energy Commission in Washington, DC, where he helped design nuclear power plants for submarines. Rickover assigned Carter to the *Seawolf*, one of the navy's first nuclear submarines; Carter had helped supervise its construction. When his father became sick and died in July 1953, Carter decided to resign from the navy and return to Plains to manage the family farm.

Back in Plains, Carter effectively managed the farm and its peanut warehouse and transformed both into a thriving business within five years. The first year was hard: a severe drought in 1954 resulted in a less than $200 profit. Rosalynn, who had opposed her husband's decision to leave the Navy, worked as a bookkeeper. The Carters found the town's attitudes slow to change in an era of increased awareness of civil rights. A segregationist organization, the White Citizens Council, spread across the South. In Plains, Carter was the only white man who refused to join and the family business was boycotted for a time as a result. When the Carter's church voted on the issue of desegregation, two of only three votes in favor of integration were cast by the Carters.

Jimmy Carter subsequently became more involved in community life, serving as deacon and Sunday school teacher at the Plains Baptist Church, which he had attended throughout his youth. Carter's first elected office was a seat on the Sumter County Board of Education (1955); he eventually became the board's chairman.

POLITICAL CAREER

In 1962 Carter ran for a newly created seat in the Georgia State Senate. Carter lost the Democratic primary, but he challenged the result on the basis of voting fraud. A judge ordered that the fraudulent votes be thrown out and Carter won the primary, followed by the general election. In the State Senate, Carter worked diligently to learn protocol and master the content of submitted legislation, and he was reelected two years later.

Carter initially decided to run for Congress in 1966, but then changed his mind, opting instead to challenge a Republican rival in his campaign for governor. The conservative backlash against the civil rights movement in the South resulted in the palpable intolerance of liberal Democrats like Carter. In the primary, he came in third, losing to segregationist Lester Maddox, who was eventually elected governor. Almost immediately, Carter announced he would run again for governor in 1970 and campaigned tirelessly across Georgia. Despite his commitment to promoting civil rights, Carter was keenly aware of his vulnerability as a liberal Democrat and challenged his opponent Carl E. Sanders, a former governor, in the Democratic primary with a more conservative platform. Carter beat Sanders in a runoff, and went on to defeat Republican Hal Suit, a television news reporter from Atlanta.

Although Carter's stance on civil rights issues during his 1970 run for governor was markedly more conservative than in his past campaigns, Carter in his 1971 inaugural address as governor asserted that "the time for racial discrimination is over," a surprise to many who had followed the candidate's campaign for office. Carter proved to be a ready reformer; he increased funding for schools that served the poor and for the disabled, recruited African Americans for state jobs, and trimmed bureaucratic waste by streamlining more than 300 state boards. He also installed a portrait of Dr. Martin Luther King, Jr. in the state capitol. In 1971 Governor Carter appeared on the cover of *Time* magazine, a representative of the "new South."

"I am a Southerner and an American, I am a farmer, an engineer, a father and husband, a Christian, a politician and former governor, a planner, a businessman, a nuclear physicist, a naval officer, a canoeist, and among other things a lover of Bob Dylan's songs and Dylan Thomas's poetry."

Jimmy Carter in his memoir, *Why Not the Best?*, 1975

During this same period, Carter jockeyed to position himself as a national figure in Democratic politics. He lobbied to become Senator George S. McGovern's vice-presidential running mate on the 1972 ticket. He spearheaded an effort to elect more Democratic governors (as chair of the Democratic Governor's Campaign Committee) and served as chairman of the Democratic National Campaign Committee.

Carter's stance in support of the Vietnam War, however, ultimately distanced him from McGovern, who chose Sargent Shriver as a running mate in his unsuccessful 1974 bid for the presidency.

When Carter first publicly announced his candidacy for the Democratic presidential nomination in December 1974, he was an obscure governor with little national recognition. America was recovering from the Watergate scandal and after-effects of the Vietnam War. Against this backdrop of disillusionment, Carter highlighted his outsider status, promising to clean up Washington if elected. His campaign slogan was, "A leader, for a change." Eventually, nine other Democrats joined the race. Carter won the Iowa caucuses and the New Hampshire primary, traditionally the first indicators of a candidate's standing in the Democratic race.

At the Democratic Convention in New York City in July 1976, Carter was nominated on the first ballot, choosing Senator Walter F. Mondale of Minnesota as his running mate. Mondale, who had served in the Senate since 1965, had an impressive prolabor record and balanced Carter geographically, providing a Northern presence on the ticket. Carter stressed diversity in his platform. He brought Wallace and King's widow, Coretta Scott King, onstage when he accepted his party's nomination. "It is time for the people to run the government," said Carter, "and not the other way around."

President Gerald R. Ford, surviving a strong challenge from former Governor Ronald Reagan for the presidential nomination, was nominated on the first ballot at the Republican National Convention. He selected Senator Robert Dole of Kansas as his running mate. The fact that Ford had not been directly elected either vice president or president (having become vice president after the resignation of Spiro T. Agnew and president on the resignation of Richard M. Nixon) worked against him. His decision to grant a full pardon to Nixon was also a huge liability for Ford, who started his campaign well behind Carter in the public opinion polls.

As the campaign progressed, Ford cut into Carter's lead, aided by an interview Carter gave to *Playboy* magazine in which the candidate admitted that he had looked on other women with lust. "I've committed adultery in my heart many times," Carter confessed. During his campaign Carter also stated that people should be allowed to preserve the "ethnic purity" of their neighborhoods, a remark for which he subsequently apologized. Ford challenged Carter to three televised debates. During one exchange Ford erroneously claimed that "there is no Soviet domination of Eastern Europe," a gross misstatement that Carter managed to effectively use against the president for the remainder of the campaign. In the end, Carter held onto his lead and won a close race, winning 297 electoral votes to Ford's 240.

PRESIDENCY

As president, Carter disdained the "imperial presidency" of his predecessors and sought to project a more casual image. Rather than riding in a limousine, he walked down Pennsylvania Avenue to his inauguration and wore a business suit for the occasion. When he addressed the nation on television for the first time, Carter wore a cardigan. He also sold off the presidential yacht, the *Sequoia*.

President Carter remained aloof from the political game in Washington by not pandering to Democratic interests, as well as opposing customary "pork barrel" legislations that were traditionally used by Congress to please special interests. He did not shy away, however, from controversial measures. On his first day in office, Carter pardoned Vietnam War draft evaders. He also withdrew funding for the B-1 bomber and, later, the neutron bomb.

Carter had difficulties establishing a productive relationship with Congress, which asserted its autonomy by blocking Carter's consumer protection bill and a labor reform package. He did influence the House and Senate to pass deregulation legislation, though: for cargo airlines in 1977; commercial airlines in 1978; the natural gas industry in 1978; and trucking in 1980. After a prolonged battle with the White House, Congress did approve in November 1978 an energy bill that encouraged fuel conservation and the development of alternative sources of energy. President Carter also worked to promote light-water nuclear power stations and created the Department of Energy with a cabinet-level secretary.

Much of the Carter presidency was spent addressing energy issues, especially those concerning oil. The United States was heavily reliant on imported oil, and the Organization of the Petroleum Exporting Countries (OPEC), formed in 1960, increased the price of oil during the Carter presidency, from $13 to $34 a barrel, which consequently led to inflation. Higher oil prices translated into long lines at the pump and general voter dissatisfaction with Carter's leadership. In July 1979 Carter retreated to Camp David for ten days to reevaluate his policies. He emerged from seclusion to deliver a nationally televised speech in which he spoke of a national "crisis of confidence." The speech failed to alleviate the malaise Carter described. By the 1980 election, the rate of inflation stood at 12 percent and interest rates hit 20 percent. The dollar also weakened during the Carter presidency and unemployment remained at high levels.

Carter moved to stockpile oil and succeeded in passing a Crude Oil Windfall Profits Tax, but Congress defeated his veto of a measure striking down an import duty on oil. In the end, Carter did succeed in reducing America's reliance on foreign oil. His programs additionally produced a larger oil reserve and greater energy supply as a result of his gas industry reforms and increased domestic oil production.

Among the other measures Carter implemented as president were a ban on dumping sewage into the ocean (1977); the Strip Mining Control and Reclamation Act (1977); and the Alaska National Interest Lands Act (1980), which designated 55 million new acres of wilderness and expanded existing national parks. Carter also made food stamps free (1977) and signed the Humphrey-Hawkins Full Employment Act (1978) establishing a goal of 4 percent unemployment by 1983.

During Carter's presidency, relations with the Soviet Union were somewhat confrontational.

On his diplomatic team were National Security Adviser Zbigniew Brzezinski, somewhat of a hard-liner on the subject of Communism, and Secretary of State Cyrus Vance, a former diplomat but strong voice for change. The Carter administration attacked human rights abuses in the Soviet bloc and took action against oppressive governments in Central America. Carter also supported increases in defense spending, and the development of the cruise missile and the MX, a mobile nuclear weapons system designed to thwart Soviet first-strike capability.

> "Because we are free we can never be indifferent to the fate of freedom elsewhere. Our moral sense dictates a clearcut preference for these societies which share with us an abiding respect for individual human rights. We do not seek to intimidate, but it is clear that a world which others can dominate with impunity would be inhospitable to decency and a threat to the well-being of all people."
>
> Jimmy Carter, from his inaugural address, January 20, 1977

In 1977 Carter announced that he had reached an agreement with Panama (in negotiation since 1964) that called for the transfer of the American-run Panama Canal to Panamanian control. The transfer would become effective in 1999 and involve the withdrawal of all US troops stationed there. The arrangement came under immediate attack, with polls showing that three-quarters of Americans opposed the transfer of the canal. A compromise was reached af-

President Jimmy Carter joining hands with President Sadat (left) and Prime Minister Begin (right) outside the White House during the official signing ceremony of the peace treaty between Egypt and Israel on March 26, 1979.

ter Cyrus Vance asserted that the United States retained the right to defend the canal, a claim that Panama initially denied. The Senate then introduced an amendment to the treaty reinstating America's ability to intervene in certain matters in order to protect the canal; Panama's President Omar Torrijos agreed to this condition. The Senate ratified the treaty in 1978 with two votes of 68-32, one vote clear of the necessary two-thirds majority. Carter later said that the vote was "the most courageous thing that the US Senate ever did in its existence."

In 1978 President Carter invited Egypt's president Anwar Sadat and Israeli prime minister Menachem Begin to Camp David in Maryland to reopen their stalled peace negotiations. Under Carter's supervision, Begin and Sadat negotiated for two weeks and produced the historic Camp David Accords that led to a signed peace treaty in 1979. It was a historic turning point for

the two nations, and the state of war that had existed between them for more than thirty years.

With Leonid Brezhnev in 1979, President Carter concluded a second Strategic Arms Limitation Treaty (SALT II) between the United States and the Soviet Union. The treaty met immediate resistance in the Senate, and after the Soviet invasion of Afghanistan in December 1979, it was never ratified. Carter responded to the invasion by halting the shipment of grain supplies and the sale of high-tech equipment to the Soviet Union and by ordering a boycott of the 1980 Moscow Olympics by American athletes.

In 1979 the United States formally recognized the People's Republic of China and established diplomatic relations with the Communist nation. This required the United States to withdraw its earlier recognition of Taiwan as the official Chinese state and remove US forces deployed there.

The most serious crisis of the Carter presidency was the hostage situation that developed in Iran and played itself out for more than a year on televisions across the land and throughout the world. After years of brutal oppression and large-scale corruption, Iranians revolted against the Western-backed Shah Mohammed Reza Pahlevi. He was forced to flee the country, and amid the ensuing civil chaos, Ayatollah Khomeini, the Islamic fundamentalist who had led the insurrection from exile in Paris, returned to power. After the United States allowed the shah to seek medical treatment for cancer in New York, militant students seized the American Embassy in Teheran and took sixty-six Americans hostages, demanding that the shah be returned to Iran to stand trial for crimes against his people.

Secret negotiations, economic sanctions, and the freezing of substantial Iranian assets in the United States failed to secure the release of the hostages. In April 1980 Carter authorized a military mission ("Desert One") that would attempt to free the hostages. The mission was an embarrassing failure, with helicopters breaking down in the Iranian desert and eight servicemen losing their lives in a crash as the rescuers were evacuated. Iran then separated and dispersed the hostages, thus ensuring that no rescue could succeed. Even the death of the shah did not lead to the hostages' release. An agreement was finally reached whereby the United States agreed to return the Iranian assets it had seized. On January 20, 1981, the day Ronald Reagan assumed office, and after 444 days in captivity, the hostages left Iran.

The hostage crisis, and Carter's perceived inability to solve it, doomed the president's hopes for a second term. Carter was consistently unable to cultivate a positive image in the media, a failure that was perhaps often exacerbated by the antics of his brother Billy (who among other media charges was accused of accepting $250,000 from the government of Libya). In September 1979 Carter was photographed in a state of near collapse while on a jog at Camp Davis, a well-known image that—fairly or not—became a metaphor for his presidency.

In the summer of 1980, Carter's approval ratings stood at a mere 21 percent, the lowest ever recorded for a sitting president (worse even than Richard Nixon's during the height of the Watergate scandal). Fearing major defeat for the Democratic Party, many Democrats were drawn to the presidential campaign mounted by Senator Edward M. Kennedy of Massachusetts. Though Kennedy initially seemed to pose a threat to Carter, controversy surrounding his past personal life (including the infamous car crash on Chappaquiddick Island in July 1969, which had resulted in the death of a young female campaign worker) soon ensured Carter's renomination. With Walter Mondale again standing at his side as the vice-presidential candidate, Carter sought reelection in 1980. However, Republican Ronald Reagan triumphed, winning a landslide victory.

POST-PRESIDENTIAL CAREER

Former President Carter has arguably had the most successful public service career of any US president after leaving office. After the 1980 election, Jimmy and Rosalynn Carter returned to Plains, Georgia. At first, Carter worked privately, writing his memoirs and teaching a course at Emory University in Atlanta. He has written numerous books since 1981, including an autobiography, poetry, and a novel.

In 1986 the Carter Center was opened in Atlanta. It was conceived by Carter as a place to promote democracy and the peaceful resolution of conflicts. In addition, President Carter has traveled frequently as the official representative of international organizations monitoring elections worldwide. In 1990, for example, he observed elections in Nicaragua, the Dominican Republic, and Haiti. In 1994 Carter returned to Haiti with former General Colin Powell and Senator Sam Nunn of Georgia to help orchestrate the peaceful transfer of power in that country after elections.

On August 9, 1999, President Bill Clinton presented both Jimmy and Rosalynn Carter with the Presidential Medal of Freedom, the highest civilian award in the United States.

Since 1984 the Carters have been associated

with Habitat for Humanity, a nonprofit organization that constructs housing for the poor worldwide. In March 1984 Carter helped construct several houses in Americus, Georgia, and later that same year he and Rosalynn volunteered to do the same in the South Bronx in New York (regarded as one of the poorest residential neighborhoods in the United States in the 1970s), traveling by bus there.

"The bond of our common humanity is stronger than the divisiveness of our fears and prejudices. God gives us the capacity for choice. We can choose to alleviate suffering. We can choose to work together for peace. We can make these changes—and we must."

Jimmy Carter, in his Nobel Lecture, October 11, 2002

On October 11, 2002, Jimmy Carter was awarded the Nobel Peace prize for "his decades of untiring effort to find peaceful solutions to international conflicts, to advance democracy and human rights, and to promote economic and social development." The Nobel Committee mentioned the Camp David Accords, the Carter Center, and Carter's long-time commitment to human rights. These remain his most significant achievements and have served to reestablish his reputation as a premier statesman.

Birthplace: Plains, GA
Residency: Georgia
Religion: Southern Baptist
Education: Georgia Southwestern College, Americus, GA (1941–1942); Georgia Institute of Technology (1942–1943); United States Naval Academy, Annapolis, MD, graduated 1946; Union College, Schenectady, NY (1952–1953)
Place of Death: n/a
Burial Site: n/a
Dates in Office: January 20, 1977–January 20, 1981 (4 years)
Age at Inauguration: 52 years, 112 days

FAMILY

Father: James Earl Carter (1894–1953)
Mother: Lillian ("Bessie") Gordy Carter (1898–1983)
Siblings: Jimmy was the eldest of four children; his siblings were Gloria Carter (1926–1990); Ruth Carter (1929–1983); William ("Billy") Alton Carter (1937–1988).
Wife: Eleanor Rosalynn Smith Carter (1927–), married on July 7, 1946, in Plains, GA
Children: John ("Jack") William Carter (1947–); James ("Chip") Earl Carter (1950–); Donnel ("Jeff") Jeffrey Carter (1952–); Amy Lynn Carter (1967–)

CAREER

Private: farmer, warehouseman, university professor
Political: GA state legislature (1963–1967); governor of GA (1971–1975); president of the United States (1977–1981)
Military: Carter graduated from the US Naval Academy in Annapolis, MD with distinction, and commissioned as ensign (1946); assigned to the USS *Wyoming* in Norfolk, VA, and later the USS *Mississippi* (1946-1948); attended the US Navy Submarine School in New London, CT (June–December 1948); assigned to the USS *Pomfret* in Pearl Harbor, HI, where he served as communications officer, sonar officer, electronics officer, gunnery officer, and supply officer (1948); promoted to lieutenant junior grade (June 1949); assigned engineering officer on the submarine chaser USS *K-1* (1951); promoted to lieutenant (1952); while serving in the Naval Reactors Branch, US Atomic Energy Commission, Carter attended Union College in Schenectady, NY to study nuclear physics and assist in training the precommissioned crew of the USS *Seawolf,* Washington, DC, one of the navy's first nuclear

submarines (1952–1953); honorably discharged on October 9, 1953.

Selected Works: *Why Not the Best?* (Nashville, TN: Broadman Books, 1975); *A Government as Good as Its People* (Fayetteville, AK: University of Arkansas Press, 1996); *The Wit and Wisdom of Jimmy Carter* (New York: Random House Value Publishing, 1980); *Sources of Strength* (New York: Times Books, 1977); *Keeping Faith* (New York: Bantam, Books, 1982); *Everything to Gain*, with Rosalynn Carter (New York: Random House, 1987); *An Outdoor Journal* (New York: Bantam Books, 1988); *Turning Point* (New York: Times Books, 1992); *The Blood of Abraham* (Fayetteville, AK: University of Arkansas Press, 1993); *Always a Reckoning and Other Poems* (New York: Crown, 1994); *Living Faith* (New York: Crown, 1996); *The Virtues of Aging* (New York: Ballantine Books, 1998); *An Hour Before Daylight* (New York: Simon & Schuster, 2001); *The Hornet's Nest* (New York: Simon & Schuster, 2003); *Sharing Good Times* (New York: Simon & Schuster, 2004).

PRESIDENCY

Nomination: 1976: The Democratic Convention was held in New York City, July 12–16, 1976. Carter won the nomination on the first vote, securing 2,238½ votes to 329½ for Representative Morris K. Udall of Arizona and 300½ for Governor Jerry Brown of California. Carter chose Senator Walter F. Mondale of Minnesota as the vice-presidential candidate.

1980: The Democratic Convention was held in New York City, August 11–14, 1980. Carter captured renomination on the first vote, receiving 2,129 votes to 1,146 cast for Senator Edward M. Kennedy of Massachusetts. Carter again picked Mondale as his running mate.

Election: 1976: elected president on November 2, 1976

1980: defeated by Ronald Reagan, November 4, 1980

Opponent: 1976: Gerald Ford, MI, Republican

1980: Ronald Reagan, CA, Republican; John Anderson, IL, Independent

Vote Totals: 1976: Carter, 40,825,839 popular,

297 electoral; Ford, 39,147,770 popular, 240 electoral. [Ronald Reagan received one electoral vote from the State of Washington.]

1980: Reagan, 43,899,248 popular, 489 electoral; Carter, 35,481,435 popular, 49 electoral; Anderson, 5,719,437 popular, 0 electoral.

Inauguration: January 20, 1977

Vice President: Walter F. Mondale, MN (1977–1981)

CABINET

Secretary of State: Cyrus R. Vance, NY (1977–1980); Edmund R. Muskie, ME (1980–1981)

Secretary of the Treasury: W. Michael Blumenthal, MI (1977–1979); G. William Miller, OK (1979–1981)

Secretary of Defense: Harold Brown, CA (1977–1981)

Attorney General: Griffin B. Bell, GA (1977–1979); Benjamin R. Civiletti, MD (1979–1981)

Secretary of Agriculture: Robert S. Bergland, MN (1977–1981)

Secretary of the Interior: Cecil D. Andrus, ID (1977–1981)

Secretary of Labor: F. Ray Marshall, TX (1977–1981)

Secretary of Commerce: Juanita M. Kreps, NC (1977–1979); Philip M. Klutznick, IL (1980–1981)

Secretary of Health, Education, and Welfare: Joseph A. Califano, Jr., Washington, DC (1977–1979); Patricia R. Harris, Washington, DC (1979–1981) [Note: In 1979 HEW was reorganized; renamed the Department of Health and Human Services, it no longer oversaw educational matters.]

Secretary of Housing and Urban Development: Patricia R. Harris, Washington, DC (1977–1979); Moon Landrieu, LA (1979–1981)

Secretary of Transportation: Brock Adams, WA (1977–1979); Neil E. Goldschmidt, OR (1979–1981)

Secretary of Energy: James R. Schlesinger, VA (1977–1979); Charles W. Duncan, Jr., TX (1979–1981) [Note: Under President Carter, this new department came into existence on October 1, 1977.]

Secretary of Education: Shirley M. Hufstedler,

CA (1979–1981) [Note: In 1979 the Department of Education was created from part of the previous Department of Health, Education, and Welfare.]

CONGRESS:
95th Congress (1977–1979); Speaker of the House: Thomas P. O'Neill, Jr. (Democrat, MA)
96th Congress (1979–1981); Speaker of the House: Thomas P. O'Neill, Jr. (Democrat, MA)

SUPREME COURT APPOINTEES
None

MAJOR EVENTS OF THE CARTER ADMINISTRATION
◆ On January 20, 1977, Jimmy Carter is inaugurated as president.
◆ On February 2, 1977, Carter signs the Emergency Natural Gas Act.
◆ By June 30, 1977, production of the B-1 bomber is completely halted in the United States.
◆ The new, cabinet-level Department of Energy is established under James Schlesinger, on August 4, 1977.
◆ On September 7, 1977, Panama and the United States reach an agreement turning over control of the US-run Panama Canal, effective 1999.
◆ On September 15, 1977 Budget Director Bert Lance appears before a Senate committee charged with using his position for personal gain. Lance resigns days later.
◆ At a press conference on October 13, 1977, Carter declares that oil companies are perpetrating "the biggest rip-off in history."
◆ On December 20, 1977, Carter signs amendments to the Social Security Act, which in turn raise federal income taxes. The changes are designed to safeguard Social Security through the year 2030.
◆ The Presidential Records Act, enacted in 1978, establishes that presidential papers are public, rather than private, property.
◆ On February 3, 1978, President Anwar Sadat of Egypt visits Washington, DC, for talks with the White House, including dialogue on the stalled Mideast peace process.

◆ The Senate ratifies the Panama Canal Treaty on March 16, 1978; it passes by a historic one-vote margin.
◆ On April 7, 1978, Carter calls for a delay in the development of the controversial enhanced radiation weapon or neutron bomb.
◆ The Senate ratifies a treaty on April 18, 1978, to transfer control of the Panama Canal to the country of Panama; the treaty also calls for the right of US troops to intervene in any future circumstances that threaten the security of the canal.
◆ By January 1, 1979, diplomatic relations with the People's Republic of China are established. As a result, the United States ceases to recognize Taiwan as the official Chinese state.
◆ On January 29, 1979, Chinese Communist premier Deng Xiaoping visits the United States.
◆ President Anwar Sadat of Egypt and Prime Minister Menachem Begin of Israel sign a historic peace treaty on March 26, 1979, in Washington, DC, following the Camp David Accords of September, 1978. The agreement brings an official end to hostilities between the two Middle Eastern nations.
◆ President Carter and Soviet Premier Leonid Brezhnev sign the SALT II arms control agreement on June 18, 1979, in Vienna. It is never ratified by the Senate.
◆ In a televised speech on July 15, 1979, Carter describes a "crisis of confidence"; it is later referred to as Carter's "malaise" speech. Two days later, Carter asks his entire cabinet to resign; five members do.
◆ On August 15, 1979, Andrew Young resigns as ambassador to the United Nations after it is revealed that he had met privately with a representative of the Palestinian Liberation Organization (PLO).
◆ Carter establishes the Department of Education on October 17, 1979.
◆ Followers of Iran's fundamentalist leader Ayatollah Khomeini seize sixty-six American hostages in Teheran on November 4, 1979.
◆ On November 6, 1979, Senator Edward M. Kennedy of Massachusetts (brother of the late US president and New York senator) formally

announces his candidacy for the Democratic presidential nomination.

◆ On December 4, 1979, Carter officially declares his intention to run for reelection.

◆ On December 25, 1979, the Soviet Union invades Afghanistan.

◆ Carter defeats Kennedy in the Iowa caucuses, January 21, 1980.

◆ In his State of the Union message on January 23, 1980, the president outlines what becomes known as the Carter Doctrine, asserting that Soviet military intervention in the Middle East is a direct threat to US national security.

◆ On March 25, 1980, Carter loses the New York primary to Kennedy.

◆ On April 24, 1980, a US military attempt to rescue the American hostages in Iran fails.

◆ On July 19, 1980, the Moscow Summer Olympics begin without the participation of US athletes; Carter had called for the boycott in protest of the Soviet invasion of Afghanistan.

◆ Ronald Reagan is nominated as the Republican candidate for president, July 28, 1980.

◆ On August 13, 1980, Carter accepts the Democratic nomination.

◆ On October 28, 1980, Carter and Reagan debate in Cleveland, Ohio. A large percentage of viewers claim Reagan is the victor in the debate, an opinion shared by most media pundits.

◆ On December 11, 1980, Carter signs the Superfund Bill, created to clean up toxic waste dumps.

MAJOR US AND WORLD EVENTS, 1977–1981

◆ On January 17, 1977, Gary Gilmore is executed by firing squad in Utah. It is the first execution in the United States in a decade.

◆ On March 17, 1977, 560 people die when two jumbo jets collide on the runway at an airport in Tenerife, Spain.

◆ Black South African leader Steve Biko dies in police custody on September 12, 1977.

◆ On November 19, 1977, Egyptian president Anwar Sadat makes a historic visit to Israel; he is the first Arab leader to ever visit the Jewish state.

◆ Silent film star Charlie Chaplin dies on December 25, 1977.

◆ Colleen McCullough publishes *The Thorn Birds*, 1977.

◆ Popular music hits of 1977 include the Eagles' "Hotel California," Fleetwood Mac's "Go Your Own Way," and Barbra Streisand and Paul Williams's duet, "Love Theme from *A Star is Born*."

◆ Notable films of 1977 include Woody Allen's *Annie Hall* with Diane Keaton, *Saturday Night Fever* with John Travolta, *Equus* with Richard Burton, Steven Spielberg's *Close Encounters of the Third Kind*, and George Lucas's *Star Wars*.

◆ Iranian Prime Minister Jaffer Sharif-Emami resigns on November 5, 1978, after severe riots break out.

◆ On December 10, 1978, the Nobel prize for Peace is awarded jointly to Egypt's President Anwar Sadat and Israeli Prime Minister Menachem Begin for their efforts to build a lasting peace in the Middle East.

◆ James Alan McPherson publishes *Elbow Room*, 1978.

◆ Barbara Tuchman publishes *A Distant Mirror*, 1978.

◆ Herman Wouk publishes *War and Remembrance*, 1978.

◆ John Irving publishes *The World According to Garp*, 1978.

◆ John Updike publishes *The Coup*, 1978.

◆ Television series debuting in 1978 include *Dallas*, *20/20*, *Mork & Mindy*, *Taxi*, and *Diff'rent Strokes*.

◆ Popular music hits of 1978 include Billy Joel's "Just the Way You Are," Barry Manilow's "Copacabana," Donna Summer's "Last Dance," and Anne Murray's "You Needed Me."

◆ Notable films of 1978 include Michael Cimino's *The Deer Hunter* with Christopher Walken, Meryl Streep, and Robert DeNiro, Warren Beatty's *Heaven Can Wait*, *Coming Home* with Jane Fonda, and *California Suite* with Jane Fonda, Alan Alda, Maggie Smith, and Michael Caine.

◆ On January 16, 1979, Shah Mohammed

Reza Pahlevi flees Iran, and the exiled religious leader Ayatollah Khomeini makes a triumphant return to Iran after 14 years in exile.

◆ On February 17, 1979, China invades Vietnam.

◆ A nuclear accident on March 28, 1979, at Three Mile Island nuclear power station in Pennsylvania leaks radioactive steam into the air.

◆ Margaret Thatcher becomes British Prime Minister following the national election in the United Kingdom, May 4, 1979.

◆ On June 2, 1979, Pope John Paul II becomes the first pope to visit a Communist country when he returns to his homeland, Poland.

◆ On July 17, 1979, Sandinista rebels seize Managua, the Nicaraguan capital.

◆ The Chrysler Loan Guarantee Bill is introduced in Congress on November 9, 1979; it signals the beginning of the government bailout of that corporation.

◆ John Cheever publishes *The Stories of John Cheever*, 1979.

◆ Penelope Fitzgerald publishes *Offshore*, 1979.

◆ William Styron publishes *Sophie's Choice*, 1979.

◆ Kurt Vonnegut publishes *Jailbird*, 1979.

◆ Television series debuting in 1979 include *The Dukes of Hazzard*, *The Facts of Life*, *Benson*, and *Knots Landing*.

◆ Andrew Lloyd Webber and Tim Rice's *Evita* debuts on Broadway, 1979.

◆ Popular music hits of 1979 include the Doobie Brothers' "What a Fool Believes," Dionne Warwick's "I'll Never Love This Way Again," Donna Summer's "Hot Stuff," and Michael Jackson's "Don't Stop 'Til You Get Enough."

◆ Notable films of 1979 include Bob Fosse's *All That Jazz*, Francis Ford Coppola's *Apocalypse Now*, *Being There* with Peter Sellers, *The China Syndrome* with Jack Lemmon and Jane Fonda, and *Kramer Versus Kramer* with Dustin Hoffman.

◆ On January 22, 1980, Soviet dissident nuclear physicist Andrei Sakharov is exiled to Gorky.

◆ Robert Mugabe becomes Zimbabwe's first black prime minister, March 4, 1980.

◆ At least nine people are killed on May 19, 1980, when Mount St. Helens erupts in Washington State.

◆ Iraq invades Iran on September 22, 1980.

◆ On December 8, 1980, Mark David Chapman shoots and kills former Beatle John Lennon outside of Lennon's home at the Dakota Apartments, off Central Park in New York City.

◆ The 1980 census estimates a US population of 226.5 million people.

◆ William Golding publishes *Rites of Passage*, 1980.

◆ Normal Mailer publishes *The Executioner's Song*, 1980.

◆ Tom Wolfe publishes *The Right Stuff*, 1980.

◆ Popular music hits of 1980 include Christopher Cross's "Sailing," Kenny Loggins's "This Is It," Bette Midler's "The Rose," and Barbra Streisand and Barry Gibbs's "Guilty."

◆ Television series debuting in 1980 include *That's Incredible!*, *Bosom Buddies*, *Solid Gold*, *Too Close for Comfort*, and *Magnum, P.I.*

◆ Notable films of 1980 include *Coal Miner's Daughter* with Cissy Spacek, David Lynch's *The Elephant Man*, *Ordinary People* with Mary Tyler Moore and Donald Sutherland, and Martin Scorcese's *Raging Bull* with Robert DeNiro.

FAST FACTS ABOUT JIMMY CARTER

◆ Jimmy Carter was the first president sworn in using his nickname.

◆ Carter was the first president who was born in a hospital.

◆ Carter was the first president to graduate from the US Naval Academy.

◆ While at Annapolis, Carter was paddled and hazed for defiantly refusing to sing General Sherman's Civil War battle hymn, "Marching Through Georgia."

◆ In 1973 then-Governor Carter appeared on the TV show *What's My Line*, and the panel failed to guess his occupation.

◆ Carter was the first president to send his mother on a diplomatic mission. He appointed Lillian Gordy Carter, who had previously served as a Peace Corps nurse in India, to head the US delegation attending the funeral of Indian President Fakhruddin Ali Ahmed on February 11, 1977, in New Delhi.

Ronald Reagan

Nickname: Dutch, the Gipper
Presidency: 40th president, 1981–1989
Party: Republican (from 1962)
Life dates: February 6, 1911–June 5, 2004 (93 years, 120 days)

EARLY LIFE AND EDUCATION

Ronald Wilson Reagan was born on February 6, 1911, in his family's home in Tampico, Illinois. He was the second son of Nelle Wilson and John Edward ("Jack") Reagan, a shoe salesman. Ronald's brother (John) Neil Reagan had been born in 1909. The young Reagan lived in seven homes by the age of eight before the family settled in Dixon, Illinois. Ronald was nicknamed "Dutch" by his father who said his infant son looked like a "fat little Dutchman" the first time he saw him.

Jack Reagan's shoe enterprises collapsed during the Depression, and Jack, a staunch Roosevelt supporter, then found employment with a variety of New Deal public works projects. He had a long-standing drinking problem. Nelle was a pious woman who told her sons their father's alcoholism was a disease. Ronald was baptized as a member of his mother's Disciples of Christ church, and as a youth, he spoke publicly about the perils of alcohol. He was also exposed to the stage at an early age as his mother often presented dramas in local prisons and hospitals.

In school, Ronald had difficulty keeping up until his chronic nearsightedness was diag-

nosed and corrected. At Dixon High School, he played on the football and basketball teams and was president of the student body. Ronald studied drama and figured prominently in school plays. In 1926 he spent his first summer as a lifeguard on the Rock River in nearby Lowell Park, and was credited over the years that followed with saving some seventy-seven lives on the river.

In June 1928 Ronald graduated from high school; he attended Eureka College near Peoria, Illinois, from 1928 to 1932 on a partial football scholarship. Working part-time as a coach and dishwasher, he was able to pay the remainder of his tuition and support himself. At college, Ronald studied economics and sociology, maintaining a C average. He played guard on the football team, and was a member of numerous student societies—including the drama club and debate team—and wrote for the student newspaper.

In his first year at Eureka, Ronald experienced a taste of political power. As freshman representative, he led a school strike against the college's president who had imposed restrictions on student dances and off-campus nighttime activities, and also reduced the number of course offerings to save money. Under mounting pressure from various interest groups, the college president was forced to resign. Ronald graduated in June 1932, in the midst of the Depression. He opted for a career in radio, drawn in part by the radio addresses of President Franklin Delano Roosevelt whom he venerated as a young man.

EARLY CAREER

In December 1932 Reagan landed a job as a part-time announcer at WOC radio in Davenport, Iowa, which soon merged with the larger WHO station in Des Moines. On the radio Reagan called Big Ten football games and recreated Cubs games. To do this, he would receive information about the Cubs game in progress via the telegraph, and then describe the plays to the listening audience as though he were watching the game live. Years later Reagan would jokingly recount the story of one afternoon when the wire service suddenly failed. He began to describe a series of foul balls hit by the batter at the plate: Six minutes later, when the ticker started up again, it turned out the same player had scored a hit on the first pitch.

While employed in radio, Reagan developed the ambition to act in feature films. In 1937 he went to Catalina Island to cover the Cubs' spring training season for WHO. He arranged to have a screen test at Warner Brothers and secured a seven-year contract with the studio, starting at $200 a week. Reagan moved to Hollywood and went on to appear in more than fifty movies. He portrayed a good guy in all but one film, his last, a TV movie entitled *The Killers* (1964); it was eventually redistributed to theaters when the network deemed the film too violent for a television audience.

The first movie Reagan appeared in was *Love Is on the Air* (1937), in which he played Andy McCaine, a radio crime reporter. In 1938 Reagan starred in *Brother Rat* with Jane Wyman, who had been under contract at Warner Brothers since 1936. At the time, she was married to Myron Futterman, but the marriage ended shortly thereafter. Wyman and Reagan were married at a chapel near Hollywood on January 26, 1940. That year, they acted opposite each other again in *Brother Rat and a Baby*. The couple had a daughter, Maureen Elizabeth, on January 4, 1941, and adopted a son, Michael Edward, in 1945.

Reagan's most successful film role was his portrayal of the Notre Dame football great, George "The Gipper" Gipp, in *Knute Rockne—All American* (1940). Legend has it that on his deathbed in 1920, Gipp had asked Rockne, his coach, to inspire his teammates to someday "go in there with all they've got and win just one for the Gipper." In the film, Coach Rockne (played by Pat O'Brien) uses these same words in a half-time speech to rally the losing Notre Dame team against Army at Yankee Stadium in 1928. Notre Dame goes on to win the game, and thereafter the phrase "Win one for the Gipper" became indelibly linked to Reagan. In *Kings Row* (1942) Reagan gave perhaps his best performance, playing Drake McHugh, a charmer who eventually loses both his legs after a rail yard accident. After awakening from his operation, McHugh cries, "Where's the rest of me?" Reagan later used this same line as the title of his 1965 autobiography. Jane Wyman enjoyed an even more storied Hollywood movie career than her husband. She appeared as Ray Milland's wife in the critically acclaimed *Lost Weekend* (1945), and won an Academy Award for her work in *Johnny Belinda* (1948), in which she played a deaf-mute.

Reagan had joined the Reserve Corps of the Cavalry as a second lieutenant in May 1937. When the United States entered World War II, Reagan was called up, but his bad eyesight precluded him from combat. Reagan instead served in the Army Air Force's First Motion Picture Unit in Culver City as the narrator of its training films. He was promoted to first lieutenant in January 1943 and to captain later that year; he received his discharge in December 1945. In 1946 Reagan resigned with Warner Brothers, negotiating a contract that paid $3,500 a week, but his postwar film career was not as successful. *Bedtime for Bonzo* (1951), in which Reagan appeared with a chimpanzee, is perhaps his most memorable movie from this period.

Before World War II Reagan had become a board member of the Screen Actors Guild (SAG). In 1947 he was elected SAG president; in this capacity he served from 1947 to 1952, and again from 1959 to 1960. Reagan appeared before the House Committee on Un-American Activities in Washington, DC, in October 1947, and voiced his strong opposition to Communism. Throughout this period he remained a Democrat, supporting, for example, Helen Gahagan Douglas's Senate campaign against Richard Nixon in 1950. By 1952, however, he was a Democrat-for-Eisenhower, and in 1960 he campaigned actively for Nixon's presidential run. Reagan officially changed his party registration to Republican in 1962.

In 1947, when Reagan was very ill with pneumonia, Jane Wyman gave birth to a premature daughter, who died after only one day. The couple eventually separated in 1948, and their divorce became final in 1949, with Wyman maintaining custody of the two Reagan children.

Shortly thereafter Reagan began dating actress Nancy Davis, and in 1952, after what the bride years later described as an on-again, off-again courtship, the two wed at the Little Brown Church in the Valley in Los Angeles. Davis was born Anne Frances Robbins in New York City in 1921, and had been under contract to MGM since 1941. She had first met Reagan in 1949 upon contacting him as SAG president. An actress who shared the same name as Davis had appeared on a Communist Party blacklist, and Nancy Davis was concerned that confusion over the names would hurt her chances of securing future acting jobs. The couple appeared together in Hellcats of the Navy (1957). Their daughter Patricia Davis was born in 1952, followed by Ronald Prescott Reagan in 1958.

In 1954 Reagan became the host of the GE Theatre. Besides introducing dramas produced for this then-popular television show, he toured the country on speaking engagements for the General Electric Corporation. Over the course of the next eight years, Reagan developed his pro-business sensibilities. Meeting and interacting with tens of thousands of Americans, he also found that he had a talent for holding a crowd's attention. Soon Reagan's appearances became more politically oriented, and GE ended its arrangement with him in 1962. In 1964 Reagan was named host of the television series Death Valley Days.

⌣

"You and I have a rendezvous with destiny. We will preserve for our children this, the last best hope of man on Earth, or we will sentence them to take the last step into a thousand years of darkness."

Ronald Reagan, in his speech supporting Barry Goldwater's presidential bid, October 27, 1964

⌣

In 1964, in a nationally televised speech paid for by Holmes P. Tuttle, a Los Angeles-based car dealer, Reagan declared his support for Barry Goldwater's run for president. The speech, known as "A Time for Choosing," made a huge impact, establishing Reagan's conservative credentials and creating his national political reputation.

POLITICAL CAREER

In 1965 businessman Tuttle formed a group to promote Reagan's candidacy for governor of California. This "kitchen cabinet" hired a campaign manager and other savvy advisers to groom Reagan for his public appearances. At their urging, Reagan wrote an autobiography, Where's the Rest of Me? (1965), to help spread his message of new conservatism. In the November 8, 1966, election, Reagan handily defeated the Democratic incumbent Edmund G. "Pat" Brown by more than a million votes.

In the race Reagan had stood on a platform of reduced government, but his actions as governor sometimes contradicted this rhetoric. He began his term by proposing 10 percent budget cuts, but state spending increased markedly throughout his tenure. In his first year as governor, Reagan enacted an $844 million state tax hike, then the largest in US history, followed by a $1 billion increase his second year. Reagan did adopt some socially conservative policies, for instance, decreasing welfare rolls by dropping 300,000 recipients and authorizing police action against student protesters on California campuses. In his 1966 campaign, Reagan had once famously remarked, "A tree is a tree. How many more do you need to look at?" But as governor, he established Redwood National Park and advocated antipollution laws. He also signed a Democratic-Party-sponsored abortion reform bill that gave California a more liberal abortion law.

In 1968 Reagan mounted a campaign for the Republican presidential nomination, but came in third behind Richard Nixon and Nelson Rockefeller. In 1970 he was reelected as governor, defeating Democratic Assembly Speaker Jesse M. Unruh. When Reagan's second term ended in January 1975, he worked for a time as a public speaker and radio commentator. He challenged sitting President Gerald R. Ford for the 1976 nomination and came to within sixty votes of beating him.

Four years later Reagan was the clear front-runner for the Republican presidential nomination. He defeated Senator Howard Baker of Tennessee, former Governor John B. Connally of Texas, Senator Robert Dole of Kansas, Congressman Philip Crane of Illinois, and John Anderson, also a congressman from Illinois, who went on to run as an independent in the general election. Former congressman and CIA director George H. W. Bush seemed to pose the only viable threat to Reagan, having won primaries in the battleground states of Pennsylvania and Michigan. On one campaign stop Bush had pointedly attacked Reagan's proposed fiscal policy, calling it "voodoo economics." By the convention, Bush's initial surge had waned and he too dropped out of contention, leaving Reagan easy grasp of the nomination at the 1980 Republican National Convention in Detroit. At first, Reagan sought to take on former President Ford as his running mate, but when the two men failed to agree on terms, Reagan selected Bush as his vice-presidential candidate.

During the campaign, Reagan embodied a kind of energized optimism that contrasted with the hand-wringing which seemed to characterize the Carter presidency, which was still struggling, in the public eye, to address inflation, gas lines, and the continued captivity of American hostages in Iran after a failed rescue effort. Reagan promised to balance the federal budget while cutting taxes and increasing defense spending, while Carter proposed a number of new economic initiatives, including jobs programs, and attacked Reagan's fiscal ideas. In a televised debate, Reagan scored heavily with voters, good-naturedly fending off Carter's attack on his record, shaking his head and asserting, "There you go again." On November 4, 1980, Ronald Reagan captured 51 percent of the popular vote to Carter's 41 percent and Anderson's 7 percent, to become the 40th president of the United States.

PRESIDENCY

After his inauguration on January 20, 1981, Reagan set about offering his new economic vision to Congress and the American people, but seventy days into office he was shot and gravely wounded by John W. Hinckley, Jr., outside the Hilton in Washington, DC. Hinckley also shot and injured police officer Tom Delahanty, Secret Service agent Tim McCarthy, and the president's press secretary, James Brady, who was paralyzed as the result of his wounds. The bullet that hit the president had cannoned off his limousine, hit a rib, passed through a lung, and come perilously close to his heart. Less than two weeks later, Reagan was back at the White House. His cheerfulness and courage in the face of adversity soon endeared him to the public. Hinckley, who claimed he had been trying to impress movie star Jodie Foster, was found not guilty by reason of insanity and confined to St. Elizabeth's Hospital in Washington, DC, where he remains to this day.

Reagan's economic policy—or "Reaganomics" as it came to be known—centered on tax cuts coupled with reductions in government spending. With congressional approval Reagan secured a 25 percent reduction in personal income tax and slashed programs other than those related to national defense. He was an advocate of a "supply-side" fiscal policy, whereby money returned to business and individual consumers is theoretically reinvested in the economy, spurring growth and raising revenues. At the same time, the Federal Reserve and its chairman, Paul Volcker, attempted to tackle inflation by more conventional means, restricting the money supply.

"Honey, I forgot to duck."

Ronald Reagan, to his wife Nancy after being shot on March 30, 1981

The United States suffered a serious recession starting in 1981, with high rates of unemployment that reached almost 11 percent in November, the highest in more than forty years. Growth anticipated from the tax cuts failed to materialize and the deficit rose dramatically—in 1982 it was $100 billion— and eventually tripled. Debt interest payments became the government's third largest bill after defense programs and entitlements such as public assistance. Reagan asked America to "stay the course" while Congress enacted a huge, $100 billion tax increase. By 1983 the economy had turned the corner, and soon the country enjoyed its most prolonged period of growth since World War II.

As president, Ronald Reagan was a hands-off manager, but that approach was not to be confused with indecisiveness. In August 1981 he responded forcefully to 11,000 striking air traffic controllers by firing and then replacing them. In foreign affairs, Reagan took a hard line against the Soviet Union. He deployed Pershing II missiles to Europe, causing the Soviets to suspend arms-reduction talks being held in Geneva. He

predicted the imminent end of Communism and in a 1983 speech described the USSR as the "evil empire." The same month he announced that America would work to develop a series of space-based systems to take down any Soviet missiles. This Strategic Defense Initiative (SDI) was denounced in Moscow for contravening existing antiballistic missile agreements. Domestically, there was fierce debate as to whether SDI, or "Star Wars" as it came to be known, could ever be successfully deployed. Tensions with the Soviet Union increased when a Soviet fighter shot down Korean Air Lines flight KAL 007 in September 1983 after the plane had strayed into Soviet airspace. The plane's 269 passengers and crew, including 61 Americans, died. The president was quick to characterize the action as a "crime against humanity."

The USSR was itself undergoing internal change. General Secretary Leonid Brezhnev died in November 1982. His successor Yuri Andropov died in early 1984 and was replaced by Konstantin Chernenko. Little more than a year later, reform-minded Mikhail Gorbachev became general secretary of the Communist Party.

In 1982, after Israel invaded Lebanon, Reagan dispatched a small US force to that country, to act as peacekeepers with the warring Christian and Muslim groups there. In April 1983 seventeen Americans were among the sixty-three deaths in a suicide attack on the US Embassy in Beirut, caused by the explosion of a truck bomb. Six months later another truck bomb was detonated, this time at a Marine barracks, killing 241. Three months later US forces were withdrawn. The day after the second Beirut bombing, US troops invaded the strife-torn Caribbean nation of Grenada. In Operation Urgent Fury, American forces secured an airstrip that was being built by Cuban operatives, unseated the Marxist government, and brought back 800 medical students who had fled from the island. Nineteen Americans died in the operation.

In the 1984 election, Reagan faced Jimmy Carter's vice president Walter Mondale, who had defeated Colorado Senator Gary Hart, the early frontrunner, and the Reverend Jesse Jackson to win the Democratic nomination. Mondale selected as his running mate Representative Geraldine Ferraro of New York, making her the first woman to run as part of a presidential ticket. At his party's convention, Mondale asserted that the president would raise taxes in a second term. But he added, "And so will I. He won't tell you. I just did," unwittingly presenting the Reagan campaign with an admission to use against him. Mondale campaigned for a reduction in the huge federal deficit and opposed some of Reagan's expensive defense projects.

Initially, President Reagan appeared vulnerable on account of his age; he would be seventy-three come election day. He performed badly during the first debate with Mondale in Louisville, but rebounded in the second in Kansas City, defusing the age issue by saying, "I will not make age an issue of this campaign. I am not going to exploit, for political purposes, my opponent's youth and inexperience."

Reagan enjoyed a commanding lead in the polls. "It's morning again in America," was the Republican slogan. Reagan did make one blunder, though, that cut into his lead. Talking into what he believed to be a closed microphone, he jokingly insisted that he had just signed legislation to outlaw Russia forever, saying, "We begin bombing in five minutes."

Despite this and a few other gaffes, Ronald Reagan won reelection by a huge margin, capturing 59 percent of the popular vote and all but thirteen electoral college votes, making it the largest-ever landslide victory in US presidential history. Mondale was the victor in only the District of Columbia and his native state of Minnesota. Reagan broke decades-old voting patterns, securing the votes of a quarter of registered Democrats, thus creating a new coalition of "Reagan Democrats" within the Republican Party.

President Reagan's second term was characterized by a number of foreign policy challenges, some self-inflicted. In May 1985 Reagan accepted an invitation from German Chancellor Helmut Kohl to visit, during an economic summit in that country, a cemetery where German World War II veterans were buried. After Reagan went to Bitburg, the media reported that forty-nine members of the Waffen SS, a Nazi organization notorious for its war crimes, were among the buried. The Reagan team quickly added a trip to the Bergen-Belsen concentration camp to the president's itinerary in an attempt to overcome severe criticism from Jewish organizations and US veterans groups.

During its first term, the Reagan administration became involved in a complex scheme, later known as the Iran-contra affair. Reagan had long opposed the Sandinista government in Nicaragua, approving covert funding for anti-Sandinista groups such as the contra rebels as early as 1981. He battled with Congress for more aid, and despite the congressional prohibition of military assistance (the so-called Boland II Amendment), the president eventually approved back-channel assistance in 1984, with this directive transmitted by National Security Adviser Robert McFarlane to Marine Lieutenant Colonel Oliver North. After the CIA head in Beirut, William Buckley, and several other Americans were kidnapped in March of 1984 by pro-Iranian groups in Lebanon, North acted as a liaison to facilitate the sale of missiles and much-needed spare parts to Iran in exchange for the hostages. North then redirected the profits of the sales, almost $4 million in total, to the contra rebels in Nicaragua, who were conducting a guerrilla war against the Sandinista government.

The sale of arms to Iran was exposed first in a Lebanese magazine, and then by the American press in November 1986. President Reagan appointed former Senator John Tower of Texas as head of a commission to investigate the media charges. The Justice Department under Attorney General Edwin Meese and Lawrence E. Walsh, who was selected by Congress as an independent prosecutor, also started their own separate investigations. Reagan summarily fired Oliver North and forced Admiral John Poindexter, who had replaced McFarlane, to resign. The investigations exposed a deeply fractured and mismanaged White House staff.

The questions of exactly how much the president knew, and when he knew it, remained unanswered. Reagan denied authorizing the

General Secretary Mikhail Gorbachev and President Ronald Reagan signing the INF Treaty on December 8, 1987, at the White House.

transfer of money from the Iran arms sales to the contra rebels. In his testimony and questioning at congressional hearings, Admiral Poindexter admitted that he had approved such a plan, and also that he had destroyed any evidence of the president assenting to the sales to Iran. In its official report, the Tower Commission seemed to blame White House Chief of Staff Donald Regan for much of what happened, referring to the "chaos" at the White House. President Reagan, in response, forced him to resign. Walsh's office indicted Poindexter and thirteen others, including McFarlane and North, on criminal charges arising from the affair, but Poindexter's and North's subsequent convictions were eventually overturned as a result of immunity agreements that were made prior to their testimonies. Defense Secretary Caspar Weinberger was charged with perjury for withholding information about the aid to contra rebels from Congress, but he was pardoned in 1992 by the next president, George H. W. Bush, before he could be tried on those charges. The commission also assailed the arms-for-

hostages policy, under which Iran received 2,000 missiles.

In addition to the attacks on American facilities in Beirut in 1983, the Reagan presidency bore witness to a number of other violent international incidents, most terrorist-instigated. A TWA airliner was hijacked between Athens and Rome in June 1985, and US Navy diver Robert Stethem was killed before the nightmare ended for the plane's passengers. Wheelchair-bound American Leon Klinghoffer was murdered by Palestinian hijackers on the *Achille Lauro* cruise ship in October of that same year.

In April 1986 two American soldiers and a Turkish woman died in the bombing of a Berlin discotheque. Intelligence reports linked the attack to Libya, with whom the United States had had tense relations for years. The US government accused Libya of sponsoring terrorism, and in 1981 expelled all Libyan diplomats in America and suspended all trade between the two nations, a condition that persisted until early 1986. Ten days after the Berlin bombing, the United States invoked Article 51 of the UN

Charter, which allowed nations to act in their own self-defense, and launched a major air strike on Tripoli and Benghazi. Libyan leader Colonel Muamar Gaddafi's residence was hit; Gaddafi was unharmed but his adopted daughter was killed.

"General Secretary Gorbachev, if you seek peace, if you seek prosperity for the Soviet Union and Eastern Europe, if you seek liberalization: Come here to this gate! Mr. Gorbachev, open this gate! Mr. Gorbachev, tear down this wall!"

Ronald Reagan, from his world-famous speech delivered at the Brandenburg Gate, Berlin, June 12, 1987

The following two years saw just as much violence. In May 1987 an Iraqi missile hit the US frigate *Stark*, on escort duty in the Persian Gulf, killing thirty-seven sailors onboard. After an Iranian attack on an oil tanker commanded by an American captain, US forces retaliated by destroying several oil platforms in the Gulf. In July 1988 an American ship shot down an Iranian airliner after mistaking it for a fighter plane. Though accidental, the act only exasperated tensions between the United States and Iran. On December 21, 1988, Pan Am Flight 103, a jumbo jet en route to New York, exploded over Lockerbie in southern Scotland. All 259 people on the plane were killed, as well as 11 people on the ground struck by falling debris. In 2001 a former Libyan intelligence agent was convicted of planting a suitcase containing a bomb on the jet.

Perhaps Reagan's most enduring achievement as president was his improvement of US relations with the Soviet Union. Reagan wanted to negotiate a reduction in nuclear weapons with the Kremlin, but to do so from a position of strength. The first of four summits between Reagan and Soviet leader Mikhail Gorbachev was held in Geneva, November 19, 1985. In return for his promise to cut nuclear stockpiles, the Soviet leader wanted Reagan to yield on the further development of the SDI initiative. Reagan and Gorbachev agreed to disagree and also to meet again.

Reagan and Gorbachev soon forged an excellent working relationship, managing to overcome their differences on SDI. In Reykjavik, Iceland, on October 12, 1986, they remained divided on SDI, but within weeks reached agreement on an Intermediate Nuclear Forces Treaty. It cut existing stockpiles of weapons and was officially signed in Washington, DC, on December 8, 1986. Reagan traveled to Moscow and met with Gorbachev three more times after he left office; the two men considered each other friends. Ronald Reagan's policy toward the Soviet Union, a combination of negotiation and pressure, is credited by some with hastening the end of Communism in Europe and terminating the Cold War. In one of the iconic moments of his presidency, Reagan visited the Berlin Wall, calling for its destruction.

When Ronald Reagan left office in January 1989, he had a job approval rating of 63 percent, twelve points higher than it had been when he first became president.

POST-PRESIDENTIAL CAREER

After leaving the White House, Reagan performed some of the customary post-presidential rituals, including writing his autobiography *An American Life* (1991). The Ronald Reagan Presidential Library opened in Simi Valley, California, in November 1991. In addition to Reagan, four other US presidents attended the dedication ceremony: President George H. W. Bush and former presidents Nixon, Ford, and Carter. In May 1992 Reagan presented the first Ronald Reagan Freedom Award to Mikhail Gorbachev. He also spoke at the Republican Convention that same summer.

Reagan's public appearances became fewer, and in early November of 1994, he published a letter announcing that he had Alzheimer's disease. He died on June 5, 2004, at the age of 93 at his home on St. Cloud Drive in Bel Air, California. Tens of thousands of people paid their respects outside the president's estate before his body was flown to Washington, DC, where more than 200,000 mourners filed past his casket in the Capitol Rotunda. After a funeral service at the National Cathedral, Ronald Reagan's body was returned home to California and buried at the Presidential Library in Simi Valley.

"We've done our part. And as I walk off into the city streets, a final word to the men and women of the Reagan revolution, the men and women across America who for eight years did the work that brought America back. My friends: We did it. We weren't just marking time. We made a difference. We made the city stronger. We made the city freer, and we left her in good hands. All in all, not bad, not bad at all."

Ronald Reagan, in his farewell address to the nation, January 11, 1989

The eulogies for Reagan stressed his tremendous likeability and the "great communicator's" skill at presenting his message to the American public. Reagan is credited with improving the nation's self-image in 1981, buoying it at a critical moment in history.

Reagan's palpable success at the polls was shared by a new generation of Republicans who entered Congress in large numbers in the 1980s and 1990s. His ability to work constructively with Republicans and Democrats alike within both divisions of Congress was a significant element behind his effectiveness as a leader. Reagan also named more federal judges than any other president in US history, thus extending the scope of his legacy. At the same time, the nation incurred huge deficits during his two terms of office. Reagan was additionally perceived as lacking social compassion in some quarters: His response to the AIDS crisis was late and insufficient. The notion that poorer Americans would be helped by wealth that "trickled down" from above was also much criticized. Nevertheless, Reagan remains an enormously popular and iconic president.

Birthplace: Tampico, IL
Residency: California
Religion: Baptized in the Disciples of Christ church (Presbyterian)
Education: Eureka College, graduated 1932
Place of Death: Bel-Air, CA
Burial Site: Ronald Reagan Presidential Library, Simi Valley, CA
Dates in Office: January 20, 1981–January 20, 1989 (eight years)
Age at Inauguration: 69 years, 349 days

FAMILY

Father: John Edward "Jack" Reagan (1883–1941)
Mother: Nelle Wilson Reagan (1883–1962)
Siblings: Reagan's only sibling was John Neil Reagan (1909–1996).
Wives: Jane Wyman (1914–), married on January 24, 1940, in Glendale, CA; Nancy Davis (1921–), married on March 4, 1952, in Los Angeles, CA
Children: With Jane Wyman, Maureen Elizabeth Reagan (1941–2001), Michael Edward Reagan (1945–), unnamed child (June 26–27, 1947); with Nancy Davis, Ronald Prescott Reagan (1958–), Patricia Ann Davis (1962–)

CAREER

Private: radio announcer (1932–1937); screen actor (1937–1964); president of Screen Actors Guild (1947–1952, 1959–1960)
Political: governor of California (1967–1974), president of the United States (1981–1989)

Military: Reagan enlisted in the Army Enlisted Reserve on April 29, 1937, and was assigned as a private to the 322nd cavalry at Des Moines, IA; appointed second lieutenant in the Officer Reserve Corps of the cavalry on May 25, 1937, and was later assigned to the 323rd cavalry; ordered to active duty on April 19, 1942 as second lieutenant of cavalry in reserve, but was disqualified from overseas combat due to poor eyesight; assigned to the San Francisco Port of Embarkation at Fort Mason, CA, as liaison officer of the Port and Transportation Office; transferred on June 9, 1942, to the Army Air Forces (AAF) and assigned to the 1st Motion Picture Unit in Culver City, CA; promoted to first lieutenant on January 14, 1943; promoted to captain on July 22, 1943; served temporary duty in New York City in January 1944; assigned to AAF Base Unit in Culver City, CA in November 1944; ordered to Fort MacArthur, CA, on September 8, 1945; discharged from active duty on December 9, 1945.

Selected Works: *An American Life* (New York: Simon & Schuster, 1990); *Dear Americans: Letters from the Desk of Ronald Reagan*, ed. by Ralph E. Weber (New York: Broadway, 2003); *The Greatest Speeches of Ronald Reagan* (Newsmax.com, 2003); *Reagan, In His Own Hand : The Writings of Ronald Reagan That Reveal His Revolutionary Vision for America* (New York: Free Press, 2001); *A Shining City: The Legacy of Ronald Reagan*, ed. by D. Erik Felten (New York: Simon & Schuster, 1998); *Speaking My Mind: Selected Speeches* (New York: Simon & Schuster, 2004); *State of the Union Addresses of Ronald Reagan* (IndyPublish.com, 2005); *Time for Choosing: The Speeches of Ronald Reagan 1961-1982* (Washington, DC: Regnery Publishing, 1983); *Where's the Rest of Me?* (New York: Duell, Sloan & Pearce, 1965)

PRESIDENCY

Nomination: 1980: The Republican Convention was held in Detroit, Michigan, July 14–18, 1980. Reagan received the nomination on the first ballot, capturing 1,939 votes to 37 for John Anderson and 13 for George H. W. Bush. Reagan chose Bush as his vice-presidential running mate.

1984: The Republican Convention was held in Dallas, Texas, August 20–24, 1984. Reagan and Bush were renominated, unopposed.

Election: 1980: elected president on November 4, 1980

1984: elected president on November 6, 1984

Opponents: 1980: Jimmy Carter, GA, Democrat; John B. Anderson, IL, Independent

1984: Walter Mondale, MN, Democrat

Vote Totals: 1980: Reagan, 43,899,248 popular, 489 electoral; Carter, 35,481,435 popular, 49 electoral; Anderson, 5,719,437 popular, 0 electoral.

1984: Reagan, 54,281,858 popular, 525 electoral; Mondale, 37,457,215 popular, 13 electoral.

Inauguration: 1980: January 20, 1981

1984: January 21, 1985

Vice President: George H. W. Bush (1981–1989)

CABINET

Secretary of State: Alexander M. Haig, PA (1981—1982); George P. Shultz, CA (1982–1989)

Secretary of the Treasury: Donald T. Regan, NY (1981–1985); James A. Baker, TX (1985–1988); Nicholas F. Brady, NJ (1988–1989)

Secretary of Defense: Caspar W. Weinberger, CA (1981–1987); Frank C. Carlucci, PA (1987–1989)

Attorney General: William French Smith, CA (1981–1985); Edwin Meese, CA (1985–1988); Richard Thornburgh, PA (1988–1989)

Secretary of Agriculture: John R. Block, IL (1981–1986); Richard E. Lyng, CA (1986–1989)

Secretary of the Interior: James G. Watt, WY (1981–1983); William P. Clark, CA (1983–1985); Donald P. Hodel, OR (1985–1989)

Secretary of Labor: Raymond J. Donovan, NJ (1981–1985); William E. Brock, TN (1985–1987); Anne Dore McLaughlin, District of Columbia (1987–1989)

Secretary of Commerce: Malcolm Baldridge, CT (1981–1987); C. William Verity, Jr., OH (1987–1989)

Secretary of Health and Human Services: Richard S. Schweiker, PA (1981–1983); Margaret M. Heckler, MA (1983–1985); Otis R. Bowen, IN (1985–1989)

Secretary of Housing and Urban Development: Samuel R. Pierce, Jr., NY (1981–1989)

Secretary of Transportation: Andrew Lewis, PA (1981–1983); Elizabeth H. Dole, KS (1983–1987); James H. Burnley, NC (1987–1989)

Secretary of Energy: James B. Edwards, SC (1981–1982); Donald P. Hodel, OR (1982–1985); John S. Herrington, CA (1985–1989)

Secretary of Education: Terrel H. Bell, UT (1981-1985); William J. Bennett, NC (1985-1988); Lauro F. Cavazos, TX (1988-1989)

CONGRESS:

97th Congress (1981–1983); Speaker of the House: Thomas P. O'Neill, Jr. (Democrat, MA)
98th Congress (1983–1985); Speaker of the House: Thomas P. O'Neill, Jr. (Democrat, MA)
99th Congress (1985–1987); Speaker of the House: Thomas P. O'Neill, Jr. (Democrat, MA)
100th Congress (1987–1989); Speaker of the House: James C. Wright, Jr. (Democrat, TX)

SUPREME COURT APPOINTEES

Sandra Day O'Connor, AZ; Associate Justice (1981–)
William H. Rehnquist, VA; Chief Justice (1986–) [Note: Rehnquist was originally named to the Court as an associate justice by President Nixon and served from 1972 to 1986 in that capacity.]
Antonin Scalia, NJ; Associate Justice (1986–)
Anthony M. Kennedy, CA; Associate Justice (1988–)

MAJOR EVENTS OF THE REAGAN ADMINISTRATION

◆ On January 20, 1981, Ronald Reagan is inaugurated as the 40th president of the United States. Minutes after Reagan is sworn in, the American hostages held in Iran are released after 444 days in captivity.

◆ On February 18, 1981, Reagan speaks to a joint session of Congress and describes his "program for economic recovery," including deep cuts in entitlement programs, a 30 percent tax cut, and increased defense spending.

◆ President Reagan and three others are shot by John Hinckley, Jr. outside a hotel in Washington, DC, March 30, 1981.

◆ On April 28, 1981, President Reagan addresses a joint session of Congress, five weeks after the attempt on his life.

◆ On July 29, 1981, Congress passes Reagan's tax bill, but with a 25 rather than 30 percent cut. Reagan signs the bill into law on August 13.

◆ President Reagan dismisses 11,000 striking air traffic controllers, August 5, 1981.

◆ On September 25, 1981, Sandra Day O'Connor, a former Arizona Appeals Court judge, becomes the first woman to be sworn in as a Supreme Court associate justice. She replaces Justice Potter Stewart.

◆ On August 25, 1982, US Marines arrive in Beirut, Lebanon, to begin peacekeeping operations.

◆ November 2, 1982: In the mid-term elections the Democrats pick up twenty-six seats in the House of Representatives. The GOP retains a Senate majority.

◆ President Reagan submits his 1984 budget to both houses of Congress on January 31, 1983. It includes a $189 billion deficit.

◆ On March 8, 1983, addressing the Annual Convention of the National Association of Evangelicals in Orlando, Reagan describes the Soviet Union as an "evil empire."

◆ President Reagan speaks to the nation and outlines the concept for a shield in space: the Strategic Defense Initiative or SDI, also known as "Star Wars," March 23, 1983.

◆ On April 18, 1983, a car bomb explodes at the US embassy in Beirut, killing 63 people.

◆ On April 20, 1983, Congress amends the Social Security Act to keep the retirement program solvent through 2050. The amendment raises the retirement age to 67 by 2027.

◆ A Soviet fighter plane shoots down Korean Airlines flight KAL 007 over Soviet airspace on September 1, 1983. Of the 269 people who perish, 61 are Americans.

◆ On October 23, 1983, a terrorist drives a truck bomb into a US Marines barracks in Lebanon, killing 241 soldiers. Fifty-eight die in a separate attack on a French barracks two miles away.

◆ On October 25, 1983, the United States invades Grenada.

◆ The birthday of fallen civil rights leader Dr. Martin Luther King, Jr., is established as a national holiday on November 2, 1983.

◆ In a May 9, 1984, address President Reagan calls for aid to the contra rebels in Nicaragua. He describes the contra rebels as "freedom fighters."

◆ June 6, 1994, Reagan attends official French ceremonies marking the fortieth anniversary of D-Day in Normandy. In his speech he pays homage to "the boys of Pointe du Hoc," US Rangers who scaled a cliff to take German positions overlooking Omaha Beach.

◆ On July 17, 1984, President Reagan signs legislation at the White House Rose Garden raising the national drinking age to 21.

◆ On August 23, 1984, Reagan accepts renomination at the Republican National Convention in Dallas.

◆ The second televised debate between Reagan and Democratic challenger Walter Mondale is held on October 21. Reagan effectively counters Mondale's strident criticisms by joking about Mondale's "youth and inexperience."

◆ Ronald Reagan is reelected, winning by the largest landslide in US election history, November 6, 1984.

◆ On January 8, 1985, Donald Regan is appointed as White House chief of staff, and Reagan nominates James Baker as Secretary of the Treasury. The two men will swap jobs.

◆ On January 20, 1985, Ronald Reagan is inaugurated for a second term. At 73, he is the oldest president ever sworn in.

◆ President Reagan visits Bitburg Cemetery and Bergen-Belsen concentration camp, May 5, 1985.

◆ On July 13, Reagan undergoes surgery for colon cancer.

◆ On July 25, 1985, Israeli representatives meet with Iranian Foreign Minister Manucher Ghorbanifar to discuss an arms deal that is part of the "arms for hostages" policy.

◆ On August 20, 1985, Israel ships ninety-six TOW antitank missiles to Iran.

◆ President Reagan and Soviet General Secretary Mikhail Gorbachev meet for the first time on November 19, 1985. The two men talk for an hour at the Hotel Fleur D'Eau in Geneva.

◆ On December 7, 1985, then Secretary of Defense Caspar Weinberger, Secretary of State George Shultz, and Chief of Staff Donald Regan advise the president to halt arms sales to Iran.

◆ January 28, 1986, the Space Shuttle *Challenger* explodes seconds after lift-off. Aboard are astronauts Michael Smith, Dick Scobee, Judith Resnik, Ronald McNair, Ellison Onizuka, Gregory Jarvis, and Christa McAuliffe. President Reagan postpones his State of the Union address and speaks to a grieving nation.

◆ A Berlin discotheque is bombed on April 5, 1986, killing two American servicemen and a Turkish woman. Intercepted embassy communications link the bombing with Libya.

◆ On April 15, 1986, US aircraft strike targets in Libya.

◆ The International Court of Justice rules that the United States has violated international law by supporting the contra rebels in Nicaragua, June 27, 1986.

◆ On September 26, 1986, Chief Justice William Rehnquist and Associate Justice Antonin Scalia are sworn in.

◆ At a summit in Reykjavik, Iceland, on October 12, 1986, President Reagan and Soviet leader Mikhail Gorbachev fail to reach an agreement on reducing nuclear stockpiles. Reagan's refusal to halt SDI development remains a sticking point.

◆ After the Iran-contra scandal breaks, the Tower Commission is appointed to investigate it, November 26, 1986.

◆ On December 8, 1986, Reagan and Gorbachev sign the Intermediate Nuclear Forces Treaty. Under its terms, missiles with a range of 300 to 3,400 miles will be destroyed.

◆ On December 19, 1986, Iran-contra Independent Counsel Lawrence E. Walsh is appointed.

◆ On February 26, 1987, the Tower Commission issues its official report, describing its findings pertaining to the Iran-contra scandal.

◆ Donald Regan resigns as chief of staff and is replaced by Howard Baker, February 27, 1987.

◆ The *USS Stark*, a guided missile frigate, is struck by two Exocet missiles fired by an Iraqi fighter jet. Thirty-seven sailors aboard the *Stark* are killed.

◆ In a June 12, 1987, speech at the Brandenburg Gate, in front of the Berlin Wall dividing East and West, Reagan asks Gorbachev to "Tear down this wall."

◆ On July 1, 1987, Judge Robert Bork, a judge on the US Appellate Court for the District of Columbia, is nominated to fill a vacancy on the Supreme Court, replacing Associate Justice Lewis Powell, who has resigned.

◆ On August 11, 1987, Alan Greenspan is sworn in as chairman of the Federal Reserve Board.

◆ On October 6, 1987, the Senate Judiciary Committee rejects Bork's nomination.

◆ On "Black Monday," October 19, 1987, the stock market crashes 508 points. The 23 percent market loss is almost twice that of the Crash of 1929, and sets off a stunning reaction in world markets, coming close to financial panic.

◆ Reagan nominates Douglas Ginsburg of the US Appellate Court for the District of Columbia to the Supreme Court on October 29, 1987.

◆ Ginsburg is forced to withdraw his nomination on November 7, 1987, after it is revealed that he smoked marijuana as a college student in the 1960s and later as a Harvard professor in the 1970s.

◆ US Circuit Court Judge Anthony Kennedy is nominated to the Supreme Court on November 11, 1987.

◆ On December 8, 1987, Reagan and Gorbachev begin a three-day summit in Washington, DC. The two men will sign the Intermediate-Range Nuclear Forces (INF) Treaty in a first attempt to reverse the nuclear arms race.

◆ On January 2, 1987, the Canada-US Free Trade Agreement is signed, reducing trade restrictions in stages over a ten-year period.

◆ Anthony Kennedy is sworn in as associate justice of the Supreme Court on February 18, 1988.

◆ On April 14, 1988, the Soviet Union agrees to withdraw its troops from Afghanistan after negotiations with the United States, Pakistan, and Afghanistan.

◆ US forces strike Iranian oil platforms in the Persian Gulf on April 18, 1988.

◆ On May 11, 1988, President Reagan endorses the candidacy of George H. W. Bush for the Republican presidential nomination.

◆ In the Gulf on July 3, 1988, Iran Air Flight 655 is shot down by the *USS Vincennes*.

◆ On August 15, 1988, Reagan addresses the Republican Party Convention in New Orleans.

◆ On January 11, 1989, President Reagan makes his farewell address to the nation.

◆ On January 20, 1989, George H. W. Bush is sworn in as the 41st president, and Ronald and Nancy Reagan return to California.

MAJOR US AND WORLD EVENTS, 1981–1989

◆ Polish Prime Minister Josef Pinkowski resigns and is replaced by General Wojciech Jaruzelski on February 9, 1981.

◆ The first Space Shuttle, the *Columbia*, is launched from the Kennedy Space Center in Cape Canaveral, Florida, on April 12, 1981.

◆ IRA leader Bobby Sands dies in a Northern Ireland prison on May 5, 1981, after refusing to eat for sixty-six days.

◆ On May 14, 1981, Pope John Paul II is shot and wounded in Vatican City by Turkish citizen Mehmet Ali Agca.

◆ On June 7, 1981, Israeli jets destroy the Osiriq nuclear reactor near Baghdad, Iraq.

◆ In a lavish ceremony televised around the globe, Charles, Prince of Wales, and Lady Diana Spencer exchange their wedding vows at St. Paul's Cathedral in London, July 29, 1981.

◆ Egyptian President Anwar Sadat is assassinated on October 6, 1981. Hosni Mubarak replaces him.

◆ On December 31, 1981, General Jaruzelski declares martial law in Poland.

◆ John Updike publishes *Rabbit Is Rich*, 1981.

◆ Tracy Kidder publishes *The Soul of a New Machine*, 1981.

◆ Martin Cruz Smith publishes *Gorky Park*, 1981.

◆ Television series debuting in 1981 include *Dynasty*, *Hill Street Blues*, *The Fall Guy*, and *Gimme a Break*.

◆ Popular music hits of 1981 include Kim Carnes's "Bette Davis Eyes," Rick Springfield's "Jesse's Girl," the Police's "Don't Stand So Close to Me," and Pat Benetar's "Fire and Ice."

◆ Notable films of 1981 include *On Golden Pond* with Henry Fonda and Katharine Hepburn, Warren Beatty's *Reds*, Steven Spielberg's *Raiders of the Lost Ark* with Harrison Ford, and *Atlantic City* with Susan Sarandon and Burt Lancaster.

◆ On April 2, 1982, Argentina invades the British-held Falkland Islands in the South Atlantic.

◆ Israeli forces enter Lebanon, June 6, 1982.

◆ On June 14, 1982, Argentina surrenders to Great Britain, bringing an end to the Falkland Islands War.

◆ US Marines join UN peacekeeping forces in Lebanon on August 25, 1982.

◆ On September 15, 1982, Princess Grace of Monaco (former Hollywood star Grace Kelly) dies from injuries sustained in a car accident along the coast of the Riviera.

◆ A Lebanese Christian militia enters the Sabra and Shatila refugee camps in West Beirut on September 16, 1982. Over the next few days, hundreds of Palestinians are massacred.

◆ Helmut Kohl replaces Helmut Schmidt as chancellor of West Germany on October 1, 1982.

◆ On October 7, 1982, Andrew Lloyd Webber's *Cats* opens at the Winter Garden Theater on Broadway. It plays for 18 years, with a record 7,485 performances.

◆ October 8, 1982, Poland outlaws Solidarity, the country's labor union.

◆ Leonid Brezhnev, general secretary of the Russian Communist Party, dies on November 10, 1982. He is replaced by Yuri Andropov.

◆ On November 12, 1982, Solidarity leader Lech Walesa is released by the Polish government after eleven months of imprisonment.

◆ Dr. Robert Jarvik implants an artificial heart in Barney Clark, 61, on December 2, 1982, in Seattle, WA. Clark survives for 112 days.

◆ Alice Walker publishes *The Color Purple*, 1982..

◆ Russell Baker publishes *Growing Up*, 1982.

◆ David McCullough publishes *Mornings on Horseback*, 1982.

◆ Television series debuting in 1982 include *Family Ties*, *Silver Spoons*, *Knight Rider*, *Square Pegs*, and *Cheers*.

◆ Popular music hits of 1982 include Toto's "Rosanna," John Cougar's "Hurts So Good," Survivor's "Eye of the Tiger," and Marvin Gaye's "Sexual Healing."

◆ Notable films of 1982 include *Gandhi* with Ben Kingsley, Steven Spielberg's *ET*, Sidney Pollack's *Tootsie* with Dustin Hoffman, and *Missing* with Jack Lemmon and Sissy Spacek.

◆ On January 19, 1983, Nazi war criminal Klaus Barbie (the "Butcher of Lyons") is arrested in Bolivia.

◆ Ariel Sharon, the defense minister of Israel, resigns on February 8, 1983, after an official inquiry finds that he did not act to prevent the Palestinian refugee camp massacres.

◆ The final episode of the popular television series *M.A.S.H.* airs on February 28, 1983. Approximately 106 million Americans watch, the largest audience of television viewers ever.

◆ On March 3, 1983, CIA station chief William Buckley is kidnapped in Lebanon. Buckley dies in captivity on June 3, 1985.

◆ Martial law is terminated in Poland on July 22, 1983.

◆ On August 21, 1983, Filipino opposition leader Benigno Aquino is killed moments after returning home to run in the upcoming national elections.

◆ On October 19, 1983, Maurice Bishop, prime minister of Grenada, is killed in a military coup staged by Communist Bernard Coard.

◆ William Kennedy publishes *Ironweed*, 1983.

◆ Umberto Eco publishes *The Name of the Rose*, 1983.

◆ Television series debuting in 1983 include *Mama's Family*, *The A-Team*, *Fraggle Rock*, and *Webster*.

◆ Popular music hits of 1983 include Michael Jackson's "Beat It," the Police's "Every Breath You Take," and Irene Cara's "Flashdance: What a Feeling."

◆ Notable films of 1983 include *The Big Chill*, *Terms of Endearment* with Shirley MacLaine and Jack Nicholson, *The Right Stuff*, *Tender Mercies* with Robert Duvall, and *Silkwood* with Meryl Streep.

◆ On February 9, 1984, Soviet leader Yuri Andropov dies of kidney failure; Konstantin Chernenko replaces him.

◆ The USSR announces that it will boycott the 1984 Summer Olympic Games to be held in Los Angeles, July 28–August 12, 1984. Fourteen Soviet bloc countries boycott, although Romania attends.

◆ On September 26, 1984, the United Kingdom agrees to return the colony of Hong Kong to the People's Republic of China in 1997.

◆ On October 31, 1984, amid growing civil unrest and the Indian government's repressive attempts to control it, Prime Minister Indira Gandhi is assassinated by two of her bodyguards.

◆ On December 3, 1984, clouds of methyl isocyanate gas escape from the Union Carbide plant in Bhopal, India. An estimated 3,000 people die that night, although unofficial reports place the death toll much higher.

◆ Alison Lurie publishes *Foreign Affairs*, 1984.

◆ Gore Vidal publishes *Lincoln: A Novel*, 1984.

◆ Lee Iacocca, with William Novak, publishes *Iacocca: An Autobiography*, 1984.

◆ Studs Terkel publishes *The Good War: An Oral History of World War Two*, 1984.

◆ Television series debuting in 1984 include *Night Court*, *Punky Brewster*, *Highway to Heaven*, and *The Cosby Show*.

◆ Popular music hits of 1984 include Tina Turner's "What's Love Got to Do with It," Prince's "I Feel for You," and Bruce Springsteen's "Dancing in the Dark."

◆ Notable films of 1984 include Milos Forman's *Amadeus*, Roland Joffe's *The Killing Fields*, David Lean's *A Passage to India* with Judy Davis, and *Places in the Heart* with Sally Field.

◆ On January 5, 1985, Israel ends its airlift of Ethiopian refugees.

◆ On March 10, 1985, Soviet leader Konstantin Chernenko, aged 73, dies.

◆ March 11, 1985, Mikhail Gorbachev becomes Soviet General Secretary.

◆ On June 14, 1985, hijackers commandeer TWA Flight 847 from Athens and force the pilot to fly to Beirut, where Navy diver Robert Dean Stethem is killed and his body thrown onto the airport tarmac. Most of the original 153 passengers are freed. Sixteen days later, the remaining 39 hostages are released.

◆ The Greenpeace flagship *Rainbow Warrior* explodes in Auckland Harbor, New Zealand, on July 10, 1985, as it prepares to protest French nuclear testing in the South Pacific. Portuguese photographer Fernando Pereira is killed. Two French government agents are later convicted of the bombing.

◆ July 13, 1985, Live Aid concerts in London and Philadelphia raise millions of dollars for famine relief in Africa.

◆ On September 4, 1985, an expedition led by Dr. Robert Ballard takes the first film footage of the wreck of the *Titanic*. The skeletal remains of the White Star Line's luxury liner (whose builders had once claimed she was "unsinkable") rest at the bottom of the North Atlantic.

◆ A chartered DC-8 carrying 248 members of the 101st Airborne returning from peacekeeping operations in the Middle East, and a crew of 8, crashes on take-off from Gander, Newfoundland, on December 12, 1985.

◆ Don DeLillo publishes *White Noise*, 1985.

◆ E. L. Doctorow publishes *World's Fair*, 1985.

◆ Larry McMurtry publishes *Lonesome Dove*, 1985.

◆ J. Anthony Lukas publishes *Common Ground: A Turbulent Decade in the Lives of Three American Families*, 1985.

◆ Television series debuting in 1985 include *Moonlighting*, *Mr. Belvedere*, *Growing Pains*, and *The Golden Girls*.

◆ Popular music hits of 1985 include "We Are the World," a group performance by various notable artists including Michael Jackson and Lionel Ritchie, Dire Straits's "Money for Nothing," and Whitney Houston's "Saving All My Love for You."

◆ Notable films of 1985 include Steven Spielberg's *The Color Purple* with Whoopi Goldberg, *Kiss of the Spider Woman* with William Hurt, *Out of Africa* with Meryl Streep and Robert Redford, and Peter Weir's *Witness* with Harrison Ford.

◆ On February 28, 1986, Swedish Prime Minister Olof Palme is assassinated and his wife shot upon leaving a cinema in Stockholm.

◆ On February 28, 1986, Corazon Aquino (widow of Benigno Aquino) becomes prime minister of the Philippines.

◆ The world's worst nuclear disaster, an accident, occurs at the Chernobyl power plant in Ukraine, April 25, 1986. Approximately thirty people are killed instantly and radioactive material spills into the atmosphere.

◆ Peter Taylor publishes *A Summons to Memphis*, 1986.

◆ Barry Lopez publishes *Arctic Dreams*, 1986.

◆ Bill Cosby publishes *Fatherhood*, 1986.

◆ Television series debuting in 1986 include *L. A. Law*, *Matlock*, *Designing Women*, and *Alf*.

◆ Popular music hits of 1986 include Steve Winwood's "Higher Love," Robert Palmer's "Addicted to Love," Prince and the Revolution's "Kiss," and the Eurythmics' "Missionary Man."

◆ Notable films of 1986 include *Children of a Lesser God* with Marlee Matlin and William Hurt, Woody Allen's *Hannah and Her Sisters* with Mia Farrow and Michael Caine, Oliver Stone's *Platoon*, and David Lynch's *Blue Velvet*.

◆ On July 3, 1987, ex-Gestapo chief Klaus Barbie is sentenced to life imprisonment in Lyons, France, for ordering the deportation of thousands of Jews to concentration camps during World War II.

◆ On August 17, 1987, Hitler deputy Rudolf Hess, who had been held at Spandau Prison in Berlin since 1946, is found dead at age 93. Hess had crash-landed in Great Britain toward the war's end, hoping to negotiate peace terms with the Allies.

◆ Lynne Cox swims the Bering Straight between the USSR and the United State on August 7, 1987.

◆ On November 11, 1987, Vincent Van Gogh's *Irises* is sold for $54 million (including commission) at Sotheby's in New York City.

◆ Saul Bellow publishes *More Die of Heartbreak*, 1987.

◆ Toni Morrison publishes *Beloved*, 1987.

◆ Richard Rhodes publishes *The Making of the Atom Bomb*, 1987.

◆ Scott Turow publishes *Presumed Innocent*, 1987.

◆ Donald J. Trump publishes *Trump: The Art of the Deal*, 1987.

◆ Bob Woodward publishes *Veil: The Secret Wars of the CIA, 1981–1987*, 1987.

◆ Television series debuting in 1987 include *Full House*, *Married...with Children*, *A Different World*, and *Star Trek: The Next Generation*.

◆ Claude-Michel Schönberg and Alain Boublil's adaptation of Victor Hugo's *Les Misérables* debuts on Broadway, 1987.

◆ Popular music hits of 1987 include Paul Simon's "Graceland," Whitney Houston's "I Wanna Dance with Somebody," Bill Medley and Jennifer Warnes's "The Time of My Life," and Jody Watley's "Looking for a New Love."

◆ Notable films of 1987 include Bernardo Bertolucci's *The Last Emperor*, Norman Jewison's *Moonstruck* with Cher, *Fatal Attraction* with Glenn Close and Michael Douglas, and *Broadcast News* with Albert Brooks and Holly Hunter.

◆ February 21, 1988, TV evangelist Jimmy Swaggart is forced to resign from his ministry after a sex scandal involving him hits the tabloids. Swaggart publicly begs for forgiveness.

◆ On March 16, 1988, an Iraqi poison gas attack on the Kurdish city of Halabja kills thousands.

◆ On September 27, 1988, Canadian sprinter Ben Johnson is stripped of the gold medal he won for the 100 meters at the Seoul Olympics when he tests positive for anabolic steroids.

◆ In the first Space Shuttle launch since the *Challenger* disaster, the *Discovery* lifts off from Cape Canaveral, September 29, 1988.

◆ On December 21, 1988, Pan Am Flight 103 explodes over the town of Lockerbie in Scotland. All 259 passengers on the plane are killed, along with 11 people on the ground. Two members of Libyan intelligence are later charged with planting explosives on the jet; one is convicted.

◆ Pete Dexter publishes *Paris Trout*, 1988.

◆ Neil Sheehan publishes *A Bright Shining Lie*, 1988.

◆ Stephen W. Hawking publishes *A Brief History of Time*, 1988.

◆ Television series debuting in 1988 include *The Wonder Years*, *Empty Nest*, *Roseanne*, and *Murphy Brown*.

◆ Andrew Lloyd Webber's *The Phantom of the Opera* debuts on Broadway, 1988.

◆ Popular music hits of 1988 include Bobby McFerrin's "Don't Worry Be Happy," George Michael's "Faith," Robert Palmer's "Simply Irresistible," and Tracy Chapman's "Fast Car."

◆ Notable films of 1988 include *Dangerous Liaisons* with Glenn Close, Barry Levinson's *Rain Man* with Dustin Hoffman and Tom Cruise, Alan Parker's *Mississippi Burning* with Gene Hackman and Willem Dafoe, and *The Accidental Tourist* with William Hurt.

FAST FACTS ABOUT RONALD REAGAN

◆ Ronald Reagan never won an Academy Award, but he did receive a Golden Globe Award for his performance in *Hollywood Citizenship*, 1957.

◆ Reagan was the first divorced man to become president.

◆ At the time of his first inauguration, Reagan was 69 years and 349 days, making him the oldest president to hold office.

◆ As the former president of the Screen Actor's Guild, Reagan was the first president to have been the head of a union.

◆ Ronald Reagan was the only president wounded during an assassination attempt who survived the ordeal.

◆ Reagan was such a fan of jelly bean candies that the Jelly Belly company created a blueberry flavor in honor of his 1981 inauguration; the president ordered three tons of its jelly beans for the occasion.

◆ On June 8, 1982, President Reagan became the first American president to address both Houses of Parliament in London.

George Herbert Walker Bush

Nickname: Poppy
Party: Republican
Presidency: 41st president, 1989–1993
Life dates: June 12, 1924–

EARLY LIFE AND EDUCATION

George Herbert Walker Bush was born on June 12, 1924, in Milton, Massachusetts. He was the second child of Prescott Bush and Dorothy Walker Bush; his older brother, Prescott, was born in 1922. The couple had married in Kennebunkport, Maine, in 1921 and moved to Massachusetts shortly thereafter.

When George was an infant, the Bush family moved from Massachusetts to Greenwich, Connecticut. Prescott Bush worked for Brown Brothers, Harriman, a prosperous investment firm in Manhattan, to which he commuted daily. He later became US Senator from Connecticut in 1952, an accomplishment that would help pave the way for the ensuing political careers of George and his own sons. George attended the Greenwich Country Day School until ninth grade. At school, he was an average student, but excelled at sports, especially baseball, and played on many sports teams. Growing up, George spent summers sailing and fishing at his maternal grandfather's compound at Walker's Point, Kennebunkport.

In 1936 Bush entered Phillips Academy, a prep school in Andover, Massachusetts. George entered the school a year early so he could be in the same class as his brother Prescott. However, he ended up repeating his junior year after developing a serious arm infection. He was president of his senior class, captain of the baseball and soccer teams, and also played basketball.

George was introduced to sixteen-year-old Barbara Pierce at a Christmas dance at a country club in Greenwich during his senior year at Andover, 1941. Barbara Pierce was born in Rye, New York, on June 8, 1925. She was a student at fashionable Ashley Hall prep school in South Carolina at the time of the couple's meeting and went on to attend Smith College. A descendent of former US President Franklin Pierce, Barbara Pierce's father Marvin served as a vice president of McCall's Publishing Company.

George Bush had been accepted at Yale University, but after the Japanese attack on Pearl Harbor and US entry into World War II, he decided to defer his college education and join the navy. George enlisted the day he graduated from Andover, on his eighteenth birthday—June 12, 1942. After preflight training in Chapel Hill, North Carolina, he received further flight instruction in Minneapolis; Corpus Christi, Texas; and Charlestown, Rhode Island. After bomber and aerial photography training, George was granted his wings and promoted to ensign, making him the youngest pilot in the Navy at that time.

MILITARY CAREER
After additional training piloting the Grumman *Avenger* torpedo bomber, Bush was assigned to the aircraft carrier *San Jacinto* in the Pacific Ocean. During his service in the Pacific campaign he participated in significant combat operations, flying missions against Japanese positions on Saipan, Guam, Iwo Jima, and Chichi Jima. On September 2, 1944, Bush's plane was hit by antiaircraft fire over Chichi Jima in the Bonin Islands. He continued toward the target, dropped his bombs, and ordered his crew to bail out over the ocean. Both his crewmates were killed, but Bush was rescued from sea by the submarine *USS Finback* that happened to be in the area. He spent a month onboard the *Finback* as it continued its own search-and-destroy mission against Japanese shipping vessels.

> "A government that remembers that the people are its master is a good and needed thing."
>
> George H. W. Bush, in his acceptance speech at the Republican National Convention, New Orleans, August 18, 1988

While home on leave, Lieutenant George Bush, then 20, married 19-year-old Barbara Pierce on January 6, 1945, at the First Presbyterian Church in Rye. Although he had accrued enough service to be discharged from the Navy, Bush chose to return to the Pacific. However, before he could return, the war against Japan ended, and Bush was discharged from the Navy on September 18, 1945. He had flown 58 missions totaling 1,228 hours of combat time. For the bravery he showed in the mission over Chichi Jima, he earned the Distinguished Flying Cross.

COLLEGE AND EARLY CAREER
Bush entered Yale in November 1945, a member of a class of 8,000, with college enrollment in general having greatly increased by returning servicemen on the GI Bill. He studied economics and sociology in an accelerated two-year program, and played first base on the university's baseball team, which reached the College World Series two years in a row (1947 and 1948). Bush was also on the school's soccer team that won the New England Collegiate championship. His father was a Yale alumnus, and like Prescott, George Bush was a member of the secret Skull and Bones Society and the Delta Kappa Epsilon fraternity, and was also elected to Phi Beta Kappa. During his sophomore year, Barbara gave birth to their first son, George, on July 6, 1946.

In 1948, Bush graduated from Yale. Through his father and grandfather, he had numerous contacts at prominent banking firms in New York, but decided to follow a different course, opting for a career in the oil industry. Prescott Bush had been a board member of Dresser Industries and its president, Neil Mallon, agreed to take on the young Bush as a trainee.

Despite Barbara's unease with this decision, she and George, along with their young son, moved to the town of Odessa in west Texas. Bush first worked at the International Derrick and Equipment Company (Ideco), earning $375 a month doing a variety of trainee's jobs like painting pumps and keeping inventory. He then moved to Pacific Pumps, a subsidiary of Dresser Industries, in Huntington Park, California, where he worked in a factory and joined the United Steelworkers Union. Bush also sold drilling equipment throughout southern California, relocating his family to towns like Whittier, Ventura, and Compton.

While in Midland, Texas, Bush resigned from Dresser in 1950, and with money secured from his uncle G. Herbert Walker, Jr., established the Bush-Overbey Oil Development Company with his friend John Overbey. In 1953, Bush-Overbey merged with another company to form Zapata Petroleum, with Bush named as a vice president. Zapata struck oil in a number of wells and eventually established a subsidiary, Zapata Off-Shore. In 1959 Bush bought out his partners in Zapata Off-Shore and moved the business to Houston. Under Bush's leadership, the company thrived, building numerous drilling platforms.

Over the course of these years, George and Barbara had five more children: Pauline Robinson, known as Robin (1949), John Ellis, known as "Jeb" (1953), Neil (1955), Marvin (1956), and Dorothy Walker (1959). Shortly after Jeb was born, Robin was diagnosed with leukemia. She was treated at New York's prestigious Sloan-Kettering Hospital but died in 1954. Thereafter, Bush carried with him a medal inscribed "for the love of Robin."

POLITICAL CAREER

In Houston George Bush began cultivating local political contacts to help firmly establish his business. In the early 1960s Texas politics were dominated by conservative Democrats. One Democrat Bush became close to was James A. Baker III, a lawyer at a prominent firm and later a Bush White House appointee. Bush campaigned for Republican candidates and became chair of the Harris County Republican Party. He was a delegate for Barry Goldwater at the 1964 Republican Convention, and that same year ran for the US Senate, facing Democrat Ralph Yarborough. Bush adopted a conservative platform designed to appeal to Goldwater supporters (speaking against the 1964 Civil Rights Act, for example). Yarborough was swept into office on the coattails of Lyndon B. Johnson, who was elected president by a huge margin; Yarborough defeated Bush by a decisive 57 to 43 percent.

In 1966 Bush sold his interests in Zapata Off-Shore and directed his full attention toward politics. In November he ran for Congress in Texas's new Seventh District in Houston. After campaigning with a more moderate platform, Bush was elected, capturing 56 percent of the vote over local District Attorney Frank Briscoe. Bush was reelected in 1968, running unopposed. When Bush served in the House of Representatives, Democrats held the majority in both branches of Congress. As a freshman rep-

resentative, Bush managed to secure a seat on the influential House Ways and Means Committee. He supported the Vietnam War, but voted for some parts of Johnson's Great Society program including the Civil Rights Act in 1968. Back home Bush met with angry constituents and told them black soldiers returning from Vietnam deserved equal treatment in housing. "I voted from conviction," Bush said, "a feeling deep in my heart that this was the right thing for me to do."

Bush submitted his name for the vice-presidential nomination in 1968. He made the short list, but was ultimately told by Richard Nixon that, as a one-term congressman, he was too inexperienced. George Bush, in fact, had a very close relationship with President Johnson, and sought that chief executive's counsel about staying in the House or risking another run for the Senate. Johnson, who had made a name for himself in the Senate, advised Bush to try his luck there again. In 1970, with the hope of adding more Republicans to the Senate, then President Nixon asked Bush to run against Yarborough, who had earlier defeated Bush. However, Yarborough, a staunch supporter of liberal policies, was unexpectedly defeated in the Democratic primary by the more conservative Lloyd Bentsen, who went on to defeat Bush in the general election.

Because Bush had relinquished a safe House seat to oppose Yarborough, Nixon promised him an important position within the White House if he lost the election. On December 11, 1970, Bush was named US Ambassador to the United Nations. Bush's tenure at the United Nations was marked by one difficult scenario, whereby he attempted to secure representation for both the People's Republic of China and Taiwan, while Nixon was secretly preparing to visit Beijing, a move that later prompted Taiwan to give up its UN seat and led to American recognition of the Communist nation.

After he was reelected in 1972, Nixon offered Bush the chairmanship of the Republican National Committee. During the Watergate crisis in this capacity, Bush was vocal in his support of the president, touring the country giving speeches and holding press conferences to rally public approval. But when the existence of White House tapes recording conversations between Nixon and his advisors became known (which clearly demonstrated the White House's attempts to conceal its connection to the break-in and subsequent cover-up), Bush was among the first to face just how damaging these revelations were to the presidency and the Republican Party. On August 7, 1974, Bush wrote Nixon a letter clarifying that the president could no longer expect his party's support in any impeachment proceeding in Congress, and Nixon soon tendered his historic resignation.

In the 1974 presidential campaign George Bush again had his sights set on the vice presidency. He was a leading candidate, but President Gerald R. Ford selected the more liberal Governor Nelson Rockefeller of New York instead, in hopes of broadening his electoral appeal. Ford offered Bush ambassadorships to Great Britain or France. Bush asked for China, and he was consequently named as Chief of the US Liaison Office in the People's Republic of China. (Bush did not receive the formal title of ambassador because the United States and China had not yet established full diplomatic ties.)

In late 1975 President Ford needed to replace the outgoing head of the Central Intelligence Agency (CIA), William Colby. The CIA had recently come under fire for various abuses of power, including its involvement in the Watergate cover-up scandal. Bush was Ford's second choice. After Edward Bennett Williams turned down the appointment, Bush was offered the position. Bush feared that accepting this role would mean the end of his political future, but he also strongly believed that it was his duty to the president and to his country to accept it.

In January 1976 Bush was confirmed as director of the CIA. One of the conditions Senate Democrats attached to Bush's appointment was that Ford not select him as a running mate in the 1976 election, in order to avoid any political conflicts of interest. Bush scrupulously maintained political neutrality while he headed the CIA. He did not attend the 1976 Republican

National Convention, for example. Bush also worked to overhaul the agency's administration, secure the funding for espionage technology, and improve its communication and sharing of information with allied agencies. His successful tenure was cut short, however, when incoming Democratic President Jimmy Carter chose to replace him with Stansfield Turner.

"My Dad inculcated into his sons a set of values that have served me well in my own short public life. One of these values quite simply is that one should serve his country and his President. And so if that is what the president wants me to do, the answer is a firm 'Yes.'"

George H. W. Bush, remarks made to Henry Kissinger, November, 1975

George Bush returned to private life in Houston, Texas. He joined the boards of several banks in Houston and was a member of the executive committee of the First International Bank. Bush was eager to return to politics, though, and in May 1979 he announced that he would seek the Republican nomination for the presidency in 1980.

Bush managed to defeat Ronald Reagan by 2,182 votes in the Iowa caucus, but was defeated badly by the former California governor in the New Hampshire primary. He rebounded to win the Republican primaries in Michigan and Pennsylvania; however, he soon ran short of money and pulled out of the race on Memorial Day. Reagan's first choice as a running mate was former President Ford. Many in the Reagan camp opposed the choice of Bush as a vice-presidential candidate, particularly due to Bush's strident attacks on Reagan's proposed economic policies (which Bush had characterized as "voodoo economics" on the campaign trail) to undercut his credentials. Nevertheless, when Ford and Reagan failed to agree on the terms of Ford's inclusion on the ticket, Bush became the obvious second choice. When Reagan decisively defeated Jimmy Carter, George H. W. Bush became the nation's vice president.

Despite their earlier rivalry for the presidential nomination, Reagan and Bush established a productive relationship as president and vice president. Bush generally maintained a low profile, and when Reagan was shot and nearly killed on March 30, 1981, Bush remained calm in a potentially chaotic situation. When he arrived at the White House after the shooting, he refused to arrive by helicopter, insisting that this was the president's privilege. Nor, during Reagan's two-week hospitalization, would he work out of the Oval Office or sit in the president's chair at cabinet meetings.

As vice president, George Bush visited the fifty states of the union and some sixty-five countries. He represented the United States at the Moscow funerals of Leonid Brezhnev and Yuri Andropov. He toured Europe to rally support for the deployment of Pershing II missiles and visited Beirut to witness the aftermath of the truck bombing of US Marines barracks. In July 1985 President Reagan underwent surgery for the removal of a cancerous polyp. Without the 25th Amendment's transfer of power having been invoked, Bush served as de facto president for a number of hours.

In 1984 the Reagan–Bush ticket was re-elected in a landslide election, handily defeating Walter Mondale and his running mate, Geraldine Ferraro. Bush was the center of attention when he debated Ferraro, but he gave an uncharacteristically impolite performance and Ferraro accused him of being patronizing.

Much of Reagan's second term was preoccupied by the Iran-contra scandal and the congressional committee hearings that followed; however, both Reagan and Bush emerged from the situation relatively unscathed. The president and vice president both claimed to have been unaware of the details of the affair, and there

was no evidence found to link either of them to any crime.

On October 13, 1987, at the Hyatt Regency Hotel in Houston, George Bush announced his candidacy for the presidential nomination. Early on, Bush's campaign seemed to falter; he finished third behind Senator Robert Dole of Kansas and the Reverend Pat Robertson in the Iowa caucuses. Prompted by campaign strategists Lee Atwater and Roger Ailes, Bush went on the offensive to counteract the perception that he was a "wimp." He charged that Dole would raise taxes and the senator's voting record rendered him "Senator Straddle." Bush's opponents soon fell by the wayside, and by the time the Republican Convention transpired in New Orleans in August 1988, Bush was unopposed. He caused a stir within party ranks, and in general, when he chose the junior senator from Indiana, James Danforth ("Dan") Quayle, as his running mate.

"The Congress will push me to raise taxes, and I'll say no, and they'll push, and I'll say no, and they'll push again. And all I can say to them is: read my lips. No new taxes."

George H. W. Bush, in his acceptance speech at the Republican National Convention, August 18, 1988

Quayle was a graduate of DePauw University and Indiana University law school. He had worked at a local newspaper owned by his father before he ran for the House in 1976. In 1980 he was elected to the Senate. Quayle had a modest record in Congress. He sponsored only one major piece of legislation. But his youth complemented Bush's experience, and he had a strong following in the Midwest where Bush was vulnerable.

Bush's opponent was Governor Michael

Dukakis of Massachusetts. Bush waged a highly negative campaign against Dukakis, relentlessly attacking him for his membership in the American Civil Liberties Union (ACLU) and for having vetoed a Massachusetts bill in 1977 that called for teachers to lead classes in the recital of the Pledge of Allegiance. The Bush campaign seized on the 1987 case of Willie Horton who, while on furlough from a Massachusetts prison where he was serving a sentence for murder, assaulted a couple in Maryland. Ads for Bush criticized Dukasis's "revolving-door" prison policy, and Bush referred to the Horton case in speeches along the campaign trail. One of the few dents the Democrats were able to make in the Bush campaign occurred during the vice-presidential debate, when Dukakis's running mate, Lloyd Bentsen, scored heavily against an inarticulate Dan Quayle.

Bush won the election comfortably, taking 54 percent of the popular vote to Dukakis's 46 percent, and 426 electoral votes to 111. The voter turnout that election year was the lowest since 1924.

PRESIDENCY

George H. W. Bush was inaugurated on January 20, 1989. Both Houses of Congress were controlled by the Democrats, which meant that many measures promoted by the president passed only after compromises were reached with congressional leaders. Bush also vetoed a lot of measures: thirty-five by late 1992. The president suffered a major setback when almost the full Senate rejected his nominee for Secretary of Defense, John Tower, in March 1989, the first such action against a cabinet appointee since 1959.

Under George Bush, inflation settled to 3 percent and interest rates fell, but unemployment and the number of Americans on the welfare rolls increased. The budget deficit also skyrocketed, forcing Bush to introduce a deficit reduction package. By June 1990 the president publicly acknowledged that he would have to go back on his campaign pledge and increase taxes. The House rejected an initial compromise, with many Republicans voting against the increase. A compromise for the 1991 fiscal year was finally reached at the very end of the 101st Congress. Taxes were raised on consumer goods like gas and cigarettes as well as a number of luxury items. Some higher-rate exemptions were also eliminated, but the capital gains tax was not reduced, as many Republicans had hoped for.

Bush was faced with a crisis in the savings and loans (S&L) industry when hundreds of such institutions became insolvent. In 1989 he signed into law a measure to bail them out. The first package provided for about $150 billion, most of it public money. New regulations were then introduced to cover them. Over time, the administration conceded that the eventual cost of the bail-out would be much higher than initially calculated.

The economy remained sluggish, and unemployment grew worse. Bush traveled through Southeast Asia, hoping to encourage trade. Toward the end of his presidency, Bush, Mexican President Carlos Salinas, and Canadian Prime Minister Brian Mulroney signed the North American Free Trade Agreement (NAFTA). According to its terms, the three countries formed a single market of 400 million people; it was formally approved and signed into law by President Bill Clinton. Bush also introduced a stimulus package in 1992, cutting the capital gains tax, decreasing regulations, and slashing federal programs, but vetoed the final bill because it raised taxes. One other domestic accomplishment of the Bush presidency was the Clean Air Act of 1990, which sought to reduce pollution by expanding regulations to control industrial pollutants, in addition to requiring most cities to meet smog reduction regulations by 2005. In 1990 the Immigration Act was passed; it increased the cap on the number of immigrants to 675,000 per year and encouraged the admission of those with job skills and financial resources as well as family ties in the United States. Bush also approved the wide-ranging Americans with Disabilities Act (ADA) in 1990.

During his term of office, George Bush filled two vacancies on the Supreme Court. David H. Souter of New Hampshire was confirmed to replace William Brennan without controversy. But the nomination of Clarence Thomas to replace Thurgood Marshall became one of the most charged episodes of the Bush presidency. Thomas was confirmed 52–48 by the Senate, barely surviving charges of sexual harassment made by a former staff member, Anita Hill, by then a professor at the University of Oklahoma, in televised proceedings.

To American foreign policy Bush brought his prior experience as a diplomat, UN ambassador, and vice president. He quickly reversed the widely discredited Reagan policy of attempting to overthrow the Sandinista government in Nicaragua. Congress approved an extension in nonmilitary aid to the Contras. Without the use of military force or violence, Violeta Chamorra led a broad coalition and defeated the Sandinistas in the February 1990 elections. Bush then lifted American economic sanctions against the country.

During this same time period American forces staged an invasion in Central America—Operation Just Cause—against Panamanian leader General Manuel Antonio Noriega. Noriega, a one-time US intelligence asset, had for years engaged in drug trafficking, charges for which he was indicted by a Florida grand jury in 1988. Noriega ignored the results of the national election held in Panama in 1989 as it would have displaced him. US forces intervened after a Marine lieutenant was killed and another tortured by Noriega supporters. As part of the attack, initiated on December 20, 1989, the 82nd Airborne made its first combat parachute jump since World War II. The United States's action was criticized abroad, and the UN General Assembly condemned the invasion in a vote of 75 to 20, with 40 abstentions. Noriega was finally captured on January 3, 1990. In 1992, found guilty of the drug trafficking and racketeering charges against him, he was sentenced to forty years in a Miami prison. Twenty-three American troops died in the Panamanian operation. Counts for the civilian casualties vary widely, from 300 to more than 4,000, as estimated by former Attorney General and peace activist Ramsey Clark.

George Bush had spent a year as US envoy in China during the Ford presidency, and personally knew the leaders who ordered troops to quell student-led public demonstrations in Beijing's historic Tiananmen Square in June 1989. The image of a single protester standing defiantly in front of an advancing column of tanks defined the event. President Bush spoke out against the Communist government's use of excessive force, and urged China to improve its human rights record.

Bush continued the Reagan policy of détente with the Soviet Union. In January 1990 Bush and Mikhail Gorbachev met in Washington, DC, and each agreed to reduce his country's nuclear stockpile. Subsequently, at a November 1990 meeting in Paris, the members of NATO and the Soviet Union signed a nonaggression pact and assented to additional arms cuts. The Cold War was officially over and the Warsaw Pact dissolved in 1991. The superpowers pulled back their forces in response: The Soviet Union withdrew from its former satellite countries, and the United States removed nuclear weapons from the United Kingdom. In July 1992 Bush and Gorbachev signed the Strategic Arms Reduction Talks (START), cutting nuclear arsenals even further.

Gradually, Communist power came to an end in the USSR. In May 1989 the first elections in seventy years established the Congress of People's Deputies, effectively ending the Communist Party's monopoly on power the following year. Gorbachev survived an attempted coup in 1991, aided by Russian President Boris Yeltsin. Yelstin led a resistance against the Committee of the State of Emergency, formed by the leaders of the coup, which sought to attain control over the government. The republics that had made up the USSR began to secede: first the Baltic nations, then Russia, Ukraine, and Belorussia. Gorbachev formally resigned on Christmas Day, 1991.

Throughout Eastern Europe popular uprisings combined with reform movements to overthrow communism. Solidarity assumed power in Poland after the 1989 elections, with Lech Walesa voted in as president. In Romania Communist dictator Nikolai Ceaucescu and his wife were tried of war crimes and executed; dissident Vaclav Havel became president of Czechoslovakia. Free elections were held in Albania, Bulgaria, and Hungary, while Yugoslavia descended into a bloody civil war. The main symbol of the Cold War, the Berlin Wall, was opened on November 9, 1989, and East and West Germany reunited in 1990.

In August 1990 Saddam Hussein's Iraq invaded the neighboring state of Kuwait. Iraq claimed Kuwait was historically part of its territory, but the unprovoked attack was seen as nothing more than an attempt to exploit Kuwait's valuable oil reserves. President Bush went to work putting together an international coalition to oust Iraq from Kuwait, while stating to Hussein that his act of aggression would not go unpunished.

The first US response was Operation Desert Shield, with General H. Norman Schwarzkopf leading US forces in Saudi Arabia to prevent further Iraqi incursions, in addition to combined diplomatic efforts against Iraq. The United Nations approved action against Iraq and on January 12, 1991, President Bush secured congressional approval for the use of military force. After a UN deadline for Iraqi withdrawal passed, the United States and its allies began Operation Desert Storm on January 16, 1991; the war's first phase consisted of a massive air assault—from aircraft and cruise missiles—on targets in Baghdad and throughout Iraq.

George Bush assembled a coalition of more than thirty nations, including Great Britain, France, and Saudi Arabia, to carry out the war against Iraq. The air war lasted through February 24, 1991, when ground forces attacked, defeating the Iraqi army in 100 hours of fighting. Kuwait was freed, but retreating Iraqi troops set hundreds of oil wells on fire, and palls of smoke soon hung over the desert.

The coalition's use of overwhelming force minimized its own casualties. Of more than 541,000 US troops dispatched to the Gulf, only 148 were killed in combat and 467 wounded. US military sources estimated that 100,000 Iraqi soldiers were killed and 300,000 wounded. Nevertheless, Saddam's regime frequently violated the terms of the UN peace agreement, and sanctions and allied air strikes continued against Iraq with the United States, France, and Britain enforcing a "no-fly zone" over the country.

President Bush's popularity soared with the swift conclusion of the Gulf War. But focus soon returned to the economy. Bush and Vice President Dan Quayle were renominated without opposition as the 1992 Republican ticket, but during the primary season Bush faced a strong challenge from conservative ideologue Pat Buchanan. At the convention itself right-wing extremists took on a prominent role and they staked out positions often at odds with the viewpoints of the party's own nominees. By the time the nominees were chosen, Democratic candidate Bill Clinton had a clear edge over Bush in public opinion polls. This lead continued to the the election and, coupled with Texan billionaire Ross Perot's independent run, resulted in Bush's defeat and a solid Democratic victory.

POST-PRESIDENTIAL CAREER

George and Barbara Bush have maintained homes in Houston and Kennebunkport since leaving Washington, DC. Bush has worked on several books, although not a comprehensive memoir. The opening ceremony for the George Bush Presidential Library and Museum, located on the campus of Texas A&M University in College Station, Texas, was held on November 6, 1997. Former US Presidents Gerald Ford and Jimmy Carter attended the event, as did then current President Bill Clinton.

Since her days as First Lady, Barbara Bush has served as a strong advocate for literacy. In 1989 she established the Barbara Bush Foundation for Family Literacy. Former President Bush and his wife have also seen their sons follow similar political paths. George W. assumed the presidency in 2000 and was reelected in 2004; brother Jeb Bush became the governor of Florida in 1998 and was reelected in 2002. Despite his age, former President Bush continues to lead a rigorously active and public life. On June 11, 2004, he delivered a eulogy for Ronald Reagan at the National Cathedral in Washington. The following day, his eightieth birthday, he went skydiving. After the tsunamis struck in Asia on December 26, 2004, President George W. Bush named his father and former President Clinton to spearhead fund-raising efforts to raise money for the survivors. The ex-presidents, who seem to interact on friendly terms, together visited the devastated region in early 2005.

As a former congressman, ambassador, party chairman, intelligence chief, vice president, and present goodwill ambassador, George H. W. Bush has one of the most extensive résumés of any US president. At the conclusion of the Gulf War, he scored the highest approval rating ever recorded for a sitting US president: 89 percent. However, a year later, with the stagnant economy once again taking centerstage, Bush captured the lowest percentage of votes cast for a president seeking reelection in eighty years.

Birthplace: Milton, MA
Residency: Texas
Religion: Episcopalian
Education: Yale University, graduated 1948
Place of Death: n/a
Burial Site: n/a
Dates in Office: January 20, 1989–January 20, 1993 (four years)
Age at Inauguration: 64 years, 222 days

FAMILY

Father: Prescott Sheldon Bush (1875–1972)
Mother: Dorothy Walker Bush (1901–1992)
Siblings: George was the second eldest son; his siblings were Prescott Sheldon Bush, Jr. (1922–); Nancy Bush (1926–); Jonathan James Bush (1931–); William Henry Trotter Bush (1938–)
Wife: Barbara Pierce (1925–), married on January 6, 1945, in Rye, NY
Children: George W. Bush (1946–); Robin Bush (1949–1953); John Ellis "Jeb" Bush (1953–); Neil Bush (1955–); Marvin Bush (1956–); Dorothy Bush (1959–)

CAREER

Private: oil worker (1948–1950); oil executive (1950–1966); banker (1977–1979)

Political: member of the US House of Representatives (1967–1971); US ambassador to the United Nations (1971–1972); chairman, Republican National Committee (1972–1974); chief of the US Liaison Office to the People's Republic of China (1974–1975); director of the Central Intelligence Agency (1976–1977); vice president under Reagan (1981–1989); president of the United States (1989–1993)

Military: enlisted in the US Navy, June 12, 1942, and attended preflight training at the University of North Carolina at Chapel Hill; commissioned as an ensign on June 9, 1943, at the US Naval Station in Fort Lauderdale, FL; assigned to a torpedo squadron based on the USS San Jacinto, 1944; promoted to lieutenant junior grade, August 1, 1944; flew a total of 58 combat missions in 1944; received the Distinguished Flying Cross for flying a mission in September, 1944, during which his plane was shot down and his two other crewmates perished; also received three Air Medals and the Presidential Unit Citation awarded to the USS San Jacinto; assigned to a training wing at the US Naval Air Station in Norfolk, VA, in December, 1944; honorably discharged in September, 1945.

Selected Works: All the Best, George Bush (New York: Scribner, 1999); George Bush, Man of Integrity, ed. by Doug Wead (Eugene, Oregon: Harvest House, 1988); Heartbeat: George Bush in His Own Words, ed. by Jim McGrath (New York: Scribner, 2001); Looking Forward (New York: Doubleday, 1987); A World Transformed, with Brent Scowcroft (New York: Knopf, 1998)

PRESIDENCY

Nomination: 1988: The Republican Convention was held in New Orleans, Louisiana, August 15–18, 1988; unopposed, George H. W. Bush was nominated on the first ballot. He selected Senator J. Danforth ("Dan") Quayle of Indiana as his vice-presidential running mate.

1992: The Republican Convention was held in Houston, Texas, August 17–20, 1992. Both Bush and Quayle were renominated, unopposed.
Election: 1988: elected on November 8, 1988

1992: defeated on November 3, 1992

Opponents: 1988: Michael Dukakis, MA, Democrat

1992: Bill Clinton, AK, Democrat; H. Ross Perot, TX, Independent

Vote Totals: 1988: Bush, 47,946,422 popular, 426 electoral; Dukakis, 41,016,429 popular, 111 electoral [A West Virginia elector cast 1 vote for Lloyd Bentsen.]

1992: Clinton, 44,908,233 popular, 370 electoral; Bush, 39,102,282 popular, 168 electoral; Perot, 19,741,048 popular, 0 electoral

Inauguration: January 20, 1989

Vice President: James Danforth ("Dan") Quayle (1989–1993)

CABINET

Secretary of State: James A. Baker, TX (1989–1992); Lawrence S. Eagleburger, WI (1992–1993)

Secretary of the Treasury: Nicholas F. Brady, NJ (1989–1993)

Secretary of Defense: Dick Cheney, WY (1989–1993)

Attorney General: Richard Thornburgh, PA (1988–1991); William P. Barr, NY (1991–1993)

Secretary of Agriculture: Clayton Yeutter, NE (1989–1991); Edward Madigan, IL (1991–1993)

Secretary of the Interior: Manuel Lujan, NM (1989–1993)

Secretary of Labor: Elizabeth H. Dole, KS (1989–1990); Lynn Martin, IL (1990–1993)

Secretary of Commerce: Robert Mosbacher, TX (1989–1992); Barbara H. Franklin, PA (1992–1993)

Secretary of Health and Human Services: Louis Sullivan, GA (1989–1993)

Secretary of Housing and Urban Development: Jack Kemp, NY (1989–1993)

Secretary of Transportation: Samuel Skinner, IL (1989–1991); Andrew Card, MA (1992–1993)

Secretary of Energy: James Watkins, CA (1989–1993)

Secretary of Education: Lauro F. Cavazos, TX (1988–1990); Lamar Alexander, TN (1991–1993)

Secretary of Veterans Affairs: Edward Derwinski, IL (1989–1992) [Note: On March 15, 1989, this department and cabinet-level position was created to replace the Veterans Administration.]

CONGRESS

101st Congress (1989–1991); Speaker of the House: James C. Wright, Jr. (TX, Democrat): Thomas S. Foley (WA, Democrat)

102nd Congress (1991–1993); Speaker of the House: Thomas S. Foley (Democrat, WA)

SUPREME COURT APPOINTEES:

David H. Souter, NH; Associate Justice (1990–)
Clarence Thomas, GA; Associate Justice (1991–)

MAJOR EVENTS OF THE BUSH ADMINISTRATION

◆ On January 20, 1989, President George H. W. Bush is sworn in as the 41st president.

◆ On February 6, 1989, President Bush announces a controversial bail-out plan for failed S&Ls, in which the newly created Office of Thrift Supervision will oversee S&L regulation and the Resolution Trust Corporation will be responsible for the resolution of insolvent S&Ls.

◆ March 9, 1989, former Texas Senator John Tower, Bush's choice for secretary of defense, is rejected 53–47 by the Senate because of concerns about his prior personal conduct, which was rumored to have included womanizing and excessive drinking.

◆ On March 14, 1989, the administration bans the import of semiautomatic rifles.

◆ President Bush signs the Whistleblower Protection Act, April 10, 1989. The act is designed to protect workers reporting fraud or abuse in federal programs.

◆ After the Tiananmen Square massacre, in which an untold number of demonstrators are killed and countless others are injured, Bush suspends arms sales to the People's Republic of China on June 5, 1989.

◆ On August 9, 1989, Bush signs the Financial Institutions Reform, Recovery, and Enforcement Act of 1989, a second aid package for S&Ls. It establishes a new regulatory body, the Resolution Trust Company.

◆ President Bush signs the Fair Labor Standards Amendments on November 17,

1989, raising the minimum wage that had existed from 1991 to $4.25 per hour.

◆ On December 2, 1989, Bush and Soviet leader Mikhail Gorbachev begin talks in Malta on nuclear disarmament.

◆ December 20, 1989, US armed forces invade Panama to capture dictator Manuel Antonio Noriega. He surrenders on January 3, 1990.

◆ Meeting in Washington, DC, on June 1, 1990, Bush and Gorbachev sign an arms reduction agreement. According to the treaty's terms, the United States will destroy 25 percent of its stockpiles and the former Soviet Union 40 percent.

◆ On June 26, 1990, the Bush White House releases a statement indicating that income taxes may have to be increased in the coming year to offset the ballooning budget deficit.

◆ Bush signs the Americans with Disabilities Act (ADA), July 26, 1990.

◆ On August 2, 1990, Iraqi forces invade neighboring Kuwait. Bush affirms that Iraq's act of aggression "will not stand."

◆ The United Nations imposes trade sanctions on Iraq, August 6, 1990.

◆ On October 31, 1990, Bush doubles the US military presence in Saudi Arabia.

◆ The 1991 budget, signed on November 5, 1990, includes a provision for $140 billion in new taxes as part of a deficit reduction package.

◆ November 15, 1990, President Bush signs the Clean Air Act.

◆ November 29, 1990, President Bush signs the Immigration Act. On the same day the UN Security Council votes to allow "all means necessary" to restore Kuwait's sovereignty.

◆ Congress authorizes the use of force in Kuwait, January 12, 1991.

◆ Operation Desert Shield and Operation Desert Storm, the so-called Gulf War, begin with air strikes on Iraq and Kuwait, January 17, 1991.

◆ On January 18, 1991, Iraq launches its first Scud missile attack on Israel.

◆ February 24, 1991, ground troops, including a large contingent of American soldiers, begin operations in Operation Desert Storm.

◆ On February 25, 1991, an Iraqi Scud missile hits a US military base in Dhahran, Saudi Arabia, killing twenty-eight American soldiers.

◆ A ceasefire is declared and Kuwait liberated, February 27, 1991.

◆ Bush lifts economic sanctions against South Africa on July 10, 1991, after that nation asserts its intention to end its long-standing apartheid policy.

◆ On July 31, 1991, Bush and Gorbachev meet in Moscow. They sign the Strategic Arms Reduction Treaty (START I) that will further reduce both superpowers' nuclear stockpiles.

◆ On October 15, 1991, the Senate confirms Supreme Court nominee Clarence Thomas in a 52–48 vote after a heated confirmation hearing, at which Thomas is charged with sexual harassment by a former employee.

◆ President Bush signs the Civil Rights Act, November 21, 1991; the act calls for the provision of damages in cases of deliberate employment discrimination.

◆ On February 1, 1992, Bush and Gorbachev meet at Camp David, with both men proclaiming an official end to the Cold War.

◆ In his reelection bid, Bush easily wins the Republican primary in New Hampshire, February 18, 1992.

◆ On April 1, 1992, Bush announces an aid package of $24 billion for the former Soviet Union.

◆ The 27th Amendment to the Constitution, originally proposed in 1789, mandates that no congressional pay raises shall take effect before an intervening election has occurred; it is ratified on May 7, 1992.

◆ On June 16, 1992, Presidents Bush and Boris Yeltsin agree to additional reductions in US and Soviet nuclear warheads.

◆ At the Republican Convention, August 17–20, 1992, President Bush and Vice President Quayle, unopposed, are renominated.

◆ In the presidential election on November 3, 1992, Democratic challenger Bill Clinton defeats Bush.

◆ On December 9, 1992, as part of Operation Restore Hope, US troops land in Somalia to ensure a safe delivery of humanitarian aid to starving Somalians.

◆ President Bush, Mexican President Salinas, and Canadian Prime Minister Mulroney officially sign the North American Free Trade Agreement (NAFTA) on December 17, 1992, in three separate ceremonies in the three capitals. The agreement proposes to eliminate significant trade restrictions between the three countries, thus creating a single and integrated North American market.

◆ On January 3, 1993, Boris Yeltsin and George Bush sign the START II arms-reduction treaty.

MAJOR US AND WORLD EVENTS, 1989–1993

◆ Serial killer Theodore "Ted" Bundy is executed in Florida, January 24, 1989.

◆ On February 14, 1989, Union Carbide settles with the Indian government for the company's liability in the 1984 chemical disaster in Bhopal. Some $470 million is to be paid to the victims.

◆ On February 14, 1989, Iran's Ayatollah Khomeini alleges that Salman Rushdie's book The Satanic Verses defames Islam, and condemns Rushdie, who resides in the West, to death.

◆ The Department of Defense sets the first of twenty-four satellites of the Global Positioning System (GPS) into orbit, also on February 14, 1989.

◆ On February 15, 1989, the USSR officially announces the withdrawal of all Soviet troops from Afghanistan, ending ten years of military occupation.

◆ The ruptured tanker Exxon Valdez spills 11 million gallons of crude oil into Alaska's Prince William Sound on March 24, 1989, after running aground on Bligh Reef, creating an ecologic disaster.

◆ On June 4, 1989, hundreds, perhaps thousands, of protesters are killed in Tiananmen Square when Chinese leaders send in troops and tanks to disperse the massive crowd gathered there. Dissident students had initiated a wave of increasingly large demonstrations starting in April.

◆ On July 5, 1989, former White House aide Oliver North is convicted on three of twelve charges arising from his role in the Iran-contra affair. He receives a three-year suspended prison sentence, plus probation, community service with an inner-city drugs project, and a $150,000 fine.

◆ Cornell University student Robert Morris, Jr., is indicted on July 26, 1989, for releasing what is considered to be the first computer worm virus.

◆ On October 17, 1989, an earthquake measuring 6.9 on the Richter scale hits San Francisco, killing nine and injuring hundreds.

◆ In Germany citizens begin to demolish the Berlin Wall, November 9, 1989.

◆ The animated television series The Simpsons premieres on December 17, 1989. The popular satire goes on to become the longest-running animated series in television history.

◆ On December 25, 1989, a firing squad executes former Romanian president Nicolae Ceausescu and his wife Elena. Under his watch, the country's Communist regime had committed incalculable atrocities.

◆ Oscar Hijuelos publishes The Mambo Kings Play Songs of Love, 1989.

◆ Tom Clancy publishes Clear and Present Danger, 1989.

◆ Television series debuting in 1989 include Seinfeld, Life Goes On, The Simpsons, Baywatch, and Family Matters.

◆ Popular music hits of 1989 include Bette Midler's "Wind Beneath My Wings," Bonnie Raitt's "Nick of Time," Young MC's "Bust a Move," and Bobby Brown's "Every Little Step."

◆ Notable films of 1989 include Field of Dreams with Kevin Costner, My Left Foot with Daniel Day-Lewis, Oliver Stone's Born on the Fourth of July with Tom Cruise, and Kenneth Branagh's Henry V.

◆ Media giants Time, Inc. and Warner Communications, Inc. merge on January 10, 1990.

◆ The Soviet Union's Communist Party agrees to give up its monopoly of power on February 7, 1990.

◆ After twenty-seven years of imprisonment, South African dissident Nelson Mandela is freed on February 11, 1990.

◆ On February 26, 1990, after ten years of rule in Nicaragua, the Sandinistas lose the national elections.

◆ Lithuania declares its independence from the Soviet Union, March 11, 1990.

◆ On April 25, 1990, the Hubble Space Telescope is lifted into orbit from the shuttle *Discovery*.

◆ Soviet leader Mikhail Gorbachev wins the Nobel Peace Prize on October 3, 1990.

◆ On October 3, 1990, East and West Germany, divided since 1945, are reunited.

◆ Conservative Margaret Thatcher resigns on November 22, 1990, after eleven years as Britain's prime minister; she is succeeded by John Major.

◆ On December 16, 1990, Jean-Bertrand Aristide, a Catholic priest, wins the presidential election in Haiti.

◆ The 1990 census estimates the US population at 248.7 million people.

◆ Charles Johnson publishes *Middle Passage*, 1990.

◆ John Updike publishes *Rabbit at Rest*, 1990.

◆ Thomas Pynchon publishes *Vineland*, 1990.

◆ Stephen King publishes *The Stand*, 1990.

◆ Television series debuting in 1990 include *Law & Order* and *In Living Color*.

◆ Popular music hits of 1990 include Phil Collins's "Another Day in Paradise," Mariah Carey's "Vision of Love," and Aerosmith's "Janie's Got a Gun."

◆ Notable films of 1990 include Kevin Costner's *Dances with* Wolves, Martin Scorsese's *Goodfellas* wth Ray Liotta and Joe Pesci, Francis Ford Coppola's *The Godfather Part III*, and *Awakenings* with Robert DeNiro and Robin Williams.

◆ On March 31, 1991, the Warsaw Pact, the Eastern bloc's response to NATO established in 1955, is dissolved.

◆ On May 21, 1991, a bomb kills India's former Prime Minister Rajiv Gandhi (son of Indira Gandhi and grandson of Jawaharlal Nehru) who is attempting a political comeback.

◆ Boris Yeltsin is elected the first president of the Russian Federation, June 12, 1991.

◆ Croatia and Slovenia declare their independence from Yugoslavia on June 25, 1991.

◆ On September 6, 1991, Russia's second largest city renames itself St. Petersburg, its original name. Since 1924 the city had been known as Leningrad.

◆ The Union of Soviet Socialist Republics is officially dissolved on December 26, 1991.

◆ Norman Rush publishes *Mating*, 1991.

◆ John Grisham publishes *The Firm*, 1991.

◆ Daniel Yergin publishes *The Prize*, 1991.

◆ Television series debuting in 1991 include *Rugrats*, *Home Improvement*, and *Sisters*.

◆ Popular music hits of 1991 include Natalie and Nat King Cole's "Unforgettable," R.E.M.'s "Losing My Religion," and Michael Bolton's "When a Man Loves a Woman."

◆ Notable films of 1991 include Jonathan Demme's *The Silence of the Lambs* with Anthony Hopkins and Jodie Foster, Ridley Scott's *Thelma and Louise* with Susan Sarandon and Geena Davis, Oliver Stone's *JFK* with Kevin Costner, and Barbra Streisand's *The Prince of Tides*.

◆ Slovenia and Croatia win their independence, January 15, 1992.

◆ On March 3, 1992, Bosnia and Herzegovina declares its sovereignty from the former Yugoslavia.

◆ On March 5, 1992, Microsoft releases the Windows 3.1 computer operating system.

◆ Riots erupt in Los Angeles on April 29, 1992, after four police officers are acquitted of assaulting a black motorist, Rodney King, an incident caught on video. Disturbances erupt in South-Central Los Angeles and soon spread throughout the city. After three days, at least 54 are killed, more than 2,000 injured, and more than 1,000 buildings destroyed.

◆ On May 22, 1992, Johnny Carson retires as host of *The Tonight Show*. Carson hosted his first episode on October 2, 1962.

◆ Cormac McCarthy publishes *All the Pretty Horses*, 1992.

◆ Terri McMillan publishes *Waiting to Exhale*, 1992.

◆ H. Norman Schwarzkopf publishes *It Doesn't Take a Hero*, 1992.

◆ David McCullough publishes *Truman*, 1992.

◆ Television series debuting in 1992 include *Barney & Friends*, *Mad About You*, and *The Real World*.

◆ Popular music hits of 1992 include Eric Clapton's "Tears in Heaven," Red Hot Chili Pepper's "Give It Away," Arrested Development's "Tennessee," and Sir Mix-A-Lot's "Baby Got Back."

◆ Notable films of 1992 include Clint Eastwood's *Unforgiven*, Robert Altman's *The Player*, *The Crying Game* with Stephen Rea, *Scent of a Woman* with Al Pacino, and *A Few Good Men* with Tom Cruise and Jack Nicholson.

FAST FACTS ABOUT GEORGE H. W. BUSH

◆ George Herbert Walker Bush was named for his maternal grandfather, from whom he also inherited the nickname "Poppy."

◆ Bush was the youngest aviator in the Navy when he completed flight training and was commissioned as an ensign in June, 1943.

◆ George H. W. Bush was the first US president to have served as chairman of a major political party, director of the Central Intelligence Agency, and ambassador to the United Nations.

◆ The tenth *Nimitz*-class aircraft carrier, set to launch in 2009, will be named the *USS George H. W. Bush*.

◆ George H. W. Bush holds his own annual fishing tournament in Islamorada, an island in the Florida Keys.

◆ When his son George W. Bush entered the White House in 2000, George H. W. Bush became the first president since John Adams to be the father of another president.

◆ On November 22, 2004, New York Governor George Pataki named former US presidents George H. W. Bush, Gerald Ford, Jimmy Carter, and Bill Clinton as honorary members of the board overseeing rebuilding at the World Trade Center, following the September 11 terrorist attacks. That same day a plane en route to pick up Bush crashed in Houston, Texas, killing three passengers.

William Jefferson Clinton

Nickname: Bill; Slick Willy
Party: Democratic
Presidency: 42nd president, 1993–2001
Life dates: August 19, 1946–

EARLY LIFE AND EDUCATION

Bill Clinton was born William Jefferson Blythe IV in Hope, Arkansas, on August 19, 1946. His father, William Jefferson Blythe III, had died at the age of twenty-eight in an auto accident on May 17 of that year, leaving his mother, Virginia Cassidy Blythe, widowed.

After the birth of her son, Virginia took baby William to her parents' home in Hope. After a year, Virginia journeyed to New Orleans to train as a nurse anesthetist, and the infant was cared for by his grandparents, Edith Grisham Cassidy, a nurse, and James Eldridge Cassidy, a night watchman who also operated a grocery store.

After completing her training, Virginia Cassidy returned to Hope and in June 1950 she married Roger Clinton, owner of the local Buick dealership. Soon after the marriage, when the couple moved into their own home on Thirteenth Street, young William began calling himself "Billy Clinton."

Billy attended Miss Marie Purkins' School for Little Folks kindergarten, where he befriended Mack McLarty, who later became his first White House chief of staff. While in kindergarten, Clinton broke his leg and spent two months recuperating in a hospital. Clinton later recalled the kindness his stepfather showed him at this time, arranging a trip to St. Louis so the two could see the Cardinals play baseball and several fishing trips. However, Roger Clinton's drinking and abusive behavior toward his wife were the larger realities of Bill Clinton's childhood. On one occasion Roger fired a gun during an argument with Virginia and ended up spending the night in jail.

The summer after Billy had completed the first grade, Roger Clinton sold the car dealership and relocated his family to a run-down farm (which included an outhouse) west of Hot Springs, Arkansas. There, Roger Clinton sold cars at his brother's Buick dealership, and Virginia worked as an anesthetist. For two years Billy attended St. John's Catholic School before the family moved again, this time to the city of Hot Springs, where they rented a large house on Park Avenue owned by Roger's brother. Billy spent many hours in the local library and attended Park Place Baptist Church at which he was later baptized.

On July 25, 1956, Billy's younger brother, Roger Cassidy Clinton, was born. Around the same time, the Clinton family purchased its first television set. Watching the Democratic and Republican National Conventions that summer, young Billy became fascinated with the political process. After Ramble Elementary School, Billy was enrolled at Central Junior High School in Hot Springs. He took up the saxophone, playing in the junior high band and attending a music camp at the University of Arkansas seven summers in a row.

Roger Clinton's violent outbursts toward his wife escalated, and young Bill would often intervene, in one instance brandishing a golf club to stop his stepfather from hitting his mother. When Bill was fifteen, Virginia moved out of the house on Park Avenue with her sons and filed for divorce. After it became final, she and Roger reconciled; they remarried and settled in a house on Scully Street in Hot Springs.

"My fellow Americans, I end tonight where it all began for me—I still believe in a place called Hope. God bless you, and God Bless America."

Governor Bill Clinton, in his acceptance speech at the Democratic National Convention, New York City, July 16, 1992

Bill was an accomplished student at Hot Springs High School. He also played saxophone on the all-state band. In 1963, after his junior year, Bill attended the American Legion Boys State program in Arkansas and was selected as one of the state's two representatives on an excursion that the Legion's "Boys Nation" made to College Park, Maryland. As part of that trip, on July 22, 1963, Bill visited Washington, D.C., and was able to meet the two US senators from his home state: J. William Fulbright and John McClellan. Two days later, the boys in the program met President John F. Kennedy in the Rose Garden. This opportunity to shake the hand of one of his heroes became a defining

moment in Bill's youth. After graduating fourth in his high school class in 1964, Bill attended the School of Foreign Service at Georgetown University, the only undergraduate program to which he had applied. He wanted to return to Washington, still buoyed by his visit there a year earlier, and, already interested in a political career, he decided that learning about international affairs would be helpful in the future. He was elected president of the freshman class and served again as class president his sophomore year. The following summer Bill worked on the ultimately unsuccessful campaign of Frank Holt to capture the Democratic nomination for governor of Arkansas.

On the recommendation of Frank Holt's brother Jack, Bill secured a part-time job as assistant clerk for the Senate Foreign Relations Committee chaired by Senator Fulbright. These earnings allowed Clinton to pay for college independently of his parents, a serious consideration as Roger Clinton had been recently diagnosed with cancer and Bill was unsure how he would be able to continue his studies at Georgetown.

Bill worked every day after class clipping noteworthy newspaper articles and typing correspondence for Senator Fulbright. By 1966 Fulbright strongly opposed American involvement in Vietnam—particularly any increase in the number of US troops deployed there—and Bill soon became immersed in the politics on Capitol Hill, concentrating less on his academic studies. During the spring of 1967, Clinton spent weekends at the Duke Medical Center in Durham, North Carolina, where his stepfather was receiving treatment. Roger Clinton died in November 1967.

Clinton graduated with a degree in international affairs from Georgetown in the spring of 1968. His graduation ceremony was overshadowed by the tumult following the assassination of Senator Robert F. Kennedy of New York. That summer Clinton returned to Arkansas to campaign for Senator Fulbright before leaving for Oxford where he had been awarded a prestigious Fulbright scholarship.

At University College, Oxford, Clinton pursued politics, philosophy and economics, concentrating mostly on politics during his second year of study. While abroad, Clinton participated in demonstrations against the Vietnam War (on one occasion, he was a steward at a protest outside the US Embassy in London) and traveled extensively in Europe, including forays to Czechoslovakia and the former Soviet Union.

While in London, Clinton reported for induction and took an army physical as part of the draft process. He was classified I-A, eligible for military service. When he returned to the United States in June 1969, he considered enrolling at the University of Arkansas law school; instead, he joined the university's Reserve Officer Training Corp (ROTC, which reclassified him as I-D, exempt from active service). Troubled by the conflict between his opposition to the war in Vietnam and his belief that avoiding the draft was wrong, Clinton changed his mind and reentered the draft. On December 1, 1969, he drew number 311, a high number, although he still worried about being drafted. In a letter that was later reprinted during his run for the presidency (and caused his campaign great embarrassment), Clinton wrote the director of the University of Arkansas ROTC, thanking him for "saving" Clinton from the draft, detailing his opposition to the war, and admitting that he had decided to submit to the draft (rather than becoming a draft resister) to "maintain my political viability within the system." He subsequently returned to Oxford for a second year.

Rather than complete a third year at Oxford, Clinton accepted a scholarship to Yale University Law School. He missed many of his classes at the beginning of his first year because he took time to work on the campaign of Joe Duffey, who was seeking a seat in the US Senate. With the incumbent Tom Dodd, a former Democrat, running as an independent, the Democratic vote was split and the election was lost to Lowell Weicker, the Republican candidate (who later became governor of Connecticut as an independent).

It was at Yale that Clinton met fellow law student Hillary Rodham. By then Clinton had had a fair number of girlfriends, but this self-assured,

bespectacled young woman captured his attention. After class one day, she finally approached him and introduced herself as Hillary Rodham. Born to an upper-middle-class family in Chicago, Hillary had graduated from Wellesley College. Before long the two became inseparable, sharing a passion for the social causes of the time and a political solution to them. Together in Texas, they worked for Senator George McGovern, the unsuccessful Democratic presidential candidate in the 1972 election.

POLITICAL CAREER

In 1973 both Bill and Hillary graduated from Yale with law degrees. Rodham took a job with the Children's Defense Fund in Massachusetts, and Clinton accepted an offer to teach law at the University of Arkansas in Fayetteville. In 1974, with the impeachment of President Richard Nixon on the horizon, the House Judiciary Committee offered him a position as assistant counsel that instead went to Rodham on his recommendation. Clinton ran for a seat in the Third Congressional District in Arkansas that year. He advanced beyond the Democratic primary, but lost to the four-term incumbent, Republican John Paul Hammerschmidt, by 52 to 48 percent in the election.

In 1974 Hillary Rodham moved to Fayetteville to teach with Clinton at the law school. The two were married on October 11, 1975, in a small ceremony at their home, with Hillary retaining her maiden name. In 1977 she joined the Rose Law Firm in Little Rock where she was highly successful. On February 27, 1980, the Clintons' daughter, and only child, Chelsea was born.

Bill Clinton became the attorney general of Arkansas in 1976; he had won the primary and ran unopposed in the general election. Clinton also worked on Jimmy Carter's presidential campaign in his home state that year. In 1978 Clinton decided to run for governor. He won the Democratic primary and then, easily, the general election, capturing some 63 percent of the vote to beat Republican Lynne Low. At thirty-two, Clinton was the youngest governor in the country and one of the youngest ever elected.

As a first-term governor, Clinton assembled an energetic coterie of advisers (Steve Clark, the new attorney general, and Paul Revere, secretary of state, were both thirty-one), but he soon ran into political difficulties, partly because of his overly ambitious agenda. He raised the gas tax and auto license fees to pay for highway improvements. This, along with his stance against clear-cutting, alienated the timber industry, a powerful interest group in the state. When hundreds of Cuban refugees the federal government had placed at Fort Chaffee in Arkansas rioted, many held Clinton personally responsible for the outbreak. In 1980 Clinton ran for reelection but he lost to Republican Frank White.

After his defeat Clinton returned to the law, and from 1981 to 1982 worked at the firm of Wright, Lindsey and Jennings in Little Rock. By 1982 Clinton was again ready to run for public office. Mounting an aggressive campaign for the Democratic nomination for governor, he publicly apologized for the mistakes of his first term, including the tax hike. Clinton won the Democratic primary and defeated Frank White in the general election, winning 55 percent of the popular vote. He subsequently defeated, in their separate bids for governor, Elwood "Woody" Freeman in 1984, Frank White in 1986, and Sheffield Nelson in 1990 (after the state legislature voted to institute a four-year term for the governorship).

In his second term as governor, Clinton introduced important educational reforms within Arkansas. He agreed to raise teachers' pay, but required them to take and pass a competency test, which many teachers actually opposed. His reforms also allowed teachers to have more say in class programs, introduced a standardized test for eighth graders, extended the drop-out age to seventeen, and withdrew driver's licenses from adolescents who left school without graduating. He also appointed his wife to a committee mandated to develop policies for further improving the quality of education throughout the state. In another important area, Clinton tried to move welfare recipients into the work world, increasing the number of job opportunities available to them by offering tax incentives to companies based in Arkansas. State programs to support minority-owned businesses were devised, and Clinton appointed a larger number of African Americans to state jobs than all his predecessors combined. As governor, Clinton also supported the death penalty.

Bill Clinton had long had his sights set on the national stage. In 1985 he delivered the Democrats' official response to President Ronald Reagan's State of the Union address. He was chair of the National Governors Association in 1986 and 1987 and was a member, then chairperson, of the Democratic Leadership Council, a moderate group within the national party. Clinton considered running for president in 1988 but decided against it. However, he did place Massachusetts Governor Michael Dukasis's name in nomination at that year's Democratic Convention, giving an overly long and rambling speech that was badly received in some quarters. Exhibiting his adeptness at overcoming adversity, Clinton made a guest appearance on the Tonight Show shortly thereafter, allowing host Johnny Carson to make fun of his long-windedness.

In October 1991 Governor Clinton, who had originally promised that he would serve out his four-year term in Little Rock, announced his candidacy for the presidency. He immediately came under close scrutiny for a number of personal issues, including his alleged use of marijuana (which led to his infamous "did not inhale" admission to the New York Times that led to many jokes and spoofs at his expense). Amid rumors concerning the candidate's private life, the Clintons together appeared on CBS News' 60 Minutes on January 23, 1992; in the interview Clinton frankly conceded that he had "caused pain" in his marriage. The next day Gennifer Flowers, a former nightclub performer, held a press conference at which she claimed to have had a twelve-year liaison with Clinton. Also during his campaign for nomination, The Wall Street Journal ran a story about Clinton's draft record, and a segment of ABC's Nightline eventually aired the contents of the letter of thanks he had written to the University of Arkansas' ROTC director, after escaping selection in the draft lottery.

Despite these revelations and the attendant media coverage, Clinton continued in his bid for the Democratic nomination. He lost the New Hampshire primary to Senator Paul Tsongas of Massachusetts, but made a strong second-place showing. Dubbing himself the "comeback kid," Clinton overcame his challengers in the ensuing primaries, and at the Democratic Convention in July he roundly defeated Tsongas and former California Governor Jerry Brown on the first ballot. Clinton chose Al Gore, US senator from Tennessee, as his running mate. Gore had a strong, knowledgeable background in national security, arms control, and foreign policy issues. In his acceptance speech (still long by traditional standards), Clinton called for a "New Covenant" between the American government and its people.

"Our democracy must be not only the envy of the world but the engine of our own renewal. There is nothing wrong with America that cannot be cured by what is right with America."

Bill Clinton, in his first inaugural address, January 20, 1993

Bill Clinton's dynamic campaign team, led by James Carville, focused the race on what the Democratic challenger insisted was the real issue: the stagnant economy. "It's the economy, stupid," asserted a sign at Clinton headquarters. In spite of the high approval ratings President George H. W. Bush had enjoyed after the Gulf War, his standing plummeted over the lack of new jobs and growth during his first term, and what the public perceived to be his passive management of a worsening situation. The Republican Convention in Houston also did not help matters for Bush; it was dominated by right-wing elements within the GOP, including ideologue Pat Buchanan, and many of the extremist speeches delivered there, carried live on television, did not sit well with an essentially moderate electorate.

Another unexpected development in the campaign was the independent candidacy of Texas billionaire H. Ross Perot and his "United We Stand" Party. Espousing a populist platform and tapping into mainstream dissatisfaction with big government, Perot actually established a lead over both major party candidates in early polls. He dropped out of the race in July (after Clinton was nominated at the Democratic Convention), but reentered it in October. On election day Perot captured 19 percent of the vote (although no electoral votes), with his candidacy possibly hurting Bush the most. Bill Clinton proved victorious, surmounting the Republican attacks on his record as governor and personal character; he won 43 percent of the popular vote, totaling 370 electoral votes, to Bush's 37 percent and 168 electoral votes.

PRESIDENCY

On January 20, 1993, Bill Clinton was sworn in as the 42nd president. He acted quickly on a number of controversial fronts; on his first day in office, he rescinded the "gag rule" preventing federally funded clinics from offering pregnant women information on abortion and also relaxed previous restrictions on military hospitals from performing abortions. Within a week Clinton appointed his wife to spearhead the national effort to reform health care. This initiative met fierce resistance almost immediately, with the effort grinding to a halt in September 1994 when it became clear that Congress was not prepared to approve sweeping reform. The first bill signed by Clinton was the Family and Medical Leave Act, a piece of legislation earlier vetoed by Presidents Reagan and Bush, which allowed unpaid leave for employees during pregnancy or illness. His first year in the Oval Office, Clinton also signed the Brady Handgun Violence Prevention Act— known as the Brady Bill—that required a five-day wait period for, and background check on, all individuals seeking to purchase a handgun. The act, named for former

White House press secretary James Brady who had been partially paralyzed in the attempted assassination of Reagan in 1981, was fiercely resisted by the gun lobby.

Perhaps the most controversial of all Clinton's initial actions was his administration's attempt, within ten days of assuming office, to lift the long-standing prohibition on gays in the military. It drew sharp opposition from the military services and conservatives. The compromise policy arrived at, dubbed "don't ask, don't tell," was also much criticized by gay rights organizations for not addressing issues of discrimination.

The Clinton administration also ran into difficulties, early on, with its appointments. Three of the president's women nominees (Zoe Baird and Kimba Wood for attorney general, and Lani Guinier for assistant attorney general for civil rights) never made it to congressional consideration after details of their personal or professional lives received extensive media coverage. Baird came under fire because she had not paid Social Security taxes for an immigrant couple under her employ; Wood then withdrew her name after admitting that she had hired an illegal alien (not against the law at the time); and Clinton himself removed Guinier from contention after some of her earlier, and controversial, legal writings on sensitive racial issues were brought to light.

Clinton's first economic initiative was a deficit reduction package that barely made its way through a Democratic-controlled Congress, with Vice President Gore casting the tie-breaking vote in the Senate. The plan sought to cut the deficit by almost $500 billion in over five years, but it involved an increase in taxes, rather than any reduction for the middle class, which Clinton had promoted in his presidential campaign.

The hearings, investigations, and scandals that would come to characterize both terms of the Clinton administration in the media started almost immediately. In May 1993 seven members of the White House Travel Office, which arranges travel for journalists covering the president, were unexpectedly fired. A week later five were reinstated, placed on administrative leave. Allegations of possible impropriety surfaced, with some suggesting that Hillary had had a hand in the flurry of firings. "Travelgate," however, was soon dwarfed by a much larger subject of scrutiny during the Clinton administration: Whitewater.

In 1978 Bill and Hillary Clinton, in partnership with Jim and Susan McDougal, had purchased 230 acres of land in northern Arkansas situated along the White River for development into vacation properties. The Madison Guaranty Savings & Loan owned by the McDougals, and which Hillary had represented while at the Rose Law Firm, became the focus of a legal investigation. In July 1993 former Rose Law Firm partner and then White House counsel Vince Foster committed suicide. He had been under intense pressure for his possible involvement in the travel office scandal and also the surreptitious review of Hillary Clinton's billing records when she represented Madison Guaranty at Rose. It was later revealed that he had been undergoing treatment for depression during this period. A cloud of suspicion hung over the Oval Office, nevertheless.

In January 1994 Clinton's attorney general, Janet Reno, appointed Republican Robert B. Fiske as special counsel to investigate various transactions involving Whitewater. A federal panel subsequently replaced Fiske with attorney Kenneth W. Starr. Starr doggedly called one Clinton associate after another as witnesses and widened the scope of his investigation. For the first time in US history, a first lady was subpoenaed when, in 1996, Starr questioned Hillary about missing Rose Law Firm billing records that had mysteriously turned up in the White House. Clinton also had to testify under oath regarding a loan made to Susan McDougal. Clinton's personal travails increased in May 1994 when Paula Jones, a state employee in Arkansas at the time Clinton served as governor, filed a lawsuit charging that Clinton had sexually harassed her in 1991. Two members of Clinton's cabinet then came under investigation on unrelated charges: Agriculture Secretary Mike Espy for wrongdoing involving the acceptance of gifts, and Housing and Urban Development Secretary Henry Cisneros for making incorrect statements about his personal expenses during his interview for the cabinet position. By the mid-term elections in 1994 Clinton's popularity was at a low point, and Republicans swept to power in both houses—the first time they had done so in forty years.

By 1994 Clinton had managed to get deficit reduction packages through Congress. When the new Republican Congress tried to slash government programs, he vetoed its proposals. Congress tried to force its budget and a balanced budget bill on the president, and the impasse led to a government shutdown in late 1995. In spite of these difficulties with Republican lawmakers on fiscal matters, the Clinton administration saw the nation through a period of economic prosperity that combined fast growth and low inflation to produce big surpluses— $124 billion in 1999 and predicted to be even greater in the twenty-first century. The healthy economy was also reflected in low unemployment levels and high levels of home ownership.

During his first presidential campaign Clinton had promised welfare reform, and in 1996 he signed a controversial and wide-ranging welfare bill that would effectively remove recipients from the rolls after two years. To balance this bill, Clinton also secured an increase in the minimum wage to $5.15 per hour. Although illegal immigrants were barred from receiving Social Security and other benefits, he vetoed Republican attempts to withhold public education from the children of illegal immigrants.

In the area of foreign affairs, several key events occurred. On September 13, 1993, the leaders of the Palestine Liberation Organization (PLO) and Israel, Yasser Arafat and Yitzhak Rabin, signed the Oslo Accords at the White House. By its terms the PLO agreed to a ceasefire in exchange for limited self-rule. In October 1993 US troops participating in a humanitarian mission in Somalia were attacked and eighteen killed. In April 1994 widespread genocide began in Rwanda, with an estimated 800,000 Tutsi killed during the Hutu rampage. Despite the magnitude of the killing, there was little international response, even from the United Nations. In his later memoirs Clinton referred to the White House's decision to not become embroiled in the conflict given the earlier disastrous events in Somalia as the single greatest foreign policy failing of his administration. In September 1994 US troops were sent to Haiti to return President Jean-Bertrand Aristide to power. When Clinton stood for reelection in 1996, public opinion polls showed that although voters did not necessarily trust the president, they believed he was doing a good job. Clinton faced Republican Senate Majority Leader Robert Dole of Kansas and, once again, Texas billionaire H. Ross Perot. To win his party's nod, Dole overcame challenges from conservative columnist Pat Buchanan and wealthy publisher Steve Forbes. At the convention Dole chose Jack Kemp, a congressman from New York, as his running mate.

Clinton adopted a more centrist position in his run against Dole. The economy was robust enough for him to propose tax cuts; it also allowed him to remind average Americans that they were doing well. On November 5, 1996, Clinton defeated Dole by 49 percent to 41 percent, capturing 370 electoral votes to Dole's 159. In his second bid for the White House Perot proved less of a factor, winning only 8 million popular votes.

During his second term Clinton became the second president, after Andrew Johnson in 1868, to be impeached. In May 1997 the Supreme Court ruled that Paula Jones's lawsuit against the president could proceed while he was in office. The Jones case soon intersected with another, that of former White House intern Monica Lewinsky. Twenty-one-year-old Lewinsky had started work at the White House in June 1995 as an intern to chief of staff Leon Panetta. In November of that same year Clinton initiated a sexual relationship with her. In April 1996 Lewinsky was abruptly transferred to a job at the Pentagon, where she met government staffer Linda Tripp. Lewinsky confided in Tripp about her relationship with the president, and Tripp began secretly taping her conversations with Lewinsky.

Beginning in January 1998, the drama un-

President Bill Clinton seated with his first-term cabinet.

folded, much of it on television. Revelations seemed to come daily amid acrimonious accusations of leaks from both sides; the first lady spoke of a "vast right-wing conspiracy" against her husband, who was then enjoying the highest approval ratings of his presidency to date. First, Lewinsky filed an affidavit denying a relationship. After Tripp communicated with Kenneth Starr's office, the FBI contacted Lewinsky and offered her immunity to testify in the Paula Jones case. As the scandal became public, Clinton, in a videotaped deposition in the Jones matter, and also on television, denied an affair, insisting, "I did not have sexual relations with that woman, Miss Lewinsky." Starr then took on the Lewinsky case, seeking to determine whether the president and his friend and close adviser Vernon Jordan had coached Lewinsky to deny the intimate relationship under oath.

In April the Paula Jones lawsuit was dismissed, with the Lewinsky affair soon ascending as the focus of national attention. When Jones's lawyers filed an appeal, the president's lawyers agreed to a monetary settlement whereby the lawsuit was dropped without Clinton admitting any guilt.

After protracted negotiations Monica Lewinsky reached an immunity agreement with Kenneth Starr in July 1998; in August both she and the president testified before a grand jury. The evening after testifying, Clinton delivered a brief televised address to the nation in which he admitted to an "inappropriate" relationship with Lewinsky. In September 1998 Starr released his official report to Congress, outlining possible impeachable offenses, and the House voted to open an impeachment inquiry. The House Judiciary Committee approved four articles of impeachment: two counts of perjury (one in the Paula Jones case and one in front of the grand jury), abuse of power, and obstruction of justice in the Lewinsky case. The House then voted to impeach Clinton on two charges: perjury and the obstruction of justice.

The impeachment trial was held in the Senate beginning on January 9, 1999. The Senate debated whether the charges against the president amounted to the "high crimes and misdemeanors" that are cited, along with treason and bribery, in the Constitution as grounds for impeachment. After a five-week trial the Senate voted. With a two-thirds majority required for conviction in the Senate, the perjury charge was defeated 45 to 55; the obstruction charge ended in a 50 to 50 split, and the president remained in office.

In September 2000 the Whitewater investigation came to a close. In his final report Ken Starr's successor, Robert Ray, announced that his office, after nearly six years of inquiry, had uncovered no evidence of wrongdoing by the Clintons that could be offered in a court of law. Clinton supporters contended then, as they still do, that many of the numerous investigations of the president and his administration were politically motivated.

As the impeachment process unfolded, Clinton tried to focus on foreign affairs. In August 1998 American embassies in Nairobi, Kenya, and Dar es Salaam, Tanzania, were destroyed by terrorist bombs. More than two hundred died in the incident in Kenya alone. Two weeks later Operation Infinite Reach was staged, as US warships launched cruise missile attacks on targets in the Sudan desert and Afghanistan, which were believed to support the al Qaeda network of Osama bin Laden, a likely suspect in the embassy bombings. In October 2000 bin Laden was linked to an attack on the USS Cole in the port of Aden, Yemen, that killed seventeen sailors.

In the Balkans US warplanes participated in NATO attacks on Bosnian Serbian forces during the civil war in Bosnia that pitted Muslims, Croats, and Serbs against each other. In November 1995 the presidents of Serbia, Croatia, and Bosnia-Herzegovina signed a peace agreement at an air base near Dayton, Ohio. US troops were part of a NATO peace-keeping contingent that arrived in Bosnia after the Dayton Accords. In March 1999 Clinton further committed US forces to a NATO campaign to stop the Serbian government's policy of "ethnic cleansing" in regard to Kosovo's Albanian population. After Serbian forces withdrew from Kosovo, NATO troops occupied the region, which later became a UN protectorate.

"I judge my presidency primarily in terms of its impact on people's lives. That is how I kept score: all the millions of people with new jobs, new homes, and college aid; the kids with health insurance and after-school programs; the people who left welfare for work; the families helped by the family leave law; the people living in safer neighborhoods—all those people have stories; and they're better ones now."

Bill Clinton, in his autobiography My Life, 2004

In his last State of the Union address in January 2000, President Clinton declared that the country was "as strong as we have ever been." In April unemployment dipped below 4 percent for the first time in thirty years. In 1999 the government enjoyed the first budget surplus in thirty years. In keeping with a presidential tradition, Clinton issued pardons during his last hours in office. Among the 140 pardoned was Marc Rich, ex-husband of a leading Democrat fund-raiser, Denise Rich. Marc Rich had fled the United States for Switzerland in 1983, owing $48 million in taxes and facing charges of trading with an enemy in the form of oil deals with Iran. As he prepared to leave office, Clinton faced possible prosecution for perjury in the Monica Lewinsky case. The day before Clinton stepped down, he and Independent Counsel Robert Ray officially ended the seven-year investigation that began with Whitewater and extended into the Lewinsky affair. Clinton admitted giving misleading testimony in a deposition for the Lewinsky case in 1998. Answering a suit brought in Arkansas, Clinton had his law license suspended for five years and paid a $25,000 fine. "I hope my actions today will help bring closure and finality to these matters," he asserted.

Despite the problems that dogged him during his presidency, Clinton has remained immensely popular with the public, including many Democrats, who nostalgically point to his accomplishments in such areas as the economy, family issues, the environment, women's rights, and strong international ties.

POST-PRESIDENTIAL CAREER

On the same day that the contested election between Clinton's vice president, Al Gore, and George W. Bush took place, Hillary Clinton was elected US Senator from New York. To establish residency in the state in time for the 2000 elections, the Clintons had bought a house in Chappaqua in Westchester County, where they moved after Bush was inaugurated. While Hillary Clinton fulfilled her congressional duties in Washington, her husband opened an office on 125th Street in the center of Harlem.

In his post-presidential activities, Clinton has remained a highly public figure. He has been the key player in the Clinton Foundation, a nonprofit organization recognized for its work on increasing awareness of HIV/AIDS worldwide, providing medication to victims of the disease, and training doctors and other medical professionals in India and Africa. In June 2004 Clinton's much anticipated autobiography My Life was published. The former president reportedly received a $10 million advance for the book. On its first day of release, an estimated 400,000 copies were sold, a record number for a work of nonfiction. Clinton has also been a frequent public speaker. His customary hectic schedule, and prior poor eating and exercise habits, eventually caught up with him, however, and in Sep-

tember 2004 Clinton underwent a quadruple coronary artery bypass operation at Columbia Presbyterian Hospital in New York City.

After leaving the White House, Clinton was actively involved in the planning and construction of his presidential library in Little Rock, Arkansas, an architecturally striking building that officially opened in November 2004 amidst much fanfare, with President George W. Bush, and former Presidents George H. W. Bush and Jimmy Carter in attendance. Clinton and Bush senior, once political adversaries, joined together to lead the US fund-raising efforts after the catastrophic December 2004 tsunami in South Asia. Recently, Clinton was named special UN envoy for tsunami relief (a role that will involve conflict resolution in the region) by Secretary-General Kofi Annan. It is rumored that the former president would one day like to head the United Nations. Many Americans also believe that Hillary Clinton will seek the presidency in 2008. If she is elected to the highest office in the land, the Clintons could set a series of new precedents in US politics.

Birthplace: Hope, Arkansas
Residency: Arkansas
Religion: Baptist
Education: Georgetown University, graduated 1968; University of Oxford, attended 1968–1970; Yale University Law School, graduated 1973
Place of Death: n/a
Burial Site: n/a
Dates in Office: January 20, 1993–January 20, 2001 (eight years)
Age at Inauguration: 46 years, 164 days

FAMILY

Father: William Jefferson Blythe, III (1917–1946)
Mother: Virginia Cassidy Blythe (1923–1994)
Siblings: Clinton was the only child of Virginia Cassidy and William Jefferson Blythe, III; his siblings are Roger Cassidy Clinton, Jr. (half-brother, 1956– ; born of Virginia Cassidy Blythe's second marriage to Roger Clinton); Henry Leon Ritzenthaler (half-brother, 1938?– ; born of William Jefferson Blythe III's first marriage to Adele Gash); Sharon Lee Blythe (half-sister,

1941– ; born of William Jefferson Blythe III's second marriage to Faye Gash)
Wife: Hillary Diane Rodham Clinton (1947–), married on October 11, 1975, in Fayetteville, AR
Children: Chelsea Victoria Clinton (1980–)

CAREER

Private: law professor (1973–1976); lawyer (1981–1982)
Political: attorney general of Arkansas (1977–1979); governor of Arkansas (1979–1981, 1983–1992); president of the United States (1993–2001)
Military: none
Selected Works: *Between Hope and History* (New York: Random House, 1996); *Clinton on Clinton: A Portrait of the President in His Own Words*, ed. by Wayne Meyer (New York: Avpm Books, 1999); *The Clinton Foreign Policy Reader: Presidential Speeches with Commentary*, ed. by Alvin Z. Rubinstein, Albina Sayevich, and Boris Zlotnikov (Armonk, NY: M. E. Sharpe, 2000); *The Impeachment and Trial of President Clinton: The Official Transcripts*, intro. by Michael R. Beschloss, ed. by Merrill McLoughlin (New York: Times Books, 1999); *My Life* (New York: Alfred A. Knopf, 2004); *Preface to the Presidency: Selected Speeches of Bill Clinton, 1974–1992*, compiled and ed. by Stephen A. Smith (Fayetteville: University of Arkansas Press, 1996); *Putting People First* (New York: Three Rivers Press, 1992)

PRESIDENCY

Nomination: 1992: The Democratic Convention was held in New York City, July 13–17, 1992. Clinton was nominated on the first ballot, receiving 3,372 votes to 596 for Jerry Brown and 209 for Paul Tsongas. He selected Senator Al Gore of Tennessee as his running mate.
    1996: The Democratic Convention was held in Chicago, August 26–30, 1996; the Clinton-Gore ticket was renominated, unopposed.
Election: 1992: elected president on November 3, 1992 1996: reelected president on November 5, 1996
Opponent: 1992: George H. W. Bush, TX, Republican; H. Ross Perot, TX, Independent

1996: Robert J. Dole, KS, Republican; H. Ross Perot, TX, Independent
Vote Totals: 1992: Clinton, 44,908,233 popular, 370 electoral; Bush, 39,102,282 popular, 168 electoral; Perot, 19,741,048 popular, 0 electoral
    1996: Clinton, 47,402,357 popular, 379 electoral; Dole, 39,198,755 popular, 159 electoral; Perot, 8,085,402, 0 electoral
Inauguration: 1992: January 20, 1993
    1996: January 20, 1997
Vice President: Albert A. Gore (1993–2001)

CABINET

Secretary of State: Warren M. Christopher, CA (1993–1997); Madeleine K. Albright, Washington, DC (1997–2001)
Secretary of the Treasury: Lloyd M. Bentsen, TX (1993–1994); Robert E. Rubin, NY (1995–1999); Lawrence H. Summers, MA (1999–2001)
Secretary of Defense: Les Aspin, WI (1993–1994); William J. Perry, CA (1994–1997); William S. Cohen, ME (1997–2001)
Attorney General: Janet Reno, FL (1993–2001)
Secretary of Agriculture: Mike Espy, MS (1993–1994); Dan Glickman, KS (1995–2001)
Secretary of the Interior: Bruce Babbitt, AZ (1993–2001)
Secretary of Labor: Robert B. Reich, MA (1993–1997); Alexis Herman, AL (1997–2001)
Secretary of Commerce: Ronald H. Brown, NY (1993–1996); Mickey Kantor, CA (1996–1997); William Daley, IL (1997–2001)
Secretary of Health and Human Services: Donna E. Shalala, WI (1993–2001)
Secretary of Housing and Urban Development: Henry G. Cisneros, TX (1993–1997); Andrew M. Cuomo, NY (1997–2001)
Secretary of Transportation: Federico F. Pena, CO (1993–1997); Rodney E. Slater, AK (1997–2001)
Secretary of Energy: Hazel R. O'Leary, MN (1993–1997); Federico F. Pena, CO (1997–1998); Bill Richardson, AZ (1998–2001)
Secretary of Education: Richard W. Riley, SC (1993–2001)
Secretary of Veterans Affairs: Jesse Brown, IL (1993–1997); Togo D. West, Washington, DC (1998–2001)

CONGRESS:

103rd Congress (1993–1995); Speaker of the House: Thomas S. Foley (Democrat, WA)
104th Congress (1995–1997); Speaker of the House: Newt Gingrich (Republican, GA)
105th Congress (1997–1999); Speaker of the House: Newt Gingrich (Republican, GA)
106th Congress (1999–2001); Speaker of the House: J. Dennis Hastert (Republican, IL)

SUPREME COURT APPOINTEES:

Ruth Bader Ginsburg, NY; Associate Justice (1993–)
Stephen G. Breyer, MA; Associate Justice (1994–)

MAJOR EVENTS OF THE CLINTON ADMINISTRATION

◆ Clinton is sworn in as the forty-second president on January 20, 1993.

◆ On January 25, 1993, Clinton appoints First Lady Hillary Rodham Clinton to lead the Task Force on National Health Care Reform. A comprehensive plan is developed and announced in September 1993, but opposition from private insurance companies and many conservatives, as well as competing plans from other Democrats, prevent its serious consideration as potential legislation.

◆ On January 29, 1993, Clinton announces a six-month policy that prohibits the military from asking recruits about their sexual orientation. According to this policy, known as "don't ask, don't tell," as long as gays do not proclaim their sexual orientation or openly engage in behavior suggesting their homosexuality, the military will not seek to uncover this information.

◆ President Clinton signs the Family and Medical Leave Act (FMLA), February 5, 1993. It provides for twelve weeks of unpaid leave for covered employees under a variety of circumstances, including the birth or adoption of a child and the serious illness of a family member.

◆ On February 28, 1993, FBI agents raid the Branch Davidian compound near Waco, Texas, to serve the religious cult leader David Koresh with an arrest warrant for illegal possession of firearms. Four agents and an undetermined number of Davidians die in the raid; a 51-day siege begins. The siege ends on April 19 when fire engulfs the compound as federal agents attempt to enter it. Eighty Davidians, including Koresh, perish in the fire.

◆ Janet Reno becomes the first female attorney general of the United States, March 11, 1993.

◆ On May 19, 1993, seven members of the White House travel office are accused of mishandling money and summarily fired, although none are ever indicted for or convicted of this offense. Opponents dub the incident "Travelgate," accusing the Clintons of firing the career staffers to replace them with political cronies.

◆ On June 14, 1993, Clinton nominates Ruth Bader Ginsburg to the Supreme Court. She is confirmed as associate justice by the Senate two months later.

◆ In retaliation for an alleged plot by Iraqi intelligence under orders of Saddam Hussein to kill former President George H. W. Bush during a visit to Kuwait in April 1993, the United States launches a missile attack on Iraq's intelligence center in Baghdad on June 26, 1993.

◆ July 20, 1993, White House lawyer and long-time Clinton associate Vince Foster is found dead in Fort Marcy Park in Washington, DC. The death is ruled a suicide by various investigators, including Independent Counsel Kenneth Starr, but conspiracy theorists postulate that either his body was moved to prevent its discovery in some location that would prove embarrassing to the administration or he was murdered to prevent his disclosure of damaging information on the Clintons.

◆ On August 10, 1993, Clinton signs the Omnibus Budget Reconciliation Act, a deficit reduction bill calling for tax increases and spending cuts. The bill had passed the House by two votes and required the vote of Vice President Gore to break the tie in the Senate.

◆ Israel's Prime Minster Yitzhak Rabin and Yasser Arafat, chairman of the Palestinian

Liberation Organization (PLO), sign the Oslo Accords at the White House, September 13, 1993. The agreement provides for five years of interim self-rule by Palestinians, during which negotiations continue for a permanent settlement of boundaries, sovereignty, security, and other issues.

◆ Three US soldiers who are part of a UN force attempting to relieve widespread famine in Somalia are killed by a landmine on October 3, 1993. The UN force subsequently attacks Somalian warlord Mohammed Farah Aidid, and in the ensuing battle twenty more US soldiers are killed. Video images of two US soldiers' naked bodies being dragged through the streets of Mogadishu (the capital) are broadcast around the world.

◆ On October 7, 1993, President Clinton orders 15,000 US reinforcements to Somalia.

◆ November 30, 1993, Clinton signs the Brady Bill into law; it establishes a five-day waiting period and background checks for handgun purchases. The bill is named for James Brady, the White House press secretary who was shot and seriously injured during a 1981 assassination attempt on President Ronald Reagan.

◆ Clinton signs the controversial North American Free Trade Agreement (NAFTA) on December 8, 1993; the agreement calls for the gradual elimination of tariffs and trade barriers between Canada, the United States, and Mexico.

◆ On January 6, 1994, Clinton's mother, Virginia Kelley, dies from breast cancer.

◆ On January 12, 1994, Attorney General Janet Reno announces the appointment of Robert Fiske, an independent counsel, to investigate Whitewater, a failed real estate development corporation in Arkansas. Despite allegations of impropriety on the part of the Clintons, who were partners in the venture, special prosecutors eventually conclude that there is insufficient evidence to charge them with any crime.

◆ The last US troops leave Somalia, March 25, 1994.

◆ On April 27, 1994, Clinton, and former Presidents Ford, Carter, Reagan, and Bush attend the funeral of former President Richard Nixon.

◆ On May 6, 1994, Paula Jones files a sexual harassment lawsuit against Clinton, alleging that when he was governor of Arkansas and she was a state employee, he had propositioned her and engaged in other sexually explicit behavior in a Little Rock hotel room. Clinton denies the charges; the case is settled out of court in 1998, with Clinton paying an $850,000 settlement without admitting guilt and Jones agreeing to drop the lawsuit.

◆ Clinton nominates Stephen Breyer to the Supreme Court, May 13, 1994. He is confirmed as associate justice by the Senate two months later.

◆ Robert Fiske deposes Bill and Hillary Clinton at the White House on June 12, 1994. The deposition is the first for a sitting president and first lady.

◆ On July 26, 1994, Congress starts its own hearings on the Whitewater scandal. On August 5 a panel of three federal judges selects Kenneth Starr to take over the official investigation.

◆ Clinton dispatches US troops to Haiti on September 15, 1994, to restore ousted President Jean-Bertrand Aristide to power.

◆ On September 26, 1994, Senate Majority Leader George Mitchell declares an official end to Clinton's health care initiative.

◆ Clinton and his Russian counterpart, Boris Yeltsin, meet in Washington on September 27, 1994, reaching agreements on disarmament and economic ties.

◆ On October 26, 1994, with Clinton looking on, Prime Minister Yitzhak Rabin of Israel and King Hussein of Jordan sign a formal treaty, ending forty-six years of conflict.

◆ In the midterm elections of November 8, 1994, the Republicans gain new majorities in both the House and the Senate. The 104th Congress selects Newt Gingrich as Speaker of the House. Gingrich mounts a congressional campaign to implement his "Contract with America," a series of detailed Republican proposals developed to reform the federal government. The Contract promises fiscal responsibility, a balanced budget, cuts in welfare, limits on litigation, and job creation.

◆ On December 9, 1994, Clinton dismisses Surgeon General Joycelyn Elders for a controversial statement on masturbation, in which she described it as "part of human sexuality."

◆ Clinton nominates Dr. Henry Foster for surgeon general on February 2, 1995. Foster, an obstetrician, is criticized by conservatives for having performed abortions; he withdraws from consideration after the Republicans lead a filibuster in the Senate.

◆ On July 7, 1995, the Clinton administration normalizes US relations with Vietnam.

◆ On July 18, 1995, the Senate Whitewater Committee begins its hearings on Whitewater and Vince Foster's suicide.

◆ On August 17, 1995, a grand jury charges James and Susan McDougal and Arkansas Governor Jim Guy Tucker with bank fraud.

◆ November 13, 1995, Clinton vetoes the balanced budget proposal submitted by the House and the federal government comes to a grinding halt. A second shutdown occurs from December through January.

◆ Hillary Clinton's billing records from the Rose Law Firm are found in the White House residence on January 4, 1996.

◆ On January 22, 1996, Independent Counsel Kenneth Starr calls upon Hillary Clinton to testify under oath about the billing records, marking the first time a first lady has ever been subpoenaed. She offers testimony before a grand jury on January 26, 1996.

◆ In his State of the Union address on January 23, 1996, Clinton declares, "The era of big government is over."

◆ April 3, 1996, Secretary of Commerce Ron Brown is killed in a plane crash in Croatia.

◆ On April 9, 1996, Clinton signs a bill granting the US chief executive the "line-item veto," the ability to veto a specific item in a budget or tax bill without vetoing the entire piece of legislation.

◆ Vice President Al Gore attends a fund-raising event at a Buddhist temple in Los Angeles, April 29, 1996. The event raises $60,000 for the Democratic National Committee, but draws instant criticism because donors are reimbursed by the temple in contravention of campaign finance laws.

◆ In May, 1996, Clinton's former business partners in the Whitewater investment scheme, Jim and Susan McDougal, and Arkansas Governor Jim Guy Tucker, are convicted of fraud in the first trial to emerge from the Whitewater investigation.

◆ On August 22, 1996, after vetoing two previous versions, Clinton signs a welfare reform bill, officially entitled the Personal Responsibility and Work Opportunity Reconciliation Act of 1996. The bill provides for "welfare to work" initiatives.

◆ On August 21, 1996, Clinton signs the Health Insurance Portability and Accountability Act (HIPAA), a compromise health care package. One of HIPAA's provisions is the greater confidentiality of a patient's medical records.

◆ December 5, 1996, Clinton nominates Madeleine Albright as secretary of state; the Senate confirms her appointment a month later.

◆ On January 20, 1997, Bill Clinton is sworn in for his second term.

◆ The Supreme Court rules that the Paula Jones case can proceed while Clinton is in office, May 27, 1997.

◆ On August 5, 1997, Clinton signs legislation that promises to balance the federal budget by 2002.

◆ On January 12, 1998, former White House employee Linda Tripp, transferred to the Pentagon when Clinton became president, gives Kenneth Starr's office tape recordings of her private conversations with Monica Lewinsky, in which Lewinsky describes the details of her affair with the president.

◆ On January 16, 1998, Kenneth Starr expands his investigation into allegations that Clinton and his close friend and adviser, Vernon Jordan, pressured Monica Lewinsky into lying under oath about her alleged relationship with the president.

◆ January 17, 1998, during a videotaped deposition in the Paula Jones lawsuit, Clinton denies having a sexual relationship with Monica Lewinsky.

◆ In a January 27, 1998, appearance on the *Today* morning show, Hillary Clinton speaks of a "vast right-wing conspiracy" to remove her husband from office. The same day Kenneth Starr begins his grand jury investigation into the Monica Lewinsky allegations.

◆ On February 2, 1998, Clinton signs the first balanced budget since 1969.

◆ Appearing on *60 Minutes*, March 18, 1998, former Clinton aide Kathleen Willey claims that the president made sexual advances toward her in 1993.

◆ On April 1, 1998, Paula Jones's sexual harassment lawsuit is dismissed.

◆ After Clinton intervenes in the negotiations, Catholic and Protestant leaders in Northern Ireland sign an agreement, the Good Friday Peace Accords, on April 10, 1998.

◆ On August 6, 1998, under the glare of unprecedented media coverage, Monica Lewinsky testifies before a federal grand jury about her prior relationship with President Clinton.

◆ President Clinton testifies the next day, on closed circuit TV, about his relationship with Lewinsky. In a televised address later that evening he admits to the nation that he had maintained a relationship with the former White House intern which was "not appropriate . . . in fact, it was wrong." He also states that he never asked her or anyone else to lie under oath.

◆ On August 20, 1998, US forces fire cruise missiles at targets in Sudan and Afghanistan following terrorist attacks on the US embassies in Kenya and Tanzania.

◆ On September 9, 1998, Kenneth Starr releases his report to Congress, citing eleven potential impeachable offenses. The report is published on September 11, with excerpts appearing in major daily newspapers.

◆ The House Judiciary Committee approves the first three articles of impeachment against President Clinton on December 11, 1998, and on the 12th, the fourth.

◆ In Operation Desert Fox, US and British forces attack Iraqi military installations on December 16, 1998, after Iraq's failure to agree to weapons inspections.

◆ On December 19, 1998, the House votes to impeach Clinton on charges of perjury and obstruction of justice.

◆ The impeachment trial of Clinton opens on January 7, 1999, in the Senate chamber.

◆ On February 12, 1999, the Senate votes 55 to 45 against the perjury charge and 50 to 50 on the obstruction of justice charge. With the impeachment effort failing to capture the two-thirds majority vote required for ouster, Clinton remains in office.

◆ NATO begins a campaign of airstrikes in Yugoslavia to quell Serbian attacks on Albanians in Kosovo, March 24, 1999.

◆ On October 18, 1999, Kenneth Starr resigns as independent counsel; he is replaced by Robert Ray.

◆ Hillary Clinton announces on February 6, 2000, that she will run for Congress.

◆ In June 2000 Clinton meets with Russian president Vladimir Putin to discuss strategic arms reductions and the planned US missile-defense system.

◆ October 12, 2000, the *USS Cole* is attacked in Yemen.

◆ On January 3, 2001, Hillary Rodham Clinton is sworn in as a US senator representing the State of New York.

MAJOR US AND WORLD EVENTS, 1993–2001

◆ A bomb planted by terrorists explodes in the garage below the North Tower of the World Trade Center on February 26, 1993, killing six and injuring more than a thousand.

◆ On April 22, 1993, the US Holocaust Memorial Museum is dedicated in Washington, D.C.

◆ In June 1993 Heidi Fleiss is arrested in Los Angeles and accused of running a high-priced call girl business, catering to the rich and famous. She allegedly has a "little black book" that will name clients. Actor Charlie Sheen admits to being one of her paying customers. Fleiss is convicted in 1997 and serves three years in prison.

◆ On June 23, 1993, Lorena Bobbitt cuts several inches from the penis of her husband,

John Wayne Bobbitt, later claiming that he abused her sexually and emotionally on a regular basis. She is acquitted of criminal charges but ordered to spend forty-five days in a mental institution.

◆ On June 25, 1993, Kim Campbell becomes the first woman prime minister of Canada, serving until November 1993.

◆ John Grisham publishes *The Client*, 1993.

◆ John Gray publishes *Men Are from Mars, Women Are from Venus*, 1993.

◆ Stephen Ambrose publishes *Band of Brothers*, 1993.

◆ E. Annie Proulx publishes *The Shipping News*, 1993.

◆ Popular music hits of 1993 include Whitney Houston's "I Will Always Love You," Sting's "If I Ever Lose My Faith in You," Dr. Dre's "Let Me Ride," and Aerosmith's "Livin' on the Edge."

◆ Television series debuting in 1993 include *Beavis and Butt-Head*, *Boy Meets World*, *Cracker*, *Diagnosis Murder*, *Dr. Quinn Medicine Woman*, *Frasier*, *Grace Under Fire*, *Homicide: Life on the Street*, *The Iron Chef* (the Japanese title is *Ryori no tetsujin*), *The Jon Stewart Show*, *Late Night with Conan O'Brien*, *Late Show with David Letterman*, *Lois & Clark*, *The Nanny*, *NYPD Blue*, *Star Trek: Deep Space Nine*, and *The X Files*.

◆ Notable films of 1993 include Steven Spielberg's *Schindler's List* with Liam Neeson and Ben Kingsley, Jane Campion's *The Piano* with Holly Hunter and Harvey Keitel, Andrew Davis's *The Fugitive* with Harrison Ford and Tommy Lee Jones, Steven Spielberg's *Jurassic Park* with Sam Neill, Laura Dern, and Jeff Goldblum, Chris Columbus's *Mrs. Doubtfire* with Robin Williams and Sally Field, Jonathan Demme's *Philadelphia* with Tom Hanks and Denzel Washington, and James Ivory's *The Remains of the Day* with Anthony Hopkins and Emma Thompson.

◆ Figure skater Nancy Kerrigan is attacked on January 6, 1994, at the US National Figure Skating Championship. Rival skater Tonya Harding's ex-husband Jeff Gillooly and two others are later found guilty of the assault, intended to disable Kerrigan before the upcoming Winter Olympics.

◆ On January 17, 1994, an earthquake measuring 6.6 on the Richter scale hits Los Angeles.

◆ On April 6, 1994, a plane carrying President Habyarimana of Rwanda, a Hutu, is shot down, setting off a hundred-day massacre during which perhaps as many as 800,000 rival Tutsi are killed.

◆ The Channel Tunnel (affectionately called the "Chunnel"), a rail tunnel under the English Channel connecting England and France, is officially opened in a ceremony held in Calais on May 6, 1994.

◆ On May 10, 1994, Nelson Mandela is inaugurated as president of South Africa, winning the country's first multiracial elections.

◆ Nicole Brown Simpson, ex-wife of football legend O. J. Simpson, and her friend Ronald Goldman are murdered outside her home in the Brentwood section of Los Angeles on the evening of June 12, 1994.

◆ On December 18, 1994, a network of caves is discovered in the south of France that contains the oldest known cave paintings, dated at 31,000 years old (from the Paleolithic era). The caves are soon named the Chauvet Caves after one of the amateur speleologists who discovered them.

◆ Jonathan Weiner publishes *The Beak of the Finch*, 1994.

◆ Mikal Gilmore publishes *Shot in the Heart*, 1994.

◆ Henry Lewis Gates publishes *Colored People*, 1994.

◆ Rick Moody publishes *The Ice Storm*, 1994.

◆ John Berendt publishes *Midnight in the Garden of Good and Evil*, 1994.

◆ Popular music hits of 1994 include Bruce Springsteen's "Streets of Philadelphia," Sheryl Crow's "All I Wanna Do," Aerosmith's "Crazy," and Babyface's "When Can I See You."

◆ Television shows debuting in 1994 include *Babylon 5*, *Chicago Hope*, *Dennis Miller Live*, *Ellen*, *ER*, *Friends*, *Inside the Actors' Studio*, *My So-Called Life*, *Party of Five*, and *Touched by an Angel*.

◆ Notable films of 1994 include Tom Shadyac's *Ace Ventura: Pet Detective* with Jim

Carrey, Tim Burton's *Ed Wood* with Johnny Depp and Martin Landau, Robert Zemeckis's *Forrest Gump* with Tom Hanks, Disney's *The Lion King*, Oliver Stone's *Natural Born Killers* with Woody Harrelson and Juliette Lewis, Quentin Tarantino's *Pulp Fiction* with John Travolta, Samuel L. Jackson, and Uma Thurman, Robert Redford's *Quiz Show* with Ralph Fiennes and Rob Morrow, Frank Darabont's *The Shawshank Redemption* with Morgan Freeman and Tim Robbins, and Krzysztof Kieslowski's *Red* with Irene Jacob and Jean-Louis Trintignant.

◆ The United Nations withdraws peacekeeping troops from Somalia on March 3, 1995.

◆ A car bomb destroys the Murrah Federal Building in Oklahoma City, Oklahoma, on April 19, 1995, killing 168 people. Police arrest Timothy McVeigh within an hour of the explosion.

◆ Jacques Chirac is elected president of France on May 17, 1995.

◆ On September 26, 1995, with his legal "dream team" having questioned the reliability of a mountain of forensic (including DNA) evidence, O. J. Simpson is found not guilty of the murders of his ex-wife Nicole and her friend Ronald Goldman. Many accuse the defense, led by controversial civil rights attorney Johnnie Cochran, of playing the race card.

◆ On November 4, 1995, Prime Minister Yitzhak Rabin of Israel is assassinated in Tel Aviv by a member of an extremist right-wing organization.

◆ The presidents of Serbia, Croatia, and Bosnia-Herzegovina sign a peace pact at Wright-Patterson Air Force Base near Dayton, Ohio, on November 21, 1995, ending four years of civil war.

◆ Richard Ford publishes *Independence Day*, 1995.

◆ Colin Powell publishes *My American Journey*, 1995.

◆ James Redfield publishes *The Celestine Prophecy*, 1995.

◆ Michael Crichton publishes *The Lost World*, 1995.

◆ John Grisham publishes *The Rainmaker*, 1995.

◆ David Herbert Donald publishes *Lincoln*, 1995.

◆ Jonathan Kozol publishes *Amazing Grace*, 1995.

◆ Popular music hits of 1995 include Alanis Morisette's "You Outta Know," Seal's "Kiss From a Rose," Blues Traveler's "Run-Around," TLC's "Creep," and Annie Lennox's "No More I Love You's."

◆ Television series debuting in 1995 include *Caroline in the City*, *The Drew Carey Show*, *Hercules: The Legendary Journeys*, *JAG*, *The Jeff Foxworthy Show*, *Murder One*, *NewsRadio*, *Real Sports with Bryant Gumbel*, *Sliders*, *Star Trek: Voyager*, and *Xena: Warrior Princess*.

◆ Notable films of 1995 include Ron Howard's *Apollo 13* with Tom Hanks, Martin Scorsese's *Casino* with Robert De Niro and Sharon Stone, Amy Heckerling's *Clueless* with Alicia Silverstone, Oliver Stone's *Nixon* with Anthony Hopkins, Ang Lee's *Sense and Sensibility* with Emma Thompson and Kate Winslet, Bryan Singer's *The Usual Suspects* with Kevin Spacey and Gabriel Byrne, Tim Robbins' *Dead Man Walking* with Susan Sarandon and Sean Penn, Mel Gibson's *Braveheart*, and Mike Figgis's *Leaving Las Vegas* with Nicolas Cage and Elizabeth Shue.

◆ On April 3, 1996, the FBI arrest the suspected "Unabomber," Theodore Kaczynski, in rural Montana after receiving a tip from his brother David.

◆ A ewe named Dolly, the first mammal to be cloned from an adult cell, is born on July 5, 1996.

◆ A bomb explodes at the Atlanta Summer Olympic games on July 27, 1996, killing two and injuring hundreds more. Two years later, Eric Rudolph is charged with the bombing as well as three others, and in April 2005, he admits to the crime as part of a plea bargain.

◆ The Taliban capture Kabul, the capital of Afghanistan, on September 27, 1996.

◆ An anonymous author (later identified as Washington columnist Joe Klein) publishes *Primary Colors*, 1996.

◆ Frank McCourt publishes *Angela's Ashes*, 1996.

◆ John le Carré publishes *The Tailor of Panama*, 1996.

◆ Tim LaHaye and Jerry B. Jenkins publish *Left Behind: A Novel of the Earth's Last Days*, 1996; it is the first book in the *Left Behind* series.

◆ Stephen Ambrose publishes *Undaunted Courage*, 1996.

◆ Jonathan Larson's *Rent* debuts on Broadway, 1996.

◆ Popular music hits of 1996 include Eric Clapton's "Change the World," Toni Braxton's "Un-Break My Heart," Dave Matthews Band's "So Much to Say," and Beck's "Where It's At."

◆ Television series debuting in 1996 include *Boston Common*, *The Daily Show*, *Everybody Loves Raymond*, *Judge Judy*, *Men Behaving Badly*, *The Rosie O'Donnell Show*, *Sabrina the Teenage Witch*, *Spin City*, *Suddenly Susan*, *3rd Rock from the Sun*, and *7th Heaven*.

◆ Notable films of 1996 include Anthony Minghella's *The English Patient* with Ralph Fiennes and Kristen Scott Thomas, Joel and Ethan Coen's *Fargo* with Frances McDormand, Douglas McGrath's *Emma* with Gwyneth Paltrow and Jeremy Northam, Cameron Crowe's *Jerry Maguire* with Tom Cruise and Renée Zellweger, Roland Emmerich's *Independence Day* with Will Smith and Jeff Goldblum, Billy Bob Thornton's *Sling Blade*, and Danny Boyle's *Trainspotting* with Ewan McGregor.

◆ Madeleine Albright, the first woman US secretary of state, is sworn in on January 23, 1997.

◆ February 19, 1997, Chinese leader Deng Xiaoping dies at the age of ninety-two.

◆ On April 13, 1997, twenty-one-year-old Tiger Woods wins the US Masters golf tournament in Augusta, Georgia. He is the youngest winner ever; he wins by twelve shots, a record, and posts the lowest score ever recorded.

◆ British Labour Party leader Tony Blair is appointed prime minister of the United Kingdom on May 2, 1997, when Labour wins a majority of the 179 seats in Parliament.

◆ On July 1, 1997, the territory of Hong Kong reverts from British to Chinese sovereignty, ending 156 years of British colonial rule.

◆ The Mars rover *Sojourner* begins its exploration of the planet's surface, July 6, 1997.

◆ On the evening of August 31, 1997, the car carrying Diana, Princess of Wales, is involved in a high-speed accident in Paris, France. The princess dies in a nearby hospital early the next morning. Her companion, Dodi Al Fayed, and the vehicle's driver, Henri Paul, are instantly killed.

◆ Mother Teresa, Nobel Peace Prize-winning champion of the poor, dies on September 5, 1997.

◆ Jon Krakauer publishes *Into Thin Air,* 1997.

◆ Toni Morrison publishes *Paradise*, 1997.

◆ Philip Roth publishes *American Pastoral*, 1997.

◆ Thomas Pynchon publishes *Mason & Dixon*, 1997.

◆ Don DeLillo publishes *Underworld*, 1997.

◆ Charles Frazier publishes *Cold Mountain*, 1997.

◆ J. K. Rowling publishes *Harry Potter and the Philosopher's Stone* (entitled *Harry Potter and the Sorcerer's Stone* in the United States), 1997.

◆ Mitch Alborn publishes *Tuesdays with Morrie*, 1997.

◆ Patricia Cornwell publishes *Unnatural Exposure*, 1997.

◆ Popular music hits of 1997 include Shawn Colvin's "Sunny Came Home," Blackstreet's "No Diggity," the Wallflowers's "One Headlight," and Jamiroquai's "Virtual Insanity."

◆ Television series debuting in 1997 include *Ally McBeal*, *Antiques Roadshow*, *Buffy the Vampire Slayer*, *Dharma & Greg*, *Emeril Live*, *Judge Joe Brown*, *Just Shoot Me!*, *King of the Hill*, *La Femme Nikita*, *The Practice*, *South Park*, *Stargate SG-1*, *Teletubbies*, and *The View*.

◆ Notable films of 1997 include James Cameron's *Titanic* with Kate Winslet and Leonardo DiCaprio, James L. Brooks's *As Good As It Gets* with Jack Nicholson, Helen Hunt, and Greg Kinnear, Peter Cattaneo's *The Full Monty* with Robert Carlyle and Tom Wilkinson,

Gus Van Sant's *Good Will Hunting* with Matt Damon and Robin Williams, Curtis Hanson's *L.A. Confidential* with Russell Crowe and Kevin Spacey, Barry Sonnenfield's *Men in Black* with Will Smith and Tommy Lee Jones, and Paul Thomas Anderson's *Boogie Nights* with Mark Wahlberg and Burt Reynolds.

◆ A new law prohibits smoking in all California bars and restaurants effective January 1, 1998.

◆ On January 8, 1998, cleric Ramzi Yousef is sentenced to 240 years in prison for masterminding the first World Trade Center bombing. Five other conspirators also receive 240-year prison sentences.

◆ The motion picture *Titanic* wins eleven Oscars at the Academy Awards on March 23, 1998.

◆ April 15, 1998, former Cambodian despot and mass murderer Pol Pot dies a peaceful death.

◆ On May 18, 1998, the US Department of Justice and twenty US states file a historic antitrust suit against Microsoft Corporation, alleging that the company abused its market power to hinder competition.

◆ After thirty-two years in power, President Suharto of Indonesia is pressured to resign on May 21, 1998, amid economic instability and charges of corruption.

◆ On August 7, 1998, bombs strike US embassies in Kenya and Tanzania. Osama bin Laden, a Saudi exile and suspected Islamic terrorist leader operating out of Afghanistan, is believed to have ordered the attacks.

◆ September 8, 1998, St. Louis Cardinals baseball player Mark McGwire breaks Roger Maris's 1961 record for single-season home runs. He finishes the season with seventy.

◆ On October 23, 1998, in Washington, Israeli Prime Minister Benjamin Netanyahu and Palestinian leader Yasser Arafat sign the Wye Memorandum authorizing Israeli troop withdrawals from parts of the West Bank. The PLO agree to stop calling for the destruction of the state of Israel.

◆ House Speaker-elect Bob Livingston resigns from Congress on December 28, 1998, under allegations of marital infidelity.

◆ Barbara Kingsolver publishes *The Poisonwood Bible*, 1998.

◆ Lorrie Moore publishes *Birds of America*, 1998.

◆ Michael Cunningham publishes *The Hours*, 1998.

◆ Tom Brokaw publishes *The Greatest Generation*, 1998.

◆ J. K. Rowling publishes *Harry Potter and the Chamber of Secrets*, 1998.

◆ Popular music hits of 1998 include Celine Dion's "My Heart Will Go On," Lauryn Hill's "Doo Wop (That Thing)," Madonna's "Ray of Light," and Lenny Kravitz's "Fly Away."

◆ Television series debuting in 1998 include *Any Day Now*, *Becker*, *Charmed*, *Dawson's Creek*, *Felicity*, *The King of Queens*, *Sex and the City*, *Sports Night*, *That '70s Show*, *Trading Places*, *Who Wants to Be a Millionaire?*, and *Will and Grace*.

◆ Notable films of 1998 include Shekhar Kapur's *Elizabeth* with Cate Blanchett, John Madden's *Shakespeare in Love* with Gwyneth Paltrow and Joseph Fiennes, Eric Darnell and Tim Johnson's *Antz*, Bill Condon's *Gods and Monsters* with Ian McKellen and Brendan Fraser, Roberto Benigni's *Life Is Beautiful*, Bobby and Peter Farrelly's *There's Something About Mary* with Cameron Diaz, Steven Spielberg's *Saving Private Ryan* with Tom Hanks, and Peter Weir's *The Truman Show* with Jim Carrey.

◆ On January 1, 1999, the euro is introduced as the common currency to be used by financial institutions of the eleven European Union (EU) member countries.

◆ Bertrand Piccard of Switzerland and Brian Jones of Great Britain complete the first successful nonstop circumnavigation of the world by hot-air balloon on March 21, 1999.

◆ On March 29, 1999, the Dow reaches 10,000 for the first time.

◆ On April 20, 1999, Dylan Klebold and Eric Harris, two teenaged students, carry out a shooting and bombing rampage at the Columbine High School in Littleton, Colorado, killing twelve students and a teacher and wounding twenty-three others before committing suicide, making it the worst instance of school violence in US history.

◆ Author Stephen King is hit by a van and seriously injured while walking on a road near his home in Maine, June 19, 1999.

◆ On the evening of July 16, 1999, John F. Kennedy, Jr., is killed along with his wife, Carolyn Bessette, and his sister-in-law, Lauren Bessette, as the single-engine plane he is piloting crashes into the sea off Martha's Vineyard.

◆ Australian voters reject replacing Britain's Queen Elizabeth with a president on November 6, 1999, thus maintaining their country's status as a constitutional monarchy.

◆ Jhumpa Lahiri publishes *Interpreter of Maladies*, 1999.

◆ Ha Jin publishes *Waiting*, 1999.

◆ Joanne Harris publishes *Chocolat*, 1999.

◆ J. K. Rowling publishes *Harry Potter and the Prisoner of Azkaban*, 1999.

◆ Popular music hits of 1999 include Carlos Santana's "Smooth," Sting's "Brand New Day," Sarah McLachlan's "I Will Remember You," and Cher's "Believe."

◆ Television series debuting in 1999 include *Angel*, *Big Brother*, *Family Guy*, *Freaks and Geeks*, *Futurama*, *Judging Amy*, *Law and Order: Special Victims Unit*, *The Man Show*, *The Naked Chef*, *Once and Again*, *Queer as Folk*, *Roswell*, *The Sopranos*, *SpongeBob SquarePants*, *Third Watch*, and *The West Wing*.

◆ Notable films of 1999 include Sam Mendes's *American Beauty* with Kevin Spacey and Annette Bening, Frank Darabont's *The Green Mile* with Tom Hanks and Michael Clarke Duncan, David Fincher's *Fight Club* with Edward Norton and Brad Pitt, Spike Jonze's *Being John Malkovich* with John Cusack and Cameron Diaz, M. Night Shyamalan's *The Sixth Sense* with Bruce Willis and Haley Joel Osment, Andy and Larry Wachowski's *The Matrix* with Keanu Reeves, Laurence Fishburne, and Carrie-Anne Moss, Tom Tykwer's *Run Lola Run* with Franka Potente, Michael Mann's *The Insider* with Russell Crowe, and Kimberly Peirce's *Boys Don't Cry* with Hilary Swank.

◆ On January 1, 2000, despite widespread concern about possible problems being triggered by computer programs that would not accept dates beyond the end of 1999, Y2K (short for "year 2000") passes with few reported problems.

◆ America Online, America's top Internet provider, announces on January 10, 2000, that it will acquire Time Warner, the world's top media conglomerate, making the merger the largest in corporate history.

◆ On February 13, 2000, the final original "Peanuts" comic strip appears in Sunday newspapers around the world, just hours after famous cartoonist Charles Schulz dies. The popular strip ran continuously from October 2, 1950.

◆ March 26, 2000, Vladimir Putin, the hand-picked successor of Boris Yeltsin, is officially elected president of Russia.

◆ On April 22, 2000, Elian Gonzalez, a six-year-old boy brought to the United States from Cuba by his mother, who died in the sea crossing, is reunited with his father at Andrews Air Force Base after US courts order him returned to his father, who wishes to take his son back to Cuba.

◆ April 25, 2000, Vermont begins issuing licenses for same-sex civil unions, providing homosexual couples with many of the same legal protections that heterosexual married couples have.

◆ Chen Shui-bian, a member of the Democratic Progressive Party, which has traditionally been supportive of Taiwan independence, is elected president of the Republic of China on May 20, 2000.

◆ The House normalizes trade relations with China on May 24, 2000.

◆ On July 25, 2000, an Air France Concorde crashes after takeoff from Paris, killing 109 people onboard and 4 on the ground.

◆ Hillary Rodham Clinton is elected US Senator from New York on November 7, 2000, becoming the only first lady ever elected to the US Senate.

◆ The 2000 census reveals a US population of 281.4 million people.

◆ Michael Chabon publishes *The Amazing Adventures of Kavalier and Klay*, 2000.

◆ Richard Ben Cramer publishes *Joe DiMaggio*, 2000.

◆ Ian Frazier publishes *On the Rez*, 2000.

◆ Philip Roth publishes *The Human Stain*, 2000.

◆ David Levering Lewis publishes *W. E. B. Du Bois: Biography of a Race 1868–1919*, 2000.

◆ Isabel Allende publishes *Daughter of Fortune*, 2000.

◆ J. K. Rowling publishes *Harry Potter and the Goblet of Fire*, 2000.

◆ Bruce Wilkinson and David Kopp publish *The Prayer of Jabez*, 2000.

◆ Popular music hits of 2000 include U2's "Beautiful Day," Macy Gray's "I Try," Faith Hill's "Breathe," and Destiny's Child's "Say My Name."

◆ Television series debuting in 2000 include *Boston Public, CSI: Crime Scene Investigation, Curb Your Enthusiasm, Dark Angel, Dora the Explorer, Ed, Gilmore Girls, Jackass, Malcolm in the Middle, Survivor*, and *Yes, Dear*.

◆ Notable films of 2000 include Stephen Soderburgh's *Erin Brockovich* with Julia Roberts, Stephen Soderburgh's *Traffic* with Michael Douglas and Benicio Del Toro, Christopher Guest's *Best in Show* with Michael McKean, Eugene Levy, and Catherine O'Hara, Joel Coen's *O Brother, Where Art Thou?* with George Clooney, Robert Zemeckis's *Cast Away* with Tom Hanks, Cameron Crowe's *Almost Famous* with Billy Crudup and Kate Hudson, Ridley Scott's *Gladiator* with Russell Crowe, and Ang Lee's *Crouching Tiger, Hidden Dragon* with Chow Yun-Fat and |Michelle Yeoh.

FAST FACTS ABOUT BILL CLINTON

◆ Clinton was the first US chief executive born after World War II, making him the first president from the "baby boom" generation.

◆ Elected governor of Arkansas in 1978 at the age of thirty-two, Clinton was the youngest governor in the country at the time and one of the youngest ever elected.

◆ During his first presidential campaign, Clinton appeared on the *Arsenio Hall Show* in 1992 and played "Heartbreak Hotel" on his saxophone.

◆ Clinton was the first president to assume power after the end of the Cold War.

◆ Clinton was only the second president ever to be impeached (the first was Andrew Johnson in 1868).

◆ Among those pardoned by Clinton in January 2001 was Patty Hearst, the newspaper heiress who was kidnapped in 1974 by the Symbionese Liberation Army (SLA), a radical group. During her captivity the indoctrinated heiress (aka "Tanya") had participated in a bank robbery with her captors.

◆ Clinton is the only US president who was a Rhodes scholar.

◆ Clinton became the first president to record his voice for the "Hall of Presidents" at Walt Disney World, to which his statue was added in 1993. (President George W. Bush has since recorded his voice for the same tourist attraction.)

◆ Hillary Clinton was the first wife of a sitting president to hold a post-graduate degree; she earned a law degree from Yale University Law School.

◆ The William J. Clinton Presidential Library, which opened in Little Rock, Arkansas, in November 2004, features the only full-scale replica of the Oval Office in a presidential library, as well as exhibits on Clinton's diplomatic efforts, Hillary Clinton's role as first lady, and the scandals that led to Clinton's impeachment and acquittal.

George W. Bush

Nickname: Dubya, Shrub, Bushie
Party: Republican
Presidency: 43rd president, 2001–
Life dates: July 6, 1946–

EARLY LIFE AND EDUCATION

George Walker Bush was born on July 6, 1946, in New Haven, Connecticut, when his father, George Herbert Walker Bush, the future 41st president, was a sophomore at Yale University. "Georgie," as the baby was known, was the first of six children of George H. W. Bush and his wife Barbara Pierce Bush. When Georgie was two, his family moved to Odessa, Texas, where George H. W. Bush started his career in the oil business. As the older Bush moved from one job in the oil industry to the next, the family followed him, moving through small towns in California before settling in Midland, Texas, in 1950, where he formed a partnership and began an oil exploration firm.

While the Bushes were in California in 1949, their daughter Robin was born. Another son, John ("Jeb"), was born in 1953. Later that year, after a long struggle with leukemia, Robin died at the age of three. The Bushes later had three more children: Neil in 1955, Marvin in 1956, and Dorothy in 1959.

With the elder Bush by then doing well in the oil business, the family moved into a large house in Midland. As a child, George enjoyed all kinds of sports, including Little League base-ball, and playing and watching football. George attended Sam Houston Elementary School in Midland, where he was known as a prankster in class. He was once punished for drawing sideburns on his face. He subsequently attended San Jacinto Junior High in Midland. When the family moved to Houston, George joined the eighth grade at the private Kinkade School.

As his father before him, George attended Phillips Academy in Andover, Massachusetts, for his high school years. There, he spent much of his time participating in extra-curricular activities. He played junior varsity basketball, was an enthusiastic cheerleader for the football team, and was "High Commissioner of Stickball," the urban street ball game that had become popular at the school.

George followed family tradition by attending Yale University beginning in 1964—his father and grandfather were both alumni. Like his father, George played baseball at the university, serving as a relief pitcher on the junior varsity team. George also joined his father's fraternity, Delta Kappa Epsilon, and was a member of the secretive Skull and Bones society, as his father had been. A history major, George was a "C" student. He was gregarious by nature and popular among his classmates, and enjoyed his share of college pranks. He was one of a group of students who tore down the Princeton goalposts after a Yale football victory, and he was also once arrested for stealing a Christmas wreath (the charges were later dropped). George became engaged to Cathryn Wolfram, a student at Rice University, in late 1966, but the engagement was called off in 1967. He graduated from college in 1968, one of the most tumultuous years in US history.

> "Americans are a free people who know that freedom is the right of every person and the future of every nation. The liberty we prize is not America's gift to the world; it is God's gift to humanity."
>
> George W. Bush, in his State of the Union address, January 28, 2003

Upon graduating from Yale, George became eligible for the draft that had been instituted to provide troops for the war in Vietnam. By his own admission, he did not want to serve as a member of the infantry fighting in Vietnam; he wanted to become a pilot, just as his father had done during World War II. In May 1968 George joined the Air National Guard, which committed him to thirty-nine days of service for each of the following six years. He enlisted in the 147th Fighter-Interceptor Group at Ellington Air Force Base in Houston. In November 1968 George started flight school at Moody Air Force Base in Valdosta, Georgia, spending a year there before returning to Ellington to train on F-102 fighter planes. He served at Ellington periodically through 1972. Between assignments George worked for the Republican Party on three Senate races: first in the 1968 campaign of Edward Gurney in Florida, then in 1970 for his father's

campaign in Texas, and next in the 1972 campaign of Winton "Red" Blount in Alabama. In 1973 George worked for the Professional United Leadership League (PULL), a program for troubled teenagers in the Houston area.

While in Montgomery, Alabama, George received permission to fulfill that year's National Guard commitment with a local unit. Many years later, during his second presidential bid, questions were raised about his service in Alabama—whether he in fact had satisfied his National Guard obligations. Although official records indicate that a year elapsed during which he did not report for duty, they also show that he was honorably discharged in October 1973.

Bush has referred to this period of his life as his "nomadic" years: He partied frequently, dated many women, drank heavily, and allegedly used cocaine. Despite his work on political campaigns, he remained largely apolitical, uninvolved with, and detached from, the many social changes sweeping America during these turbulent years. After first being denied admission to the University of Texas Law School, George attended Harvard Business School, beginning his studies there in 1973 and receiving an MBA in 1975.

EARLY CAREER

After securing his MBA, Bush returned to Midland to try his hand at the oil business. He began as a "landman," a go-between who researched mineral rights and tried to lease them. He had a little money—about $13,000— left over from a trust fund he had lived on while at Yale and Harvard. Bush lived modestly at first, in an apartment over a garage. In 1977 he established the Arbusto Energy Company (*arbusto* is the Spanish word for "bush"), opening an office in the Petroleum Building in Midland, the same building in which his father had set up shop in 1950.

Before starting up Arbusto, Bush ran for Congress, vying for a seat vacated by George Mahon, a conservative Democrat, who had served for forty-three years. Bush adopted a conservative, pro-business, antiregulation platform. He defeated the favorite, Jim Reese, in the Republican run-off, but lost to the Democratic candidate, State Senator Kent Hance, by 53 percent to 47 percent in the 1978 election. Both Reese and Hance attacked Bush as a carpetbagger from the Northeast who was an interloper in Texas politics.

While campaigning for Congress, Bush met thirty-year-old librarian Laura Welch at a cookout hosted by mutual friends in Midland. Laura had grown up in Midland, the only daughter of Harold Welch, a house builder, and Jenna Welch. She had attended Southern Methodist University, where she received a degree in education, and the University of Texas, where she earned a master's degree in library science. Laura had worked at public schools in Dallas and Houston, and was living in Austin, where she was employed as a librarian, when she met Bush during a visit back home. After a three-month courtship, on November 5, 1977, the couple married. George Bush promised his wife that she would not have to make political speeches, but when she joined him on the campaign trail throughout the Midland area, she did just that. Laura Bush gave birth to twin girls, Jenna Welch Bush and Barbara Pierce Bush, on November 25, 1981.

At Arbusto, beginning in 1979, George Bush sought investors in oil and gas drilling. Oil prices were rising fast; Bush's uncle Jonathan helped him find investors; Bush also called on his own contacts from Yale and Harvard. He raised some money with an otherwise unsuccessful public offering in 1982. The company's prospecting hit oil or gas at a rate of nearly 50 percent, but it showed a poor return on its investments. Bush changed Arbusto's name to the Bush Exploration Company later that year.

In 1984 Bush Exploration merged with a company called Spectrum 7, and Bush became chairman of the new enterprise, with a $75,000 salary. Investment in oil fell off precipitously when prices collapsed in 1986. Spectrum 7 ran up debts of $3 million, and in September 1986 it was taken over by a Dallas firm, Harken Oil and Gas, whose biggest stockholder was billionaire George Soros. George Bush received $300,000

in Harken stock and a seat on the board, and was paid as a consultant, but with the sale of Spectrum 7, he was effectively out of the oil business. It was during this phase of his career that Bush, who was a heavy drinker, decided to give up alcohol after raucously celebrating his fortieth birthday with family and friends in Colorado Springs. Around the same time, Bush also became a born-again Christian.

In 1988 Bush relocated with his family to Washington, DC, to help support his father's bid for the presidency. When he moved back to Texas in 1989, Bush considered running for office again. Instead, he organized a group of investors that purchased the Texas Rangers, a major league baseball team, from Eddie Chiles, a Bush family friend. Of the $89 million asking price, Bush put up $500,000, later raising his stake to slightly more than $600,000. He became managing general partner and the public face of the team. In order to pay off the money he borrowed to help purchase the Rangers, Bush sold his 212,140 shares in Harken Oil and Gas at $4 a share. Two weeks later the publication of poor earning results for Karken caused a sharp drop in the value of its stock. In 1991 the Securities and Exchange Commission investigated the sale and determined that Bush had filed the necessary paperwork but beyond the required deadline; the inquiry, however, was closed with no formal action taken.

POLITICAL CAREER

George Bush's prominent position with the Rangers helped raise his profile in Texas, and in 1993 he announced his candidacy for the Republican gubernatorial nomination. Former President George H. W. Bush helped his son raise a large campaign fund. After winning the primary and backed by a team of skilled advisers including Karl Rove, Bush challenged the incumbent, Democrat Ann Richards, with a concise four-point manifesto on education, stricter penalties for juvenile crime, tort reform, and welfare reform. With his campaign machine effectively hammering away at these issues, Bush was elected governor with more than 53 percent of the vote.

Before he took office in Austin, Bush relinquished his role as managing partner of the Texas Rangers. In 1998, when the team was sold to a group headed by Thomas O. Hicks for $250 million, Bush's original investment of $606,000 was parlayed into almost $15 million.

As governor, Bush quickly moved to make good on his four campaign promises. He forged important relationships with key Democrats, including House Speaker Pete Laney and Lieutenant Governor Bob Bullock, thus ensuring broader support for his sweeping reforms in the State Senate. Bush toughened incarceration guidelines for juvenile offenders and lowered the age that they could be tried as adults. He also signed into law a statute permitting gun owners to carry a concealed weapon. In the area of education, school administrators' salaries were linked to student performance, and statewide standards improved as a result. Bush also instituted limited tort reform and subjected those receiving public assistance to work requirements.

Bush was overwhelmingly reelected in November 1998, capturing 69 percent of the vote against Land Commissioner Gary Mauro, which translated into 1.4 million votes and 239 of Texas's 254 counties. His popularity made him an immediate front-runner for the 2000 Republican nomination for president. In March 1999 Bush formed a presidential exploratory committee and started raising money, and by the time of the general election, he had amassed a record war chest of $175 million.

In the early primaries, the Republican field was crowded. Bush won the Iowa caucuses in January 2000, beating wealthy publisher Steve Forbes. But in February Arizona Senator John McCain defeated Bush in the New Hampshire primary, forcing a key fight between the two in South Carolina, which Bush won but at the expense of soured relations with McCain. McCain, viewed as more of a moderate, held on and won primaries in Michigan and his home state of Arizona. However, George Bush prevailed on "Super Tuesday," the busiest day of the primary season, with the key support of California, New York, and Ohio, causing McCain to withdraw

from the race and publicly endorse Bush. At the Republican Convention in Philadelphia, Bush was formally nominated; he chose former Wyoming Congressman and Secretary of Defense (under George H. W. Bush) Dick Cheney as his running mate for his long-running political experience and military knowledge.

George Bush faced Bill Clinton's two-term vice president, Al Gore, who overcame an early challenge by Senator Bill Bradley of New Jersey. Gore had selected Senator Joseph Lieberman of Connecticut, a devoutly Jewish moderate, as his running mate. Although Gore started his campaign with a lead over Bush in public opinion polls, he soon sought to distance himself from the Clinton presidency, no doubt because of its many scandals. Many Democrats later regarded this as a serious tactical error on the part of Gore's campaign team, given the strong appeal the former president still had for many voters. Bush meanwhile, though backed by powerful conservative groups within the country, began to increasingly position himself as a moderate candidate with the electorate. Describing himself as a "compassionate conservative," he promised to unite what seemed like an often bitterly divided nation if elected and implement tax cuts, welfare, Social Security, and Medicare reform, as well as strengthen the military. In the days leading up to the election, the media revealed that Bush had been arrested for driving under the influence in Kennebunkport, Maine, in 1976. He had pleaded guilty to a misdemeanor and paid a fine. The Bush camp acknowledged the arrest, but declined to discuss it beyond a simple admission, rendering the police record a non-issue for many voters.

The election took place on November 7, 2000, and became one of the most bitterly contested elections in US history. On election night several major media outlets projected Gore to be the winner, whereas others declared Bush the victor. Based on initial tallies, Gore conceded the election to his opponent, but then retracted his concession when it became clear that the electoral college vote count hinged on the outcome in Florida, and the vote in that state remained too close to call.

On November 9, with the election still undecided, Bush led in Florida by about 2,000 votes; after a machine recount, as mandated by state law, his lead fell to 327. Democrats called for manual recounts in four counties, where there were numerous irregularities and some voters alleged tactics intended to disenfranchise them. Florida's Secretary of State Kathleen Harris (a Republican and chairman of the Bush-Cheney campaign in Florida) ruled that the hand recounts would not be included, but on appeal, the Florida Supreme Court decided in favor of Gore, asserting that recounts must be included in the certified result. As absentee votes were tallied, vote totals continued to change on a daily basis. By November 18 Bush led in Florida by 930 votes, but the result had not been certified. The Florida Supreme Court set a deadline of November 26 for all recounts to be included; that date passed with some counties not yet able to finish their recounts. More lawsuits and counter-lawsuits were filed, with Bush calling for a result and Gore requesting an extension so all recounts could be completed and included in the total. The Florida Supreme Court ruled in favor of Gore, leading some representatives in the Florida state legislature to threaten to appoint the state's electors.

Finally, the US Supreme Court agreed to hear Bush's appeal of the Florida decision. On December 12, 2000, the Court issued its now historic decision, voting 5 to 4 that there was insufficient time to establish a uniform standard for recounts. The recounts came to a halt, and the election result was certified. On December 13 Gore decided to accept the Court's decision as final and conceded the election to Bush. Many breathed a sigh of relief—with the nation spared a constitutional crisis—but others viewed the Supreme Court's decision as an improper intrusion on a state's right to formulate its own election policy. To some of these embittered voters, it seemed as if the Court had handed down the presidency to Bush without regard for the will of the electorate.

By last count Bush won Florida by 537 votes, or 0.009 percent of the popular vote. Green Party candidate Ralph Nader made a strong showing in the election, winning almost three million votes, including 90,000 in Florida. His candidacy definitely hurt Gore the most. As it was, though, Al Gore bested George W. Bush in the popular tally by some 500,000 votes. For the fourth time in US history, a president who had failed to win the popular vote was elected; the other three instances occurred in 1824 with John Quincy Adams, in 1876 with Rutherford B. Hayes, and in 1888 with Benjamin Harrison.

PRESIDENCY

Amid continuing controversy regarding the election result, George W. Bush was sworn in as the 43rd president on January 20, 2001. He quickly went to work to implement the tax cuts he had promised during the campaign. A complex series of tax measures passed the House and Senate and were signed into law by Bush in June 2001. New tax regulations included relief for low-wage earners and reduced rates for those falling in the top income brackets.

In 2001 Congress passed legislation reducing federal restrictions on religious organizations and their charitable activities. By executive order, Bush established a new White House Office of Faith-Based and Community Initiatives, to evaluate and fund the proposals of national religious groups and community organizations.

The course of Bush's first term was dramatically altered on September 11, 2001. Shortly after its take-off, hijackers seized control of American Airlines Flight 11 (which had left Boston en route to Los Angeles) and at 8.47 a.m. crashed the jet into the North Tower of the World Trade Center in New York City. At 9:02, a second hijacked plane, United Airlines Flight 175 (also seized after departing from Boston), slammed into the South Tower of the World Trade Center. At 9:41, American Airlines Flight 77, commandeered after take-off from Dulles Airport, crashed into the Pentagon in Washington, DC. Both towers in New York City remained ablaze for approximately an hour, until 9:50 when the South Tower collapsed, followed by the North Tower nearly forty minutes later. A fourth hijacked plane, United Airlines Flight 93, crashed into an open field in Shanksville, Pennsylvania (southeast of Pittsburgh), around 10 a.m. It was later learned that the passengers on-board Flight 93, by then aware of the devastation at the World Trade Center, recognized the intent of their hijackers—with the plane on course to Washington, DC, to possibly destroy the US Capitol or the White House—and decided to prevent its use against another target on the ground.

> "The pictures of airplanes flying into buildings, fires burning, huge structures collapsing, have filled us with disbelief, terrible sadness, and a quiet, unyielding anger. These acts of mass murder were intended to frighten our nation into chaos and retreat. But they have failed; our country is strong. A great people has been moved to defend a great nation. Terrorist attacks can shake the foundations of our biggest buildings, but they cannot touch the foundation of America. These acts shattered steel, but they cannot dent the steel of American resolve."
>
> George W. Bush, in his evening address to the nation after the terrorist attacks, September 11, 2001

As the tragic situation unfolded that morning, Bush was making a previously scheduled appearance at the Emma E. Booker Elementary School in Sarasota, Florida. After learning of the attacks, he made a short public statement be-fore boarding Air Force One. That night the president returned to Washington, DC and addressed the nation.

Rescue efforts continued at the World Trade Center site—termed Ground Zero—for many days until it became a somber recovery operation. Among those lost were hundreds of fire-fighters, police officers, and emergency medical technicians who had responded to the catastrophe. Close to 3,000 people died in the 9/11 attacks.

The Bush administration prepared its response to the worst attack on US soil since Pearl Harbor. Quickly, the focus of blame fell on the al Qaeda terrorist network of Osama bin Laden, which had already been connected with the attacks on US embassies in Kenya and Tanzania in 1998, and on the USS Cole in 2000. The United States' first retaliatory military actions focused on Afghanistan, where the Taliban regime was thought to be sheltering bin Laden and al Qaeda training camps. Before a joint session of Congress, Bush demanded that the Taliban hand over bin Laden and close al Qaeda camps operating within its borders. Bush also established a new Office of Homeland Security, naming former Pennsylvania Governor Tom Ridge as its head. In November 2002 this office became the Department of Homeland Security, with cabinet-level status, and consolidating 22 agencies and 180,000 employees with responsibility for intelligence gathering, border security and immigration, counterterrorism, and emergency preparedness and response.

Just a few short weeks after the World Trade Center attacks, letters tainted with anthrax began to circulate through the US mail. The first were addressed to NBC Nightly News then anchor Tom Brokaw and the New York Post. In early October Robert Stevens, a photo editor, died after inhaling anthrax at his workplace, the American Media office in Delray Beach, Florida. Several members of Congress (including then Senate Democratic Majority Leader Tom Daschle of South Dakota) also received mail contaminated with anthrax, and government offices and postal facilities were periodically closed and evacuated so they could be searched

President George Bush at the scene of the World Trade Center disaster ("Ground Zero"), on September 14, 2001.

for the potentially lethal bacteria. Five people, including postal workers who had handled tainted mail, died in the anthrax incidents, but no explanation for their occurrence has ever been determined.

On October 7, 2001, the United States and Great Britain commenced their full-scale war on terrorism, launching Operation Enduring Freedom with air strikes on Taliban targets in Afghanistan. Anti-Taliban forces in Afghanistan, the Northern Alliance, staged offensives, first seizing the city of Mazar-e Sharif before moving toward the capital of Kabul. Taliban forces dispersed in the face of penetrated US bombing and the Northern Alliance advanced. Somewhere along the remote border between Afghanistan and Pakistan, site of the rugged Hindu Kush mountain range, Osama bin Laden escaped, and to this date he has eluded capture. The United States, in December 2001, appointed Hamid Karzai, leader of Afghanistan's largest ethnic group, the Pashtun, as head of a new interim government.

October 2001 also witnessed passage of wide-ranging legislation known as the USA-PA-TRIOT Act (also commonly referred to as the "Patriot Act") in both houses of Congress without debate or dissent. The law, designed to assist the government's counterterrorism efforts, includes a number of controversial provisions, such as "sneak and peek" and secret search warrants, widely expanded wiretap and surveillance powers, and the securing of personal information, such as phone, medical, and travel records, extending to borrowing history at a local library. Under the Patriot Act, aliens can be detained without judicial review if they are deemed a threat to national security. Then Attorney General John Ashcroft additionally extended the FBI's powers in domestic security cases. Critics, whose numbers have steadily increased since the act's implementation, maintain that these provisions represent a threat to US civil liberties and are contrary to the protections provided by the Constitution and the Bill of Rights. Within the United States, hundreds of arrests have been made under the provisions of the Patriot Act. Only one person, Zacarias Moussaoui (a French terrorist of Moroccan descent who was believed to be an intended hijacker on one of the airplanes seized), has ever been formally charged in relation to the 9/11 terrorist attacks.

> **"Intelligence gathered by this and other governments leaves no doubt that the Iraq regime continues to possess and conceal some of the most lethal weapons ever devised."**
>
> George W. Bush, in a nationally televised address, March 17, 2003

In January 2002 the US government began moving Taliban and Al Qaeda prisoners to the Guantánamo Bay Naval Base in Cuba, to a facility known as Camp X-Ray. The Bush administration was quick to identify these prisoners as "unlawful combatants" rather than prisoners of war, and claim that they were not covered by the provisions of the Geneva Conventions or other international laws. As such, the detainees were denied legal representation and contact with their families, and held without formal charges or trials. By the summer of 2003 up to 680 suspected Taliban and Al Qaeda members from more than forty countries were reportedly being held at Camp X-Ray. In July 2004, after the petitioning of more than 60 detainees, the Supreme Court ruled that all the detainees were entitled to file the petitions necessary in order to contest the United States' right to hold them without charge.

By the fall of 2002 the foreign policy focus of

the Bush administration had shifted from the war on terror to Iraq. Under the terms of the Gulf War ceasefire, special UN inspectors had been mandated to supervise Iraq's destruction of any remaining nuclear, biological, and chemical weapons. Until they could verify the nonexistence of all such capabilities, economic sanctions against Iraq and a no-fly air zone were maintained. In 1998 UN inspectors departed from Iraq after Saddam Hussein made no effort to comply with disarmament, and the United States next launched a series of air strikes, Operation Desert Fox, as punishment. In 1999 the United Nations established a new monitoring commission; its inspectors arrived in Baghdad in November 2002.

By this time many important figures within the administration—notably Vice President Dick Cheney, Defense Secretary Donald Rumsfeld, and Deputy Defense Secretary Paul Wolfowitz—were campaigning hard for military action to remove Hussein. Citing intelligence reports that confirmed the likelihood of weapons of mass destruction within Iraq's borders, and drawing a connection between Iraq and the events of 9/11, the White House was able to prevail on both houses of Congress to pass a resolution, in October 2002, authorizing the president to use force, if necessary, should diplomatic negotiations break down and Hussein refuse to surrender his stockpile of weapons. In his January State of the Union address, President Bush referred to North Korea, Iran, and Iraq as an "axis of evil," identifying them as countries that actively support terrorism.

In February 2003 then Secretary of State Colin Powell delivered a formal address to the UN Security Council in which he provided US intelligence information that allegedly documented the presence of weapons of mass destruction in Iraq. Unswayed by this address and still insistent on a diplomatic solution, France, Germany, and Russia moved to block US action through the United Nations. Only Great Britain, Spain, Australia, and Poland agreed to participate in any land invasion should Hussein not accede to US demands.

On March 17, 2003, President Bush gave

Saddam Hussein and his two sons (Uday and Qusay) forty-eight hours to leave Iraq. When that deadline passed, on March 19, the United States initiated a massive air strike designed to swiftly break Iraqi resistance. On March 20 the so-called coalition of the willing began its ground invasion, consisting of troops from the U.S., Great Britain, Poland, and Australia, as well as naval support from Spain and Denmark. Supported by massive air power and encountering only intermittent resistance along the route from Kuwait, coalition forces reached Bagdad in early April. By April 15, 2003, Bush declared that the "regime of Saddam Hussein is no more."

Nevertheless, the occupation and rebuilding of Iraq proved to be a greater challenge than the invasion itself. With the country's infrastructure effectively destroyed, chaos soon engulfed many major regions and cities. Looting became widespread, and Iraqi civilians found themselves without basic services, including electrical power, clean water, or phone service. Bush appointed the head of the US counterterrorism office, Paul Bremer, as Iraq's civil administrator, but he struggled in the face of a growing anti-American insurgency that was able to appeal to disenfranchised Iraqis and utilize guerrilla tactics against coalition forces. Though some segments of society seemed willing to ally themselves with US efforts to rebuild (such as the Sunni in large cities and the Kurds in the north), others, especially Shia, rejected the notion of an occupying force and cooperation with the United States. Several Shia Muslim leaders, including Muqtada al-Sadr, organized radical opposition movements that were difficult to suppress. Before long Westerners in Iraq—both civilian contractors and those there to offer humanitarian assistance—became the victims of random kidnappings, some even ending in gruesome executions that were filmed and seen worldwide on the Internet.

The coalition did succeed in removing the most prominent members of Saddam Hussein's regime. Hussein's sons were also killed in a gun battle inside Mosul in July 2003, and Saddam himself was captured in his hometown of Tikrit by members of the US 4th Infantry Divi-

sion in December. And a month beforehand Bush had received congressional funding for the occupation, a record $87.5 billion. But public opinion polls within the United States showed that the president's approval ratings were sliding. To some it seemed as if the administration had no clear plan for the reconstruction of Iraq or exit strategy, even an effective response to the ever-growing insurgency. Critics also pointed to the fact that ground forces had not uncovered weapons of mass destruction, and questioned whether the American people had been misled by the administration into a war on spurious grounds. Despite mounting opposition, Bush remained resolute in his prosecution of the war in Iraq.

Against the backdrop of the war on terror and the occupation of Iraq, Bush's domestic agenda continued. In January 2002 the No Child Left Behind Act passed Congress with bipartisan support. The legislation mandated a program of student testing to which local funding would be tied, although critics still maintain that the act imposes educational requirements for which funding is inadequate. Congress also passed, in March 2002, long-discussed campaign finance reforms in the form of the McCain-Feingold bill, which banned "soft" money contributions, the unlimited and unregulated donations to political parties, for candidates running for federal office.

President Bush joined the debate on affirmative action in early 2003 when he stated that his administration would support a challenge to the University of Michigan's admissions policy. He also signed the US Medicare Prescription Drug, Improvement, and Modernization Act on December 8, 2003. The $400 billion measure, which made its way through the Senate and House with both Democratic and Republican approval, included a prescription-drug benefit for seniors, thus fulfilling another earlier campaign pledge. The issue of prescription drug costs—specifically for seniors—had been a much debated issue; spending on prescription drugs had twice as much as total national heath expenditures between the years 1990 and 2000. However, this period saw no initiative on the issue of health care coverage, with record numbers of working Americans and families among the uninsured.

Despite record budget deficits to contrast the budget surplus that had existed when Bush entered office, the White House followed through on its policy of tax cuts. Three such measures were signed during Bush's first term, including in May 2003 the third largest cut in US history, mandating $330 billion in cuts. The economy, though, continued to exhibit slow growth in the jobs sector, with overseas outsourcing becoming a more prevalent policy among traditional employers.

In April 2004 photographs that showed US military personnel torturing and sexually humiliating prisoners at the Abu Ghraib prison in Iraq appeared on television around the world. While a Pentagon investigation acknowledged patterns of abuse at Abu Ghraib, it sought to characterize these incidents as isolated and the actions of a small group of rogue soldiers. National leaders and the media, however, sought to determine if these incidents were based on a larger policy of permissible torture as defined by the Department of Defense (and possibly emanating from the White House) in regard to the war on terror. Congressional hearings ensued, with Secretary of Defense Donald Rumsfeld and military commanders called to testify. In July 2004 the International Committee of the Red Cross issued an official report accusing the US military of routinely using torture and other unlawful measures against detainees, a charge that the Bush administration continues to deny.

With the public outcry over these events growing and no end to the hostilities in Iraq in sight, the 2004 presidential campaign unfolded. In the spring Senator John Kerry of Massachusetts appeared to be a virtual shoe-in for the Democratic nomination. Though Kerry, like the overwhelming majority of the Senate, had voted to give Bush the authority to invade Iraq if necessary, he soon questioned the president's long-term motives and strategy. The challenger's campaign also attempted to make much of the major domestic issues facing the nation: with the ballooning national debt, poor job growth,

high unemployment, outsourcing, and health care reform at the top of the list. These issues soon took a back seat, however, as the campaign—and its coverage—became increasingly mired in personal attacks and unsubstantiated allegations. The details of President Bush's service in the Air National Guard came under question in a *60 Minutes* broadcast later condemned for its bogus evidence, which CBS had failed to verify. A monied special interest group, the Swift Boat Veterans for Truth (later connected with the Republican Party), ran a series of high-profile ads challenging Kerry's naval record during the Vietnam War, as a result of which he had received several medals for heroism.

Although the American public was dissatisfied with the lack of progress in Iraq and not necessarily in agreement with some of the Bush administration's more conservative views, it also seemed reluctant to switch presidents during a time of war. Kerry and his vice-presidential running mate, former Senator John Edwards of North Carolina (who had challenged Kerry for the presidential nomination during the primary season and made a surprisingly strong showing with a populist platform), left the Democratic Convention in Boston with little improvement in their poll ratings. Pegging Kerry as a "flip flopper" with no consistent record and weak on defense, Bush and the Republicans gathered a month later in New York City. There, amid a huge antiwar march that drew several hundred thousand protesters from around the country, the president spoke of 9/11 and his administration's commitment to the war on terror.

As the campaign evolved, the race between Bush and Kerry tightened. Established by the White House in 2002 with some reluctance but under intense pressure from surviving family members, and chaired by former Governor Thomas Kean of New Jersey, the National Commission on Terrorist Attacks Upon the United States, or the 9/11 Commission, began its public hearings in the spring of 2004. Startling among the many sworn statements were those of Richard Clark, former counterintelligence czar for both the Clinton and Bush administrations, who asserted that the Bush White House had paid little heed to his warning on the growing al Qaeda threat in the months leading up to the terrorist attacks. The commission's official report, issued in July 2004, confirmed multiple intelligence failures related to the attacks. The Bush administration received a further blow when the 9/11 Commission rejected any link between al Qaeda and Iraq, what had been cited as part of the justification for the invasion of Iraq. And in October 2004 an official CIA report concluded that Iraq had not, in fact, possessed weapons of mass destruction in March 2003, although it did have the capability to produce such weapons in the future.

> **"I believe the most solemn duty of the American president is to protect the American people. If America shows uncertainty and weakness in this decade the world will drift towards tragedy. This will not happen on my watch."**
>
> George Bush, at the Republican National Convention in New York City, September 2, 2004

As the gap between Bush and Kerry narrowed, the Kerry camp attempted to draw voter attention to the economy and health care, and the worsening situation in Iraq, with now almost daily insurgent attacks on coalition forces and civilians. In the country's "swing states," where the Democrats had concentrated much of their time and money, the Bush camp emphasized the Republican Party's conservative stands on issues such as abortion and gay marriage, hoping to mobilize its base. The president, in fact, voiced support for a constitutional amendment that would ban gay marriage, thus rendering the same-sex unions that some communities had already started to permit as illegal.

On an election day with record turnout, more Americans voted for George W. Bush, and John Kerry, than any prior presidential candidate. With the election again coming down to the results in one state—in this instance, Ohio—Bush proved the victor, capturing 286 electoral college votes and 51 percent of the popular vote to Kerry's 254 votes and 48 percent. Reported irregularities in Ohio, including alleged voter suppression in minority neighborhoods and the utilization of unfair standards in discarding voter ballots, once more drew attention to the often political nature of the election process (Ohio's Secretary of State, Kenneth Blackwell, was also the chair of the 2004 Bush-Cheney campaign in that state), the possible inadequacies of the electoral system, and the absence of a paper trail with electronic voting machines. Although the votes of the electoral college proclaiming Bush president were later entered into the official congressional record, one US senator, Democrat Barbara Boxer of California, did step forward to force a debate in the Senate regarding the election results.

At his January 2005 inauguration, an event marked by unprecedented security, President Bush spoke in bold, sweeping terms, declaring the "spreading of democracy" to be America's noble mission. Referring in a White House news conference to the "political capital" he had gained in his reelection, Bush seemed poised to spend it in his second term, announcing immediately his plans to overhaul Social Security; impose tort reforms, especially in the area of medical malpractice; make permanent the tax cuts from his first term that are due to expire in 2010; and implement immigration reforms, including a guest-worker program. In January his administration could also point to the successful national elections in Iraq, which insurgents remained unable to derail, and the training of a greater number of security forces in that besieged country. As well, the FBI and CIA were reorganized in accordance with some of the 9/11 Commission's recommendations, and a Director of National Intelligence was named in February 2005: John Negroponte, the former US ambassador to Iraq.

The late twentieth and early twenty-first centuries in US politics have seen the increasing polarization of liberals and Democrats on one side and conservatives and Republicans on the other. Those most critical of the Clinton presidency tend to be most enthusiastically supportive of the Bush presidency, and Democrats often feel they have little common ground with Bush supporters. A majority of Americans supported Bush in the dark days following the terrorist attacks of September 11, 2001, when he was perceived as a strong and unifying leader, and few found fault with the attacks on Afghanistan in pursuit of Osama bin Laden and Al Qaeda. However, questions about the justification for the invasion of Iraq (further raised by the insider Downing Street memo released in June 2005 that suggested US intelligence was being "fixed" to support an invasion months beforehand), coupled with the mounting losses in that war, the enormous budget deficits it has caused ($427 million at last count), and the absence of any clear timetable for the withdrawal of US troops, have eroded much of the bipartisan support Bush once enjoyed. Media revelations on what many claim to be commonplace tactics at Guantánamo (for instance, the desecration of the Koran) persist, and several congressional leaders, including a handful of Republicans, have called on the US government to shut down the facility. Some of the ambitious domestic agenda unveiled just six months ago (principally, changes to the Social Security system) has come to a halt. In mid-2005 Americans continue to express concern and doubts about Iraq, the state of the economy, and many of George W. Bush's social programs.

Birthplace: New Haven, CT
Residency: Texas
Religion: Methodist
Education: Yale University, graduated 1968; Harvard University, graduated 1975
Place of Death: n/a
Burial Site: n/a
Dates in Office: January 20, 2001–
Age at Inauguration: 55 years, 198 days

FAMILY

Father: George Herbert Walker Bush (1924–)
Mother: Barbara Pierce Bush (1925–)
Siblings: George is the eldest of six children; the next born was Pauline Robinson ("Robin") Bush (1949–1953); his other siblings are John Ellis ("Jeb") Bush (1953–), Neil Mallon Bush (1955–), Marvin Pierce Bush (1956–), Dorothy Walker Bush (1959–)
Wife: Laura Lane Welch Bush (1946–), married on November 5, 1977, in Midland, TX
Children: Twins Barbara Pierce and Jenna Welch Bush (1981–)

CAREER

Private: oil executive; part-owner and managing partner of the Texas Rangers baseball team
Political: governor of Texas (1995–2000); president of the United States (2001–)
Military: Bush trained as F-102 fighter pilot in the Texas Air National Guard (1968–1973), attaining the rank of lieutenant.
Selected Works: *A Charge to Keep* (New York: William Morrow, 1999); *The Deluxe Election-Edition Bushisms: The First Term, in His Own Special Words*, compiled by Jacob Weisberg (New York: Fireside, 2004); *The George W. Bush Foreign Policy Reader: Presidential Speeches and Commentary*, ed. by John W. Dietrich (Armonk, NY: M. E. Sharpe, 2005); *George W. Bush on God and Country*, ed. by Thomas M. Freiling (Fairfax, VA: Allegiance Press, 2004); *We Will Prevail: President George W. Bush on War, Terrorism, and Freedom*, selected and ed. by the *National Review* (New York: Continuum, 2003)

PRESIDENCY

Nomination: 2000: The Republican Convention was held in Philadelphia, July 31–August 3, 2000. Bush secured the nomination on the first ballot and chose Dick Cheney as his running mate.

2004: The Republican Convention was held in New York City, August 30–September 2, 2004. Bush and Cheney were renominated, unopposed.
Election: 2000: elected president on November 7, 2000

2004: reelected president on November 2, 2004

Opponents: 2000: Al Gore, TN, Democratic; Ralph Nader, CT, Green Party; Patrick Buchanan, VA, Reform Party

2004: John Kerry, MA, Democratic; Ralph Nader, CT, Independent

Vote Totals: 2000: Bush, 50,460,110 popular, 271 electoral; Gore, 51,003,926 popular, 266 electoral; Nader, 2,883,105 popular, o electoral; Buchanan, 449,225 popular, o electoral. One elector from the District of Columbia abstained in the electoral college vote.

2004: Bush, 62,040,610 popular, 286 electoral; Kerry, 59,028,111 popular, 251 electoral; Nader, 463,653 popular, o electoral

Inauguration: 2000: January 20, 2001

2004: January 20, 2005

Vice President: Richard ("Dick") Cheney (2001–)

CABINET

Secretary of State: Colin L. Powell, NY (2001–2004); Condoleezza Rice, AL (2005–)

Secretary of the Treasury: Paul H. O'Neill, NY (2001–2003); John W. Snow, VA (2004–)

Secretary of Defense: Donald H. Rumsfeld, IL (2001–)

Attorney General: John Ashcroft, MO (2001–2004); Alberto Gonzales, TX (2005–)

Secretary of Agriculture: Ann M. Veneman, CA (2001–2004); Mike Johanns, NE (2005–)

Secretary of the Interior: Gale Norton, CO (2001–)

Secretary of Labor: Elaine Chao, CA/KY (2001–)

Secretary of Commerce: Donald Evans, TX (2001–2004); Carlos Gutierrez, MI (2005–)

Secretary of Health and Human Services: Tommy G. Thompson, WI (2001–2004); Michael O. Leavitt, UT (2005–)

Secretary of Housing and Urban Development: Melquiades Martinez, FL (2001–2003); Alphonso Jackson, TX (2004–)

Secretary of Transportation: Norman Y. Mineta, CA (2001–)

Secretary of Energy: Spencer Abraham, MI (2001–2004); Samuel W. Bodman, MA (2005–)

Secretary of Education: Rod Paige, TX (2001–2004); Margaret Spellings, TX (2005–)

Secretary of Veterans Affairs: Anthony Principi, CA (2001–)

Secretary of Homeland Security: Tom Ridge, PA (2003–2004); Michael Chertoff, NJ (2005–) [Note: Under President Bush, this new department came into existence on January 24, 2003.]

CONGRESS:

107th Congress (2001–2003); Speaker of the House: J. Dennis Hastert (Republican, IL)108th Congress (2003–2005); Speaker of the House: J. Dennis Hastert (Republican, IL)109th Congress (2005–2007); Speaker of the House: J. Dennis Hastert (Republican, IL)

SUPREME COURT APPOINTEES:

None at the time of publication; however, a new justice will replace Sandra Day O'Connor, who resigned on July 1, 2005.

MAJOR EVENTS OF THE BUSH ADMINISTRATION

❖ On January 21, 2001, amid lingering acrimony over the Supreme Court's controversial decision on the November election results, George W. Bush is sworn in as the 43rd president.

❖ On March 5, 2001, Vice President Dick Cheney undergoes surgery to clear a blocked artery.

❖ Vermont Senator Jim Jeffords resigns his membership in the Republican Party on June 5, 2001, and the Democrats assume control of the US Senate.

❖ On June 7, 2001, Bush signs the first of three tax cuts implemented in his first term: the Economic Growth and Tax Relief Reconciliation Act (EGTRRA).

❖ On September 11, 2001, Islamic terrorists attack the World Trade Center in New York City and the Pentagon in Washington, DC. Four airplanes are hijacked: Two fly into the World Trade Center; one smashes into the Pentagon; and the fourth crashes in rural Pennsylvania without reaching its intended target, thought to be the US Capitol or the White House. All passengers onboard the hijacked jets are killed, and over 2,000 civilians on the ground perish.

◆ On September 17, 2001, the New York Stock Exchange reopens following the terrorist attacks. In the third quarter of the year, the Dow falls 16 percent and the Nasdaq 31 percent.

◆ In a nationally televised joint session of Congress on September 20, 2002, President Bush demands that the Taliban regime in Afghanistan hand over Osama bin Laden, head of al Qaeda, to the US government.

◆ On October 5, 2001, Robert Stevens, a sixty-three-year-old photo editor at American Media, in Florida, dies from exposure to inhalation anthrax.

◆ US and British forces begin their attack on Afghanistan, October 7, 2001.

◆ On October 26, 2001, Bush signs the USA-PATRIOT ACT, after this measure granting the government new authority to investigate and obstruct terrorism is passed in the Congress.

◆ November 13, 2001, Bush signs an executive order permitting secret military tribunals against any foreigners suspected of having connections to terrorist acts.

◆ On November 19, 2001, Bush signs a bill that federalizes airport security services, a measure affecting all 28,000 airport screeners. Regulations on baggage search, and passenger check-in, are also further tightened.

◆ The US government indicts Zacarias Moussaoui, a French citizen, on December 11, 2001, for his involvement in the 9/11 terrorist attacks.

◆ On December 13, 2001, Bush announces that the United States will withdraw from the Anti-Ballistic Missile Treaty and pursue a missile defense system. Russian President Vladimir Putin characterizes the decision as a mistake.

◆ On December 22, 2001, a flight from Paris to Miami is diverted to Boston after passenger Richard Reid attempts to detonate a bomb hidden in his shoe. Reid is subdued by fellow passengers and the crew.

◆ Bush signs the No Child Left Behind Act into law at a Cincinnati high school on January

8, 2002. The act calls for broad reform of the nation's educational system, including the requirement of school districts to provide annual report cards informing parents and communities of their progress; additionally, schools that do not show progress must provide supplemental services such as tutoring or after-school assistance.

◆ On January 13, 2002, Bush faints and collapses, suffering a bruise to his face after almost choking on a pretzel at the White House while watching a football game.

◆ On January 23, 2002, *Wall Street Journal* reporter Daniel Pearl is kidnapped in Pakistan by a militant Islamic group describing itself as the National Movement for the Restoration of Pakistani Sovereignty. Days later Pearl is decapitiated. His body is found on the outskirts of Karachi on May 16.

◆ In eastern Afghanistan, the US combat attempt against al Qaeda and Taliban forces, known as Operation Anaconda, begins on March 1, 2002.

◆ On March 9, 2002, the president signs the Job Creation and Workers Assistance Act. The act is designed to help workers and businesses affected by the 9/11 terrorist attacks, extending unemployment and tax benefits.

◆ On March 12, 2002, Homeland Security head Tom Ridge announces the formulation of a color-coded, nationwide terror alert system to describe the level of potential threat: severe (red), high (orange), elevated (yellow), guarded (blue), and low (green).

◆ Bush signs the McCain-Feingold campaign finance bill into law on March 27, 2002, which bans the contribution of soft money to candidates campaigning for federal positions.

◆ US officials announce the capture of Osama bin Laden's top deputy, Abu Zubaydah, on April 1, 2002.

◆ August 2, 2002, Bagdad invites UN chief weapons inspector Hans Blix to Iraq.

◆ At the United Nations on September 12, 2002, citing US intelligence allegedly confirming the existence of weapons of mass destruction, Bush asks member nations to confront the "grave and gathering danger" in

Iraq or allow the United States to initiate military action.

◆ On October 2, 2002, a joint resolution of Congress gives the president authority to use force against Iraq if weapons violations cannot be resolved through diplomatic channels.

◆ Bush signs the Iraq war resolution on October 16, 2002.

◆ On November 8, 2002, the UN Security Council unanimously approves Resolution 1441, requiring Saddam Hussein to disarm or face "serious consequences."

◆ On November 18, 2002, Hans Blix's inspectors arrive in Iraq.

◆ November 25, 2002, Bush signs the Homeland Security Act into law, establishing the Department of Homeland Security as the largest new government department since the creation of the Department of Defense in 1947.

◆ Iraq files a 12,000-page weapons declaration with the UN Security Council on December 7, 2002. The declaration is deemed incomplete by the Security Council and weapons inspectors.

◆ On December 19, 2002, the United States accuses Iraq of being in "material breach" of the UN resolution.

◆ Saddam Hussein, on February 27, 2003, agrees to destroy Samoud 2 missiles discovered by weapons inspectors. US and British leaders dismiss the move, claiming it is a ruse to conceal the true extent of Iraq's stockpiled arsenal and buy time.

◆ Beginning on March 16, 2003, the leaders of the United States, Great Britain, Portugal, and Spain meet at a summit in the Azores Islands. Bush calls Monday, March 17th, the "moment of truth," meaning that his so-called coalition of the willing would make one last-ditch effort to extract a resolution from the UN Security Council giving Iraq an ultimatum to disarm immediately or be disarmed by force.

◆ Bush issues the final US ultimatum to Saddam Hussein on March 17, 2003. With his sons Uday and Qusay, Hussein must depart from Iraq or face US military action.

◆ On March 19, 2003, the deadline passes and the United States begins its first airstrikes on Bagdad.

◆ On March 20, 2003, ground forces of the United States, the United Kingdom, Australia, and Poland invade Iraq.

◆ The United States and the United Kingdom launch a massive air strike on military targets in Bagdad on March 22, 2003. Secretary of Defense Donald Rumsfeld refers to the campaign as "shock and awe" at a White House press briefing.

◆ Private First Class Jessica Lynch is rescued by US special forces from an Iraqi hospital on April 1, 2003. Lynch later criticized the Pentagon for releasing false information about her capture and exploiting her rescue for propaganda purposes.

◆ On April 9, 2003, US forces seize control of Bagdad, bringing the regime of Saddam Hussein to an end.

◆ On May 1, 2003, Bush lands on the aircraft carrier USS *Abraham Lincoln* in a Lockheed S-3 *Viking* that he has co-piloted. To the cheers of soldiers and sailors, he declares "mission accomplished," announcing the end of major combat in Iraq.

◆ On June 4, 2003, Bush travels to Jordan and Egypt to win support among leaders there for his "road map" to peace in the Middle East.

◆ Bush signs the US Medicare Prescription Drug, Improvement, and Modernization Act on December 8, 2003. The $400 billion measure, which is passed in Congress with bipartisan support, includes a prescription-drug benefit for seniors.

◆ On December 13, 2003, Saddam Hussein, former president of Iraq, is captured in Tikrit, his hometown, by the US 4th Infantry Division.

◆ On January 14, 2004, Bush announces significant increases in NASA's budget, thus ensuring that the United States will be able to return to the moon by 2020, as well as build a space station and investigate landing humans on the surface of Mars.

◆ March 2, 2004, John Kerry wins nine out of ten "Super Tuesday" primaries and caucuses, effectively clinching the 2004 Democratic Party presidential nomination.

◆ Heavy fighting breaks out in Najaf, Sadr City, and Basra, Iraq, on April 4, 2004, as Shia insurgents supporting Muqtada al-Sadr rise against coalition forces.

◆ On April 28, 2004, *60 Minutes II* airs a segment on the abuse of prisoners at the Abu Ghraib prison in Iraq.

◆ Nick Berg, a civilian contractor working in Iraq, is decapitated by a group claiming links to Al Qaeda. A chilling video of the beheading makes its way onto the Internet on May 12, 2004.

◆ On June 28, 2004, the US-led coalition transfers sovereignty in Iraq to a provisional government headed by interim Prime Minister Ayad Allawi.

◆ The 9/11 Commission issues its final report on July 22, 2004, citing massive intelligence failures prior to the terrorist attacks.

◆ On September 8, 2004, Internet sources challenge the authenticity of documents CBS had used in an earlier *60 Minutes* segment in which Dan Rather questioned the veracity of records released on President Bush's National Guard service. The typewritten memos purportedly dating to the 1970s appear to have been produced using a modern word processing system. A senior producer and two others within the news organization are summarily fired. Rather resigns as the anchor of *CBS Nightly News* several months later.

◆ On October 27, 2004, a CIA report, authored by analyst Charles Duelfer, concludes that Saddam Hussein did not possess weapons of mass destruction when the United States invaded Iraq in 2003.

◆ November 2, 2004, with the largest recorded voter turnout in US history, Bush defeats John Kerry to win a second term in office.

◆ On November 7, 2004, approximately two months before the scheduled national election in Iraq, US forces launch a major assault on Fallujah. The city, a former stronghold of insurgents, is virtually destroyed.

◆ Secretary of State Colin Powell submits his resignation on November 14, 2004. Bush names national security adviser Condoleezza Rice to replace him; after a somewhat acrimonious hearing on the Hill in which she is closely pressed about various statements

issued by the White House, the Senate confirms her appointment on January 26, 2005.

◆ On January 20, 2005, at a lavish inauguration with unprecedented security, Bush takes the oath of office for a second time.

◆ Bush's nominee for attorney general, Alberto Gonzales, is grilled by a Senate committee about his role in the alleged torture policy in the war on terror. In a memo written while he was still White House counsel, Gonzalez had offered legal advice on how the US military could circumvent the Geneva Conventions in its treatment of detainees. On February 4, 2005, the Senate confirms Gonzalez' appointment by a vote of 60 to 36.

◆ Supreme Court Justice Sandra Day O'Connor, the first female to be appointed to the US Supreme Court, announces her resignation on July 1, 2005.

MAJOR US AND WORLD EVENTS, 2001–

◆ On January 31, 2001, a Scottish court sitting in the Netherlands convicts one Libyan and acquits another for their part in the 1988 explosion of Pan Am Flight 103 over Lockerbie, Scotland.

◆ On April 28, 2001, Dennis Tito, a billionaire California businessman, becomes the first "space tourist" when he blasts off from Kazakhstan to spend eight days aboard a space station. Tito pays $20 million for his trip.

◆ When the *NEAR Shoemaker* touches down on 433 Eros on February 12, 2001, it becomes the first spacecraft to land on an asteroid.

◆ On February 20, 2001, CIA agent Robert Hanssen is arrested and charged with spying for the Soviet Union over a fifteen-year period. In May 2001 he is sentenced to life in prison without the possibility of parole.

◆ A US spy plane collides with a Chinese fighter jet on April 1, 2001. The US plane makes an emergency landing in Hainan, China, and its crew is detained for ten days by Chinese authorities.

◆ May 7, 2001, Pope John Paul II begins his historic visit to Syria.

◆ On June 1, 2001, Crown Prince Dipendra, heir to the throne of the Kingdom of Nepal, goes on a violent rampage, killing his parents (the king and queen) and other members of the royal family before turning a gun on himself. It is alleged that he had been in dispute with his parents over their choice of a bride for him.

◆ On June 11, 2001, Timothy McVeigh is excuted by lethal injection at the Federal Penitentiary in Terre Haute, Indiana, for his role as the principal perpetrator of the Oklahoma City bombing in 1995.

◆ The anti-Taliban Afghan leader General Ahmad Shah Massoud, known as the "Lion of Panjshir," is assassinated on September 9, 2001.

◆ On November 12, 2001, American Airlines Flight 587 crashes after take-off from New York's John F. Kennedy Airport, killing all 260 onboard.

◆ On December 12, 2001, Enron files for Chapter 11 bankruptcy protection.

◆ The trial of former Yugoslav President Slobodan Milosevic begins at the United Nations war crimes tribunal in the Hague on December 12, 2001.

◆ Jonathan Franzen publishes *The Corrections*, 2001.

◆ W. G. Sebald publishes *Austerlitz*, 2001.

◆ Richard Russo publishes *Empire Falls*, 2001.

◆ Yann Martel publishes *The Life of Pi*, 2001.

◆ Laura Hillenbrand publishes *Seabiscuit: An American Legend*, 2001.

◆ Popular music hits of 2001 include Christina Aguilera, Lil' Kim, Mya, and Pink's "Lady Marmalade," Alicia Keys's "Fallin," Outkast's "Ms. Jackson," and Usher's "U Remind Me."

◆ Television series debuting in 2001 include *According to Jim*, *Alias*, *The Amazing Race*, *The Bernie Mac Show*, *The Chris Isaak Show*, *Crossing Jordan*, *Enterprise*, *Fear Factor*, *Law and Order: Criminal Intent*, *The Office*, *Reba*, *Six Feet Under*, *Smallville*, and *24*.

◆ Notable films of 2001 include Ron Howard's *A Beautiful Mind* with Russell Crowe, Robert Altman's *Gosford Park* with Maggie Smith, Baz Luhrmann's *Moulin Rouge* with Nicole Kidman, Peter Jackson's *The Lord of the Rings: The Fellowship of the Ring* with Elijah Wood and Viggo Mortensen, Steven Soderbergh's *Ocean's Eleven* with George Clooney, Julia Roberts, and Brad Pitt, and David Lynch's *Mulholland Drive* with Naomi Watts.

◆ On March 21, 2002, in Pakistan, Ahmed Omar Saeed Sheikh and three other suspects are charged with murder for their part in the kidnapping and killing of *Wall Street Journal* reporter Daniel Pearl who was covering the rise of Islamic fundamentalists in the region.

◆ On May 22, 2002, the remains of Chandra Levy, a former congressional intern missing for thirteen months, are found in Rock Creek Park in Washington, DC. Levy had been romantically linked to Congressman Gary Condit from her hometown of Modesto, California, and her disappearance was the subject of intense media speculation.

◆ John Walker Lindh, an American captured with Taliban forces in Afghanistan, pleads guilty on July 15, 2002, to abetting the enemy and possessing explosives during the commission of a felony. Given Lindh's youth and his cooperation with US intelligence after capture, the judge sentences him to only ten years of imprisonment.

◆ Terrorist bombs explode in a crowded tourist district the Indonesian island of Bali on October 12, 2002, killing 202. A third bomb goes off near the US consulate.

◆ On October 24, 2002, suspects in a string of sniper shootings in the Washington, DC, area, John Allen Muhammad and Lee Boyd Malvo, are apprehended. Muhammad, a former US serviceman, is later sentenced to death; Malvo, a seventeen-year-old immigrant from Jamaica, to life in prison.

◆ US Senator Paul Wellstone, his wife Sheila, daughter Marcia, three staff members, and two pilots are killed in a plane crash near Eveleth, Minnesota, on October 25, 2002.

◆ On November 5, 2002, midterm elections see the Republicans maintain control of the House of Representatives and regain control of the Senate.

◆ On November 16, 2002, the first outbreak of severe acute respiratory syndrome (SARS) is reported in Guangdong province, China.

◆ Rick Warren publishes *The Purpose Driven Life*, 2002.

◆ Jeffrey Eugenides publishes *Middlesex*, 2002.

◆ Robert Caro publishes *Master of the Senate*, 2002.

◆ Julia Glass publishes *Three Junes*, 2002.

◆ Ian McEwan publishes *Atonement*, 2002.

◆ Popular music hits of 2002 include Norah Jones's "Don't Know Why," the Dixie Chicks's "Long Time Gone," the Foo Fighters' "All My Life," and Nelly's "Hot in Herre."

◆ Television series debuting in 2002 include *American Dreams, American Idol, The Bachelor, CSI: Miami, The Dead Zone, Dr. Phil, 8 Simple Rules, Everwood, Firefly, George Lopez, Last Call with Carson Daly, Monk, The Osbournes, The Shield,* and *Without a Trace.*

◆ Notable films of 2002 include Rob Marshall's *Chicago* with Renée Zellweger, Catherine Zeta-Jones, and Richard Gere, Spike Jonze's *Adaptation* with Nicholas Cage, Todd Haynes's *Far from Heaven* with Julianne Moore and Dennis Quaid, Steven Spielberg's *Catch Me If You Can* with Leonardo DiCaprio and Tom Hanks, Roman Polanski's *The Pianist* with Adrien Brody, and Stephen Daldry's *The Hours* with Nicole Kidman, Julianne Moore, and Meryl Streep.

◆ On February 1, 2003, the Space Shuttle *Columbia* disintegrates over Texas upon reentry, killing the seven astronauts onboard.

◆ June 4, 2003, lifestyle guru Martha Stewart and her Wall Street broker are indicted for using insider information to sell off stock and subsequently obstructing a federal investigation of the trade.

◆ Self-styled terrorist Eric Rudolph, on the FBI's Most Wanted list in connection with the 1996 Centennial Olympic Park bombing in Atlanta, is captured in North Carolina on May 31, 2003.

◆ On August 15, 2003, the power grid for the Northeast overloads, and a massive blackout spreads from New England to as far west as Michigan, affecting more than 50 million people in high heat and humidity weather conditions.

◆ After recalling Democratic Governor Gray Davis, California's voters elect as their new governor Republican Arnold Schwarzenegger, former muscleman and mega-Hollywood movie star, on October 7, 2003.

◆ The Concorde, the Anglo-French supersonic airliner, makes its last commercial flight on October 24, 2003.

◆ An earthquake devastates the Iranian city of Bam on December 26, 2003. Over 40,000 casualties are reported.

◆ Dan Brown publishes *The Da Vinci Code*, 2003.

◆ Anne Applebaum publishes *Gulag*, 2003.

◆ Jonathan Lethem publishes *The Fortress of Solitude*, 2003.

◆ Michael Moore publishes *Dude, Where's My Country*, 2003.

◆ Mitch Alborn publishes *The Five People You Meet in Heaven*, 2003.

◆ J. K. Rowling publishes *Harry Potter and the Order of the Phoenix*, 2003.

◆ Popular music hits of 2003 include Coldplay's "Clocks," Justin Timberlake's "Cry Me a River," Eminem's "Lose Yourself," and No Doubt's "Underneath It All."

◆ Television series debuting in 2003 include *Arrested Development, America's Next Top Model, The Bachelorette, Carnivàle, Celebrity Poker Showdown, Cold Case, Extreme Makeover: Home Edition, Fear Factor, Joan of Arcadia, Las Vegas, Navy NCIS, Nip/Tuck, The O.C., Queer Eye for the Straight Guy, The Simple Life,* and *Two and a Half Men.*

◆ Notable films of 2003 include Anthony Minghella's *Cold Mountain* with Nicole Kidman and Renée Zellweger, Clint Eastwood's *Mystic River* with Sean Penn and Tim Robbins, Peter Jackson's *Lord of the Rings: The Return of the King* with Elijah Wood and Viggo Mortensen, Gore Verbinski's *Pirates of the Caribbean* with Johnny Depp, and Sofia Coppola's *Lost in Translation* with Bill Murray.

◆ In January 2004 NASA lands two rovers, MER-A (*Spirit*) and MER-B (*Opportunity*), on Mars to search for proof of the past presence of water on the red planet.

◆ February 12, 2004, as an act of civil disobedience, the City and County of San Francisco begin issuing marriage licenses to same-sex couples.

◆ Bush announces on February 24, 2004, that he would support a constitutional amendment defining marriage as the union of a man and woman, thus barring same-sex marriages.

◆ On February 29, 2004, a rebellion breaks out in Haiti, and Boniface Alexandre replaces President Jean-Bertrand Aristide; Aristide asserts that he was forced from power and "kidnapped" by the United States, a claim the US State Department denies.

◆ On March 11, 2004, terrorist bombs explode on morning rush-hour commuter trains in Madrid, Spain, killing 190 people on their way to work and injuring hundreds of others. Within days Spanish voters elect a socialist government, and on March 15 Spain announces that it will withdraw all of its troops from Iraq.

◆ In its largest single expansion, NATO, on March 29, 2004, admits Bulgaria, Estonia, Latvia, Lithuania, Romania, Slovakia, and Slovenia.

◆ On May 1, 2004, the number of member states in the European Union increases by ten with the admission of Poland, Lithuania, Latvia, Estonia, the Czech Republic, Slovakia, Slovenia, Hungary, Malta, and Cyprus.

◆ After the first presidential state funeral in Washington, DC, since 1973, former President Ronald Reagan is laid to rest on June 11, 2004, in Simi Valley, California, at the site of the Reagan Presidential Library.

◆ On July 16, 2004, businesswoman Martha Stewart is sentenced to five months in prison for obstructing a federal securities investigation of insider trading.

◆ On August 13, 2004, Hurricane Charley, a category 4 hurricane, kills twenty-seven people in Florida after resulting in four fatalities in Cuba and one in Jamaica.

◆ August 22, 2004, thieves steal Edvard Munch's The Scream from a museum in Oslo, Norway.

◆ Chechen rebels seize more than a thousand hostages, mostly children, at a school in Beslan, Northern Ossetia, on September 1, 2004. When Russian forces end the siege on September 3, at least 335 people, including 32 of the approximately 40 hostage-takers, are killed.

◆ On October 9, 2004, Hamid Karzai is elected president of Afghanistan.

◆ Yasser Arafat, president of the Palestinian Authority and long-time head of the Palestine Liberation Organization (PLO), dies on November 11, 2004, in France.

◆ On December 13, 2004, doctors in Vienna confirm that Ukrainian presidential candidate Viktor Yushchenko has been poisoned with dioxin. Yushchenko becomes president of Ukraine in January 2005 after the highest court in that land deems the results of the prior election (in which Yushchenko was defeated) invalid and a new election is held.

◆ On December 26, 2004, an earthquake in the Indian Ocean, measuring 9.0 on the Richter scale, triggers tsunamis in Indonesia, Thailand, Malaysia, India, Sri Lanka, and neighboring countries, as well as the eastern coast of Africa. The disaster is the worst tsunami in recorded history; more than 220,000 people are killed and the devastation in the region is estimated at $675 million.

◆ Steve Coll publishes Ghost Wars, 2004.

◆ Marilynne Robinson publishes Gilead, 2004.

◆ Philip Roth publishes The Plot Against America, 2004.

◆ Stephen Greenblatt publishes Will in the World, 2004.

◆ Bob Dylan publishes Chronicles, Vol. I, 2004.

◆ Popular music hits of 2004 include Britney Spears's "Toxic," Jay-Z's "99 Problems," Prince's "Musicology," and Norah Jones's "Here We Go Again" by Ray Charles.

◆ Television series debuting in 2004 include The Apprentice, Boston Legal, CSI: NY, Deadwood, Desperate Housewives, House, Joey, Kevin Hill, Lost, Nanny 911, Project Runway, Rescue Me, Stargate: Atlantis, Veronica Mars, and The 4400.

◆ Notable films of 2004 include Sam Raimi's Spider-Man 2 with Tobey Maguire, Mel Gibson's The Passion of the Christ with James Caviezel, Michael Moore's Fahrenheit 9/11, Martin Scorsese's The Aviator with Leonardo DiCaprio, Alexander Payne's Sideways with Paul

Giamatti, Thomas Hayden Church, Virginia Madsen, and Sandra Oh, Terry George's *Hotel Rwanda* with Don Cheadle, and Clint Eastwood's *Million Dollar Baby* with Hilary Swank and Morgan Freeman.

◆ On January 9, 2005, Mahmoud Abbas is elected to succeed Yasser Arafat as Palestinian Authority president.

◆ On February 10, 2005, North Korea announces that it possesses nuclear weapons, in part to protect itself from any US threat.

◆ March 31, 2005, two weeks after her feeding tube is removed, forty-one-year-old Terri Schiavo, who has been on life support since 1990, dies in Florida. She was the center of a years-long legal struggle between her parents and husband who claimed it was his wife's final wish to not persist in a vegetative state.

◆ Pope John Paul II dies at age eighty-four in his Vatican apartment on April 2, 2004. The Polish-born Karol Wojtyla was elected pope in 1978. Millions of mourners from around the world flock to Rome for his funeral.

◆ On April 19, 2005, German Cardinal Joseph Ratzinger, seventy-eight and a close confidante of Pope John Paul II, is elected pope on the second day of the papal enclave. He takes the name Benedict XVI.

◆ On July 7, 2005, three bombs explode in London's underground subway system and one detonates aboard a bus; there are more than 700 injuries, and more than 50 deaths. British authorities believe it to be an act of terrorism.

FAST FACTS ABOUT GEORGE W. BUSH

◆ Bush was the first governor of Texas to be elected to two four-year terms.

◆ Like his father, Bush was a member of Skull and Bones, a secret society of Yale students.

◆ Although both George Bush and Laura Welch simultaneously attended the same junior high school, they did not meet, and get to know each other, until years later.

◆ George H. W. Bush and George W. Bush are only the second father and son to serve as US presidents; the first were John Adams and John Quincy Adams.

◆ When Bush asked Condoleezza Rice and Alberto Gonzales to join his cabinet at the start of his second term, he became the first president to have an African American woman to serve as secretary of state, and the first president to have an Hispanic to serve as attorney general.

◆ The Bush family moved into the White House with their aging English springer spaniel, Spot, who had been born there to Millie, the pet dog of George and Barbara Bush. Spot died at age fifteen; the other Bush family pets include Barney, a black Scottish terrier, and India (called "Willy"), a black cat.

◆ Bush formerly enjoyed jogging for exercise, but knee troubles have made mountain biking his new outdoor activity of choice, especially when at home on his ranch in Crawford, Texas. He is known to be an aggressive cyclist and has been the victim of several spills, including a recent one at the G8 summit near Edinburgh, Scotland.

◆ Bush banned the wearing of jeans in the Oval Office (which had become something of a standard during the Clinton administration).

◆ Bush does not always express himself well in public, especially when being questioned at press conferences. This has given rise to the term "Bushisms" to describe his malapropisms, among them, "I understand small business growth. I was one"; "You teach a child to read, and he or her will be able to pass a literacy test"; and "I was raised in the West. The west of Texas. It's pretty close to California, in more ways than Washington, DC, is close to California."

◆ Bush refers to the swimming pool at his Texas ranch as the "whining pool," maintaining that it was installed only because of his daughters' persistent requests.

◆ On November 17, 2001, Laura Bush became the first person other than a president to deliver the weekly presidential radio remarks.

◆ In April 2005, at the annual White House Correspondents dinner, Laura Bush delivered a surprisingly comedic "roast" of her husband, calling him "Mr. Excitement" because of his early bedtime and joking that he had once tried to milk a horse—a male horse.

Index